Coding
ALL-IN-ONE

Coding
ALL-IN-ONE

by Nikhil Abraham, Andy Harris,
Eva Holland, Joris Meys, Luca Massaron,
Chris Minnick, John Paul Mueller,
and Andrie de Vries

Coding All-in-One For Dummies®

Published by: **John Wiley & Sons, Inc.**, 111 River Street, Hoboken, NJ 07030-5774, www.wiley.com

Copyright © 2017 by John Wiley & Sons, Inc., Hoboken, New Jersey

Media and software compilation copyright © 2017 by John Wiley & Sons, Inc. All rights reserved.

Published simultaneously in Canada

No part of this publication may be reproduced, stored in a retrieval system or transmitted in any form or by any means, electronic, mechanical, photocopying, recording, scanning or otherwise, except as permitted under Sections 107 or 108 of the 1976 United States Copyright Act, without the prior written permission of the Publisher. Requests to the Publisher for permission should be addressed to the Permissions Department, John Wiley & Sons, Inc., 111 River Street, Hoboken, NJ 07030, (201) 748-6011, fax (201) 748-6008, or online at http://www.wiley.com/go/permissions.

Trademarks: Wiley, For Dummies, the Dummies Man logo, Dummies.com, Making Everything Easier, and related trade dress are trademarks or registered trademarks of John Wiley & Sons, Inc. and may not be used without written permission. All trademarks are the property of their respective owners. John Wiley & Sons, Inc. is not associated with any product or vendor mentioned in this book.

LIMIT OF LIABILITY/DISCLAIMER OF WARRANTY: THE PUBLISHER AND THE AUTHOR MAKE NO REPRESENTATIONS OR WARRANTIES WITH RESPECT TO THE ACCURACY OR COMPLETENESS OF THE CONTENTS OF THIS WORK AND SPECIFICALLY DISCLAIM ALL WARRANTIES, INCLUDING WITHOUT LIMITATION WARRANTIES OF FITNESS FOR A PARTICULAR PURPOSE. NO WARRANTY MAY BE CREATED OR EXTENDED BY SALES OR PROMOTIONAL MATERIALS. THE ADVICE AND STRATEGIES CONTAINED HEREIN MAY NOT BE SUITABLE FOR EVERY SITUATION. THIS WORK IS SOLD WITH THE UNDERSTANDING THAT THE PUBLISHER IS NOT ENGAGED IN RENDERING LEGAL, ACCOUNTING, OR OTHER PROFESSIONAL SERVICES. IF PROFESSIONAL ASSISTANCE IS REQUIRED, THE SERVICES OF A COMPETENT PROFESSIONAL PERSON SHOULD BE SOUGHT. NEITHER THE PUBLISHER NOR THE AUTHOR SHALL BE LIABLE FOR DAMAGES ARISING HEREFROM. THE FACT THAT AN ORGANIZATION OR WEBSITE IS REFERRED TO IN THIS WORK AS A CITATION AND/OR A POTENTIAL SOURCE OF FURTHER INFORMATION DOES NOT MEAN THAT THE AUTHOR OR THE PUBLISHER ENDORSES THE INFORMATION THE ORGANIZATION OR WEBSITE MAY PROVIDE OR RECOMMENDATIONS IT MAY MAKE. FURTHER, READERS SHOULD BE AWARE THAT INTERNET WEBSITES LISTED IN THIS WORK MAY HAVE CHANGED OR DISAPPEARED BETWEEN WHEN THIS WORK WAS WRITTEN AND WHEN IT IS READ.

For general information on our other products and services, please contact our Customer Care Department within the U.S. at 877-762-2974, outside the U.S. at 317-572-3993, or fax 317-572-4002. For technical support, please visit https://hub.wiley.com/community/support/dummies.

Wiley publishes in a variety of print and electronic formats and by print-on-demand. Some material included with standard print versions of this book may not be included in e-books or in print-on-demand. If this book refers to media such as a CD or DVD that is not included in the version you purchased, you may download this material at http://booksupport.wiley.com. For more information about Wiley products, visit www.wiley.com.

Library of Congress Control Number: 2017935595

ISBN 978-1-119-36302-6 (pbk); 978-1-119-36303-3 (epub); 978-1-119-36305-7 (epdf)

Manufactured in the United States of America

10 9 8 7 6 5 4 3 2 1

Contents at a Glance

Introduction ... 1

Book 1: Getting Started with Coding 5
- **CHAPTER 1:** What Is Coding? ... 7
- **CHAPTER 2:** Programming for the Web 19
- **CHAPTER 3:** Becoming a Programmer 33

Book 2: Career Building with Coding 43
- **CHAPTER 1:** Exploring Coding Career Paths 45
- **CHAPTER 2:** Exploring Undergraduate and Graduate Degrees .. 59
- **CHAPTER 3:** Training on the Job ... 73
- **CHAPTER 4:** Coding Career Myths 83

Book 3: Basic Web Coding .. 93
- **CHAPTER 1:** Exploring Basic HTML 95
- **CHAPTER 2:** Getting More Out of HTML 113
- **CHAPTER 3:** Getting Stylish with CSS 129
- **CHAPTER 4:** Next Steps with CSS 151
- **CHAPTER 5:** Building Floating Page Layouts 173
- **CHAPTER 6:** Using Alternative Positioning 201

Book 4: Advanced Web Coding 231
- **CHAPTER 1:** Working Faster with Twitter Bootstrap 233
- **CHAPTER 2:** Adding in JavaScript 249
- **CHAPTER 3:** Understanding Callbacks and Closures 269
- **CHAPTER 4:** Embracing AJAX and JSON 279
- **CHAPTER 5:** jQuery .. 295

Book 5: Creating Web Applications 311
- **CHAPTER 1:** Building Your Own App 313
- **CHAPTER 2:** Researching Your First Web Application 325
- **CHAPTER 3:** Coding and Debugging Your First Web Application .. 341

Book 6: Selecting Data Analysis Tools 351
- **CHAPTER 1:** Wrapping Your Head around Python 353
- **CHAPTER 2:** Installing a Python Distribution 367
- **CHAPTER 3:** Working with Real Data 387

Book 7: Evaluating Data 405
- **CHAPTER 1:** Conditioning Your Data 407
- **CHAPTER 2:** Shaping Data 433
- **CHAPTER 3:** Getting a Crash Course in MatPlotLib 451
- **CHAPTER 4:** Visualizing the Data 467
- **CHAPTER 5:** Exploring Data Analysis 489
- **CHAPTER 6:** Exploring Four Simple and Effective Algorithms 511

Book 8: Essentials of Machine Learning 527
- **CHAPTER 1:** Introducing How Machines Learn 529
- **CHAPTER 2:** Demystifying the Math behind Machine Learning 553
- **CHAPTER 3:** Descending the Right Curve 571
- **CHAPTER 4:** Validating Machine Learning 585

Book 9: Applying Machine Learning 603
- **CHAPTER 1:** Starting with Simple Learners 605
- **CHAPTER 2:** Leveraging Similarity 623
- **CHAPTER 3:** Hitting Complexity with Neural Networks 643
- **CHAPTER 4:** Resorting to Ensembles of Learners 661
- **CHAPTER 5:** Real-World Applications 677

Index 725

Table of Contents

INTRODUCTION .. 1
 About This Book...2
 Foolish Assumptions...2
 Icons Used in This Book3
 Beyond the Book..4
 Where to Go from Here4

BOOK 1: GETTING STARTED WITH CODING5

CHAPTER 1: What Is Coding?.......................................7
 Defining What Code Is8
 Following instructions...................................8
 Writing code with some Angry Birds......................9
 Understanding What Coding Can Do for You9
 Eating the world with software10
 Coding on the job11
 Scratching your own itch (and becoming rich and famous)12
 Surveying the Types of Programming Languages13
 Comparing low-level and high-level programming languages....14
 Contrasting compiled code and interpreted code15
 Programming for the web16
 Taking a Tour of a Web App Built with Code.................16
 Defining the app's purpose and scope.....................16
 Standing on the shoulders of giants......................17

CHAPTER 2: Programming for the Web19
 Displaying Web Pages on Your Desktop and Mobile Device.........20
 Hacking your favorite news website.......................20
 Understanding how the World Wide Web works23
 Watching out for your front end and back end..............24
 Defining web and mobile applications.....................25
 Coding Web Applications26
 Starting with HTML, CSS, and JavaScript26
 Adding logic with Python, Ruby, or PHP....................27
 Coding Mobile Applications28
 Building mobile web apps29
 Building native mobile apps.............................30

CHAPTER 3: Becoming a Programmer ... 33
Writing Code Using a Process ... 33
- Researching what you want to build ... 35
- Designing your app ... 36
- Coding your app ... 37
- Debugging your code ... 38

Picking Tools for the Job ... 38
- Working offline ... 39
- Working online with Codecademy.com ... 39

BOOK 2: CAREER BUILDING WITH CODING ... 43

CHAPTER 1: Exploring Coding Career Paths ... 45
Augmenting Your Existing Job ... 46
- Creative design ... 46
- Content and editorial ... 47
- Human resources ... 48
- Product management ... 49
- Sales and marketing ... 50
- Legal ... 51

Finding a New Coding Job ... 52
- Front-end web development ... 53
- Back-end web development ... 54
- Mobile application development ... 56
- Data analysis ... 57

CHAPTER 2: Exploring Undergraduate and Graduate Degrees ... 59
Getting a College Degree ... 60
- College computer science curriculum ... 60
- Doing extracurricular activities ... 61
- Two-year versus four-year school ... 64

Enrolling in an Advanced Degree Program ... 65
- Graduate school computer science curriculum ... 66
- Performing research ... 68

Interning to Build Credibility ... 68
- Types of internship programs ... 69
- Securing an internship ... 71

CHAPTER 3: Training on the Job ... 73
Taking a Work Project to the Next Level ... 74
Learning on the Job and after Work ... 75
- Training on the job ... 76
- Learning after work ... 77

Freelancing to Build Confidence and Skills ... 79

Transitioning to a New Role..80
 Assessing your current role...................................81
 Networking with developers..................................81
 Identifying roles that match your interest and skills..........82

CHAPTER 4: Coding Career Myths..83
Educational Myths...83
 You must be good at math....................................84
 You must have studied engineering...........................84
 You can learn coding in a few weeks..........................85
 You need a great idea to start coding........................85
 Ruby is better than Python...................................86
Career Myths..87
 Only college graduates receive coding offers..................87
 You must have experience....................................88
 Tech companies don't hire women or minorities...............89
 The highest paying coding jobs are in San Francisco...........90
 Your previous experience isn't relevant.......................91

BOOK 3: BASIC WEB CODING .. 93

CHAPTER 1: Exploring Basic HTML..95
What Does HTML Do?..95
Understanding HTML Structure..96
 Identifying elements..97
 Featuring your best attribute.................................98
 Standing head, title, and body above the rest................100
Getting Familiar with Common HTML Tasks and Tags..................102
 Writing headlines..103
 Organizing text in paragraphs................................104
 Linking to your (heart's) content.............................104
 Adding images...106
Styling Me Pretty...107
 Highlighting with bold, italics, underline, and strikethrough....107
 Raising and lowering text with superscript and subscript......108
Building Your First Website Using HTML...............................109

CHAPTER 2: Getting More Out of HTML.....................................113
Organizing Content on the Page......................................113
Listing Data..115
 Creating ordered and unordered lists.........................116
 Nesting lists...117

Putting Data in Tables..118
 Basic table structuring......................................118
 Stretching table columns and rows.........................120
 Aligning tables and cells....................................121
Filling Out Forms..124
 Understanding how forms work............................125
 Creating basic forms..126
Practicing More with HTML..127

CHAPTER 3: Getting Stylish with CSS129
What Does CSS Do?...129
CSS Structure..131
 Choosing the element to style..............................131
 My property has value......................................133
 Hacking the CSS on your favorite website.................133
Common CSS Tasks and Selectors................................135
 Font gymnastics: Size, color, style, family, and decoration......135
 Customizing links..139
 Adding background images and styling foreground images....142
Styling Me Pretty..146
 Adding CSS to your HTML.................................146
 Building your first web page...............................148

CHAPTER 4: Next Steps with CSS ...151
Styling (More) Elements on Your Page............................152
 Styling lists...152
 Designing tables...155
Selecting Elements to Style.......................................157
 Styling specific elements..................................158
 Naming HTML elements...................................161
Aligning and Laying Out Your Elements.........................163
 Organizing data on the page..............................163
 Shaping the div..165
 Understanding the box model............................167
 Positioning the boxes.....................................169
Writing More Advanced CSS.....................................172

CHAPTER 5: Building Floating Page Layouts173
Creating a Basic Two-Column Design............................173
 Designing the page..173
 Building the HTML..175
 Using temporary background colors.....................177
 Setting up the floating columns..........................179
 Tuning up the borders....................................180

Advantages of a fluid layout..................................181
Using semantic tags182
Building a Three-Column Design..................................185
Styling the three-column page186
Problems with the floating layout..........................188
Specifying a min-height189
Using height and overflow..................................191
Building a Fixed-Width Layout....................................193
Setting up the HTML..193
Fixing the width with CSS..................................194
Building a Centered Fixed-Width Layout...........................196
Making a surrogate body with an all div197
How the jello layout works.................................198
Limitations of the jello layout............................199

CHAPTER 6: Using Alternative Positioning201

Working with Absolute Positioning................................201
Setting up the HTML..202
Adding position guidelines.................................203
Making absolute positioning work204
Managing z-index...206
Handling depth...206
Working with z-index.......................................207
Building a Page Layout with Absolute Positioning.................208
Overview of absolute layout209
Writing the HTML...210
Adding the CSS...210
Creating a More Flexible Layout..................................212
Designing with percentages.................................213
Building the layout..215
Exploring Other Types of Positioning.............................216
Creating a fixed menu system...............................216
Setting up the HTML..218
Setting the CSS values.....................................219
Flexible Box Layout Model..221
Creating a flexible box layout.............................222
Viewing a flexible box layout..............................223
...And now for a little reality............................225

BOOK 4: ADVANCED WEB CODING231

CHAPTER 1: Working Faster with Twitter Bootstrap233

Figuring Out What Bootstrap Does.................................234
Installing Bootstrap...235

Understanding the Layout Options .236
 Lining up on the grid system .236
 Dragging and dropping to a website .239
 Using predefined templates .240
 Adapting layout for mobile, tablet, and desktop241
Coding Basic Web Page Elements. .243
 Designing buttons .243
 Navigating with toolbars. .244
 Adding icons. .246
Build the Airbnb Home Page .247

CHAPTER 2: Adding in JavaScript . 249

What Does JavaScript Do? .249
Understanding JavaScript Structure .251
 Using semicolons, quotes, parentheses, and braces.252
Coding Common JavaScript Tasks. .253
 Storing data with variables. .253
 Making decisions with if-else statements254
 Working with string and number methods258
 Alerting users and prompting them for input.259
 Naming code with functions .260
 Adding JavaScript to the web page .261
Writing Your First JavaScript Program .263
Working with APIs .263
 What do APIs do?. .264
 Scraping data without an API. .266
 Researching and choosing an API. .267
Using JavaScript Libraries. .267
 jQuery .267
 D3.js. .268

CHAPTER 3: Understanding Callbacks and Closures. 269

What Are Callbacks? .269
 Passing functions as arguments .270
 Writing functions with callbacks .270
 Using named callback functions .271
Understanding Closures. .274
Using Closures .277

CHAPTER 4: Embracing AJAX and JSON .279

Working behind the Scenes with AJAX .279
 AJAX examples .280
 Viewing AJAX in action. .282
 Using the XMLHttpRequest object .285

Working with the same-origin policy287
Using CORS, the silver bullet for AJAX requests288
Putting Objects in Motion with JSON289

CHAPTER 5: jQuery ...295

Writing More and Doing Less295
Getting Started with jQuery296
The jQuery Object297
Is Your Document Ready?298
Using jQuery Selectors298
Changing Things with jQuery300
 Getting and setting attributes300
 Changing CSS300
 Manipulating elements in the DOM301
Events ...302
 Using on() to attach events302
 Detaching with off()304
 Binding to events that don't exist yet304
 Other event methods305
Effects ..305
 Basic effects306
 Fading effects306
 Sliding effects306
 Setting arguments for animation methods307
 Custom effects with animate()307
 Playing with jQuery animations308
AJAX ..309
 Using the ajax() method309
 Shorthand AJAX methods310

BOOK 5: CREATING WEB APPLICATIONS311

CHAPTER 1: Building Your Own App313

Building a Location-Based Offer App313
 Understanding the situation314
 Plotting your next steps314
Following an App Development Process315
Planning Your First Web Application316
Exploring the Overall Process317
Meeting the People Who Bring a Web App to Life319
 Creating with designers319
 Coding with front- and back-end developers321
 Managing with product managers322
 Testing with quality assurance322

CHAPTER 2: Researching Your First Web Application325
- Dividing the App into Steps326
 - Finding your app's functionality326
 - Finding your app's functionality: My version.................326
 - Finding your app's form328
 - Finding your app's form: The McDuck's Offer App design.......332
- Identifying Research Sources.........................333
- Researching the Steps in the McDuck's Offer App335
- Choosing a Solution for Each Step338

CHAPTER 3: Coding and Debugging Your First Web Application ..341
- Getting Ready to Code342
- Coding Your First Web Application342
 - Development environment343
 - Prewritten code343
 - Coding steps for you to follow....................347
- Debugging Your App.............................350

BOOK 6: SELECTING DATA ANALYSIS TOOLS351

CHAPTER 1: Wrapping Your Head around Python353
- What Does Python Do?..............................354
- Defining Python Structure355
 - Understanding the Zen of Python.........................355
 - Styling and spacing356
- Coding Common Python Tasks and Commands357
 - Defining data types and variables..................357
 - Computing simple and advanced math..................358
 - Using strings and special characters360
 - Deciding with conditionals: if, elif, else..........................361
 - Input and output362
- Shaping Your Strings..................................363
 - Dot notation with upper(), lower(), capitalize(), and strip()363
 - String formatting with %............................364
- Building a Simple Tip Calculator Using Python.....................365

CHAPTER 2: Installing a Python Distribution367
- Choosing a Python Distribution with Machine Learning in Mind....368
 - Getting Continuum Analytics Anaconda369
 - Getting Enthought Canopy Express370
 - Getting Python(x,y)371
 - Getting WinPython371

Installing Python on Linux..371
Installing Python on Mac OS X....................................372
Installing Python on Windows.....................................374
Downloading the Data Sets and Example Code..................378
 Using Jupyter Notebook..378
 Defining the code repository...................................379
 Understanding the data sets used in this book................385

CHAPTER 3: Working with Real Data387
Uploading, Streaming, and Sampling Data.......................388
 Uploading small amounts of data into memory..............388
 Streaming large amounts of data into memory.............390
 Sampling data..391
Accessing Data in Structured Flat-File Form.....................392
 Reading from a text file.......................................393
 Reading CSV delimited format................................394
 Reading Excel and other Microsoft Office files..............396
Sending Data in Unstructured File Form..........................397
Managing Data from Relational Databases......................400
Interacting with Data from NoSQL Databases...................401
Accessing Data from the Web....................................402

BOOK 7: EVALUATING DATA405

CHAPTER 1: Conditioning Your Data407
Juggling between NumPy and pandas............................408
 Knowing when to use NumPy.................................408
 Knowing when to use pandas................................408
Validating Your Data..409
 Figuring out what's in your data.............................410
 Removing duplicates..411
 Creating a data map and data plan..........................412
Manipulating Categorical Variables..............................414
 Creating categorical variables................................415
 Renaming levels...417
 Combining levels..417
Dealing with Dates in Your Data..................................419
 Formatting date and time values............................419
 Using the right time transformation.........................420
Dealing with Missing Data..421
 Finding the missing data.....................................421
 Encoding missingness..422
 Imputing missing data..423

Slicing and Dicing: Filtering and Selecting Data424
 Slicing rows..424
 Slicing columns ..425
 Dicing...426
Concatenating and Transforming..............................426
 Adding new cases and variables427
 Removing data...428
 Sorting and shuffling....................................429
Aggregating Data at Any Level................................430

CHAPTER 2: Shaping Data433
Working with HTML Pages434
 Parsing XML and HTML..................................434
 Using XPath for data extraction435
Working with Raw Text......................................436
 Dealing with Unicode436
 Stemming and removing stop words438
 Introducing regular expressions440
Using the Bag of Words Model and Beyond442
 Understanding the bag of words model443
 Working with n-grams...................................445
 Implementing TF-IDF transformations.....................446
Working with Graph Data....................................447
 Understanding the adjacency matrix448
 Using NetworkX basics..................................448

CHAPTER 3: Getting a Crash Course in MatPlotLib...............451
Starting with a Graph452
 Defining the plot452
 Drawing multiple lines and plots..........................453
 Saving your work454
Setting the Axis, Ticks, Grids455
 Getting the axes..455
 Formatting the axes456
 Adding grids ..457
Defining the Line Appearance.................................458
 Working with line styles458
 Using colors ...459
 Adding markers ..460
Using Labels, Annotations, and Legends........................462
 Adding labels ...463
 Annotating the chart....................................464
 Creating a legend......................................465

CHAPTER 4: Visualizing the Data ... 467

- Choosing the Right Graph ... 468
 - Showing parts of a whole with pie charts ... 468
 - Creating comparisons with bar charts ... 470
 - Showing distributions using histograms ... 471
 - Depicting groups using boxplots ... 472
 - Seeing data patterns using scatterplots ... 474
- Creating Advanced Scatterplots ... 475
 - Depicting groups ... 476
 - Showing correlations ... 477
- Plotting Time Series ... 478
 - Representing time on axes ... 478
 - Plotting trends over time ... 480
- Plotting Geographical Data ... 481
- Visualizing Graphs ... 483
 - Developing undirected graphs ... 484
 - Developing directed graphs ... 485

CHAPTER 5: Exploring Data Analysis ... 489

- The EDA Approach ... 490
- Defining Descriptive Statistics for Numeric Data ... 491
 - Measuring central tendency ... 492
 - Measuring variance and range ... 493
 - Working with percentiles ... 494
 - Defining measures of normality ... 494
- Counting for Categorical Data ... 495
 - Understanding frequencies ... 496
 - Creating contingency tables ... 497
- Creating Applied Visualization for EDA ... 498
 - Inspecting boxplots ... 498
 - Performing t-tests after boxplots ... 499
 - Observing parallel coordinates ... 500
 - Graphing distributions ... 501
 - Plotting scatterplots ... 502
- Understanding Correlation ... 504
 - Using covariance and correlation ... 504
 - Using nonparametric correlation ... 507
 - Considering chi-square for tables ... 507
- Modifying Data Distributions ... 508
 - Using the normal distribution ... 508
 - Creating a z-score standardization ... 509
 - Transforming other notable distributions ... 509

CHAPTER 6: Exploring Four Simple and Effective Algorithms ... 511
Guessing the Number: Linear Regression ... 512
 Defining the family of linear models ... 512
 Using more variables ... 513
 Understanding limitations and problems ... 514
Moving to Logistic Regression ... 515
 Applying logistic regression ... 516
 Considering when classes are more ... 517
Making Things as Simple as Naïve Bayes ... 518
 Finding out that Naïve Bayes isn't so naïve ... 519
 Predicting text classifications ... 521
Learning Lazily with Nearest Neighbors ... 522
 Predicting after observing neighbors ... 523
 Choosing your k parameter wisely ... 525

BOOK 8: ESSENTIALS OF MACHINE LEARNING ... 527

CHAPTER 1: Introducing How Machines Learn ... 529
Getting the Real Story about AI ... 530
 Moving beyond the hype ... 530
 Dreaming of electric sheep ... 532
 Overcoming AI fantasies ... 535
 Considering the relationship between AI and machine learning ... 538
 Considering AI and machine learning specifications ... 539
 Defining the divide between art and engineering ... 540
Learning in the Age of Big Data ... 541
 Defining big data ... 542
 Considering the sources of big data ... 543
 Specifying the role of statistics in machine learning ... 546
 Understanding the role of algorithms ... 547
 Defining what training means ... 550

CHAPTER 2: Demystifying the Math behind Machine Learning ... 553
Working with Data ... 554
 Creating a matrix ... 556
 Understanding basic operations ... 558
 Performing matrix multiplication ... 558
 Glancing at advanced matrix operations ... 561
 Using vectorization effectively ... 561
Exploring the World of Probabilities ... 563
 Operating on probabilities ... 564
 Conditioning chance by Bayes' theorem ... 565
Describing the Use of Statistics ... 568

CHAPTER 3: Descending the Right Curve 571
Interpreting Learning as Optimization 572
 Supervised learning 572
 Unsupervised learning 573
 Reinforcement learning 573
 The learning process 573
Exploring Cost Functions 576
Descending the Error Curve 578
Updating by Mini-Batch and Online 581

CHAPTER 4: Validating Machine Learning 585
Checking Out-of-Sample Errors 586
 Looking for generalization 587
Getting to Know the Limits of Bias 589
Keeping Model Complexity in Mind 591
Keeping Solutions Balanced 592
 Depicting learning curves 593
Training, Validating, and Testing 595
Resorting to Cross-Validation 596
Looking for Alternatives in Validation 597
Optimizing Cross-Validation Choices 598
 Exploring the space of hyper-parameters 599
Avoiding Sample Bias and Leakage Traps 601
 Watching out for snooping 602

BOOK 9: APPLYING MACHINE LEARNING 603

CHAPTER 1: Starting with Simple Learners 605
Discovering the Incredible Perceptron 606
 Falling short of a miracle 606
 Touching the nonseparability limit 608
Growing Greedy Classification Trees 610
 Predicting outcomes by splitting data 610
 Pruning overgrown trees 614
Taking a Probabilistic Turn 615
 Understanding Naïve Bayes 615
 Estimating response with Naïve Bayes 618

CHAPTER 2: Leveraging Similarity 623
Measuring Similarity between Vectors 624
 Understanding similarity 624
 Computing distances for learning 625

Using Distances to Locate Clusters..........................626
 Checking assumptions and expectations....................628
 Inspecting the gears of the algorithm......................629
Tuning the K-Means Algorithm..............................630
 Experimenting K-means reliability........................631
 Experimenting with how centroids converge...............634
Searching for Classification by k-Nearest Neighbors............637
Leveraging the Correct K Parameter..........................638
 Understanding the k parameter..........................638
 Experimenting with a flexible algorithm...................639

CHAPTER 3: Hitting Complexity with Neural Networks........643

Learning and Imitating from Nature..........................644
 Going forth with feed-forward............................645
 Going even deeper down the rabbit hole...................647
 Getting back with backpropagation.......................650
Struggling with Overfitting..................................653
 Understanding the problem.............................653
 Opening the black box..................................654
Introducing Deep Learning..................................657

CHAPTER 4: Resorting to Ensembles of Learners.................661

Leveraging Decision Trees...................................662
 Growing a forest of trees................................663
 Understanding the importance measures...................667
Working with Almost Random Guesses........................670
 Bagging predictors with Adaboost........................670
Boosting Smart Predictors..................................673
 Meeting again with gradient descent......................674
Averaging Different Predictors...............................676

CHAPTER 5: Real-World Applications.............................677

Classifying Images..677
 Working with a set of images.............................678
 Extracting visual features................................683
 Recognizing faces using eigenfaces.......................684
 Classifying images......................................688
Scoring Opinions and Sentiments............................691
 Introducing natural language processing..................691
 Understanding how machines read.......................692
 Processing and enhancing text...........................694
 Scraping textual data sets from the web...................699

- Handling problems with raw text 702
- Using Scoring and Classification 703
 - Performing classification tasks 704
 - Analyzing reviews from e-commerce 706
- Recommending Products and Movies 710
 - Realizing the revolution 711
 - Downloading rating data 712
 - Trudging through the MovieLens data set. 712
 - Navigating through anonymous web data 714
 - Encountering the limits of rating data 715
 - Leveraging SVD ... 716

INDEX ... 725

Introduction

The ability to read, write, and understand code has never been more important, useful, or lucrative than it is today. Computer code has forever changed our lives. Many people can't even make it through the day without interacting with something built with code. Even so, for many people, the world of coding seems complex and inaccessible. Maybe you participated in a tech-related business meeting and did not fully understand the conversation. Perhaps you tried to build a web page for your family and friends, but ran into problems displaying pictures or aligning text. Maybe you're even intimidated by the unrecognizable words on the covers of books about coding, words such as HTML, CSS, JavaScript, Python, or Ruby.

If you've previously been in these situations, then *Coding All-in-One For Dummies* is for you. This book explains basic concepts so you can participate in technical conversations and ask the right questions, and it goes even further than *Coding For Dummies* by covering additional topics in data science, machine learning, and coding careers. Don't worry — this book assumes you're starting with little to no previous coding knowledge, and I haven't tried to cram every possible coding concept into these pages. Additionally, I encourage you here to learn by doing and by actually creating your own programs. Instead of a website, imagine that you want to build a house. You could spend eight years studying to be an architect, or you could start today by learning a little bit about foundations and framing. This book kick-starts your coding journey today.

The importance of coding is ever-increasing. As author and technologist Douglas Rushkoff famously said, "program or be programmed." When humans invented languages and then the alphabet, people learned to listen and speak, and then read and write. In our increasingly digital world, it's important to learn not just how to use programs but also how to make them. For example, observe this transition in music. For over a century, music labels decided what songs the public could listen to and purchase. In 2005, three coders created YouTube, which allowed anyone to release songs. Today more songs have been uploaded to YouTube than have been released by all the record labels combined in the past century.

Accompanying this book are examples at www.codecademy.com, whose exercises are one of the easiest ways to learn how to code without installing or downloading anything. The Codecademy website includes examples and exercises from this book, along with projects and examples for additional practice.

About This Book

This book is designed for readers with little to no coding experience, and gives an overview of programming to non-programmers. In plain English, you learn how code is used to create web programs, who makes those programs, and the processes they use. The topics covered include

- » Explaining what coding is and answering the common questions related to code
- » Building basic websites using the three most common languages: HTML, CSS, and JavaScript
- » Surveying other programming languages such as Python
- » Creating an application using HTML, CSS, and JavaScript
- » Analyzing data using machine learning algorithms and techniques
- » Exploring coding careers paths and different ways to learn how to code

As you read this book, keep the following in mind:

- » The book can be read from beginning to end, but feel free to skip around if you like. If a topic interests you, start there. You can always return to the previous chapters, if necessary.
- » At some point, you will get stuck, and the code you write will not work as intended. Do not fear! There are many resources to help you, including support forums, others on the Internet, and me! Using Twitter, you can send me a public message at @nikhilgabraham with the hashtag #codingFD. Additionally, you can sign up for book updates and explanations for changes to programming language commands by visiting http://tinyletter.com/codingfordummies.
- » Code in the book will appear in a monospaced font like this: <h1>Hi there!</h1>.

Foolish Assumptions

I do not make many assumptions about you, the reader, but I do make a few.

I assume you don't have previous programming experience. To follow along, then, you only need to be able to read, type, and follow directions. I try to explain as many concepts as possible using examples and analogies you already know.

I assume you have a computer running the latest version of Google Chrome. The examples in the book have been tested and optimized for the Chrome browser, which is available for free from Google. Even so, the examples may also work in the latest version of Firefox. Using Internet Explorer for the examples in this book, however, is discouraged.

I assume you have access to an Internet connection. Some of the examples in the book can be done without an Internet connection, but most require one so that you can access and complete the exercises on www.codecademy.com.

For the books on data analysis and machine learning, I assume you are able to download and install the Python programming language and associated programming libraries, both of which are available for free. I also assume you have some math background and understand how algorithms work.

Icons Used in This Book

Here are the icons used in the book to flag text that should be given extra attention or that can be skipped.

This icon flags useful information or explains a shortcut to help you understand a concept.

This icon explains technical details about the concept being explained. The details might be informative or interesting, but are not essential to your understanding of the concept at this stage.

Try not to forget the material marked with this icon. It signals an important concept or process that you should keep in mind.

Watch out! This icon flags common mistakes and problems that can be avoided if you heed the warning.

Beyond the Book

A lot of extra content that you won't find in this book is available at www.dummies.com. Go online to find the following:

- **The source code for the examples in this book:** You can find it at

 www.dummies.com/go/codingaiodownloads.

 The source code is organized by chapter. The best way to work with a chapter is to download all the source code for it at one time.

- **The links to the Codecademy and other exercises:** You can find these at

 www.dummies.com/go/codingaiolinks.

- **Cheat Sheet:** You can find a list of common HTML, CSS, and JavaScript commands, among other useful information.

 To view this book's Cheat Sheet, simply go to www.dummies.com and search for "Coding For Dummies All-in-One Cheat Sheet" in the Search box.

- **Updates:** Code and specifications are constantly changing, so the commands and syntax that work today may not work tomorrow. You can find any updates or corrections by visiting

 http://tinyletter.com/codingfordummies.

Where to Go from Here

All right, now that all the administrative stuff is out of the way, it's time to get started. You can totally do this. Congratulations on taking your first step into the world of coding!

1
Getting Started with Coding

Contents at a Glance

CHAPTER 1: What Is Coding? .. 7
 Defining What Code Is .. 8
 Understanding What Coding Can Do for You 9
 Surveying the Types of Programming Languages 13
 Taking a Tour of a Web App Built with Code 16

CHAPTER 2: Programming for the Web 19
 Displaying Web Pages on Your Desktop and Mobile Device 20
 Coding Web Applications 26
 Coding Mobile Applications 28

CHAPTER 3: Becoming a Programmer 33
 Writing Code Using a Process 33
 Picking Tools for the Job 38

IN THIS CHAPTER

» Seeing what code is and what it can do

» Touring your first program using code

» Understanding programming languages used to write code

Chapter 1
What Is Coding?

"A million dollars isn't cool, you know what's cool? A billion dollars."
— SEAN PARKER, *The Social Network*

Every week the newspapers report on another technology company that has raised capital or sold for millions of dollars. Sometimes, in the case of companies like Instagram, WhatsApp, and Uber, the amount in the headline is for billions of dollars. These articles may pique your curiosity, and you may want to see how code is used to build the applications that experience these financial outcomes. Alternatively, your interests may lie closer to work. Perhaps you work in an industry in decline, like print media, or in a function that technology is rapidly changing, like marketing. Whether you are thinking about switching to a new career or improving your current career, understanding computer programming or "coding" can help with your professional development. Finally, your interest may be more personal — perhaps you have an idea, a burning desire to create something, a website or an app, to solve a problem you have experienced, and you know reading and writing code is the first step to building your solution. Whatever your motivation, this book will shed light on coding and programmers, and help you think of both not as mysterious and complex but approachable and something you can do yourself.

In this chapter, you will understand what code is, what industries are affected by computer software, the different types of programming languages used to write code, and take a tour of a web app built with code.

CHAPTER 1 **What Is Coding?** 7

Defining What Code Is

Computer code is not a cryptic activity reserved for geniuses and oracles. In fact, in a few minutes you will be writing some computer code yourself! Most computer code performs a range of tasks in our lives from the mundane to the extraordinary. Code runs our traffic lights and pedestrian signals, the elevators in our buildings, the cell phone towers that transmit our phone signals, and the space ships headed for outer space. We also interact with code on a more personal level, on our phones and computers, and usually to check email or the weather.

Following instructions

Computer code is a set of statements, like sentences in English, and each statement directs the computer to perform a single step or instruction. Each of these steps is very precise, and followed to the letter. For example, if you are in a restaurant and ask a waiter to direct you to the restroom, he might say, "head to the back, and try the middle door." To a computer, these directions are so vague as to be unusable. Instead, if the waiter gave instructions to you as if you were a computer program he might say, "From this table, walk northeast for 40 paces. Then turn right 90 degrees, walk 5 paces, turn left 90 degrees, and walk 5 paces. Open the door directly in front of you, and enter the restroom." Figure 1-1 shows lines of code from the popular game, Pong. Do not worry about trying to understand what every single line does, and don't feel intimated. You will soon be reading and writing your own code.

```
1   launchPong(function () {
2       function colour_random() {
3           var num = Math.floor(Math.random() * Math.pow(2, 24));
4           return '#' + ('00000' + num.toString(16)).substr(-6);
5       }
6
7
8       pongSettings.ball.size = 15;
9       pongSettings.ball.color = colour_random();
10      pongSettings.ball.velocity[0] = 15;
11      pongSettings.ball.velocity[1] = 15;
12
13  });
14
15
```

FIGURE 1-1: Computer code from the game Pong.

One rough way to measure a program's complexity is to count its statements or lines of code. Basic applications like the Pong game have 5,000 lines of code, while more complex applications like Facebook currently have over 10 million lines of code. Whether few or many lines of code, the computer follows each instruction exactly and effortlessly, never tiring like the waiter might when asked the hundredth time for the location of the restroom.

TIP

Be careful of only using lines of code as a measure for a program's complexity. Just like when writing in English, 100 well written lines of code can perform the same functionality as 1,000 poorly written lines of code.

Writing code with some Angry Birds

If you've never written code before, now is your chance to try! Go to http://csedweek.org/learn, where you will see a beginner student experience, scroll down the page, and click the tile labeled "Write Your First Computer Program," the link with the Angry Birds icon, as shown in Figure 1-2. This tutorial is meant for those with no previous computer programming experience, and it introduces the basic building blocks used by all computer programs. *You can also click the tile labeled "Star Wars: Building a Galaxy with Code."* The most important takeaway from these tutorials is to understand that computer programs use code to literally and exactly tell the computer to execute a set of instructions.

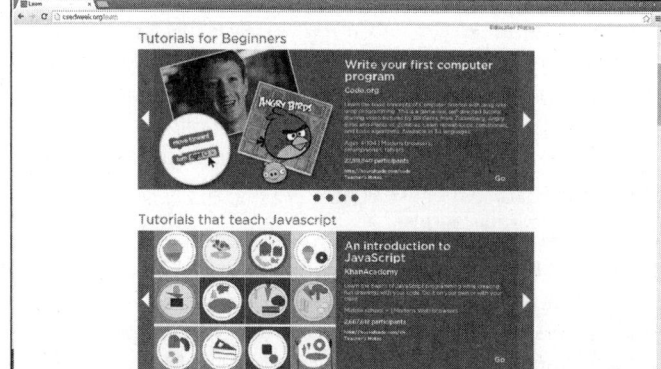

FIGURE 1-2: Write your first computer program with a gamelike tutorial using Angry Birds.

TIP

Computer Science Education Week is an annual program dedicated to elevating the profile of computer science during one week in December. In the past, President Obama, Bill Gates, basketball player Chris Bosh, and singer Shakira, among others, have supported and encouraged people from the United States and around the world to participate.

Understanding What Coding Can Do for You

Coding can be used to perform tasks and solve problems that you experience every day. The "everyday" situations in which programs or apps can provide assistance

CHAPTER 1 **What Is Coding?** 9

continue to grow at an exponential pace, but this was not always the case. The rise of web applications, Internet connectivity, and mobile phones inserted software programs into daily life, and lowered the barrier for you to become a creator, solving personal and professional problems with code.

Eating the world with software

In 2011, Marc Andreessen, creator of Netscape Navigator and now venture capitalist, noted that "software is eating the world." He predicted that new software companies would disrupt existing tech companies at a rapid pace. Traditionally, code-powered software used on desktops and laptops had to first be installed, and then you had to supply data to the program. However, three trends have dramatically increased the use of code in everyday life:

» **Web-based software:** This software operates in the browser without requiring installation. For example, to check your email, you previously had to install an email client either by downloading the software or from a CD-ROM. Sometimes issues arose when the software wasn't available for your operating system, or conflicted with your operating system version. Hotmail, a web-based email client, rose to popularity, in part, because it allowed users visiting www.hotmail.com to instantly check their email without worrying about installation issues or software incompatibility. Web applications increased consumer appetite to try more applications, and developers in turn were incentivized to write more applications.

» **Internet broadband connectivity:** Broadband connectivity has increased, providing a fast Internet connection to more people in the last few years than in the previous decade. Today more than 2 billion people can access web-based software, up from approximately 50 million only a decade ago.

» **Mobile phones:** Today's smartphones bring programs with you wherever you go, and help supply data to programs. Many software programs became more useful when accessed on-the-go than when limited to a desktop computer. For instance, use of maps applications greatly increased thanks to mobile phones, which makes sense, because users need directions the most when lost, not just when planning a trip at home on the computer. In addition, through GPS technology, mobile phones are equipped with sensors that measure and supply data to programs like orientation, acceleration, and current location. Now instead of having to input all the data to programs yourself, mobile devices can help. For instance, a fitness application like RunKeeper doesn't require you to input start and end times in order to keep track of your runs. You can press Start at the beginning of your run, and the phone will automatically track your distance, speed, and time.

The combination of these trends have created software companies that have upended incumbents in almost every industry, especially those typically immune to technology. Here are some notable examples:

- **Airbnb:** Airbnb is a peer-to-peer lodging company that owns no rooms, yet books more nights than the Hilton and Intercontinental, the largest hotel chains in the world. (See Figure 1-3.)
- **Uber:** Uber is a car transportation company that owns no vehicles, books more trips, and has more drivers in the largest 200 cities than any other car or taxi service.
- **Groupon:** Groupon, the daily deals company, generated almost $1 billion after just two years in business, growing faster than any other company in history, let alone any other traditional direct marketing company.

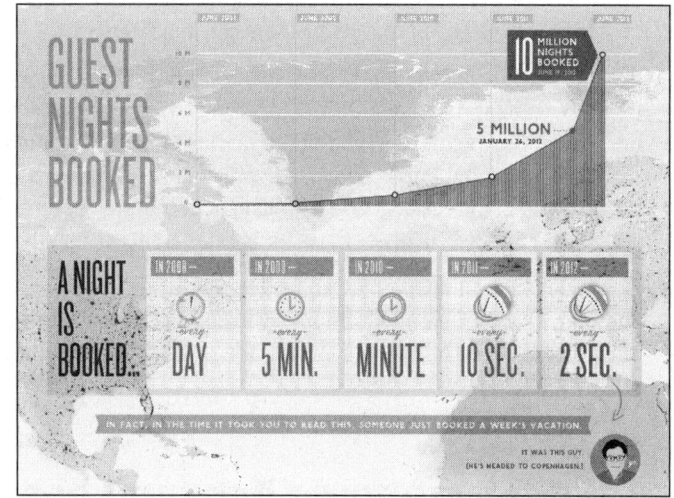

FIGURE 1-3: Airbnb booked 5 million nights after 3.5 years, and its next 5 million nights 6 months later.

Coding on the job

Coding can be useful in the workplace as well. Outside the technology sector, coding in the workplace is common for some professions like financial traders, economists, and scientists. However, for most professionals outside the technology sector, coding is just beginning to penetrate the workplace, and gradually starting to increase in relevance. Here are areas where coding is playing a larger role on the job:

- **Advertising:** Spend is shifting from print and TV to digital campaigns, and search engine advertising and optimization rely on keywords to bring visitors

to websites. Advertisers who understand code see successful keywords used by competitors, and use that data to create more effective campaigns.

» **Marketing:** When promoting products, personalizing communication is one strategy that often increases results. Marketers who code can query customer databases and create personalized communications that include customer names and products tailored to specific interests.

» **Sales:** The sales process always starts with leads. Salespeople who code retrieve their own leads from web pages and directories and then sort and quantify those leads.

TIP

Retrieving information by copying text on web pages and in directories is referred to as *scraping*.

» **Design:** After creating a web page or a digital design, designers must persuade other designers and eventually developers to actually program their drawings into a product. Designers who code can more easily bring their designs to life and can more effectively advocate for specific designs by creating working prototypes that others can interact with.

» **Public relations:** Companies constantly measure how customers and the public react to announcements and news. For instance, if a celebrity spokesperson for a company does or says something offensive, should the company dump the celebrity? Public relations people who code query social media networks like Twitter or Facebook and analyze hundreds of thousands of individual messages in order to understand market sentiment.

» **Operations:** Additional profit can be generated, in part, by analyzing a company's costs. Operations people who code write programs to try millions of combinations in an attempt to optimize packaging methods, loading routines, and delivery routes.

Scratching your own itch (and becoming rich and famous)

Using code built by others and coding in the workplace may cause you to think of problems you personally face that you could solve with code of your own. You may have an idea for a social network website, a better fitness app, or something new altogether. The path from idea to functioning prototype used by others involves a good amount of time and work, but might be more achievable than you think. For example, take Coffitivity, a productivity website that streams ambient coffee shop sounds to create white noise. The website was created by two people who had just learned how to program a few months prior. Shortly after Coffitivity launched, *Time* magazine named the website as one of 50 Best Websites of 2013, and the *Wall Street Journal* also reviewed the website. While not every startup or app will

initially receive this much media coverage, it can be helpful to know what is possible when a solution really solves a problem.

Having a goal, like a website or app you want to build, is one of the best ways to learn how to code. When facing a difficult bug or a hard concept, the idea of bringing your website to life will provide the motivation you need to keep going. Just as important, do not learn how to code to become rich and famous, as the probability of your website or app becoming successful is largely due to factors out of your control.

TIP

The characteristics that make a website or app addictive are described using the "hook model" at http://techcrunch.com/2012/03/04/how-to-manufacture-desire. Products are usually made by companies, and the characteristics of an enduring company are described at http://www.sequoiacap.com/grove/posts/ya16/elements-of-enduring-companies, which is based on a review of companies funded by Sequoia, one of the most successful venture capital firms in the world and an early investor in Apple, Google, and PayPal.

Surveying the Types of Programming Languages

Code comes in different flavors called *programming languages.* Some popular programing languages are shown in Figure 1-4.

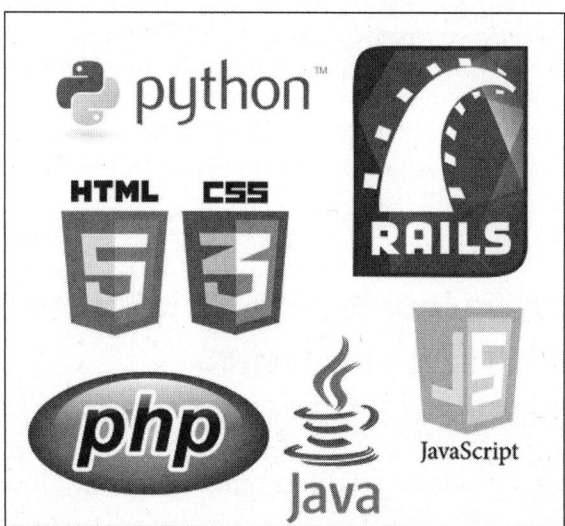

FIGURE 1-4: Some popular programming languages.

CHAPTER 1 **What Is Coding?** 13

You can think of programming languages as being similar to spoken languages because they both share many of the same characteristics, such as the following:

» **Functionality across languages:** Programming languages can all create the same functionality similar to how spoken languages can all express the same objects, phrases, and emotions.

» **Syntax and structure:** Commands in programming languages can overlap just like words in spoken languages overlap. To output text to a screen in Python or Ruby, you use the Print command, just like *imprimer* and *imprimir* are the verbs for "print" in French and Spanish.

» **Natural lifespan:** Programming languages are "born" when a programmer thinks of a new or easier way to express a computational concept. If other programmers agree, they adopt the language for their own programs, and the programming language spreads. However, just like Latin or Aramaic, if the programming language is not adopted by other programmers or a better language comes along, then the programming language slowly dies from lack of use.

Despite these similarities, programming languages also differ from spoken languages in a few key ways:

» **One creator:** Unlike spoken languages, programming languages can be created by one person in a short period of time, sometimes in just a few days.

Popular languages with a single creator include JavaScript (Brendan Eich), Python (Guido van Rossum), and Ruby (Yukihiro Matsumoto).

» **Written in English:** Unlike spoken languages (except, of course, English), almost all programming languages are written in English. Whether they're programming in HTML, JavaScript, Python, or Ruby, Brazilian, French, or Chinese, almost all programmers use the same English keywords and syntax in their code. Some non-English programming languages do exist, such as languages in Hindi or Arabic, but none of these programming languages are widespread or mainstream.

Comparing low-level and high-level programming languages

One way to classify programming languages is as either low-level languages or high-level languages. Low-level languages interact directly with the computer processor or CPU, are capable of performing very basic commands, and are generally hard to read. Machine code, one example of a low-level language, uses

code that consists of just two numbers, 0 and 1. Figure 1-5 shows an example of machine code. Assembly language, another low-level language, uses keywords to perform basic commands, such as read data, move data, and store data.

FIGURE 1-5: Machine code consists of 0s and 1s.

By contrast, high-level languages use natural language, so it is easier for people to read and write. Once code is written in a high-level language, like C++, Python, or Ruby, an interpreter or compiler must translate this high-level language into low-level code that a computer can understand.

Contrasting compiled code and interpreted code

Interpreted languages are considered more portable than compiled languages, while compiled languages execute faster than interpreted languages. However, the speed advantage compiled languages have is starting to fade in importance as improving processor speeds make performance differences between interpreted and compiled languages negligible.

High-level programming languages like JavaScript, Python, and Ruby are interpreted. For these languages, the interpreter executes the program directly, translating each statement *one line at a time* into machine code. High-level programming languages like C++, COBOL, and Visual Basic are compiled. For these languages, after the code is written, a compiler translates *all* the code into machine code, and an executable file is created. This executable file is then distributed via the Internet, CD-ROMs, or other media and run. Software you install on your computer, like Microsoft Windows or Mac OS X, are coded using compiled languages, usually C or C++.

Programming for the web

Software accessible on websites is gradually starting to take over installed software. Think of the last time you downloaded and installed software for your computer — you may not even remember! Installed software like Windows Media Player and Winamp that play music and movies have been replaced with websites like YouTube and Netflix. Traditional installed word processor and spreadsheet software like Microsoft Word and Excel is starting to see competition from web software like Google Docs and Sheets. Google is even selling laptops called Chromebooks that contain no installed software, and instead rely exclusively on web software to provide functionality.

The remainder of this book focuses on developing and creating web software, not just because web software is growing rapidly but also because programs for the web are easier to learn and launch than traditional installed software.

Taking a Tour of a Web App Built with Code

With all this talk of programming, let us actually take a look at a web application built with code. Yelp.com is a website that allows you to search and find crowd-sourced reviews for local businesses like restaurants, nightlife, and shopping. As shown in Figure 1-6, Yelp did not always look as polished as it does today, but its purpose has stayed relatively constant over the years.

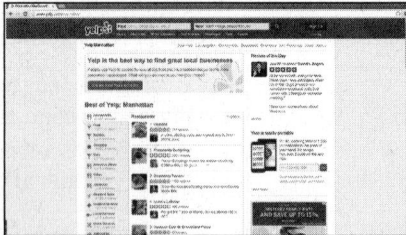

FIGURE 1-6:
Yelp's website in 2004 and in 2014.

Defining the app's purpose and scope

Once you understand an app's purpose, you can identify a few actionable tasks a user should be able to perform to achieve that purpose. Regardless of design, the Yelp's website has always allowed users to do the following:

- » Search local listings based on venue type and location.
- » Browse listing results for address, hours, reviews, photos, and location on a map.

Successful web applications generally allow for completing only a few key tasks when using the app. Adding too many features to an app is called scope *creep*, which dilutes the strength of the existing features, and so is avoided by most developers. For example, it took Yelp, which has 30,000 restaurant reviews, exactly one decade after its founding to allow users to make reservations at those restaurants directly on its website.

REMEMBER

Whether you're using or building an app, have a clear sense of the app's purpose.

Standing on the shoulders of giants

Developers make strategic choices and decide which parts of the app to code themselves, and on which parts of the app to use code built by others. Developers often turn to third-party providers for functionality that is either not core to the business or not an area of strength. In this way, apps stand on the shoulders of others, and benefit from others who have come before and solved challenging problems.

Yelp, for instance, displays local listing reviews and places every listing on a map. While Yelp solicits the reviews and writes the code to display basic listing data, it is Google, as shown in Figure 1-7, that develops the maps used on Yelp's website. By using Google's map application instead of building its own, Yelp created the first version of the app with fewer engineers than otherwise would have been required.

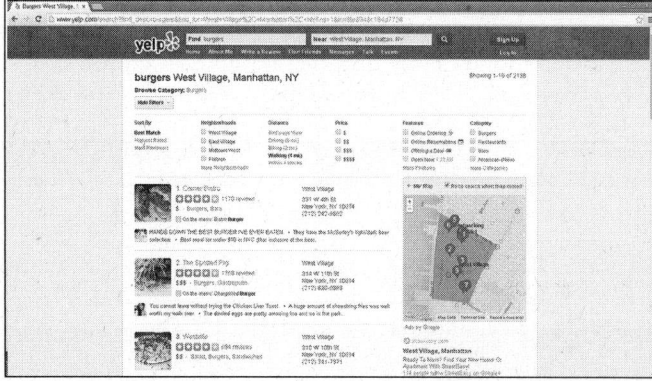

FIGURE 1-7: Google maps used for the Yelp web application.

CHAPTER 1 **What Is Coding?** 17

IN THIS CHAPTER

» Seeing the code powering websites you use every day

» Understanding the languages used to make websites

» Finding out how applications are created for mobile devices

Chapter 2
Programming for the Web

"To think you can start something in your college dorm room . . . and build something a billion people use is crazy to think about. It's amazing."
— MARK ZUCKERBERG

Programming for the web allows you to reach massive audiences around the world faster than ever before. Four years after its 2004 launch, Facebook had 100 million users, and by 2012 it had over a billion. By contrast, it took desktop software years to reach even one million people. These days, mobile phones are increasing the reach of web applications. Although roughly 300 million desktop computers are sold every year, almost two billion mobile phones are sold in that time — and the number is steadily increasing.

In this chapter, you discover how websites are displayed on your computer or mobile device. I introduce the languages used to program websites and show you how mobile-device applications are made.

Displaying Web Pages on Your Desktop and Mobile Device

On desktop computers and mobile devices, web pages are displayed by applications called *browsers*. The most popular web browsers include Google Chrome, Mozilla Firefox (formerly Netscape Navigator), Microsoft Internet Explorer, and Apple Safari. Until now, you have likely interacted with websites you visit as an obedient user, and followed the rules the website has created by pointing and clicking when allowed. The first step to becoming a producer and programmer of websites is to peel back the web page, and see and play with the code underneath it all.

Hacking your favorite news website

What's your favorite news website? By following a few steps, you can see and even modify the code used to create that website. (No need to worry; you won't be breaking any rules by following these instructions.)

Although you can use almost any modern browser to inspect a website's code, these instructions assume you're using the Google Chrome browser. Install the latest version by going to www.google.com/chrome/browser.

To "hack" your favorite news website, follow these steps:

1. **Open your favorite news website using the Chrome browser.**

 In this example, I use www.huffingtonpost.com.

2. **Place your mouse cursor over any static fixed headline and right-click once, which opens a contextual menu.**

3. **Then left-click once on the Inspect Element menu choice. (See Figure 2-1.)**

 If using a Macintosh computer, you can right-click by holding down the Control key and clicking once.

 The Developer Tools panel opens at the bottom of your browser. This panel shows you the code used to create this web page! Highlighted in blue is the specific code used to create the headline where you originally put your mouse cursor. (See Figure 2-2.)

 Look at the left edge of the highlighted code. If you see a right-pointing arrow, left-click once on the arrow to expand the code.

FIGURE 2-1: Right-click a headline and select Inspect Element from the menu that appears.

FIGURE 2-2: The blue highlighted code is used to create the web page headline.

4. **Scan the highlighted code carefully for the text of your headline. When you find it, double-click the headline text.**

 This allows you to edit the headline. (See Figure 2-3.)

WARNING

 Be careful not to click anything that begins with http, which is the headline link. Clicking a headline link will open a new window or tab and loads the link.

5. **Insert your name in the headline and press Enter.**

 Your name now appears on the actual web page. (See Figure 2-4.) Enjoy your newfound fame!

CHAPTER 2 **Programming for the Web** 21

FIGURE 2-3: Double-click the headline text to edit it with your own headline.

TIP

If you were unable to edit the headline after following these steps, visit `http://goggles.webmaker.org` for an easier, more guided tutorial. It's a foolproof teaching aid that shows that any code on the Internet can be edited and modified. On that page, follow the instructions to add the bookmark to your web browser bookmark toolbar, and click the "Sample activity page" button to try a step-by-step tutorial. Try again to hack your favorite news website by following the "Remix the News" activity instructions.

FIGURE 2-4: You successfully changed the headline of a major news website.

If you successfully completed the preceding steps and changed the original headline, it's time for your 15 minutes of fame to come to an end. Reload the web page, and the original headline reappears. What just happened? Did your changes appear to everyone visiting the web page? And why did your edited headline disappear?

To answer these questions, you first need to understand how the Internet delivers web pages to your computer.

Understanding how the World Wide Web works

After you type a URL, such as huffingtonpost.com, into your browser, the following steps happen behind the scenes in the seconds before your page loads (see Figure 2-5):

1. Your computer sends your request for the web page to a router. The router distributes Internet access throughout your home or workplace.

2. The router passes your request on to your Internet service provider (ISP).

 In the United States, your ISP is a company like Comcast, Time Warner, AT&T, or Verizon.

3. Your ISP then converts the words and characters in your URL — "huffington-post.com," in my example — into a numerical address called the *Internet Protocol address* (or, more commonly, *IP address*).

 An IP address is a set of four numbers separated by periods (such as 192.168.1.1). Just like your physical address, this number is unique, and every computer has one. Your ISP has a digital phone book, similar to a physical phonebook, called a *domain name server* that's used to convert text URLs into IP addresses.

4. With the IP address located, your ISP knows which server on the Internet to forward your request to, and your personal IP address is included in this request.

5. The website server receives your request and sends a copy of the web page code to your computer for your browser to display.

6. Your web browser renders the code onto the screen.

When you edited the website code using the Developer Tools, you modified only the copy of the website code that exists on your computer, so only you could see the change. When you reloaded the page, you started Steps 1 through 6 again, and retrieved a fresh copy of the code from the server, overwriting any changes you made on your computer.

TIP

You may have heard of a software tool called an *ad blocker*. Ad blockers work by editing the local copy of website code, as you just did, to remove website advertisements. Ad blockers are controversial because websites use advertising revenue to pay for operating costs. If ad blockers continue rising in popularity, ad revenue could dry up, and websites may demand that readers pay to see their content.

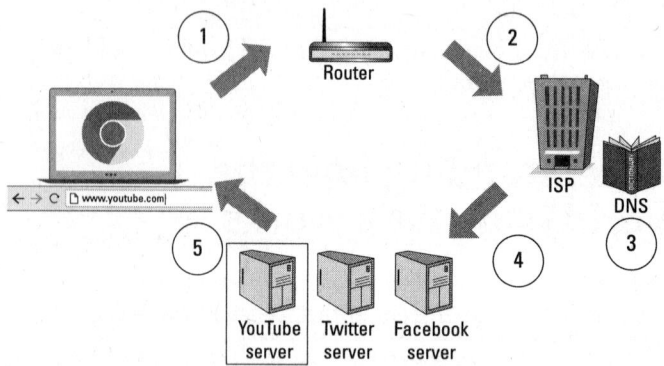

FIGURE 2-5: Steps followed to deliver a website to your browser.

Watching out for your front end and back end

Now that you know how your browser accesses websites, let us dive deeper into the way the actual website is constructed. As shown in Figure 2-6, the code for websites, and for programs in general, can be divided into four categories, according to the code's function:

- **Appearance:** Appearance is the visible part of the website, including content layout and any applied styling, such as font size, font typeface, and image size. This category is called the *front end* and is created using languages like HTML, CSS, and JavaScript.

- **Logic:** Logic determines what content to show and when. For example, a New Yorker accessing a news website should see New York weather, whereas Chicagoans accessing the same site should see Chicago weather. This category is part of the group called the *back end* and is created using languages like Ruby, Python, and PHP. These back end languages can modify the HTML, CSS, and JavaScript that is displayed to the user.

- **Storage:** Storage saves any data generated by the site and its users. User-generated content, preferences, and profile data must be stored for retrieval later. This category is part of the back end and is stored in databases like MongoDB and MySQL.

- **Infrastructure:** Infrastructure delivers the website from the server to you, the client machine. When the infrastructure is properly configured, no one notices it, but it can become noticeable when a website becomes unavailable because of high traffic from events like presidential elections, the Super Bowl, and natural disasters.

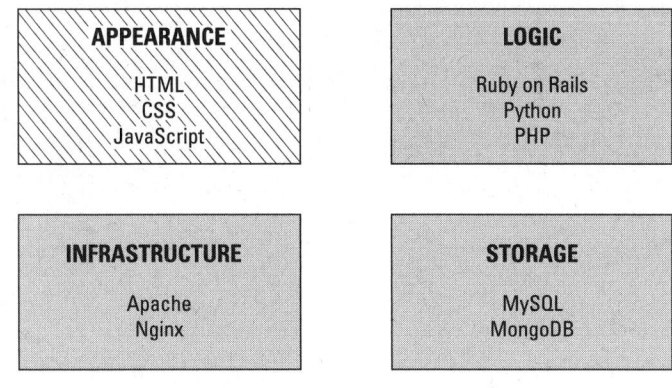

FIGURE 2-6: Every website is made up of four different parts.

Usually, website developers specialize in one or at most two of these categories. For example, an engineer might really understand the front end and logic languages or specialize only in databases. Website developers have strengths and specializations, and outside these areas their expertise is limited, much in the same way that Jerry Seinfeld, a terrific comedy writer, would likely make a terrible romance novelist.

TECHNICAL STUFF

The rare website developer proficient in all four categories is referred to as a *full stack developer*. Usually, smaller companies hire full stack developers, whereas larger companies require the expertise that comes with specialization.

Defining web and mobile applications

Web applications are websites you visit using a web browser on any device. Websites optimized for use on a mobile device, like a phone or tablet, are called *mobile web applications*. By contrast, *native mobile applications* cannot be viewed using a web browser. Instead, native mobile applications are downloaded from an app store like the Apple App Store or Google Play and are designed to run on a specific device such as an iPhone or an Android tablet. Historically, desktop computers outnumbered and outsold mobile devices, but recently two major trends in mobile usage have occurred:

>> In 2014, people with mobile devices outnumbered people with desktop computers. This gap is projected to continue increasing, as shown in Figure 2-7.

>> Mobile-device users spend 80 percent of their time using native mobile applications and 20 percent of their time browsing mobile websites.

CHAPTER 2 **Programming for the Web** 25

FIGURE 2-7: Mobile devices have increased at a faster pace than desktops.

The increase in mobile devices happened so quickly over the past 10 years that many companies are becoming "mobile first," designing and developing the mobile version of their applications before the desktop version. WhatsApp and Instagram, two popular mobile applications, first built mobile applications, which continue to have more functionality than their regular websites.

Coding Web Applications

Web applications are easier to build than mobile applications, require little to no additional software to develop and test, and run on all devices, including desktops, laptops, and mobile devices. Although mobile applications can perform many common web-application tasks, such as email, some tasks are still easier to perform using web applications. For example, booking travel is easier using web applications, especially since the steps necessary — reviewing flights, hotels, and rental cars, and then purchasing all three — are best achieved with multiple windows, access to a calendar, and the entry of substantial personal and payment information.

The programming languages used to code basic web applications, further defined in the following sections, include HTML (Hypertext Markup Language), CSS (Cascading Style Sheets), and JavaScript. Additional features can be added to these websites using languages like Python, Ruby, or PHP.

Starting with HTML, CSS, and JavaScript

Simple websites, such as the one shown in Figure 2-8, are coded using HTML, CSS, and JavaScript:

» HTML is used to place text on the page.

» CSS is used to style that text.

>> JavaScript is used to add interactive effects like the Twitter or Facebook Share button that allows you to share content on social networks and updates the number of other people who have shared the same content.

Websites conveying mainly static, unchanging information are often coded only in these three languages. You read about each of these languages in Book 3.

FIGURE 2-8:
The lindaliukas.fi website, built with HTML, CSS, and JavaScript.

Adding logic with Python, Ruby, or PHP

Websites with more advanced functionality, such as user accounts, file uploads, and e-commerce, typically require a programming language to implement these features. Although Python, Ruby, and PHP aren't the only programming languages these sites can use, they are among the most popular ones. This popularity means that there are large online communities of online developers who program in these languages, freely post code that you can copy to build common features, and host public online discussions that you can read for solutions to common issues.

Each of these languages also has popular and well-documented frameworks. A *framework* is a collection of generic components, such as user accounts and authentication schemes that are reused frequently, allowing developers to build, test, and launch websites more quickly.

TIP

Think of a framework as being similar to the collection of templates that comes with a word processor. You can design your resume, greeting card, or calendar from scratch, but using the built-in template for each of these document types helps you create your document faster and with greater consistency.

Popular frameworks for these languages include

- Django and Flask for Python
- Rails and Sinatra for Ruby
- Zend and Laravel for PHP

Coding Mobile Applications

Mobile applications are hot topics today, in part because mobile apps such as WhatsApp and Instagram were acquired for billions of dollars, and mobile app companies like Rovio, makers of Angry Birds, and King Digital, makers of Candy Crush, generate annual revenues of hundreds of millions to billions of dollars.

When coding mobile applications, developers can build in one of the following ways:

- Mobile web applications, using HTML, CSS, and JavaScript.
- Native mobile applications using a specific language. For example, Apple devices are programmed using Objective-C or Swift, and Android devices are programmed using Java.

The choice between these two options may seem simple, but there are a few factors at play. Consider the following:

- Companies developing mobile web applications must make sure the mobile version works across different browsers, different screen sizes, and even different manufacturers, such as Apple, Samsung, RIM, and Microsoft. This requirement results in thousands of possible phone combinations, which can greatly increase the complexity of testing needed before launch. Native mobile apps run on only one phone platform, so there is less variation to account for.
- Despite running on only one platform, native mobile apps are more expensive and take longer to build than mobile web apps.
- Some developers have reported that mobile web applications have more performance issues and load more slowly than native mobile applications.

- » As mentioned earlier, users are spending more time using native mobile applications and less time using browser-based mobile web apps.

- » Native mobile apps are distributed through an app store, which may require approval from the app store owner, whereas mobile web apps are accessible from any web browser. For example, Apple has a strict approval policy and takes up to six days to approve an app for inclusion in the Apple App Store, while Google has a more relaxed approval policy and takes two hours to approve an app.

TECHNICAL STUFF

In one famous example of an app rejected from an app store, Apple blocked Google from launching the Google Voice app in the Apple App Store because it overlapped with Apple's own phone functionality. Google responded by creating a mobile web app accessible from any browser, and Apple could do nothing to block it.

If you're making this choice, consider the complexity of your application. Simple applications, like schedules or menus, can likely be cheaply developed with a mobile web app, whereas more complex applications, like messaging and social networking, may benefit from having a native mobile app. Even well-established technology companies struggle with this choice. Initially, Facebook and LinkedIn created mobile web applications, but both have since shifted to primarily promoting and supporting native mobile apps. The companies cited better speed, memory management, and developer tools as some of the reasons for making the switch.

Building mobile web apps

Although any website can be viewed with a mobile browser, those websites not optimized for mobile devices look a little weird; that is, they look as though the regular website font size and image dimensions are decreased to fit on a mobile screen. (See Figure 2-9.) By contrast, websites optimized for mobile devices have fonts that are readable, images that scale to the mobile device screen, and a vertical layout suitable for a mobile phone.

Building mobile web apps is done using HTML, CSS, and JavaScript. CSS controls the website appearance across devices based on the screen width. Screens with a small width, such as those on phones, are assigned one vertically based layout, whereas screens with a larger width, like those on tablets, are assigned a horizontally based layout. Because mobile web apps are accessed from the browser and aren't installed on the user's device, these web apps can't send push notifications (alerts) to your phone, run in the background while the browser is minimized, or communicate with other apps.

 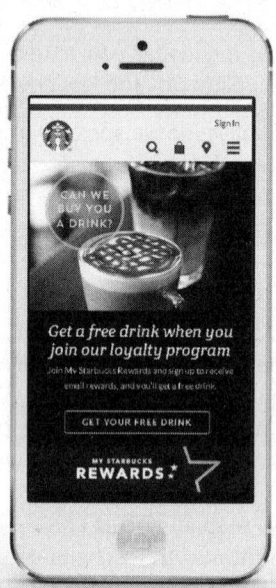

FIGURE 2-9: Left: starbucks.com not optimized for mobile. Right: starbucks.com optimized for mobile.

Although you can write HTML, CSS, and JavaScript for your mobile web app from scratch, mobile web frameworks allow you to develop from a base of prewritten code, much like the frameworks for programming languages I mention earlier. These mobile web frameworks include a collection of generic components that are reused frequently and allow developers to build, test, and launch websites more quickly. Twitter's Bootstrap is one such mobile web framework, which I introduce in Book 4, Chapter 1.

Building native mobile apps

Native mobile apps can be faster and more reliable and can look more polished than mobile web apps, as shown in Figure 2-10. Built using Java for use on Android devices, and Objective-C or Swift for use on Apple devices (iOS), native mobile apps must be uploaded to an app store, which may require approvals. The main benefit of an app store is its centralized distribution, and the app may be featured in parts of the app store that can drive downloads. Also, since native mobile applications are programs that are installed on the mobile device, they can be used in more situations without an Internet connection. Finally, and most importantly, users appear to prefer native mobile apps to mobile web apps by a wide margin, one that continues to increase.

Native mobile apps can take advantage of features that run in the background while the app is minimized, such as push notifications, and communicate with other apps, and these features aren't available when you're creating a mobile web app.

Additionally, native mobile apps perform better when handling graphics-intensive applications, such as games. To be clear, native mobile apps offer better performance and a greater number of features, but they require longer development times and are more expensive to build than mobile web apps.

FIGURE 2-10: Left: facebook.com native mobile app. Right: facebook.com mobile web app.

There is an alternative way to build a native mobile app—a hybrid approach that involves building an app using HTML, CSS, and JavaScript, packaging that code using a "wrapper," and then running the code inside a native mobile app container. The most popular "wrapper" is a product called PhoneGap, and it recognizes specific JavaScript commands that allow access to device-level functionality that's normally inaccessible to mobile web applications. After one version of the app is built, native mobile app containers can be launched for up to nine platforms, including Apple, Android, BlackBerry, and Windows Phone. The major advantage to using this hybrid approach is building your app once, and then releasing it to many platforms simultaneously.

TIP

Imagine you knew how to play the piano, but you wanted to also learn how to play the violin. One way you could do this is to buy a violin and start learning how to play. Another option is to buy a synthesizer keyboard, set the tone to violin, and play the keyboard to sound like a violin. This is similar to the hybrid approach, except in this example, the piano is HTML, CSS, and JavaScript, the violin is a native iOS app, and the synthesizer keyboard is a wrapper like PhoneGap. Just like the synthesizer keyboard can be set to violin, cello, or guitar, so too can PhoneGap create native apps for Apple, Android, and other platforms.

CHAPTER 2 **Programming for the Web** 31

WHAT ABOUT ALL THOSE OTHER PROGRAMMING LANGUAGES? (C, JAVA, AND SO ON)

You may wonder why so many languages exist, and what they all do. Programming languages are created when a developer sees a need not addressed by the current languages. For example, Apple recently created the Swift programming language to make developing iPhone and iPad apps easier than Objective-C, the current programming language used. After they're created, programming languages are very similar to spoken languages, like English or Latin. If developers code using the new language, then it thrives and grows in popularity, like English has over the past six centuries; otherwise, the programming language suffers the same fate as Latin, and becomes a dead language.

You may remember languages like C++, Java, and FORTRAN. These languages still exist today, and they're used in more places than you might think. C++ is preferred when speed and performance are extremely important and is used to program web browsers, such as Chrome, Firefox, and Safari, along with games like Call of Duty and Counter Strike. Java is preferred by many large-scale businesses and is also the language used to program apps for the Android phone. Finally, FORTRAN isn't as widespread or popular as it once was, but it is popular within the scientific community, and it powers some functionality in the financial sector, especially at some of the largest banks in the world, many of which continue to have old code.

As long as programmers think of faster and better ways to program, new programming languages will continue to be created, while older languages will fall out of favor.

IN THIS CHAPTER

» Discovering the process programmers follow when coding

» Understanding the different roles people play to create a program

» Picking tools to start coding offline or online

Chapter 3
Becoming a Programmer

"The way to get started is to quit talking and begin doing."
— WALT DISNEY

Programming is a skill that can be learned by anyone. You might be a student in college wondering how to start learning or a professional hoping to find a new job or improve your performance at your current job. In just about every case, the best way to grasp how to code is pretty straightforward:

» Have a goal of what you would like to build.

» Actually start coding.

In this chapter, you discover the process every programmer follows when programming, and the different roles programmers play to create a program (or, more commonly these days, to create an app). You also find out about the tools to use when coding either offline or online.

Writing Code Using a Process

Writing code is much like painting, furniture making, or cooking — it isn't always obvious how the end product was created. However, all programs, even mysterious

ones, are created using a process. Here are two of the most popular processes used today:

» **Waterfall:** A set of *sequential* steps followed to create a program.

» **Agile:** A set of *iterative* steps followed to create a program. (See Figure 3-1.)

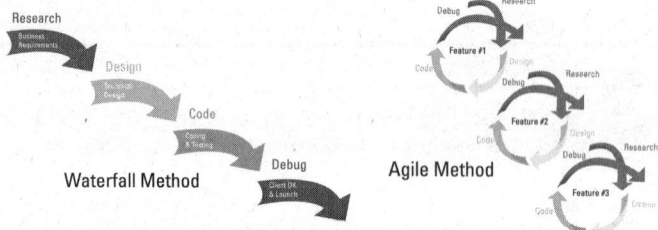

FIGURE 3-1: The waterfall and agile processes are two different ways of creating software.

Let me describe a specific scenario to explain how these two processes work. Imagine that you want to build a restaurant app that does the following two things:

» It displays restaurant information, such as the hours of operation and the menu.

» It allows users to make or cancel reservations.

Using the waterfall method, you define everything the app needs to do: You design both the information-display and the reservation parts of the app, code the entire app, and then release the app to users. In contrast, using the agile method, you define, design, and code only the information-display portion of the app, release it to users, and collect feedback. Based on the feedback collected, you then redesign and make changes to the information-display to address major concerns. When you're satisfied with the information-display piece, you then define, design, and build the reservation part of the app. Again, you collect feedback and refine the reservation feature to address major concerns.

The agile methodology stresses shorter development times and has increased in popularity as the pace of technological change has increased. The waterfall approach, on the other hand, demands that the developer code and release the entire app at once, but since completing a large project takes an enormous amount of time, changes in technology may occur before the finished product arrives. If you use the waterfall method to create the restaurant-app example, the technology needed to take reservations may change by the time you get around to coding that portion of the app. Still, the waterfall approach remains popular in certain contexts, such as with financial and government software, where requirements

and approval are obtained at the beginning of a project, and whose documentation of a project must be complete.

The healthcare.gov website, released in October 2013, was developed using a waterfall style process. Testing of all the code occurred in September 2013, when the entire system was assembled. Unfortunately, the tests occurred too late and weren't comprehensive, resulting in not enough time to fix errors before launching the site publicly.

Regardless of whether you pick the agile or waterfall methodology, coding an app involves four steps:

1. Researching what you want to build
2. Designing your app
3. Coding your app
4. Debugging your code

On average, you'll spend much more time researching, designing, and debugging your app than doing the actual coding, which is the opposite of what you might expect.

These steps are described in the sections that follow. You'll use this process when you create your own app in Book 5, Chapter 1.

Researching what you want to build

You have an idea for a web or mobile application, and usually it starts with, "Wouldn't it be great if. . . ." Before writing any code, it helps to do some investigating. Consider the possibilities in your project as you answer the following questions:

» What similar website/app already exists? What technology was used to build it?

» Which features should I include — and more importantly exclude — in my app?

» Which providers can help create these features? For example, companies like Google, Yahoo, Microsoft, or others may have software already built that you could incorporate into your app.

To illustrate, consider the restaurant app I discussed earlier. When conducting market research and answering the three preceding questions, using Google to search is usually the best choice. Searching for *restaurant reservation app* shows

CHAPTER 3 **Becoming a Programmer** 35

existing restaurant apps that include OpenTable, SeatMe, and Livebookings. OpenTable, for example, allows users to reserve a table from restaurants displayed on a map using Google Maps.

In the restaurant app example, you want to research exactly what kinds of restaurant information you need to provide and how extensive the reservation system portion of the app should be. In addition, for each of these questions, you must decide whether to build the feature from scratch or to use an existing provider. For example, when providing restaurant information, do you want to show only name, cuisine, address, telephone number, and hours of operation, or do you also want to show restaurant menus? When showing restaurant data, do you prefer extensive coverage of a single geographical area, or do you want national coverage even if that means you cover fewer restaurants in any specific area?

Designing your app

Your app's visual design incorporates all of your research and describes exactly how your users will interact with every page and feature. Because your users will be accessing your site from desktop, laptop, and mobile devices, you want to make sure you create a responsive (multi-device) design and carefully consider how your site will look on all these devices. At this stage of the process, a general web designer, illustrator, or user interface specialist will help create visual designs for the app.

Many responsive app designs and templates can be found on the Internet and used freely. For specific examples, see Book 4, Chapter 1, or search Google using the query *responsive website design examples*.

There are two types of visual designs (see Figure 3-2):

>> **Wireframes:** These are low-fidelity website drawings that show structurally the ways your content and your site's interface interact.

>> **Mockups:** These are high-fidelity website previews that include colors, images, and logos.

Balsamiq is a popular tool used to create wireframes, and Photoshop is a popular tool to create mockups. However, you can avoid paying for additional software by using PowerPoint (PC), Keynote (Mac), or the free and open-source OpenOffice to create your app designs.

Professional designers create mockups with Adobe Photoshop and use *layers*, which isolate individual site elements. A properly created layered Photoshop file helps developers more easily write the code for those website elements.

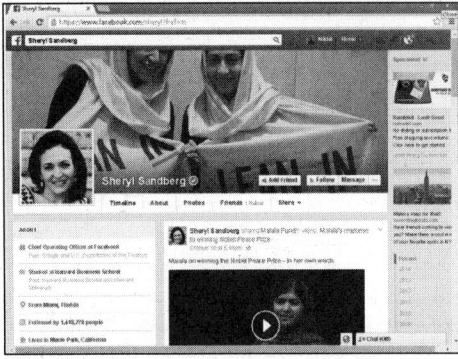

FIGURE 3-2: Wireframes (left) are simple site renderings, whereas mockups (right) show full site previews.

In addition to visual design, complex apps also have technical designs and decisions to finalize. For example, if your app stores and retrieves user data, you need a database to perform these tasks. Initial decisions here include the type of database to add, the specific database provider to use, and the best way to integrate the database into the application. Additionally, developers must design the database by choosing the fields to store. The process is similar to the process of creating a spreadsheet to model a company's income — you first decide the number of columns to use, whether you'll include fields as a percentage of revenue or a numerical value, and so on. Similarly, other features like user logins or credit card payments all require you to make choices for how to implement these features.

Coding your app

With research and design done, you're now ready to code your application. In everyday web development, you begin by choosing which pages and features to start coding. As you work through the projects in this book, however, I will guide you on what to code first.

Knowing how much to code and when to stop can be tough. Developers call the first iteration of an app the *minimum viable product* — meaning you've coded just enough to test your app with real users and receive feedback. If no one likes your app or thinks it's useful, it's best to find out as soon as possible.

An app is the sum of its features, and for any individual feature, it's a good idea to write the minimum code necessary and then add to it. For example, your restaurant app may have a toolbar at the top of the page with drop-down menus. Instead of trying to create the whole menu at once, it's better to just create the main menu and then later create the drop-down menu.

Projects can involve front-end developers, who write code to design the appearance of the app, and back-end developers, who code the logic and create databases. A "full stack developer" is one who can do both front-end and back-end development. On large projects, it's more common to see specialized front-end and back-end developers, along with project managers who ensure everyone is communicating with each other and adhering to the schedule so that the project finishes on time.

Debugging your code

Debugging is going to be a natural part of creating an application. The computer always follows your instructions exactly, yet no program ever works as you expect it to. Debugging can be frustrating. Three of the more common mistakes to watch out for are

» **Syntax errors:** These are errors caused by misspelling words/commands, by omitting characters, or by including extra characters. Some languages, such as HTML and CSS, are forgiving of these errors, and your code will still work even with some syntax errors; whereas other languages, such as JavaScript, are more particular, and your code won't run when even one such error is present.

» **Logic errors:** These are harder to fix. With logic errors, your syntax is correct, but the program behaves differently than you expected, such as when the prices of the items in the shopping cart of an e-commerce site don't add up to the correct total.

» **Display errors:** These are common mainly in web applications. With display errors, your program might run and work properly, but it won't appear properly. Web apps today run on many devices, browsers, and screen sizes, so extensive testing is the only way to catch these types of errors.

The word *debugging* was popularized in the 1940s by Grace Hopper, who fixed a computer error by literally removing a moth from a computer.

Picking Tools for the Job

Now you're ready to actually start coding. You can develop websites either offline, by working with an editor, or online, with a web service such as Codecademy.com.

Especially if you haven't done any coding before, I strongly recommend that you code with access to an Internet connection using the Codecademy.com platform, because you don't have to download and install any software to start coding, you don't have to find a web host to serve your web pages, and you don't need to upload your web page to a web host. As you code, the Codecademy.com platform does these tasks for you automatically.

Working offline

To code offline, you need the following:

>> **Editor:** This refers to the text editor you use to write all the code this book covers, including HTML, CSS, JavaScript, Ruby, Python, and PHP.

 The editor you use will depend on the type of computer you have:

 - *PC:* Use the preinstalled Notepad or install Notepad++, a free editor available for download at http://notepad-plus-plus.org.

 - *Mac:* Use the preinstalled TextEdit or install TextMate 2.0, an open-source editor available for download at http://macromates.com.

>> **Browser:** Many browsers exist, including Firefox, Safari, Internet Explorer, and Opera.

 I recommend you use Chrome, because it offers the most support for the latest HTML standards. It's available for download at www.google.com/chrome/browser.

>> **Web host:** In order for your website code to be accessible to everyone on the Internet, you need to host your website online. Freemium web hosts include Weebly (www.weebly.com) and Wix (www.wix.com); these sites offer basic hosting but charge for additional features such as additional storage or removal of ads. Google provides free web hosting through Google Sites (http://sites.google.com) and Google Drive (http://drive.google.com).

Working online with Codecademy.com

Codecademy.com is the easiest way to start coding online, and lessons from the site form the basis for this book. The site doesn't require you to install a code editor or sign up for a web host before you start coding, and it's free to individual users like you.

The site can be accessed using any up-to-date modern browser, but Google Chrome or Mozilla Firefox are recommended. After you access the site, you can

CHAPTER 3 **Becoming a Programmer** 39

sign up for a free account that will save your course progress and allow you to access more advanced content. As you use the site, you may see offers to upgrade to Codecademy Pro, which includes extra quizzes, projects, and live help. For the purposes of completing this book, purchasing a Codecademy Pro subscription is completely optional.

Touring the learning environment

After signing up or signing into the site, you will see either an interactive card or the coding interface, depending on the content you learn. (See Figure 3-3.)

 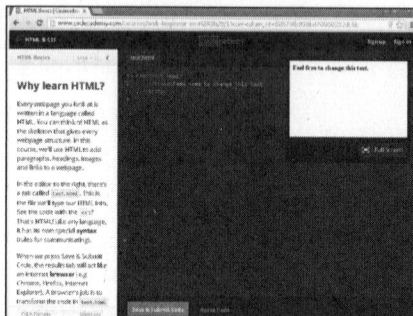

FIGURE 3-3: Codecademy.com interactive cards (left) and the coding interface (right).

The interactive cards allow you to click toggle buttons to demonstrate effects of prewritten code, whereas the coding interface has a coding editor and a live preview window that shows you the effects of the code entered into the coding editor.

The coding interface has four parts:

» Background information on the upper-left side of the screen tells you about the coding task you're about to do.

» The lower-left side of the screen shows instructions to complete in the coding window.

» The coding window allows you to follow the exercise's instructions and write code. The coding window also includes a preview screen that shows a live preview of your code as you type.

» After completing the coding instructions, press Save & Submit, Next, or Run. If you successfully followed the instructions, you advance to the next exercise; otherwise, the site will give you an error message along with a helpful hint for correcting it.

The interactive cards have three parts:

- Background information about a coding concept.
- A coding window to complete one simple coding task. A preview window also shows a live preview of your code as you type.
- After completing the coding instructions, press the Got It button. You can review any previous interactive cards by clicking the Go Back button.

Receiving support from the community

If you run into a problem or have a bug you cannot fix, try the following steps:

- Click the hint below the instructions.
- Use the Q&A Forums to post your problem or question or to review questions others have posted.
- Subscribe to this book's mailing list at http://tinyletter.com/coding fordummies for book updates and explanations for changes to programming language commands.
- Tweet me at @nikhilgabraham with your question or problem, and include the hashtag #codingFD at the end of your tweet.

Career Building with Coding

Contents at a Glance

CHAPTER 1: Exploring Coding Career Paths 45
 Augmenting Your Existing Job 46
 Finding a New Coding Job 52

CHAPTER 2: Exploring Undergraduate and Graduate Degrees 59
 Getting a College Degree 60
 Enrolling in an Advanced Degree Program 65
 Interning to Build Credibility 68

CHAPTER 3: Training on the Job 73
 Taking a Work Project to the Next Level 74
 Learning on the Job and after Work 75
 Freelancing to Build Confidence and Skills 79
 Transitioning to a New Role 80

CHAPTER 4: Coding Career Myths 83
 Educational Myths .. 83
 Career Myths ... 87

IN THIS CHAPTER

» Using coding in your existing job

» Exploring entry-level full-time coding roles

» Understanding skills and tasks in various coding roles

Chapter 1
Exploring Coding Career Paths

"We shall not cease from exploration, and the end of all our exploring will be to arrive where we started and know the place for the first time."

— T.S. ELIOT

For many people, the words "coding career" evoke an image of a person sitting in a dimly lit room typing incomprehensible commands into a computer. The stereotype has persisted for decades — just watch actors such as Matthew Broderick in *War Games* (1983), Keanu Reeves in *The Matrix* (1999), or Jesse Eisenberg in *The Social Network* (2010). Fortunately, these movies are not accurate representations of reality. Just like a career in medicine can lead to psychiatry, gynecology, or surgery, a career in coding can lead to an equally broad range of options.

In this chapter, you see how coding can augment your existing job across a mix of functions, and you explore increasingly popular careers based primarily on coding.

Augmenting Your Existing Job

Many people find coding opportunities in their existing job. It usually starts innocently enough, and with something small. For example, you may need a change made to the text on the company's website, but the person who would normally do that is unavailable before your deadline. If you knew how to alter the website's code, you could perform your job faster or more easily. This section explores how coding might augment your existing job.

Creative design

Professionals in creative design include those who

- Shape how messages are delivered to clients.
- Create print media such as brochures and catalogs.
- Design for digital media such as websites and mobile applications.

> **CHOOSING A CAREER PATH**
>
> Coding career paths are extremely varied. For some people, the path starts with using code to more efficiently perform an existing job. For others, coding is a way to transition to a new career. As varied as the career path is, so too are the types of companies that need coders.
>
> As more people carry Internet-capable mobile phones, businesses of every type are turning to coders to reach customers and to optimize existing operations. No business is immune. For example, FarmLogs is a company that collects data from farm equipment to help farmers increase crop yields and forecast profits. FarmLogs needs coders to build the software that collects and analyzes data, and farmers with large operations may need coders to customize the software.
>
> To build or customize software, you'll need to learn new skills. Surprisingly, the time required to learn and start coding can range from an afternoon of lessons to a ten-week crash course to more time-intensive options, such as a four-year undergraduate degree in computer science.

Traditionally, digital designers, also known as visual designers, created *mockups*, static illustrations detailing layout, images, and interactions, and then sent these mockups to developers who would create the web or mobile product. This process worked reasonably well for everyday projects, but feedback loops started becoming longer as mockups became more complex. For example, a designer would create multiple mockups of a website, and then the developer would implement them to create working prototypes, after which the winning mockup would be selected. As another example, the rise of mobile devices has led to literally thousands of screen variations between mobile phones and tablets created by Apple, Samsung, and others. Project timelines increased because designers had to create five or more mockups to cover the most popular devices and screen sizes.

As a designer, one way to speed up this process is to know just enough code to create working prototypes of the initial mockups that are responsive, which means one prototype renders on both desktop and mobile devices. Then project managers, developers, and clients can use these early prototypes to decide which versions to further develop and which to discard. Additionally, because responsive prototypes follow a predictable set of rules across all devices, creating additional mockups for each device is unnecessary, which further decreases design time. As mobile devices have become more popular, the demand for designers who understand how to create good user interactions (UI) and user experiences (UX) has greatly increased.

Prototyping tools such as InVision and Axure provide a middle option between creating static illustrations and coding clickable prototypes by allowing designers to create working prototypes without much coding. Still, a person with basic coding skills can improve a prototype generated with these tools by making it more interactive and realistic. Designers who can design and code proficiently are referred to as "unicorns" because they are rare and in high demand.

Content and editorial

Professionals in content and editorial perform tasks such as the following:

>> Maintain the company's presence on social networks such as Twitter and Facebook.

>> Create short posts for the company blog and for email campaigns.

>> Write longer pieces for articles or presentations.

At smaller companies, content creation is usually mixed with other responsibilities. At larger companies, creating content is a full-time job. Whether you're blogging for a startup or reporting for *The Wall Street Journal*, writers of all types face the same challenges of identifying relevant topics and backing it up with data.

CHAPTER 1 **Exploring Coding Career Paths** 47

Traditionally, content was written based on a writer's investigation and leads from a small group of people. For example, you might write a blog post about a specific product's feature because a major customer asked about it during a sales call. But what if most of your smaller customers, whom you don't speak with regularly, would benefit from a blog post about some other product feature?

As a writer, you can produce more relevant content by writing code to analyze measurable data and use the conclusions to author content. I Quant NY (http://iquantny.tumblr.com), an online blog, is one shining example of data driving content creation. In 2014, the site's author, Ben Wellington, analyzed public data on New York City parking tickets, bike usage, and traffic crashes, and wrote about his conclusions. His analysis led to original stories and headlines in major newspapers such as *The New York Times* and *New York Post* (see Figure 1-1).

FIGURE 1-1: Article about a ticket-generating fire hydrant.

Human resources

Those who work in human resources might be expected to do the following:

- » Source and screen candidates for open company jobs.
- » Manage payroll, benefits, performance, and training for employees.
- » Ensure company compliance with relevant laws, and resolve disputes.

Traditionally, HR professionals have not performed much coding in the workplace. The human- and process-driven components of the job generally outweighed the need for automation that coding typically provides. For example, a dispute between coworkers is usually resolved with an in-person meeting organized by

HR, not by a computer program. However, the recruiting function in HR may benefit from coding. Hiring employees has always been challenging, especially for technical positions where the demand for employees far exceeds the supply of available and qualified candidates.

If you're responsible for technical recruiting and want to increase the number of candidates you reach out to and source, one solution is to develop some coding experience that enables you to discover people who may not meet the traditional hiring criteria. For example, a company might ordinarily look for developers from a specific university with at least a 3.0 grade point average.

However, increasingly developers are self-taught and may have dropped out or not attended university at all. A technical recruiter who can evaluate code that self-taught developers have written and made publicly available on sites such as GitHub or Bitbucket can qualify candidates who previously would have been rejected. Additionally, recruiters working with technical candidates improve outcomes by being able to speak their language.

Companies such as Google and Facebook have taken a technical approach to managing the expensive and difficult problem of finding and retaining employees. These companies perform people analytics on their employees by looking at everyone who applies and analyzing factors that contribute to hiring, promotion, and departure, such as undergraduate GPA, previous employer, interview performance, and on-the-job reviews. At Google, this analysis requires some serious coding because more than two million people apply each year.

Product management

Product managers, especially those working on software and hardware products, perform tasks like the following:

- » Manage processes and people to launch products on time and on budget, maintain existing products, and retire old products.
- » Connect all departments that create a product, including sales, engineering, marketing, design, operations, and quality control.
- » Guide the product definition, roadmap, and business model based on understanding the target market and customers.

The product manager's role can vary greatly because it is a function of the company culture and the product being built. This is especially true for technical products; in some companies, product managers define the problem and engineers design hardware and software to solve those problems. In other companies,

product managers not only define the problem but also help design the technical solution.

One of the hardest challenges and main responsibilities of a product manager is to deliver a product on time and within budget. Timelines can be difficult to estimate, especially when new technology is used or existing technology is used in a new way. When you manufacture, say, a chair, it has a set product definition. For a product with a technical component, additional features can creep into the project late in development, or a single feature might be responsible for the majority of time or cost overruns. The product manager helps to keep these variables in check.

The product manager working on a technical product who has some coding skill will be able to better estimate development cycles and anticipate the moving pieces that must come together. In addition, solving technical challenges that arise and understanding the tradeoffs of one solution versus another are easier with some coding background.

Business analysts or integration specialists translate business requirements from customers into technical requirements that are delivered to project managers and that are eventually implemented by back-end engineers.

Sales and marketing

Sales and marketing professionals perform tasks such as

>> Segment existing customers and identify new potential customers.

>> Generate and convert prospective leads into sold customers.

>> Craft product and brand images to reflect company and customer values.

Salespeople and marketers expend a great deal of effort placing the right message at the right time before the right customer. For decades, these messages were delivered in newspapers, in magazines, and on television and radio. Measuring their effect in these channels was difficult, part art and part science. With the movement of messages to the Internet, we can now measure and analyze every customer view and click. Online marketing has created another problem: Online customers generate so much data that much of it goes unanalyzed.

The salesperson or marketer who can code is able to better target customers online. If you're a salesperson, generating leads is the start of the sales funnel, and coding enables you to find and prioritize online website visitors as potential customers. For example, when Uber launched their mobile application, it was available only in San Francisco. The company tracked and analyzed the location of users who opened the app to decide which city to launch in next.

If you're in marketing, identifying *whom* to market to is as important as identifying *what* message to market. Website visitors reveal behavioral and demographic data about themselves, including location, web pages visited, visit duration, and often gender, age, employer, and past online purchases. Even moderately successful websites generate tens of millions of records a month, and coding can help spot trends such as the 25-to-29-year-old females in Nebraska who are suddenly interested in but aren't purchasing your product. Marketing messages become more efficient when you know the segments you're targeting and how they are responding.

Legal

Professionals providing legal services might perform the following tasks:

- Identify and manage legal risks in agreements and transactions.
- Ensure ongoing compliance with relevant laws and regulations.
- Review documents such as prior cases, business records, and legal filings.
- Resolve disputes through litigation, mediation, and arbitration.

Historically, the legal profession has been resilient to advances in technology. I include it here because if lawyers who code are able to more efficiently perform their jobs, professionals in any other industry should be able to benefit from coding as well.

Coding knowledge may not assist a lawyer with delivering a passionate argument in court or finalizing a transaction between two Fortune 500 companies, but the bulk of a lawyer's time is spent on document review, a task that could benefit from coding knowledge.

When reviewing legal documents, a lawyer might read previous cases in a litigation, check existing patent filings before filing a new patent, or examine a company's contracts in preparation for a merger. All these tasks involve processing large amounts of text, and current legal tools enable, for example, wildcard searching (such as using *new** to find New York, New Jersey, and New Hampshire).

However, the use of *regular expressions* — code that searches for patterns in text — could help lawyers review documents faster and more efficiently. See Figure 1-2.

For example, suppose you are a government lawyer investigating an investment bank for fraudulently selling low-quality mortgages. The investment bank has produced two million documents, and you want to find every email address mentioned in these documents. You could spend months reviewing every page and noting the email addresses, or you could spend a few minutes writing a regular expression that returns every email address automatically.

CHAPTER 1 **Exploring Coding Career Paths** 51

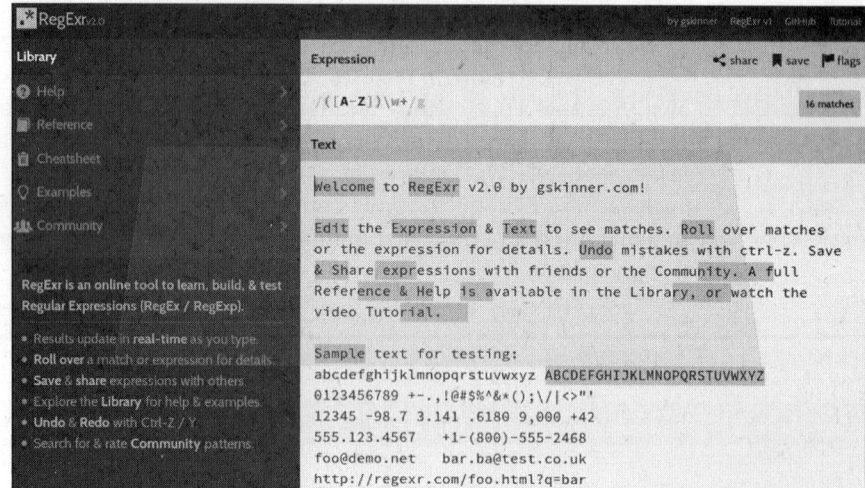

FIGURE 1-2:
Use RegExr.com to practice searching with regular expressions.

As the government lawyer reviewing those documents, one of many regular expressions you could use to find email addresses is .+@.+\..+. Much like the * wildcard character, each symbol represents a pattern to match. I show it here only as an example, so don't let the code intimidate you. This regular expression first looks for a least one character before and after the @ symbol, and at least one character before and after a period that appears following the @ symbol. This pattern matches the username@domain.com email address format.

David Zvenyach, a government lawyer and computer programmer, has created two websites of interest to lawyers:

>> The first site, SCOTUS Servo, logs a message whenever the Supreme Court changes an already issued opinion and is available at `https://twitter.com/scotus_servo`.

>> The second site, Coding for Lawyers, teaches lawyers code that could be helpful in the practice of law and is available at `http://codingforlawyers.com`.

Finding a New Coding Job

The career changer looking to transition to a coding job can choose from a variety of roles. This section describes the most popular coding jobs today. In these roles at the entry level, your coding knowledge will be used daily. As you become more skilled and senior, however, your people-management responsibilities will increase while the number of lines of code you write will decrease. For example, Mark Zuckerberg wrote the code for the initial version of Facebook and continued

to write code for two years after the website launched, after which he stopped coding for almost six years to focus on managing the team's growth.

Some coding roles may appeal to you to more than others. In addition to understanding jobs available in the market, some self-reflection can help you make the best choice possible. As you review the role descriptions in this section, take a personal inventory of

- Tasks you enjoy and dislike in your current role
- Skills you already possess, and the skills you will need to learn
- Interests you want to pursue that will make you excited about working every day

Although no job is completely secure, the demand for technical roles is high and continues to grow. The US government estimates that by 2020, more than 1 million computer science-related jobs will be unfilled, with 1.4 million available jobs and only 400,000 computer science students trained to fill them.

Front-end web development

Web developers create websites. There are two types of web developers: front-end developers and back-end developers. Each requires different skills and tasks, which are discussed in this section.

Front-end web developers code everything visible on the web page, such as the layout, image placement and sizing, input features including buttons and text boxes, and the site's general look and feel. These effects are created with three major programming languages: HTML (Hypertext Markup Language), which is used to place text on the page, CSS (Cascading Style Sheet), which styles the text and further contributes to its appearance, and JavaScript, which adds interactivity.

In addition to these three languages, front-end developer job postings reveal a common set of skills that employers are looking for:

- **SEO (search engine optimization):** Creating web pages for humans might seem like the only goal, but machines, specifically search engines, are the primary way most users find websites. Search engines "view" web pages differently than humans, and certain coding techniques can make it easier for search engines to index an individual web page or an entire website.
- **Cross-browser testing:** Users navigate web pages by using four major browsers (Chrome, Firefox, Internet Explorer, and Safari), each with two or three active versions. As a result, a web developer must be skilled in testing

websites across eight or more browser versions. Developing for older browsers is typically more difficult because they support fewer features and require more code to achieve the same effect as modern browsers.

» **CSS tools:** Developers use precompilers and CSS frameworks to make coding in CSS easier:

- *Precompilers* extend CSS functionality with features such as variables and functions, which make it easier to read and maintain CSS code.

- *CSS frameworks,* such as Bootstrap and Base, provide prewritten HTML and CSS code that makes it easier to develop a website with a consistent look across desktop and mobile devices.

Proficiency in all precompilers and frameworks is unnecessary, but knowledge of one precompiler and framework can be helpful.

» **JavaScript frameworks:** Developers use prewritten JavaScript code called a *JavaScript framework* to add features to web pages. Some popular JavaScript frameworks are Angular.js and Ember.js. Proficiency in the over 30 JavaScript frameworks is unnecessary, but knowing one or two can be helpful.

Words like HTML, CSS, and JavaScript might seem intimidating at first, especially if you have no prior experience in web development. I mention some terminology here and also in the glossary because knowing the names of these programming language is the first step to learning more about each of them.

None of the work a web developer does would be possible without product managers and designers. Developers work with product managers to ensure that the product scope and timelines are reasonable. Additionally, product managers make sure that the technical and nontechnical teams are communicating and aligned. Developers also work with designers who create *mockups*, or illustrations of the website, images, and the flow users take to move between web pages. After the mockups are created, front-end developers code the website to match the mockups as closely as possible.

Back-end web development

Back-end web developers code everything that is not visible on the web page but is necessary to support the front-end developer's work. Back-end development happens in the following three places:

» **Server:** The *server* is the computer hosting the coding files that include the website application and the database. When you visit www.google.com, for example, your web browser requests the web page from Google servers, which respond with a copy of the web page you see in your browser.

» **Application:** The *application* handles the content in web pages sent to users and the changes made to the database. Applications are written using programming languages like Ruby, Python, and PHP, and run only on the server. Proficiency in one language is usually sufficient.

» **Database:** The *database* stores website and user data so it is available for future browsing sessions. The simplest database is an Excel spreadsheet, which is ill suited for web development. Databases such as PostgreSQL and MongoDB are optimized for website use; usually only one these databases is used per website.

As an example of back-end web development, suppose that you visit www.amazon.com using your web browser. Your computer makes a request to the Amazon server, which runs an application to determine what web content to serve you. The application queries a database, and past purchases and browsing show that you have an interest in technology, legal, and travel books. The application creates a web page that displays books matching your interests, and sends it to your computer. You see a book on bike trails in New York, and click to purchase it. After you enter your credit card and shipping details, the application stores the information in a database on the server for easy checkout in the future.

For back-end developers, one major part of the job is writing code for the application and database to render web pages in the browser. Employers are interested in additional skills such as these:

» **Scaling:** Back-end developers must change and optimize application code, servers, and databases to respond to increases in website traffic. Without the right planning, a mention of your website on a morning talk show or in the newspaper could result in a "website not available" error message instead of thousands of new customers. *Scaling* involves balancing the cost of optimizing the website with leaving the configuration as-is.

» **Analytics:** Every online business, whether large or small, has key website performance indicators, such as new user signups and retention of existing users. Back-end developers can implement and track these metrics by querying information from the website database.

» **Security:** Websites with a substantial number of users become a target for all types of security risks. Attackers may automate signups, in which fake profiles post spam that promotes unrelated products. Additionally, you may receive a massive amount of traffic in a short period of time, called a *denial of service attack,* which prevents legitimate customers from accessing your website. Or attackers might try to detect weaknesses in your servers to gain unauthorized access to sensitive information such as email addresses, passwords, and

credit card numbers. In 2014, major data breaches were uncovered at large corporations including Sony, Target, and JP Morgan. Prevention of these attacks rests, in part, with back-end developers.

The back-end developer is a part of the product team and works closely with front-end developers and product managers. Unlike front-end developers, back-end developers do not interact frequently with designers because the job is not as visual or based on website appearance.

Mobile application development

Mobile application developers create applications that run on cell phones, tablets, and other mobile devices. Mobile applications can be more challenging to create than browser-based websites because users expect the same functionality on a device without a dedicated keyboard and with a smaller screen.

In 2014, users purchased and spent more time on mobile devices than traditional PC desktops, marking a major milestone and the continuation of a trend years in the making.

Users today prefer to download and use native mobile applications from an app store, though it is possible to create mobile optimized websites that run in the browser using HTML, CSS, and JavaScript. The two most popular app stores are

- » The Apple App Store, which hosts apps for iOS devices such as iPhones and iPads
- » The Google Play Store, which hosts apps for phones and tablets running the Android operating system

Developers code apps for iOS devices by using the Objective-C and Swift programming languages, and they code apps for Android devices by using Java.

Objective-C, which was invented in 1983, is traditionally and currently used to create iOS apps. Swift is a new programming language that Apple created and released in 2014. This programming language was designed from the ground up as a replacement for Objective-C.

Mobile developers are in high demand as mobile usage overtakes browsing on traditional PCs. In addition to creating apps, employers also value these skills:

- » **Location services:** The service most frequently integrated into and used in mobile applications is location. Maps, reservation, and transportation applications all become more useful when they take into account your current location.

TIP

Location services consume battery life rapidly, although specialized techniques can reduce battery drain. Mobile developers who understand these techniques will have a leg up on the competition.

» **Application testing:** The number of devices that a mobile developer has to consider is staggering. In addition, an errant line of code can cause a mobile application to install incorrectly or to leak memory until the application crashes. Mobile application-testing software automates the process of testing your application across a variety of device types, saving a huge amount of time and a drawer full of phones. Mobile developers who can integrate testing software such as Crashlytics into their applications will get the data needed to continuously improve their application code.

Mobile application developers work with designers to create easy and intuitive mobile experiences, with back-end developers to ensure that data submitted by or received from the phone is in sync with data on the website, and with product managers so that the application launches smoothly.

Data analysis

Data analysts sift through large volumes of data, looking for insights that help drive the product or business forward. This role marries programming and statistics in the search for patterns in the data. Popular examples of data analysis in action include the recommendation engines used by Amazon to make product suggestions to users based on previous purchases and by Netflix to make movie suggestions based on movies watched.

The data analyst's first challenge is simply importing, cleaning, and processing the data. A website can generate daily millions of database entries of users' data, requiring the use of complicated techniques, referred to as *machine learning*, to create classifications and predictions from the data. For example, half a billion messages are sent per day using Twitter; some hedge funds analyze this data and classify whether a person talking about a stock is expressing a positive or negative sentiment. These sentiments are then aggregated to see whether a company has a positive or negative public opinion before the hedge fund purchases or sells any stock.

Any programming language can be used to analyze data, but the most popular programming languages used for the task are R, Python, and SQL. Publicly shared code in these three languages makes it easier for individuals entering the field to build on another person's work. While crunching the data is important, employers also look for data analysts with skills in the following:

» **Visualization:** Just as important as finding insight in the data is communicating that insight. Data visualization uses charts, graphs, dashboards, infographics,

and maps, which can be interactive, to display data and reduce the complexity such that one or two conclusions appear obvious, as shown in Figure 1-3 (courtesy of I Quant NY). Common data visualization tools include D3.js, a JavaScript graphing library, and ArcGIS for geographic data.

FIGURE 1-3: The two Manhattan addresses farthest away from Starbucks.

» **Distributed storage and processing:** Processing large amounts of data on one computer can be time-intensive. One option is to purchase a single faster computer. Another option, called *distributed storage and processing*, is to purchase multiple machines and divide the work. For example, imagine that we want to count the number of people living in Manhattan. In the distributed storage and processing approach, you might ring odd-numbered homes, I would ring even-numbered homes, and when we finished, we would total our counts.

Data analysts work with back-end developers to gather data needed for their work. After the data analysts have drawn conclusions from the data and come up with ideas on improving the existing product, they meet with the entire team to help design prototypes to test the ideas on existing customers.

> **IN THIS CHAPTER**
>
> » Learning to code with a bachelor's or master's degree
>
> » Coding outside class in clubs and hackathons
>
> » Securing an internship to learn on the job

Chapter 2
Exploring Undergraduate and Graduate Degrees

"When I was in college, I wanted to be involved in things that would change the world."

— ELON MUSK

Going to college to learn how to code is probably the most traditional and expensive path you can take. A bachelor's degree, designed to take four years, is rooted in the tradition of the English university system and was made popular by the GI Bill after World War II. More recently, the two-year associate degree has become more popular. It costs less than a bachelor's degree, but many are designed as a way to eventually transfer to a four-year bachelor degree program.

But when it comes to computer programmers, you likely know more people who didn't graduate from college than did. Entrepreneurs such as Bill Gates, Steve Jobs, Mark Zuckerberg, and Larry Ellison dropped out of college to create technology companies worth billions of dollars. Still, the world's biggest technology companies continue to hire mainly college graduates.

Whether you're thinking about going to college, are already in college, or attended college and want another degree, this chapter is for you. I explore learning to code in college or graduate school, and then building your credibility with an internship.

Getting a College Degree

The recent media attention on coding, with movies such as *The Social Network* and TV shows such as *Silicon Valley*, might make it seem like everyone in college is learning how to program. Although computer science (CS) graduates earn some of the highest salaries in the United States (see Figure 2-1), less than 3 percent of students major in computer science, and less than 1 percent of AP exams taken in high school are in computer science.

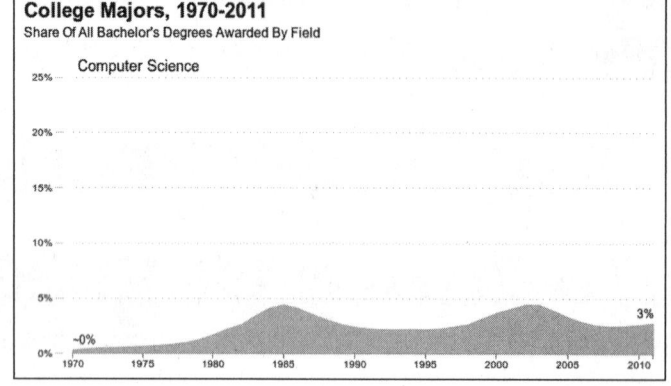

FIGURE 2-1: Bachelor's degrees awarded in CS over the past 40 years, courtesy of NPR.

Source: Digest of Educational Statistics; credit: Quoctrung Bui/NPR

The supply of students is low but is improving relative to the jobs that are available. Companies such as Apple, Microsoft, Yahoo!, Facebook, and Twitter recruit computer science engineers from schools such as Carnegie Mellon, MIT, and Stanford. It's not just the companies you read about in the news that are hiring either. CS graduates are in high demand — the Bureau of Labor Statistics estimates that by 2020, there will be 1.4 million computing jobs but only 400,000 trained computer science students to fill those jobs.

Yet far more important to employers than the name of the school you went to is what you did while you were in school. Employers will ask how you challenged yourself with your course load, and the applications you built and why.

College computer science curriculum

College CS courses offer a sweeping survey of entire computer systems from the hardware used to allocate memory to the high-level software that runs programs and the theories used to write that software. As a result, you gain a great sense of why computer systems behave as they do, which gives you the foundation to advance a technology or a programming language when the need arises.

This approach differs dramatically from the learning you'd typically do by yourself or in a boot camp, where the focus is only on software development in a specific language such as Python or Ruby. Given the typical 12-week duration of a boot camp, there isn't much time for anything else.

The core CS curriculum across universities is similar. Table 2-1 compares select core curriculum classes required as part of the Computer Science degree at Stanford and Penn State — a private university on the West Coast and a public university on the East Coast, respectively. Both have introductory classes to acquaint you with programming topics, math classes that cover probability, hardware classes for low-level programming and memory storage, software classes for designing algorithms, and higher level classes that cover advanced topics such as artificial intelligence and networking.

Until recently, universities generally did not teach web programming courses. As web programming has increased in popularity, this has begun to change — for example, Stanford offers a web programming class (CS 142) that teaches HTML, CSS, and Ruby on Rails, and Penn State has a similar class that teaches web programming with Java.

Doing extracurricular activities

Many students complement their coursework by applying what they've learned in a tangible way. Your coursework will include project work, but projects assigned in class may not have changed in a few years to make it easier for the instructor to provide support and grade your work. Also, with so many technologies constantly popping up, using your coding skills outside the classroom will help build confidence and skill.

One option is to code side projects, which are personal coding projects that perform some small basic utility and can be built in a short amount of time, over a weekend to a few months at most. For example, not many people know that before Mark Zuckerberg built Facebook, he had coded many side projects, including an instant messaging client for his dad's dental practice, an MP3 player that suggested the next song to listen to, and a tool that helped students choose their semester schedule based on which classes their friends were enrolling in. In another example, three students at Tufts University wanted an easy way to find the cheapest place to buy all their textbooks. They created a site called Getcha-Books, which lets students select the classes they would be taking in a semester and then retrieved the full list of books needed and the total prices across many stores to find the cheapest price. Although the site is no longer actively developed, all the code is open sourced and can be viewed either at getchabooks.com or github.com/getchabooks/getchabooks.

TABLE 2-1 CS Select Core Curriculum at Stanford and Penn State

Course name	Course description	Stanford	Penn State
Programming Abstractions	Intro to programming using C++ with sorting and searching	CS 106B	CMPSC 121
Programming with Web Applications	Intro to graphics, virtual machines, and programming concepts using Java	N/A	CMPSC 221
Math Foundations of Computing	Topics include proofs, logic, induction, sets, and functions	CS 103	CMPSC 360
Probability	Probability and statistics relevant to computer science	CS 109	STAT 318
Algorithms	Algorithm types (e.g., random) and complexity	CS 161	CMPSC 465
Hardware systems	Machine registers, assembly language, and compilation	CS 107	CMPSC 311
Computer systems	Storage and file management, networking, and distributed systems	CS 110	N/A
Operating systems	Designing and managing operating and system tasks	CS 140	CMPSC 473
Computer and network security	Principles of building and breaking secure systems	CS 155	CMPSC 443
Intro to Artificial Intelligence	AI concepts such as searching, planning, and learning	CS 121	CMPSC 448
Intro to Databases	Database design and using SQL and NoSQL systems	CS 145	CMPSC 431W

In addition to coding on your own, coding and discussing technology topics with others can be more engaging. On-campus clubs are usually formed by students and cater to almost every interest. You can find clubs on robotics, financial technologies such as bitcoin, technology investing from the venture capital stage to the public equities stage, and more.

TIP

The Dorm Room Fund is a student-run venture capital firm with locations in San Francisco, Boston, New York, and Philadelphia that invests in student-run companies. Backed by First Round Capital, the goal is to nurture and support young technology companies, teach students how to evaluate and invest in technology companies, and find the next billion-dollar company on a college campus.

TECHNICAL VERSUS PRACTICAL EDUCATION

As you look at the courses offered in the Stanford and Penn State CS programs, you'll notice that the overwhelming majority speak to the theory of computer science and aren't always used every day. For example, as a person interested in software development, you likely aren't going to use much if any of your hardware systems courses. Note that some classes will be very relevant — algorithms and databases are two topics frequently used in web programming.

However, understanding the theory is useful. For example, database systems were initially created assuming that storage was expensive and the amount of data that needed to be stored would grow linearly. The reality turned out to be different — the cost of hardware plummeted and hard drives became bigger and cheaper, while people generated more data at a faster pace than ever before. Computer scientists, with a solid understanding of databases, took advantage of cheap hardware and created distributed databases, which store data across multiple computers instead of a single one.

Whether or not you should learn programming in college comes down to your goal. If you want to one day be in a position to change the industry or work on cutting-edge technology, the theory you learn studying computer science is without substitute or comparison. There are few other places where you can engage with a professional, in this case a professor, of a high caliber to push the limits of fundamental understanding. Also, specific programming languages and technologies are constantly changing, while the underlying concepts and theories stay the same. Python and Ruby, for example, are only 20 years old.

On the other hand, if your goal is to use these concepts to make a living in the industry instead of trying to change the industry, you could learn to code in a less expensive and less time-intensive way than obtaining a computer science degree.

The most intense extracurricular pursuit for a student is participating in hackathons. A *hackathon* is a one-day to weekend-long event with the goal of brainstorming, designing, and building a small useful app. Hackathons are most popular among students, who often stay up all night coding their apps, while the hosts are often technology companies. However, some of the largest hackathons, such as Cal Hacks, which is hosted by UC Berkeley, and PennApps, which is hosted by the University of Pennsylvania (see Figure 2-2), are organized by students and attended by thousands of students from schools around the country.

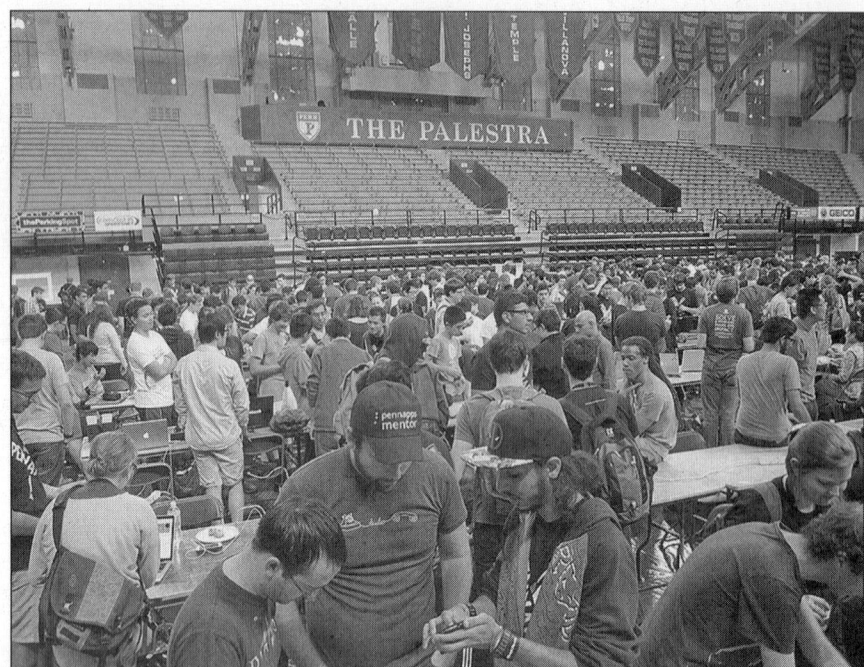

FIGURE 2-2: Students show a mentor their mobile application at PennApps.

Credit: Andrew Mager via Flickr

Two-year versus four-year school

You may not be able to afford the time, expense, or commitment demanded by a four-year degree. Even though some colleges offer financial aid, not earning money for four years or earning a far-reduced wage may not be feasible, especially if you have to support yourself or family members.

One alternative to the Bachelor of Arts (BA) degree is the Associate of Arts (AA) degree, which is typically granted by community colleges or technical schools. You can complete an AA degree in two years. In addition to taking less time, according to the College Board, tuition and fees are on average $3,200 per year, compared to $9,000 per year at public four-year institutions. Courses are also offered during evenings and on weekends, so students can work while attending school. When evaluating an institution that grants the AA degree, review the instructors teaching the courses and make sure they are experienced practitioners in the field. Additionally, see the types of jobs recent graduates went on to do and the employers they worked for to make sure that both match with your goals.

A close relative of the AA degree is a certificate granted by a school of continuing education. Certificates are noncredit offerings completed within a year. They usually cost less than $10,000 but don't result in a degree. To get the most bang for your buck, get your certificate from a school with a good regional or even

national reputation. For example, NYU has a Certificate in Web Development that teaches web development basics with HTML, CSS, and JavaScript along with more advanced topics such as PHP, a popular programming language for the web, and SQL, a language used to query databases. (See Figure 2-3.) Learning these topics in a structured way from an instructor can help jumpstart your learning so you can teach yourself additional topics on your own.

FIGURE 2-3: NYU's Certificate in Web Development offers classes in SQL and PHP.

When enrolling in a certificate program, keep in mind that instructor quality can be highly variable. Make sure you talk to current students or find some student reviews before signing up for either the certificate program or courses that the certificate requires.

Enrolling in an Advanced Degree Program

The options for learning how to code never seem to end, and advanced degrees typically appeal to a particular group of people. While not necessary for either learning to code or obtaining a coding job, an advanced degree can help accelerate your learning and differentiate you from other job candidates. Here are the two types of advanced degree programs:

>> **Master's degree:** A technical degree that allows you to explore and specialize in a particular area of computer science such as artificial intelligence, security, database systems, or machine learning. Based on the course load, the degree typically takes one or two years of full-time, in-person instruction to complete.

CHAPTER 2 **Exploring Undergraduate and Graduate Degrees** 65

Upon completion, the degree can be a way for a student who pursued a nontechnical major to transition into the field and pursue a coding job. Alternatively, some students use the master's degree experience as a way to gauge their interest in or improve their candidacy for a PhD program.

A growing number of part-time online master's degree programs are becoming available. For example, Stanford and Johns Hopkins both offer a master's degree in Computer Science with a concentration in one of ten topics as part of an online part-time degree that takes on average three to five years to complete. Similarly, Northwestern University offers a master's degree in Predictive Analytics, an online part-time program in big data that teaches students SQL, NoSQL, Python, and R.

» **Doctorate degree:** A program typically for people interested in conducting research into a specialized topic. PhD candidates can take six to eight years to earn their degree, so it's not the most timely way to learn how to code. PhD graduates, especially those with cutting-edge research topics, differentiate themselves in the market and generally work on the toughest problems in computer science. For example, Google's core search algorithm is technically challenging in a number of ways — it takes your search request, compares it against billions of indexed web pages, and returns a result in less than a second. Teams of PhD computer scientists work to write algorithms that predict what you're going to search for, index more data (such as from social networks), and return results to you five to ten milliseconds faster than before.

Students who enroll and drop out of PhD programs early have often done enough coursework to earn a master's degree, usually at no cost to the student because PhD programs are typically funded by the school.

Graduate school computer science curriculum

The master's degree school curriculum for computer science usually consists of 10 to 12 computer science and math classes. You start with a few foundational classes, and then specialize by focusing on a specific computer science topic. The PhD curriculum follows the same path, except after completing the coursework, you propose a previously unexplored topic to further research, spend three to five years conducting original research, and then present and defend your results before other professors appointed to evaluate your work.

Table 2-2 is a sample curriculum to earn a master's degree in CS with a concentration in Machine Learning from Columbia University. Multiple courses can be used to meet the degree requirements, and the courses offered vary by semester.

TABLE 2-2 Columbia University MS in Computer Science

Course Number	Course Name	Course Description
W4118	Operating Systems I	Design and implementation of operating systems including topics such as process management and synchronization
W4231	Analysis of Algorithms I	Design and analysis of efficient algorithms including sorting and searching
W4705	Natural Language Processing	Natural language extraction, summarization, and analysis of emotional speech
W4252	Computational Learning Theory	Computational and statistical possibilities and limitations of learning
W4771	Machine Learning	Machine learning with classification, regression, and inference models
W4111	Intro to Databases	Understanding of how to design and build relational databases
W4246	Algorithms for Data Science	Methods for organizing, sorting, and searching data
W4772	Advanced Machine Learning	Advanced machine learning tools with applications in perception and behavior modeling
E6232	Analysis of Algorithms II	Graduate course on design and analysis of efficient approximation algorithms for optimization problems
E6998	Advanced Topic in Machine Learning	Graduate course covers current research on Bayesian networks, inference, Markov models, and regression

The curriculum, which in this case consists of ten classes, begins with three foundational classes, and then quickly focuses on an area of concentration. Concentrations vary across programs, but generally include the following:

>> **Security:** Assigning user permissions and preventing unauthorized access, such as preventing users from accessing your credit card details on an e-commerce site

>> **Machine learning:** Finding patterns in data, and making future predictions, such as predicting what movie you should watch next based on the movies you've already seen and liked

>> **Network systems:** Protocols, principles, and algorithms for how computers communicate with each other, such as setting up wireless networks that work well for hundreds of thousands of users

- **Computer vision:** Duplicating the ability of the human eye to process and analyze images, such as counting the number of people who enter or exit a store based on a program analyzing a live video feed
- **Natural language processing:** Automating the analysis of text and speech, such as using voice commands to convert speech to text

Performing research

Students are encouraged in master's degree programs and required in PhD programs to conduct original research. Research topics vary from the theoretical, such as estimating how long an algorithm will take to find a solution, to the practical, such optimizing a delivery route given a set of points.

Sometimes this academic research is commercialized to create products and companies worth hundreds of millions to billions of dollars. For example, in 2003 university researchers created an algorithm called Farecast that analyzed 12,000 airline ticket prices. Later, it could analyze billions of ticket prices in real time, and predict whether the price of your airline ticket would increase, decrease, or stay the same. Microsoft purchased the technology for $100 million and incorporated it into its Bing search engine.

In another example, Shazam was based on an academic paper that analyzed how to identify an audio recording based on a short, low-quality sample, usually an audio recording from a mobile phone. Today, Shazam lets a user record a short snippet of a song, identifies the song title, and offers the song for purchase. The company has raised over $100 million in funding for operations and is privately valued at over $1 billion. Both products were based on published research papers that identified a problem that could be addressed with technology and presented a technology solution that solved existing constraints with high accuracy.

Your own research may not lead to the creation of a billion-dollar company, but it should advance, even incrementally, a solution for a computer science problem or help eliminate an existing constraint.

Interning to Build Credibility

Your classroom work helps create a theoretical foundation but can be divorced from the real world. Actual real-world problems often have inaccurate or incomplete data and a lack of obvious solutions. One way to bridge the gap from the classroom to the real world is to take on an internship.

Internships are 10- to 12-week engagements, usually over the summer, with an employer on a discrete project. The experience is meant to help an intern assess whether the company and the role are a good fit for permanent employment and for the company to assess the intern's abilities.

The competition for interns is just as strong as it is for full-time employees, so interns can expect to be paid. Top tech companies pay interns between $6,000 and $8,000 per month, with Palantir, LinkedIn, and Twitter topping the list. After the internship is finished, companies offer successful interns anywhere from $5,000 to $100,000 signing bonuses to return to the firm to work full time.

Types of internship programs

Companies structure their internship program differently, but the following configurations are more common than others:

- » **Summer internship:** The majority of internships happen during the summer. Because of the work involved in organizing an intern class, larger companies usually have a formal process with application deadlines and fixed dates when interviews for the internship are conducted. After offers are extended, companies ideally screen projects given to interns to make sure the work is interesting and substantive. There are also a significant number of social events so that full-time employees and interns can meet in an environment outside work.

- » **School-year internship:** Some internships take place during the school year, from September to May. These programs are usually smaller, hiring is on an as-needed basis, and the entire process is less formalized. Usually, the intern does more work to find divisions who need extra help, networks with managers of those divisions, and then finally interviews for and accepts an internship position. You can get a more realistic view of what working at the company is like because there likely aren't many other interns working with you, and you might be able to integrate more closely with the team.

- » **Fellowship:** Many students get the itch to try a longer professional experience before graduation. These experiences, called fellowship programs, last six to twelve months and give a person enough time to work on a project to make a substantive contribution. For undergraduates, the work confirms an existing interest or creates an interest in a new area of technology. For graduate students, the work can highlight the difference between theory and practice, inform an area of research, or help them break into a new industry.

HOW BOB REN LEARNED TO CODE

Between classes, clubs, hackathons, and internships, the possibilities seem endless for students in college or graduate school to learn how to code. Here is how Bob Ren, a college senior, stitched together his learning experiences while in school.

Bob attended the University of Illinois at Urbana-Champaign. After his first two years, he decided to take a break from school and gain some real-world experience at a technology company. He applied to and joined the fellowship program at Codecademy, a startup in New York. As a Codecademy fellow, Bob worked at the startup for one year as a full-time employee, was paid $80,000, and contributed to product development as an engineer. While at Codecademy, Bob contributed to a number of projects and wrote code to redesign the main website, add language support for Spanish and French, and develop an open-source platform called EventHub, which allows companies to understand various actions that visitors perform on a website.

While at Codecademy, Bob also kept busy outside work. A few months into his fellowship, he attended the Techcrunch Disrupt hackathon, and created a common application for startups based on issues he faced applying for jobs at startups. Like the common application for college, the app was designed so students could enter their information once and apply to multiple startups at the same time. TechCrunch, the startup blog and event organizer, wrote about the project at www.techcrunch.com/2013/04/28/startup_common_application_hackathon.

After the Disrupt Hackathon, Bob continued coding and built the following, either by himself or with a team before eventually joining Facebook as a software engineer:

- **LivingLanguage:** A Chrome extension that translates random words on any web page into a foreign language you want to learn. The app won first place at the Facebook Summer Hackathon in 2013.

- **SnapMeNow:** Like Snapchat for your computer, this web app uses your computer's camera to create images that self-destruct after up to 10 seconds. Bob released the app on Reddit, where it was barely noticed. After ten months, however, the app was reposted to HackerNews and ProductHunt, went viral with hundreds of thousands of people using the product, and was covered by media outlets such as MTV and BuzzFeed.

- **ClassTranscribe:** An open-source project that uses crowdsourcing to quickly and accurately transcribe college lectures. After the lectures are transcribed, students can search for keywords in the lectures to better understand concepts presented in class. The app is available at http://classtranscribe.com.

TIP

Positions for internships are often more selective than positions for full-time jobs, so apply early and for more than one internship position. If you don't receive an internship, try again for a full-time position. Companies have large hiring needs, and one purpose for hiring summer interns is to ensure that the interns have a great time at the company so when they return to campus they tell other students, who then feel more comfortable applying.

Securing an internship

Much of the advice in Book 2 for obtaining a full-time job applies to securing an internship offer as well. There are a few strategies to keep in mind when pursuing an internship.

Choose products and companies you're passionate about. As an intern, you join a company for three months at most, and much of that time is spent meeting new people, understanding the company, and fitting into existing processes. As a passionate power user of the product, your excitement will naturally show, and your ideas will give the company a sense for what you want to work on and provide a fresh and valuable perspective to the team, which likely feels that they have already explored every possible idea. Be able to describe how you use the product and what additional features would help increase your engagement or retention.

TIP

For any product that has a public profile, link to your profile so team members can easily see how frequently you use the product.

After you've chosen a few companies, start looking for current students who have worked at the company as well as school alumni who currently work at the company. Reach out by email and schedule short phone calls or a coffee chat no longer than 30 minutes to try and build a connection. Current students can share information about their experience, tell you which groups have the greatest need, and share some of the company culture, such as what the company values. Alumni will be able to share much of the same information, but they can also send a recommendation to HR on your behalf or may be able to hire you.

TIP

There is a balance between the response rate, ability to help, and seniority of a person you reach out to. Try to reach for the most senior alumni you can find at a company, because a quick email from them to HR will guarantee an interview, but recognize that they may not always have the time to respond. Alternatively, more junior employees will likely have more time to chat with you but likely do not have as much influence over interview or hiring decisions.

CHAPTER 2 **Exploring Undergraduate and Graduate Degrees** 71

Finally, include a mix of startups and more established companies in your search process. Given the number of interviews they do, established companies can be formulaic in their interview and hiring decisions, often looking for candidates from specific schools with a minimum GPA. If you aren't attending a top school or have below a 3.0 (out of 4.0) GPA, you should still apply to the larger companies and include an explanation for your lower GPA if one applies. Another option is to apply to startups, which will likely care more about the products you've built than your grade in chemistry. The trade-off is that startups likely have less time and people to help train you and a smaller selection of projects for you to choose from. After you join a company and finish a brief orientation period, you'll often need to start coding right away and contributing to the product.

WARNING

Be careful of startups formed by a nontechnical founder who has not yet built a product. Sometimes these companies are looking for cheap labor to help build the first version — the experience can involve many hours, unreasonable deadlines, and low to no compensation, especially if you're paid in equity. As an example, you can see a sample of recruiting pitches for coders that nontechnical founders sent to the University of Pennsylvania CS mailing list at `http://whartonite seekscodemonkey-blog.tumblr.com`.

IN THIS CHAPTER

» Choosing a task to practice coding at work

» Learning to code during and after work

» Transitioning to a coding role

Chapter 3
Training on the Job

"I hated every minute of training, but I said, 'Don't quit. Suffer now and live the rest of your life as a champion.'"

— MUHAMMAD ALI

As an employee, whether you're a marketer, a sales person, or a designer, you likely find that technology dominates more and more of your conversations with your boss, coworkers, and clients. Perhaps your boss wants to know which customer segments the company should target with online advertising, and you need to analyze millions of customer records to provide an answer. Or maybe a client wants to add or change a feature and will double the contract if the process can be done in six weeks, and you need to know whether it's possible. More tangibly, you might find yourself performing mundane and repetitive tasks that you know a computer could do.

You have probably found that an ability to code could help you perform your current job more efficiently. Companies are also noticing the value of having non-technical employees learn to code, and offering various on-site training options and support. This chapter shows you how to learn to code on the job and ways to incorporate what you've learned into your job.

Taking a Work Project to the Next Level

As a busy professional with a full work schedule, you need a tangible project to work toward to keep you motivated while you find out how to code. Think of all the tasks you perform during the week — how many could be automated if you had the right tools and skills?

The following sample tasks can be done more efficiently with some coding and could help you think of a goal of your own:

- **Spreadsheet consolidation:** You have 15 team members who submit timesheets to you using spreadsheets, and you create a consolidated weekly report by manually cutting and pasting entries from each spreadsheet.
- **Content updates:** You cut and paste the latest press stories every week into a content management system to update the company's website.
- **Data retrieval:** You work for a financial services company, and monitor acquisitions and sales made by ten private equity firms. Every day you visit each firm's website to look for updates.
- **Quality assurance:** You test updates made to the company's website by clicking the same set of links to make sure they work as expected.
- **Prototyping designs:** You create website designs, but it's difficult to explain to clients the user experience and interactions through static illustrations.

Whatever task you choose, make sure that you can describe how to complete it from start to finish. For example, the steps to complete the data retrieval task might be listed as follows:

1. Visit the first firm's website, and download the list of companies on the acquisitions page.
2. Permanently store the list. If the acquisition list has previously been retrieved, compare the list downloaded today with yesterday's version, and note any additions or deletions.
3. Display the additions or deletions.
4. Repeat Steps 1–3 for the next firm, until all the firm websites have been visited.
5. Repeat Steps 1–4 daily.

You may be part of a technical process, such as a designer who hands off mockups to a developer to create. Instead of automating your existing work, you could try to complete work the technical team normally does after you. For example, if you

do customer or sales support, you regularly receive customer and client feedback and file support tickets for issues that require an engineer. The number of support tickets always exceeds the number of engineers, so choose a low-priority non-mission-critical issue to fix.

Don't worry about choosing a task that seems too simple. Fixing an issue on a live site currently in use is always more complex than it initially appears. However, try to choose a work-related task so you can ask for help from coworkers.

Learning on the Job and after Work

After you've selected a task, you need to learn some coding to be able to fix the issue. Given that you're already working, going back to school or taking a hiatus from work to learn full-time is likely not feasible. Your next best option is to learn coding on the job, ideally with your company's support. Companies are increasingly supporting employees who want to expand their technical skill-set by providing resources to help them learn and by incentivizing those who learn tangible skills.

WISTIA CODE SCHOOL

Companies are starting to recognize the demand for coding education and the benefits of having more employees who can code. Wistia, a video-hosting and analytics company, hosts a code school so that nontechnical employees can learn how to code. Employees work as customer champions, or customer support agents, and are paired with a developer who conducts an hourly mentoring session every week for five to six months.

Normally, people learning to code practice their skills on personal projects. One advantage Wistia employees have is that the programming skills they learn are used to solve real problems that customers are experiencing. Solving coding issues, no matter how small, for a live website is difficult because the fix will immediately affect customers using the website.

As employees learn more, they still refer complex issues to the technical staff but are able to handle the easier technical problems themselves, resulting in quicker resolution times.

CHAPTER 3 **Training on the Job** 75

Training on the job

You are likely familiar with the compliance and leadership training available at your company, especially in medium- to large-sized firms. However, you may have never looked for the technical training options available to you. Here are some tips for getting started learning on the job:

» **Virtual training resources:** Corporate training libraries such as Safari, Skillsoft, Lynda, and Pluralsight are popular among companies, and are a good place to start learning programming fundamentals. (See Figure 3-1.) Each provider has a mix of text and video content, which you can read and view on-demand. Additionally, look for company-generated wikis and other training resources that describe internal programming tools and procedures.

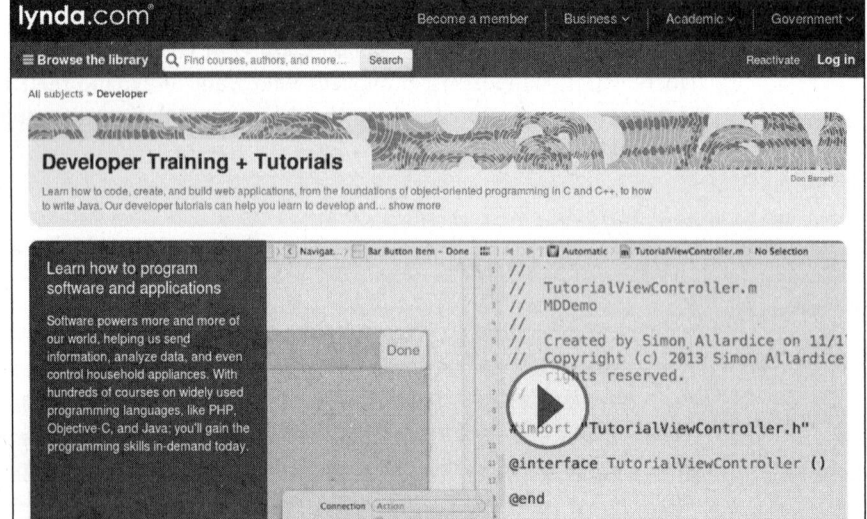

FIGURE 3-1: Lynda.com is a popular online training tool used in companies.

» **In-person training programs:** Company employees often teach orientation training courses to introduce new engineers to basic concepts and the way to code in the company. Additionally, outside vendors may occasionally conduct specific training courses on more advanced programming topics and languages. Ask whether you can view the list of training topics typically made available to engineers, and then attend introductory training sessions.

TIP

Let your supervisor know that learning to code is a development goal, and include it in any reviews. Your supervisor can help you access training programs not traditionally offered to nontechnical employees. Additionally, letting as many coworkers as possible know about your goals will increase your accountability and motivation.

» **Support from company developers:** Your company likely has developers who already assist you with the technical side of your projects. Whether you've chosen a project to improve the efficiency of your own workflow or are trying to complete work a developer would typically do, make sure to recruit a developer, usually one you already have a relationship with, so you have a resource to help you answer questions when you get stuck.

TIP

Your coworkers, especially on technical teams, are just as busy as you are. Before asking for help, try finding the answer by reviewing internal materials, using a search engine, or posting a question on a question-and-answer site such as Stack Overflow. Include where you looked because developers might use the same resources to answer questions.

Learning after work

Your company may be too small to have on-site technical training, or your office may not have any developers. Don't fret! You can take classes after work to learn how to code. Look for classes that meet twice a week in the evenings, and set aside time to do coursework during the weekend.

Companies often partially or fully reimburse the cost for employees who successfully complete a job-related course. Think of a few tangible ways that learning to code would help you do your job better, or take on a new project and then make the pitch to your manager. If you receive approval, make sure to keep up with the coursework so you're ready to contribute at work after the class is over.

A few places teach in-person coding classes designed for working professionals. Because a live instructor is teaching and assisting you, many charge a fee.

TIP

Lower cost and free options are usually taught exclusively online, though completion rates for in-person classes are usually higher than online classes. Examples of online coding websites include www.codecademy.com and www.udacity.com.

Here are some places where you can learn to code from a live instructor:

» **General Assembly:** Teaches part-time, in-person classes across a range of subjects, and has a presence in major cities in the United States and internationally. Topics include front-end, back-end, data science, and mobile development.

CHAPTER 3 **Training on the Job** 77

Classes typically meet twice a week for three hours over 12 weeks. General Assembly is one of the largest companies teaching coding classes. You can view their classes at www.generalassemb.ly.

» **Local boot camps:** As coding has become more popular, coding boot camps have sprung up in many cities around the world. Many of these boot camps offer part-time programs that don't require you to quit your job. You can search boot camps by subject, location, and cost by using Course Report, available at www.coursereport.com, and CourseHorse, available at www.coursehorse.com.

TIP

Before signing up, make sure you review the instructor, the physical location, and the cost, which should be no more than $4,000 for a part-time program with 70 hours of instruction. Course Report profiles ten part-time boot camps at www.coursereport.com/blog/learn-web-development-at-these-10-part-time-bootcamps.

CODING ON THE JOB WITH KELSEY MANNING

Kelsey Manning worked in media during and immediately after graduating from college. At Notre Dame, she was a sports editor for the school newspaper and wrote blog posts for various outlets. In addition to writing, she also did marketing and publicity for a PR agency and then Hachette, a book publisher. Hachette needed a developer to design responsive web pages, ones that display correctly on desktop and mobile devices, and hired Kelsey for the job.

Without any previous coding experience, Kelsey had to learn to code on the job to complete her work. During her first few weeks, she had to redesign real pages being used on the website. She tackled the problem by first taking online classes at Codecademy, and solving as many problems as she could on her own by searching with Google. When she hit a wall, she would ask coworkers how to solve her problem. She also kept learning and supplemented her learning with in-person coding classes taught locally in New York.

Kelsey's journey has been far from easy, but it appears to have paid off. You probably will have more time to learn with less pressure than she did, but I hope her story gives you confidence that it's possible to learn to code while working a full-time job. You can read more about Kelsey's journey at www.levo.com/articles/skills/learning-to-code-on-the-job.

78 BOOK 2 **Career Building with Coding**

» **College courses:** Traditionally, college computer science courses were theoretical, but colleges have recently started offering more applied web development and data science courses. Check your local university or community college's continuing education departments to see what's offered. For example, the City College of New York offers an Intro to Web Development class with 16 hours of instruction for $280.

» **Library classes:** Public libraries offer desktop productivity and other computer classes, and have recently started offering web development classes as well. For example, the New York Public Library has a free, ten-week program called Project_<code>, in which you build a website for a small business.

Freelancing to Build Confidence and Skills

You've taken training classes at work, found a coding mentor, and solved your first problem by using code. Congratulations! So where do you go from here? Like a foreign language, if you stop coding, you'll forget what you've learned. The most important thing is to keep coding and building your confidence and skills.

Here are a few ideas for you to practice coding in the workplace:

» **Clone a website:** Unlike programs that may have code you can't access, company websites allow you to see and save text and images. You may not be able to re-create all the functionality, but choose a specific company's web page and try creating a copy of the layout, images, and text. This process will help you practice your HTML, CSS, and JavaScript skills.

» **Build a mobile app:** People purchase more mobile devices and spend more time on them than on desktops and laptops. Still, some companies have been slow to adapt, and don't have a mobile presence. Create a mobile website using HTML and CSS, or a native application using Swift for the iPhone or Java for Android devices.

» **Code a small workplace utility app:** There are many tasks that everyone at your company and in your office performs. Your coworkers come to the office around the same time, eat lunch at the same places, and leave work using the same modes of transportation. They also share the same frustrations, some of which might be solved with a simple program. Try building an app that solves a small workplace annoyance — no one knows what would appeal to your coworkers better than you. For example, build a website that sends an email to those who opt-in whenever there is a traffic jam on the highway that

CHAPTER 3 **Training on the Job** 79

everyone uses to leave work. Similarly, you could build an app that sends an alert if any of the restaurants close to work fails a health inspection. The goal here is to learn a new technology to solve a problem, and get real feedback from other users.

After you've practiced and built a few things, publish your code on a hosting service such as GitHub and create a portfolio website pulling everything you've built into one place. You'll be able to share and others will be able to find your work, and the progression in your coding skills will be visible for anyone to see.

If you are stuck and can't think of anything to build, try freeCodeCamp, available at www.freecodecamp.com. The website, shown in Figure 3-2, connects working professionals with nonprofits that need a website or app built. After you complete the challenges, you'll start working on a vetted nonprofit project. Current projects include an animal adoption database for Latin America through the nonprofit People Saving Animals, and a charity fundraiser website for the Save a Child's Heart Foundation.

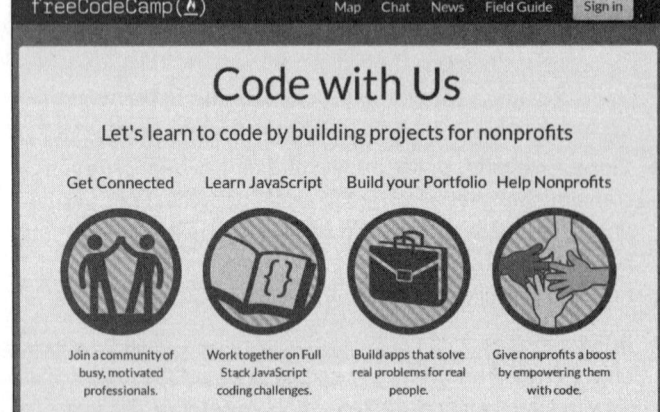

FIGURE 3-2: freeCodeCamp connects professionals who code together for nonprofits.

Transitioning to a New Role

Like any skill, coding can take a lifetime to master, but after you learn a little, you may find that you want to move into a technology-based role. The first step is to do a self-assessment and evaluate what you like and dislike about your current role, and how that matches with the technology role you want. You'll likely also need input from others; networking and chatting with developers you trust will help give you a balanced view of the job. If you decide to take the leap, you have the big advantage of being inside a company, so you'll know what they need before a job posting is ever written.

Assessing your current role

You've worked hard to get to where you are — perhaps you just landed a job in a competitive industry or have been working and advancing in your role for a few years. In either case, if you're thinking about switching to a coding job, you should do a self-assessment and decide whether a new role would be a better fit for you.

Think about what you like and dislike about your current job. For some people, the issue is office politics or poor team dynamics, but these are present in every role that involves working with other people, and switching to a coding job carries the risk of seeing the same issues. On the other hand, if you're ready to learn a new topic or have limited advancement opportunities, switching roles could be a good idea.

After evaluating your current job, think about what you would like or dislike about a coding job. For some, tech jobs seem attractive because companies overnight can become worth billions of dollars and employee salaries are reportedly in the millions. It is true that companies such as Facebook and Twitter are worth billions of dollars, and engineers at these companies are well compensated, but these are the exceptions not the rule. According to the federal Bureau of Labor Statistics, web developers and computer programmers make on average between $65,000 and $75,000, which is higher than many jobs but will not make you a millionaire overnight.

Networking with developers

One major benefit you have over other job seekers is that you probably work with developers who hold the position you're trying to obtain. Seek out some of these developers, either from people you already work with or in a department that you think is interesting.

After you connect with a few people, ask them how they spend their days, what they enjoy and what they would change about their job, and for any advice they have for you on how to make the transition. These types of conversations happen less frequently than you might think, so don't be shy about reaching out — you might be surprised to find that some developers are happy to chat with you because they are wondering how to transition into a nontechnical or business role.

The biggest constraint any company faces when hiring externally is not finding people who are technically capable of doing the job but finding people who will fit in with the company and the team culturally. As a current employee, you've already passed one culture screen, and you're in a good position to learn about how you might fit in with the existing developer culture at the company. After you build relationships with developers, maintain them and keep them updated on your goals. At some point, they'll likely be asked how serious you are and whether you'd be a good fit.

Identifying roles that match your interest and skills

Technical roles are just as numerous and varied as nontechnical roles. The positions include data analysts who analyze big data, traffic analysts who monitor website traffic and patterns, web developers who create website front ends and back ends, app developers who create mobile web apps and native apps for mobile devices, and quality assurance testers who test for and help solve bugs in new releases.

Apply for roles in which you have a strong interest. If you like working with statistics and math, a data analyst or traffic analytics role might suit you best. Or if you're a visual person and like creating experiences others can see, consider a front-end developer role.

No matter the role, you should aim for a junior title and be committed to learning a lot on the job. Don't be afraid of starting over. For example, if you've been in marketing for four years and are interested in being a web developer, you will likely start as a junior developer. Your previous job experience will help you be a better team member and manager, which could help you advance more quickly, but you'll need to show that you're able to complete basic technical tasks first. Also, no matter the role, you'll be spending a lot of time learning on the job, and will be relying on your coworkers to teach you, so choose your role and team carefully.

IN THIS CHAPTER

» Understanding myths about how to learn to code

» Reviewing myths related to securing a career in coding

» Developing a response to myths that may apply to you

Chapter 4
Coding Career Myths

"Nothing is more difficult than competing with a myth."
— FRANÇOISE GIROUD

The tech profession is filled with myths and rumors. It can be hard to separate fact from fiction, especially given the reports of eye-popping salaries and prices for company acquisitions in the news. After you cut through the hype, the tech industry is like any other, with demand for talent far exceeding supply.

The following myths about coding just aren't true. These myths mainly apply to people learning to code for the first time. Read on to separate myth from reality.

Educational Myths

It's common to think that coding careers are reserved for the few technical wizards in the world. In fact, it's a regular job for regular folks. If you're persistent, conscientious, and curious, I'll bet you can do it. Don't sell yourself short by buying into ideas that just aren't true.

You must be good at math

Developers who are building cutting-edge games, data scientists trying to create the next big machine-learning algorithm, or engineers working in the financial services industry likely need some proficiency in physics, statistics, or financial math. However, many developers, such as those building e-commerce applications or typical web pages, do not need much more math than basic addition and subtraction and high school algebra.

A good deal of math operates and powers applications, but there often isn't a need to understand everything that is happening. Computer languages and programs are designed to manage complexity by requiring that you understand the inputs and outputs — but not what happens in between, a concept called *abstraction*. For example, when driving a car, you don't need to understand how the internal combustion engine works or the physics behind converting the energy from the piston to the wheels. To drive a car, you need to understand how to operate the accelerator, the brake, and the clutch for stick-shift cars. Similarly, programs have functions that perform operations, but you need to understand only the inputs you send a function and the output it returns.

In other words, you need to be able to understand math and have some basic math skills, but you do not need to be the next Einstein to be able to program.

You must have studied engineering

Many people who study engineering learn how to program, but you do not need to be an engineer to learn how to code. Engineering teaches skills that are useful to programmers, such as how to solve a problem step-by-step as well as working within and then designing around real-world constraints. These are useful skills, but you can learn them outside the engineering curriculum.

Many topics that are part of an engineering curriculum vary in usefulness for learning how to code. Topics such as algorithms can be directly applicable, especially if you're working on cutting-edge problems. Other topics, such as assembly language and computational theory, provide a good background but are rarely used by most coders.

If your goal is to push the cutting edge of computer programs, a degree in computer engineering might be useful. However, if you want to create a website to solve a problem, learning to code in three to six months is probably sufficient to start.

TIP

Many colleges offer scholarships that can subsidize or completely cover the cost of attendance for women and minorities pursuing science and engineering degrees.

You can learn coding in a few weeks

Like any passion or profession, coding is an art, and coders hone their skills over decades. Although you don't need decades of study to start coding, the amount of time needed to learn depends on your goals. For example:

» **One week:** Learn enough HTML to put text, images, and other basic content on the page. You'll be able to operate site builders to create and customize informational websites.

» **One month:** Develop your front-end CSS skills so you can position and style elements on the page. You'll also be able to edit sites built with website builders such as Wix, Weebly, and SquareSpace. For data science, you can learn to import and handle large data sets and use Python or R to find insights about the data.

» **Three to six months:** Learn front-end and back-end development skills to take a concept, build a working prototype that can store data in a database, and then code a version that can handle hundreds of thousands of users. In addition, learn how to use a programming language's external libraries to add additional functionality, user management, and version control systems such as Git so multiple people can work on a project at the same time. For data science, you'll be able to build an interactive visualization using a JavaScript library such as d3.js. Whether learning web development or data science, it will take approximately 800 hours of effort to be proficient enough to be hired for a job.

You need a great idea to start coding

Learning to code is a lengthy process, filled with ups and downs. You might get stuck for days and not see much progress. During periods of inevitable frustration, having a bigger idea or a concrete reason to motivate you to keep learning can be helpful. Instead of trying to build the next Facebook, YouTube, or Google, try to build something that solves a problem you've personally faced. Here are people who learned to code and remained motivated with a project:

» **Coffitivity.com:** Four college students wanted to fight writer's block by listening to ambient sound. While learning to code, Tommy Nicholas built a site that streams coffee shop sounds to add background noise to otherwise silent offices and workspaces.

» **Outgrow.me:** Sam Fellig is a Kickstarter enthusiast who wanted a simple way to browse and purchase items from successful crowdfunded projects. He took the leap and learned to code so he could build his website, shown in Figure 4-1, which turned into one of *Time* magazine's Top 50 websites of 2013.

CHAPTER 4 **Coding Career Myths** 85

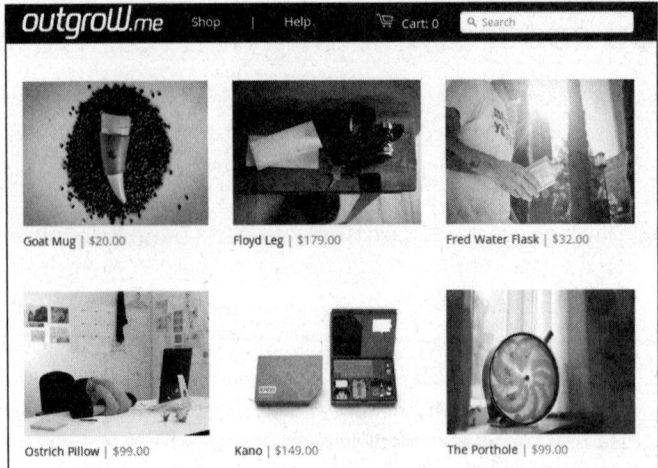

FIGURE 4-1:
Outgrow.me sells products from successful crowdfunded projects.

>> **Sworkit:** Ryan Hanna liked to work out but often became bored at the gym. While learning JavaScript and Ruby, he built an app that guided users through military-style workouts in five minutes or less. The app had over one million downloads, and Ryan eventually sold it to Nexercise, an exercise company.

Each of these sites enjoyed a degree of popularity and was noticed by a huge number of users. If something similar happens with a site you design, it serves as a nice bonus. But even if it doesn't, you'll feel satisfied having solved your own problem.

Ruby is better than Python

You might wonder what language to learn first, especially given all the choices out there. You could start with Ruby, Python, JavaScript, PHP, Swift, Objective-C — the list goes on. To resolve this debate, you might search for which language is the best, or which language to learn first. You'll find articles and posts advocating one language or another. Unlike comparing TVs or toasters, a clear winner is unlikely to emerge. Sometimes you can spend more time deciding which language to learn first than getting down to learning the language.

The most important thing is to learn a few easy scripting languages first and then choose one all-purpose beginner programming language to learn thoroughly.

Usually, beginners start with HTML, CSS, and JavaScript. These languages are the most forgiving of syntax mistakes and the easiest to learn. Then, after you learn these basics, choose Python or Ruby if you're interested in web development. You'll find many online tutorials and help for both.

If you plan on doing work with a content management system such as WordPress or Drupal, consider learning PHP.

Don't spend too much time deciding which language to learn first, and don't try to learn all of them at the same time. Sometimes people hit a roadblock with one language, give up, and start learning another language. However, the end result is learning a little bit about many languages, instead of mastering a single language and being able to build a complete and functioning website.

Career Myths

Like careers in medicine or law, a career in coding was often a long road. Much has changed in the industry, and today it's possible to get started without being accepted at a prestigious university or working for years on an advanced degree. In fact, you can probably go to work right away after learning the skills that employers require. Don't sell yourself short with these common misbeliefs.

Only college graduates receive coding offers

Both Bill Gates and Mark Zuckerberg left college before graduating to start their own technology companies. To encourage more college dropouts, Peter Thiel, the billionaire founder of PayPal and investor in Facebook, created a fellowship to pay students $100,000 to start businesses and forgo school. Still, whether you can get a coding offer without a degree varies by company type:

>> **Elite technology companies:** Google, Apple, Facebook, Microsoft, Twitter, and Yahoo! are some of the world's most elite technology companies. Because of their sheer size and name recognition, they employ recruiters who screen for certain attributes, such as college affiliation. College graduates from top schools apply to these companies in overwhelming numbers. Although it is not impossible to be hired at one of these companies without a college degree, it is very difficult.

TIP

To find out which colleges serve as feeder schools for the top technology companies, read the *Wired* article at www.wired.com/2014/05/alumni-network-2.

>> **Fortune 1000 companies:** Large companies such as Verizon and AT&T hire thousands of engineers a year, making their initial requirements for hiring slightly more flexible. These companies typically look for a college degree or two to three years of relevant experience with a specific programming language.

CHAPTER 4 **Coding Career Myths** 87

- » **Startups and small companies:** Startups are sympathetic to nondegree holders, and many startup employees are currently in college or are college dropouts. Although startups don't require a college degree, a great deal of emphasis is put on what you've built previously and your ability to code under tight deadlines. Well-funded startups are often a good place to gain experience because they need talent to keep growing and often compensate employees as well as the more mature companies do.

- » **Freelancing and contracting:** When working for contracting websites such as Upwork or for yourself, the main consideration is whether you can complete the job. Few employers check whether you have a college degree; a portfolio of past work, even if it was unpaid, is much more important to securing the job and conveying the confidence that you'll be able to deliver the project on time and within budget.

Interest in nontraditional candidates is growing. Companies such as www.entelo.com specialize in sourcing and scoring candidates with nontraditional markers of success, such as blog posts, Stack Exchange answers, Twitter comments, and code posted to GitHub.

You must have experience

Studies have shown that there is no correlation between experience and performance in software development. For the new programmer, after you master some basic skills, your performance is affected by much more than the amount of time you've spent on a job. Despite the research, however, some companies still screen for years of experience when filling open positions.

Much of the same logic that applies to getting a coding job without a college degree applies here as well. Elite technology companies receive so many resumes and are in such high demand that they can be more selective and look first at experienced candidates. Fortune 1000 companies usually take one of two approaches: They look for a minimum one to two years of experience, or they understand that as a new hire, you'll need training and use existing staff to help support you.

Startups and small companies typically pay the least attention to the number of years of experience and more attention to your previous projects. Your contributions to an open-source project or a weekend project that attracted real users will generate plenty of interest and enthusiasm for you as a candidate. Although it can be easier to get your foot in the door at a startup, remember that the company's small size likely means there are fewer people and less money to devote to your training and support, so much of your learning will be self-supported.

Companies of any size willing to invest in developing your programming abilities will typically look for a positive attitude, a willingness to learn, and the persistence to keep trying to solve problems and overcome obstacles.

Tech companies don't hire women or minorities

Whether in the *Law and Order: SVU* portrayal of women in technology or the national media reports of the high-powered lawsuit filed by Ellen Pao about her treatment in the technology industry, the tech industry has not had the best year for welcoming women and minorities.

Admittedly, the numbers show a story that has improved but still has plenty of room to grow, with the tech industry workforce made up of 25 percent women and 5 percent minority workers, which is below the national averages for both groups.

TIP

The Wall Street Journal has compiled publicly released diversity data from top tech companies broken down by leadership and technology positions (see Figure 4-2). To see the report, go to http://graphics.wsj.com/diversity-in-tech-companies.

FIGURE 4-2: *WSJ* compilation of diversity in tech companies based on public filings.

Although many contributing causes have been identified, including the lack of a pipeline of candidates studying computer science or applying to tech firms, many leading companies and nonprofits are actively trying to increase the recruitment and support of women and minorities in the workplace.

CHAPTER 4 **Coding Career Myths** 89

On the corporate side, larger companies are creating programs that train and increase the number of pathways to join the workforce. For example, Google recently launched a $50 million campaign called Made with Code to highlight women in tech and provide opportunities for girls to learn to code.

Similarly, nonprofit organizations such as Code 2040 connect Black and Latino talent to companies. On the training side, nonprofits such as Yes We Code, Girls Who Code, Black Girls Who Code, and Women Who Code teach technical skills to increase the number of women and minorities entering the jobs pipeline.

The highest paying coding jobs are in San Francisco

Many of the most famous tech companies, including Apple, Facebook, Google, Twitter, and Yahoo!, are located in Silicon Valley. While these and other companies in the San Francisco and Silicon Valley area hire a large number of tech workers each year, that paints only part of the picture.

Cities across the United States pay tech salaries comparable to San Francisco but have a much lower cost of living, as shown in Table 4-1. Two numbers to keep in mind when evaluating a city are the average salaries paid to tech workers and the average cost of living. Salary minus rent provides a simple and rough estimate of take-home pay, though it doesn't take into account taxes, transportation, and cost of goods and services.

TABLE 4-1 Salary and Median Rent by City

City	Annual Salary	Annual Rent	Salary Less Rent
Austin, TX	$98,672	$16,200	$82,472
New York, NY	$106,263	$25,856	$80,407
Seattle, WA	$103,309	$23,400	$79,909
Washington, D.C.	$102,873	$24,000	$78,873
Houston, TX	$95,575	$17,000	$78,575
St. Louis, MO	$83,582	$11,700	$71,882
San Francisco, CA	$118,243	$50,400	$67,843

Sources: Dice.com Annual Salary Survey, Zillow.com median rent prices

Although San Francisco does pay the most of any city in the country, it looks less attractive after subtracting the cost of rent from annual pay. By contrast, cities such as St. Louis and Seattle offer strong salaries with a much lower cost of living.

A cost of living calculator will help you compare salaries in different cities. See, for example, the PayScale cost of living calculator by visiting `www.payscale.com/cost-of-living-calculator`.

Your previous experience isn't relevant

Coding skill is one important factor that tech companies evaluate when hiring coders. But just as important is your domain knowledge and ability to work and lead a team. For example, perhaps you're a lawyer looking to switch careers and become a coder. Your legal knowledge will far exceed that of the average programmer, and if you target companies making software for lawyers, your perspective will be valuable.

Similarly, whether you previously were in finance or marketing, the issues around managing and leading teams are similar. It is natural for a team of people to disagree, have trouble communicating, and end up short of the intended goal. Your previous experiences handling this type of situation and turning it into a positive outcome will be valued in a tech company, where much of the coding is performed in teams.

Finally, your current or previous job might not seem technical, but others like you have made the transition into a coding job. People from a variety of professions — such as lawyers, teachers, and financial analysts — have learned how to code, and found ways to incorporate their past work experiences into their current coding careers.

3 Basic Web Coding

Contents at a Glance

CHAPTER 1: Exploring Basic HTML 95
- What Does HTML Do? ... 95
- Understanding HTML Structure 96
- Getting Familiar with Common HTML Tasks and Tags 102
- Styling Me Pretty ... 107
- Building Your First Website Using HTML 109

CHAPTER 2: Getting More Out of HTML 113
- Organizing Content on the Page 113
- Listing Data ... 115
- Putting Data in Tables .. 118
- Filling Out Forms ... 124
- Practicing More with HTML 127

CHAPTER 3: Getting Stylish with CSS 129
- What Does CSS Do? ... 129
- CSS Structure ... 131
- Common CSS Tasks and Selectors 135
- Styling Me Pretty ... 146

CHAPTER 4: Next Steps with CSS 151
- Styling (More) Elements on Your Page 152
- Selecting Elements to Style 157
- Aligning and Laying Out Your Elements 163
- Writing More Advanced CSS 172

CHAPTER 5: Building Floating Page Layouts 173
- Creating a Basic Two-Column Design 173
- Building a Three-Column Design 185
- Building a Fixed-Width Layout 193
- Building a Centered Fixed-Width Layout 196

CHAPTER 6: Using Alternative Positioning 201
- Working with Absolute Positioning 201
- Managing z-index ... 206
- Building a Page Layout with Absolute Positioning 208
- Creating a More Flexible Layout 212
- Exploring Other Types of Positioning 216
- Flexible Box Layout Model 221

IN THIS CHAPTER

» Learning the purpose of HTML

» Understanding basic HTML structure

» Adding headlines, paragraphs, hyperlinks, and images

» Formatting web page text

» Creating a basic HTML website

Chapter 1
Exploring Basic HTML

"You affect the world by what you browse."

— TIM BERNERS-LEE

HTML, or *HyperText Markup Language*, is used in every single web page you browse on the Internet. Because the language is so foundational, a good first step for you is to start learning HTML.

In this chapter, you discover the HTML basics, including basic HTML structure and how to make text appear in the browser. Next, you find out how to format text and display images in a web browser. Finally, you create your own, and possibly first, HTML website. You may find that HTML without any additional styling appears to be very plain, and doesn't look like the websites you normally visit on the Internet. After you code a basic website using HTML, you will use additional languages in later chapters to add even more style to your websites.

What Does HTML Do?

HTML instructs the browser on how to display text and images in a web page. Recall the last time you created a document with a word processor. Whether you use Microsoft Word or WordPad, Apple Pages, or another application, your word processor has a main window in which you type text, and a menu or toolbar with multiple options to structure and style that text (see Figure 1-1). Using your word

processor, you can create headings, write paragraphs, insert pictures, or underline text. Similarly, you can use HTML to structure and style text that appears on websites.

FIGURE 1-1:
The layout of a word processor.

Markup language documents, like HTML documents, are just plain text files. Unlike documents created with a word processor, you can view an HTML file using any web browser on any type of computer.

REMEMBER

HTML files are plain text files that appear styled only when viewed with a browser. By contrast, the rich text file format used by word processors add unseen formatting commands to the file. As a result, HTML written in a rich text file won't render correctly in the browser.

Understanding HTML Structure

HTML follows a few rules to ensure that a website always displays in the same way no matter which browser or computer is used. Once you understand these rules, you'll be better able to predict how the browser will display your HTML pages, and to diagnose your mistakes when (not if!) the browser displays your web page differently than you expected. Since its creation, HTML has evolved to include more effects, but the following basic structural elements remain unchanged.

TIP

You can use any browser to display your HTML files, though I strongly recommend you download, install, and use Chrome or Firefox. Both of these browsers are updated often, are generally fast, and support and consistently render the widest variety of HTML tags.

96 BOOK 3 **Basic Web Coding**

Identifying elements

HTML uses special text keywords called *elements* to structure and style a website. The browser recognizes an element and applies its effect if the following three conditions exist:

>> The element is a letter, word, or phrase with special meaning. For example, h1 is an element recognized by the browser to apply a header effect, with bold text and an enlarged font size.

>> The element is enclosed with a left-angle bracket (<) and right-angle bracket (>). An element enclosed in this way is called a *tag* (such as, for example, <h1>).

>> An opening tag (<element>) is followed by a closing tag (</element>). Note that the closing tag differs from the opening tag by the addition of a forward slash after the first left bracket and before the element (such as, for example, </h1>).

REMEMBER

Some HTML tags are self-closing, and don't need separate closing tags, only a forward slash in the opening tag. For more about this topic, see the section, "Getting Familiar with Common HTML Tasks and Tags," later in this chapter.

When all three conditions are met, the text between the opening and closing tags is styled with the tag's defined effect. If even one of these conditions is not met, the browser just displays plain text.

For a better understanding of these three conditions, see the following example code:

```
<h1>This is a big heading with all three conditions</h1>
h1 This is text without the < and > sign surrounding the tag /h1
<rockstar>This is text with a tag that has no meaning to the browser</rockstar>
This is regular text
```

You can see how a browser displays this code in Figure 1-2.

FIGURE 1-2:
The example code displayed in a browser.

CHAPTER 1 **Exploring Basic HTML** 97

The browser applies a header effect to "This is a big heading with all three conditions" because h1 is a header tag and all three conditions for a valid HTML tag exist:

» The browser recognizes the h1 element.

» The h1 element is surrounded with a left (<) and right angle bracket (>).

» The opening tag (<h1>) is followed by text and then a closing tag (</h1>).

Notice how the h1 tag itself does not display in the heading. The browser will never display the actual text of an element in a properly formatted HTML tag.

The remaining lines of code display as plain text because they each are missing one of the conditions. On the second line of code, the <h1> tag is missing the left and right brackets, which violates the second condition. The third line of code violates the first condition because rockstar is not a recognized HTML element. (Once you finish this chapter, however, you may feel like a rockstar!) Finally, the fourth line of code displays as plain text because it has no opening tag preceding the text, and no closing tag following the text, which violates the third condition.

Every left angle-bracket must be followed after the element with a right angle-bracket. In addition, every opening HTML tag must be followed with a closing HTML tag.

Over 100 HTML elements exist, and I cover the most important elements in the following sections. For now, don't worry about memorizing individual element names.

HTML is a forgiving language, and may properly apply an effect even if you're missing pieces of code, like a closing tag. However, if you leave in too many errors, your page won't display correctly.

Featuring your best attribute

Attributes provide additional ways to modify the behavior of an element or specify additional information. Usually, but not always, you set an attribute equal to a value enclosed in quotes. Here's an example using the title attribute and the hidden attribute:

```
<h1 title="United States of America">USA</h1>
<h1 hidden>New York City</h1>
```

The title attribute provides advisory information about the element that appears when the mouse cursor hovers over the affected text (in other words, a *tooltip*). In

this example, the word USA is styled as a header using the <h1> tag with a title attribute set equal to "United States of America". In a browser, then when you place your mouse cursor over the word USA, the text United States of America displays as a tooltip. (See Figure 1-3.)

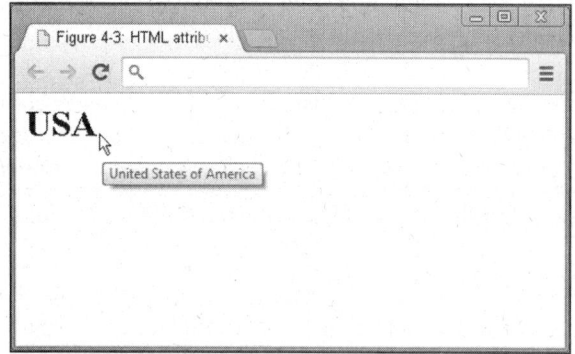

FIGURE 1-3: A heading with title attribute has a tooltip.

The hidden attribute indicates that the element is not relevant, so the browser won't render any elements with this attribute. In this example, the words New York City never appear in the browser window because the hidden attribute is in the opening <h1> tag. More practically, hidden attributes are often used to hide fields from users so they can't edit them. For example, an RSVP website may want to include but hide from users' view a date and time field.

TECHNICAL STUFF

The hidden attribute is new in HTML5, which means it may not work on some older browsers.

You don't have to use one attribute at a time. You can include multiple attributes in the opening HTML tag, like this:

```
<h1 title="United States of America" lang="en">USA</h1>
```

In this example, I used the title attribute, and the lang attribute, setting it equal to "en" to specify that the content of the element is in the English language.

REMEMBER

When including multiple attributes, separate each attribute with one space.

Keep the following rules in mind when using attributes:

» If using an attribute, always include the attribute in the opening HTML tag.

» Multiple attributes can modify a single element.

» If the attribute has a value, then use the equal sign (=) and enclose the value in quotes.

CHAPTER 1 **Exploring Basic HTML** 99

Standing head, title, and body above the rest

HTML files are structured in a specific way so browsers can correctly interpret the file's information. Every HTML file has the same five elements: four whose opening and closing tags appear once and only once, and one that appears once and doesn't need a closing tag. These are as follows:

- » `!DOCTYPE html` must appear first in your HTML file, and it appears only once. This tag lets browsers know which version of HTML you're using. In this case, it's the latest version, HTML5. No closing tag is necessary for this element.

 For HTML4 websites, the first line in the HTML file reads `<!DOCTYPE HTML PUBLIC "-//W3C//DTD HTML 4.01//EN" "http://www.w3.org/TR/html4/strict.dtd">`

- » `html` represents the *root* or beginning of an HTML document. The `<html>` tag is followed by first an opening and closing `<head>` tag, and then an opening and closing `<body>` tag.

- » `head` contains other elements, which specify general information about the page, including the title.

- » `title` defines the title in the browser's title bar or page tab.

 Search engines like Google use `title` to rank websites in search results.

- » `body` contains the main content of an HTML document. Text, images, and other content listed between the opening and closing body tag is displayed by the browser.

Here is an example of a properly structured HTML file with these five tags (see Figure 1-4):

```
<!DOCTYPE html>
<html>
<head>
    <title>Favorite Movie Quotes</title>
</head>
<body>
    <h1>"I'm going to make him an offer he can't refuse"</h1>
    <h1>"Houston, we have a problem"</h1>
    <h1>"May the Force be with you"</h1>
    <h1>"You talking to me?"</h1>
</body>
</html>
```

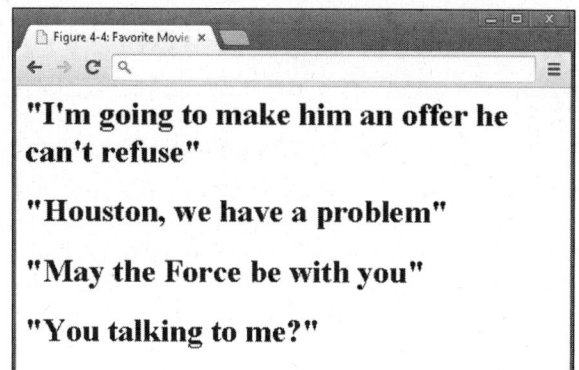

FIGURE 1-4:
A web page created with basic HTML elements.

TIP

Using spaces to indent and separate your tags is highly recommended. It helps you and others read and understand your code. These spaces are only for you and any other human that reads the code, however. Your browser won't care. As far as your browser is concerned, you could run all your tags together on one line. (Don't do this, though. The next person who reads your code will be most unhappy.) HTML does recognize and display the first whitespace character in text between opening and closing HTML tags.

REMEMBER

The example had many h1 tags but only one opening and closing `html`, `head`, `title`, and `body` tag.

HISTORY OF HTML

A computer engineer, Tim Berners-Lee, wanted academics to easily access academic papers and collaborate with each other. To accomplish this goal, in 1989 Mr. Berners-Lee created the first version of HTML, which had the same hyperlink elements you find in this chapter, and hosted the first website in 1991. Unlike with most other computer software, Mr. Berners-Lee made HTML available royalty-free, allowing widespread adoption and use around the world. Shortly after creating the first iteration of HTML, Mr. Berners-Lee formed the W3C (World Wide Web Consortium), which is a group of people from academic institutions and corporations who define and maintain the HTML language. The W3C continues to develop the HTML language, and has defined more than 100 HTML elements, far more than the 18 that Mr. Berners-Lee originally created. The latest version of HTML is HTML5, and it has considerable new functionality. In addition to supporting elements from previous HTML versions, HTML5 allows developers to write code for browsers to play audio and video files, easily locate a user's physical location, and build charts and graphs.

Getting Familiar with Common HTML Tasks and Tags

Your browser can interpret over a hundred HTML tags, but most websites use just a few tags to do most of the work within the browser. To understand this, let's try a little exercise: Think of your favorite news website. Have one in mind? Now connect to the Internet, open your browser, and type the address of that website. Bring this book with you, and take your time — I can wait!

In the event you can't access the Internet right now, take a look at the article from my favorite news website, *The New York Times*, found in Figure 1-5.

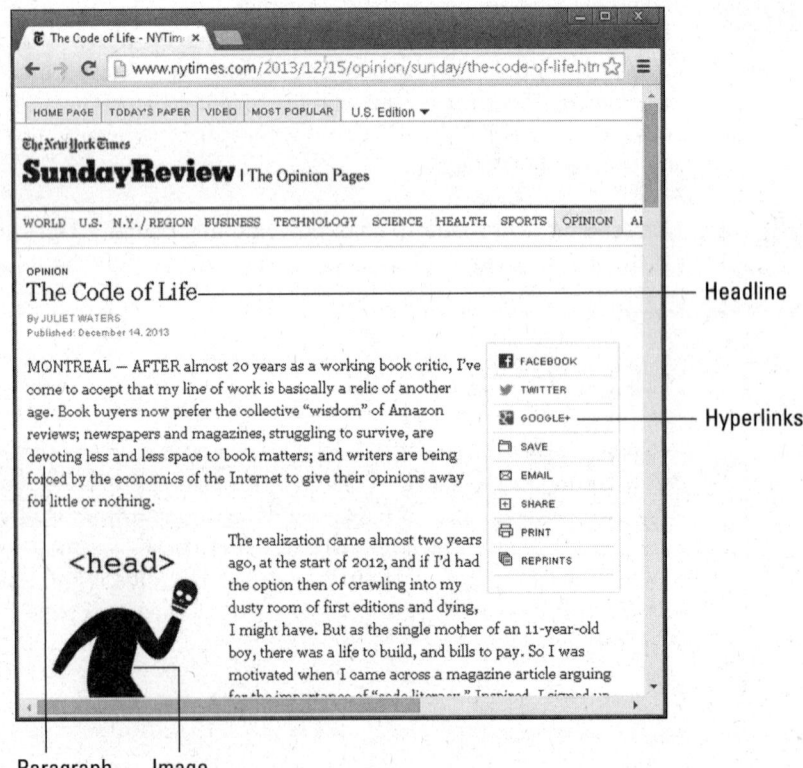

FIGURE 1-5: A *New York Times* article with headline, paragraphs, hyperlinks, and images.

Look closely at the news website on your screen (or look at mine). Four HTML elements are used to create the majority of the page:

>> **Headlines:** Headlines are displayed in bold and have a larger font size than the surrounding text.

102 BOOK 3 **Basic Web Coding**

» **Paragraphs:** Each story is organized into paragraphs with white space dividing each paragraph.

» **Hyperlinks:** The site's homepage and article pages have links to other stories, and links to share the story on social networks like Facebook, Twitter, and Google+.

» **Images:** Writers place images throughout the story, but also look for site images like icons and logos.

In the following sections, I explain how to write code to create these common HTML features.

Writing headlines

Use headlines to describe a section of your page. HTML has six levels of headings (see Figure 1-6):

» h1, which is used for the most important headings

» h2, which is used for subheadings

» h3 to h6, which are used for less important headings

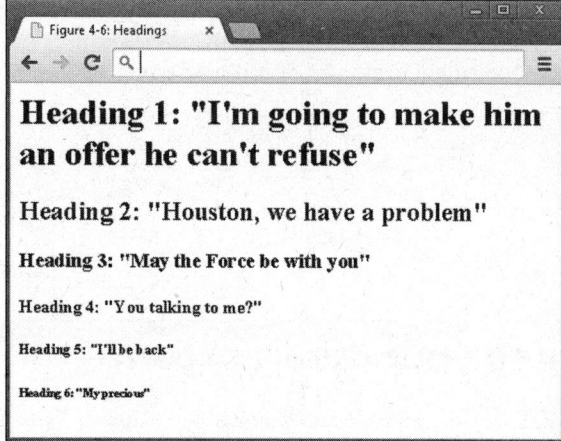

FIGURE 1-6: Headings created using elements h1 through h6.

The browser renders h1 headings with a font size larger than h2's, which in turn is larger than h3's. Headings start with an opening heading tag, the heading text, and then the closing heading tag, as follows:

```
<h1>Heading text here</h1>
```

CHAPTER 1 **Exploring Basic HTML** 103

Here are some additional code examples showing various headings:

```
<h1>Heading 1: "I'm going to make him an offer he can't refuse"</h1>
<h2>Heading 2: "Houston, we have a problem"</h2>
<h3>Heading 3: "May the Force be with you"</h3>
<h4>Heading 4: "You talking to me?"</h4>
<h5>Heading 5: "I'll be back"</h5>
<h6>Heading 6: "My precious"</h6>
```

Always close what you open. With headings, remember to include a closing heading tag, such as </h1>.

Organizing text in paragraphs

To display text in paragraphs, you can use the p element: Place an opening <p> tag before the paragraph, and a closing tag after it. The p element takes text and inserts a line break after the closing tag.

To insert a single line break after any element, use the
 tag. The
 tag is self-closing so no closing tag is needed, and </br> isn't used.

Paragraphs start with an opening paragraph tag, the paragraph text, and then the closing paragraph tag:

```
<p>Paragraph text here</p>
```

Here are some additional examples of coding a paragraph (see Figure 1-7):

```
<p>Armstrong: Okay. I'm going to step off the LM now.</p>
<p>Armstrong: That's one small step for man; one giant leap for mankind.</p>
<p>Armstrong: Yes, the surface is fine and powdery. I can kick it up loosely
with my toe. It does adhere in fine layers, like powdered charcoal, to the
sole and sides of my boots.</p>
```

Linking to your (heart's) content

Hyperlinks are one of HTML's most valuable features. Web pages that include hyperlinked references to other sources allow the reader to access those sources with just a click, a big advantage over printed pages.

FIGURE 1-7:
Text displayed in paragraphs using the p element.

Hyperlinks have two parts:

» **Link destination:** The web page the browser visits once the link is clicked.

To define the link destination in HTML, start with an opening anchor tag (`<a>`) that has an `href` attribute. Then add the value of the `href` attribute, which is the website the browser will go to once the link is clicked.

» **Link description:** The words used to describe the link.

To create a hyperlink, add text to describe the link after the opening anchor tag, and then add the closing anchor tag.

The resulting HTML should look something like this:

```
<a href="website url">Link description</a>
```

Here are three more examples of coding a hyperlink (see Figure 1-8):

```
<a href="http://www.amazon.com">Purchase anything</a>
<a href="http://www.airbnb.com">Rent a place to stay from a local host</a>
<a href="http://www.techcrunch.com">Tech industry blog</a>
```

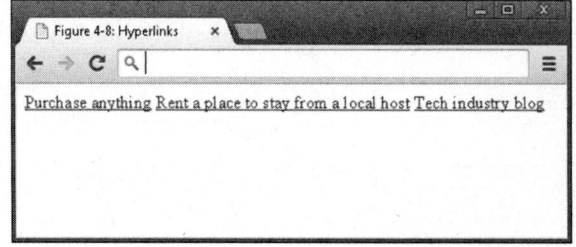

FIGURE 1-8:
Three hyperlinks created using the a element.

CHAPTER 1 **Exploring Basic HTML** 105

When rendering hyperlinks, the browser, by default, will underline the link and color the link blue. To change these default properties, see Book 3, Chapter 3.

The `<a>` tag does not include a line break after the link.

Google's search engine ranks web pages based on the words used to describe a web page between the opening and closing `<a>` tags. This improved on search results from previous methods, which relied primarily on analyzing page content.

Adding images

Images spruce up otherwise plain HTML text pages. To include an image on your web page — your own or someone else's — you must obtain the image's web address. Websites like Google Images (`images.google.com`) and Flickr (`www.flickr.com`) allow you to search for online images based on keywords. When you find an image you like, right-click on the image, and select Copy Image URL.

Make sure you have permission to use an online image. Flickr has tools that allow you to search for images with few to no license restrictions. Additionally, websites pay to host images, and incur charges when a website directly links to an image. For this reason, some websites do not allow *hotlinking*, or linking directly from third-party websites (like you) to an image.

If you want to use an image that has not already been uploaded to the Internet, you can use a site like `www.imgur.com` to upload the image. After uploading, you will be able to copy the image URL and use it in your HTML.

To include an image, start with an opening image tag ``, define the source of the image using the `src` attribute, and include a forward slash at the end of the opening tag to close the tag (see Figure 1-9):

```
<img src="http://upload.wikimedia.org/wikipedia/commons/5/55/
Grace_Hopper.jpg"/>
<img src="http://upload.wikimedia.org/wikipedia/commons/b/bd/
Dts_news_bill_gates.jpg"/>
```

The image tag is self-closing, which means a separate `` closing image tag is not used. The image tag is one of the exceptions to the always-close-what-you-open rule!

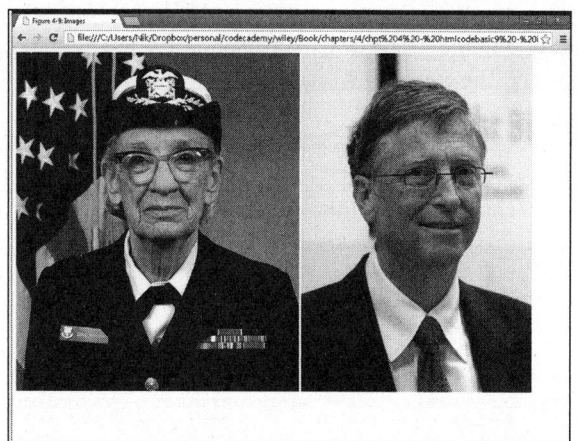

FIGURE 1-9: Images of Grace Hopper, a US Navy rear admiral, and Bill Gates, the cofounder of Microsoft, rendered using ``.

Bill Gates photo credit https://commons.wikimedia.org/wiki/File:Dts_news_bill_gates_wikipedia.JPG

Styling Me Pretty

Now that you know how to display basic text and images in a browser, you should understand how to further customize and style them. HTML has basic capabilities to style content, and later chapters show you how to use CSS to style and position your content down to the last pixel. Here, however, I explain how to do some basic text formatting in HTML, and then you'll build your first web page.

Highlighting with bold, italics, underline, and strikethrough

HTML allows for basic text styling using the following elements:

- `strong` marks important text, which the browser displays as bold
- `em` marks emphasized text, which the browser displays as italicized
- `u` marks text as underlined
- `del` marks deleted text, which the browser displays as strikethrough

REMEMBER

The underline element is not typically used for text because it can lead to confusion. Hyperlinks, after all, are underlined by default.

CHAPTER 1 **Exploring Basic HTML** 107

To use these elements, start with the element's opening tag, followed by the affected text, and then a closing tag, as follows:

```
<element name>Affected text</element name>
```

Here are some examples (see Figure 1-10):

```
Grace Hopper, <strong> a US Navy rear admiral </strong>, popularized the term
"debugging."
Bill Gates co-founded a company called <em>Microsoft</em>.
Stuart Russell and Peter Norvig wrote a book called <u>Artificial Intelligence:
A Modern Approach</u>.
Mark Zuckerberg created a website called <del>Nosebook</del> Facebook.
Steve Jobs co-founded a company called <del><em>Peach</em></del> <em>Apple</em>
```

FIGURE 1-10: Sentences formatted using bold, italics, underline, and strikethrough.

TIP

You can apply multiple effects to text by using multiple HTML tags. Always close the most recently opened tag first and then the next most recently used tag. For an example, look at the last line of code in Figure 1-10, and the tags applied to the word Peach.

Raising and lowering text with superscript and subscript

Reference works like *Wikipedia* and technical papers often use superscript for footnotes and subscript for chemical names. To apply these styles, use the elements

- » sup for text marked as superscript
- » sub for text marked as subscript

To use these elements, start with the element's opening tag, followed by the affected text, and then a closing tag as follows:

```
<element name>Affected text</element name>
```

Here are two examples (see Figure 1-11):

```
<p>The University of Pennsylvania announced to the public the first electronic
general-purpose computer, named ENIAC, on February 14, 1946.<sup>1</sup></p>
<p>The Centers for Disease Control and Prevention recommends drinking several
glasses of H<sub>2</sub>0 per day.</p>
```

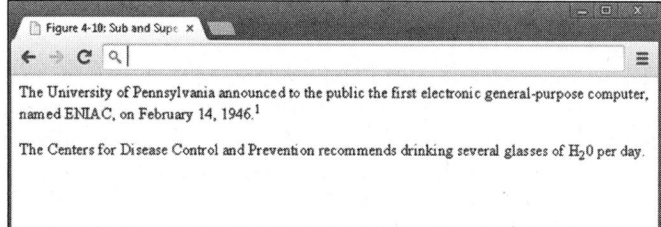

FIGURE 1-11: Text formatted to show superscript and subscript effects.

TIP

When using the superscript element to mark footnotes, use an `<a>` anchor tag to link directly to the footnote so the reader can view the footnote easily.

Building Your First Website Using HTML

Now that you understand the basics, you can put that knowledge to use. You can practice directly on your computer by following these steps:

1. **Open any text editor, such as Notepad (on a PC) or TextEdit (on a Mac).**

 On a PC running Microsoft Windows, you can access Notepad by clicking the Start button and selecting Run; in the search box, type **Notepad**.

 On a Macintosh, select the Spotlight Search (hourglass icon on the top-right corner of the toolbar), and type **TextEdit**.

CHAPTER 1 Exploring Basic HTML 109

2. **Enter into the text editor any of the code samples you have seen in this chapter, or create your own combination of the code.**

3. **Once you have finished, save the file and make sure to include ".html" at the end of the filename.**

4. **Double-click the file to open in your default browser.**

You can download at no cost specialized text editors created specifically for writing code:

» For PCs, you can download Notepad++ at www.notepad-plus-plus.org.

» For Mac computers, you can download TextMate at http://macromates.com/download.

If you want to practice your HTML online, you can use the Codecademy website. Codecademy is a free website created in 2011 to allow anyone to learn how to code right in the browser, without installing or downloading any software. (See Figure 1-12.) Practice all the tags (and a few more) that you find in this chapter by following these steps:

1. **Open your browser, go to** www.dummies.com/go/codingaiolinks, **and click the Codecademy link.**

2. **If you have a Codecademy account, sign in.**

 Signing up is discussed in Book 1, Chapter 3.

 Creating an account allows you to save your progress as you work, but it's optional.

3. **Navigate to and click HTML Basics.**

 Background information is presented in the upper-left portion of the site, and instructions are presented in the lower-left portion of the site.

4. **Complete the instructions in the main coding window.**

 As you type, a live preview of your code is generated.

5. **After you have finished completing the instructions, click the Save and Submit Code button.**

 If you followed the instructions correctly, a green checkmark appears, and you proceed to the next exercise. If an error exists in your code, a warning appears

with a suggested fix. If you run into a problem, or have a bug you cannot fix, click the hint, use the Q&A Forums, or tweet me at @nikhilgabraham and include the hashtag #codingFD. Additionally, you can sign up for book updates and explanations for changes to programming language commands by visiting http://tinyletter.com/codingfordummies.

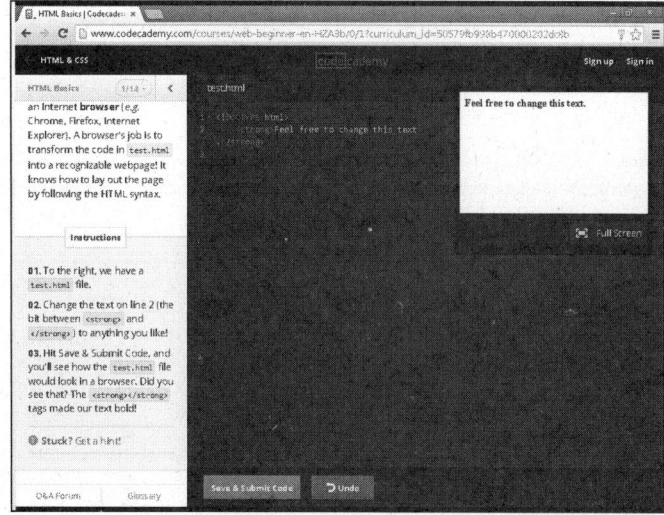

FIGURE 1-12: Codecademy in-browser exercises.

IN THIS CHAPTER

» Organizing content in a web page

» Writing HTML lists

» Creating HTML tables

» Filling out HTML forms

Chapter **2**

Getting More Out of HTML

"I'm controlling, and I want everything orderly, and I need lists."
— SANDRA BULLOCK

Even your best content needs structure to increase readability for your users. This book is no exception. Consider the "In This Chapter" bulleted list of items at the top of this chapter, or the table of contents at the beginning of the book. Lists and tables make things easier for you to understand at a glance. By mirroring the structure you find in a book or magazine, web elements let you precisely define how content, such as text and images, appear on the web.

In this chapter, you find out how to use HTML elements such as lists, tables, and forms, and how to know when these elements are appropriate for your content.

Organizing Content on the Page

Readability is the most important principle for organizing and displaying content on your web page. Your web page should allow visitors to easily read, understand, and act on your content. The desired action you have in mind for your visitors may be to click on and read additional content, share the content with others, or

perhaps make a purchase. Poorly organized content will lead users to leave your website before engaging with your content long enough to complete the desired action.

Figures 2-1 and 2-2 show two examples of website readability. In Figure 2-1, I searched Craigslist.org for an apartment in New York. The search results are structured like a list, and you can limit the content displayed using the filters and search forms. Each listing has multiple attributes, such as a description, the number of bedrooms, the neighborhood, and, most importantly, the price. Comparing similar attributes from different listings takes some effort — notice the jagged line your eye must follow.

FIGURE 2-1:
A Craigslist.org listing of apartments in New York (2014).

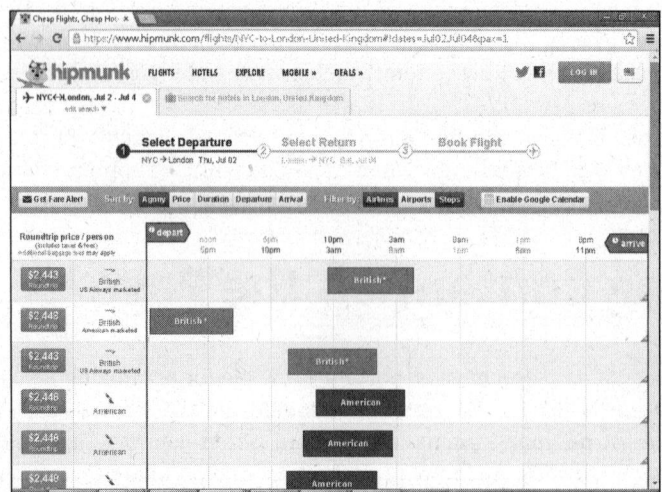

FIGURE 2-2:
A Hipmunk.com listing of flights from New York to London (2014).

114 BOOK 3 **Basic Web Coding**

Figure 2-2 shows the results of a search I conducted at Hipmunk.com for flights from New York to London. As with the Craigslist search results, you can limit the content displayed using the filters and search forms. Additionally, each flight listing has multiple attributes, including price, carrier, departure time, landing time, and duration, which are similar to the attributes of the apartment listings. Comparing similar attributes from different flights is much easier with the Hipmunk layout, however. Notice how the content, in contrast to Craigslist's, has a layout that allows your eye to follow a straight line down the page, so you can easily rank and compare different options.

TIP

Don't underestimate the power of simplicity when displaying content. Although Craigslist's content layout may look almost too simple, the site is one of the top 50 most visited websites in the world. Reddit.com is another example of a top 50 website with a simple layout.

Before displaying your content, ask yourself a few questions first:

» **Does your content have one attribute with related data, or does it follow sequential steps?** If so, consider using lists.

» **Does your content have multiple attributes suitable for comparison?** If so, consider using tables.

» **Do you need to collect input from the visitor?** If so, consider using forms.

Don't let these choices overwhelm you. Pick one, see how your visitors react, and if necessary change how you display the content. The process of evaluating one version against another version of the same web page is called *A/B testing*.

Listing Data

Websites have used lists for decades to convey related or hierarchical information. In Figure 2-3, you can see an older version of Yahoo.com that uses bulleted lists to display various categories and today's Allrecipes.com recipe page, which uses lists to display various ingredients.

Lists begin with a symbol, an indentation, and then the list item. The symbol used can be a number, letter, bullet, or no symbol at all.

 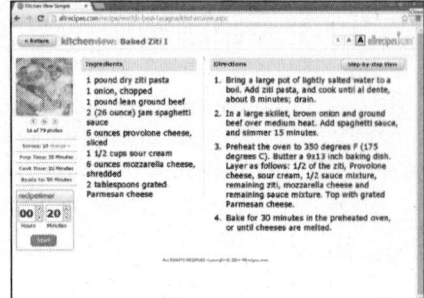

FIGURE 2-3: Yahoo!'s 1997 homepage using an unordered list (left) and Allrecipes.com's 2014 recipe using an ordered list (right).

Creating ordered and unordered lists

Here are the two most popular types of lists:

» **Ordered:** Ordered lists are numerical or alphabetical lists in which the sequence of list items is important.

» **Unordered:** These lists are usually bulleted lists in which the sequence of list items has no importance.

You create lists by specifying the type of list as ordered or unordered and then adding each list item using the `li` tag, as shown in the following steps:

1. **Specify the type of list.**

 Add opening and closing list tags that specify either an ordered (ol) or unordered (ul) list, as follows:

 - ol to specify the beginning and end of an ordered list
 - ul to specify the beginning and end of an unordered list

2. **Add an opening and closing tag (that is, `` and ``) for each item in the list.**

 For example, here's an ordered list:

   ```
   <ol>
       <li> List item #1 </li>
       <li> List item #2 </li>
       <li> List item #3 </li>
   </ol>
   ```

Nesting lists

Additionally, you can nest lists within lists. A list of any type can be nested inside another list; to nest a list, replace the list item tag `` with a list type tag, either `` or ``.

The example code in Figure 2-4 shows various list types including a nested list. (See Figures 2-4 and 2-5.)

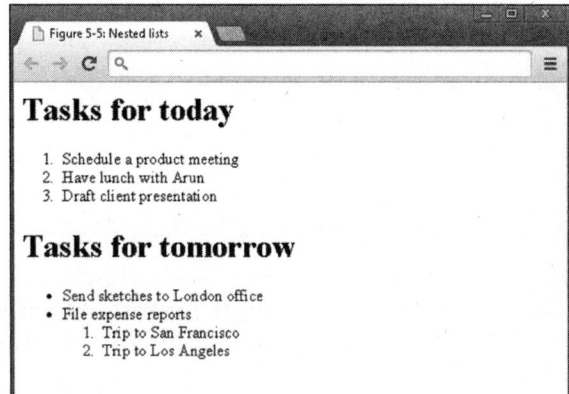

FIGURE 2-4: Coding an ordered list and a nested list.

FIGURE 2-5: The page produced by the code in Figure 2-4.

TIP

The `<h1>` tag shown in this code sample is not necessary to create a list. I use it here only to name each list.

Every opening list or list item tag must be followed with a closing list or list item tag.

CHAPTER 2 **Getting More Out of HTML** 117

Putting Data in Tables

Tables help further organize text and tabular data on the page. (See Figure 2-6.) The table format is especially appropriate when displaying pricing information, comparing features across products, or in any situation where the columns or rows share a common attribute. Tables act as containers, and can hold and display any type of content, including text, such as heading and lists and images. For example, the table in Figure 2-6 includes additional content and styling like icons at the top of each column, gray background shading, and rounded buttons. This content and styling can make tables you see online differ from tables you ordinarily see in books.

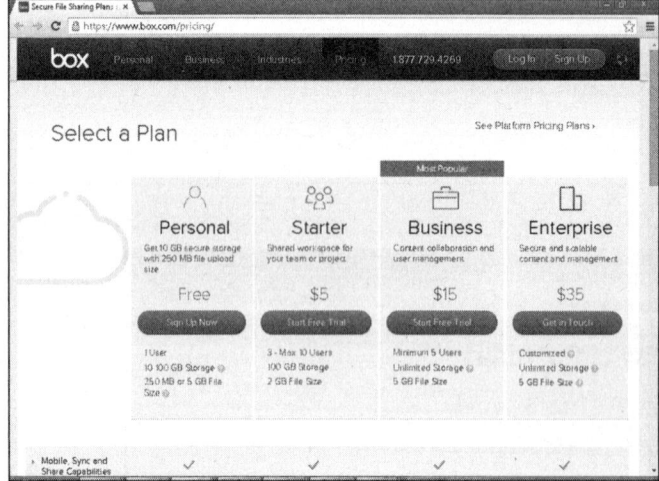

FIGURE 2-6: Box.net uses tables to display pricing information.

Avoid using tables to create page layouts. In the past, developers created multi-column layouts using tables, but today developers use CSS (see Book 3, Chapter 4) for layout-related tasks.

Basic table structuring

Tables comprise several parts, like the one shown in Figure 2-7.

You create a table by following these steps:

1. **Define a table with the** `table` **element.**

 To do this, add the opening and closing `<table>` tags.

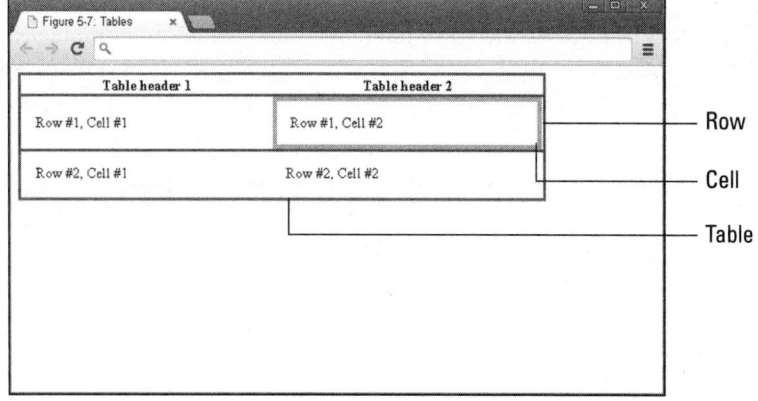

FIGURE 2-7:
The different parts of a table.

2. **Divide the table into rows with the** `tr` **element.**

 Between the opening and closing `table` tags, create opening `<tr>` tags and closing `</tr>` tags for each row of your table.

3. **Divide rows into cells using the** `td` **element.**

 Between the opening and closing `tr` tags, create opening and closing `td` tags for each cell in the row.

4. **Highlight cells that are headers using the** `th` **element.**

 Finally, specify any cells that are headers by replacing the `td` element with a `th` element.

REMEMBER

Your table will have only one opening and closing `<table>` tag; however, you can have one or more table rows (`tr`) and cells (`td`).

The following example code shows the syntax for creating the table shown in Figure 2-7.

```
<table>
   <tr>
     <th>Table header 1</th>
     <th>Table header 2</th>
   </tr>
   <tr>
     <td>Row #1, Cell #1</td>
     <td>Row #1, Cell #2</td>
   </tr>
   <tr>
     <td>Row #2, Cell #1</td>
     <td>Row #2, Cell #2</td>
   </tr>
</table>
```

CHAPTER 2 **Getting More Out of HTML**

TIP

After you've decided how many rows and columns your table will have, make sure to use an opening and closing `<tr>` tag for each row and an opening and closing `<td>` tag for each cell in the row.

Stretching table columns and rows

Take a look at the table describing Facebook's income statement in Figure 2-8. Data for 2011, 2012, and 2013 appears in individual columns of equal-sized width. Now look at Total Revenue, which appears in a cell that stretches or spans across several columns.

FIGURE 2-8: An income statement in a table with columns of different sizes.

TECHNICAL STUFF

Stretching a cell across columns or rows is called *spanning*.

The `colspan` attribute spans a column over subsequent vertical columns. The value of the `colspan` attribute is set equal to the number of columns you want to span. You always span a column from left to right. Similarly, the `rowspan` attribute spans a row over subsequent horizontal rows. Set `rowspan` equal to the number of rows you want to span.

The following code generates a part of the table shown in Figure 2-8. You can see the `colspan` attribute spans the Total Revenue cell across two columns. As

described in Book 3, Chapter 1, the `` tag is used to mark important text, and is shown as bold by the browser.

```
<tr>
    <td colspan="2">
        <strong>Total Revenue</strong>
    </td>
    <td>
        <strong>7,872,000</strong>
    </td>
    <td>
        <strong>5,089,000</strong>
    </td>
    <td>
        <strong>3,711,000</strong>
    </td>
</tr>
```

If you set a column or row to span by more columns or rows than are actually present in the table, the browser will insert additional columns or rows, changing your table layout.

CSS helps size individual columns and rows, as well as entire tables. See Book 3, Chapter 4.

Aligning tables and cells

The latest version of HTML does not support the tags and attributes in this section. Although your browser may correctly render this code, there is no guarantee your browser will correctly render it in the future. I include these attributes because, as of this writing, HTML code on the Internet, including the Yahoo! Finance site in the previous examples, still uses these deprecated (older) attributes in tables. This code is similar to expletives — recognize them but try not to use them. Refer to Book 3, Chapter 3 to see modern techniques using Cascading Style Sheets (CSS) for achieving the identical effects.

The `table` element has three deprecated attributes you need to know — `align`, `width`, and `border`. These attributes are described in Table 2-1.

TABLE 2-1 **Table Attributes Replaced by CSS**

Attribute Name	Possible Values	Description
align	left center right	Position of table relative to the containing document according to the value of the attribute. For example, align="right" positions the table on the right side of the web page.
width	pixels (#) %	Width of table measured either in pixels on-screen or as a percentage of the browser window or container tag.
border	pixels (#)	Width of table border in pixels.

The following example code shows the syntax for creating the table in Figure 2-9 with align, width, and border attributes.

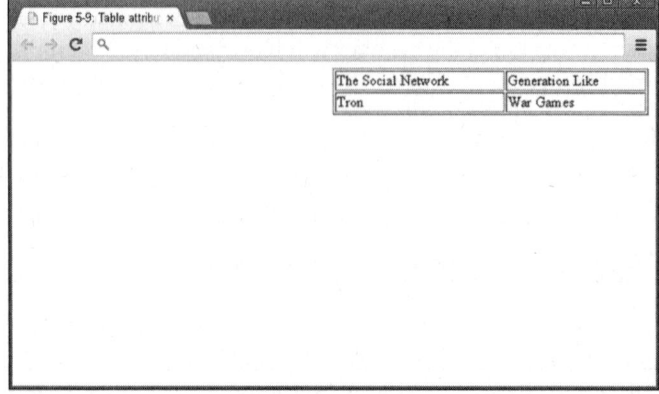

FIGURE 2-9: A table with deprecated align, width, and border attributes.

```
<table align="right" width=50% border=1>
   <tr>
     <td>The Social Network</td>
     <td>Generation Like</td>
   </tr>
   <tr>
     <td>Tron</td>
    <td>War Games</td>
   </tr>
</table>
```

Always insert attributes inside the opening <html> tag, and enclose words in quotes.

REMEMBER

122 BOOK 3 **Basic Web Coding**

The `tr` element has two deprecated attributes you need to know — `align` and `valign`. These are described in Table 2-2.

TABLE 2-2 Table Row Attributes Replaced by CSS

Attribute Name	Possible Values	Description
`align`	`left` `right` `center` `justify`	Horizontal alignment of a row's cell contents according to the value of the attribute. For example, `align="right"` positions a row's cell contents on the right side of each cell.
`valign`	`top` `middle` `bottom`	Vertical alignment of a row's cell contents according to the value of the attribute. For example, `align="bottom"` positions a row's cell contents on the bottom of each cell.

The `td` element has four deprecated attributes you need to know — `align`, `valign`, `width`, and `height`. These are described in Table 2-3.

TABLE 2-3 Table Cell Attributes Replaced by CSS

Attribute Name	Possible Values	Description
`align`	`left` `right` `center` `justify`	Horizontal alignment of a cell's contents according to the value of the attribute. For example, `align="center"` positions the cell's contents in the center of the cell.
`valign`	`top` `middle` `bottom`	Vertical alignment of a cell's contents according to the value of the attribute. For example, `align="middle"` positions a cell's contents in the middle of the cell.
`width`	`pixels (#)` `%`	Width of a cell measured either in pixels on-screen or as a percentage of the table width.
`height`	`pixels (#)` `%`	Height of a cell measured either in pixels on-screen or as a percentage of the table width.

CHAPTER 2 **Getting More Out of HTML**

The following example code shows the syntax for creating the table in Figure 2-10 with `align`, `valign`, `width`, and `height` attributes.

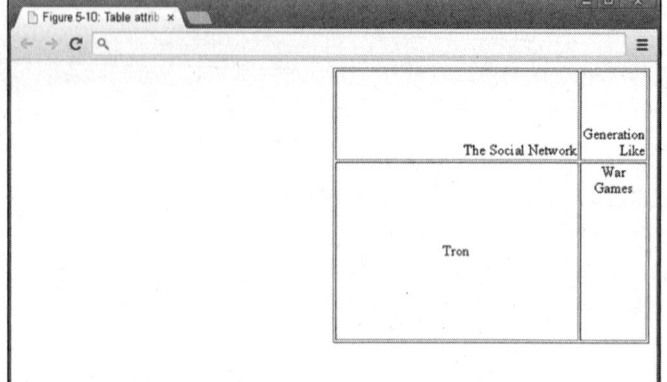

FIGURE 2-10: A table with deprecated `align`, `valign`, `width`, and `height` attributes.

```
<table align="right" width=50% border=1>
   <tr align="right" valign="bottom">
      <td height=100>The Social Network</td>
      <td>Generation Like</td>
   </tr>
   <tr>
      <td height=200 align="center" valign="middle">Tron</td>
      <td align="center" valign="top" width=20%>War Games</td>
   </tr>
</table>
```

WARNING

Remember, these attributes are no longer supported and should not be used in your code.

Filling Out Forms

Forms allow you to capture input from your website visitors. Until now we have displayed content as-is, but capturing input from visitors allows you to do the following:

» **Modify existing content on the page.** For example, price and date filters on airline websites allow for finding a desired flight more quickly.

» **Store the input for later use.** For example, a website may use a registration form to collect your email, username, and password information to allow you to access it at a later date.

Understanding how forms work

Forms pass information entered by a user to a server by using the following process:

1. The browser displays a form on the client machine.
2. The user completes the form and presses the Submit button.
3. The browser submits the data collected from the form to a server.
4. The server processes and stores the data and sends a response to the client machine.
5. The browser displays the response, usually indicating whether the submission was successful.

TIP

See Book 1, Chapter 2 for an additional discussion about the relationship between the client and server.

REMEMBER

A full description of how the server receives and stores data (Steps 3 to 5) is beyond the scope of this book. For now, all you need to know is that server-side programming languages such as Python, PHP, and Ruby are used to write scripts that receive and store form submissions.

Forms are very flexible, and can record a variety of user inputs. Input fields used in forms can include free text fields, radio buttons, check boxes, drop-down menus, range sliders, dates, phone numbers, and more. (See Table 2-4.) Additionally, input fields can be set to initial default values without any user input.

TABLE 2-4 Selected Form Attributes

Attribute Name	Possible Values	Description
type	checkbox email submit text password radio (a complete list of values has been omitted here for brevity)	Defines the type of input field to display in the form. For example, text is used for free text fields, and submit is used to create a Submit button.
value	text	The initial value of the input control.

CHAPTER 2 **Getting More Out of HTML** 125

View the entire list of form input types and example code at `www.w3schools.com/tags/att_input_type.asp`.

Creating basic forms

You create a basic form by

1. **Defining a form with the** `form` **element.**

 Start by adding an opening `<form>` tag and closing `</form>` tag.

2. **Using the** `action` **attribute, specify in the** `form` **element where to send form data.**

 Add an `action` attribute to your opening `<form>` tag and set it equal to the URL of a script that will process and store the user input.

3. **Using the** `method` **attribute, specify in the** `form` **element how to send form data.**

 Add a `method` attribute to your opening `<form>` tag and set it equal to `POST`.

 The `method` attribute is set equal to `GET` or `POST`. The technicalities of each are beyond the scope of this book, but, in general, `POST` is used for storing sensitive information (such as credit card numbers), whereas `GET` is used to allow users to bookmark or share with others the results of a submitted form (for example, airline flight listings).

4. **Providing a way for users to input and submit responses with the** `input` **element.**

 Between the opening `<form>` and closing `</form>` tags, create one `<input>` tag.

 Your form will have only one opening and closing `<form>` tag; however, you will have at least two `<input>` tags to collect and submit user data.

5. **Specify input types using the** `type` **attribute in the** `input` **element.**

 For this example, set the `type` attribute equal to `"text"`.

 The `<input>` tag doesn't have a closing tag, which is an exception to the "close every tag you open" rule. These tags are called self-closing tags, and you can see more examples in Book 3, Chapter 1.

6. **Finally, create another** `<input>` **tag and set the** `type` **attribute equal to** `submit`**.**

126 BOOK 3 **Basic Web Coding**

The following example code shows the syntax for creating the form shown in Figure 2-11.

FIGURE 2-11: A form with one user input and a Submit button.

```
<form action="mailto:nikhil.abraham@gmail.com" method="POST">
    <input type="text" value="Type a short message here">
    <input type="submit">
</form>
```

TECHNICAL STUFF

The action attribute in this form is set equal to mailto, which signals to the browser to send an email using your default mail client (such as Outlook or Gmail). If your browser isn't configured to handle email links, then this form won't work. Ordinarily, forms are submitted to a server to process and store the form's contents, but in this example form, the contents are submitted to the user's email application.

Practicing More with HTML

Practice your HTML online using the Codecademy website. Codecademy is a free website created in 2011 to allow anyone to learn how to code right in the browser, without installing or downloading any software. Practice all the tags (and a few more) that you find in this chapter by following these steps:

1. **Open your browser, go to www.dummies.com/go/codingaiolinks, and click the link to Codecademy.**

2. **If you have a Codecademy account, sign in.**

 Signing up is discussed in Book 1, Chapter 3. Creating an account allows you to save your progress as you work, but it's optional.

3. **Navigate to and click HTML Basics II to practice creating lists, and HTML Basics III to practice creating tables.**

 Background information is presented in the upper-left portion of the site, and instructions are presented in the lower-left portion of the site.

4. **Complete the instructions in the main coding window.**

 As you type, a live preview of your code is generated.

5. **After you have finished completing the instructions, click the Save and Submit Code button.**

 If you followed the instructions correctly, a green checkmark appears, and you proceed to the next exercise. If an error exists in your code, a warning appears with a suggested fix. If you run into a problem or a bug you cannot fix, click the hint, use the Q&A Forum, or tweet me at `@nikhilgabraham` and include the hashtag `#codingFD`. Additionally, you can sign up for book updates and explanations for changes to programming language commands by visiting `http://tinyletter.com/codingfordummies`.

IN THIS CHAPTER

» Understanding CSS and its structure

» Formatting text size, color, and style

» Styling images

» Using CSS in three different contexts

Chapter 3
Getting Stylish with CSS

"Create your own style . . . let it be unique for yourself and yet identifiable for others."

— ANNA WINTOUR

The website code examples I show in the preceding chapters resemble websites you may have seen from a previous era. Websites you browse today are different, and they have a more polished look and feel. Numerous factors enabled this change. Twenty years ago you might have browsed the Internet with a dial-up modem, but today you likely use a very fast Internet connection and a more powerful computer. Programmers have used this extra bandwidth and speed to write code to further customize and style websites.

In this chapter you discover modern techniques to style websites using Cascading Style Sheets (CSS). First, I discuss basic CSS structure and then the CSS rules to style your content. Finally, I show you how to apply these rules to your websites.

What Does CSS Do?

CSS styles HTML elements with greater control than HTML does. Take a look at Figure 3-1. On the left, Facebook appears as it currently exists; on the right, however, the same Facebook page is shown without all the CSS styling. Without the CSS, all the images and text appear left-justified, borders and shading disappear, and text has minimal formatting.

 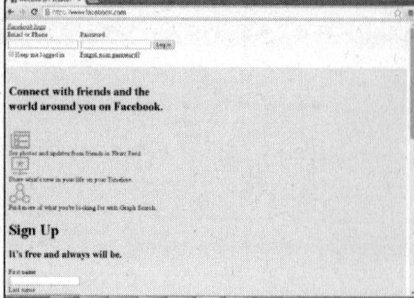

FIGURE 3-1:
Left Facebook with CSS. Right: Facebook without CSS.

CSS can style almost any HTML tag that creates a visible element on the page, including all the HTML tags used to create headings, paragraphs, links, images, lists, and tables that I showed you in previous chapters. Specifically, CSS allows you to style

- » Text size, color, style, typeface, and alignment
- » Link color and style
- » Image size and alignment
- » List bullet styles and indentation
- » Table size, shading, borders, and alignment

REMEMBER

CSS styles and positions the HTML elements that appear on a web page. However, some HTML elements (for example, `<head>`) aren't visible on the page and aren't styled using CSS.

You may wonder why creating a separate language like CSS to handle styling was considered a better approach than expanding the capabilities of HTML. There are three reasons:

- » **History:** CSS was created four years after HTML as an experiment to see whether developers and consumers wanted extra styling effects. At the time, it was unclear whether CSS would be useful, and only some major browsers supported it. As a result, CSS was created separately from HTML to allow developers to build sites using just HTML.

- » **Code management:** Initially, some CSS functionality overlapped with existing HTML functionality. However, specifying styling effects in HTML results in cluttered and messy code. For example, specifying a particular font typeface in HTML requires that you include the font typeface attribute in every paragraph (`<p>`) tag. Styling a single paragraph this way is easy, but applying the font to a series of paragraphs (or an entire page or website) quickly becomes tedious. By contrast, CSS requires the typeface to be specified only

once, and it automatically applies to all paragraphs. This feature makes it easier for developers to write and maintain code. In addition, separating the styling of the content from the actual content itself has allowed search engines and other automated website agents to more easily process the content on web pages.

» **Inertia:** Currently millions of web pages use HTML and CSS separately, and every day that number grows. CSS started as a separate language for preceding reasons, and it remains a separate language because its popularity continues to grow.

CSS Structure

CSS follows a set of rules to ensure that websites will be displayed in the same way no matter the browser or computer used. Sometimes, because of varying support of the CSS standard, browsers can and do display web pages differently. Nevertheless, generally speaking, CSS ensures that users have a consistent experience across all browsers.

TIP

Every web browser will interpret CSS rules to style your HTML, though I strongly recommend you download, install, and use Chrome or Firefox.

Choosing the element to style

CSS continues to evolve and support increased functionality, but the basic syntax for defining CSS rules remains the same. CSS modifies HTML elements with rules that apply to each element. These rules are written as follows:

```
selector {
property: value;
}
```

A CSS rule is comprised of three parts:

» **Selector:** The HTML element you want to style.

» **Property:** The feature of the HTML element you want to style, for example, font typeface, image height, or color.

» **Value:** The options for the property that the CSS rule sets. For example, if `color` were the property, the value would be `red`.

The selector identifies which HTML element you want to style. In HTML, an element is surrounded by angle brackets, but in CSS, the selector stands alone. The selector is followed by a space, an opening left curly bracket ({), property with a value, and then a closing right curly bracket (}). The line break after the opening curly bracket, and before the closing curly bracket is not required by CSS — in fact, you could put all your code on one line with no line breaks or spaces. Using line breaks is the convention followed by developers to make CSS easier to modify and read.

TIP

You can find curly brackets on most keyboards to the right of the P key.

The following code shows you an example of CSS modifying a specific HTML element. The CSS code appears first, followed by the HTML code that it modifies:

The CSS:

```
h1 {
    font-family: cursive;
}
```

And now the HTML:

```
<h1>
    Largest IPOs in US History
</h1>
<ul>
    <li>2014: Alibaba - $20B</li>
    <li>2008: Visa - $18B</li>
</ul>
```

The CSS selector targets and styles the HTML element with the same name (in this case, <h1> tags). For example, in Figure 3-2, the heading "Largest IPOs in US History," created using the opening and closing <h1> tag is styled using the h1 selector, and the font-family property with cursive value.

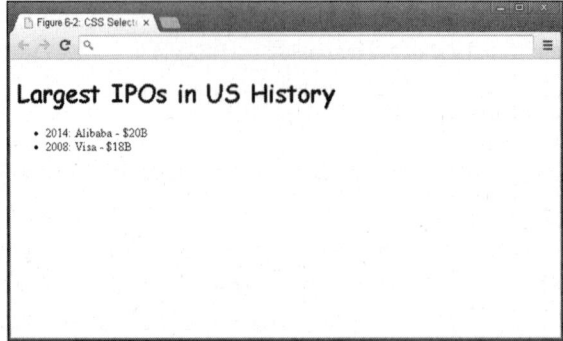

FIGURE 3-2:
CSS targeting the heading h1 element.

132 BOOK 3 **Basic Web Coding**

REMEMBER CSS uses a colon instead of the equal sign (=) to set values against properties.

TIP The font in Figure 3-2 likely doesn't appear to be cursive, as defined in the preceding code, because cursive is the name of a generic font family, not a specific font. Generic font families are described later in this chapter.

My property has value

CSS syntax requires that a CSS property and its value appear within opening and closing curly brackets. After each property is a colon, and after each value is a semicolon. This combination of property and value together is called a *declaration*, and a group of properties and values is called a *declaration block*.

Let us look at a specific example with multiple properties and values:

```
h1 {
   font-size: 15px;
   color: blue;
}
```

In this example, CSS styles the h1 element, changing the font-size property to 15px, and the color property to blue.

TIP You can improve the readability of your code by putting each declaration (each property/value combination) on its own line. Additionally, adding spaces or tabs to indent the declarations also improves the readability. Adding these line breaks and indentions doesn't affect browser performance in any way, but it will make it easier for you and others to read your code.

Hacking the CSS on your favorite website

In Book 1, Chapter 2, you modified a news website's HTML code. In this chapter, you modify its CSS. Let's take a look at some CSS rules in the wild. In this example, you change the CSS on huffingtonpost.com (or your news website of choice) using the Chrome browser. Just follow these steps:

1. **Using a Chrome browser, navigate to your favorite news website, ideally one with many headlines. (See Figure 3-3.)**

2. **Place your mouse pointer over a headline, right-click, and from the menu that appears select Inspect.**

 A window opens at the bottom of your browser.

3. **Click the Styles tab on the right side of this window to see the CSS rules being applied to HTML elements. (See Figure 3-4.)**

CHAPTER 3 **Getting Stylish with CSS** 133

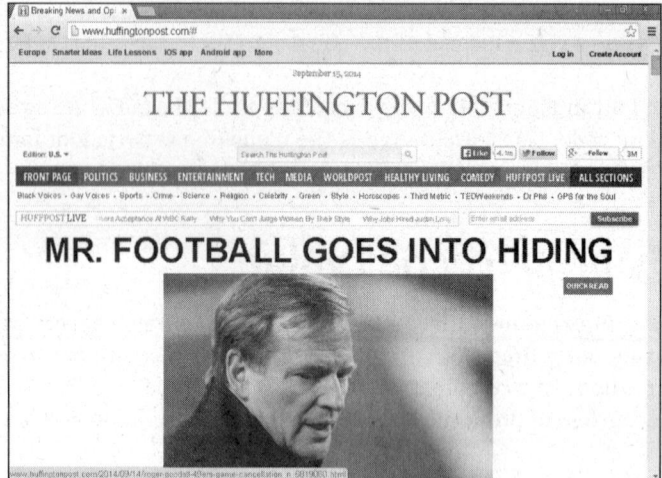

FIGURE 3-3:
The Huffington Post website before modification.

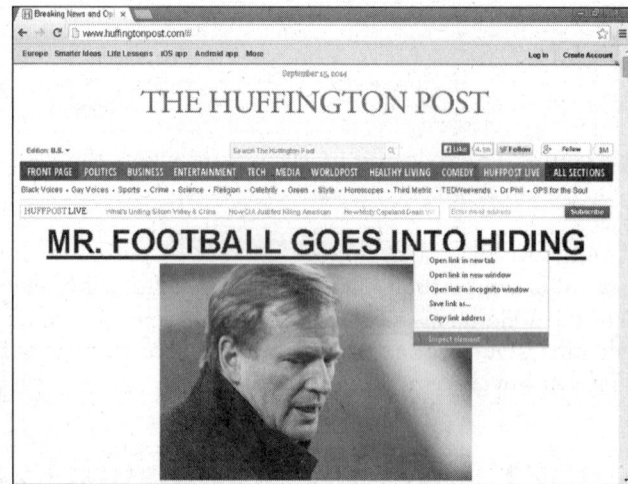

FIGURE 3-4:
The CSS rules that style the Huffington Post website.

4. **Change the color of the headline using CSS.**

 To do this, first find the `color` property in the `element.style` section; note the square color box within that property that displays a sample of the current color. Click this box and change the value by selecting a new color from the pop-up menu, and then press Enter.

 Your headline now appears in the color you picked. (See Figure 3-5.)

 TIP

 If the `element.style` section is blank and no `color` property appears, you can still add it manually. To do so, click once in the `element.style` section, and when the blinking cursor appears, type **color: purple**. The headline changes to purple.

134 BOOK 3 **Basic Web Coding**

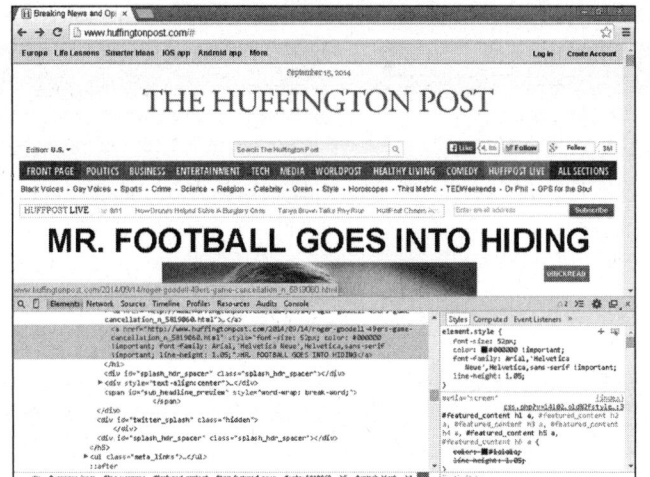

FIGURE 3-5: Changing the CSS changes the color of the headline.

TIP

As with HTML, you can modify any website's CSS using Chrome's Inspect Element feature, also known as Developer Tools. Most modern browsers, including Firefox, Safari, and Opera, have a similar feature.

Common CSS Tasks and Selectors

Although CSS includes over 150 properties and many values for each property, on modern websites, a handful of CSS properties and values do the majority of the work. In the previous section, when you "hacked" the CSS on a live website, you changed the heading color — a common task in CSS. Other common tasks performed with CSS include

- » Changing font size, style, font family, and decoration
- » Customizing links including color, background color, and link state
- » Adding background images and formatting foreground images

Font gymnastics: Size, color, style, family, and decoration

CSS lets you control text in many HTML elements. The most common text-related CSS properties and values are shown in Table 3-1. I describe these properties and values more fully in the sections that follow.

CHAPTER 3 **Getting Stylish with CSS** 135

TABLE 3-1 **Common CSS Properties and Values for Styling Text**

Property Name	Possible Values	Description
font-size	pixels (#px) % em (#em)	Specifies the size of text measured either in pixels, as a percentage of the containing element's font size, or with an em value which is calculated by desired pixel value divided by containing element font size in pixels. Example: font-size: 16px;
color	name hex code rgb value	Changes the color of the text specified using names (color: blue;), hexadecimal code (color: #0000FF;), or RGB (red, green, and blue) value (color: rgb(0,0,255);).
font-style	normal italic	Sets font to appear in italics (or not).
font-weight	normal bold	Sets font to appear as bold (or not).
font-family	font name	Sets the font typeface. Example: font-family: serif;
text-decoration	none underline line-through	Sets font to have an underline or strikethrough (or not).

Setting the font-size

As in a word processor, you can set the size of the font you're using with CSS's `font-size` property. You have a few options for setting the font size, and the most common one is to use pixels, as in the following:

```
p {
   font-size: 16px;
}
```

In this example, I used the p selector to size the paragraph text to 16 pixels. One disadvantage of using pixels to size your font occurs when users who prefer a large font size for readability have changed their browser settings to a default font size value that's larger than the one you specify on your site. In these situations, the font size specified in the browser takes precedence, and the fonts on your site will not scale to adjust to these preferences.

Percentage-sizing and em values, the other options to size your fonts, are considered more accessibility-friendly. The default browser font size of normal text is

16 pixels. With percentage-sizing and em values, fonts can be sized relative to the user-specified default. For example, the CSS for percentage-sizing looks like this:

```
p {
   font-size: 150%;
}
```

In this example, I used the `p` selector to size the paragraph text to 150 percent of the default size. If the browser's default font size was set at 16 pixels, this paragraph's font would appear sized at 24 pixels (150 percent of 16).

A `font-size` equal to `1px` is equivalent to one pixel on your monitor, so the actual size of the text displayed varies according to the size of the monitor. Accordingly, for a fixed font size in pixels, the text appears smaller as you increase the screen resolution.

Setting the color

The `color` property sets the color in one of three ways:

» **Name:** One hundred forty-seven colors can be referenced by name. You can reference common colors, such as black, blue, and red, along with uncommon colors, such as burlywood, lemon chiffon, thistle, and rebeccapurple.

Rebecca Meyer, the daughter of prominent CSS standards author Eric Meyer, passed away in 2014 from brain cancer at the age of six. In response, the CSS standardization committee approved adding a shade of purple called rebeccapurple to the CSS specification in Rebecca's honor. All major Internet browsers have implemented support for the color.

» **Hex code:** Colors can be defined by component parts of red, green, and blue, and when hexadecimal code is used, over 16 million colors can be referenced. In the code example, I set the `h1` color equal to `#FF0000`. After the hashtag, the first two digits (FF) refer to the red in the color, the next two digits (00) refer to the green in the color, and the final two digits (00) refer to the blue in the color.

» **RGB value:** Just like hex codes, RGB values specify the red, green, and blue component parts for over 16 million colors. RGB values are the decimal equivalent to hexadecimal values.

Don't worry about trying to remember hex codes or RGB values. You can easily identify colors using an online color picker such as the one at www.w3schools.com/colors/colors_picker.asp.

The following example shows all three types of color changes:

```
p {
  color: red
}
h1 {
  color: #FF0000
}
li {
  color: rgb(255,0,0)
}
```

li is the element name for a list item in ordered and unordered lists.

All three colors in the preceding code example reference the same shade of red. For the full list of colors that can be referenced by name go to www.w3.org/TR/css3-color/#svg-color.

Setting the font-style and font-weight

The `font-style` property can set text to italics, and the `font-weight` property can set text to bold. For each of these properties, the default is `normal`, which doesn't need to be specified. In the following example, the paragraph is styled so that the font appears italicized and bold. Here's an example of each:

```
p {
  font-style: italics;
  font-weight: bold;
}
```

Setting the font-family

The `font-family` property sets the typeface used for text. The property is set equal to one font, or to a list of fonts separated by commas. Your website visitors will have a variety of different fonts installed on their computers, but the `font-family` property displays your specified font only if that font is already installed on their system.

The `font-family` property can be set equal to two types of values:

» **Font name:** Specific font names such as Times New Roman, Arial, and Courier.

» **Generic font family:** Modern browsers usually define one installed font for each generic font family. These five generic font families include

- **Serif** (Times New Roman, Palantino)
- **Sans-serif** (Helvetica, Verdana)
- **Monospace** (Courier, Andale Mono)
- **Cursive** (Comic Sans, Florence)
- **Fantasy** (Impact, Oldtown)

When using `font-family`, it's best to define two or three specific fonts followed by a generic font family as a fallback in case the fonts you specify aren't installed, as in the following example:

```
p {
    font-family: "Times New Roman", Helvetica, serif;
}
```

In this example, the paragraph's font family is defined as Times New Roman. If Times New Roman isn't installed on the user's computer, the browser then uses Helvetica. If Helvetica isn't installed, the browser will use any available font in the generic serif font family.

TIP

When using a font name with multiple words (such as Times New Roman), enclose the font name in quotes.

Setting the text-decoration

The `text-decoration` property sets any font underlining or strikethrough. By default, the property is equal to none, which doesn't have to be specified. In the following example, any text with an h1 heading is underlined, whereas any text inside a paragraph tag is made strikethrough:

```
h1 {
    text-decoration: underline;
}
p {
    text-decoration: line-through;
}
```

Customizing links

In general, browsers display links as blue underlined text. Originally, this default behavior minimized the confusion between content on the page and an interactive link. Today, almost every website styles links in its own way. Some websites don't

underline links; others retain the underlining but style links in colors other than blue; and so on.

REMEMBER

The HTML anchor element (a) is used to create links. The text between the opening and closing anchor tag is the link description, and the URL set in the href attribute is the address the browser visits when the link is clicked.

The anchor tag has evolved over time and today has four states:

- » link: A link that a user hasn't clicked or visited
- » visited: A link that a user has clicked or visited
- » hover: A link that the user hovers the mouse cursor over without clicking
- » active: A link the user has begun to click but hasn't yet released the mouse button

CSS can style each of these four states, most often by using the properties and values shown in Table 3-2.

TABLE 3-2 Common CSS Properties and Values for Styling Links

Property Name	Possible Values	Description
color	name hex code rgb value	Link color specified using names (color: blue;), hexadecimal code (color: #0000FF;), or RGB value (color: rgb(0,0,255);).
text-decoration	none underline	Sets link to have an underline (or not).

The following example styles links in a way that's similar to the way they're styled in articles at Wikipedia, where links appear blue by default, underlined on mouse hover, and orange when active. As shown in Figure 3-6, the first link to Chief Technology Officer of the United States appears underlined as it would if my mouse was hovering over it. Also, the link to Google appears orange as it would if active and my mouse were clicking it.

```
a:link{
    color: rgb(6,69,173);
    text-decoration: none;
}
```

140 BOOK 3 **Basic Web Coding**

```
a:visited {
   color: rgb(11,0,128)
}
a:hover {
   text-decoration: underline
}
a:active {
   color: rgb(250,167,0)
}
```

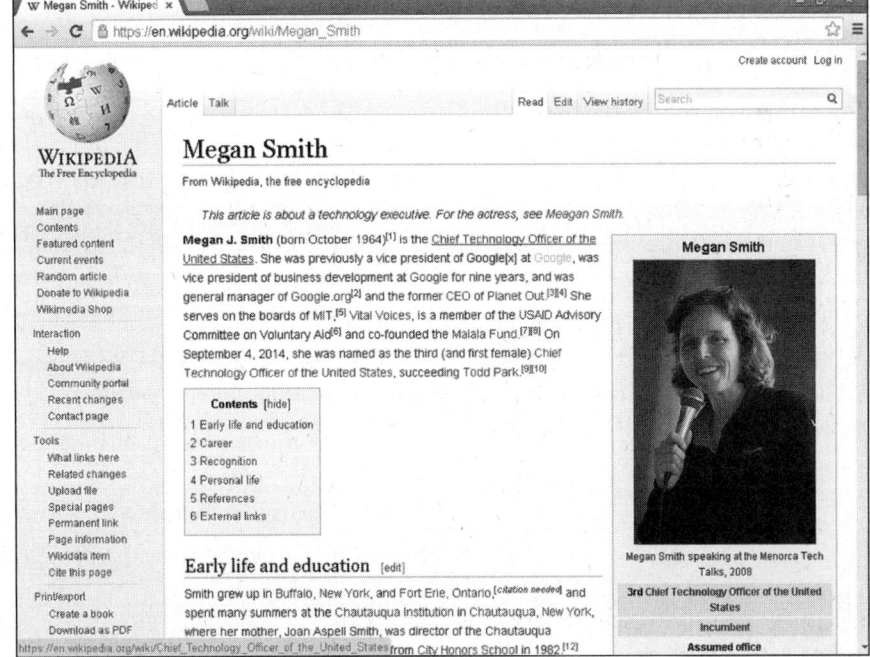

FIGURE 3-6: Wikipedia.org page showing link, visited, hover, and active states.

Remember to include the colon between the a selector and the link state.

Although explaining why is beyond the scope of this book, CSS specifications insist that you define the various link states in the order shown here — link, visited, hover, and then active. However, it is acceptable to not define a link state, as long as this order is preserved.

The various link states are known as *pseudo-class selectors*. Pseudo-class selectors add a keyword to CSS selectors and allow you to style a special state of the selected element.

CHAPTER 3 **Getting Stylish with CSS** 141

Adding background images and styling foreground images

You can use CSS to add background images behind HTML elements. Most commonly, the background-image property is used to add background images to individual HTML elements such as div, table, and p, or (when applied to the body element) to entire web pages.

TIP

Background images with smaller file sizes load more quickly than larger images. This is especially important if your visitors commonly browse your website using a mobile phone, which typically has a slower data connection.

The properties and values in Table 3-3 show the options for adding background images.

TABLE 3-3 CSS Properties and Values for Background Images

Property Name	Possible Values	Description
background-image	url("URL")	Adds a background image from the image link specified at *URL*.
background-size	auto contain cover width height (#px, %)	Sets background size according to the value: auto (default value) displays the image as originally sized. contain scales the image's width and height so that it fits inside element. cover scales the image so element background isn't visible. Background size can also be set by specifying width and height in pixels or as a percentage.
background-position	keywords position (#px, %)	Positions the background in element using keywords or exact position. *Keywords* comprise horizontal keywords (left, right, center) and vertical keywords (top, center, and bottom). The placement of the background can also be exactly defined using pixels or a percentage to describe the horizontal and vertical position relative to the element.
background-repeat	repeat repeat-x repeat-y no-repeat	Sets the background image to *tile*, or repeat, as follows: horizontally (repeat-x) vertically (repeat-y) horizontally and vertically (repeat) don't repeat at all (no-repeat).
background-attachment	scroll fixed	Sets the background to scroll with other content (scroll), or to remain fixed (fixed).

Setting the background-image

As shown in the following example, the `background-image` property can set the background image for the entire web page or a specific element.

```
body {
    background-image:
    url("http://upload.wikimedia.org/wikipedia/commons/e/e5/
    Chrysler_Building_Midtown_Manhattan_New_York_City_1932.jpg
    ");
}
```

TIP

You can find background images at sites such as `images.google.com`, `www.flickr.com`, or `publicdomainarchive.com`.

WARNING

Check image copyright information to see if you have permission to use the image, and comply with image's licensing terms, which can include attributing or identifying the author. Additionally, directly linking to images on other servers is called *hotlinking*. It is preferable to download the image and host and link to the image on your own server.

TIP

If you prefer a single-color background instead of an image, use the `background-color` property. This property is defined in much the same way as the `background-image` property. Just set it equal to a color name, RGB value, or hex code, as I describe earlier in this chapter in the section "Setting the color."

Setting the background-size

By specifying exact dimensions using pixels or percentages, the `background-size` property can scale background images to be smaller or larger, as needed. In addition, this property has three dimensions commonly used on web pages, as follows (see Figure 3-7):

>> `auto`: This value maintains the original dimensions of an image.

>> `cover`: This value scales an image so all dimensions are greater than or equal to the size of the container or HTML element.

>> `contain`: This value scales an image so all dimensions are less than or equal to the size of the container or HTML element.

FIGURE 3-7: Setting the background size to three different values.

Setting the background-position

The `background-position` property sets the initial position of the background image. The default initial position is in the top-left corner of the web page or specific element. You change the default position by specifying a pair of keywords or position values, as follows:

» **Keywords:** The first keyword (`left`, `center`, or `right`) represents the horizontal position, and the second keyword (`top`, `center`, or `bottom`) represents the vertical position.

» **Position:** The first position value represents the horizontal position, and the second value represents the vertical. Each value is defined using pixels or percentages, representing the distance from the top-left of the browser or the specified element. For example, `background-position: center center` is equal to `background-position: 50% 50%`. (See Figure 3-8.)

Setting the background-repeat

The `background-repeat` property sets the direction the background will tile as follows:

» `repeat`: This value (the default) repeats the background image both horizontally and vertically.

» `repeat-x`: This value repeats the background image only horizontally.

» `repeat-y`: This repeats the background image only vertically.

» `no-repeat`: This value prevents the background from repeating at all.

Setting the background-attachment

The `background-attachment` property sets the background image to move (or not) when the user scrolls through content on the page. The property can be set to

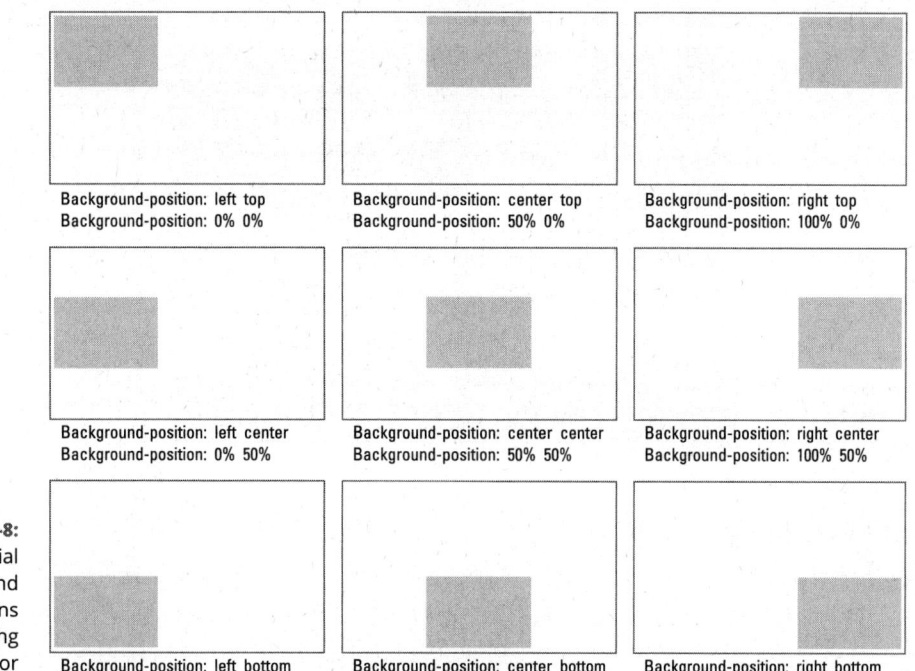

FIGURE 3-8: The initial background image positions specified using keywords or position.

» `scroll`: The background image moves when the user scrolls.

» `fixed`: The background image doesn't move when the user scrolls.

The following code segment uses several of the properties discussed earlier to add a background image that stretches across the entire web page, is aligned in the center, does not repeat, and does not move when the user scrolls. (See Figure 3-9.)

```
body {
    background-image:
    "http://upload.wikimedia.org/wikipedia/commons/thumb/a/a0/
    USMC-090807-M-8097K-022.jpg/640px-USMC-090807-M-8097K-022.jpg");
    background-size: cover;
    background-position: center center;
    background-repeat: no-repeat;
    background-attachment: fixed;
}
```

CHAPTER 3 **Getting Stylish with CSS** 145

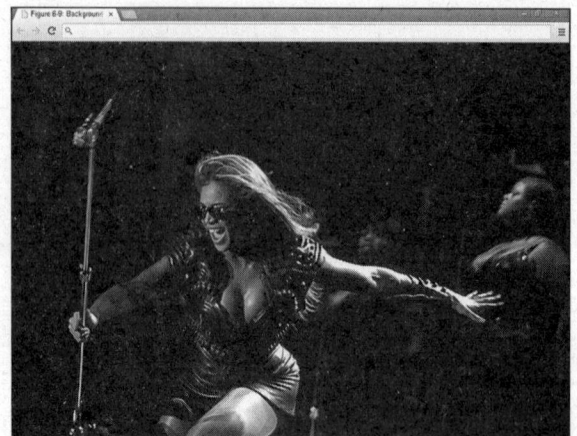

FIGURE 3-9: An image set as the background for entire page.

Styling Me Pretty

The CSS rules discussed in this chapter give you a taste of a few common styling properties and values. Although you aren't likely to remember every property and value, with practice, the property and value names will come to you naturally. After you understand the basic syntax, the next step is to actually incorporate CSS into your web page and try your hand at styling HTML elements.

Adding CSS to your HTML

There are three ways to apply CSS to a website to style HTML elements:

» **In-line CSS:** CSS can be specified within an HTML file on the same line as the HTML element it styles. This method requires placing the `style` attribute inside the opening HTML tag. Generally, in-line CSS is the least preferred way of styling a website because the styling rules are frequently repeated. Here's an example of in-line CSS:

```
<!DOCTYPE html>
<html>
<head>
   <title>Record IPOs</title>
</head>
<body>
   <h1 style="color: red;">Alibaba IPO expected to be biggest IPO of all time</h1>
</body>
</html>
```

146 BOOK 3 **Basic Web Coding**

» **Embedded CSS:** With this approach, CSS appears within the HTML file, but separated from the HTML tags it modifies. The CSS code appears within the HTML file between an opening and closing `<style>` tag, which itself is located between an opening and closing `<head>` tag. Embedded CSS is usually used when styling a single HTML page differently than the rest of your website.

In this example, the embedded CSS styles the header red, just like the preceding in-line CSS does.

```
<!DOCTYPE html>
<html>
<head>
  <title>Record IPOs</title>
  <style type="text/css">
  h1 {
      color: red;
  }
  </style>
</head>
<body>
  <h1>Alibaba IPO expected to be biggest IPO of all time</h1>
</body>
</html>
```

» **Separate style sheets:** CSS can be specified in a separate *style sheet* — that is, in a separate file. Using a separate style sheet is the preferred approach to storing your CSS because it makes maintaining the HTML file easier and allows you to quickly make changes. In the HTML file, the `<link>` tag is used to refer to the separate style sheet, and has three attributes:

- `href`: Specifies the CSS filename.
- `rel`: Should be set equal to `"stylesheet"`.
- `type`: Should be set equal to `"text/css"`.

TECHNICAL STUFF

With three different ways of styling HTML elements with CSS, all three ways could be used with contradictory styles. For example, say your in-line CSS styles h1 elements as red, whereas embedded CSS styles them as blue, and a separate style sheet styles them as green. To resolve these conflicts, in-line CSS has the highest priority and overrides all other CSS rules. If no in-line CSS is specified, then embedded CSS has the next highest priority, and finally in the absence of in-line or embedded CSS, the styles in a separate style sheet are used. In the example, with the presence of all three styles, the h1 element text would appear red because in-line CSS has the highest priority and overrides the embedded CSS blue styling and the separate CSS green styling.

The following example uses a separate CSS style sheet to style the header red, as in the previous two examples:

CSS: style.css

```
h1 {
    color: red;
}
```

HTML: index.html

```
<DOCTYPE html>
<html>
<head>
 <title>Record IPOs</title>
 <link href="style.css" text="text/css" rel="stylesheet">
</head>
<body>
  <h1>Alibaba IPO expected to be biggest IPO of all time</h1>
</body>
</html>
```

Building your first web page

Practice your HTML online using the Codecademy website. Codecademy is a free website created in 2011 to allow anyone to learn how to code right in the browser, without installing or downloading any software. You can practice all of the tags (and a few more) discussed in this chapter by following these steps:

1. **Open your browser, go to www.dummies.com/go/codingaiolinks, and click the Codecademy link.**

2. **If you have a Codecademy account, sign in.**

 Signing up is discussed in Book 1, Chapter 3. Creating an account allows you to save your progress as you work, but it's optional.

3. **Navigate to and click About You.**

 Background information is presented in the upper-left portion of the site, and instructions are presented in the lower-left portion of the site.

4. **Complete the instructions in the main coding window.**

 As you type, a live preview of your code is generated.

5. **After you have finished completing the instructions, click the Save and Submit Code button.**

If you followed the instructions correctly, a green checkmark appears, and you proceed to the next exercise. If an error exists in your code, a warning appears with a suggested fix. If you run into a problem, or have a bug you cannot fix, click the hint, use the Q&A Forums, or tweet me at `@nikhilgabraham` and include the hashtag `#codingFD`. Additionally, you can sign up for book updates and explanations for changes to programming language commands by visiting `http://tinyletter.com/codingfordummies`.

> **IN THIS CHAPTER**
>
> » Formatting lists and tables
>
> » Styling web pages using parent and child selectors
>
> » Naming pieces of code using `id` and `class`
>
> » Using the box model to position HTML elements on the page

Chapter **4**

Next Steps with CSS

"Design is not just what it looks like and feels like. Design is how it works."
— STEVE JOBS

In this chapter, you continue building on the CSS you worked with in Book 3, Chapter 3. So far, the CSS rules you've seen in the previous chapter applied to the entire web page, but now they get more specific. You find out how to style several more HTML elements, including lists, tables, and forms, and how to select and style specific parts of a web page, such as the first paragraph in a story or the last row of a table. Finally, you read about how professional web developers use CSS and the box model to control, down to the pixel, the positioning of elements on the page. Understanding the box model is not necessary to build your app in Book 5.

Before diving in, remember the big picture: HTML puts content on the web page, and CSS further styles and positions that content. Instead of trying to memorize every rule, use this chapter to understand CSS basics. CSS selectors have properties and values that modify HTML elements.

TIP

There is no better way to learn than by doing, so feel free to skip ahead to the Codecademy practice lessons at the end of the chapter. Then use this chapter as a reference when you have questions about specific elements you're trying to style.

CHAPTER 4 **Next Steps with CSS** 151

Styling (More) Elements on Your Page

In this section, you discover common ways to style lists and tables. In the previous chapter, the CSS properties and rules you saw, like `color` and `font-family`, can apply to any HTML element containing text. By contrast, some of the CSS shown here is used only to style lists, tables, and forms.

Styling lists

In Book 3, Chapter 2 you created ordered lists, which start with markers like letters or numbers, and unordered lists, which start with markers like bullet points. By default, list items in an ordered list use numbers (for example, 1, 2, 3), whereas list items in unordered lists use a solid black circle (●).

These defaults may not be appropriate for all circumstances. In fact, the two most common tasks when styling a list include the following:

>> **Changing the marker used to create a list:** For unordered lists, like this one, you can use a solid disc, empty circle, or square bullet point. For ordered lists, you can use numbers, Roman numerals (upper or lower case), or case letters (upper or lower).

>> **Specifying an image to use as the bullet point:** You can create your own marker for ordered and unordered lists instead of using the default option. For example, if you create an unordered bulleted list for a burger restaurant, instead of using a solid circle as a bullet point, you could use a color hamburger icon image.

You can accomplish either of these tasks by using the properties in Table 4-1 with an `ol` or `ul` selector to modify the list type.

TABLE 4-1 Common CSS Properties and Values for Styling Lists

Property Name	Possible Values	Description
`list-style-type` (unordered list)	disc circle square none	Sets the markers used to create list items in an unordered list to disc (●), circle (o), square (■), or none.

152 BOOK 3 Basic Web Coding

Property Name	Possible Values	Description
`list-style-type` (ordered list)	`decimal` `upper-roman` `lower-roman` `upper-alpha` `lower-alpha`	Sets the markers used to create list items in an ordered list to decimal (1, 2, 3), uppercase Roman numerals (I, II, III), lowercase Roman numerals (i, ii, iii), uppercase letters (A, B, C), or lowercase letters (a, b, c).
`list-style-image`	`url("URL")`	When *URL* is replaced with the image link, the property sets an image as the marker used to create a list item.

REMEMBER

CSS selectors using properties and rules modify HTML elements by the same name. For example, Figure 4-1 has HTML `` tags that are referred to in CSS with the `ul` selector, and styled using the properties and rules in Table 4-1.

FIGURE 4-1: Embedded and in-line CSS.

TIP

Many text website navigation bars are created using unordered bulleted lists with the marker set to *none*. You can see an example in the Codecademy CSS Positioning course starting with Exercise 21.

CSS properties and values apply to a CSS selector and modify an HTML element. In the following example, embedded CSS (between the opening and closing `<style>` tags) and in-line CSS (defined with the `style` attribute in the HTML) is used to

CHAPTER 4 **Next Steps with CSS** 153

- » Change the marker in an unordered list to a square using `list-style-type`.
- » Change the marker in an ordered list to uppercase Roman numerals again using `list-style-type`.
- » Set a custom marker to an icon using `list-style-image`.

The code for embedded and in-line CSS is shown next and in Figure 4-1. Figure 4-2 shows this code rendered in the browser.

```html
<html>
<head>
<title>Figure 4-1: Lists</title>
<style>
ul {
    list-style-type: square;
}

ol {
    list-style-type: upper-roman;
}

li {
    font-size: 27px;
}

</style>
</head>
<body>

<h1>Ridesharing startups</h1>
<ul>
    <li>Hailo: book a taxi on your phone</li>
    <li>Lyft: request a peer-to-peer ride</li>
    <li style="list-style-image: url('car.png');">Uber: hire a driver</li>
</ul>

<h1>Food startups</h1>
<ol>
    <li>Grubhub: order takeout food online</li>
    <li style="list-style-image: url('burger.png');">Blue Apron: subscribe to
    weekly meal delivery</li>
    <li>Instacart: request groceries delivered the same day</li>
</ol>
</body>
</html>
```

FIGURE 4-2:
Ordered and unordered lists modified to change the marker type.

> **Ridesharing startups**
>
> - Hailo: book a taxi on your phone
> - Lyft: request a peer-to-peer ride
> - Uber: request a driver for hire
>
> **Food startups**
>
> I. Grubhub: order takeout food online
> - Blue Apron: subscribe to weekly meal delivery
> III. Instacart: request groceries delivered the same day

TIP

If the custom image for your marker is larger than the text, your text may not align vertically with the marker. To fix this problem, you can either increase the font size of each list item using `font-size` (as shown in the example) and increase the margin between each list item using `margin`, or you can set `list-style-type` to none and set a background image on the `ul` element using `background-image`.

REMEMBER

There are three ways to apply CSS — with inline CSS using the `style` attribute, with embedded CSS using an opening and closing `<style>` tag, and in a separate CSS style sheet.

Designing tables

In Book 3, Chapter 2, you found out how to create basic tables. By default, the width of these tables expands to fit content inside the table, content in individual cells is left-aligned, and no borders are displayed.

These defaults may not be appropriate for all circumstances. Deprecated (unsupported) HTML attributes can modify these defaults, but if at any time, browsers stop recognizing these attributes, tables created with these attributes will display incorrectly. As a safer alternative, CSS can style tables with greater control. Three common tasks CSS can perform for tables include the following:

» Setting the width of a table, table row, or individual table cell with the `width` property

» Aligning text within the table with the `text-align` property

» Displaying borders within the table with the `border` property (See Table 4-2.)

CHAPTER 4 **Next Steps with CSS** 155

TABLE 4-2 **Common CSS Properties and Values for Styling Tables**

Property Name	Possible Values	Description
Width	*pixels* (#px) %	Width of table measured either in pixels on-screen or as a percentage of the browser window or container tag.
text-align	left right center justify	Position of text relative to the table according to the value of the attribute. For example, text-align="center" positions the text in the center of the table cell.
Border	width style color	Defines three properties in one — border-width, border-style, and border-color. The values must be specified in this order: Width (pixel), style (none, dotted, dashed, solid), and color (name, hexadecimal code, RBG value). For example, border: 1px solid red.

In the following example, the table is wider than the text in any cell, the text in each cell is centered, and the table border is applied to header cells:

```
<html>
<head>
<title>Figure 4-2: Tables</title>
<style>
   table {
      width: 700px;
   }

   table, td {
      text-align: center;
      border: 1px solid black;
      border-collapse: collapse;
   }

</style>
</head>
<body>
 <table>
   <caption>Desktop browser market share (August 2014)</caption>
   <tr>
     <th>Source</th>
     <th>Chrome</th>
     <th>IE</th>
     <th>Firefox</th>
     <th>Safari</th>
     <th>Other</th>
```

```
        </tr>
        <tr>
          <td>StatCounter</td>
          <td>50%</td>
          <td>22%</td>
          <td>19%</td>
          <td>5%</td>
          <td>4%</td>
        </tr>
        <tr>
          <td>W3Counter</td>
          <td>38%</td>
          <td>21%</td>
          <td>16%</td>
          <td>16%</td>
          <td>9%</td>
        </tr>
      </table>
    </body>
</html>
```

TIP

The HTML tag `<caption>` and the CSS property `border-collapse` further style the preceding table. The `<caption>` tag adds a title to the table. Although you can create a similar effect using the `<h1>` tag, `<caption>` associates the title with the table. The CSS `border-collapse` property can have a value of `separate` or `collapse`. The `separate` value renders each border separately (refer to Book 3, Chapter 2, Figure 2-9), whereas `collapse` draws a single border when possible (see Figure 4-3).

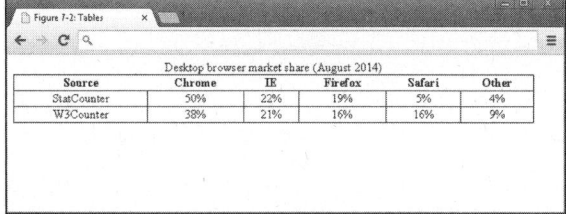

FIGURE 4-3: Table with width, text alignment, and border modified using CSS.

Selecting Elements to Style

Currently, the CSS you have seen styles every HTML element that matches the CSS selector. For example, in Figure 4-3 the `table` and `td` selectors have a `text-align` property that centers text in every table cell. Depending on the content, you may

CHAPTER 4 **Next Steps with CSS** 157

want to center only the text in the header row, but left-align text in subsequent rows. Here are two ways to do so:

» Styling specific HTML elements based on position to other elements

» Naming HTML elements, and styling elements only by name

Styling specific elements

When styling specific elements, it is helpful to visualize the HTML code as a family tree with parents, children, and siblings. In the following code example (also shown in Figure 4-4), the tree starts with the html element, which has two children head and body. The head has a child element called title. The body has h1, ul, and p elements as children. Finally, the ul element has li elements as children, and the p element has a elements as children. Figure 4-4 shows how the following code appears in the browser, and Figure 4-5 shows a depiction of the following code using the tree metaphor. Note that Figure 4-6 shows each relationship once. For example, in the following code, an a element is inside each of three li elements, and Figure 4-6 shows this ul li a relationship once.

```
<html>
<head>
    <title>Figure 4-3: DOM</title>
</head>
<body>

<h1>Parody Tech Twitter Accounts</h1>
<ul>
    <li>
    <a href="http://twitter.com/BoredElonMusk">Bored Elon Musk</a>
    </li>
    <li>
    <a href="http://twitter.com/VinodColeslaw">Vinod Coleslaw</a>
    </li>
    <li>
    <a href="http://twitter.com/Horse_ebooks">horse ebooks</a>
    </li>
</ul>

<h1>Parody Non-Tech Twitter Accounts</h1>
<p><a href="http://twitter.com/SeinfeldToday">Modern Seinfeld</a></p>
<p><a href="http://twitter.com/Lord_Voldemort7">Lord_Voldemort7</a></p>

</body>
</html>
```

FIGURE 4-4: Styling a family tree of elements.

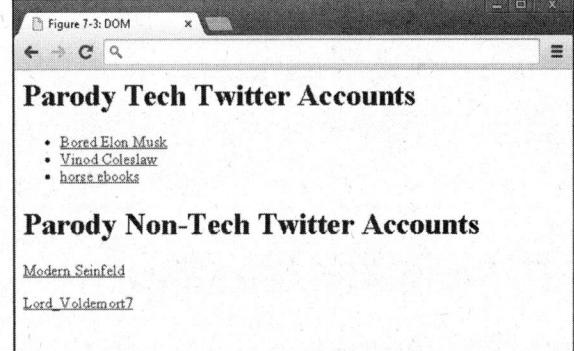

FIGURE 4-5: Parody Tech and Non-Tech Twitter accounts (browser view).

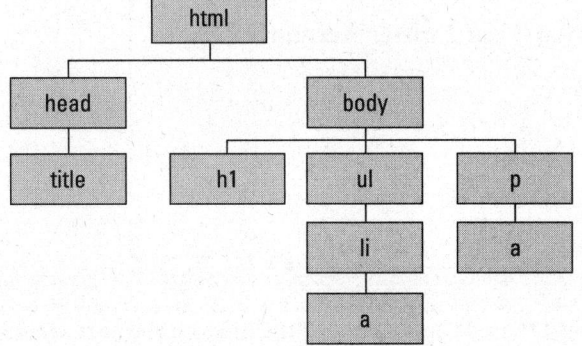

FIGURE 4-6: Parody Tech and Non-Tech Twitter account (HTML tree or Document Object Model view).

TIP

Bored Elon Musk is a parody of Elon Musk, the founder of PayPal, Tesla, and SpaceX. Vinod Coleslaw is a parody of Vinod Khosla, the Sun Microsystems cofounder and venture capitalist. Horse ebooks is a spambot that became an Internet phenomenon.

CHAPTER 4 Next Steps with CSS 159

 The HTML tree is called the *DOM* or *document object model*.

Child selector

The Parody Non-Tech Twitter account anchor tags are immediate children of the paragraph tags. If you want to style just the Parody Non-Tech Twitter accounts, you can use the *child selector*, which selects the immediate children of a specified element. A child selector is created by first listing the parent selector, then a greater-than sign (›), and finally the child selector.

In the following example, the anchor tags that are immediate children of the paragraph tags are selected, and those hyperlinks are styled with a red font color and without any underline. The Parody Tech Twitter accounts are not styled because they are direct children of the list item tag. (See Figure 4-7.)

```
p › a {
    color: red;
    text-decoration: none;
}
```

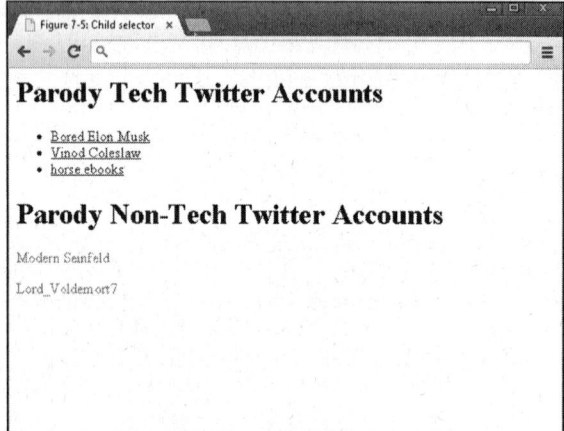

FIGURE 4-7: Child selector used to style the Parody Non-Tech Twitter accounts.

 If you use just the a selector here, all the links on the page would be styled instead of just a selection.

Descendant selector

The Parody Tech Twitter account anchor tags are descendants, or located within, the unordered list. If you want to style just the Parody Tech Twitter accounts, you can use the *descendant selector*, which selects not just immediate children of a

specified element but all elements nested within the specified element. A descendant selector is created by first listing the parent selector, a space, and finally the descendant selector you want to target.

In the following example, as shown in Figure 4-8, the anchor tags that are descendants of the unordered list are selected, and those hyperlinks are styled with a blue font color and are crossed out. The Parody Non-Tech Twitter accounts aren't styled because they aren't descendants of an unordered list.

```
ul a {
    color: blue;
    text-decoration: line-through;
}
```

FIGURE 4-8: Child selector used to style the Parody Tech Twitter accounts.

TIP

Interested in styling just the first anchor tag within a list, like the Modern Seinfeld Twitter account, or the second list item, like the Vinod Coleslaw Twitter account? Go to w3schools.com and read more about the `first-child` (www.w3schools.com/cssref/sel_firstchild.asp), and `nth-child` selectors (www.w3schools.com/cssref/sel_nth-child.asp).

Naming HTML elements

The other way of styling specific elements in CSS is to name your HTML elements. You name your code by using either the `id` or `class` attribute, and then style your code by referring to the `id` or `class` selector.

CHAPTER 4 Next Steps with CSS 161

Naming your code using the id attribute

Use the `id` attribute to style one specific element on your web page. The `id` attribute can name any HTML element, and is always placed in the opening HTML tag. Additionally, each element can have only one `id` attribute value, and the attribute value must appear only once within the HTML file. After you define the attribute in the HTML file, you refer to the HTML element in your CSS by writing a hashtag (#) followed by the attribute value.

Using the `id` attribute, the following code styles the Modern Seinfeld Twitter link the color red with a yellow background:

HTML:

```html
<p><a href="http://twitter.com/SeinfeldToday" id="jerry">Modern Seinfeld</a></p>
```

CSS:

```css
#jerry {
    color: red;
    background-color: yellow;
}
```

Naming your code using the class attribute

Use the `class` attribute to style multiple elements on your web page. The `class` attribute can name any HTML element and is always placed in the opening HTML tag. The attribute value need not be unique within the HTML file. After you define the attribute in the HTML file, you refer to the HTML element by writing a period (.) followed by the attribute value.

With the `class` attribute, the following code styles all the Parody Tech Twitter account links the color red with no underline:

HTML:

```html
<ul>
<li>
<a href="http://twitter.com/BoredElonMusk" class="tech">Bored Elon Musk</a>
</li>
<li>
<a href="http://twitter.com/VinodColeslaw" class="tech">Vinod Coleslaw</a>
</li>
```

```
<li>
<a href="http://twitter.com/Horse_ebooks" class="tech">Horse ebooks</a>
</li>
</ul>
```

CSS:

```
.tech {
    color: red;
    text-decoration: none;
}
```

TIP

Proactively use a search engine, such as Google, to search for additional CSS effects. For example, if you want to increase the spacing between each list item, open your browser and search for *list item line spacing css*. Links appearing in the top ten results should include:

» `www.w3schools.com`: A beginner tutorial site

» `www.stackoverflow.com`: A discussion board for experienced developers

» `www.mozilla.org`: A reference guide initially created by the foundation that maintains the Firefox browser and now maintained by a community of developers

Each of these sites is a good place to start; be sure to look for answers that include example code.

Aligning and Laying Out Your Elements

CSS not only allows control over the formatting of HTML elements, it also allows control over the placement of these elements on the page, known as *page layout*. Historically, developers used HTML tables to create page layouts. HTML table page layouts were tedious to create, and required that developers write a great deal of code to ensure consistency across browsers. CSS eliminated the need to use tables to create layouts, helped reduce code bloat, and increased control of page layouts.

Organizing data on the page

Before diving into code, let's look at Figure 4-9 and review some of the basic ways we can structure the page and the content on it. Layouts have evolved over time, with some layouts working well on desktop computers but not displaying optimally on tablet or mobile devices.

FIGURE 4-9: Vertical and horizontal navigation layouts.

TIP

Always ask yourself how your intended layout will appear on desktop, tablet, and mobile devices.

Hundreds of different layouts exist, and a few selected page layouts appear here along with example websites.

TIP

Left and right navigation toolbars aren't usually seen on mobile devices. Top navigation toolbars are used on both desktop and mobile devices, and bottom navigation toolbars are most common on mobile devices.

The following examples show real websites with these layouts:

» Vertical navigation, as shown in Figure 4-10, aids reader understanding when a hierarchy or relationship exists between navigational topics.

In the w3schools.com example, HTML, JavaScript, Server Side, and XML relate to one another, and underneath each topic heading are related subtopics.

» Horizontal or menu navigation, as shown in Figure 4-11, helps reader navigation with weak or disparate relationships between navigational topics.

In the eBay example, the Motors, Fashion, and Electronics menu items have different products and appeal to different audiences.

FIGURE 4-10:
Use of left and right navigation toolbar on w3schools.com (left) and hunterwalk.com (right).

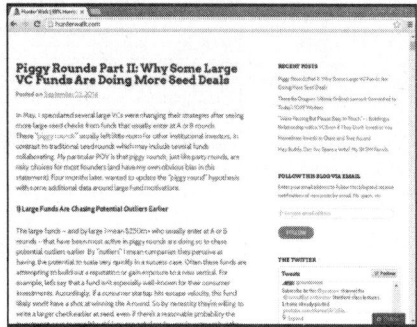

FIGURE 4-11:
Use of top and bottom navigation toolbar on ebay.com (left) and moma.org (right).

TIP

Don't spend too much time worrying about what layout to pick. You can always pick one, observe whether your visitors can navigate your website quickly and easily, and change the layout if necessary.

Shaping the div

The preceding page layouts are collections of elements grouped together. These elements are grouped together using rectangular containers created with an opening and closing `<div>` tag, and all of the layouts can be created with these `<div>` tags. By itself, the `<div>` tag doesn't render anything on the screen, but instead serves as a container for content of any type, such as HTML headings, lists, tables, or images. To see the `<div>` tag in action, take a look at the Codecademy.com home page in Figure 4-12.

Notice how the page can be divided into three parts — the navigation header, the middle video testimonial, and then additional text user testimonials. `<div>` tags are used to outline these major content areas, and additional nested `<div>` tags within each part are used to group content such as images and text.

CHAPTER 4 Next Steps with CSS 165

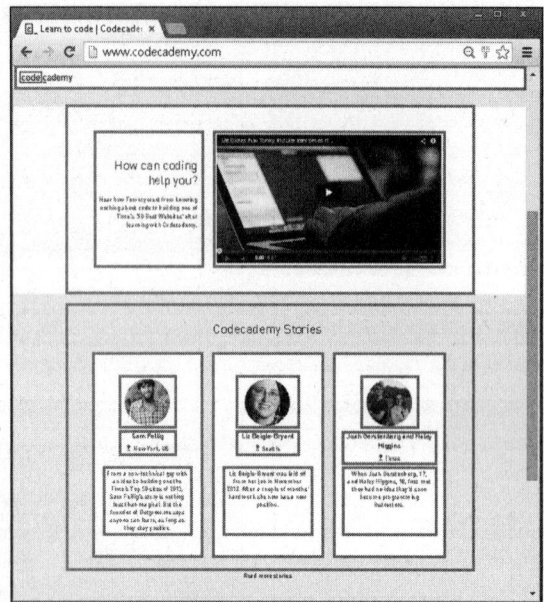

FIGURE 4-12: Codecademy.com homepage with visible borders for the <div> tags.

In the following example, as shown in Figure 4-13, HTML code is used to create two containers using <div> tags, the id attribute names each div, and CSS sizes and colors the div.

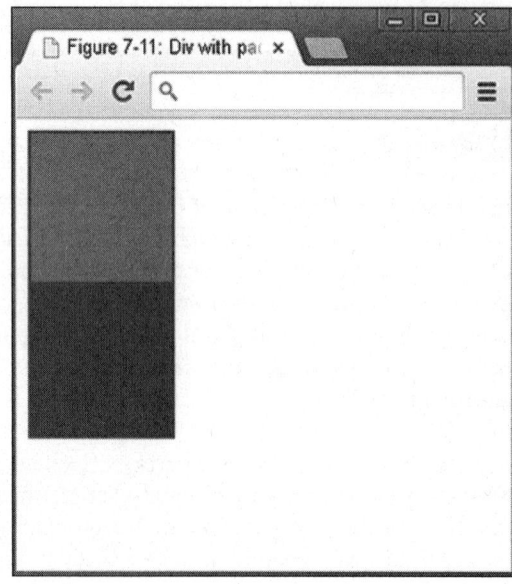

FIGURE 4-13: Two boxes created with HTML <div> tag and styled using CSS.

HTML:

```
<div id="first"/></div>
<div id="second"/></div>
```

CSS:

```
div {
    height: 100px;
    width: 100px;
    border: 2px solid purple;
}

#first {
    background-color: red;
}

#second {
    background-color: blue;
}
```

Understanding the box model

Just as we created boxes with the preceding tags, CSS creates a box around each and every single element on the page, even text. Figure 4-14 shows the box model for an image that says "This is an element." These boxes may not always be visible, but comprise four parts:

» `content`: HTML tag that is rendered in the browser

» `padding`: Optional spacing between content and the border

» `border`: Marks the edge of the padding, and varies in width and visibility

» `margin`: Transparent optional spacing surrounding the border

TIP

Using the Chrome browser, navigate to your favorite news website, then right-click an image and in the context menu choose Inspect Element. On the right side of the screen, you see three tabs; click the Computed tab. The box model is displayed for the image you right-clicked, showing the content dimensions, and then dimensions for the padding, border, and margin.

CHAPTER 4 **Next Steps with CSS** 167

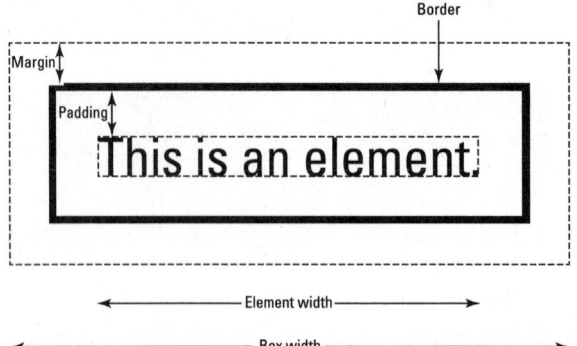

FIGURE 4-14: Box model for img element.

The padding, border, and margin are CSS properties, and the value is usually expressed in pixels. In the following code, shown in Figure 4-15, padding and margins are added to separate each `div`.

```
div {
    height: 100px;
    width: 100px;
    border: 1px solid black;
    padding: 10px;
    margin: 10px;
}
```

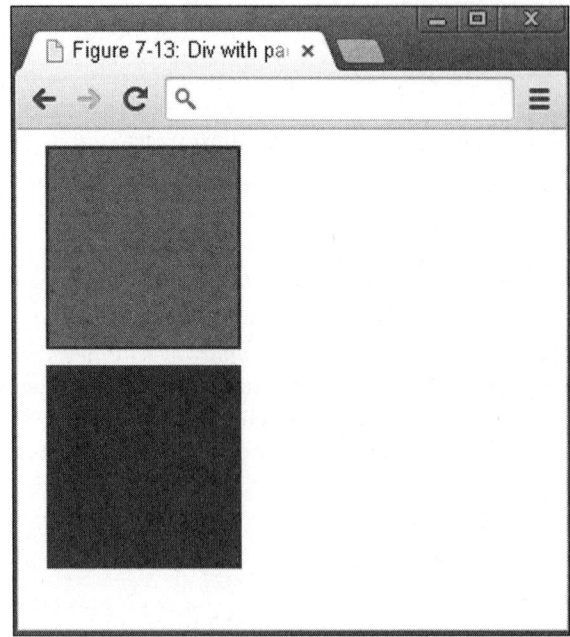

FIGURE 4-15: Padding and margin added to separate each `div`.

168 BOOK 3 **Basic Web Coding**

Positioning the boxes

Now that you understand how to group elements using HTML and how CSS views elements, the final piece is to position these elements on the page. Various techniques can be used for page layouts, and a comprehensive overview of each technique is beyond the scope of this book. However, one technique to create the layouts shown in Figure 4-16 is to use the `float` and `clear` properties (as described in Table 4-3).

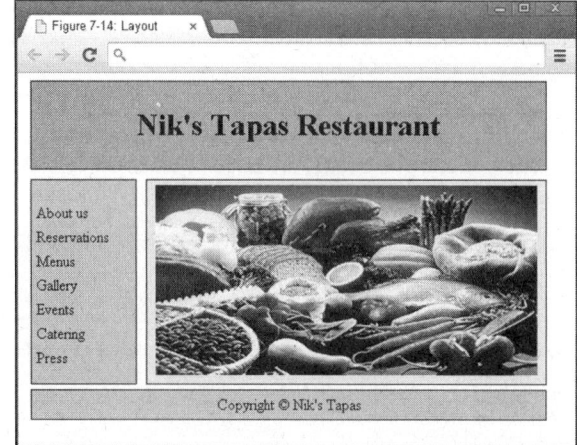

FIGURE 4-16: Left navigation web page layout created using `<div>` tags.

TABLE 4-3 Select CSS Properties and Values for Page Layouts

Property Name	Possible Values	Description
float	left right none	Sends an element to the `left` or `right` of the container it is in. The none value specifies that the element should not float.
clear	Left right both none	Specifies on which side of an element not to have other floating elements.

If the width of an element is specified, the `float` property allows elements that would normally appear on separate lines to appear next to each other, such as navigation toolbars and a main content window. The `clear` property is used to prevent any other elements from floating on one or both sides of current element, and the property is commonly set to `both` to place web page footers below other elements.

CHAPTER 4 **Next Steps with CSS** 169

The following example code uses `<div>` tags, `float`, and `clear` to create a simple left navigation layout. (See Figure 4-16.) Typically, after grouping your content using `<div>` tags, you name each `<div>` tag using `class` or `id` attributes, and then style the `div` in CSS. A lot of code follows, so let's break it down into segments:

- » The CSS is embedded between the opening and closing `<style>` tags, and the HTML is between the opening and closing `<body>` tags.
- » Between the opening and closing `<body>` tags, using `<div>` tags, the page is divided into four parts with header, navigation bar, content, and footer.
- » The navigation menu is created with an unordered list, which is left-aligned, with no marker.
- » CSS styles size and color and aligns each `<div>` tag.
- » CSS properties, `float` and `clear`, are used to place the left navigation layout to the left, and the footer below the other elements.

```html
<!DOCTYPE html>
<html>
<head>
<title>Figure 4-14: Layout</title>
<style>
  #header{
    background-color: #FF8C8C;
    border: 1px solid black;
    padding: 5px;
    margin: 5px;
    text-align: center;
  }

  #navbar {
    background-color: #00E0FF;
    height: 200px;
    width: 100px;
    float: left;
    border: 1px solid black;
    padding: 5px;
    margin: 5px;
    text-align: left;
  }

  #content {
    background-color: #EEEEEE;
    height: 200px;
```

```
        width: 412px;
        float: left;
        border: 1px solid black;
        padding: 5px;
        margin: 5px;
        text-align: center;
      }

      #footer{
        background-color: #FFBD47;
        clear: both;
        text-align: center;
        border: 1px solid black;
        padding: 5px;
        margin: 5px;
      }

      ul {
        list-style-type: none;
        line-height: 25px;
        padding: 0px;
      }
    </style>
  </head>
  <body>
    <div id="header"><h1>Nik's Tapas Restaurant</h1></div>

    <div id="navbar">
      <ul>
        <li>About us</li>
        <li>Reservations</li>
        <li>Menus</li>
        <li>Gallery</li>
        <li>Events</li>
        <li>Catering</li>
        <li>Press</li>
      </ul>
    </div>

    <div id="content"><img src="food.jpg" alt="Nik's Tapas"></div>

    <div id="footer">Copyright &copy; Nik's Tapas</div>
  </body>
</html>
```

Writing More Advanced CSS

Practice your CSS online using the Codecademy website. Codecademy is a free website created in 2011 to allow anyone to learn how to code right in the browser, without installing or downloading any software. Practice all of the tags (and a few more) that you find in this chapter by following these steps:

1. **Open your browser, go to www.dummies.com/go/codingaiolinks, and click the Codecademy link.**

2. **If you have a Codecademy account, sign in.**

 Signing up is discussed in Book 1, Chapter 3. Creating an account allows you to save your progress as you work, but it's optional.

3. **Navigate to and click CSS: An Overview, CSS Selectors, and CSS Positioning to practice CSS styling and positioning.**

 Background information is presented in the upper-left portion of the site, and instructions are presented in the lower-left portion of the site.

4. **Complete the instructions in the main coding window.**

 As you type, a live preview of your code is generated.

5. **After you have finished completing the instructions, click the Save and Submit Code button.**

If you followed the instructions correctly, a green checkmark appears, and you proceed to the next exercise. If an error exists in your code, a warning appears with a suggested fix. If you run into a problem, or have a bug you cannot fix, click the hint, use the Q&A Forums, or tweet me at @nikhilgabraham and include hashtag #codingFD. Additionally, you can sign up for book updates and explanations for changes to programming language commands by visiting http://tinyletter.com/codingfordummies.

IN THIS CHAPTER

» Creating a classic two-column page

» Creating a page-design diagram

» Using temporary background colors

» Creating fluid layouts and three-column layouts

» Working with and centering fixed-width layouts

Chapter 5

Building Floating Page Layouts

"Perfection of planned layout is achieved only by institutions on the point of collapse."

— C. NORTHCOTE PARKINSON

The floating layout technique provides a good alternative to tables, frames, and other layout tricks formerly used. You can build many elegant multi-column page layouts with ordinary HTML and CSS styles.

Creating a Basic Two-Column Design

Many pages today use a two-column design with a header and footer. Such a page is quite easy to build with the techniques you read about in this chapter.

Designing the page

It's best to do your basic design work on paper, not on the computer. Here's my original sketch in Figure 5-1.

```
┌─────────────────────────────────────────┐
│        Header - centered text           │
├──────────┬──────────────────────────────┤
│ Left     │ Right                        │
│          │                              │
│ 20%      │ 80% wide                     │
│ wide     │ Newspaper style -            │
│          │ all grayscale, single and    │
│          │ double borders               │
│          │                              │
│          │                              │
│          │                              │
├──────────┴──────────────────────────────┤
│        Footer - centered text           │
└─────────────────────────────────────────┘
```

FIGURE 5-1: This is a very standard two-column style.

Draw the sketch first so you have some idea what you're aiming for. Your sketch should include the following information:

- » **Overall page flow:** How many columns do you want? Will it have a header and footer?

- » **Section names:** Each section needs an ID, which will be used in both the HTML and the CSS.

- » **Width indicators:** How wide will each column be? (Of course, these widths should add up to 100 percent or less.)

- » **Fixed or percentage widths:** Are the widths measured in percentages (of the browser size) or in a fixed measurement (pixels)? This has important implications. For this example, I'm using a dynamic width with percentage measurements.

- » **Font considerations:** Do any of the sections require any specific font styles, faces, or colors?

- » **Color scheme:** What are the main colors of your site? What will be the color and background color of each section?

This particular sketch (in Figure 5-1) is very simple because the page will use default colors and fonts. For a more complex job, you need a much more detailed sketch. The point of the sketch is to separate design decisions from coding problems. Solve as much of the design stuff as possible first so you can concentrate on building the design with HTML and CSS.

A NOTE TO PERFECTIONISTS

If you're really into detail and control, you'll find this chapter frustrating. People accustomed to having complete control of a design (as you often do in the print world) tend to get really stressed when they realize how little actual control they have over the appearance of a web page.

Really, it's okay. This is a good thing. When you design for the web, you give up absolute control, but you gain unbelievable flexibility. Use the ideas outlined in this chapter to get your page looking right on a standards-compliant browser. Take a deep breath and look at it on something else (like Internet Explorer 6 if you want to suffer a heart attack!). Everything you positioned so carefully is all messed up. Take another deep breath and use conditional comments to fix the offending code without changing how it works in those browsers that do things correctly. It is now becoming reasonable to expect most users to have a browser that is at least partially HTML5-compliant.

Building the HTML

After you have a basic design in place, you're ready to start building the HTML code that will be the framework. Start with basic CSS, but create a `div` for each section that will be in your final work. You can put a placeholder for the CSS, but don't add any CSS yet. Here's my basic code. I removed some of the redundant text to save space:

```
<!DOCTYPE html>
<html lang = "en-US">

  <head>
    <meta charset = "UTF-8">
    <title>twoColumn.html</title>
    <link rel = "stylesheet"
          type = "text/css"
          href = "twoCol.css"/>
  </head>
  <body>
    <div id = "head">
      <h1>Two Columns with Float</h1>
    </div>
    <div id = "left">
      <h2>Left Column</h2>
      <p>
        Lorem ipsum dolor sit amet, consectetuer adipiscing elit. Vivamus dui.
      </p>
```

```html
      </div>
      <div id = "right">
        <h2>Right Column</h2>
        <p>
          Lorem ipsum dolor sit amet, consectetuer adipiscing elit. Vivamus dui.
        </p>
      </div>
      <div id = "footer">
        <h3>Footer</h3>
      </div>
  </body>
</html>
```

Nothing at all is remarkable about this HTML code, but it has a few important features, such as the following:

- » **It's standards-compliant.** It's good to check and make sure the basic HTML code is well formed before you do a lot of CSS work with it. Sloppy HTML can cause you major headaches later.

WHAT'S UP WITH THE LATIN?

The flexible layouts built throughout this chapter require some kind of text so the browser knows how big to make things. The actual text isn't important, but something needs to be there.

Typesetters have a long tradition of using phony Latin phrases as filler text. Traditionally, this text has begun with the words "Lorem Ipsum," so it's called *Lorem Ipsum* text.

This particular version is semi-randomly generated from a database of Latin words.

If you want, you can also use Lorem Ipsum in your page layout exercises. Conduct a search for Lorem Ipsum generators on the web to get as much fake text as you want for your mockup pages.

Although Lorem Ipsum text is useful in the screen shots, it adds nothing to the code listings. Throughout this chapter, I remove the Lorem Ipsum text from the code listings to save space. See the original files on the website for the full pages. This book's Introduction explains how to access the companion website at www.dummies.com/go/codingaiodownloads.

- » **It contains four divs.** The parts of the page that will be moved later are all encased in `div` elements.
- » **Each div has an ID.** All the divs have an ID determined from the sketch.
- » **No formatting is in the HTML.** The HTML code contains no formatting at all. That's left to the CSS.
- » **It has no style yet.** Although a `<link>` tag is pointing to a style sheet, the style is currently empty.

Figure 5-2 shows what the page looks like before you add any CSS to it.

FIGURE 5-2: The plain HTML is plain indeed; some CSS will come in handy.

Using temporary background colors

Before doing anything else, create a selector for each of the named divs and add a temporary background color to each div. Make each div a different color. The CSS might look like this:

```
#head {
  background-color: lightblue;
}

#left {
  background-color: yellow;
}
```

CHAPTER 5 **Building Floating Page Layouts** 177

```
#right {
  background-color: green;
}

#footer {
  background-color: orange;
}
```

You won't keep these background colors, but they provide some very useful cues while you're working with the layout:

- **Testing the selectors:** While you change the background of each selector, you can see whether you've remembered the selector's name correctly. It's amazing how many times I've written code that I thought was broken just because I didn't write the selector properly.

- **Identifying the divs:** If you make each div a different color, it'll be easier to see which div is which when they aren't acting the way you want.

- **Specifying the size of each div:** The text inside a div isn't always a good indicator of the actual size. The background color tells you what's really going on.

Of course, you won't leave these colors in place. They're just helpful tools for seeing what's going on during the design process. Look at bg.html and bg.css files for complete code available on the website at www.dummies.com/go/codingaiodownloads.

Figure 5-3 displays how the page looks with the background colors turned on.

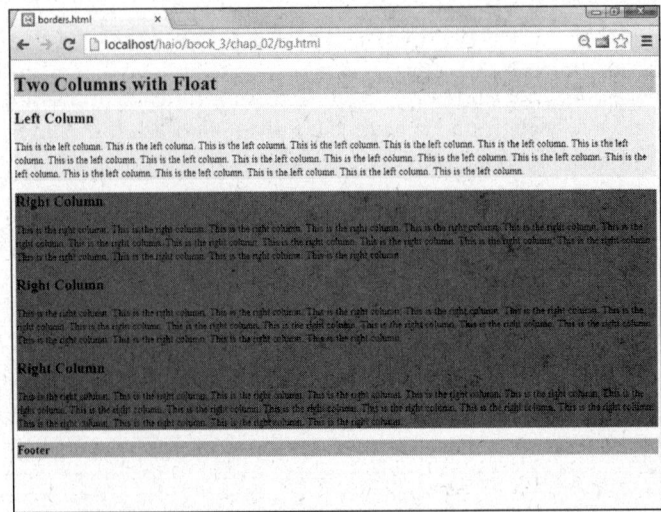

FIGURE 5-3: Colored backgrounds make it easier to manipulate the divs.

REMEMBER It's fine that you can't see the actual colors in the black-and-white image in Figure 5-3. Just appreciate that when you see the page in its full-color splendor, the various colors will help you see what's going on.

Setting up the floating columns

This particular layout doesn't require major transformation. A few CSS rules will do the trick:

```
#head {
  border: 3px black solid;
}

#left {
  border: 3px red solid;
  float: left;
  width: 20%;
}

#right {
  border: 3px blue solid;
  float: left;
  width: 75%
}

#footer {
  border: 3px green solid;
  clear: both;
}
```

I made the following changes to the CSS:

» **Floated the** `#left` **div.** Set the `#left` div's `float` property to `left` so other divs (specifically the `#right` div) are moved to the right of it.

» **Set the** `#left` **width.** When you float a div, you must also set its width. I've set the left div width to 20 percent of the page width as a starting point.

» **Floated the** `#right` **div, too.** The right div can also be floated left, and it'll end up snug to the left div. Don't forget to add a width. I set the width of `#right` to 75 percent, leaving another 5 percent available for padding, margins, and borders.

» **Cleared the footer.** The footer should take up the entire width of the page, so set its `clear` property to both.

CHAPTER 5 **Building Floating Page Layouts** 179

Figure 5-4 shows how the page looks with this style sheet in place (see floated.html and floated.css for complete code available on the website at www.dummies.com/go/codingaiodownloads).

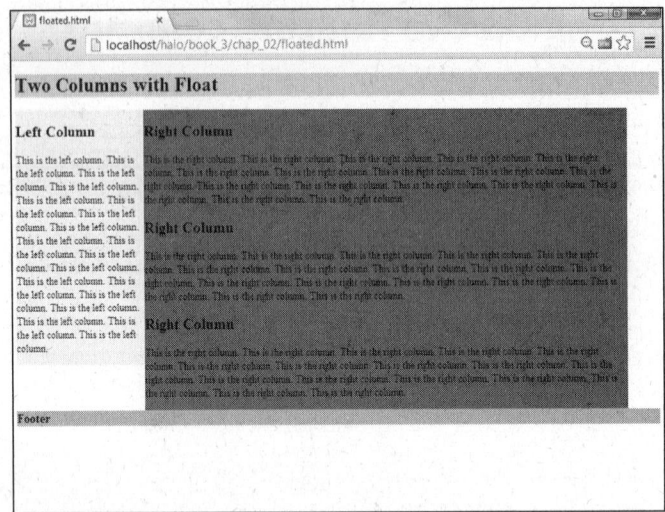

FIGURE 5-4: Now the left column is floated.

Tuning up the borders

The different backgrounds in Figure 5-4 point out some important features of this layout scheme. For instance, the two columns aren't the same height. This can have important implications.

You can change the borders to make the page look more like a column layout. I'm going for a newspaper-style look, so I use simple double borders. I put a black border under the header, a gray border to the left of the right column, and a gray border on top of the bottom segment. Tweaking the padding and centering the footer complete the look. Here's the complete CSS:

```
#head {
  border-bottom: 3px double black;
}
#left {
  float: left;
  width: 20%;
}
#right {
  float: left;
  width: 75%;
  border-left: 3px double gray;
}
```

```
#footer {
  clear: both;
  text-align: center;
  border-top: 3px double gray;
}
```

The final effect is shown in Figure 5-5.

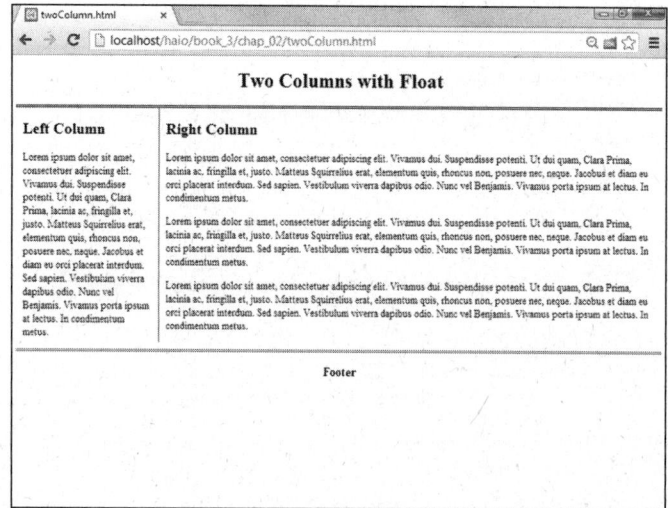

FIGURE 5-5: This is a decent design, which adjusts with the page width.

Advantages of a fluid layout

This type of layout scheme (with floats and variable widths) is often called a *fluid* layout because it has columns, but the sizes of the columns are dependent on the browser width. This is an important issue because, unlike layout in the print world, you really have no idea what size the browser window that displays your page will be. Even if the user has a widescreen monitor, the browser may be in a much smaller window. Fluid layouts can adapt to this situation quite well.

Fluid layouts (and indeed all other float-based layouts) have another great advantage. If the user turns off CSS or can't use it, the page still displays. The elements will simply be printed in order vertically, rather than in the intended layout. This can be especially handy for screen readers or devices with exceptionally small screens, like phones.

Using semantic tags

As web developers began using floating layout techniques, they almost always created divs called `nav`, `header`, and `footer`. The developers of HTML5 decided to create new elements with these names. Take a look at the following code to see the semantic tags in action.

```html
<!DOCTYPE HTML>
<html lang="en">
<head>
  <title>semantic</title>
  <meta charset="UTF-8">
  <style type = "text/css">
  header {
    border-bottom: 5px double black;
  }

  nav {
    float: left;
    width: 20%;
    clear: left;
    min-height: 400px;
    border-right: 1px solid black;
  }

  section {
    float: left;
    width: 75%;
    padding-left: 1em;
  }

  article {
    float: left;
    width: 75%;
    padding-left: 1em;
  }

  footer {
    clear: both;
    border-top: 5px double black;
    text-align: center;
  }

  </style>
</head>
```

```html
<body>
  <header>
    <h1>This is my header</h1>
  </header>

  <nav>
    <h2>Navigation</h2>
    <ul>
      <li><a href="#">link a</a></li>
      <li><a href="#">link b</a></li>
      <li><a href="#">link c</a></li>
      <li><a href="#">link d</a></li>
      <li><a href="#">link e</a></li>
    </ul>
  </nav>

  <section id = "1">
    <h2>Section 1</h2>
    <p>Section body...</p>
  </section>

  <section id = "2">
    <h2>Section 2</h2>
    <p>Section body...</p>
  </section>
  <article>
    <h2>Article</h2>
    <p>Article body...</p>
  </article>

  <footer>
    <h2>Footer</h2>
    <address>
      Nik Abraham <br/>
      <a href = "http://www.twitter.com/nikhilgabraham">
      Tweet me @nikhilgabraham</a>
    </address>
  </footer>

</body>
</html>
```

As you can see, there are a number of new semantic markup tags in HTML5:

- » `header`: This is not the same as the h1-h6 tags. It denotes a chunk of the page that will contain a header for the page. Often the header will fill up the page width and will have some sort of banner image. It frequently contains h1 content.

- » `nav`: This tag indicates some kind of navigation section. It has no particular style of its own, but it is frequently used as either a horizontal or vertical menu for site navigation.

- » `section`: A section is used to specify a generic part of the page. You can have multiple sections on the same page.

MORE FUN WITH SEMANTIC TAGS

HTML5 introduced a number of other semantic tags. Most of them have no specific formatting. Still, you will run across them, so here are a few that seem likely to make the cut:

- `address`: Holds contact information.
- `aside`: Indicates a page fragment that is related to but separate from the main content.
- `menu/command`: Eventually, will allow a pop-up menu or toolbar to be defined in the page, and commands will be embedded inside that menu. Not supported yet.
- `figure`: Incorporates an image and a caption.
- `figcaption`: Describes an image, normally enclosed within a figure tag.
- `time`: Display dates or times.
- `summary/detail`: A summary is visible at all times, and when it is clicked, the detail appears. Not supported yet.
- `svg`: Allows you to use the SVG language to describe a vector image through code.
- `meter`: Indicates a numeric value falling within a specific range.
- `output`: Intended for output in interactive applications.
- `progress`: Should indicate progress of a task (but it doesn't look like a progress bar yet).

- » `article`: An article is like a section, but it's intended for use with external resources. Many pages are built automatically by software, and when these pages integrate content from other sources, the `article` tag is used to integrate this content.

- » `footer`: A footer displays footer contents at the bottom of a page. Typically a footer covers the bottom of a page, although this isn't the default behavior.

Note that none of these elements have any specific formatting. It's up to you to provide formatting through CSS code. Each of the elements can be formatted directly as an HTML element (because that's what it is). All of the latest versions of browsers support the semantic markup tags, but if you want to support older browsers (especially IE before version 8), you still need to use divs.

Building a Three-Column Design

Sometimes, you'll prefer a three-column design. It's a simple variation of the two-column approach. Figure 5-6 shows a simple three-column layout.

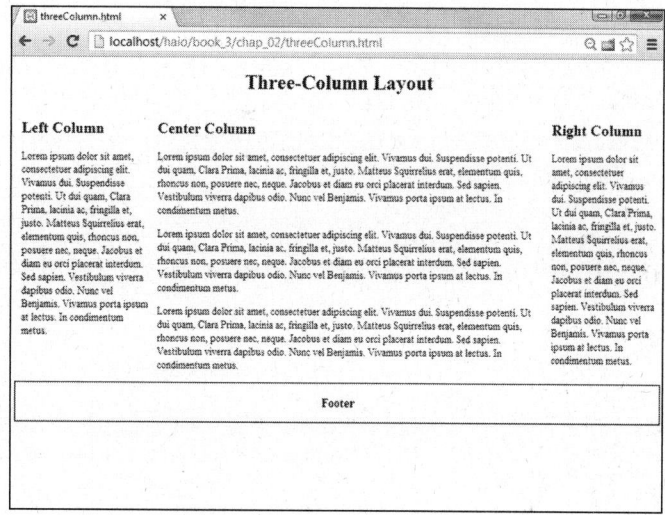

FIGURE 5-6: This is a three-column floating layout.

This design uses very basic CSS with five named divs. Here's the code (with the dummy paragraph text removed for space):

```html
<!DOCTYPE html>
<html lang = "en-US">

  <head>
    <meta charset = "UTF-8">
    <title>threeColumn.html</title>
    <link rel = "stylesheet"
          type = "text/css"
          href = "threeColumn.css"/>
  </head>
  <body>
    <div id = "head">
      <h1>Three-Column Layout</h1>
    </div>
    <div id = "left">
      <h2>Left Column</h2>
      <p>
        Lorem ipsum dolor sit amet, consectetuer adipiscing elit. Vivamus dui.
      </p>
    </div>
    <div id = "center">
      <h2>Center Column</h2>
      <p>
        Lorem ipsum dolor sit amet, consectetuer adipiscing elit. Vivamus dui.
      </p>
    </div>
    <div id = "right">
      <h2>Right Column</h2>
      <p>
        Lorem ipsum dolor sit amet, consectetuer adipiscing elit. Vivamus dui.
      </p>
    </div>
    <div id = "footer">
      <h3>Footer</h3>
    </div>
  </body>
</html>
```

Styling the three-column page

As you can see from the HTML, there isn't really much to this page. It has five named divs, and that's about it. All the really exciting stuff happens in the CSS:

```css
#head {
  text-align: center;
}

#left {
  float: left;
  width: 20%;
  padding-left: 1%;
}

#center {
  float: left;
  width: 60%;
  padding-left: 1%;
}

#right {
  float: left;
  width: 17%;
  padding-left: 1%;
}

#footer {
  border: 1px black solid;
  float: left;
  width: 100%;
  clear: both;
  text-align: center;
}
```

Each element (except the head) is floated with an appropriate width. The process for generating this page is similar to the two-column layout:

1. **Diagram the layout.**

 Begin with a general sense of how the page will look and the relative width of the columns. Include the names of all segments in this diagram.

2. **Create the HTML framework.**

 Create all the necessary divs, including `id` attributes.

 Add representative text so you can see the overall texture of the page.

TIP

3. **Add temporary background colors.**

 Add a temporary background color to each element so you can see what's going on when you start messing with `float` attributes.

 This also ensures you have all the selectors spelled properly.

4. **Float the leftmost element.**

 Add the `float` attribute to the leftmost column.

 Don't forget to specify a width (in percentage).

5. **Check your work.**

 Frequently save your work and view it in a browser.

 Use the browser's F5 key for a quick reload after you've saved the page.

6. **Float the center element.**

 Add `float` and `width` attributes to the center element.

7. **Float the rightmost element.**

 Incorporate `float` and `width` in the right element.

8. **Ensure that the widths total around 95 percent.**

 You want the sum of the widths to be nearly 100 percent but not quite.

 Generally, you need a little space for margins and padding. Final adjustments come later, but you certainly don't want to take up more than 100 percent of the available real estate.

9. **Float and clear the footer.**

 To get the footer acting right, you need to float it and clear it on both margins. Set its width to 100 percent, if you want.

10. **Tune up.**

 Remove the temporary borders, adjust the margins and padding, and set the alignment as desired. Use percentages for margins and padding, and then adjust so all percentages equal 100 percent.

Problems with the floating layout

The floating layout solution is very elegant, but it does have one drawback. Figure 5-7 shows the three-column page with the background colors for each element.

188 BOOK 3 **Basic Web Coding**

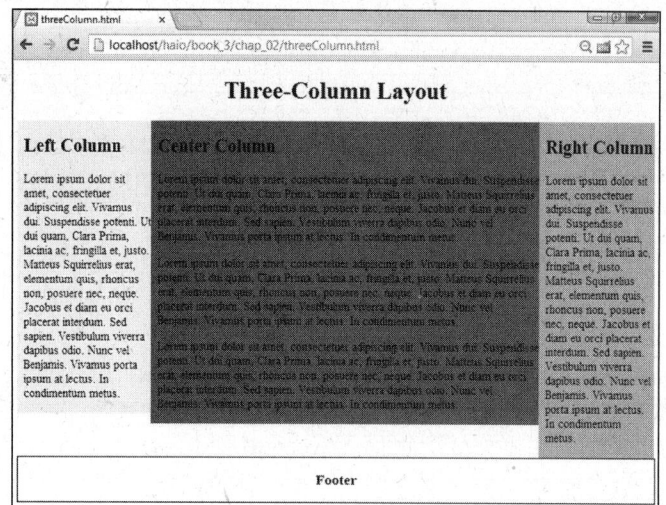

FIGURE 5-7:
The columns aren't really columns; each is a different height.

Figure 5-7 shows an important aspect of this type of layout. The columns are actually blocks, and each is a different height. Typically, I think of a column as stretching the entire height of a page, but this isn't how CSS does it. If you want to give each column a different background color, for example, you'll want each column to be the same height. This can be done with a CSS trick (at least, for the compliant browsers).

Specifying a min-height

The standards-compliant browsers (all versions of Firefox and Opera, and IE 7+) support a `min-height` property, which specifies a minimum height for an element.

TIP

You can use this property to force all columns to the same height. Figure 5-8 illustrates this effect.

The CSS code simply adds the `min-height` attribute to all the column elements:

```
#head {
   text-align: center;
   border-bottom: 3px double gray;
}

#left {
   float: left;
   width: 20%;
   min-height: 30em;
   background-color: #EEEEEE;
}
```

CHAPTER 5 **Building Floating Page Layouts** 189

```
#center {
  float: left;
  width: 60%;
  padding-left: 1%;
  padding-right: 1%;
  min-height: 30em;
}

#right {
  float: left;
  width: 17%;
  padding-left: 1%;
  min-height: 30em;
  background-color: #EEEEEE;
}

#footer {
  border: 1px black solid;
  float: left;
  width: 100%;
  clear: both;
  text-align: center;
}
```

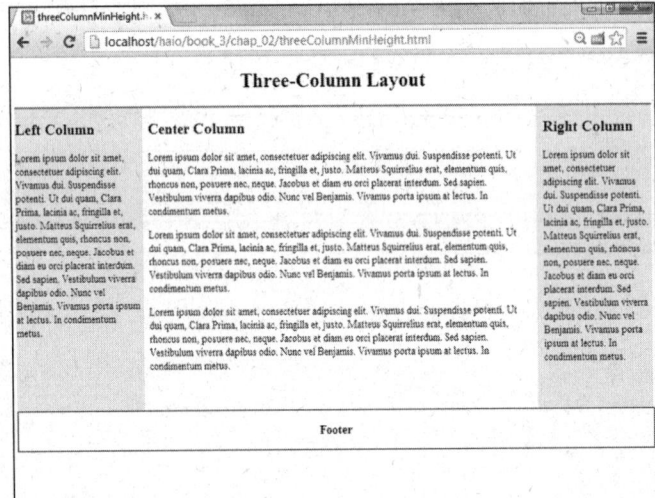

FIGURE 5-8: The min-height attribute forces all columns to be the same height.

Some guesswork is still involved. You have to experiment a bit to determine what the min-height should be. If you guess too short, one column will be longer than the min-height, and the columns won't appear correctly. If you guess too tall, you'll have a lot of empty space at the bottom of the screen.

All modern browsers support `min-height`, but a few of the older browsers may not support this attribute.

Using height and overflow

The `min-height` trick is ideal if you know the size of your content, but modern web development is all about multiple screen sizes. It's hard to predict how your page will look on a smart phone or other smaller browsers. If you use `min-height` and the text is too large to fit the screen, you can use another strategy. You can set the height of each element if you wish using the height rule. Like all CSS, the height is a suggestion. The question is what to do when content that fits fine in a large browser is forced to fit in a smaller space. The answer is a range of techniques popularly called *responsive design*. The basic idea of responsive design is to design a page so it naturally adjusts to a good view regardless of the device it's on.

One very basic approach to responsive design is to specify both width and height for a page element, but then allow the browser to manage overflow conditions. Figure 5-9 illustrates a page that is shrunk below the minimum size needed to display the text.

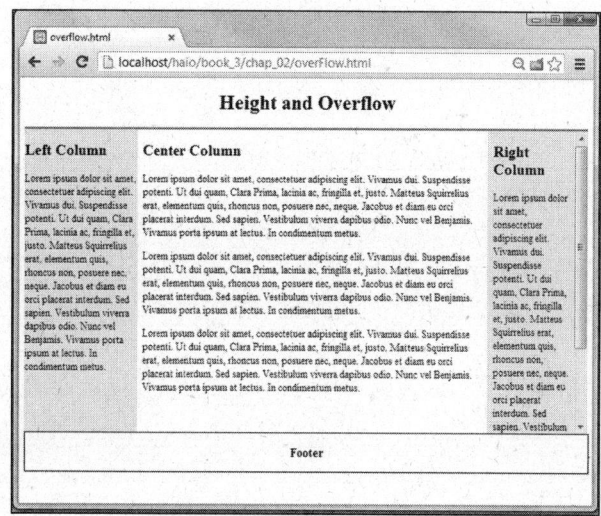

FIGURE 5-9: The page is too small to hold the text. Note the scroll bar.

If you set the height and width to a specific percentage of the page width, there is a danger the text will not fit. You can resolve this by adding an `overflow` rule in your CSS.

CHAPTER 5 **Building Floating Page Layouts** 191

Take a look at the CSS code used in overflow.html:

```
#head {
  text-align: center;
  border-bottom: 3px double gray;
}

#left {
  float: left;
  width: 20%;
  height: 30em;
  overflow: auto;
  background-color: #EEEEEE;
}

#center {
  float: left;
  width: 60%;
  padding-left: 1%;
  padding-right: 1%;
  height: 30em;
  overflow: auto;
}

#right {
  float: left;
  width: 17%;
  padding-left: 1%;
  height: 30em;
  overflow: auto;
  background-color: #EEEEEE;
}

#footer {
  border: 1px black solid;
  float: left;
  width: 100%;
  clear: both;
  text-align: center;
}
```

Setting the overflow property tells the browser what to do if it cannot place the text in the indicated space.

TIP

Use `overflow: auto` to place scrollbars only when necessary. Other options for the `overflow` rule are `visible` (text flows outside the box — the default value), `hidden` (overflow is not shown), and `scroll` (always place a scrollbar). I prefer `auto`.

192 BOOK 3 **Basic Web Coding**

Building a Fixed-Width Layout

Fluid layouts are terrific. They're very flexible, and they're not hard to build. Sometimes, though, it's nice to use a fixed-width layout, particularly if you want your layout to conform to a particular background image.

The primary attribute of a fixed-width layout is the use of a fixed measurement (almost always pixels), rather than the percentage measurements used in a fluid layout.

Figure 5-10 shows a two-column page.

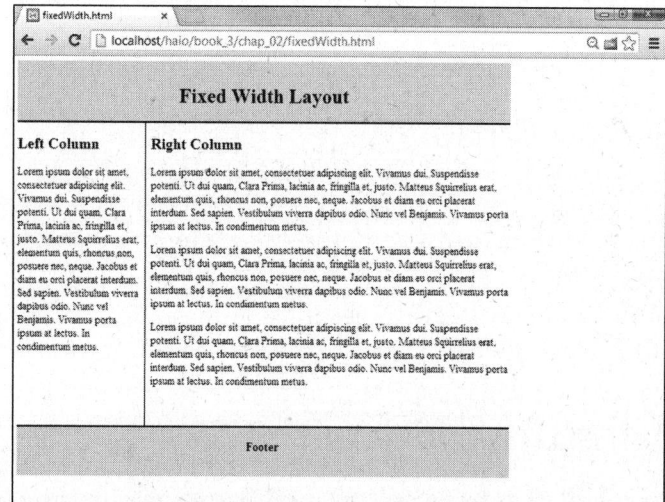

FIGURE 5-10: A fixed-width layout can work well but looks off-center.

The next examples will look off-center. Follow along to see what's going on, and see how to center a floated layout in the "Building a Centered Fixed-Width Layout" section later in this chapter.

Setting up the HTML

As usual, the HTML code is minimal. It contains a few named divs, and I've removed filler text for space reasons.

CHAPTER 5 Building Floating Page Layouts 193

```
<!DOCTYPE html>
<html lang = "en-US">

  <head>
    <meta charset = "UTF-8">
    <title>fixedWidth.html</title>
    <link rel = "stylesheet"
          type = "text/css"
          href = "fixedWidth.css"/>
  </head>

<body>
    <div id = "header">
      <h1>Fixed Width Layout</h1>
    </div>
    <div id = "left">
      <h2>Left Column</h2>
    </div>
    <div id = "right">
      <h2>Right Column</h2>
    </div>
    <div id = "footer">
      <h3>Footer</h3>
    </div>
  </body>
</html>
```

Fixing the width with CSS

After the HTML is set up, you can use CSS to enforce the two-column scheme.

Here's the CSS code:

```
#header {
  background-color: #e2e393;
  border-bottom: 3px solid black;
  text-align: center;
  width: 800px;
  padding-top: 1em;
}

#left {
  float: left;
  width: 200px;
  clear: left;
  border-right: 1px solid black;
```

```css
  height: 30em;
  overflow: auto;
  padding-right: .5em;
}

#right {
  float: left;
  width: 570px;
  height: 30em;
  overflow: auto;
  padding-left: .5em;
}

#footer {
  width: 800px;
  text-align: center;
  background-color: #e2e393;
  border-top: 3px double black;
  clear: both;
}
```

It's all part of a process:

1. **Color each element to see what's happening.**

 Begin by giving each div a different background color so you can see what is happening.

2. **Determine the overall width of the layout.**

 Pick a target width for the entire layout. I chose 800 pixels because it's a reasonably standard width.

3. **Adjust the widths of the page-wide elements.**

 It's often easiest to start with elements like the header and footer that often take up the entire width of the design.

4. **Float the columns.**

 The columns are floated as described throughout this chapter. Float each column to the left.

5. **Set the column widths.**

 Begin by making the column widths add up to the width of the entire design (in my case, 800 pixels). Later you'll adjust a bit for margins and borders.

6. **Clear the left column.**

 Ensure the left column has the `clear: left` rule applied.

CHAPTER 5 Building Floating Page Layouts 195

7. **Set column heights.**

 Give each column the same height. This makes things look right if you add borders or background colors to the columns.

8. **Adjust borders and padding.**

 Use borders, padding, and margins to adjust your page to get the look you want. In my case, I added a border to the left column to separate the columns, and I added padding to keep the text from sitting right on the border.

9. **Adjust widths again.**

 Adding borders, padding, and margins can change the widths of the existing elements. After you've modified these attributes, take a careful look at your layout to be sure it didn't get messed up, and modify the various widths if necessary.

Building a Centered Fixed-Width Layout

Fixed-width layouts are common, but they look a little strange if the browser isn't the width specified in the CSS. If the browser is too narrow, the layout won't work, and the second column will (usually) drop down to the next line.

If the browser is too wide, the page appears to be scrunched onto the left margin with a great deal of white space on the right.

The natural solution is to make a relatively narrow fixed-width design that's centered inside the entire page. Figure 5-11 illustrates a page with this technique.

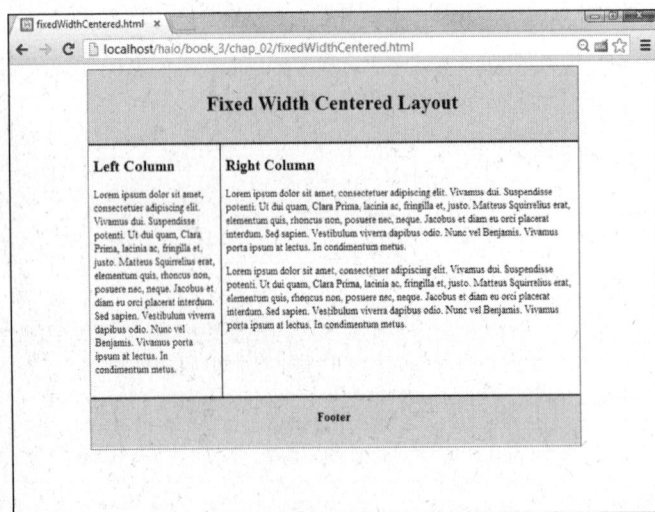

FIGURE 5-11: Now the fixed-width layout is centered in the browser.

196 BOOK 3 **Basic Web Coding**

 Some have called this type of design (fixed-width floating centered in the browser) a *jello* layout because it's not quite fluid and not quite fixed.

Making a surrogate body with an all div

In any case, the HTML requires only one new element, an `all` div that encases everything else inside the body (as usual, I removed the placeholder text):

```
<!DOCTYPE html>
<html lang = "en-US">

  <head>
    <meta charset = "UTF-8">
    <title>fixedWidthCentered.html</title>
    <link rel = "stylesheet"
          type = "text/css"
          href = "fixedWidthCentered.css"/>
  </head>
  <body>
    <div id = "all">
      <div id = "header">
        <h1>Fixed Width Centered Layout</h1>
      </div>
      <div id = "left">
        <h2>Left Column</h2>
      </div>
      <div id = "right">
        <h2>Right Column</h2>
      </div>
      <div id = "footer">
        <h3>Footer</h3>
      </div>
    </div>
  </body>
</html>
```

The entire page contents are now encapsulated in a special `all` div. This div will be resized to a standard width (typically 640 or 800 pixels). The `all` element will be centered in the body, and the other elements will be placed inside `all` as if it were the body:

```
#all {
  width: 800px;
  height: 600px;
  margin-left: auto;
```

```css
    margin-right: auto;
    border: 1px solid gray;
}

#header {
    background-color: #e2e393;
    border-bottom: 3px solid black;
    text-align: center;
    width: 800px;
    height: 100px;
    padding-top: 1em;
}

#left {
    float: left;
    width: 200px;
    clear: left;
    border-right: 1px solid black;
    height: 400px;
    padding-right: .5em;
}

#right {
    float: left;
    width: 580px;
    height: 400px;
    padding-left: .5em;
}

#footer {
    width: 800px;
    height: 60px;
    text-align: center;
    background-color: #e2e393;
    border-top: 3px double black;
    padding-bottom: 1em;
    clear: both;
}
```

How the jello layout works

This code is very similar to the `fixedWidth.css` style, but it has some important new features:

> » **The `all` element has a fixed width.** This element's width will determine the width of the fixed part of the page.

- » **all also needs a fixed height.** If you don't specify a height, all will be 0 pixels tall because all the elements inside it are floated.

- » **Center** all. Remember, to center divs (or any other block-level elements), you set margin-left and margin-right both to auto.

- » **Do *not* float** all. The margin: auto trick doesn't work on floated elements. all shouldn't have a float attribute set.

- » **Ensure that the interior widths add up to** all**'s width.** If all has a width of 800 pixels, be sure that the widths, borders, and margins of all the elements inside all add up to exactly 800 pixels.

WARNING

If you go even one pixel over, something will spill over and mess up the effect. You may have to fiddle with the widths to make everything work.

- » **Adjust the heights:** If your design has a fixed height, you'll also need to fiddle with the heights to get everything to look exactly right. Calculations will get you close, but you'll usually need to spend some quality time fiddling with exact measurements to get everything just right.

Limitations of the jello layout

Jello layouts represent a compromise between fixed and fluid layouts, but they aren't perfect:

- » **Implicit minimum width:** Very narrow browsers (like cell phones) can't render the layout the way you want. Fortunately, the content will still be visible, but not in exactly the format you wanted.

- » **Wasted screen space:** If you make the rendered part of the page narrow, a lot of space isn't being used in higher-resolution browsers. This can be frustrating.

- » **Complexity:** Although this layout technique is far simpler than table-based layouts, it's still a bit involved. You do have to plan your divs to make this type of layout work.

You can investigate a number of other layout techniques in Chapter 6 of this minibook.

DOESN'T CSS3 SUPPORT COLUMNS?

If you've been looking through the CSS3 specifications (and what better bedtime reading is there?), you may have discovered the new column rule. I was pretty excited when I found support for columns because it seemed like the answer to the complexities of floating layouts. Unfortunately, the column mechanism isn't really useful for page layout. The columns are all exactly the same width, and there's no way to determine exactly which content is displayed in which column. It's useful if you want to have a magazine-style layout with text that flows in columns, but for page layout, CSS3 has a better new tool, the flexible box layout model (described in Book 3, Chapter 6).

> **IN THIS CHAPTER**
> » Setting position to absolute
> » Managing z-index
> » Creating fixed and flexible layouts
> » Working with fixed and relative positioning
> » Using the new flexbox model

Chapter 6
Using Alternative Positioning

"The absence of alternatives clears the mind marvelously."

— HENRY A. KISSINGER

Floating layouts (described in Book 3, Chapter 5) are the preferred way to set up page layouts today, but sometimes other alternatives are useful. You can use *absolute, relative,* or *fixed positioning* techniques to put all your page elements exactly where you want them. Well, *almost* exactly. It's still web development, where nothing's exact. Because none of these alternatives are completely satisfying, the W3C (web standards body) has introduced a very promising new layout model called the *flexbox model.*

The techniques described in this chapter will give you even more capabilities when it comes to setting up great-looking websites.

Working with Absolute Positioning

Begin by considering the default layout mechanism. Figure 6-1 shows a page with two paragraphs on it.

FIGURE 6-1: These two paragraphs have a set height and width, but default positioning.

I used CSS to give each paragraph a different color (to aid in discussion later) and to set a specific height and width. The positioning is left to the default layout manager, which positions the second paragraph directly below the first one.

Setting up the HTML

The code behaves as we expect:

```
<!DOCTYPE html>
<html lang = "en-US">
 <head>
    <meta charset = "UTF-8">
    <title>boxes.html</title>
    <style type = "text/css">
      #blueBox {
         background-color: blue;
         width: 100px;
         height: 100px;
      }
      #blackBox {
         background-color: black;
         width: 100px;
         height: 100px;
      }
    </style>
 </head>
```

```
<body>
    <p id = "blueBox"></p>
    <p id = "blackBox"></p>
</body>
</html>
```

If you provide no further guidance, paragraphs (like other block-level elements) tend to provide carriage returns before and after themselves, stacking on top of each other. The default layout techniques ensure that nothing ever overlaps.

Adding position guidelines

Figure 6-2 shows something new: The paragraphs are overlapping!

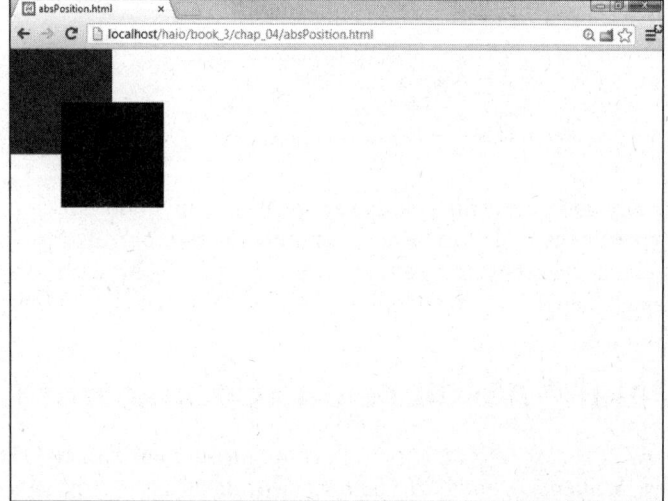

FIGURE 6-2: Now the paragraphs overlap each other.

This feat is accomplished through some new CSS attributes:

```
<!DOCTYPE html>
<html lang = "en-US">

  <head>
    <meta charset = "UTF-8">
    <title>absPosition.html</title>
    <style type = "text/css">
      #blueBox {
        background-color: blue;
        width: 100px;
```

CHAPTER 6 **Using Alternative Positioning** 203

```
            height: 100px;
            position: absolute;
            left: 0px;
            top: 0px;
            margin: 0px;
        }
        #blackBox {
            background-color: black;
            width: 100px;
            height: 100px;
            position: absolute;
            left: 50px;
            top: 50px;
            margin: 0px;
        }
    </style>
  </head>
<body>
    <p id = "blueBox"></p>
    <p id = "blackBox"></p>
</body>
</html>
```

TIP

So, why do I care if the boxes overlap? Well, you might not care, but the interesting part is this: You can have much more precise control over where elements live and what size they are. You can even override the browser's normal tendency to keep elements from overlapping, which gives you some interesting options.

Making absolute positioning work

A few new parts of CSS allow this more direct control of the size and position of these elements. Here's the CSS for one of the boxes:

```
#blueBox {
    background-color: blue;
    width: 100px;
    height: 100px;
    position: absolute;
    left: 0px;
    top: 0px;
    margin: 0px;
}
```

The following steps show how to style the blue box with absolute positioning:

1. **Set the** `position` **attribute to** `absolute`.

 Absolute positioning can be used to determine exactly (more or less) where the element will be placed on the screen:

    ```
    position: absolute;
    ```

2. **Specify a** `left` **position in the CSS.**

 After you determine that an element will have `absolute` position, it's removed from the normal flow, so you're obligated to fix its position. The `left` attribute determines where the left edge of the element will go. This can be specified with any of the measurement units, but it's typically measured in pixels:

    ```
    left: 0px;
    ```

3. **Specify a** `top` **position with CSS.**

 The `top` attribute indicates where the top of the element will go. Again, this is usually specified in pixels:

    ```
    top: 0px;
    ```

4. **Use the** `height` **and** `width` **attributes to determine the size.**

 Normally, when you specify a position, you also want to determine the size:

    ```
    width: 100px;
    height: 100px;
    ```

5. **Set the margins to 0.**

 When you're using absolute positioning, you're exercising quite a bit of control. Because browsers don't treat margins identically, you're better off setting margins to 0 and controlling the spacing between elements manually:

    ```
    margin: 0px;
    ```

TIP

Generally, you use absolute positioning only on named elements, rather than classes or general element types. For example, you will not want all the paragraphs on a page to have the same size and position, or you couldn't see them all. Absolute positioning works on only one element at a time.

CHAPTER 6 **Using Alternative Positioning** 205

Managing z-index

When you use absolute positioning, you can determine exactly where things are placed, so it's possible for them to overlap. By default, elements described later in HTML are positioned on top of elements described earlier.

Handling depth

You can use a special CSS attribute called z-index to change this default behavior. The z-axis refers to how close an element appears to be to the viewer. Figure 6-3 demonstrates how this works.

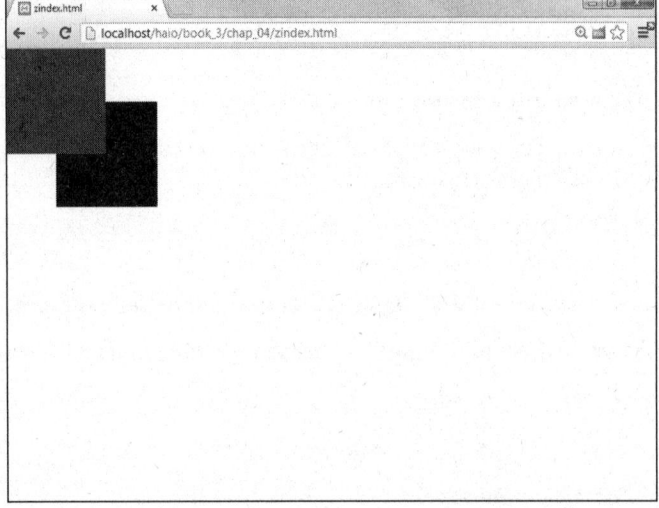

FIGURE 6-3: The z-index allows you to change which elements appear closer to the user.

The z-index attribute requires a numeric value. Higher numbers mean the element is closer to the user (or on *top*). Any value for z-index places the element higher than elements with the default z-index. This can be very useful when you have elements that you want to appear on top of other elements (for example, menus that temporarily appear on top of other text).

Here's the code illustrating the z-index effect:

```
<!DOCTYPE html>
<html lang = "en-US">

    <head>
```

```html
    <meta charset = "UTF-8">
    <title>zindex.html</title>
    <style type = "text/css">
      #blueBox {
        background-color: blue;
        width: 100px;
        height: 100px;
        position: absolute;
        left: 0px;
        top: 0px;
        margin: 0px;
        z-index: 1;
      }
      #blackBox {
        background-color: black;
        width: 100px;
        height: 100px;
        position: absolute;
        left: 50px;
        top: 50px;
        margin: 0px;
      }
    </style>
  </head>
<body>
    <p id = "blueBox"></p>
    <p id = "blackBox"></p>
  </body>
</html>
```

Working with z-index

The only change in this code is the addition of the z-index property. The higher a z-index value is, the closer that object appears to be to the user.

Here are a couple things to keep in mind when using z-index:

- **One element can totally conceal another.** When you start positioning things absolutely, one element can seem to disappear because it's completely covered by another. The z-index attribute is a good way to check for this situation.

- **Negative z-index can be problematic.** The value for z-index should be positive. Although negative values are supported, some browsers (notably older versions of Firefox) don't handle them well and may cause your element to disappear.

» **It may be best to give all values a** `z-index`. If you define the `z-index` for some elements and leave the `z-index` undefined for others, you have no guarantee exactly what will happen. If in doubt, just give every value its own `z-index`, and you'll know exactly what should overlap what.

» **Don't give two elements the same** `z-index`. The point of the `z-index` is to clearly define which element should appear closer. Don't defeat this purpose by assigning the same `z-index` value to two different elements on the same page.

Building a Page Layout with Absolute Positioning

You can use absolute positioning to create a page layout. This process involves some trade-offs. You tend to get better control of your page with absolute positioning (compared to floating techniques), but absolute layout requires more planning and more attention to detail. Figure 6-4 shows a page layout created with absolute positioning techniques.

The technique for creating an absolutely positioned layout is similar to the floating technique (in the general sense).

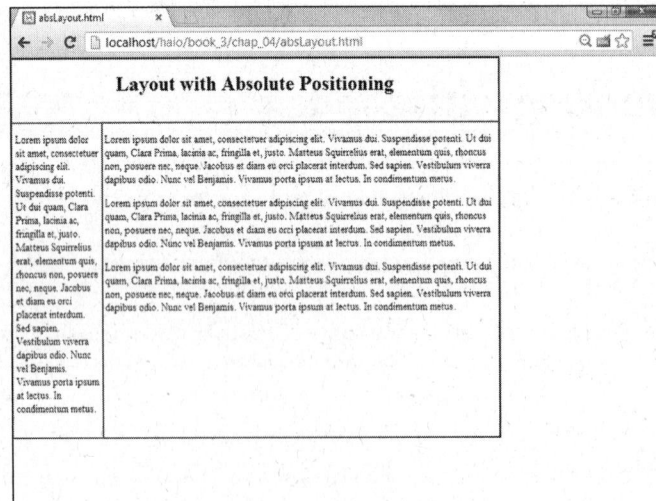

FIGURE 6-4: This layout was created with absolute positioning.

208 BOOK 3 Basic Web Coding

Overview of absolute layout

Before you begin putting your page together with absolute positioning, it's good to plan the entire process. Here's an example of how the process should go:

1. **Plan the site.**

 Having a drawing that specifies how your site layout will look is really important. In absolute positioning, your planning is even more important than the floating designs because you'll need to specify the size and position of every element.

2. **Specify an overall size.**

 This particular type of layout has a fixed size. Create an `all` div for all the other elements and specify the size of this div (in a fixed unit for now, usually px or em).

3. **Create the HTML.**

 The HTML page should have a named div for each part of the page (so if you have headers, columns, and footers, you need a div for each).

4. **Build a CSS style sheet.**

 The CSS styles can be internal or linked, but because absolute positioning tends to require a little more markup than floating, external styles are preferred.

5. **Identify each element.**

 It's easier to see what's going on if you assign a different colored border to each element.

6. **Make each element absolutely positioned.**

 Set `position: absolute` in the CSS for each element in the layout.

7. **Specify the size of each element.**

 Set the `height` and `width` of each element according to your diagram. (You *did* make a diagram, right?)

8. **Determine the position of each element.**

 Use the `left` and `top` attributes to determine where each element goes in the layout.

9. **Tune-up your layout.**

 You'll probably want to adjust margins and borders. You may need to do some adjustments to make it all work. For example, the menu is 150px wide, but I added `padding-left` and `padding-right` of 5px each. This means the width of the menu needs to be adjusted to 140px to make everything still fit.

Writing the HTML

The HTML code is pretty straightforward:

```html
<!DOCTYPE html>
<html lang = "en-US">

  <head>
    <meta charset = "UTF-8">
    <title>absLayout.html</title>
    <link rel = "stylesheet"
          type = "text/css"
          href = "absLayout.css"/>
  </head>
  <body>
    <div id = "all">
      <div id = "head">
        <h1>Layout with Absolute Positioning</h1>
      </div>

      <div id = "menu">
      </div>

      <div id = "content">
      </div>

    </div>
  </body>
</html>
```

As is typical for layout examples, I removed the lorem text from this code listing for clarity.

The HTML file calls an external style sheet called absLayout.css.

Adding the CSS

The CSS code is a bit lengthy but not too difficult:

```css
/* absLayout.css */
#all {
  border: 1px solid black;
  width: 800px;
  height: 600px;
  position: absolute;
```

```
    left: 0px;
    top: 0px;
}

#head {
    border: 1px solid green;
    position: absolute;
    width: 800px;
    height: 100px;
    top: 0px;
    left: 0px;
    text-align: center;
}

#menu {
    border: 1px solid red;
    position: absolute;
    width: 140px;
    height: 500px;
    top: 100px;
    left: 0px;
    padding-left: 5px;
    padding-right: 5px;
}

#content{
    border: 1px solid blue;
    position: absolute;
    width: 645px;
    height: 500px;
    top: 100px;
    left: 150px;
    padding-left: 5px;
}
```

A static layout created with absolute positioning has a few important features to keep in mind:

» **You're committed to position everything.** After you start using absolute positioning, you need to use it throughout your site. All the main page elements require absolute positioning because the normal flow mechanism is no longer in place.

You can still use floating layout *inside* an element with absolute position, but all your main elements (heading, columns, and footing) need to have absolute position if one of them does.

- » **You should specify size and position.** With a floating layout, you're still encouraging a certain amount of fluidity. Absolute positioning means you're taking the responsibility for both the shape and size of *each* element in the layout.

- » **Absolute positioning is less adaptable.** With this technique, you're pretty much bound to a specific screen width and height. You'll have trouble adapting to tablets and cellphones.

A more flexible alternative is shown in the next section.

- » **All the widths and heights have to add up.** When you determine the size of your display, all the heights, widths, margins, padding, and borders have to add up, or you'll get some strange results.

When you use absolute positioning, you're also likely to spend some quality time with your calculator, figuring out all the widths and the heights.

Creating a More Flexible Layout

You can build a layout with absolute positioning and some flexibility. Figure 6-5 illustrates such a design.

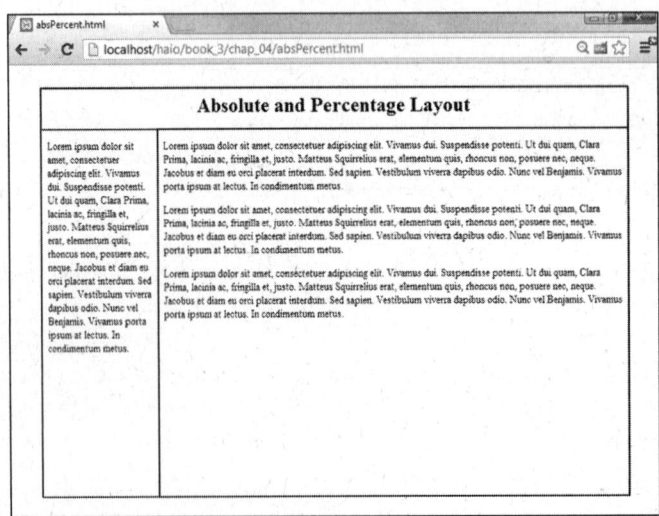

FIGURE 6-5: This page uses absolute layout, but it doesn't have a fixed size.

The size of this layout is attached to the size of the browser screen. It attempts to adjust to the browser while it's resized. You can see this effect in Figure 6-6.

212 BOOK 3 **Basic Web Coding**

FIGURE 6-6:
The layout resizes in proportion to the browser window.

The page simply takes up a fixed percentage of the browser screen. The proportions are all maintained, no matter what the screen size is.

WARNING

Having the page resize with the browser works, but it's not a complete solution. When the browser window is small enough, the text will no longer fit without some ugly bleed-over effects. You can fix this with the overflow attribute, but then you will have scrollbars in your smaller elements.

Designing with percentages

This *absolute but flexible* trick is achieved by using percentage measurements. The position is still set to absolute, but rather than defining size and position with pixels, you use percentages instead. Here's the CSS:

```
/* absPercent.css */
#all {
  border: 1px black solid;
  position: absolute;
  left: 5%;
  top: 5%;
  width: 90%;
```

CHAPTER 6 **Using Alternative Positioning** 213

```css
    height: 90%;
}

#head {
    border: 1px black solid;
    position: absolute;
    left: 0%;
    top: 0%;
    width: 100%;
    height: 10%;
    text-align: center;
}

#head h1 {
    margin-top: 1%;
}

#menu {
    border: 1px green solid;
    position: absolute;
    left: 0%;
    top: 10%;
    width: 18%;
    height: 90%;
    padding-left: 1%;
    padding-right: 1%;
    overflow: auto;
}

#content {
    border: 1px black solid;
    position: absolute;
    left: 20%;
    top: 10%;
    width: 78%;
    height: 90%;
    padding-left: 1%;
    padding-right: 1%;
    overflow: auto;
}
```

The key to any absolute positioning (even this flexible kind) is math. When you just look at the code, it isn't clear where all those numbers come from. Look at the diagram for the page in Figure 6-7 to see how all the values are derived.

FIGURE 6-7: The diagram is the key to a successful layout.

Building the layout

Here's how the layout works:

1. **Create an `all` container by building a div with the `all` ID.**

 The `all` container will hold *all* the contents of the page. It isn't absolutely necessary in this type of layout, but it does allow for a centering effect.

2. **Specify the size and position of `all`.**

 I want the content of the page to be centered in the browser window, so I set its height and width to 90 percent, and its `margin-left` and `margin-top` to 5 percent. This sets the `margin-right` and `margin-bottom` to 5 percent also. These percentages refer to the `all` div's container element, which is the body, with the same size as the browser window.

3. **Other percentages are in relationship to the `all` container.**

 Because all the other elements are placed inside `all`, the percentage values are no longer referring to the entire browser window. The widths and heights for the menu and content areas are calculated as percentages of their container, which is `all`.

4. **Determine the heights.**

 Height is usually pretty straightforward because you don't usually have to change the margins. Remember, though, that the head accounts for 10 percent of the page space, so the height of both the menu and content needs to be 90 percent.

5. **Figure the general widths.**

 In principle, the width of the menu column is 20 percent, and the content column is 80 percent. This isn't perfectly accurate, though.

CHAPTER 6 **Using Alternative Positioning**

6. **Compensate for margins.**

 You probably want some margins, or the text looks cramped. If you want 1 percent margin-left and 1 percent margin-right on the menu column, you have to set the menu's width to 18 percent to compensate for the margins. Likewise, set the content width to 78 percent to compensate for margins.

As if this weren't complex enough, remember that Internet Explorer 6 (IE6) and earlier browsers calculate margins differently! In these browsers, the margin happens *inside* the content, so you don't have to compensate for them (but you have to remember that they make the useable content area smaller). You'll probably have to make a conditional comment style sheet to handle IE6 if you use absolute positioning.

Exploring Other Types of Positioning

If you use the position attribute, you're most likely to use absolute. However, here are other positioning techniques that can be handy in certain circumstances:

» **Relative:** Set position: relative when you want to move an element from its default position. For example, if you set position to relative and top: -10px, the element would be placed 10 pixels higher on the screen than normal.

» **Fixed:** Use fixed position when you want an element to stay in the same place, even when the page is scrolled. This is sometimes used to keep a menu on the screen when the contents are longer than the screen width.

If you use fixed positioning, be sure you're not overwriting something already on the screen.

The real trick is to use appropriate combinations of positioning schemes to solve interesting problems.

Creating a fixed menu system

Figure 6-8 illustrates a very common type of web page — one with a menu on the left and a number of stories or topics in the main area.

Something is interesting about this particular design. The button list on the left refers to specific segments of the page. When you click one of these buttons (say, the Gamma button), the appropriate part of the page is called up, as shown in Figure 6-9.

FIGURE 6-8: At first glance, this is yet another two-column layout.

FIGURE 6-9: The page scrolls to the Gamma content, but the menu stays put.

Normally, when you scroll down the page, things on the top of the page (like the menu) disappear. In this case, the menu stays on the screen, even though the part of the page where it was originally placed is now off the screen.

TIP

Gamma isn't necessarily moved to the top of the page. Linking to an element ensures that it's visible but doesn't guarantee where it will appear.

You can achieve this effect using a combination of positioning techniques.

CHAPTER 6 **Using Alternative Positioning** 217

Setting up the HTML

The HTML for the fixed menu page is simple (as you'd expect by now):

```html
<!DOCTYPE html>
<html lang = "en-US">

  <head>
    <meta charset = "UTF-8">
    <title>fixedRelative.html</title>
    <link rel = "stylesheet"
          type = "text/css"
          href = "fixedRelative.css"/>
  </head>
  <body>
    <h1>Fixed Position</h1>
    <div id = "menu">
      <h2>Menu</h2>
      <ul>
        <li><a href = "#alpha">Alpha</a></li>
        <li><a href = "#beta">Beta</a></li>
        <li><a href = "#gamma">Gamma</a></li>
        <li><a href = "#delta">Delta</a></li>
      </ul>
    </div>

    <div class = "content"
         id = "alpha">
      <h2>Alpha</h2>
    </div>

    <div class = "content"
         id = "beta">
      <h2>Beta</h2>
    </div>

    <div class = "content"
         id = "gamma">
      <h2>Gamma</h2>
    </div>

    <div class = "content"
         id = "delta">
      <h2>Delta</h2>
    </div>
  </body>
</html>
```

The HTML has only a few noteworthy characteristics:

» **It has a menu.** The div named menu contains a list of links (like most menus).

» **The menu has internal links.** A menu can contain links to external documents or (like this one) links inside the current document. The `Alpha` code means create a link to the element in this page with the ID alpha.

» **The page has a series of** content **divs.** Most of the page's content appears in one of the several divs with the content class. This class indicates all these divs will share some formatting.

» **The** content **divs have separate IDs.** Although all the content divs are part of the same class, each has its own ID. This allows the menu to select individual items (and would also allow individual styling, if desired).

TIP

As normal for this type of code, I left out the filler paragraphs from the code listing.

Setting the CSS values

The interesting work happens in CSS. Here's an overview of the code:

```
/* fixedRelative.css */

body {
  background-color: #fff9bf;
}

h1 {
 text-align: center;
}

#menu {
  position: fixed;
  width: 18%;
}

#menu li {
  list-style-type: none;
  margin-left: -2em;
  text-align: center;
}
```

```css
#menu a{
  display: block;
  border: 2px gray outset;
  text-decoration: none;
  color: black;
}

#menu a:hover{
  color: white;
  background-color: black;
  border: 2px gray inset;
}

#menu h2 {
  text-align: center;
}

.content {
  position: relative;
  left: 20%;
  width: 80%;
}

.content h2 {
  border-top: 3px black double;
}
```

I changed the menu list to make it look like a set of buttons, and I added some basic formatting to the headings and borders. The interesting thing here is how I positioned various elements.

Here's how you build a fixed menu:

1. **Set the menu position to** `fixed` **by setting the** `position` **attribute to** `fixed`.

 The menu div should stay on the same spot, even while the rest of the page scrolls. Fixed positioning causes the menu to stay put, no matter what else happens on the page.

2. **Give the menu a width with the** `width` **attribute.**

 It's important that the width of the menu be predictable, both for aesthetic reasons and to make sure the content isn't overwritten by the menu. In this example, I set the menu width to 18 percent of the page width (20 percent minus some margin space).

3. **Consider the menu position by explicitly setting the** `top` **and** `left` **attributes.**

 When you specify a fixed position, you can determine where the element is placed on the screen with the `left` and `top` attributes. I felt that the default position was fine, so I didn't change it.

4. **Set** content **position to** `relative`.

 By default, all members of the content class will fill out the entire page width. Because the menu needs the leftmost 20 percent of the page, set the content class position to `relative`.

5. **Change** content**'s** `left` **attribute to 20 percent.**

 Because content has `relative` positioning, setting the left to 20 percent will add 20 percent of the parent element to each content's `left` value. This will ensure that there's room for the menu to the left of all the content panes.

6. **Give** content **a** `width` **property.**

 If you don't define the width, content panels may bleed off the right side of the page. Use the `width` property to ensure this doesn't happen.

REMEMBER

In reality, I rarely use absolute positioning for page layout. It's just too difficult to get working and too inflexible for the range of modern browsers. However, it is still used in certain specialty situations like web game development where the programmer is deliberately subverting normal layout schemes for more control of the visual interface.

Flexible Box Layout Model

Page layout has been a constant concern in web development. There have been many different approaches to page layout, and all have weaknesses. The current standard is the floating mechanism. While this works quite well, it has two major weaknesses.

» **It can be hard to understand.** The various parts of the float specification can be difficult to follow, and the behavior is not intuitive. The relationship between `width`, `clear`, and `float` attributes can be difficult to follow.

» **The page order matters.** One goal of semantic layout is to completely divorce the way the page is created from how it is displayed. With the floating layout, the order in which various elements are written in the HTML document influences how they are placed. An ideal layout solution would allow any kind of placement through CSS, even after the HTML is finished.

CHAPTER 6 **Using Alternative Positioning** 221

Absolute positioning seems great at first, but it has its own problems:

» **It's a lot more detail-oriented.** Absolute positioning is a commitment. You often end up having to directly control the size and position of every element on the screen, which is tedious and difficult.

» **It's not as flexible.** With responsive design (creating a page that can adapt to the many different devices available) all the rage today, the absolute position scheme simply doesn't deliver the flexibility needed in modern web development.

There are some other layout mechanisms (tables and frames) that have already been rejected as viable layout options, which seems to leave web programmers without an ideal solution.

Creating a flexible box layout

CSS3 proposes a new layout mechanism that aims to solve a lot of the layout problems that have plagued web development. The flexible box layout scheme (sometimes called *flexbox*) shows a lot of promise. Here's essentially how it works:

1. **Designate a page segment as a box.**

 The `display` attribute of most elements can be set to various types. CSS3 introduces a new display type: box. Setting the display of an element to box makes it capable of holding other elements with the flexible box mechanism.

2. **Determine the orientation of child elements.**

 Use a new attribute called `box-orient` to determine if the child elements of the current element will be placed vertically or horizontally inside the main element.

3. **Specify the weight of child elements.**

 Each child element can be given a numeric weight. The weight determines how much space that element takes up. If the weight is zero, the element takes as little space as possible. If the weight of all the elements is one, they all take up the same amount of space. If one element has a weight of two and the others all have a weight of one, the larger element has twice the size of the others, and so on. Weight is determined through the `box-flex` attribute.

4. **Nest another box inside the first.**

 You can nest flexboxes inside each other. Simply apply the box display type to inner elements that will show the display.

5. **Modify the order in which elements appear.**

 Normally elements appear in the order in which they were placed on the page, but you can use the `box-ordinal-group` attribute to adjust the placement order.

Viewing a flexible box layout

As an example, take a look at the following HTML code:

```
<div id = "a">
  <div id = "b">b</div>
  <div id = "c">c</div>
  <div id = "d">
     <div id = "e">e</div>
     <div id = "f">f</div>
  </div>
</div>
```

Although this is a clearly made-up example, it shows a complex structure that could be difficult to style using standard layout techniques. Figure 6-10 illustrates a complex nested style that would be difficult to achieve through traditional layout techniques:

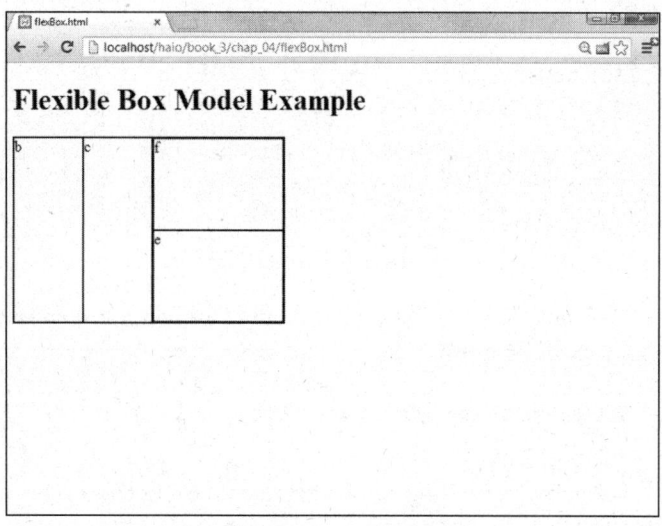

FIGURE 6-10: This structure would not be easy to build with CSS2.

CHAPTER 6 **Using Alternative Positioning** 223

The following style sheet is used to apply a flex grid style to this page:

```css
div {
  border: 1px solid black;
}

#a {
  width: 300px;
  height: 200px;
  display: box;
  box-orient: horizontal;
}

#b {
  box-flex: 1;
}

#c {
  box-flex: 1;
}

#d {
  display: box;
  box-orient: vertical;
  box-flex: 2;
}

#e {
  box-flex: 1;
    box-ordinal-group: 2;
}

#f {
  box-flex: 1;
}
```

The CSS looks complex, but there are only four new CSS elements. Here's how this specific example works:

1. Set up a to be the primary container.

The a div is the primary container, so give it a height and width. It will contain flex boxes, so set the `display` attribute to `box`. Determine how you want the children of this box to be lined up by setting the `box-orient` attribute to `vertical` or `horizontal`.

2. **Specify the weights of** b, c, **and** d.

 In my example, I want elements b and c to take up half the space, and d to fill up the remainder of the space. To get this behavior, set the box-flex value of b and c to 1, and the box-flex value of d to 2.

3. **Set up** d **as another container.**

 The d element will contain e and f. Use display: box to make d a flex container, and box-orient to vertical to make the elements line up vertically. (Normally nested elements will switch between horizontal and vertical.)

4. **Elements** e **and** f **should each take half of** d.

 Use the box-flex attribute to give these elements equal weight.

5. **Change the ordinal group of** e **so it appears after** f.

 The box-ordinal-group attribute indicates the order in which an element will be displayed inside its group. Normally, all items have a default value of 1, so they appear in the order they are written. You can demote an element by setting its box-ordinal-group value to a higher number, causing that element to be displayed later than normal. I set e to ordinal group 2, so it is displayed after element f.

. . . And now for a little reality

The flexbox system seems perfect. It's much more sensible than the Byzantine layout techniques that are currently in use. However, the flexible box system isn't ready for common use yet.

Right now, not a single browser implements the flexbox attributes directly. However, special vendor-specific versions are available:

» WebKit-based browsers (primarily Safari and Chrome) use variations that begin with -webkit-.

» Gecko-based browsers (Firefox and Mozilla) use the -moz- prefix.

» Microsoft requires -ms-.

To make the example in this chapter work in modern browsers, you need to include -ms-, -webkit-, and -moz- versions of all the attributes, like this:

```
#a {
    width: 300px;
    height: 200px;
```

```
    box-orient: horizontal;
    display: box;

    -moz-box-orient: horizontal;
    display: -moz-box;

    -webkit-box-orient: horizontal;
    display: -webkit-box;

    -ms-box-orient: horizontal;
    display: -ms-box;
}

#b {
    box-flex: 1;
    -moz-box-flex: 1;
    -webkit-box-flex: 1;
    -ms-box-flex: 1;
}
```

None of the browsers currently support the vanilla version, but I put it in anyway because hopefully in the near future only that version will be necessary. This technique is worth learning about because it may well become the preferred layout technique in the future.

For a complete example, take a look at Figure 6-11, which shows a standard two-column page.

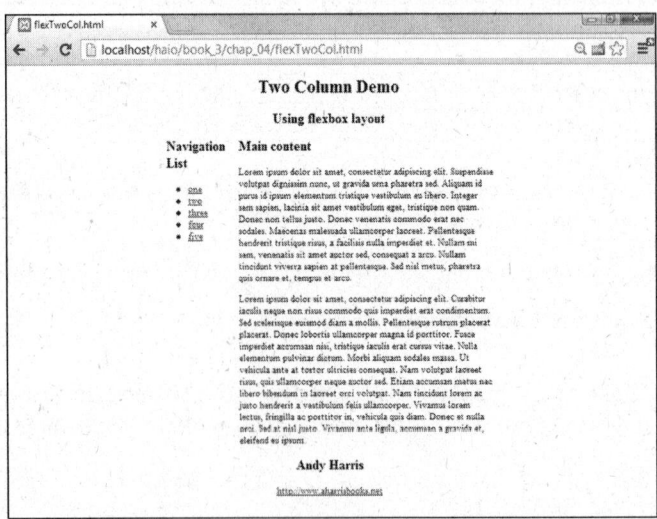

FIGURE 6-11: This standard layout uses flexbox.

Though you can't tell from the screen shot, this page uses HTML5 throughout, including the new semantic tags (see the sidebar at the end of this chapter for a discussion of semantic tags) and a flexbox layout model.

Although the CSS code may look complex, it's just repeated four times to handle all the various browser prefixes:

```html
<!DOCTYPE HTML>
  <html lang = "en">
  <head>
    <title>flexTwoCol.html</title>
    <meta charset = "UTF-8"/>
    <style type = "text/css">
      #all {
        display: box;
        display: -moz-box;
        display: -wekbit-box;
        display: -ms-box;

        box-orient: vertical;
        -moz-box-orient: vertical;
        -webkit-box-orient: vertical;
        -ms-box-orient: vertical;

        height: 600px;
        width: 600px;
        margin-right: auto;
        margin-left: auto;
      }

      #main {
        display: box;
        display: -moz-box;
        display: -webkit-box;
        display: -ms-box;
        box-orient: horizontal;

        -moz-box-orient: horizontal;
        -webkit-box-orient: horizontal;
        -ms-box-orient: horizontal;
      }

      #nav {
        box-flex: 1;
        -moz-box-flex: 1;
        -webkit-box-flex: 1;
```

CHAPTER 6 **Using Alternative Positioning** 227

```
      -ms-box-flex: 1;
    }

    #article {
      box-flex: 6;
      -moz-box-flex: 6;
      -webkit-box-flex: 6;
      -ms-box-flex: 6;
    }

    header, footer {
      display:block;
      text-align: center;
    }
  </style>
</head>

<body>
  <div id = "all">
    <header>
      <hgroup>
        <h1>Two Column Demo</h1>
        <h2>Using flexbox layout</h2>
      </hgroup>
    </header>

    <div id = "main">

      <div id = "nav">
        <h2>Navigation List</h2>
        <ul>
          <li><a href = "#">one</a></li>
          <li><a href = "#">two</a></li>
          <li><a href = "#">three</a></li>
          <li><a href = "#">four</a></li>
          <li><a href = "#">five</a></li>
        </ul>
      </div>

      <div id = "article">
        <h2>Main content</h2>
      </div>
    </div>
```

```
        <footer>
          <h2>Nik Abraham</h2>
          <a href = "http://www.twitter.com/nikhilgabraham">
            Tweet @nikhilgabraham</a>
        </footer>
      </div>
    </body>
</html>
```

The flexbox approach is really promising. When you get used to it, flexbox is less mysterious than the `float` approach, and far more flexible than absolute positioning. Essentially, my page uses a fixed width div and places a flexbox inside it. There's no need to worry about `float`, `clear`, or any specific measurements except the one for the `all` div. The only downside is the need to code the CSS for all the browser prefixes. For now, I fix that with macros in my text editor.

INTRODUCING SEMANTIC LAYOUT TAGS

Web developers embraced the idea of semantic markup, which is all about labeling things based on their *meaning*. "Within a short time, nearly every page had a number of divs with the same name: div id = "header", div id = "navigation", div id = "footer", and so on.

HTML5 finally released a set of semantic markup elements to describe the standard page elements. Here's a list of the most important ones:

- `<header>`: Describes the header area of your page.
- `<nav>`: Navigation element, often contains some sort of menu system.
- `<section>`: Contains a section of content.
- `<article>`: Contains an article — typically generated from an external source.
- `<footer>`: Contains the footer elements.

The semantic elements are useful because they simplify markup. Unfortunately, not all browsers recognize these elements yet. They will render just fine, but it may be a while before CSS can be used with these elements with confidence.

4
Advanced Web Coding

Contents at a Glance

CHAPTER 1: Working Faster with Twitter Bootstrap 233
- Figuring Out What Bootstrap Does............................ 234
- Installing Bootstrap... 235
- Understanding the Layout Options 236
- Coding Basic Web Page Elements............................. 243
- Build the Airbnb Home Page 247

CHAPTER 2: Adding in JavaScript................................ 249
- What Does JavaScript Do? 249
- Understanding JavaScript Structure 251
- Coding Common JavaScript Tasks............................. 253
- Writing Your First JavaScript Program 263
- Working with APIs... 263
- Using JavaScript Libraries.................................. 267

CHAPTER 3: Understanding Callbacks and Closures 269
- What Are Callbacks?... 269
- Understanding Closures...................................... 274
- Using Closures.. 277

CHAPTER 4: Embracing AJAX and JSON........................... 279
- Working behind the Scenes with AJAX 279
- Putting Objects in Motion with JSON 289

CHAPTER 5: jQuery... 295
- Writing More and Doing Less 295
- Getting Started with jQuery................................. 296
- The jQuery Object .. 297
- Is Your Document Ready?..................................... 298
- Using jQuery Selectors...................................... 298
- Changing Things with jQuery................................. 300
- Events ... 302
- Effects .. 305
- AJAX ... 309

IN THIS CHAPTER

» Understanding what Twitter Bootstrap does

» Viewing layouts created with Twitter Bootstrap

» Creating web page elements using Twitter Bootstrap

Chapter 1
Working Faster with Twitter Bootstrap

"Speed, it seems to me, provides the one genuinely modern pleasure."
— ALDOUS HUXLEY

Twitter Bootstrap is a free toolkit that allows users to create web pages quickly and with great consistency. In 2011 two Twitter developers, Mark Otto and Jacob Thornton, created the toolkit for internal use at Twitter and soon afterward released it to the general public. Before Bootstrap, developers would create common web page features over and over again and each time slightly differently, leading to increased time spent on maintenance. Bootstrap has become one of the most popular tools used in creating websites and is used by NASA and *Newsweek* for their websites. With a basic understanding of HTML and CSS, you can use and customize Bootstrap layouts and elements for your own projects.

In this chapter, you discover what Bootstrap does and how to use it. You also discover the various layouts and elements that you can quickly and easily create when using Bootstrap.

Figuring Out What Bootstrap Does

Imagine you're the online layout developer for *The Washington Post*, responsible for coding the front page of the print newspaper (see Figure 1-1) into a digital website version. The newspaper consistently uses the same font size and typeface for the main headline, captions, and bylines. Similarly, there are a set number of layouts to choose from, usually with the main headline at the top of the page accompanied by a photo.

FIGURE 1-1: The front page of *The Washington Post* (June 7, 2013).

Every day you could write your CSS code from scratch, defining font typeface, sizes, paragraph layouts, and the like. However, given that the newspaper follows a largely defined format, it would be easier to define this styling ahead of time in your CSS file with class names, and when necessary refer to the styling you want by name. At its core, this is how Bootstrap functions.

Bootstrap is a collection of standardized prewritten HTML, CSS, and JavaScript code that you can reference using class names (for a refresher, see Book 3, Chapter 4) and then further customize. Bootstrap allows you to create and gives you the following:

>> **Layouts:** Define your web page content and elements in a grid pattern.

» **Components:** Use existing buttons, menus, and icons that have been tested on hundreds of millions of users.

» **Responsiveness:** A fancy word for whether your site will work on mobile phones and tablets in addition to desktop computers. Ordinarily, you would write additional code so your website appears properly on these different screen sizes, but Bootstrap code is already optimized to do this for you, as shown in Figure 1-2.

» **Cross-browser compatibility:** Chrome, Firefox, Safari, Internet Explorer, and other browsers all vary in the way they render certain HTML elements and CSS properties. Bootstrap code is optimized so your web page appears consistently no matter the browser used.

FIGURE 1-2: The Angry Birds Star Wars page optimized for desktop, tablet, and mobile using Bootstrap.

Installing Bootstrap

Install and add Bootstrap to your HTML file by following these two steps:

1. Include this code between your opening and closing `<head>` tag:

```
<link rel="stylesheet"
      href="http://maxcdn.bootstrapcdn.com/bootstrap/3.2.0/css/bootstrap.min.css">
```

TIP

The `<link>` tag refers to version 3.2.0 of the Bootstrap CSS file hosted on the Internet, so you must be connected to the Internet for this method to work.

2. Include these lines of code immediately before your closing HTML `</body>` tag.

```
<!--jQuery (needed for Bootstrap's JavaScript plugins) -->
<script
        src="http://ajax.googleapis.com/ajax/libs/jquery/1.11.1/jquery.min.
```

CHAPTER 1 **Working Faster with Twitter Bootstrap** 235

```
js"></script>
<!--Bootstrap Javascript plugin file -->
<script src="http://maxcdn.bootstrapcdn.com/bootstrap/3.2.0/js/bootstrap.
```

```
min.js"></script>
```

The first `<script>` tag references a JavaScript library called jQuery. JavaScript is covered in Book 4, Chapter 2, and jQuery is covered in Book 4, Chapter 5. At a high level, jQuery simplifies tasks performed using JavaScript. The second `<script>` tag references Bootstrap JavaScript plugins, including animated effects such as drop-down menus. If your website doesn't use animated effects or Bootstrap JavaScript plugins, you don't need to include this file.

Bootstrap is free to use for personal and commercial purposes, but does require including the Bootstrap license and copyright notice.

If you don't have reliable access to an Internet connection, you can also download and locally host the Bootstrap CSS and JavaScript files. To do this, after unzipping the Bootstrap file, use the `<link>` and `<script>` tags to link to the local version of your file. Visit www.getbootstrap.com/getting-started to download the files and to access additional instructions and examples.

Understanding the Layout Options

Bootstrap allows you to quickly and easily lay out content on the page using a grid system. You have three options when using this grid system:

- » **Code yourself.** After you learn how the grid is organized, you can write code to create any layout you wish.
- » **Code with a Bootstrap editor.** Instead of writing code in a text editor, drag and drop components and elements to generate Bootstrap code. You can then download and use this code.
- » **Code with a prebuilt theme.** Download free Bootstrap themes or buy a theme where the website has already been created, and you fill in your own content.

Lining up on the grid system

Bootstrap divides the screen into a grid system of 12 equally sized columns. These columns follow a few rules:

» **Columns must sum to a width of 12 columns.** You can use one column that is 12 columns wide, 12 columns that are each one column wide, or anything in between.

» **Columns can contain content or spaces.** For example, you could have a 4-column-wide column, a space of 4 columns, and another 4-column-wide column.

Unless you specify otherwise, these columns will automatically stack into a single column on smaller browser sizes or screens like mobile devices, and expand horizontally on larger browser sizes or screens like laptop and desktop screens. (See Figure 1-3.)

FIGURE 1-3: Sample Bootstrap layouts.

Now that you have a sense for how these layouts appear on the screen, take a look at example code used to generate these layouts. To create any layout, follow these steps:

1. **Create a `<div>` tag with the attribute** `class="container"`.

2. **Inside the first `<div>` tag, create another nested `<div>` tag with the attribute** `class="row"`.

3. **For each row you want to create, create another `<div>` tag with the attribute** `class="col-md-X"`. **Set X equal to the number of columns you want the row to span.**

 For example, to have a row span 4 columns, write `<div class= "col-md-4">`. The `md` targets the column width for desktops, and I show you how to target other devices later in this section.

WARNING

You must include `<div class="container">` at the beginning of your page and have a closing `</div>` tag, or your page will not render properly.

CHAPTER 1 Working Faster with Twitter Bootstrap 237

The following code, as shown in Figure 1-4, creates a simple three-column centered layout:

```
<div class="container">
 <!-- Example row of columns -->
 <div class="row">
  <div class="col-md-4">
   <h2>Heading</h2>
   <p>Lorem ipsum dolor sit amet, consectetur adipisicing elit, sed do
   eiusmod tempor incididunt ut labore et dolore magna aliqua. Ut enim
   ad minim veniam, quis nostrud exercitation ullamco laboris nisi ut
   aliquip ex ea commodo consequat.
   </p>
  </div>
  <div class="col-md-4">
   <h2>Heading</h2>
   <p>Lorem ipsum dolor sit amet, consectetur adipisicing elit, sed do
       eiusmod
   Tempor incididunt ut labore et dolore magna aliqua. Ut enim ad minim
       veniam,
   quis nostrud exercitation ullamco laboris nisi ut aliquip ex ea commodo
   consequat.
   </p>
  </div>
  <div class="col-md-4">
   <h2>Heading</h2>
   <p>Lorem ipsum dolor sit amet, consectetur adipisicing elit, sed do
       eiusmod
   tempor incididunt ut labore et dolore magna aliqua. Ut enim ad minim
       veniam,
   quis nostrud exercitation ullamco laboris nisi ut aliquip ex ea commodo
   consequat.
   </p>
  </div>
 </div>
</div>
```

To see another example, go to the Codecademy site, and resize the browser window. You will notice that as you make the browser window smaller, the columns automatically stack on top of one another in order to be readable. Also, the columns are automatically centered. Without Bootstrap, you would need more code to achieve these same effects.

TECHNICAL STUFF

The Lorem Ipsum text you see in the preceding code is commonly used to create filler text. Although the words don't mean anything, the quotation originates from a first-century BC Latin text by Cicero. You can generate filler text when creating your own websites by using the dummy text you find at www.lipsum.org.

238 BOOK 4 **Advanced Web Coding**

FIGURE 1-4: Bootstrap three-column layout with desktop (left) and mobile (right) versions.

Dragging and dropping to a website

After looking at the preceding code, you may want an even easier way to generate the code without having to type it yourself. Bootstrap editors allow you to drag and drop components to create a layout, after which the editor will generate Bootstrap code for your use.

Bootstrap editors that you can use include the following:

» **Layoutit.com:** Free online Bootstrap editor (as shown in Figure 1-5) that allows you to drag and drop components and then download the source code

» **Jetstrap.com:** Paid online drag-and-drop Bootstrap editor

» **Pingendo.com:** Free downloadable drag-and-drop Bootstrap editor

» **Bootply.com:** Free online Bootstrap editor with built-in templates to modify

FIGURE 1-5: Layoutit.com interface with drag-and-drop Bootstrap components.

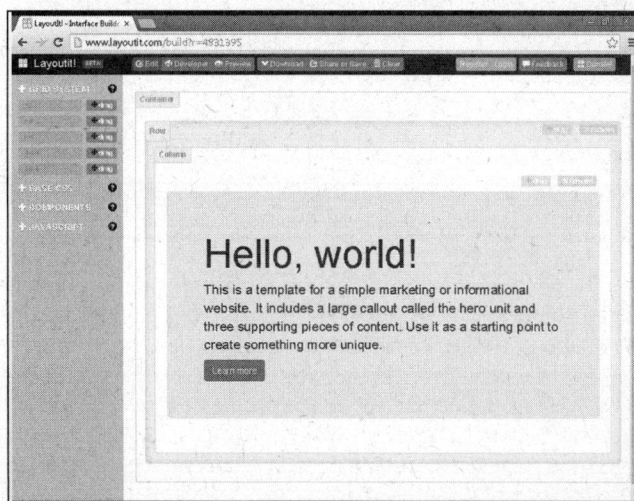

CHAPTER 1 **Working Faster with Twitter Bootstrap** 239

TIP

These sites are free, and may stop working without notice. You can find additional options by using any search engine to search for *Bootstrap editors*.

Using predefined templates

Sites exist with ready-to-use Bootstrap themes; all you need to do is add your own content. Of course, you can also modify the theme if you wish. Here are some of these Bootstrap theme websites:

» www.blacktie.co: Free Bootstrap themes (shown in Figure 1-6), all created by one designer

» www.bootstrapzero.com: Collection of free, open-source Bootstrap templates

» www.bootswatch.com and www.bootsnipp.com: Includes pre built Bootstrap components that you can assemble for your own site

» www.wrapbootstrap.com: Bootstrap templates available for purchase

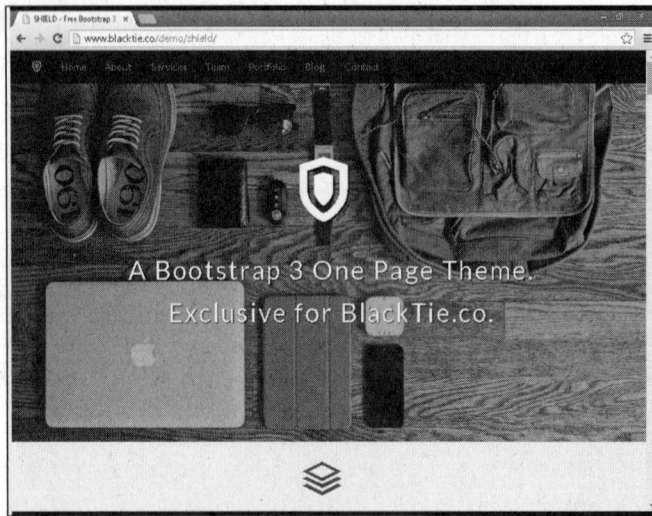

FIGURE 1-6: One-page Bootstrap template from blacktie.co.

TIP

Bootstrap themes may be available for free, but follow the licensing terms. The author may require attribution, email registration, or a tweet.

Adapting layout for mobile, tablet, and desktop

On smaller screens, Bootstrap will automatically stack the columns you create for your website. However, you can exercise more control than just relying on the default behavior over how these columns appear. There are four device screen sizes you can target — phones, tablets, desktops, and large desktops. As shown in Table 1-1, Bootstrap uses a different class prefix to target each device.

TABLE 1-1 Bootstrap Code for Various Screen Sizes

	Phones (<768px)	Tablets (≥768px)	Desktops (≥992px)	Large desktops (≥1200 px)
Class prefix	col-sx-	col-sm-	col-md-	col-lg-
Max container width	None (auto)	750px	970px	1170px
Max column width	Auto	~62px	~81px	~97px

Based on Table 1-1, if you want your website to have two equally sized columns on tablets, desktops, and large desktops, you use the `col-sm-` class name as follows:

```
<div class="container">
 <div class="row">
  <div class="col-sm-6">Column 1</div>
  <div class="col-sm-6">Column 2</div>
 </div>
</div>
```

After viewing your code on all three devices, you decide that on desktops you prefer unequal instead of equal columns such that the left column is half the size of the right column. You target desktop devices using the `col-md-` class name and add it to the class name immediately after `col-sm-`:

```
<div class="container">
 <div class="row">
  <div class="col-sm-6 col-md-4">Column 1</div>
  <div class="col-sm-6 col-md-8">Column 2</div>
 </div>
</div>
```

TIP

Some elements, such as the preceding `<div>` tag, can have multiple classes. This allows you to add multiple effects, such as changing the way a column is displayed, to the element. To define multiple classes, use the `class` attribute and set it equal to each class; separate each class with a space. For an example, refer to the preceding code: The third `<div>` element has two classes, `col-sm-6` and `col-md-4`.

Finally, you decide that on large desktop screens, you want the left column to be two columns wide. You target large desktop screens using the `col-lg-` class name, as shown in Figure 1-7, and add to your existing class attribute values:

```
<div class="container">
  <div class="row">
    <div class="col-sm-6 col-md-4 col-lg-2">Column 1</div>
    <div class="col-sm-6 col-md-8 col-lg-10">Column 2</div>
  </div>
</div>
```

FIGURE 1-7:
A two-column site displayed on tablet, desktop, and large desktop.

242 BOOK 4 **Advanced Web Coding**

Coding Basic Web Page Elements

In addition to pure layouts, Bootstrap can also create web page components found on almost every website. The idea here is the same as when working with layouts — instead of re-creating the wheel every time by designing your own button or toolbar, it would be better to use prebuilt code, which has already been tested across multiple browsers and devices.

The following examples show how to quickly create common web components.

Designing buttons

Buttons are a basic element on many web pages, but usually can be difficult to set up and style. As shown in Table 1-2, buttons can have various types and sizes.

TABLE 1-2 Bootstrap Code for Creating Buttons

Attribute	Class Prefix	Description
Button type	`btn-default btn-primary btn-success btn-danger`	Standard button type with hover effect
		Blue button with hover effect
		Green button with hover effect
		Red button with hover effect
Button size	`btn-lg btn-default btn-sm`	Large button size
		Default button size
		Small button size

To create a button, write the following HTML:

1. **Begin with the** `button` **HTML element.**
2. **In the opening** `<button>` **tag include** `type="button"`.
3. **Include the** `class` **attribute with the** `btn` **class attribute value, and add additional class prefixes based on the effect you want.**
4. **To add additional styles, continue adding the class prefix name into the HTML** `class` **attribute.**

As shown in Figure 1-8, the following code combines both button type and button size:

```
<p>
  <button type="button" class="btn btn-primary btn-lg">Large primary button
  </button>
  <button type="button" class="btn btn-default btn-lg">Large default button
  </button>
</p>
<p>
  <button type="button" class="btn btn-success">Default Success button</
          button>
  <button type="button" class="btn btn-default">Default default button</
          button>
</p>
<p>
  <button type="button" class="btn btn-danger btn-sm">Small danger button
  </button>
  <button type="button" class="btn btn-default btn-sm">Small default button
  </button>
</p>
```

FIGURE 1-8: Bootstrap button types and sizes.

TIP

For additional button type, button size, and other button options, see www.getbootstrap.com/css/#buttons.

Navigating with toolbars

Web pages with multiple pages or views usually have one or more toolbars to help users with navigation. Some toolbar options are shown in Table 1-3.

TABLE 1-3 **Bootstrap Code for Creating Navigation Toolbars**

Attribute	Class Prefix	Description
Toolbar type	nav-tabs	Tabbed navigation toolbar
	nav-pills	Pill, or solid button navigation toolbar
Toolbar button type	dropdown	Button or tab as drop-down menu
	caret dropdown-menu	Down-arrow drop-down menu icon
		Drop-down menu items

To create a pill or solid button navigation toolbar, write the following HTML:

1. **Begin an unordered list using the** ul **element.**
2. **In the opening** **tag, include** class="nav nav-pills".
3. **Create buttons using the** **tag. Include** class="active" **in one opening** **tag to designate which tab on the main toolbar should appear as visually highlighted when the mouse hovers over the button.**
4. **To create a drop-down menu, nest an unordered list. See the code next to "More" with class prefixes** "dropdown", "caret", **and** "dropdown-menu".

You can link to other web pages in your drop-down menu by using the <a> tag.

The following code, as shown in Figure 1-9, creates a toolbar using Bootstrap:

```
<ul class="nav nav-pills">
   <li class="active"><a href="timeline.html">Timeline</a></li>
   <li><a href="about.html">About</a></li>
   <li><a href="photos.html">Photos</a></li>
   <li><a href="friends.html">Friends</a></li>
   <li class="dropdown">
      <a class="dropdown-toggle" data-toggle="dropdown" href="#">More
      <span class="caret"></span>
      </a>
        <ul class="dropdown-menu">
           <li><a href="places.html">Places</a></li>
           <li><a href="sports.html">Sports</a></li>
           <li><a href="music.html">Music</a></li>
        </ul>
   </li>
</ul>
```

TIP

The dropdown-toggle class and the data-toggle="dropdown" attribute and value work together to add drop-down menus to elements such as links. For additional toolbar options, see www.getbootstrap.com/components/#nav.

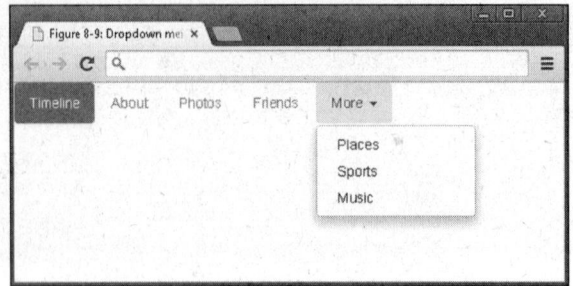

FIGURE 1-9:
Bootstrap toolbar with drop-down menus.

Adding icons

Icons are frequently used with buttons to help convey some type of action. For example, your email program likely uses a button with a trash can icon to delete emails. Icons quickly communicate a suggested action to users without much explanation.

TECHNICAL STUFF

These icons are called *glyphs*, and `www.glyphicons.com` provides the glyphs used in Bootstrap.

Bootstrap supports more than 200 glyphs, which you can add to buttons or toolbars using the `` tag. As shown in Figure 1-10, the following example code creates three buttons with a star, paperclip, and trash can glyph.

```
<button type="button" class="btn btn-default">Star
  <span class="glyphicon glyphicon-star"></star>
</button>
<button type="button" class="btn btn-default">Attach
  <span class="glyphicon glyphicon-paperclip"></star>
</button>
<button type="button" class="btn btn-default">Trash
  <span class="glyphicon glyphicon-trash"></star>
</button>
```

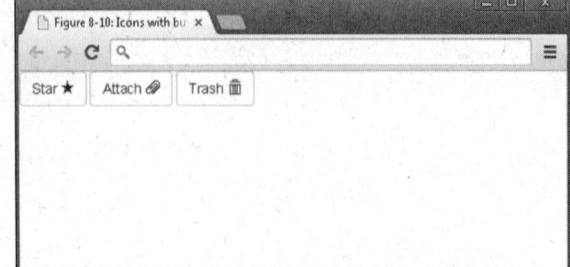

FIGURE 1-10:
Bootstrap buttons with icons.

TIP For the names of all the Bootstrap glyphs, see www.getbootstrap.com/components/#glyphicons.

Build the Airbnb Home Page

Practice Bootstrap online using the Codecademy website. Codecademy is a free website created in 2011 to allow anyone to learn how to code right in the browser, without installing or downloading any software. Practice all the tags (and a few more) that you find in this chapter by following these steps:

1. **Open your browser, go to** www.dummies.com/go/codingaiolinks, **and click the link to Codecademy.**

2. **If you have a Codecademy account, sign in.**

 Signing up is discussed in Book 1, Chapter 3. Creating an account allows you to save your progress as you work, but it's optional.

3. **Navigate to and click Make a Website to practice Bootstrap.**

 Background information is presented, and instructions are presented on the site.

4. **Complete the instructions in the main coding window.**

5. **After you have finished completing the instructions, click the Got It or Save and Submit Code button.**

If you followed the instructions correctly, a green checkmark appears, and you proceed to the next exercise. If an error exists in your code, a warning appears with a suggested fix. If you run into a problem, or have a bug you cannot fix, click the hint, use the Q&A Forum, or tweet me at @nikhilgabraham and include the hashtag #codingFD. Additionally, you can sign up for book updates and explanations for changes to programming language commands by visiting http://tinyletter.com/codingfordummies.

IN THIS CHAPTER

» Understanding JavaScript basics and structure

» Coding with variables, conditional statements, and functions

» Learning about API basics and structure

» Viewing an API request and response

Chapter 2
Adding in JavaScript

"The best teacher is very interactive."

— BILL GATES

JavaScript, one of the most popular and versatile programming languages on the Internet, adds interactivity to websites. You have probably seen JavaScript in action and not even realized it, perhaps while clicking buttons that change color, viewing image galleries with thumbnail previews, or analyzing charts that display customized data based on your input. These website features and more can be created and customized using JavaScript.

JavaScript is an extremely powerful programming language, and this entire book could have been devoted to the topic. In this chapter, you find JavaScript basics, including how to write JavaScript code to perform basic tasks, access data using an API, and program faster using a framework.

What Does JavaScript Do?

JavaScript creates and modifies web page elements and works with the existing web page HTML and CSS to achieve these effects. When you visit a web page with

JavaScript, your browser downloads the JavaScript code and runs it client-side, on your machine. JavaScript can perform tasks to do any of the following:

» Control web page appearance and layout by changing HTML attributes and CSS styles.

» Easily create web page elements like date pickers, as shown in Figure 2-1, and drop-down menus.

» Take user input in forms, and check for errors before submission.

» Display and visualize data using complex charts and graphs.

» Import and analyze data from other websites.

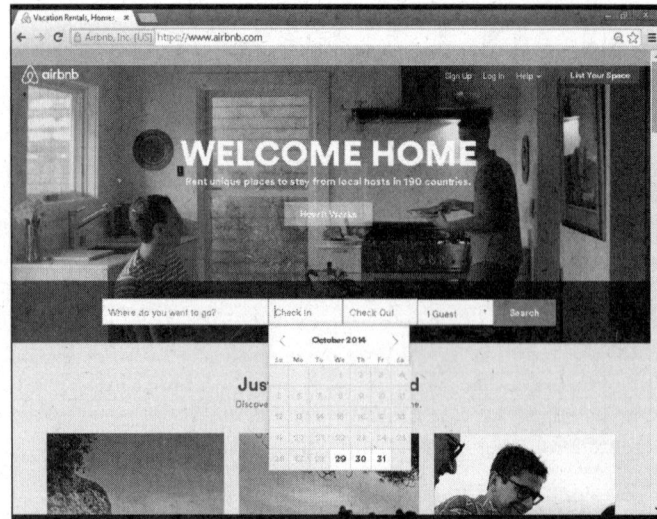

FIGURE 2-1:
JavaScript can create the date picker found on every travel website.

TECHNICAL STUFF

JavaScript is different from another programming language called Java. In 1996 Brendan Eich, at the time a Netscape engineer, created JavaScript, which was originally called LiveScript. As part of a marketing decision, LiveScript was renamed to JavaScript to try and benefit from the reputation of then-popular Java.

JavaScript was created 20 years ago, and the language has continued to evolve since then. In the past decade, its most important innovation has allowed developers to add content to web pages without requiring the user to reload the page. This technique, called *AJAX* (asynchronous JavaScript), probably sounds trivial, but has led to the creation of cutting-edge browser experiences such as Gmail (shown in Figure 2-2).

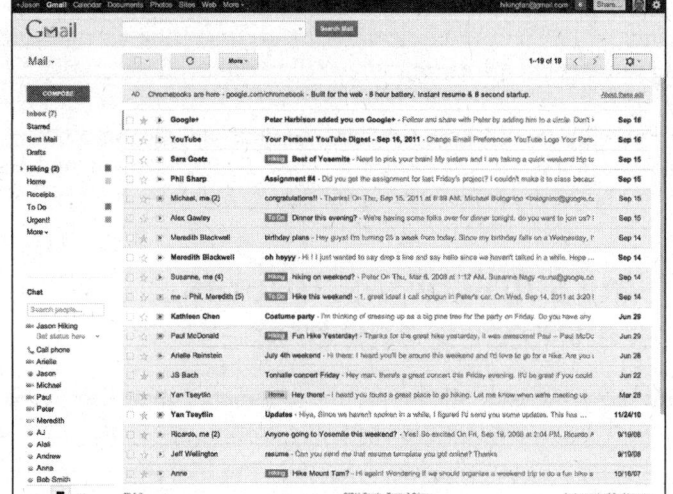

FIGURE 2-2:
Gmail uses AJAX, which lets users read new emails without reloading the web page.

Before AJAX, the browser would display new data on a web page only after waiting for the entire web page to reload. However, this slowed down the user experience, especially when viewing web pages that had frequent real-time updates such as web pages with news stories, sports updates, and stock information. JavaScript, specifically AJAX, created a way for your browser to communicate with a server in the background and to update your current web page with this new information.

TIP

Here is an easy way to think about AJAX: Imagine you're at a coffee shop and just ordered a coffee after waiting in a really long line. Before asynchronous JavaScript, you had to wait patiently at the coffee bar until you received your coffee before doing anything else. With asynchronous JavaScript, you can read the newspaper, find a table, phone a friend, and do multiple other tasks until the barista calls your name alerting you that your coffee is ready.

Understanding JavaScript Structure

JavaScript has a different structure and format from HTML and CSS. JavaScript allows you to do more than position and style text on a web page — with JavaScript, you can store numbers and text for later use, decide what code to run based on conditions within your program, and even name pieces of your code so you can easily reference them later. As with HTML and CSS, JavaScript has special keywords and syntax that allow the computer to recognize what you're trying to do. Unlike HTML and CSS, however, JavaScript is intolerant of syntax mistakes. If you forget to close an HTML tag or to include a closing curly brace in CSS, your code may still run, and your browser will try its best to display your code. When

coding in JavaScript, on the other hand, forgetting a single quote or parenthesis can cause your entire program to fail to run at all.

HTML applies an effect between opening and closing tags — `<h1>This is a header`. CSS uses the same HTML element and has properties and values between opening and closing curly braces — `h1 { color: red; }`.

Using semicolons, quotes, parentheses, and braces

The following code illustrates the common punctuation used in JavaScript — semicolons, quotes, parentheses, and braces (also called curly brackets):

```
var age=22;
var planet="Earth";
if (age>=18)
{
  console.log("You are an adult");
  console.log("You are over 18");

}
else
{
  console.log("You are not an adult");
  console.log("You are not over 18");
}
```

Here are some general rules of thumb to know while programming in JavaScript:

- Semicolons separate JavaScript statements.

- Quotes enclose text characters or *strings* (sequences of characters). Any opening quote must have a closing quote.

- Parentheses are used to modify commands with additional information called *arguments*. Any opening parenthesis must have a closing parenthesis.

- Braces group JavaScript statements into blocks so they execute together. Any opening brace must have a closing brace.

These syntax rules can feel arbitrary and may be difficult to remember initially. With some practice, however, these rules will feel like second nature to you.

Coding Common JavaScript Tasks

JavaScript can be used to perform many tasks, from simple variable assignments to complex data visualizations. The following tasks, here explained within a JavaScript context, are core programming concepts that haven't changed in the past 20 years and won't change in the next 20. They're applicable to any programming language. Finally, I've listed instructions on how to perform these tasks, but if you prefer, you can also practice these skills right away by jumping ahead to the "Writing Your First JavaScript Program" section, later in this chapter.

Storing data with variables

Variables, like those in algebra, are keywords used to store data values for later use. Though the data stored in a variable may change, the variable name remains the same. Think of a variable as being like a gym locker — what you store in the locker changes, but the locker number always stays the same. The variable name usually starts with a letter, and Table 2-1 lists some types of data that JavaScript variables can store.

TABLE 2-1 **Data Stored by a Variable**

Data Type	Description	Examples
Numbers	Positive or negative numbers with or without decimals.	156 -101.96
Strings	Printable characters.	Holly Novak Señor
Boolean	Value can be either true or false.	true false

For a list of rules on variable names see the "JavaScript Variables" section at www.w3schools.com/js/js_variables.asp.

The first time you use a variable name, you use the word var to declare the variable name. Then you can optionally assign a value to the variable using the equal sign. In the following code example, I declare three variables and assign values to those variables:

```
var myName="Nik";
var pizzaCost=10;
var totalCost=pizzaCost * 2;
```

CHAPTER 2 **Adding in JavaScript** 253

Programmers say you have declared a variable when you first define it using the `var` keyword. "Declaring" a variable tells the computer to reserve space in memory and to permanently store values using the variable name. View these values by using the `console.log` statement. For example, after running the preceding example code, running statement `console.log(totalCost)` returns the value 20.

After declaring a variable, you change its value by referring to just the variable name and using the equal sign, as shown in the following examples:

```
myName="Steve";
pizzaCost=15;
```

Variable names are case-sensitive, so when referring to a variable in your program, remember that `MyName` is a different variable from `myname`. In general, it's a good idea to give your variable a name that describes the data being stored.

Making decisions with if-else statements

After you have stored data in a variable, it is common to compare the variable's value to other variable values or to a fixed value, and then to make a decision based on the outcome of the comparison. In JavaScript, these comparisons are done using a *conditional statement*. The `if-else` statement is a type of conditional. Its general syntax is as follows:

```
if (condition) {
    statement1 to execute if condition is true
}
else {
    statement2 to execute if condition is false
}
```

In this statement, the `if` is followed by a space, and a condition enclosed in parentheses evaluates to `true` or `false`. If the condition is `true`, then `statement1`, located between the first set of curly brackets, is executed. If the condition is `false` and if I include the `else`, which is optional, then `statement2`, located between the second set of curly brackets, is executed. Note that when the `else` is not included and the condition is `false`, the conditional statement simply ends.

Notice there are no parentheses after the `else` — the `else` line has no condition. JavaScript executes the statement after `else` only when the preceding conditions are `false`.

The condition in an `if-else` statement is a comparison of values using operators, and common operators are described in Table 2-2.

TABLE 2-2 **Common JavaScript Operators**

Type	Operator	Description	Example
Less than	<	Evaluates whether one value is less than another value.	(x < 55)
Greater than	>	Evaluates whether one value is greater than another value.	(x > 55)
Equality	===	Evaluates whether two values are equal.	(x === 55)
Less than or equal to	<=	Evaluates whether one value is less than or equal to another value.	(x <= 55)
Greater than or equal to	>=	Evaluates whether one value is greater than or equal to another value.	(x >= 55)
Inequality	!=	Evaluates whether two values are not equal.	(x != 55)

Here is a simple if statement, without the else:

```
var carSpeed=70;
if (carSpeed > 55) {
    alert("You are over the speed limit!");
}
```

In this statement, I declare a variable called carSpeed and set it equal to 70. Then an if statement with a condition compares whether the value in the variable carSpeed is greater than 55. If the condition is true, an alert, which is a pop-up box, states "You are over the speed limit!" (See Figure 2-3.) In this case, the value of carSpeed is 70, which is greater than 55, so the condition is true and the alert is displayed. If the first line of code instead was var carSpeed=40;, then the condition is false because 40 is less than 55, and no alert would be displayed.

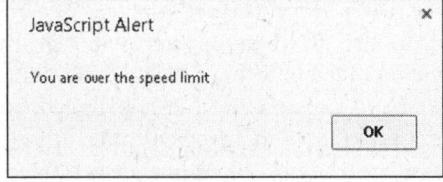

FIGURE 2-3: The alert pop-up box.

Let us expand the if statement by adding else to create an if-else, as shown in this code:

```
var carSpeed=40;
if (carSpeed > 55) {
    alert("You are over the speed limit!");
```

CHAPTER 2 **Adding in JavaScript** 255

```
}
else {
    alert("You are under the speed limit!");
}
```

In addition to the `else`, I added an `alert` statement inside the curly brackets following the `else`, and set carSpeed equal to 40. When this `if-else` statement executes, carSpeed is equal to 40, which is less than 55, so the condition is false, and because the `else` has been added, an alert appears stating "You are under the speed limit!" If the first line of code instead was `var carSpeed=70;` as before, then the condition is true, because 70 is greater than 55, and the first alert would be displayed.

Our current `if-else` statement allows us to test for one condition and to show different results depending on whether the condition is true or false. To test for two or more conditions, you can add one or more `else if` statements after the original `if` statement. The general syntax for this is as follows:

```
if (condition1) {
    statement1 to execute if condition1 is true
}
else if (condition2) {
    statement2 to execute if condition2 is true
}
else {
    statement3 to execute if all previous conditions are false
}
```

The `if-else` is written as before, and the `else if` is followed by a space, and then a condition enclosed in parentheses that evaluates to either `true` or `false`. If condition1 is `true`, then statement1, located between the first set of curly brackets, is executed. If the condition1 is `false`, then condition2 is evaluated and is found to be either `true` or `false`. If condition2 is `true`, then statement2, located between the second set of curly brackets, is executed. At this point, additional `else if` statements could be added to test additional conditions. Only when all `if` and `else if` conditions are `false`, and an `else` is included, is statement3 executed. Only one statement is executed in a block of code, after which the remaining statements are ignored and the next block of code is executed.

TIP

When writing the `if-else`, you must have one and only one `if` statement and, if you so choose, one and only one `else` statement. The `else if` is optional, can be used multiple times within a single `if-else` statement, and must come after the original `if` statement and before the `else`. You cannot have an `else if` or an `else` by itself, without a preceding `if` statement.

Here is another example `else if` statement:

```
var carSpeed=40;
if (carSpeed > 55) {
   alert("You are over the speed limit!");
}
else if (carSpeed === 55) {
   alert("You are at the speed limit!");
}
```

When this `if` statement executes, `carSpeed` is equal to 40, which is less than 55, so the condition is `false`, and then the `else if` condition is evaluated. The value of `carSpeed` is not exactly equal to 55, so this condition is also `false`, and no alert of any kind is shown, and the statement ends. If the first line of code were instead `var carSpeed=55;`, then the first condition is `false`, because 55 is not greater than 55. Then the `else if` condition is evaluated, and because 55 is exactly equal to 55, the second alert is displayed, stating "You are at the speed limit!"

REMEMBER

Look carefully at the preceding code — when setting the value of a variable, one equal sign is used, but when comparing whether two values are equal, then three equal signs (===) are used.

As a final example, here is an `if-else` statement with an `else if` statement:

```
var carSpeed=40;
if (carSpeed > 55) {
   alert("You are over the speed limit!");
}
else if (carSpeed === 55) {
   alert("You are at the speed limit!");
}
else {
   alert("You are under the speed limit!");
}
```

As the diagram in Figure 2-4 shows, two conditions, which appear in the figure as diamonds, are evaluated in sequence. In this example, the `carSpeed` is equal to 40, so the two conditions are `false`, and the statement after the `else` is executed, showing an alert that says "You are under the speed limit!" Here `carSpeed` is initially set to 40, but depending on the initial `carSpeed` variable value, any one of the three alerts could be displayed.

REMEMBER

The condition is always evaluated first, and every condition must either be `true` or `false`. Independent from the condition is the statement that executes if the condition is `true`.

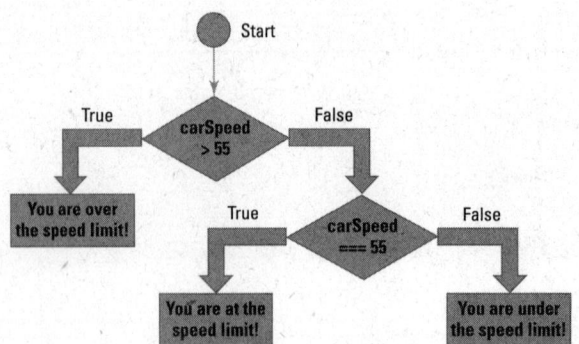

FIGURE 2-4:
if-else with an else if statement.

Working with string and number methods

The most basic data types, usually stored in variables, are strings and numbers. Programmers often need to manipulate strings and numbers to perform basic tasks such as the following:

» Determining the *length* of a string, as for a password

» Selecting part (or *substring*) of a string, as when choosing the first name in a string that includes the first and last name

» Rounding a number *to fixed* numbers of decimal points, as when taking a subtotal in an online shopping cart, calculating the tax, rounding the tax to two decimal points, and adding the tax to the subtotal

These tasks are so common that JavaScript includes shortcuts called *methods* (italicized in the preceding bullets) that make performing tasks like these easier. The general syntax to perform these tasks is to follow the affected variable's name or value with a period and the name of the method, as follows for values and variables:

```
value.method;
variable.method;
```

Table 2-3 shows examples of JavaScript methods for the basic tasks previously discussed. Examples include methods applied to values, such as strings, and to variables.

REMEMBER

When using a string, or assigning a variable to a value that is a string, always enclose the string in quotes.

258 BOOK 4 **Advanced Web Coding**

TABLE 2-3 **Common JavaScript Methods**

Method	Description	Example	Result
.toFixed(n)	Rounds a number to n decimal places.	var jenny= 8.675309; jenny.toFixed(2);	8.68
.length	Represents the number of characters in a string.	"Nik".length;	3
.substring (start, end)	Extracts portion of the string beginning from position start to end. Position refers to the location between each character, and starts before the first character with zero.	var name= "Inbox";name.substring (2,5);	Box

The .toFixed and .length methods are relatively straightforward, but the .substring method can be a little confusing. The starting and ending positions used in .substring(start, end) do not reference actual characters, but instead reference the space between each character. Figure 2-5 shows how the start and end position works. The statement "Inbox".substring(2,5) starts at position 2, which is between "n" and "b", and ends at position 5, which is after the "x".

FIGURE 2-5: The .substring method references positions that are between characters in a string.

TIP

For a list of additional string and number methods, see W3Schools at www.w3schools.com/js/js_number_methods.asp and www.w3schools.com/js/js_string_methods.asp.

Alerting users and prompting them for input

Displaying messages to the user and collecting input are the beginnings of the interactivity that JavaScript provides. Although more sophisticated techniques exist today, the alert() method and prompt() method are easy ways to show a pop-up box with a message and prompt the user for input.

The syntax for creating an alert or a prompt is to write the method with text in quotes placed inside the parentheses like so:

```
alert("You have mail");
prompt("What do you want for dinner?");
```

Figure 2-6 shows the alert pop-up box created by the `alert()` method, and the prompt for user input created by the `prompt()` method.

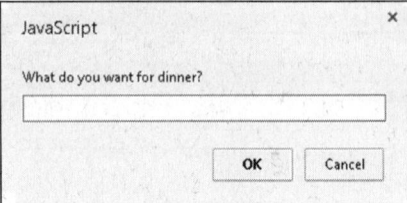

FIGURE 2-6: A JavaScript alert pop-up box and a user prompt.

Naming code with functions

Functions provide a way to group JavaScript statements and to name that group of statements for easy reference with a function name. These statements are typically grouped together because they achieve a specific coding goal. You can use the statements repeatedly just by writing the function name instead of writing the statements over and over again. Functions prevent repetition and make your code easier to maintain.

When I was younger, every Saturday morning my mother would tell me to brush my teeth, fold the laundry, vacuum my room, and mow the lawn. Eventually, my mother tired of repeating the same list over and over again, wrote the list of chores on paper, titled it "Saturday chores," and put it on the fridge. A function names a group of statements, just like "Saturday chores" named my list of chores.

Functions are defined once using the word `function`, followed by a function name, and then a set of statements inside curly brackets. This is called a *function declaration*. The statements in the function are executed only when the function is called by name. In the following example, I declared a function called `greeting` that asks for your name using the `prompt()` method, returns the name you entered storing it in a variable called `name`, and displays a message with the `name` variable using the `alert()` method:

```
function greeting() {
    var name=prompt("What is your name?");
    alert("Welcome to this website " + name);
}
```

```
greeting();
greeting();
```

Beneath the function declaration, I called the function twice, and so I will trigger two prompts for my name, which are stored in the variable name, and two messages welcoming the value in the variable name to this website.

TIP

The "+" operator is used to *concatenate* (combine) strings with other strings, values, or variables.

Functions can take inputs, called *parameters,* to help the function run, and can return a value when the function is complete. After writing my list of chores, each Saturday morning my mother would say "Nik, do the Saturday chores," and when my brother was old enough, she would say "Neel, do the Saturday chores." If the list of chores is the function declaration, and "Saturday chores" is the function name, then "Nik" and "Neel" are the parameters. Finally, after I was finished, I would let my mom know the chores were complete, much as a function returns values.

In the following example, I declared a function called amountdue, which takes price and quantity as parameters. The function, when called, calculates the subtotal, adds the tax due, and then returns the total. The function amount due(10,3) returns 31.5.

```
function amountdue(price, quantity) {
    var subtotal=price * quantity;
    var tax = 1.05;
    var total = subtotal * tax;
    return total;
}

alert("The amount due is $" + amountdue(10,3));
```

REMEMBER

Every opening parenthesis has a closing parenthesis, every opening curly bracket has a closing curly bracket, and every opening double quote has a closing double quote. Can you find all the opening and closing pairs in the preceding example?

Adding JavaScript to the web page

The two ways to add JavaScript to the web page are

>> Embed JavaScript code in an HTML file using the script tag.

>> Link to a separate JavaScript file from the HTML file using the script tag.

To embed JavaScript code in an HTML file, use an opening and closing `<script>` tag, and write your JavaScript statements between the two tags, as shown in the following example:

```
<!DOCTYPE html>
<html>
    <head>
        <title>Embedded JavaScript</title>
        <script>
            alert("This is embedded JavaScript");
        </script>
    </head>
    <body>
        <h1>Example of embedded JavaScript</h1>
    </body>
</html>
```

TIP

The `<script>` tag can be placed inside the opening and closing `<head>` tag, as shown in the preceding code, or inside the opening and closing `<body>` tag. There are some performance advantages when choosing one approach over the other, and you can read more at http://stackoverflow.com/questions/436411/where-is-the-best-place-to-put-script-tags-in-html-markup.

The `<script>` tag is also used when linking to a separate JavaScript file, which is the recommended approach. The `<script>` tag includes

» A type attribute, which for JavaScript is always set equal to "text/javascript"

» A src attribute, which is set equal to the location of the JavaScript file

```
<!DOCTYPE html>
<html>
    <head>
        <title>Linking to a separate JavaScript file</title>
        <script type="text/javascript" src="script.js"></script>
    </head>
    <body>
        <h1>Linking to a separate JavaScript file</h1>
    </body>
</html>
```

REMEMBER

The `<script>` tag has an opening and closing tag, whether the code is embedded between the tags or linked to separate file using the `src` attribute.

262 BOOK 4 **Advanced Web Coding**

Writing Your First JavaScript Program

Practice your JavaScript online using the Codecademy website. Codecademy is a free website created in 2011 to allow anyone to learn how to code right in the browser, without installing or downloading any software. Practice all of the tags (and a few more) that you find in this chapter by following these steps:

1. **Open your browser, go to** www.dummies.com/go/codingaiolinks, **and click the link to Codecademy.**

2. **If you have a Codecademy account, sign in.**

 Signing up is discussed in Book 1, Chapter 3. Creating an account allows you to save your progress as you work, but it's optional.

3. **Navigate to and click Getting Started with Programming.**

 Background information is presented in the upper-left portion of the site, and instructions are presented in the lower-left portion of the site.

4. **Complete the instructions in the main coding window.**

5. **After you have finished completing the instructions, click the Save and Submit Code button.**

If you followed the instructions correctly, a green checkmark appears and you proceed to the next exercise. If an error exists in your code, a warning appears with a suggested fix. If you run into a problem, or have a bug you cannot fix, click the hint, use the Q&A Forums, or tweet me at @nikhilgabraham and include the hashtag #codingFD. Additionally, you can sign up for book updates and explanations for changes to programming language commands by visiting http://tinyletter.com/codingfordummies.

Working with APIs

Although *APIs (application programming interfaces)* have existed for decades, the term has become popular over the past few years as I hear more conversation and promotion around their use. *Use the Facebook API! Why doesn't Craigslist have an API? Stripe's entire business is to allow developers to accept payments online using its payments API.*

Many people use the term API, but few understand its meaning. This section will help clarify what APIs do and how they can be used.

What do APIs do?

An API allows Program A to access select functions of another separate Program B. Program B grants access by allowing Program A to make a data request in a structured, predictable, documented way; Program B responds to this data request with a structured, predictable, documented response, as follows (see Figure 2-7):

>> It's *structured* because the fields in the request and the data in the response follow an easy-to-read standardized format. For example, the Yahoo Weather API data response includes these selected structured data fields:

```
"location": {
  "city": "New York",
  "region": "NY"
},
"units": {
  "temperature": "F"
},
"forecast": {
    "date": "29 Oct 2014",
    "high": "68",
    "low": "48",
    "text": "PM Showers"
    }
```

See the full Yahoo Weather API response by visiting https://developer.yahoo.com/weather.

>> It's *predictable* because the fields that must be included and can be included in the request are prespecified, and the response to a successful request will always include the same field types.

>> It's *documented* because the API is explained in detail. Any changes usually are communicated through the website, social media, and email; even after the API changes, there is often a period of backward compatibility when the old API requests will receive a response. For example, when Google Maps issued version 3 of its API, version 2 still operated for a certain grace period.

FIGURE 2-7: An API allows two separate programs to talk to each other.

264 BOOK 4 **Advanced Web Coding**

In the preceding code, you saw a weather API response, so what would you include in a request to a weather API? The following fields are likely important to include:

- Location, which can potentially be specified by using zip code, city and state, current location in latitude and longitude coordinates, or IP address
- Relevant time period, which could include the instant, daily, three-day, weekly, or ten-day forecast
- Units for temperature (Fahrenheit or Celsius) and precipitation (inches or centimeters)

REMEMBER

These fields in our request just specify the desired type and data format. The actual weather data would be sent after the API knows your data preferences.

Can you think of any other factors to consider when making the request? Here is one clue — imagine you work for Al Roker on NBC's *Today* TV show, and you're responsible for updating the weather on the show's website for one million visitors each morning. Meanwhile, I have a website, NikWeather, which averages ten daily visitors who check the weather there. The *Today* website and my website both make a request to the same weather API at the same time. Who should receive their data first? It seems intuitive that the needs of one million visitors on the *Today* website should outweigh the needs of my website's ten visitors. An API can prioritize which request to serve first, when the request includes an API key. An *API key* is a unique value, usually a long alpha-numeric string, which identifies the requestor and is included in the API request. Depending on your agreement with the API provider, your API key can entitle you to receive prioritized responses, additional data, or extra support.

Can you think of any other factors to consider when making the request? Here is another clue — is there any difference in working with weather data versus financial data? The other factor to keep in mind is frequency of data requests and updates. APIs will generally limit the number of times you can request data. In the case of a weather API, maybe the request limit is once every minute. Related to how often you can request the data is how often the data is refreshed. There are two considerations — how often the underlying data changes, and how often the API provider updates the data. For example, except in extreme circumstances, the weather generally changes every 15 minutes. Our specific weather API provider may update its weather data every 30 minutes. Therefore you would send an API request only once every 30 minutes, because sending more frequent requests wouldn't result in updated data. By contrast, financial data such as stock prices and many public APIs, which change multiple times per second, allow one request per second.

CHAPTER 2 **Adding in JavaScript** 265

Scraping data without an API

In the absence of an API, those who want data from a third-party website create processes to browse the website, search and copy data, and store it for later use. This method of data retrieval is commonly referred to as *screen scraping* or *web scraping*. These processes, which vary in sophistication from simple to complex, include

- » **People manually copying and pasting data from websites into a database:** Crowdsourced websites, such as www.retailmenot.com recently listed on the NASDAQ stock exchange, obtain some data in this way.

- » **Code snippets written to find and copy data that match preset patterns:** The preset patterns are also called *regular expressions*, which match character and string combinations, and can be written using web languages like JavaScript or Python.

- » **Automated software tools that allow you to point-and-click the fields you want to retrieve from a website:** For example, www.import.io is one point-and-click solution, and when the FIFA World Cup 2014 site lacked a structured API, a similar solution was used to extract data, such as scores, and made it easily accessible.

The advantage of screen scraping is that the data is likely to be available and with fewer restrictions because it is content that regular users see. If an API fails, it may go unnoticed and depending on the site take time to fix. By contrast, the main website failing is usually a top priority item and needs fixing as soon as possible. Additionally, companies may enforce limits on data retrieved from the API that are rarely seen and harder to enforce when screen scraping.

The disadvantage of screen scraping is that the code written to capture data from a website must be precise and can break easily. For example, a stock price is on a web page in the second paragraph, on the third line, and is the fourth word. The screen scraping code is programmed to extract the stock price from that location, but unexpectedly the website changes its layout so the stock price is now in the fifth paragraph. Suddenly, the data is inaccurate. Additionally, there may be legal concerns with extracting data in this way, especially if the website terms and conditions prohibit screen scraping. In one example, Craigslist terms and conditions prohibited data extraction through screen scraping, and after litigation, a court banned a company that accessed Craigslist data using this technique.

Researching and choosing an API

For any particular data task, there may be multiple APIs that can provide you with the data you seek. The following are some factors to consider when selecting an API for use in your programs:

» **Data availability:** Make a wish list of fields you want to use with the API, and compare it to fields actually offered by various API providers.

» **Data quality:** Benchmark how various API providers gather data, and the frequency with which the data is refreshed.

» **Site reliability:** Measure site uptime because regardless of how good the data may be, the website needs to stay online to provide API data. Site reliability is a major factor in industries like finance and health care.

» **Documentation:** Review the API documentation for reading ease and detail so you can easily understand the API features and limitations before you begin.

» **Support:** Call support to see response times and customer support knowledgeability. Something will go wrong, and when it does you want to be well supported to quickly diagnose and solve any issues.

» **Cost:** Many APIs provide free access below a certain request threshold. Investigate cost structures if you exceed those levels so you can properly budget for access to your API.

Using JavaScript Libraries

A JavaScript *library* is prewritten JavaScript code that makes the development process easier. The library includes code for common tasks that has already been tested and implemented by others. To use the code for these common tasks, you only need to call the function or method as defined in the library. Two of the most popular JavaScript libraries are jQuery and D3.js.

jQuery

jQuery uses JavaScript code to animate web pages by modifying CSS on the page, and to provide a library of commonly used functions. Although you could write JavaScript code to accomplish any jQuery effect, jQuery's biggest advantage is completing tasks by writing fewer lines of code. As the most popular JavaScript library today, jQuery is used on the majority of the top 10,000 most visited websites. Figure 2-8 shows a photo gallery with jQuery transition image effects.

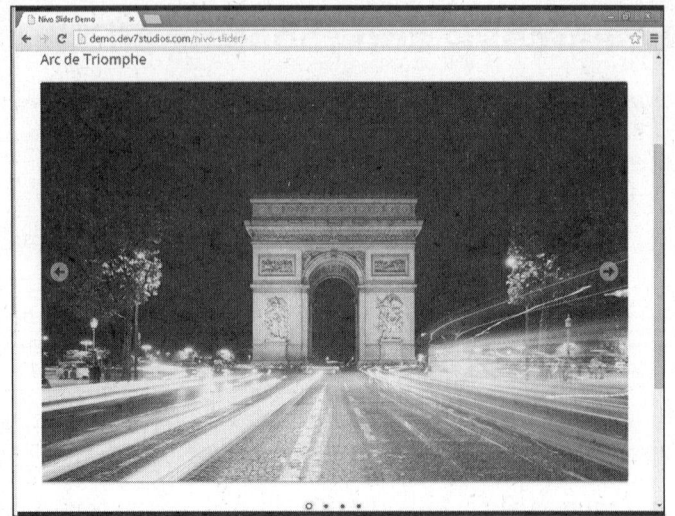

FIGURE 2-8: Photo gallery with jQuery transition image effects triggered by navigation arrows.

D3.js

D3.js is a JavaScript library for visualizing data. Just like with jQuery, similar effects could be achieved using JavaScript, but only after writing many more lines of code. The library is particularly adept at showing data across multiple dimensions and creating interactive visualizations of datasets. The creator of D3.js is currently employed at *The New York Times*, which extensively uses D3.js to create charts and graphs for online articles. Figure 2-9 is an interactive chart showing technology company IPO value and performance over time.

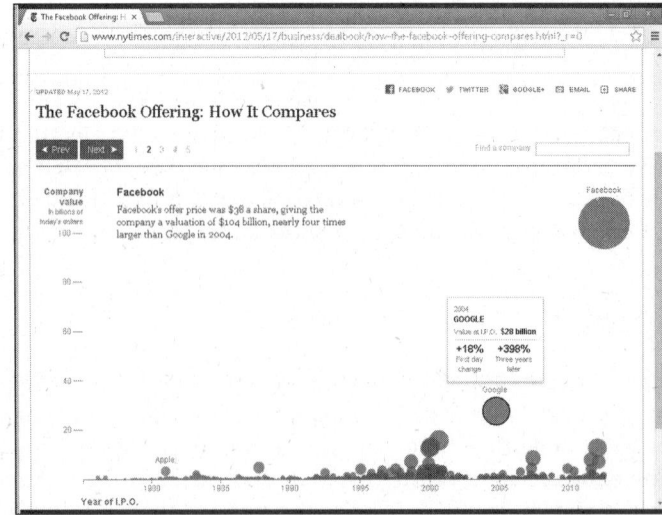

FIGURE 2-9: An IPO chart showing the valuation of the Facebook IPO relative to other technology IPOs.

> IN THIS CHAPTER
>
> » Understanding callback functions
>
> » Using callbacks
>
> » Creating closures

Chapter **3**

Understanding Callbacks and Closures

"O, call back yesterday, bid time return."
— EARL OF SALISBURY, RICHARD II

Callbacks and closures are two of the most useful and widely used techniques in JavaScript. In this chapter, you find out how and why to pass functions as parameters to other functions.

What Are Callbacks?

REMEMBER

JavaScript functions are objects. This statement is the key to understanding many of the more advanced JavaScript topics, including callback functions.

Functions, like any other object, can be assigned to variables, be passed as arguments to other functions, and created within and returned from functions.

Passing functions as arguments

A *callback function* is a function that is passed as an argument to another function. Callback functions are a technique that's possible in JavaScript because of the fact that functions are objects.

Function objects contain a string with the code of the function. When you call a function by naming the function, followed by (), you're telling the function to execute its code. When you name a function or pass a function without the (), the function does not execute.

Here is an example of a callback function using the addEventListener method:

```
document.addEventListener('click',doSomething,false);
```

This method takes an event (click) and a Function object (doSomething) as arguments. The callback function doesn't execute right away. Instead, the addEventListener method executes the function when the event occurs.

Writing functions with callbacks

Here's a simple example function, doMath, that accepts a callback function as an argument:

```
function doMath(number1,number2,callback) {
   var result = callback(number1,number2);
   document.write ("The result is: ": + result);
}
```

This function is a generic function for returning the result of any math operation involving two operands. The callback function that you pass to it specifies what actual operations will be done.

To call our doMath function, pass two number arguments and then a function as the third argument:

```
doMath(5,2,function(number1,number2){
   var calculation = number1 * number2 / 6;
   return calculation;
});
```

Listing 3-1 is a complete web page that contains the doMath function and then invokes it several times with different callback functions.

LISTING 3-1: **Calling a Function with Different Callback Functions**

```html
<html>
<head>
<title>Introducing the doMath function</title>
<script>
  function doMath(number1,number2,callback){
    var result = callback(number1,number2);
    document.getElementById("theResult").innerHTML +=
    ("The result is: " + result + "<br>");
  }

  document.addEventListener('DOMContentLoaded', function() {

    doMath(5,2,function(number1,number2){
     var calculation = number1 * number2;
     return calculation;
    });
    doMath(10,3,function(number1,number2){
     var calculation = number1 / number2;
     return calculation;
    });
    doMath(81,9,function(number1,number2){
     var calculation = number1 % number2;
     return calculation;
    });
  }, false);
</script>
</head>
<body>
  <h1>Do the Math</h1>
  <div id="theResult"></div>
</body>
</html>
```

The result of running Listing 3-1 in a browser is shown in Figure 3-1.

Using named callback functions

In the examples in the preceding section, the callback functions were all written as anonymous functions. It's also possible to define named functions and then pass the name of the function as a callback function.

Anonymous functions are functions that you create without giving them names.

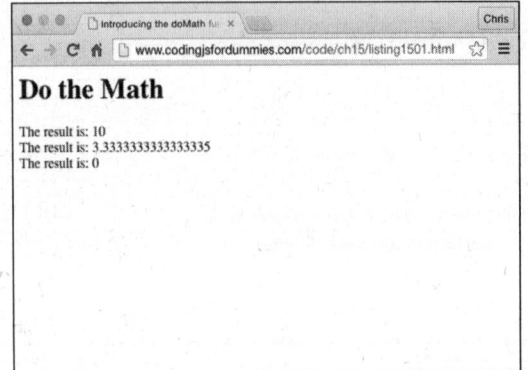

FIGURE 3-1:
Doing calculations using callbacks.

Using named functions as callbacks can reduce the visual code clutter that can come with using anonymous functions. Listing 3-2 shows an example of how to use a named function as a callback. This example also features the following two improvements over Listing 3-1:

» A test has been added to the doMath function to make sure that the callback argument is actually a function.

» It prints the code of the callback function before displaying the result of running it.

LISTING 3-2: Using Named Functions as Callbacks

```
<html>
<head>
  <title>doMath with Named Functions</title>
  <script>
    function doMath(number1,number2,callback){
      if (typeof callback === "function") {

      var result = callback(number1,number2);
      document.getElementById("theResult").innerHTML += (callback.toString() +
      "<br><br>The result is: " + result + "<br><br>");
      }
    }

    function multiplyThem(number1,number2){
      var calculation = number1 * number2;
      return calculation;
    }
    function divideThem(number1,number2){
      var calculation = number1 / number2;
      return calculation;
```

```
      }
      function modThem(number1,number2){
        var calculation = number1 % number2;
        return calculation;
      }
      document.addEventListener('DOMContentLoaded', function() {
        doMath(5,2,multiplyThem);
        doMath(10,3,divideThem);
        doMath(81,9,modThem);
      }, false);
    </script>
  </head>
  <body>
    <h1>Do the Math</h1>
    <div id="theResult"></div>
  </body>
</html>
```

The result of running Listing 3-2 in a browser is shown in Figure 3-2.

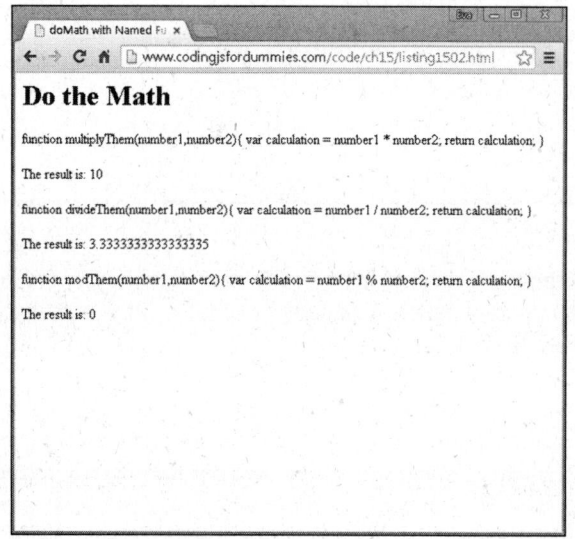

FIGURE 3-2: Doing math with named callbacks.

Using named functions for callbacks has two advantages over using anonymous functions for callbacks:

» It makes your code easier to read.

» Named functions are multipurpose and can be used on their own or as callbacks.

Understanding Closures

A *closure* is the local variable for a function, kept alive after the function has returned.

Take a look at the example in Listing 3-3. In this example, an inner function is defined within an outer function. When the outer function returns a reference to the inner function, the returned reference can still access the local data from the outer function.

In Listing 3-3, the `greetVisitor` function returns a function that is created within it called `sayWelcome`. Notice that the return statement doesn't use () after `sayWelcome`. That's because you don't want to return the value of running the function, but rather the code of the actual function.

LISTING 3-3: Creating a Function Using a Function

```
function greetVisitor(phrase) {
  var welcome = phrase + ". Great to see you!"; // Local variable
  var sayWelcome = function() {
  alert(welcome);
  }
  return sayWelcome;
}
var personalGreeting = greetVisitor('Hola Amiga');
personalGreeting(); // alerts "Hola Amiga. Great to see you!"
```

The useful thing about Listing 3-3 is that it uses the `greetVisitor` function to create a new custom function called `personalGreeting` that can still access the variables from the original function.

Normally, when a function has finished executing, the local variables within it are inaccessible. By returning a function reference (`sayWelcome`), however, the `greetVisitor` function's internal data becomes accessible to the outside world.

TIP

The keys to understanding closures are to understand variable scope in JavaScript and to understand the difference between executing a function and a function reference. By assigning the return value of the `greetVisitor` function to the new `personalGreeting` function, the program stores the code of the `sayWelcome` function. You can test this by using the `toString()` method:

```
personalGreeting.toString()
```

If you add to Listing 3-3 an alert statement to output the `toString()` value of `personalGreeting`, you get the result shown in Figure 3-3.

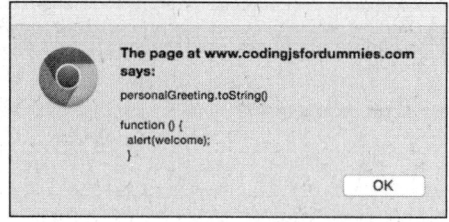

FIGURE 3-3:
A closure includes the code of the returned inner function.

In Figure 3-3, the variable `welcome` is a copy of the variable `welcome` from the original `greetVisitor` function at the time that the closure was created.

In Listing 3-4, a new closure is created using a different argument to the `greetVisitor` function. Even though calling `greetVisitor()` changes the value of the `welcome` variable, the result of calling the first function (`personalGreeting`) remains the same.

LISTING 3-4: **Closures Contain Secret References to Outer Function Variables**

```html
<html>
<head>
  <title>Using Closures</title>
  <script>
    function greetVisitor(phrase) {
      var welcome = phrase + ". Great to see you!<br><br>"; // Local variable
      var sayWelcome = function() {
      document.getElementById("greeting").innerHTML += welcome;
      }
      return sayWelcome;
    }
    // wait until the document is loaded
    document.addEventListener('DOMContentLoaded', function() {
    // make a function
    var personalGreeting = greetVisitor("Hola Amiga");
    // make another function
    var anotherGreeting = greetVisitor("Howdy, Friend");
    // look at the code of the first function
    document.getElementById("greeting").innerHTML +=
    "personalGreeting.toString() <br>" + personalGreeting.toString() + "<br>";
    // run the first function
    personalGreeting(); // alerts "Hola Amiga. Great to see you!""
    // look at the code of the 2nd function
```

(continued)

LISTING 3-4: *(continued)*

```
        document.getElementById("greeting").innerHTML +=
        "anotherGreeting.toString() <br>" + anotherGreeting.toString() + "<br>";
        // run the 2nd function
        anotherGreeting(); // alerts "Howdy, Friend. Great to see you!"
        // check the first function
        personalGreeting(); // alerts "Hola Amiga. Great to see you!""
        // finish the addEventListener method
        }, false);
    </script>
</head>
<body>
    <p id="greeting"></p>
</body>
</html>
```

The result of running Listing 3-4 in a web browser is shown in Figure 3-4.

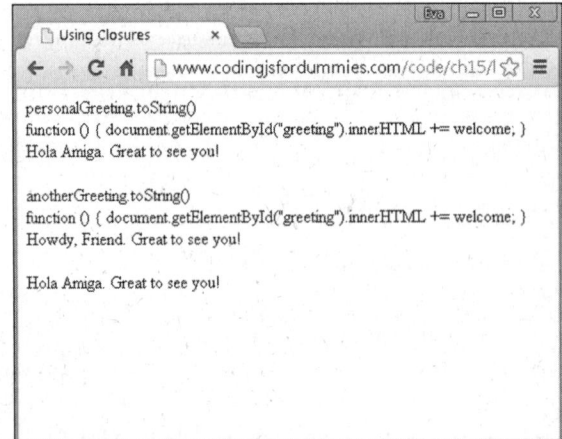

FIGURE 3-4: Creating customized greetings with closures.

TIP

Closures are not hard to understand after you know the underlying concepts and have a need for them. Don't worry if you don't feel totally comfortable with them just yet. It's fully possible to code in JavaScript without using closures, but once you do understand them, they can be quite useful and will make you a better programmer.

Using Closures

A closure is like keeping a copy of the local variables of a function as they were when the closure was created.

In web programming, closures are frequently used to eliminate the duplication of effort within a program or to hold values that need to be reused throughout a program so that the program doesn't need to recalculate the value each time it's used.

Another use for closures is to create customized versions of functions for specific uses.

In Listing 3-5, closures are used to create functions with error messages specific to different problems that may occur in the program. All the error messages get created using the same function.

TECHNICAL STUFF

When a function's purpose is to create other functions, it's known as a *function factory*.

LISTING 3-5: **Using a Function to Create Functions**

```
<html>
<head>
  <title>function factory</title>
  <script>
    function createMessageAlert(theMessage){
      return function() {
        alert (theMessage);
      }
    }

    var badEmailError = createMessageAlert("Unknown email address!");
    var wrongPasswordError = createMessageAlert("That's not your password!");

    window.addEventListener('load', loader, false);
    function loader(){
      document.login.yourEmail.addEventListener('change',badEmailError);
      document.login.yourEmail.addEventListener('change',wrongPasswordError);
    }
  </script>
</head>
<body>
  <form name="login" id="loginform">
    <p>
      <label>Enter Your Email Address:
        <input type="text" name="yourEmail">
```

(continued)

LISTING 3-5: *(continued)*

```
      </label>
    </p>
    <p>
      <label>Enter Your Password:
        <input type="text" name="yourPassword">
      </label>
    </p>
    <button>Submit</button>
  </body>
</html>
```

The key to understanding Listing 3-5 is the factory function.

```
function createMessageAlert(theMessage){
    return function() {
      alert (theMessage);
    }
}
```

To use this function factory, assign its return value to a variable, as in the following statement:

```
var badEmailError = createMessageAlert("Unknown email address!");
```

The preceding statement creates a closure that can be used elsewhere in the program just by running `badEmailError` as a function, as in the following event handler:

```
document.login.yourEmail.addEventListener('change',badEmailError);
```

IN THIS CHAPTER

» **Reading and writing JSON**

» **Understanding AJAX**

» **Using AJAX**

Chapter 4
Embracing AJAX and JSON

"The Web does not just connect machines, it connects people."
— TIM BERNERS-LEE

AJAX is a technique for making web pages more dynamic by sending and receiving data in the background while the user interacts with the pages. JSON has become the standard data format used by AJAX applications. In this chapter, you find out how to use AJAX techniques to make your site sparkle!

Working behind the Scenes with AJAX

Asynchronous JavaScript + XML (AJAX) is a term that's used to describe a method of using JavaScript, the DOM, HTML, and the XMLHttpRequest object together to refresh parts of a web page with live data without needing to refresh the entire page.

TECHNICAL
STUFF

AJAX was first implemented on a large scale by Google's Gmail in 2004 and then was given its name by Jesse James Garret in 2005.

CHAPTER 4 **Embracing AJAX and JSON** 279

The HTML DOM changes the page dynamically. The important innovation that AJAX made was to use the XMLHttpRequest object to retrieve data from the server asynchronously (in the background) without blocking the execution of the rest of the JavaScript on the web page.

Although AJAX originally relied on data formatted as XML (hence the X in the name), it's much more common today for AJAX applications to use a data format called JavaScript Object Notation (JSON). Most people still call applications that get JSON data asynchronously from a server AJAX, but a more technically accurate (but less memorable) acronym would be AJAJ.

AJAX examples

When web developers first started to use AJAX, it became one of the hallmarks of what was labeled Web 2.0. The most common way for web pages to show dynamic data prior to AJAX was by downloading a new web page from the server. For example, consider craigslist.org, shown in Figure 4-1.

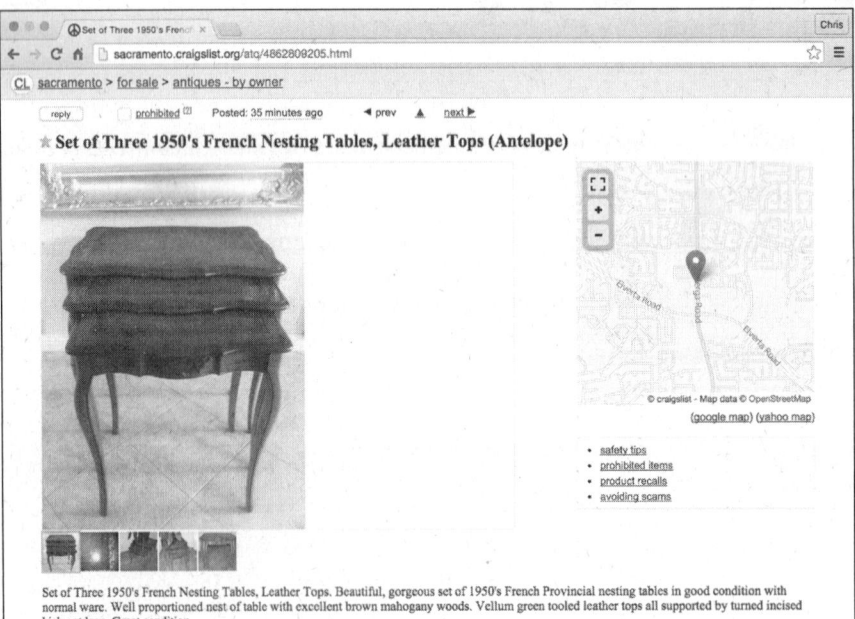

FIGURE 4-1: Craigslist.org is quite happy with Web 1.0, thank you very much.

To navigate through the categories of listings or search results on Craigslist, you click links that cause the entire page to refresh and reveal the content of the page you requested.

While still very common, refreshing the entire page to display new data in just part of the page is unnecessarily slow and can provide a less smooth user experience.

Compare the craigslist-style navigation with the more application-like navigation of Google Plus, shown in Figure 4-2, which uses AJAX to load new content into part of the screen while the navigation bar remains static.

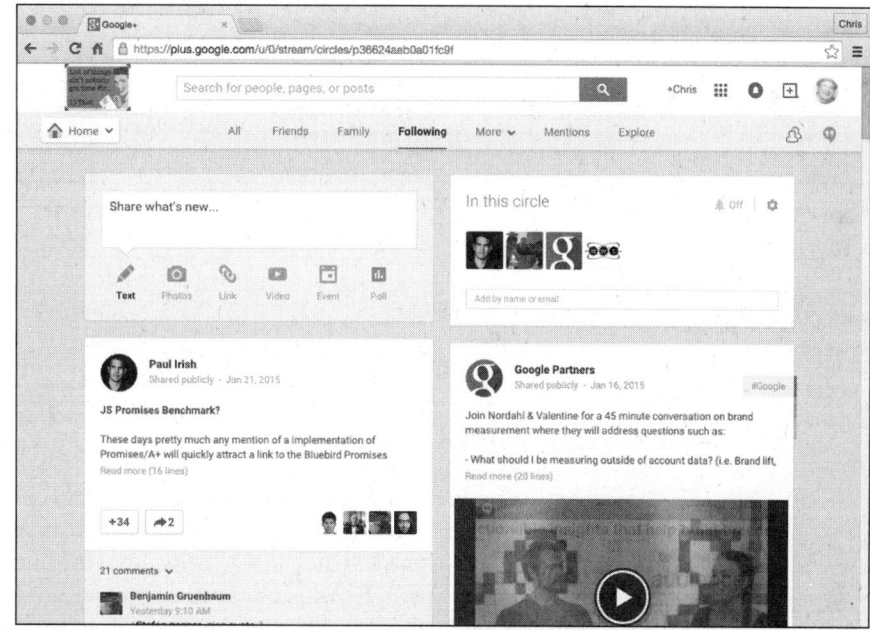

FIGURE 4-2: Google Plus uses AJAX to provide a modern user experience.

In addition to making web page navigation smoother, AJAX is also great for creating live data elements in a web page. Prior to AJAX, if you wanted to display live data, a chart, or an up-to-date view of an email inbox, you either needed to use a plug-in (such as Adobe Flash) or periodically cause the web page to automatically refresh.

With AJAX, it's possible to periodically refresh data through an asynchronous process that runs in the background and then update only the elements of the page that need to be modified.

Weather Underground's Wundermap, shown in Figure 4-3, shows a weather map with constantly changing and updating data overlays. The data for the map is retrieved from remote servers using AJAX.

CHAPTER 4 Embracing AJAX and JSON 281

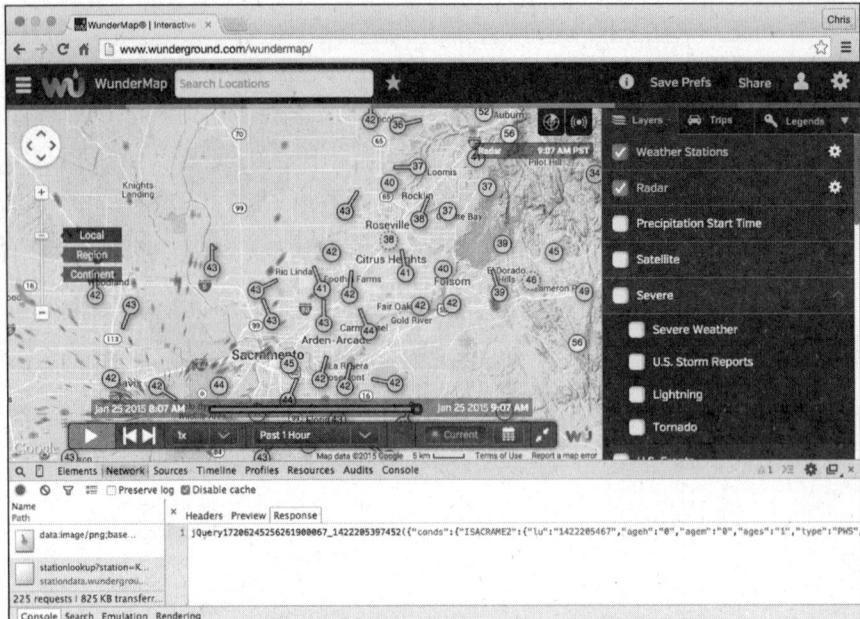

FIGURE 4-3:
Wundermap uses AJAX to display live weather data.

Viewing AJAX in action

In Figure 4-3, shown in the preceding section, the Chrome Developer Tools window is open to the Network tab. The Network tab shows all network activity involving the current web page. When a page is loading, this includes the requests and downloads of the page's HTML, CSS, JavaScript, and images. After the page is loaded, the Network tab also displays the asynchronous HTTP requests and responses that make AJAX possible.

Follow these steps to view AJAX requests and responses in Chrome:

1. **Open your Chrome web browser and navigate to** www.wunderground.com/wundermap.

2. **Open your Chrome Developer Tools by using the Chrome menu or by pressing Cmd+Option+I (on Mac) or Ctrl+Shift+I (on Windows).**

3. **Open the Network tab.**

 Your Developer Tools window should now resemble Figure 4-4. You may want to drag the top border of the Developer Tools to make it larger at this point. Don't worry if this makes the content area of the browser too small to use. What's going on in the Developer Tools is the important thing right now.

 Notice that new items are periodically appearing in the Network tab. These are the AJAX requests and responses. Some of them are images returned from the server, and some are data for use by the client-side JavaScript.

282 BOOK 4 **Advanced Web Coding**

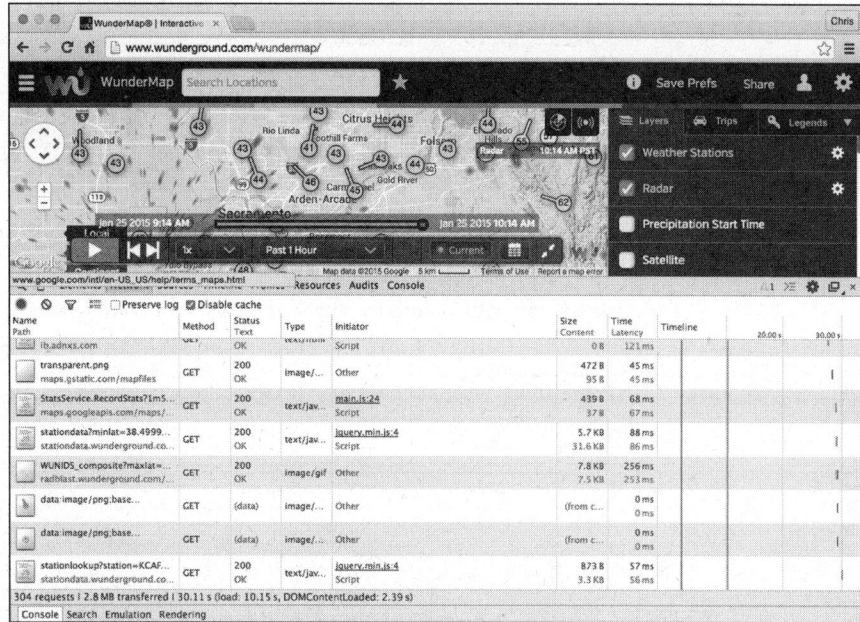

FIGURE 4-4:
The Network tab of the Developer Tools.

4. **Click one of the rows in the Name column of the Networks tab.**

 Additional data will be displayed about that particular item, as shown in Figure 4-5.

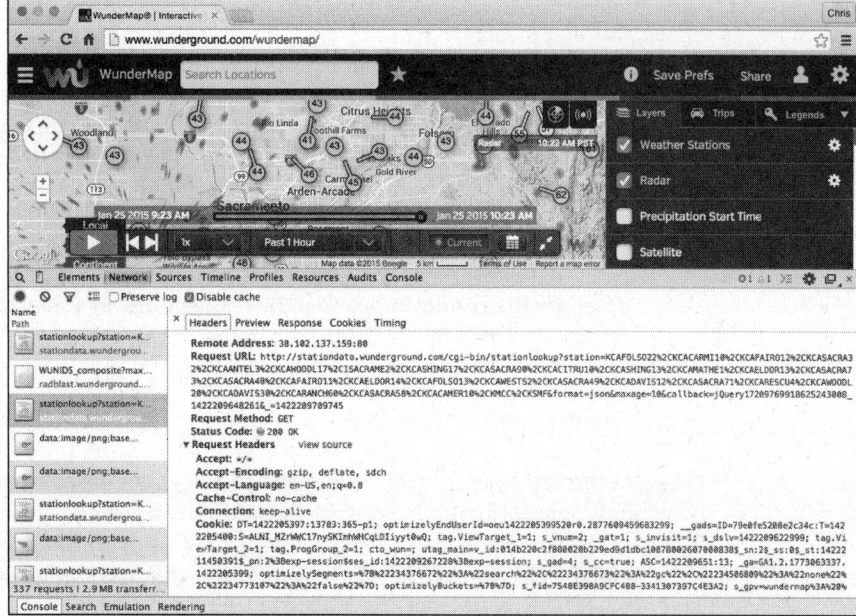

FIGURE 4-5:
Viewing additional information about a particular record in the Network tab.

CHAPTER 4 Embracing AJAX and JSON 283

5. **Click through the tabs (Headers, Preview, Response and so on) in the detailed data pane and examine the data.**

 The first tab, Headers, displays the HTTP request that was sent to the remote server. Take a look in particular at the Request URL. This is a standard website address that passes data to a remote server.

6. **Select and copy the value of the Request URL from one of the items you inspected.**

7. **Open a new tab in your browser and paste the entire Request URL into the address bar.**

 A page containing data or an image opens, as in Figure 4-6.

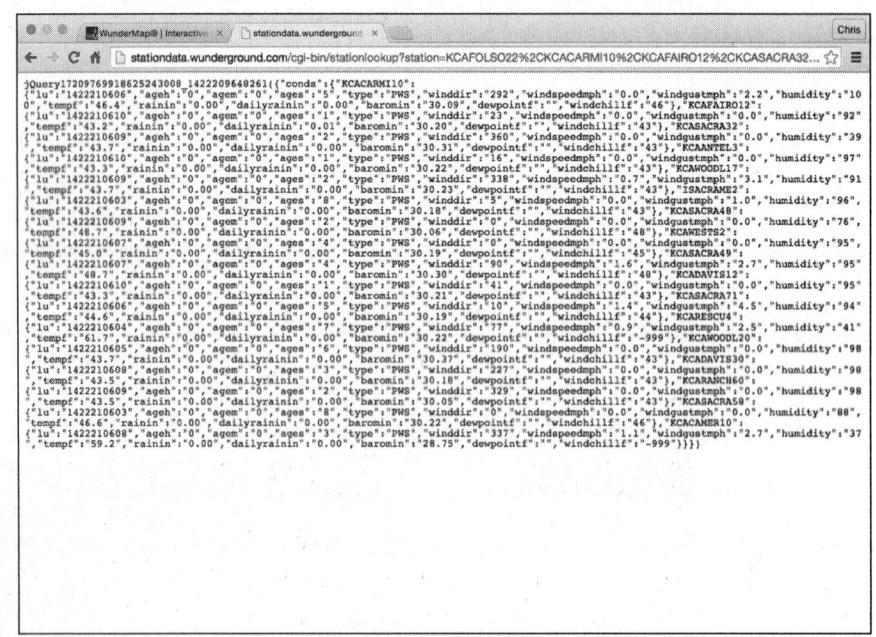

FIGURE 4-6: The result of copying an HTTP Request URL from the Network tab.

8. **Compare the results of opening the Request URL in a new tab with the results shown in the Response tab in the Developer Tools.**

 They should be similar, although they may not look identical because they weren't run at the same time.

As you can see, there's really no magic to AJAX. The JavaScript on the web page is simply requesting and receiving data from a server. Everything that happens behind the scenes is open to inspection through the Chrome Developer Tools (or the similar tools that are available with most other web browsers today).

Using the XMLHttpRequest object

The XMLHttpRequest object provides a way for web browsers to request data from a URL without having to refresh the page.

The XMLHttpRequest object was created and implemented first by Microsoft in its Internet Explorer browser and has since become a web standard that has been adopted by every modern web browser.

You can use the methods and properties of the XMLHttpRequest object to retrieve data from a remote server or your local server. Despite its name, the XMLHttpRequest object can get other types of data besides XML, and it can even use different protocols to get data besides HTTP.

Listing 4-1 shows how you can use XMLHttpRequest to load the contents of an external text document containing HTML into the current HTML document.

LISTING 4-1: Using XMLHttpRequest to Load External Data

```html
<html>
<head>
 <title>Loading External Data</title>
 <script>
 window.addEventListener('load',init,false);
 function init(e){

            document.getElementById('myButton').addEventListener('click',
            documentLoader,false);
 }
 function reqListener () {
   console.log(this.responseText);
   document.getElementById('content').innerHTML = this.responseText;
 }
   function documentLoader(){
   var oReq = new XMLHttpRequest();
   oReq.onload = reqListener;
   oReq.open("get", "loadme.txt", true);
   oReq.send();
  }
 </script>
</head>
<body>
 <form id="myForm">
  <button id="myButton" type="button">Click to Load</button>
 </form>
 <div id="content"></div>
</body>
</html>
```

The heart of this document is the `documentLoader` function:

```
function documentLoader(){
  var oReq = new XMLHttpRequest();
  oReq.onload = reqListener;
  oReq.open("get", "loadme.txt", true);
  oReq.send();
}
```

The first line of code inside the function creates the new `XMLHttpRequest` object and gives it the name of `oReq`:

```
var oReq = new XMLHttpRequest();
```

The methods and properties of the `XMLHttpRequest` object are accessible through the `oReq` object.

This second line assigns a function, `reqListener`, to the `onload` event of the `oReq` object. The purpose of this is to cause the `reqListener` function to be called when `oReq` loads a document:

```
oReq.onload = reqListener;
```

The third line uses the open method to create a request:

```
oReq.open("get", "loadme.txt", true);
```

In this case, the function uses the HTTP GET method to load the file called `loadme.txt`. The third parameter is the `async` argument. It specifies whether the request should be asynchronous. If it's set to false, the `send` method won't return until the request is complete. If it's set to true, notifications about the completion of the request will be provided through event listeners. Because the event listener is set to listen for the `load` event, an asynchronous request is what's desired.

WARNING

It's unlikely that you'll run into a situation where you'll want to set the `async` argument to false. In fact, some browsers have begun to just ignore this argument if it's set to false and to treat it as if it's true either way because of the bad effect on the user experience that synchronous requests have.

The last line in the `documentLoader` function actually sends the requests that you created with the open method:

```
oReq.send();
```

TECHNICAL STUFF

The .open method will get the latest version of the requested file. So-called live-data applications often use loops to repeatedly request updated data from a server using AJAX.

Working with the same-origin policy

If you save the HTML document in Listing 4-1 to your computer and open it in a web browser, more than likely, you won't get the results that you'd expect. If you load the document from your computer and then open the Chrome Developer Tools JavaScript console, you will see a couple of error messages similar to the error in Figure 4-7.

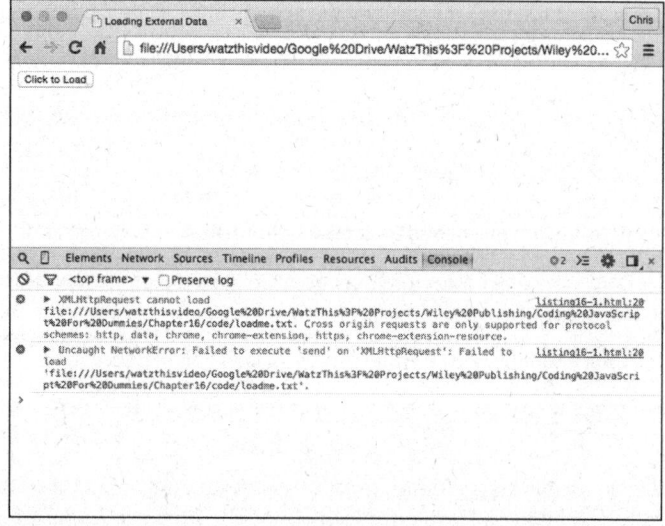

FIGURE 4-7: Errors when trying to use XMLHttp Request on a local file.

The problem here is what's called the *same-origin policy*. In order to prevent web pages from causing users to unknowingly download code that may be malicious using XMLHttpRequest, browsers will return an error by default whenever a script tries to load a URL that doesn't have the same origin. If you load a web page from www.example.com and a script on that page tries to retrieve data from www.watzthis.com, the browser will prevent the request with a similar error to the one you see in Figure 4-7.

The same-origin policy also applies to files on your local computer. If it didn't, XMLHttpRequest could be used to compromise the security of your computer.

There's no reason to worry about the examples in this book negatively affecting your computer. However, in order for the examples in this chapter to work correctly on your computer, a way around the same-origin policy is needed.

CHAPTER 4 Embracing AJAX and JSON 287

The first way around the same-origin policy is to put the HTML file containing the `documentLoader` function and the text file together onto the same web server.

The other way around the same-origin policy is to start up your browser with the same-origin policy restrictions temporarily disabled.

WARNING

These instructions are to allow you to test your own files on your local computer only. Do not surf the web with the same-origin policy disabled. You may expose your computer to malicious code.

To disable the same-origin policy on a Mac:

1. **If your Chrome browser is open, close it.**
2. **Open the Terminal app and launch Chrome using the following command:**

   ```
   /Applications/Google\ Chrome.app/Contents/MacOS/Google\ Chrome --disable-web-
            security
   ```

To disable the same-origin policy on Windows:

1. **If your Chrome browser is open, close it.**
2. **Open the Command prompt and navigate to the folder where you installed Chrome.**
3. **Type the following command to launch the browser:**

   ```
   Chrome.exe --disable-web-security
   ```

Once the browser starts up, you'll be able to run files containing AJAX requests locally until you close the browser. Once the browser is closed and reopened, the security restrictions will be re-enabled automatically.

Figure 4-8 shows the result of running Listing 4-1 in a browser without the same-origin policy errors.

Using CORS, the silver bullet for AJAX requests

It's quite common for a web application to make requests to a different server in order to retrieve data. For example, Google provides map data for free to third-party applications.

In order for the transactions between servers to be secure, mechanisms have been created for browsers and servers to work out their differences and establish trust.

FIGURE 4-8:
Listing 4-1 run in a browser with the same-origin policy disabled.

Currently, the best method for allowing and restricting access to resources between servers is the standard called *Cross-Origin Resource Sharing* (CORS).

To see CORS in action, using the Chrome web browser visit the Weather Underground's Wundermap (www.wunderground.com/wundermap). When the page has loaded, right-click and select Inspect to open the Chrome Developer Tools, then select the Network tab. Click one of the requests where the Name starts with "stationdata?" and the Type is xhr.

Click the Headers tab, and you'll see the following text within the HTTP header:

```
Access-Control-Allow-Origin: *
```

This is the CORS response header that this particular server is configured to send. The asterisk value after the colon indicates that this server will accept requests from any origin. If the owners of wunderground.com wanted to restrict access to the data at this script to only specific servers or authenticated users, they could do so using CORS.

Putting Objects in Motion with JSON

In Listing 4-1, you use AJAX to open and display a text document containing a snippet of HTML. Another common use for AJAX is to request and receive data for processing by the browser.

For example, gasbuddy.com uses a map from Google along with data about gas prices, to present a simple and up-to-date view of gas prices in different locations, as shown in Figure 4-9.

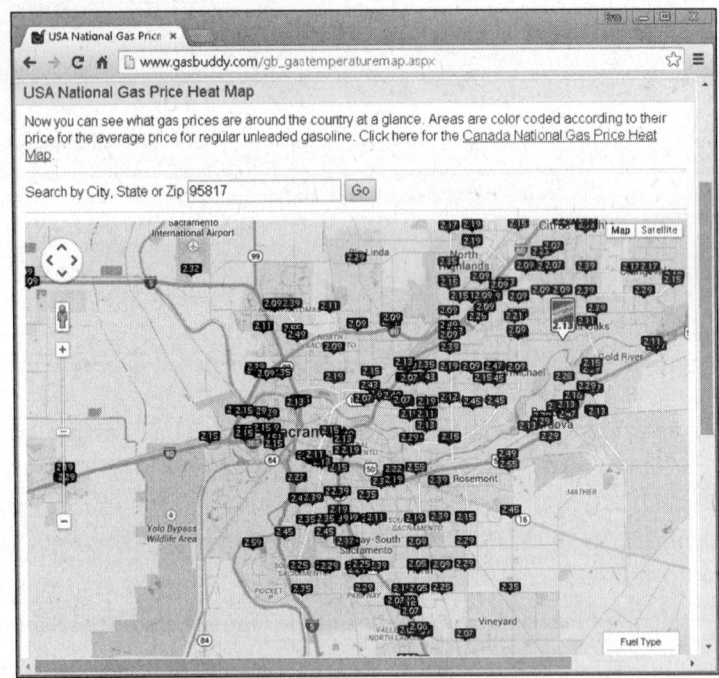

FIGURE 4-9: gasbuddy.com uses AJAX to display gas prices on a map.

If you examine gasbuddy.com in the Network tab, you'll find that some requests have responses that look something like the code shown in Listing 4-2.

LISTING 4-2: Part of a Response to an AJAX Request on gasbuddy.com

```
([{id:"tuwtvtuvvvv",base:[351289344,822599680],zrange:[11,11],
layer:"m@288429816",features:[{
id:"17243857463485476481",a:[0,0],bb:[-8,-8,7,7,-47,7,48,22,-41,19,41,34],c:"{1:
{title:\"Folsom Lake State Recreation Area\"},4:{type:1}}"}]},{id:"tuwtvtuvvvw",zrange:
[11,11],layer:"m@288429816"},{id:"tuwtvtuvvwv",base:[351506432,824291328],zrange:
[11,11],layer:"m@288429816",features:[{id:"8748558518353272790",a:[0,0],bb:[-8,-8,
7,7,-41,7,41,22],c:"{1:{title:\"Deer Creek Hills\"},4:{type:1}}"}]},{id:"tuwtvtu
vvww",zrange:[11,11],layer:"m@288429816"}])
```

If you take a small piece of data out of this block of code and reformat it, you get something like Listing 4-3, which should look more familiar to you.

LISTING 4-3: gasbuddy.com Response Data, Reformatted

```
{id:"tuwtvtuvvvv",
base:[351289344,822599680],
zrange:[11,11],
layer:"m@288429816",
features:[{
id:"17243857463485476481",
a:[0,0],
bb:[-8,-8,7,7,-47,7,48,22,-41,19,41,34],
c:"{
1:{title:\"Folsom Lake State Recreation Area\"},
4:{type:1}
}"
]}
}
```

By looking at the format of the data, you can see that it looks suspiciously like the `name:value` format of a JavaScript object literal, also known as a comma-separated list of name-value pairs enclosed in curly braces.

The main reason JSON is so easy to use is because it's already in a format that JavaScript can work with, so no conversion is necessary. For example, Listing 4-4 shows a JSON file containing information about this book.

LISTING 4-4: JSON Data Describing Coding For Dummies

```
{ "book_title": "Coding For Dummies",
  "book_author": "Nikhil Abraham",
  "summary": "Everything beginners need to know to start coding.",
  "isbn":"9781119363026"
}
```

Listing 4-5 shows how this data can be loaded into a web page using JavaScript and then used to display its data in HTML.

LISTING 4-5: **Displaying JSON Data with JavaScript**

```html
<html>
<head>
 <title>Displaying JSON Data</title>
 <script>
  window.addEventListener('load',init,false);
  function init(e){

          document.getElementById('myButton').addEventListener('click',
          documentLoader,false);
  }
  function reqListener () {
    // convert the string from the file to an object with JSON.parse
    var obj = JSON.parse(this.responseText);
    // display the object's data like any object
    document.getElementById('book_title').innerHTML = obj.book_title;
    document.getElementById('book_author').innerHTML = obj.book_author;
    document.getElementById('summary').innerHTML = obj.summary;
  }
  function documentLoader(){
    var oReq = new XMLHttpRequest();
    oReq.onload = reqListener;
    oReq.open("get", "listing4-5.json", true);
    oReq.send();
  }
 </script>
</head>
<body>
 <form id="myForm">
  <button id="myButton" type="button">Click to Load</button>
 </form>
 <h1>Book Title</h1>
 <div id="book_title"></div>
 <h2>Authors</h2>
 <div id="book_author"></div>
 <h2>Summary</h2>
 <div id="summary"></div>
</body>
</html>
```

The key to displaying any JSON data that's brought into a JavaScript document from an external source is to convert it from a string to an object using the JSON.parse method. After you do that, you can access the values within the JSON file using dot notation or bracket notation as you would access the properties of any JavaScript object.

Figure 4-10 shows the results of running Listing 4-5 in a web browser and pressing the button to load the JSON data.

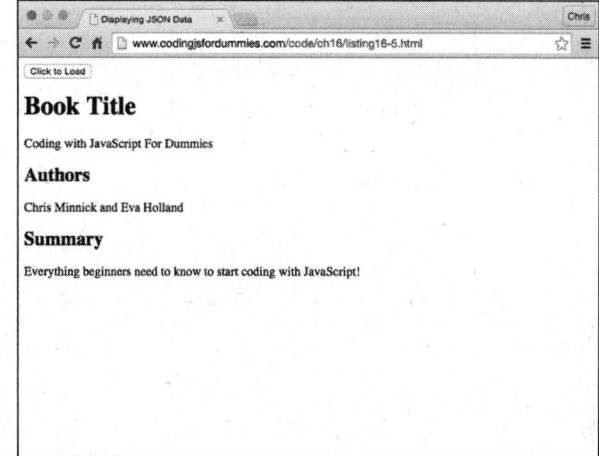

FIGURE 4-10: Displaying JSON data within an HTML page.

CHAPTER 4 **Embracing AJAX and JSON** 293

IN THIS CHAPTER

» Understanding jQuery

» Selecting elements

» Creating animations and transitions with jQuery

Chapter 5
jQuery

"It's best to have your tools with you. If you don't, you're apt to find something you didn't expect and get discouraged."

— STEPHEN KING

Query is the most popular JavaScript framework around and is used by nearly every JavaScript programmer in order to speed up and simplify JavaScript development. In this chapter, you discover the basics of jQuery and see why it's so popular.

Writing More and Doing Less

jQuery is currently used by more than 61 percent of the top 100,000 websites. It's so widely used that many people see it as an essential tool for doing JavaScript coding.

jQuery smoothes out some of the rough spots in JavaScript, such as problems with browser compatibilities, and makes selecting and changing parts of an HTML document easier. jQuery also includes some tools that you can use to add animation and interactivity to your web pages.

The basics of jQuery are easy to grasp once you know JavaScript.

Getting Started with jQuery

To get started with jQuery, you first need to include the jQuery library in your web pages. The easiest way to do this is to use a version hosted on a content delivery network (CDN). The other method for including jQuery is to download the library from the jQuery website and host it on your server. Listing 5-1 shows markup for a simple web page that includes jQuery.

TIP

Google has hosted versions of many different JavaScript libraries, and you can find links and include tags for them at https://developers.google.com/speed/libraries/#jquery.

Once you've found a link for a CDN-hosted version, include it between your `<head>` and `</head>` tags in every page that will use jQuery functionality.

WARNING

There are currently two branches of jQuery: the 1.x branch and the 2.x branch. The difference between the latest versions of the 1.x branch and the latest versions of the 2.x branch is that the 1.x branch works in Internet Explorer 6-8, while the 2.x branch eliminated support for these old and buggy browsers.

LISTING 5-1: Your First Web Page with jQuery

```
<html>
<head>
  <title>Hello JQuery</title>
  <style>
    #helloDiv {
      background: #333;
      color: #fff;
      font-size: 24px;
      text-align: center;
      border-radius: 3px;
      width: 200px;
      height: 200px;
      display: none;
    }
  </style>
  <script src="http://code.jquery.com/jquery-1.11.2.min.js"></script>
</head>
<body>
  <button id="clickme">Click me!</button>
  <div id="helloDiv">Hello, JQuery!</div>
  <script>
  $( "#clickme" ).click(function () {
    if ( $( "#helloDiv" ).is( ":hidden" ) ) {
      $( "#helloDiv" ).slideDown( "slow" );
```

```
    } else {
      $( "div" ).hide();
    }
  });
  </script>
</body>
</html>
```

The jQuery Object

All of jQuery's functionality is enabled by the `jQuery` object. The `jQuery` object can be referenced using two different methods: the `jQuery` keyword or the `$` alias. Both methods work exactly the same. The difference is that `$` is shorter, and so it's become programmers' preferred method for using jQuery.

The basic syntax for using jQuery is the following:

```
$("selector").method();
```

The first part (in parentheses) indicates what elements you want to affect, and the second part indicates what should be done to those elements.

In reality, jQuery statements often perform multiple actions on selected elements by using a technique called *chaining*, which just attaches more methods to the selector with additional periods. For example, in Listing 5-2, chaining is used to first select a single element (with the ID of `pageHeader`) and then to style it.

LISTING 5-2: **Using Chaining**

```
<html>
<head>
  <title>JQuery Chaining Example</title>
  <script src="http://code.jquery.com/jquery-1.11.2.min.js"></script>
</head>
<body>
  <div id="pageHeader"/>
  <script type="text/javascript">
    $("#pageHeader").text("Hello, world!").css("color", "red").css("font-size",
    "60px");
  </script>
</body>
</html>
```

Chained `jQuery` methods can get pretty long and confusing after you put just a couple of them together. However, keep in mind, JavaScript doesn't really care much about whitespace. It's possible to reformat the chained statement from Listing 5-2 into the following, much more readable, statement:

```
$("#pageHeader")
   .text("Hello, world!")
   .css("color", "red")
   .css("font-size", "60px");
```

Is Your Document Ready?

jQuery has its own way to indicate that everything is loaded and ready to go: the document ready event. To avoid errors caused by the DOM or jQuery not being loaded when the scripts run, it's important to use document ready, unless you put all your jQuery at the very bottom of your HTML document enclosed in script tags (as shown earlier in Listing 5-1 and Listing 5-2).

Here's the syntax for using document ready:

```
$(document).ready(function(){
   // jQuery methods go here...
});
```

Any jQuery that you want to be executed upon loading of the page needs to be inside a document ready statement. Named functions can go outside document ready, of course, because they don't run until they're called.

Using jQuery Selectors

Unlike the complicated ways that JavaScript provides for selecting elements, jQuery makes element selection simple. In jQuery, programmers can use the same techniques they use for selecting elements with CSS. Table 5-1 lists the most frequently used jQuery and CSS selectors.

TABLE 5-1 **The Common jQuery/CSS Selectors**

Selector	HTML Example	jQuery Example
Element	`<p></p>`	`$('p').css('font-size','12')`
.class	`<p class="redtext"></p>`	`$('.redtext').css`
#id	`<p id="intro"></p>`	`$('#intro').fadeIn('slow')`
[attribute]	`<p data-role="content"></p>`	`$('[data-role]').show()`

In addition to these basic selectors, you can modify a section or combine selections in many different ways. For example, to select the first p element in a document, you can use

```
$('p:first')
```

To select the last p element, you can use

```
$('p:last')
```

To select the even numbered elements, you can use

```
$('li:even')
```

To select the odd numbered elements, you can use

```
$('li:odd')
```

To combine multiple selections, you can use commas. For example, the following selector selects all the p, h1, h2, and h3 elements in a document.

```
$('p,h1,h2,h3')
```

You can select elements in many more ways with jQuery than with plain JavaScript. To see a complete list, visit http://api.jquery.com/category/selectors.

CHAPTER 5 jQuery 299

Changing Things with jQuery

After you make a selection, the next step is to start changing some things. The three main categories of things you can change with jQuery are attributes, CSS, and elements.

Getting and setting attributes

The `attr()` method gives you access to attribute values. All that you need in order to use `attr()` is the name of the attribute whose value you want to get or set. In the following code, the `attr()` method is used to change the value of the `href` attribute of an element with an id of `"homepage-link"`.

```
$('a#homepage-link').attr('href') =
"http://www.techcrunch.com/";
```

The result of running this statement is that the selected element's `href` attribute will be changed in the DOM to the new value. When a user clicks the modified link, the browser will open the web page at the specified address, rather than the one that was originally written in the `img` element.

REMEMBER

Modifying an element using jQuery changes only the element's representation in the DOM (and therefore on the user's screen). jQuery doesn't modify the actual web page on the server, and if you view the source of the web page, you won't see any changes.

Changing CSS

Changing CSS using jQuery is very similar to the technique just described for modifying an object's properties. jQuery makes modifying the style properties much easier than standard JavaScript, and the style properties are spelled exactly the same as in CSS.

Listing 5-3 combines live CSS style changes with form events to give the user control over how large the text is.

LISTING 5-3: **Manipulating Styles with jQuery**

```
<html>
<head>
  <title>JQuery CSS</title>
  <script src="http://code.jquery.com/
  jquery-1.11.2.min.js"></script>
```

```
<script type="text/javascript">
  $(document).ready(function(){

  $('#sizer').change(function() {
    $('#theText').css('font-size',$('#sizer').val());
  });
  });
  </script>
</head>
<body>
  <div id="theText">Hello!</div>
  <form id="controller">
    <input type="range" id="sizer" min="10" max="100">
  </form>
</body>
</html>
```

Figure 5-1 shows the results of running Listing 5-3 in a browser.

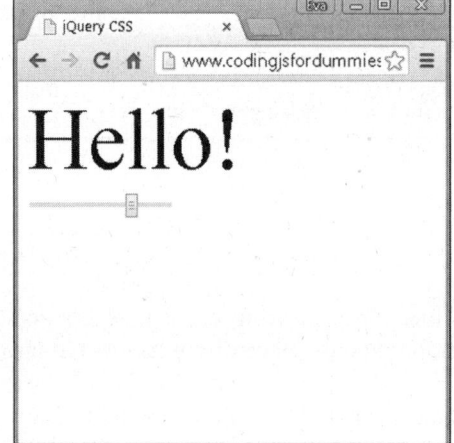

FIGURE 5-1:
Changing CSS with an input element.

Manipulating elements in the DOM

jQuery features several methods for changing the content of elements, moving elements, adding elements, removing elements, and much more. Table 5-2 lists all the available methods for manipulating elements within the DOM.

TABLE 5-2 Manipulating Elements within the DOM

Method	Description	Example
text()	Get the combined text content of the matched elements, or sets the text content of the matched elements.	`$('p').text('hello!')`
html()	Get the value of the first matched element, or set the contents of every matched element.	`$('div').html('<p>hi</p>')`
val()	Get the value of the first matched element, or set the value of every matched element.	`$('select#choices').val()`
append()	Insert content to the end of the matched elements.	`$('div #closing')` `append('<p>Thank You</p>')`
prepend()	Insert content at the beginning of the matched elements.	`$('dive #introduction')` `prepend('<p>Dear Aiden:</p>')`
before()	Insert content before the matched elements.	`$('#letter').` `before(header)`
after()	Insert content after the matched elements.	`$('#letter').after(footer)`
remove()	Remove the matched elements.	`$('.phonenumber').remove()`
empty()	Remove all of the child nodes of the matched elements.	`$('.blackout').empty()`

Events

jQuery has its own syntax for registering event listeners and handling events, which differs slightly from how these events are handled in JavaScript.

jQuery's event method, on(), handles all of the complexity of ensuring that all browsers will handle events in the same way, and it also requires far less typing than the pure JavaScript solutions.

Using on() to attach events

The jQuery on() method takes an event and a function definition as arguments. When the event happens on the selected element (or elements), the function is executed. Listing 5-4 uses on() and a jQuery selector to change the color of every other row in a table when a button is clicked.

LISTING 5-4: Changing Table Colors with the Click of a Button

```html
<html>
<head>
  <title>jQuery CSS</title>
  <style>
    td {
      border: 1px solid black;
    }
  </style>
  <script src="http://code.jquery.com/jquery-1.11.2.min.js"></script>
  <script type="text/javascript">
    $(document).ready(function(){

      $('#colorizer').on('click',function() {
        $('#things tr:even').css('background','#ffeb3b');
      });
    });
  </script>
</head>
<body>
  <table id="things">
    <tr>
      <td>item1</td>
      <td>item2</td>
      <td>item3</td>
    </tr>
    <tr>
      <td>apples</td>
      <td>oranges</td>
      <td>lemons</td>
    </tr>
    <tr>
      <td>merlot</td>
      <td>malbec</td>
      <td>cabernet sauvignon</td>
    </tr>
  </table>
  <form id="tableControl">
    <button type="button" id="colorizer">Colorize</button>
  </form>
</body>
</html>
```

Figure 5-2 shows the alternating table formatting after the button is clicked.

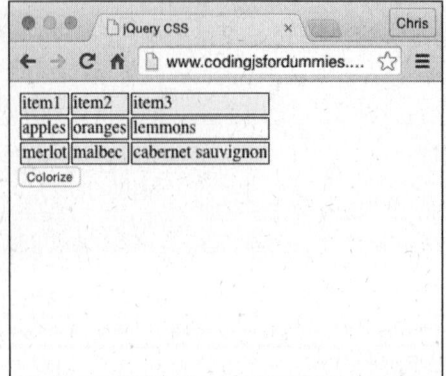

FIGURE 5-2: Alternating table colors.

TIP

Do you notice something seemingly odd about the shaded rows in Figure 5-2? The first and third rows of the table are shaded, but the code told jQuery to shade the even numbered rows. The explanation is simple: The even and odd determinations are based on the index number of the tr elements, which always start with 0. So the colorized ones are the first (index number 0) and the third (index number 2).

Detaching with off()

The off() method can be used to unregister a previously set event listener. For example, if you want to disable the button in Listing 5-4 (maybe until the user paid for the use of this feature), you use the following statement:

```
$('#colorizer').off('click');
```

Or, if you want to remove all event listeners on an element, you can do so by calling off with no arguments:

```
$('colorizer').off();
```

Binding to events that don't exist yet

With the dynamic nature of today's web, you sometimes need to register an event listener to an element that is created dynamically after the HTML loads.

To add event listeners to elements that are created dynamically, you can pass a selector that should be monitored for new elements to the on() method. For example, if you want to make sure that all rows, and all future rows, in the table are clickable, you can use the following statement:

```
$(document).on('click','tr',function(){
  alert("Thanks for clicking!");
}
```

Other event methods

Besides on(), jQuery also has a simplified shortcut syntax for attaching event listeners to selected elements. jQuery has methods with the same names as the events that you can just pass the event handler to. For example, both of these statements accomplish the same thing:

```
$('#myButton').on('click',function() {
 alert('Thanks!');
}
$('#myButton').click(function() {
 alert('Thanks!');
}
```

Other shortcut event methods include

- change()
- click()
- dblclick()
- focus()
- hover()
- keypress()
- load()

For a complete list of event methods, visit the jQuery website at http://api.jquery.com/category/events.

Effects

jQuery makes a JavaScript programmer's life much easier. It even makes simple animations and effects easier.

WARNING

jQuery effects are so simple that they're often overused. Once you see what can be done and have played with each of the different variations, it would probably be a good idea to build one web app that uses them all every time any event happens. Then delete this file and consider this urge to overuse effects to be out of your system.

Basic effects

jQuery's basic effects simply control whether selected elements are displayed or not. The basic effects are

- » `hide()`: The `hide` method hides the matched elements.
- » `show()`: The `show` method shows the matched elements
- » `toggle()`: The `toggle` method toggles between hiding and showing the matched elements:
 - If the matched element is hidden, `toggle` will cause it to be shown.
 - If the element is shown, `toggle` will cause it to be hidden.

Fading effects

You can transition selected elements between displaying and hiding by using a fade effect. The fading effects are

- » `fadeIn()`: Causes the matched element to fade into view over a specified amount of time (become opaque)
- » `fadeOut()`: Causes the matched element to fade out over a specified amount of time (become transparent)
- » `fadeTo()`: Adjusts the opacity of elements to a specified level over a specified amount of time
- » `fadeToggle()`: Fades matched elements in or out over a specified amount of time

Sliding effects

The sliding effects transition selected elements between showing and hiding by using an animated slide effect. The sliding effects are

- `slideDown()`: Displays the matched elements with an upward sliding motion
- `slideUp()`: Hides the matched elements with an upward sliding motion
- `slideToggle()`: Toggles between sliding up and sliding down

Setting arguments for animation methods

Each of the jQuery animation methods has a set of optional arguments that control the details of how the animation takes places and when.

The arguments of the basic, fading, and sliding methods are

- `duration`: A numeric value indicating how long (in milliseconds) the animation should take.
- `easing`: A string value defining what easing function should be used to do the animation. An easing function determines how the element animates. For example, it may start slow and speed up or start fast and slow down.

 jQuery has two easing functions built-in:
 - `swing` (default): Progress slightly lower at the beginning and end than in the middle.
 - `linear`: Progress at a constant rate through the animation.
- `complete`: Specifies a function to execute when the current animation is finished.

Custom effects with animate()

The `animate` method performs a custom animation of CSS properties. To specify the animation, you pass a set of properties to the `animate` method. When it runs, the animation will move toward the values you set for each property. For example, to animate increasing with width and color of a `div`, you could use this statement:

```
('div #myDiv').animate(
{
 width: 800,
 color: 'blue'
}, 5000);
```

In addition to the required CSS properties argument, the `animate` method takes the same optional arguments as the other animation methods.

Playing with jQuery animations

Listing 5-5 implements several of the jQuery animation methods. Try changing values and experimenting with the different settings for each of these methods and see what you come up with!

LISTING 5-5: Fun with jQuery Animations

```html
<html>
<head>
  <title>JQuery CSS</title>
  <style>
    td {
      border: 1px solid black;
    }
  </style>
  <script src="http://code.jquery.com/jquery-1.11.2.min.js"></script>
  <script type="text/javascript">
    // wait for the DOM to be ready
    $(document).ready(function(){
      // when the animator button is clicked, start doing things
      $('#animator').on('click',function() {
        $('#items').fadeToggle(200);
        $('#fruits').slideUp(500);
        $('#wines').toggle(400,'swing',function(){
          $('#wines').toggle(400,'swing');
        });
        $('h1').hide();
        $('h1').slideDown(1000).animate({
          'color': 'red',
          'font-size': '100px'},1000);
      });
    });
  </script>
</head>
<body>
  <h1>Here are a bunch of things!</h1>
  <table id="things">
    <tr id="items">
      <td>item1</td>
      <td>item2</td>
      <td>item3</td>
    </tr>
    <tr id="fruits">
```

```
        <td>apples</td>
        <td>oranges</td>
        <td>lemons</td>
    </tr>
    <tr id="wines">
        <td>merlot</td>
        <td>malbec</td>
        <td>cabernet sauvignon</td>
    </tr>
  </table>
  <form id="tableControl">
    <button type="button" id="animator">Animate Stuff!</button>
  </form>
</body>
</html>
```

AJAX

One of the most useful things about jQuery is how it simplifies AJAX and makes working with external data easier.

Book 4, Chapter 4 discusses AJAX, the technique of loading new data into a web page without refreshing the page. It also covers how to use JSON data in JavaScript.

Using the ajax() method

At the head of jQuery's AJAX capabilities lies the ajax() method. The ajax() method is the low-level way to send and retrieve data from an external file. At its simplest level, the AJAX method can take just a filename or URL as an argument, and it will load the indicated file. Your script can then assign the content of that file to a variable.

You can also specify many different options about how the external URL should be called and loaded, and you can set functions that should run if the request succeeds or fails.

For a complete list of the optional arguments of the ajax() method, visit http://api.jquery.com/jQuery.ajax.

Shorthand AJAX methods

jQuery also has several shorthand methods for handling AJAX. The syntax for these is simplified because they're designed for specific tasks. The shorthand AJAX methods are as follows:

» .get(): Loads data from a server using an HTTP GET request

» .getJSON(): Loads JSON data from a server using an HTTP GET request

» .getScript(): Loads a JavaScript file from a server using an HTTP GET request and then executes it

» .post(): Loads data from a server and places the returned HTML into the matched element

To use the shorthand methods, you can pass them a URL and, optionally, a success handler. For example, to get a file from a server using the get() method and then insert it into the page, you can do the following:

```
$.get( "getdata.html", function( data ) {
 $( ".result" ).html( data );
});
```

The preceding example is equivalent to the following full .ajax() statement:

```
$.ajax({
 url: getdata.html,
 success: function( data ) {
 $( ".result" ).html( data );
 }
});
```

The savings in effort isn't enormous in this example. With more complex AJAX requests, understanding and using the shorthand AJAX can result in more understandable and concise code.

5
Creating Web Applications

Contents at a Glance

CHAPTER 1: Building Your Own App 313
 Building a Location-Based Offer App 313
 Following an App Development Process 315
 Planning Your First Web Application 316
 Exploring the Overall Process 317
 Meeting the People Who Bring a Web App to Life 319

CHAPTER 2: Researching Your First Web Application 325
 Dividing the App into Steps 326
 Identifying Research Sources 333
 Researching the Steps in the McDuck's Offer App 335
 Choosing a Solution for Each Step 338

CHAPTER 3: Coding and Debugging Your First Web Application 341
 Getting Ready to Code 342
 Coding Your First Web Application 342
 Debugging Your App 350

IN THIS CHAPTER

» Completing a case study using an app

» Understanding the process of creating an app to solve a problem

» Discovering the various people who help create an app

Chapter 1
Building Your Own App

"If you have a dream, you can spend a lifetime . . . getting ready for it. What you should be doing is getting started."

— DREW HOUSTON

If you have read (or skimmed) the previous minibooks, you now have enough HTML, CSS, and JavaScript knowledge to write your own web application. To review, HTML puts content on the web page, CSS styles that content, and JavaScript allows for interaction with that content.

You may feel like you don't have enough coding knowledge to create an app, but I promise that you do. Besides, the only way to know for certain is to get started and try. In Book 5, you come to better understand a location-based app, and the basic steps to create that app. Developers often begin with just the information presented in this chapter and are expected to create a prototype. After reading this chapter, think about how you would build the app, and then refer to chapters that follow for more details on each step.

Building a Location-Based Offer App

Technology can provide developers (like you) one of the most valuable pieces of information about your users — their current location. With mobile devices, such as cell phones and tablets, you can even find users' location when they are on the go.

Although you likely have used an app to retrieve the time, weather, or even driving directions, you may never have received an offer on your phone to come into a store while walking down the street or driving in a car. Imagine passing by a Mexican restaurant during lunch time and receiving an offer for a free taco. I'm hungry, so let's get started!

Understanding the situation

The following is a fictitious case study. Any resemblance to real companies or events is coincidental.

The McDuck's Corporation is one of the largest fast food restaurants in the world, specializing in selling hamburgers in a restaurant called McDuck's. The company has 35,000 of these restaurants, which serve 6.5 million burgers every day to 70 million people in over 100 countries. In September 2014, McDuck's experienced its worst sales decline in over a decade. After many meetings, the executive team decided that the key to improving sales would be increasing restaurant foot traffic. "Our restaurant experience, with burger visuals and french-fry aromas, is the best in the industry — once a customer comes in, it is a guaranteed sale," says McDuck's CEO Duck Corleone. To promote restaurant visits, McDuck's wants a web application so customers can check into their favorite store, and receive an offer or coupon if they are close to a restaurant. "Giving customers who are five or ten minutes away from a restaurant an extra nudge may result in a visit. Even if customers use this app while at the restaurant, this will allow us to maintain a relationship with them long after they have left," says Corleone.

The McDuck's Corporation wants to run a pilot to better understand whether location-based offers will increase sales. Your task is to

» Create an app that will prove whether location-based offers are effective.

» Limit the app to work on just one McDuck's store of your choice.

» Obtain the location of customers using the app.

» Show offers to those customers who are five or ten minutes from the store.

McDuck's currently has a website and a mobile app, but both show only menu and store location information. If this pilot is successful, McDuck's will incorporate your code into its website and mobile app.

Plotting your next steps

Now that you understand McDuck's request, you likely have many questions:

- » What will the app look like?
- » What programming languages will I use to create the app?
- » How will I write code to locate a user's present location?
- » What offer will I show to a user who is five to ten minutes away?

These are natural questions to ask, and to make sure you are asking all the necessary questions upfront in an organized way, you will follow a standard development process.

Following an App Development Process

Building an app can take as little time as an hour or as long as decades. For most startups, the development processes for the initial product prototype averages one or two months to complete, whereas enterprise development processes for commercial grade software take six months to a few years to complete, depending on the industry and the project's complexity. A brief overview of the entire process is described here, and then each step is covered in additional detail as you build the app for McDuck's.

REMEMBER

An app can be a software program that runs on desktop or mobile devices.

The four steps you will follow when building your app are

- » Planning and discovery of app requirements
- » Researching of technology needed to build the app, and designing the app's look and feel
- » Coding your app using a programming language
- » Debugging and testing your code when it behaves differently than you intended

In total, you should plan to spend between two to five hours building this app. As shown in Figure 1-1, planning and research alone will take more than half your time, especially if this is the first time you're building an app. You might be surprised to learn that actually writing code will take a relatively small amount of time, with the rest of your time spent debugging your code to correct syntax and logic errors.

CHAPTER 1 **Building Your Own App** 315

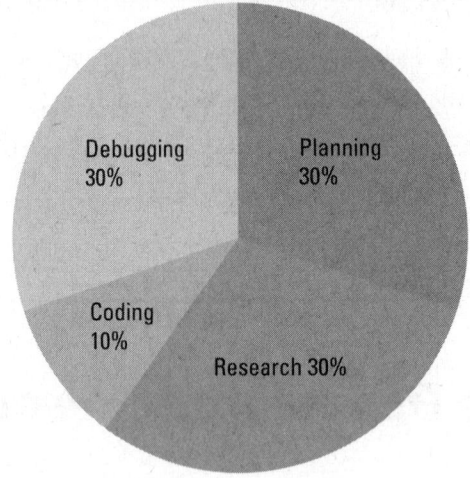

FIGURE 1-1: Time allocated to complete the four steps in the app development process.

TECHNICAL STUFF

App development processes have different names, and the two biggest processes are called *waterfall* and *agile*. Waterfall is a set of sequential steps followed to create a program, whereas agile is a set of iterative steps followed to create a program. Additional discussion can be found in Book 1, Chapter 3.

Planning Your First Web Application

You or your client has a web app idea, and planning is the process of putting those ideas down on paper. Documenting all the features that will go into the app is so important, because as the cartoon in Figure 1-2 shows for web development, and in computer science generally, it can be difficult to understand upfront what features are technically easy versus difficult to implement.

The planning phase also facilitates an up-front conversation around time, project scope, and budget, where a common saying is to "pick two out of the three." In some situations, such as with projects for finance companies, timelines and project scope may be legally mandated or tied to a big client and cannot be changed, so additional budgeting may be required to meet both. In other situations, such as projects for small startups, resources are scarce, so it's more common to adjust the project scope or extend the timeline than to increase the project's budget. Before writing any code, it will be helpful to understand which dimensions can be flexed and which are fixed.

FIGURE 1-2:
It can be difficult to separate technically easy from difficult projects.

Finally, although you will likely play multiple roles in the creation of this web app, in real life teams of people help bring to life the web apps you use every day. You will see the roles people play, and how they all work together.

Exploring the Overall Process

The purpose of the planning phase is to

- » **Understand the client goals.** Some clients may want to be the first to enter an industry with an app, even if it means sacrificing quality. Other clients may require the highest standards of quality, reliability, and stability. Similarly, others may prioritize retaining existing customers, while others want to attract new customers. All these motivations affect the product design and implementation in big and small ways.

TIP

If you're a developer in a large company, your client is usually not the end user but whoever in your internal team must greenlight the app before it is released to the public. At many companies, such as Google, Yahoo!, and Facebook, most projects do not pass internal review and are never released to the public.

» **Document product and feature requests.** Clients usually have an overall product vision, a list of tasks the user must be able to complete with the app. Often, clients have features in mind that will help accomplish those tasks.

» **Agree on deliverables and a timeline.** Almost every client will imagine a much bigger product than you have time to build. For a developer, it is extremely important to understand what features are absolutely necessary and must be built, and what features are "nice to have" if there is time remaining at the end of the project. If every feature is a "must have," you need to either push the client to prioritize something or make sure you have given yourself enough time.

TIP

Estimating the time to complete software projects is one of the most difficult project management tasks because there is greater variability and uncertainty than with physical construction projects, like building a house, or intellectual projects, like writing a memo. The most experienced developers at the world's best software companies routinely miss estimates, so don't feel bad if completion takes longer than you think it will. Your estimation skills will improve with time and practice.

After separating the necessary features from the "nice to have," you need to decide which features are easy to accomplish and which are complex. Without previous experience, this might seem difficult, but think about whether other applications have similar functionality. You need to also try searching the web for forum posts or for products that have the feature. If no product implements the feature, and all online discussions portray the task as difficult, it would be worthwhile to agree upfront on an alternative.

» **Discuss tools and software that you will use to complete the project and that your users will use to consume the project.** Take the time to understand your client and user's workflow to avoid surprises from incompatible software. Web software usually works across a variety of devices, but older operating systems and browsers can cause problems. Defining at the start of the project exactly which browser versions you will support (such as Internet Explorer 9 and later), and which devices (such as desktop and iPhone only) will save development and testing time. Usually, these decisions are based on how many existing users are on those platforms, and many organizations will support a browser version if used by a substantial part of the user base — usually at least five percent.

TIP

Browser incompatibilities are decreasing as the latest desktop and mobile browsers update themselves, and are now easier to keep up to date.

Meeting the People Who Bring a Web App to Life

You will be able to complete the app in this book by yourself, but the apps you build at work or use every day, like Google Maps or Instagram, are created by teams of people. Teams for a single product can vary in size, reaching to upward of 50 people, and each person plays a specific role across areas like design, development, product management, and testing. In smaller companies, the same person may perform multiple roles, while at larger companies, the roles become more specialized, and individual people perform each role.

Creating with designers

Before any code is written, designers work to create the site's look and feel through layout, visuals, and interactions. Designers answer simple questions like "Should the navigational menu be at the top of the page or the bottom?" to more complex questions like "How can we convey a sense of simplicity, creativity, and playfulness?" In general, designers answer these types of questions by interviewing users, creating many designs of the same product idea, and then making a final decision by choosing one design. Good design can greatly increase adoption of a product or use of a site, and products like Apple's iPhone and Airbnb.com. (See Figure 1-3.)

FIGURE 1-3: Jonathan Ive, SVP of Design at Apple, is credited for Apple's design successes.

CHAPTER 1 **Building Your Own App** 319

When building a website or app, you may decide you need a designer, but keep in mind that within design, there are multiple roles that designers play. The following roles are complementary, and may all be done by one person or by separate people:

- » **User interface (UI) and user experience (UX) designers** deal primarily with "look and feel" and with layout. When you browse a website, for example Amazon, you may notice that across all pages, the navigation menus and content are in the same place and use identical or very similar font, buttons, input boxes, and images. The UI/UX designer thinks about the order in which screens are displayed to the user, along with where and how the user clicks, enters text, and otherwise interacts with the website. If you were to eavesdrop on UI/UX designers, you might hear conversation like, "His page is too busy with too many calls to action. Our users don't make this many decisions anywhere else on the site. Let's simplify the layout by having just a single Buy button, so anyone can order with just one click."

- » **Visual designers** deal primarily with creating the final graphics used on a website, and this role is most closely associated with "designer." The visual designer creates final versions of icons, logos, buttons, typography, and images. For example, look at your Internet browser — the browser icon, the Back, Reload, and Bookmark buttons are all created by a visual designer, and anyone using the browser for the first time will know what the icons mean without explanation. If you were to eavesdrop on visual designers, you might hear conversation like, "The color contrast on these icons is too light to be readable, and if including text with the icon, let's center-align the text below the icon instead of above it."

- » **Interaction designers** deal primarily with interactions and animations based on user input and the situation. Initially, interaction designs were limited to keyboard and mouse interactions, but today touch sensors on mobile devices have created many more potential user interactions. The interaction designer thinks about how to use the best interaction so the user is able to complete a task as easily as possible. For example, think about how you check your email on your mobile phone. For many years, the traditional interaction was to see a list of messages, click a message, and then click a button to reply, flag, save to a folder, or delete the message. In 2013, interaction designers rethought the email app interaction and created an interaction so users could swipe their finger left or right to delete or reply to email messages instead of having to click through multiple menus. If you were to eavesdrop on interaction designers, you might hear conversation like, "While users are navigating with our maps app, instead of letting us know they are lost by clicking or swiping, maybe they could shake the phone and we could instantly have a location specialist call them."

 If creating an app were like making a movie, designers would be screenwriters.

Coding with front- and back-end developers

After the design is complete, the front-end and back-end developers make those designs a reality. Front-end developers, such as Mark Otto and Jacob Thornton (see Figure 1-4), code in HTML, CSS, and JavaScript, and convert the design into a user interface. These developers write the same code that you have been learning throughout this book and ensure that the website looks consistent across devices (desktop, laptop, and mobile), browsers (Chrome, Firefox, Safari, and so on), and operating systems (Windows, Mac, and so on). All these factors, especially increased adoption of mobile device, result in thousands of combinations that must be coded for and tested because every device, browser, and operating system renders HTML and CSS differently.

FIGURE 1-4: Mark Otto and Jacob Thornton created Bootstrap, the most popular front-end framework.

TIP

If creating an app were like making a movie, front-end developers would be the starring actors.

Back-end developers such as Yukihiro Matsumoto (see Figure 1-5) add functionality to the user interface created by the front-end developers. Back-end developers ensure that everything that's not visible to the user and behind the scenes is in place for the product to work as expected. Back-end developers use server-side languages like Python, PHP, and Ruby to add logic around what content to show, when, and to whom. In addition, they use databases to store user data, and create servers to serve all of this code to the users.

TIP

If creating an app were like making a movie, back-end developers would be the cinematographers, stunt coordinators, makeup artists, and set designers.

CHAPTER 1 **Building Your Own App** 321

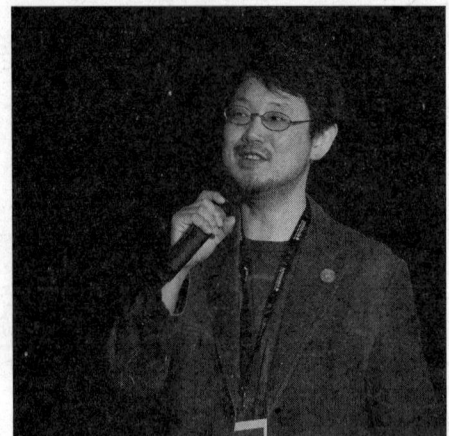

FIGURE 1-5: Yukihiro Matsumoto created Ruby, a popular server-side language used to create websites.

Managing with product managers

Product managers help define the product to be built and manage the product development process. When engineering teams are small (such as 14 people or fewer), communication, roles, and accountability are easily managed internally without much formal oversight. As engineering teams grow, the overhead of everyone communicating with each other also grows, and without some process, the interactions can become unmanageable, leading to miscommunication and missed deadlines. Product managers serve to lessen the communication overhead, and when issues arise as products are being built, these managers decide whether to extend timelines, cut scope, or add more resources to the team.

Product managers are often former engineers, who have a natural advantage in helping solve technical challenges that arise, but nontechnical people are also assuming these roles with success. Usually, no engineers report to the product manager, causing some to comment that product managers have "all of the responsibility, and none of the authority." One product manager wielding great responsibility and authority is Sundar Pichai, who originally was a product manager for the Google toolbar and recently was appointed to oversee many of Google's products, including search, Android, Chrome, maps, ads, and Google+. (See Figure 1-6.)

Testing with quality assurance

Testing is the final step of the journey after an app or website has been built. As a result of the many hands that helped with production, the newly created product will inevitably have bugs. Lists are made of all the core app user tasks and flows, and human testers along with automated programs go through the list over and over again on different browsers, devices, and operating systems to find errors.

Testers compile the newly discovered bugs and send them back to the developers, who prioritize which bugs to squash first. Trade-offs are always made between how many users are affected by a bug, the time it takes to fix the bug, and the time left until the product must be released. The most important bugs are fixed immediately, and minor bugs are scheduled to be fixed with updates or later releases. Today, companies also rely on feedback systems and collect error reports from users, with feedback forms and in some cases through automated reporting.

FIGURE 1-6: Sundar Pichai oversees almost every major Google product.

> **IN THIS CHAPTER**
>
> » **Dividing an app into smaller pieces, or steps**
>
> » **Using code from various sources to perform those steps**
>
> » **Creating app designs by reviewing and improving upon existing solutions**

Chapter 2
Researching Your First Web Application

"If we knew what it was we were doing, it would not be called research."
— ALBERT EINSTEIN

With the basic requirements defined, the next step is researching how to build the application. Apps consist of two main parts: functionality and form (design). For each of these parts, you must

» **Divide the app into steps.** Although it's good practice to divide anything you're going to build into steps, dividing apps into manageable pieces is an absolute necessity for large software projects with many people working across multiple teams.

» **Research each step.** When doing your research, the first question to ask is whether you must build a solution yourself or use an existing solution built by someone else. Building your own solution usually is the best way to directly address your need, but it takes time, whereas implementing someone else's solution is fast but may meet only part of your needs.

» **Choose a solution for each step.** You should have all the solutions selected before writing any code. For each step, decide whether you're writing your own code, or using prebuilt code. If you're not writing the code yourself, compare a few options so you can pick one with confidence.

Dividing the App into Steps

The biggest challenge with dividing an app into steps is knowing how big or small to make each step. The key is to make sure each step is discrete and independent. To test whether you have the right number of steps, ask yourself if someone else could solve and complete the step with minimal guidance.

Finding your app's functionality

Recall, from Book 5, Chapter 1, that McDuck's wants to promote restaurant visits by using a web application that sends customers an offer or coupon if they're close to a restaurant. To make this job easier, you are to create the app for customers visiting just one store.

Your first move is to break down this app into steps needed for the app to function. These steps should not be too specific. Think of them in broad terms, as if you were explaining the process to a kindergartner. With a pen and paper, write down these steps in order. Don't worry about whether each step is correct, as your skill will improve with practice and time. To help you start, here are some clues:

» Assume the McDuck's app activates when the customer presses a button in the app to check into a store.

» When the button is pressed, what are the two locations that the app must be aware of?

» When the app is aware of these two locations, what calculation involving these two locations must the computer make?

» After computing this calculation, what effect will the computer show?

Fill out your list now, and don't continue reading until you've completed it.

Finding your app's functionality: My version

The following is my version of the steps needed to make the app function according to McDuck's specifications. My steps may differ from yours, of course, and this variation is completely fine. The important lesson here is that you understand why each of these steps is necessary for the app to work.

1. **The customer presses a button on the app.**

 The preceding instructions said to initiate the app with the press of a button. That being said, there are two other options for launching the app:

- Executing the steps only when the customer opens the app
- Executing the steps continuously in the background, regularly checking the customer's location

WARNING

Currently, this technique places a heavy drain on the battery, and is not usually recommended.

2. **After the button is pressed, find the customer's current location.**

 The customer's location is one of the two locations you need to identify. The customer's current location is not fixed, and it changes, for example, when the customer is walking or driving.

3. **Find the fixed location of a McDuck's store.**

 The McDuck's restaurant location is the other location you need to identify. Because this is a pilot, you only need to identify the location for one McDuck's restaurant, a fixed location that will not change. Hypothetically, assuming that the pilot is successful and that McDuck's wants to implement this app for users visiting all 35,000 restaurants, you'd have to track many more restaurant locations. Additionally, in a larger rollout, the locations would need to be updated regularly, as new restaurants open and as existing restaurants move or close.

4. **Calculate the distance between the customer's current location and the McDuck's restaurant, and name this distance Customer Distance.**

 This step calculates how far away the customer is from the McDuck's restaurant. One complexity to be aware of — but not to worry about right now — is the direction in which the customer is moving. Although McDuck's did not specify whether it wants to display offers to customers heading both toward and away from their store, this may be a question worth asking anyway.

5. **Convert five to ten minutes of customer travel into a distance called Threshold Distance.**

 McDuck's CEO, Duck Corleone, wants to target customers who are five to ten minutes away from the store. Distance, in this sense, can be measured in both time and units of distance such as miles. For consistency, however, plan to convert time into distance — translate those five to ten minutes into miles. The number of miles traveled in this time will vary by common mode of transportation and by location, because five to ten minutes of travel in New York City won't get you as far as five to ten minutes of travel in Houston, Texas.

6. **If the Customer Distance is less than the Threshold Distance, then show an offer to the customer.**

 Following McDuck's specifications, the app should attract customers to come to the store, so the app only shows offers to customers who are close to the restaurant. Another complexity to be aware of — but not to worry about right now — is that the Customer Distance can change quickly. Customers traveling

CHAPTER 2 **Researching Your First Web Application** 327

by car could easily be outside the Threshold Distance one minute and inside it the next. Figure 2-1 shows the customers we want to target, relative to a fixed restaurant location.

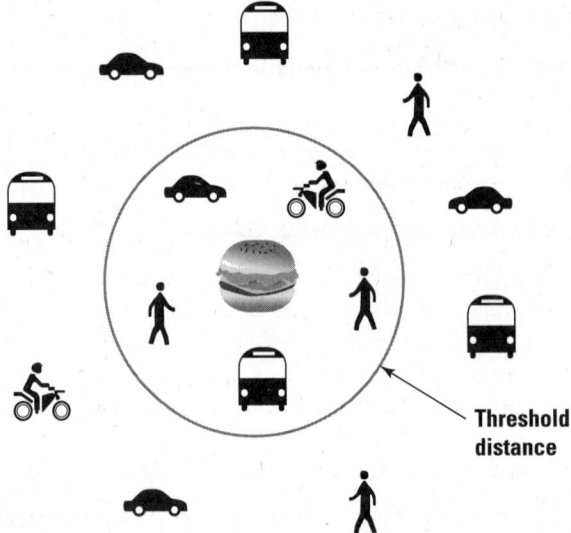

FIGURE 2-1: Customers we want to target based on a fixed restaurant location.

Many software logic mistakes happen at this stage, because the programmer forgets to include a step. Take your time reviewing these steps and understanding why each step is essential, and why this list of steps is the minimum necessary to operate the app.

Finding your app's form

After you settle on what the app will do, you must find the best way to present this functionality to users. Users can interact with your app's functionality many ways, so picking out the right approach can be tricky. Designing an app can be fun and rewarding, but it's hard work. After the first iteration of an app's design, developers are often disappointed: Users will rarely use the product as intended and will find many parts of the app confusing. This is natural — especially because at this stage you're often creating something or having the user do something that hasn't been done before. Your only choice is to keep trying and to keep testing, modifying, and creating new designs until your app is easy for everyone to use. Although the iPod is a hardware product, the approach Apple took to perfect it was basically the same. Figure 2-2 shows how the design can change over time, with the button layout changing from the original click-wheel to individual horizontal buttons, and finally back to the click-wheel again.

FIGURE 2-2: Apple's iPod design changes over multiple product releases.

(1st Gen)　　(2nd/3rd Gen)　　(4th Gen)

(4th Gen w/Color)　　(5th Gen, Video)　　(Classic)

The following list describes a basic design process to create the look and feel of your app:

1. **Define the main goals of your app.**

 If you were at a party, and you had to explain what your app did in one sentence, what would it be? Some apps help you hail a taxi, reserve a table at a restaurant, or book a flight. Famously, the goal for the iPod was 1,000 songs in your pocket accessible within three clicks, which helped create an easy-to-use user interface. An explicitly defined goal will serve as your north star, helping you to resolve questions and forcing you to keep trying.

2. **Break these goals into tasks.**

 Each goal is the sum of many tasks, and listing them will help you design the shortest path to completing each task and ultimately the goal. For instance, if your app's goal is for a user to book a flight, then the app will likely need to record desired flying times and destinations, search and select flights departing during those times, record personal and payment information, present seats for selection, and confirm payment of the flight. Sometimes designers will segment tasks by user persona, another name for the person completing the task. For example, this app may be used by business and leisure travelers. Leisure travelers may need to do heavy searching and pick flights based on price, while business travelers mostly rebook completed flights and pick flights based on schedule.

CHAPTER 2 **Researching Your First Web Application**　　329

3. **Research the flows and interactions necessary to accomplish these tasks.**

 For example, our flight app requires the user to select dates and times. One immediate question is whether the date and time should be two separate fields or one field, and on a different or same screen as the destination. Try to sketch what feels intuitive for you, and research how others have solved this problem. You can use Google to find other travel apps, list all the various designs, and either pick or improve upon the design you like best. Figure 2-3 shows two different approaches to flight search. Similarly, you can also use design-centric sites, such as www.dribbble.com, to search designer portfolios for features and commentary.

 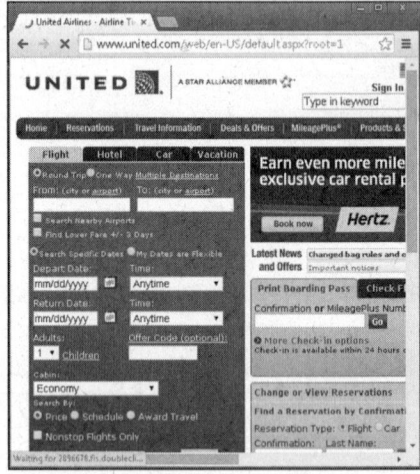

FIGURE 2-3: Different designs for flight reservation from Hipmunk.com and United Airlines.

4. **Create basic designs, called wireframes, and collect feedback.**

 Wireframes, as shown in Figure 2-4, are low-fidelity website drawings that show structurally how site content and interface interact. Wireframes are simple to create, but should have enough detail to elicit feedback from others. Many wireframe tools use a simple almost pencil-like drawing to help anyone providing comments to focus on the structural and bigger picture design, instead of smaller details like button colors or border thicknesses. Feedback at this stage to refine design is so important because the first wireframe likely doesn't address users' main concerns and overcomplicates the tasks a user needs to do.

TIP

 With mobile devices increasing in popularity relative to desktop devices, remember to create mobile and desktop versions of your wireframes.

330 BOOK 5 **Creating Web Applications**

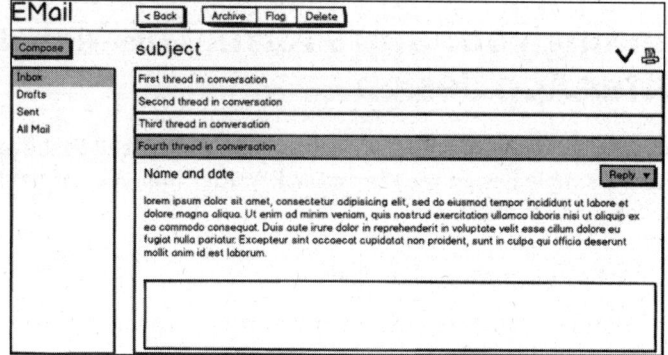

FIGURE 2-4:
A wireframe for an email client.

5. **Create mockups and collect more feedback. (See Figure 2-5.)**

 After you have finished talking to your client and to users, it is time to create mockups, which are high-fidelity website previews. These designs have all the details a developer needs to create the website, including final layout, colors, images, logos, and sequences of screens to show when the user interacts with the web page. After creating a mockup, plan to collect more feedback.

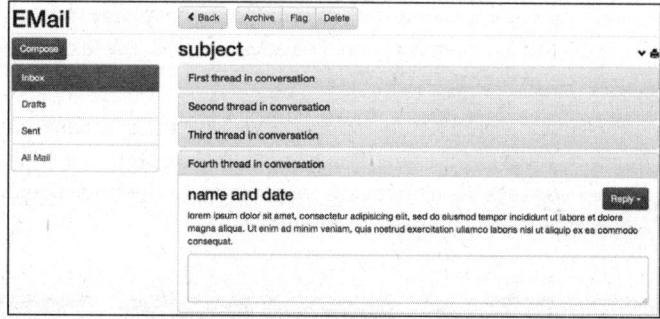

FIGURE 2-5:
A mockup for an email client.

TIP

Collecting feedback at every stage of the design process might seem unnecessary, but it is much easier to explore different designs and make changes before any code has been written.

6. **Send the final file to the developers.**

 After the mockup has been created and approved, you typically send a final image file to the developer. Although this file could be in any image file format, like PNG or JPG, the most popular file format used by designers is PSD, created using Adobe Photoshop.

CHAPTER 2 **Researching Your First Web Application** 331

Finding your app's form: The McDuck's Offer App design

In this section, you follow the design process described in the previous section to create a simple design for the McDuck's Offer App. As part of the design, you do the following things:

1. **Define the main goals of your app.**

 The main goal for McDuck's is to use offers to attract customers to restaurants.

2. **Break these goals into tasks.**

 Customers need to view the offer, navigate to the store, and use the offer.

3. **Research the flows and interactions needed to accomplish these tasks.**

 Because this is the first iteration of the app, let's focus on just allowing the customer to view the offer.

 One function that McDuck's did not specify is the ability to save single-use coupons and to share general-use coupons. However, when looking at other apps, like the ones in Figure 2-6, the need for this becomes more obvious. Also, some similar apps allow the customer to spend money to *buy* coupons — maybe this functionality should be added as well. These questions would be great to present to McDuck's later.

 The apps in Figure 2-6 also all display various "call to action" buttons to the user before displaying the deal. Some apps ask the user to check into a location, other apps ask the user to purchase the coupon, and still others show a collection of new or trending coupons today.

 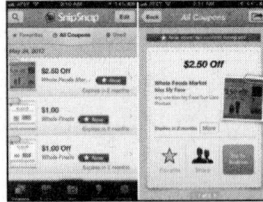

FIGURE 2-6: Example flow from deals and offer apps currently in the market.

For now, and to keep things simple, let's assume that our McDuck's app has a button that allows customers to check into their favorite McDuck's location, and when clicked within the target distance, the app displays a general-use coupon that customers receive for free.

4. **Create basic designs, called wireframes, and collect feedback.**

 A sample design for the app, based on the look and feel of other apps, appears in Figure 2-7.

FIGURE 2-7: A sample wireframe for the McDuck's offer app.

5. **Create mockups and collect more feedback.**

 Ordinarily, you would create *mockups*, which are more polished designs with real images, from the wireframes and present them to customers for feedback. In this case, however, the app is simple enough that you can just start coding.

Identifying Research Sources

Now that you know *what* your app will do, you can focus on *how* your app will do it. After breaking down your app into steps, you go over each step to determine how to accomplish it. For more complicated apps, developers first decide which of these two methods is the best way to complete each step:

» **Building code from scratch:** This is the best option if the functionality in a particular step is unique or strategically important, an area of strength for the app, and existing solutions are expensive or nonexistent. With this option, you and developers within the company write the code.

» **Buying or using a preexisting solution:** This is the best option if the functionality in a particular step is a common, noncore technical area for the app, and existing solutions are competitively priced. With this option, you and developers working on the app use code written by external third-party developers.

CHAPTER 2 **Researching Your First Web Application** 333

One company that recently made this decision — publicly and painfully — is Apple with its Maps product. In 2012, after years of using Google Maps on its mobile devices, Apple decided to introduce its own mapping application that it had been developing for two years. Although the Maps product Apple built internally turned out to initially be a failure, Apple decided to build its own mapping application because it viewed mapping capabilities as strategically important and because turn-by-turn navigation solutions were not available in the solution provided by Google.

Whether you're building or buying, research is your next step. Here are some sources to consider when researching:

TIP

» **Search engines:** Use Google.com or another search engine to type in what you're trying to accomplish with each step. One challenge can be discovering how the task you're trying to achieve is referred to by programmers. For instance, if I want to find my current location, I might enter *show my location in an app* into a search engine, but this results in a list of location-sharing apps. After reading a few of the top-ten results, I see that location-tracking is also referred to as *geolocation*. When I search again for geolocation, the top results include many examples of code that show my current location.

For more generic searches for code examples, try including the name of the computer language and the word *syntax*. For example, if you want to insert an image on a web page, search for *image html syntax* to find code examples.

» **Prior commercial and open-source apps:** Examining how others built their apps can give you ideas on how to improve upon what already exists, and insight into pushing existing technology to the limit to achieve an interesting effect. For instance, say you wanted to build a mobile app that recognized TV ads from the "audio fingerprint" of those ads and directed viewers to a product page on a mobile device. To create this app, you could build your own audio fingerprinting technology, which would likely take months or longer to build, or you could partner with Shazam, a commercial application, or Echoprint, an open-source music fingerprinting service. Either app can record a 10- to 20-second audio sample, create a digital fingerprint after overcoming background noise and poor microphone quality, compare the fingerprint to a large audio database, and then return identification information for the audio sample.

» **Industry news and blogs:** Traditional newspapers, like *The Wall Street Journal*, and tech blogs, like TechCrunch.com, report on the latest innovations in technology. Regularly reading or searching through these sites is a good way to find others who have launched apps in your space.

» **API directories:** You can easily search thousands of APIs for the functionality you need to implement. For example, if you were creating an app that used

face recognition instead of a password, you could search for *face detection APIs* and use an API you find instead of trying to build a face detection algorithm from scratch. Popular API directories include www.programmableweb.com and www.mashape.com.

TIP

As discussed in Book 4, Chapter 2, APIs are a way for you to request and receive data from other programs in a structured, predictable, documented way.

» **User-generated coding websites:** Developers in different companies frequently face the same questions on how to implement functionality for features. Communities of developers online talk about shared problems and contribute code so anyone can see how these problems have been solved in the past. You can participate in developer conversations and see the code other developers have written by using www.stackoverflow.com and www.github.com.

Researching the Steps in the McDuck's Offer App

To implement the functionality in the McDuck's Offer App, you broke down the app into six steps using plain English. Each step is an item in the bulleted list that follows, and you will research how to accomplish each step using code. Your app will require HTML to put content on the page, CSS to style that content, and JavaScript for the more interactive effects. Research the steps on your own before looking over the suggested code in the next section:

» **"The customer presses a button on the app."** This code creates a button that triggers every subsequent step. Creating a button on a web page is a very common task, so to narrow the results, search for *html button tag*. Review some of the links in the top-ten search results, and then write down the HTML tag syntax to create a button that says "McDuck's Check-in."

TIP

In your search results, sites like w3schools.com are designed for beginners, and will include example code and simple explanations.

» **"After the button is pressed, find the customer's current location."** In web lingo, finding a user's location is called *geolocation*. I will provide you with JavaScript geolocation code, along with an explanation for how it works and where I found it. To trigger this JavaScript code, you need to add an attribute to the HTML button tag to call a JavaScript function named getlocation().

TIP

As described in Book 3, Chapter 1, HTML attributes are inserted in the opening HTML tag.

CHAPTER 2 **Researching Your First Web Application** 335

Search for *html button javascript button on click* to find out how to insert the `onclick` attribute to your button HTML code. Review the search results, and then write down the HTML syntax for your button code.

» **"Find the fixed location of a McDuck's store."** You'll need a real-world address to serve as the McDuck's store. Use a mapping website like `http://maps.google.com` to find the street address of a burger restaurant near you. Computers typically represent physical addresses using latitude and longitude numbers instead of street addresses. You can search for websites that convert street addresses into latitude and longitude numbers, or if you're using Google Maps, you can find the numbers in the URL, as shown in Figure 2-8. The first number after the @ sign and up to the comma is the latitude, and the second number between the two commas is the longitude. Figure 2-8 shows a McDonald's store in New York City, where the latitude is 40.7410344 and the longitude is –73.9880763.

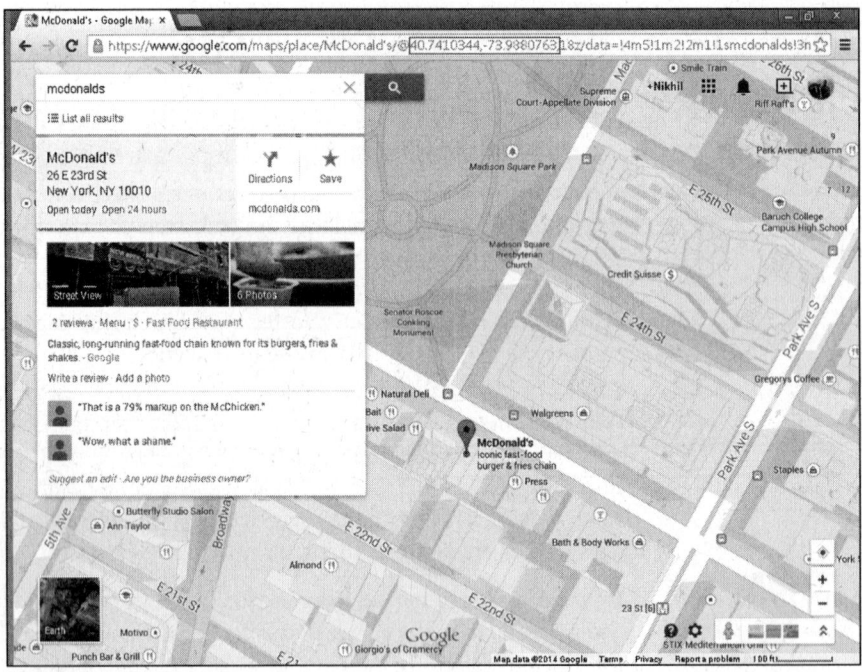

FIGURE 2-8: Latitude and longitude of a McDonald's in New York City.

Track down the latitude and longitude numbers for the burger restaurant of your choice, up to seven decimal places, and write them on a piece of paper.

Include a negative sign if you see one, and all seven decimal places for the greatest accuracy.

TIP

336　BOOK 5 **Creating Web Applications**

» **"Calculate the distance between the customer's current location and the McDuck's restaurant, and name this distance Customer Distance."** Latitude and longitude are coordinates that represent a location on a sphere. The distance along the surface of the sphere between two sets of latitude and longitude coordinates is calculated using the Haversine formula. You can find a JavaScript version of the formula at `http://stackoverflow.com/questions/27928/how-do-i-calculate-distance-between-two-latitude-longitude-points`. This is the formula you will use to calculate distance when creating the McDuck's app, and I will include this code for you.

TIP

Don't get bogged down in the details of how the Haversine formula works. Abstraction is an important concept to remember when programming, and this basically means that as long as you understand the inputs to a system and the outputs, you don't really need to understand the system itself, much as you don't need to understand the mechanics of the internal combustion engine in order to drive a car.

» **"Convert five to ten minutes of customer travel into a distance called Threshold Distance."** Using the most common method of transportation in your current city, write down the number of miles you could you travel, on average, in five to ten minutes.

» **"If the Customer Distance is less than the Threshold Distance, then show an offer to the customer."** The two pieces to research for this step are the conditional statement that decides when to show the offer to the consumer and the actual offer:

- *The conditional statement:* This is written in JavaScript using an `if-else` statement. If the customer is within the threshold distance, then it shows the offer; otherwise (else), it shows another message. To review the if-else syntax, search Google or another search engine for *JavaScript if-else statement syntax* (or refer to Book 4, Chapter 2 to review the coverage of the `if-else` statement syntax there).

- *The offer to show to the consumer:* The easiest way to show an offer is to use the JavaScript `alert()`. Search for *JavaScript alert syntax*.

After you've conducted your searches, write down your `if-else` statement with a text `alert()` for a free burger if the customer is within the Threshold Distance, and a text `alert()` notifying the customer he or she has checked in.

TIP

When you have the `if-else` statement working, you can replace the text `alert()` with an image. Search `https://images.google.com` for a burger coupon image. After you find the image, left-click it from the image grid in the search results, and left-click again the View Image button. When the image loads, the direct link to the image will be in the URL address bar in the browser. The code to insert the image is shown in Book 3, Chapter 1.

Choosing a Solution for Each Step

With your research finished, it's time to find the best solution. If multiple solutions exist for each step, you now need to choose one. To help you choose, weigh each of your multiple solutions across a variety of factors, such as these:

» **Functionality:** Will the code you write or the prebuilt solution you found do everything you need?

» **Documentation:** Is there documentation for the prebuilt solution, like instructions or a manual, that is well written with examples?

» **Community and support:** If something goes wrong while writing your code, is there a community you can turn to for help? Similarly, does the prebuilt solution have support options you can turn to if needed?

» **Ease of implementation:** Is implementation as simple as copying a few lines of code? Or is a more complex setup or an installation of other supporting software necessary?

» **Price:** Every solution has a price, whether it is the time spent coding your own solution or the money paid for someone else's prebuilt code. Think carefully about whether your time or your money is more important to you at this stage.

The following are suggested solutions for the previous McDuck's Offer App research questions. Your answers may vary, so review each answer to see where your code differs from mine:

» **"The customer presses a button on the app."** The HTML tag syntax to create a button that says "McDuck's Check-in" is

```
<button>McDuck's Check-in</button>
```

TIP

The syntax for an HTML button is available here www.w3schools.com/tags/tag_button.asp.

» **"After the button is pressed, find the customer's current location."** The HTML syntax for your button code is

```
<button onclick="getLocation()">McDuck's Check-in</button>
```

TIP

The syntax for calling a JavaScript function by pressing a button is available here: www.w3schools.com/jsref/event_onclick.asp.

» **"Find the fixed location of a McDuck's store."** I picked a McDonald's store in New York City near Madison Square Park whose latitude is 40.7410344 and longitude is -73.9880763. The latitude and longitude for your restaurant, of course, will likely differ.

» **"Calculate the distance between the customer's current location and the McDuck's restaurant, and name this distance Customer Distance."** The following is the actual code for the Haversine formula, used to calculate the distance between two location coordinates, found on Stackoverflow at http://stackoverflow.com/questions/27928/how-do-i-calculate-distance-between-two-latitude-longitude-points. I modified this code slightly so that it returned miles instead of kilometers:

```
function getDistanceFromLatLonInKm(lat1,lon1,lat2,lon2) {
  var R = 6371; // Radius of the earth in km
  var dLat = deg2rad(lat2-lat1);  // deg2rad below
  var dLon = deg2rad(lon2-lon1);
  var a =
    Math.sin(dLat/2) * Math.sin(dLat/2) +
    Math.cos(deg2rad(lat1)) * Math.cos(deg2rad(lat2)) *
    Math.sin(dLon/2) * Math.sin(dLon/2)
    ;
  var c = 2 * Math.atan2(Math.sqrt(a), Math.sqrt(1-a));
  var d = R * c * 0.621371; // Distance in miles
  return d;
}

function deg2rad(deg) {
  return deg * (Math.PI/180);
}
```

TIP

An explanation of how this formula works is outside the scope of this book, but make sure you understand the formula's inputs (latitude and longitude) and the output (distance between two points in miles).

» **"Convert five to ten minutes of customer travel into a distance called Threshold Distance."** In New York City, people usually walk, so traveling for five to ten minutes would take you 0.5 mile, which is my Threshold Distance.

» **"If the Customer Distance is less than the Threshold Distance, then display an offer to the customer."** The syntax for the if-else statement with the two text alert() methods is

```
If (distance < 0.5) {
    alert("You get a free burger");
}
else {
    alert("Thanks for checking in!");
}
```

TIP

The syntax for a JavaScript if-else statement is available at www.w3schools.com/js/js_if_else.asp.

IN THIS CHAPTER

» Reviewing code to see preexisting functionality

» Writing code by following steps to create your app

» Debugging your code by looking for common syntax errors

Chapter 3
Coding and Debugging Your First Web Application

"Talk is cheap. Show me the code."

— LINUS TORVALDS

It may not feel like it, but you've already done the majority of work toward creating your first web application. You painfully broke down your app into steps, and researched each step to determine functionality and design. As Linus Torvalds, creator of the Linux operator system, said, "Talk is cheap." So let's start actually coding.

Getting Ready to Code

Before you start coding, do a few housekeeping items. First, ensure that you are doing all of the following:

» **Using the Chrome browser:** Download and install the latest version of Chrome, as it offers the most support for the latest HTML standards and is available for download at www.google.com/chrome/browser.

» **Working on a desktop or laptop computer:** Although it is possible to code on a mobile device, it can be more difficult and all layouts may not appear properly.

» **Remembering to indent your code to make it easier to read:** One main source of mistakes is forgetting to close a tag or curly brace, and indenting your code will make spotting these errors easier.

» **Remembering to enable location services on your browser and computer:** To enable location services within Chrome, click on the settings icon (three horizontal lines on the top right of the browser), and click on Settings. Then click on the Settings tab, and at the bottom of the screen click on "Show Advanced settings . . ." Under the Privacy menu heading, click on "Content settings . . ." and scroll down to Location and make sure that "Ask when a site tries to track your physical location" is selected. You can read more here: support.google.com/chrome/answer/142065.

To enable location services on a PC no additional setting is necessary, but on a Mac using OS X Mountain Lion or later, from the Apple menu choose System Preferences, then click on the Security & Privacy icon, and click the Privacy tab. Click the padlock icon on the lower left, and select Location Services, and check Enable Location Services. You can read more here: support.apple.com/en-us/ht5403.

Finally, you need to set up your development environment. To emulate a development environment without instructional content use Codepen.io. Codepen.io offers a free stand-alone development environment, and makes it easy to share your code. Open this URL in in your browser: codepen.io/nabraham/pen/ExnsA.

Coding Your First Web Application

With the Codepen.io URL loaded, let us review the development environment, the prewritten code, and the coding steps for you to follow.

Development environment

The Codepen.io development environment, as shown in Figure 3-1, has three coding panels, one each for HTML, CSS, and JavaScript. There is also a preview pane to see the live results of your code. Using the button at the bottom of the screen, you can hide any coding panel you aren't using, and the layout of the coding panels can be changed.

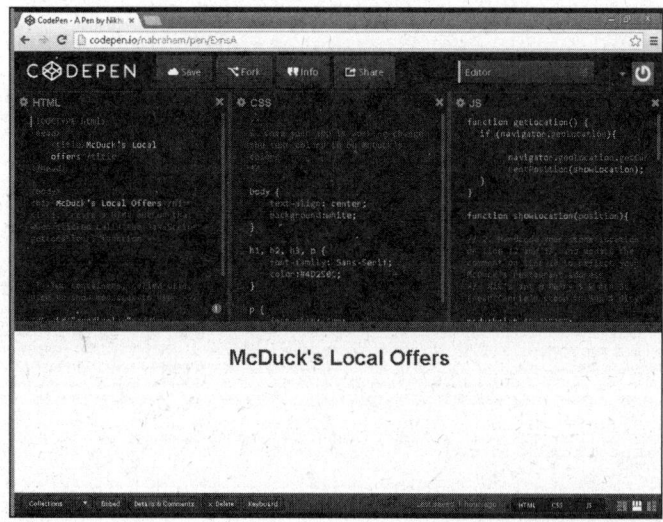

FIGURE 3-1: The Codepen.io development environment.

Signing up for a Codepen.io account is completely optional, and allows you to *fork* or save the code you have written, and share it with others.

Prewritten code

The Codepen.io development environment includes some prewritten HTML, CSS, and JavaScript code for the McDuck's app. The prewritten code includes code you have seen in previous chapters, and new code that is explained in the following sections.

HTML

The HTML code for the McDuck's app follows, and includes

» Two sections:
- An opening and closing `<head>` tag
- An opening and closing `<body>` tag

CHAPTER 3 **Coding and Debugging Your First Web Application** 343

- » Inside the `<body>` tags are `<h1>` tags to create a heading and `<div>` tags.
- » Additional `<div>` tags to display messages created in the JavaScript file. The `<div>` tag is a container that can hold content of any type:
 - The first `<div>` tag is used to display your current longitude and latitude.
 - The second `<div>` tag can be used to display additional content to the user.
- » Instructions to insert the HTML button and `onclick` attribute code, which you researched in Book 5, Chapter 2.

Here's the HTML code:

```
<!DOCTYPE html>
<html>
<head>
  <title>McDuck's App</title>
</head>
<body>
  <h1> McDuck's Local Offers</h1>
<!--1. Create a HTML button that when clicked calls the JavaScript
getLocation() function -->

<!--Two containers, called divs, used to show messages to user -->

  <div id="geodisplay"></div>
  <div id="effect"></div>
</body>
</html>
```

CSS

The CSS code for the McDuck's app follows, and includes:

- » Selectors for the body, heading, and paragraph tags
- » Properties and values that set the text alignment, background color, font family, font color, and font size

Once your app is functioning, style the app by adding a McDuck's color scheme and background image logo.

Here's the CSS:

```
body {
    text-align: center;
    background: white;
}

h1, h2, h3, p {
    font-family: Sans-Serif;
    color: black;
}

p {
    font-size: 1em;
}
```

JavaScript

The JavaScript code for the McDuck's app follows. This prewritten code is a little complex, because it calculates the current location of the user using the HTML Geolocation API. In this section, I review the code at a high level so you can understand how it works and where it came from.

The Geolocation API is the product of billions of dollars of research and is available to you for free. The most recent browsers support geolocation, though some older browsers do not. At a basic level, code is written to ask whether the browser supports the Geolocation API, and, if yes, to return the current location of the user. When called, the Geolocation API balances a number of data inputs to determine the user's current location. These data inputs include GPS, wireless network connection strength, cell tower and signal strength, and IP address.

With this in mind, let's look at the JavaScript code. The JavaScript code includes two functions, as follows:

» *The* getLocation() *function:* This function determines whether the browser supports geolocation. It does this by using an if statement and navigator.geolocation, which is recognized by the browser as part of the Geolocation API and which returns a true value if geolocation is supported.

Here is the getLocation() function:

```
function getLocation() {
    if (navigator.geolocation){
        navigator.geolocation.getCurrentPosition(showLocation);
    }
}
```

» *The* `showLocation()` *function:* When the browser supports geolocation, the next step is to call the `showlocation` function, which calculates and displays the user's location.

And here is the `showLocation()` function:

```
function showLocation(position){
// 2. Hardcode your store location on line 12 and 13, and update the comment to
// reflect your McDuck's restaurant address
//   Nik's apt @ Perry & W 4th St (change to your restaurant location)

var mcduckslat=40.735383;
var mcduckslon=-74.002994;

// current location
var currentpositionlat=position.coords.latitude;
var currentpositionlon=position.coords.longitude;

// calculate the distance between current location and McDuck's location
var distance=getDistanceFromLatLonInMiles(mcduckslat, mcduckslon,currentpositionlat,
    currentpositionlon);

// Displays the location using .innerHTML property and the lat & long coordinates
// for your current location
document.getElementById("geodisplay").innerHTML="Latitude: " + currentpositionlat +
    "<br>Longitude: " + currentpositionlon;
}

// haversine distance formula
The rest omitted for brevity because it's shown in Book 5, Chapter 2.
```

The `showLocation()` function performs the following tasks:

» Assigns the McDuck longitude and latitude to `mduckslat` and `mcduckslon` (Lines 12 and 13 of the code).

» Assigns the longitude and latitude of the customer's current location to `currentpositionlat` and `currentpositionlon` (Lines 16 and 17 of the code).

» Calculates the distance in miles between those two points and assigns that distance to a variable called `distance` (Line 20 of the code).

The Haversine formula calculates the distance between two points on a sphere, in this case the earth, and the code is shown online but omitted here for brevity.

» After the button is clicked, the `getElementByID` and `.innerHTML` methods display the customer's current longitude and latitude in an HTML tag named "geodisplay" using the `id` attribute.

REMEMBER

JavaScript functions are case-sensitive, so `getLocation()` differs from `get location()`. The letter L is uppercase in the first function, and lowercase in the second function. Similarly, `showLocation()` differs from `showlocation()` for the same reason.

Coding steps for you to follow

With some of the code already written, and with research in the previous chapter, follow these steps to insert the code:

1. **Insert the HTML `button` code below with `onclick` attribute calling the `getLocation()` function after line 8 in the HTML file.**

   ```
   <button onclick="getLocation()">McDuck's Check-in</button>
   ```

 After you insert this code, press the button. If your location settings are enabled and you inserted the code properly, you will see a dialog box asking for your permission to share your computer's location. As shown in Figure 3-2, look at the top of your browser window and click Allow.

2. **Update lines 12 and 13 in the JavaScript file with the latitude and longitude of the restaurant near you serving as the McDuck's store.**

 After you have updated the location, make sure to change the comment in line 10 to reflect the address of your restaurant (instead of my apartment).

3. **Add an alert that displays the distance between your location and the restaurant.**

 The `distance` variable stores the miles from your current location to the restaurant. Make a rough estimate — or use a map for greater precision — of your current distance from the restaurant you picked. Then using an alert, show the distance by inserting this code below in line 23.

   ```
   alert(distance);
   ```

 If the distance in the alert is larger or smaller than you expected, you likely entered in incorrect values for the latitude or longitude. If the distance matches your estimate, insert two slashes ("//") before the alert and comment it out.

CHAPTER 3 **Coding and Debugging Your First Web Application** 347

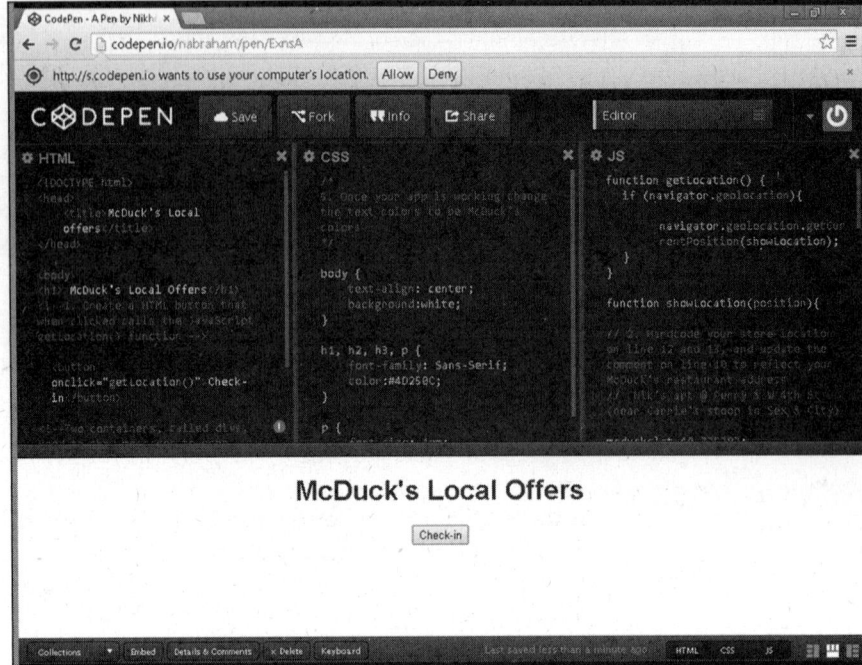

FIGURE 3-2:
The browser asks for your permission before sharing your location.

4. **Write an if-else statement on line 26 to show an alert if you are within your threshold distance to the restaurant.**

 My code, based on a half-mile threshold distance, is displayed below — yours may vary depending on your alert text and threshold distance. (See Figure 3-3.)

   ```
   if (distance < 0.5) {
       alert("You get a free burger");
   }
   else {
       alert("Thanks for checking in!");
   }
   ```

TIP

When your app logic is working, you can change `alert("You get a free burger");` to an actual picture of a coupon or burger. To do so, replace the entire line the alert is on with the following code:

   ```
   document.getElementById("effect").innerHTML="&lt;img src'http://www.image.com/image.jpg'>";
   ```

Replace the URL after `src` and within the single quotes to your own image URL. Be sure to keep the double quotation marks after the first equal sign and before the semicolon, and the single quotation marks after the second equal sign and before the right angle bracket.

348 BOOK 5 **Creating Web Applications**

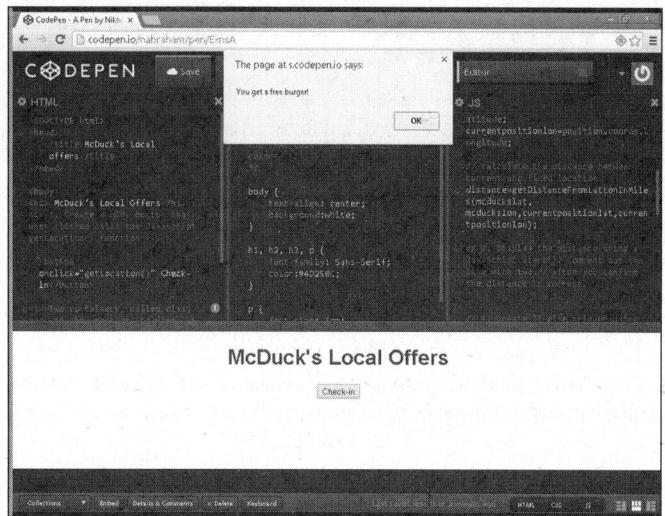

FIGURE 3-3:
The McDuck's app displaying an offer to come to the store.

5. **(Optional) When the app is working, change the text colors and insert background images to make the app look more professional.**

 Use hex-values or color names, as discussed in Book 3, Chapter 3, to change the text and background colors. Additionally, you can insert a background image, as you did in the Codecademy About You exercise, using the following code (see Figure 3-4):

   ```
   background-image: url("http://www.image.com/image.jpg");
   ```

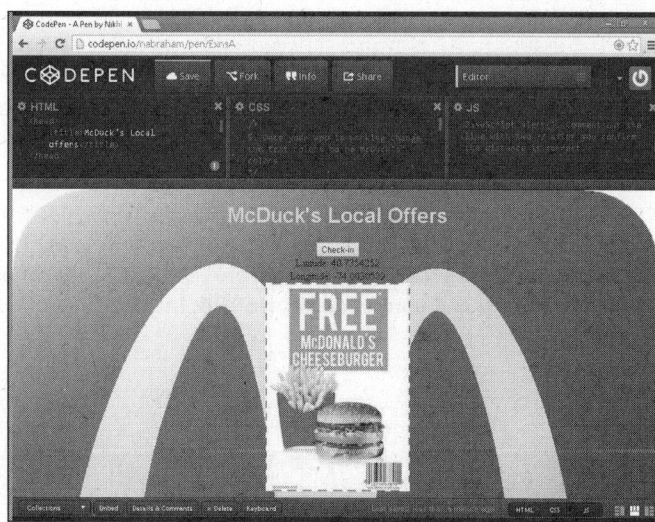

FIGURE 3-4:
The completed McDuck's app with styled content displaying an image to the user.

CHAPTER 3 **Coding and Debugging Your First Web Application** 349

Debugging Your App

When coding your app, you will almost inevitably write code that does not behave as you intended. HTML and CSS are relatively forgiving, with the browser even going so far as to insert tags so the page renders properly. However, JavaScript isn't so forgiving, and the smallest error, such as a missing quotation mark, can cause the page to not render properly.

Errors in web applications can consist of syntax errors, logic errors, and display errors. Given that we worked through the logic together, the most likely culprit causing errors in your code will be syntax related. Here are some common errors to check when debugging your code:

» **Opening and closing tags:** In HTML, every opening tag has a closing tag, and you always close the most recently opened tag first.

» **Right and left angle brackets:** In HTML, every left angle bracket ‹ has a right angle bracket ›.

» **Right and left curly brackets:** In CSS and JavaScript, every left curly bracket must have a right curly bracket. It can be easy to accidentally delete it or forget to include it.

» **Indentation:** Indent your code and use plenty of tabs and returns to make your code as readable as possible. Proper indentation will make it easier for you to identify missing tags, angle brackets, and curly brackets.

» **Misspelled statements:** Tags in any language can be misspelled, or spelled correctly but not part of the specification. For example, in HTML, `` is incorrect because `scr` should really be `src` for the image to render properly. Similarly, in CSS `font-color` looks like it is spelled correctly but no such property exists. The correct property to set font color is just `color`.

Keep these errors in mind when debugging — they may not solve all your problems, but they should solve many of them. If you have tried the steps above and still cannot debug your code, tweet me at @nikhilgabraham and include the #codingFD hashtag and your `codepen.io` URL in your tweet.

6 Selecting Data Analysis Tools

Contents at a Glance

CHAPTER 1: Wrapping Your Head around Python 353
 What Does Python Do?.................................. 354
 Defining Python Structure 355
 Coding Common Python Tasks and Commands 357
 Shaping Your Strings................................... 363
 Building a Simple Tip Calculator Using Python 365

CHAPTER 2: Installing a Python Distribution 367
 Choosing a Python Distribution with
 Machine Learning in Mind 368
 Installing Python on Linux 371
 Installing Python on Mac OS X........................... 372
 Installing Python on Windows........................... 374
 Downloading the Data Sets and Example Code 378

CHAPTER 3: Working with Real Data 387
 Uploading, Streaming, and Sampling Data 388
 Accessing Data in Structured Flat-File Form 392
 Sending Data in Unstructured File Form 397
 Managing Data from Relational Databases.................. 400
 Interacting with Data from NoSQL Databases 401
 Accessing Data from the Web 402

IN THIS CHAPTER

» Understanding Python principles and style

» Practicing Python code, such as assigning variables and using `if` statements

» Producing a simple Python project

Chapter 1
Wrapping Your Head around Python

> "I chose Python as a working title for the project, being in a slightly irreverent mood and a big fan of Monty Python's Flying Circus."
>
> — GUIDO VAN ROSSUM

Python is a server-side language created by Guido van Rossum, a developer who was bored during the winter of 1989 and looking for a project to do. At the time, van Rossum had already helped create one language, called ABC, and the experience had given him many ideas that he thought would appeal to programmers. He executed these ideas when he created Python. Although ABC never achieved popularity with programmers, Python was a runaway success. Python is one of the world's most popular programming languages, used by beginners just starting out and professionals building heavy-duty applications.

In this chapter, you deal with Python basics, including the design philosophy behind Python, how to write Python code to perform basic tasks, and steps to create your first Python program.

What Does Python Do?

Python is a general-purpose programming language typically used for web development. Python allows for storing data after the user has navigated away from the page or closed the browser, unlike HTML, CSS, and JavaScript. Using Python commands, you can create, update, store, and retrieve this data in a database. For example, imagine I wanted to create a local search and ratings site like Yelp.com. The reviews users write are stored in a central database. Review authors can exit the browser, turn off the computer, and come back to the website later to find their reviews. Additionally, when others search for venues, this same central database is queried, and the same reviews are displayed. Storing data in a database is a common task for Python developers, and existing Python libraries include prebuilt code that makes it easy to create and query databases.

SQLite is one free, lightweight database commonly used by Python programmers to store data.

Many highly trafficked websites, such as YouTube, are created with Python. Other websites currently using Python include

- » Quora for its community question and answer site
- » Spotify for internal data analysis
- » Dropbox for its desktop client software
- » Reddit for generating crowd-sourced news
- » Industrial Light & Magic and Disney Animation for creating film special effects

From websites to software to special effects, Python is an extremely versatile language, powerful enough to support a range of applications. In addition, to help spread Python code, Python programmers create libraries, which are stand-alone prewritten sets of code that do certain tasks, and make them publicly available for others to use and improve. For example, a library called Scrapy performs web scraping, while another library called SciPy performs math functions used by scientists and mathematicians. The Python community maintains thousands of libraries like these, and most are free and open-source software.

You can generally confirm the front-end programming language used by any major website with BuiltWith available at www.builtwith.com. After entering the website address in the search bar, look under the Frameworks section for Python. Note that websites may use Python for back-end services not visible to BuiltWith.

Defining Python Structure

Python has its own set of design principles that guide how the rest of the language is structured. To implement these principles, every language has its own conventions, such as curly braces in JavaScript or opening and closing tags in HTML. Python is no different, and I cover both design principles and conventions so you can understand what Python code looks like, understand Python's style, and know the special keywords and syntax that allow the computer to recognize what you're trying to do. Python, like JavaScript, can be very particular about syntax, and misspelling a keyword or forgetting a necessary character will result in the program not running.

Understanding the Zen of Python

Nineteen design principles describe how the Python language is organized. Some of the most important principles include

» **Readability counts.** This is possibly Python's most important design principle. Python code looks almost like English, and even enforces certain formatting, such as indenting, to make the code easier to read. Highly readable code means that six months from now when you revisit your code to fix a bug or add a feature, you will be able to jump in without trying too hard to remember what you did. Readable code also means others can use your code or help debug your code with ease.

TECHNICAL STUFF

Reddit.com is among the top 10 most visited websites in the United States and the top 50 most visited websites in the world. Its cofounder, Steve Huffman, initially coded the website in Lisp and switched to Python because Python is "extremely readable, and extremely writeable."

» **There should be one — and preferably *only* one — obvious way to do it.** This principle is directly opposite to Perl's motto, "There's more than one way to do it." In Python, two different programmers may approach the same problem and write two different programs, but the ideal is that the code will be similar and easy to read, adopt, and understand. Although Python does allow multiple ways to do a task — as, for example, when combining two strings — if an obvious and common option exists, it should be used.

» **If the implementation is hard to explain, it's a bad idea.** Historically, programmers were known to write esoteric code to increase performance. However, Python was designed not to be the fastest language, and this principle reminds programmers that easy-to-understand implementations are preferable over faster but harder-to-explain ones.

CHAPTER 1 **Wrapping Your Head around Python** 355

TIP

Access the full list by design principles, which is in the form of a poem, by typing **import this;** into any Python interpreter, or by visiting www.python.org/dev/peps/pep-0020. These principles, written by Tim Peters, a Python community member, were meant to describe the intentions of Python's creator, van Rossum, who is also referred to as the Benevolent Dictator for Life (BDFL).

Styling and spacing

Python generally uses less punctuation than other programming languages you may have previously tried. Some sample code is included here:

```
first_name=raw_input("What's your first name?")
first_name=first_name.upper()

if first_name=="NIK":
    print "You may enter!"
else:
    print "Nothing to see here."
```

TECHNICAL STUFF

The examples in this book are written for Python 2.7. Two popular versions of Python are currently in use — Python 2.7 and Python 3. Python 3 is the latest version of the language, but it isn't backward-compatible, so code written using Python 2.7 syntax doesn't work when using a Python 3 interpreter. Initially, Python 2.7 had more external libraries and support than Python 3, but this is changing. For more about the differences between versions see https://wiki.python.org/moin/Python2orPython3.

If you were to run this code, it would do the following:

- » Print a line asking for your first name.
- » Take user input (raw_input(What's your first name?)) and save it to the first_name variable.
- » Transform any input text into uppercase.
- » Test the user input. If it equals "NIK," then the code will print "You may enter!" Otherwise it will print "Nothing to see here."

Each of these statement types is covered in more detail later in this chapter. For now, as you look at the code, notice some of its styling characteristics:

- » **Uses less punctuation.** Unlike JavaScript, Python has no curly braces, and unlike HTML, no angle brackets.

» **Whitespace matters.** Statements indented to the same level are grouped together. In the preceding example, notice how the `if` and `else` align, and the `print` statements underneath each are indented the same amount. You can decide on the amount of indentation and whether to use tabs or spaces as long as you're consistent. Generally, four spaces from the left margin is considered the style norm.

See Python style suggestions on indentation, whitespace, and commenting by visiting `https://www.python.org/dev/peps/pep-0008`.

» **Newlines indicate the end of statements.** Although you can use semicolons to put more than one statement on a line, the preferred and more common method is to put each statement on its own line.

» **Colons separate code blocks.** New Python programmers sometimes ask why using colons to indicate code blocks, like the one at the end of the `if` statement, is necessary when newlines would suffice. Early user testing with and without the colons showed that beginner programmers better understood the code with the colon.

Coding Common Python Tasks and Commands

Python, as with other programming languages, can do everything from simple text manipulation to designing complex graphics in games. The following basic tasks are explained within a Python context, but they're foundational to understanding any programming language. Even experienced developers learning a new language, like Apple's recently released Swift programming language, start by learning these foundational tasks.

Start using some basic Python now, or practice these skills right away by jumping ahead to the "Building a Simple Tip Calculator Using Python" section, later in this chapter.

Millions of people have used Python, so it's easy to find answers to questions that might arise while learning simply by conducting an Internet search. The odds are in your favor that someone has asked your question before.

Defining data types and variables

Variables, like the ones in algebra, are keywords used to store data values for later use. Though the data stored in a variable may change, the variable name will

CHAPTER 1 **Wrapping Your Head around Python** 357

always be the same. Think of a variable as a gym locker — what you store in the locker changes, but the locker number always stays the same.

Variables in Python are named using alphanumeric characters and the underscore (_) character, and they must start with a letter or an underscore. Table 1-1 lists some of the data types that Python can store.

TABLE 1-1 **Data Stored by a Variable**

Data Type	Description	Example
Numbers	Positive or negative numbers with or without decimals	156
		-101.96
Strings	Printable characters	Holly Novak
		Señor
Boolean	Value can either be true or false	true
		false

To initially set or change a variable's value, write the variable name, a single equal sign, and the variable value, as shown in the following example:

```
myName = "Nik"
pizzaCost = 10
totalCost = pizzaCost * 2
```

TIP

Avoid starting your variable names with the number one (1), a lowercase "L" (l), or uppercase i (I). Depending on the font used, these characters can all look the same, causing confusion for you or others later!

Variable names are case-sensitive, so when referring to a variable in your program, remember that `MyName` is a different variable than `myname`. In general, give your variable a name that describes the data being stored.

Computing simple and advanced math

After you create variables, you may want to do some math on the numerical values stored in those variables. Simple math like addition, subtraction, multiplication, and division is done using operators you already know. Exponentiation (for example, 2 to the power of 3) is done differently in Python than in JavaScript and uses two asterisks. Examples are shown here:

```
num1 = 1+1  #equals 2
num2 = 5-1  #equals 4
num3 = 3*4  #equals 12
num4 = 9/3  #equals 3
num5 = 2**3 #equals 8
```

The # symbol indicates a comment in Python.

Don't just read these commands, try them! Go to http://repl.it/languages/Python for a lightweight in-browser Python interpreter that you can use right in your browser without downloading or installing any software.

Advanced math like absolute value, rounding to the nearest decimal, rounding up, or rounding down can be performed by using math functions. Python has some functions that are built-in prewritten code that can be referenced to make performing certain tasks easier. The general syntax to use Python math functions is to list the function name, followed by the variable name or value as an argument, as follows:

```
method(value)
method(variable)
```

The math functions for absolute value and rounding follow the preceding syntax, but some math functions, like rounding up or rounding down, are stored in a separate math module. To use these math functions you must

» Write the statement import math just once in your code before using the math functions in the math module.

» Reference the math module, as follows: math.method(value) or math.method(variable).

See these math functions with examples in Table 1-2.

TABLE 1-2 Common Python Math Functions

Function Name	Description	Example	Result
abs(n)	Return the absolute value of a number (n).	abs(-99)	99
round (n, d)	Round a number (n) to a number of decimal points (d).	round (3.1415, 2)	3.14
math.floor(n)	Round down to the nearest integer.	math.floor(4.7)	4.0
math.ceil(n)	Round up to the nearest integer.	math.ceil(7.3)	8.0

CHAPTER 1 **Wrapping Your Head around Python**

TECHNICAL STUFF

Modules are separate files that contain Python code, and the module must be referenced or imported before any code from the module can be used.

See all the function in the math module by visiting https://docs.python.org/2/library/math.html.

TIP

Using strings and special characters

Along with numbers, variables in Python can also store strings. To assign a value to a string, you can use single or double quotation marks, as follows:

```
firstname = "Travis"
lastname = 'Kalanick'
```

REMEMBER

Variables can also store numbers as strings instead of numbers. However, even though the string looks like a number, Python will not be able to add, subtract, or divide strings and numbers. For example, consider amountdue = "18" + 24 — running this code as is would result in an error. Python does multiply strings but in an interesting way — print 'Ha' * 3 results in 'HaHaHa'.

Including a single or double quote in your string can be problematic because the quotes inside your string will terminate the string definition prematurely. For example, if I want to store a string with the value 'I'm on my way home' Python will assume the ' after the first letter I is the end of the variable assignment, and the remaining characters will cause an error. The solution is to use special characters called escape sequences to indicate when you want to use characters like quotation marks, which normally signal the beginning or end of a string, or other nonprintable characters like tabs. Table 1-3 shows some examples of escape sequences.

TABLE 1-3 **Common Python Escape Sequences**

Special Character	Description	Example	Result
\' or \"	Quotation marks	print "You had me at \"Hello\""	You had me at "Hello"
\t	Tab	print "Item\tUnits \tPrice"	Item Units Price
\n	Newline	print "Anheuser?\nBusch?\nBueller? Bueller?"	Anheuser? Busch? Bueller? Bueller?

360 BOOK 6 **Selecting Data Analysis Tools**

Escape sequences are interpreted only for strings with double quotation marks. For a full list of escape sequences, see the table under Section 2.4 "Literals" at http://docs.python.org/2/reference/lexical_analysis.html.

Deciding with conditionals: if, elif, else

With data stored in a variable, one common task is to compare the variable's value to a fixed value or another variable's value, and then make a decision based on the comparison. If you previously read the chapters on JavaScript, the discussion and concepts here are very similar. The general syntax for an if-elif-else statement is as follows:

```
if conditional1:
    statement1 to execute if conditional1 is true
elif conditional2:
    statement2 to execute if conditional2 is true
else:
    statement3 to run if all previous conditional are false
```

Notice there are no curly brackets or semicolons, but don't forget the colons and to indent your statements!

The initial if statement will evaluate to true or false. When conditional1 is true, then statement1 is executed. This is the minimum necessary syntax needed for an if-statement, and the elif and else are optional. When present, the elif tests for an additional condition when conditional1 is false. You can test for as many conditions as you like using elif. Specifying every condition to test for can become tedious, so having a "catchall" is useful. When present, the else serves as the "catchall" and executes when all previous conditionals are false.

You cannot have an elif or an else by itself, without a preceding if statement. You can include many elif statements, but one and only one else statement.

The conditional in an if statement compares values using comparison operators, and common comparison operators are described in Table 1-4.

Here is an example if statement:

```
carSpeed=55
if carSpeed > 55:
    print "You are over the speed limit!"
elif carSpeed == 55:
    print "You are at the speed limit!"
else:
    print "You are under the speed limit!"
```

TABLE 1-4 Common Python Comparison Operators

Type	Operator	Description	Example
Less than	<	Evaluates whether one value is less than another value.	x < 55
Greater than	>	Evaluates whether one value is greater than another value.	x > 55
Equality	==	Evaluates whether two values are equal.	x == 55
Less than or equal to	<=	Evaluates whether one value is less than or equal to another value.	x <= 55
Greater than or equal to	>=	Evaluates whether one value is greater than or equal to another value.	x >= 55
Inequality	!=	Evaluates whether two values are not equal.	x != 55

As the diagram in Figure 1-1 shows, there are two conditions, each signaled by the diamond, which are evaluated in sequence. In this example, carSpeed is equal to 55, so the first condition (carSpeed > 55) is false, the second conditional (carSpeed==55) is true, and the statement executes printing "You are at the speed limit!" When a conditional is true, the if statement stops executing, and the else is never reached.

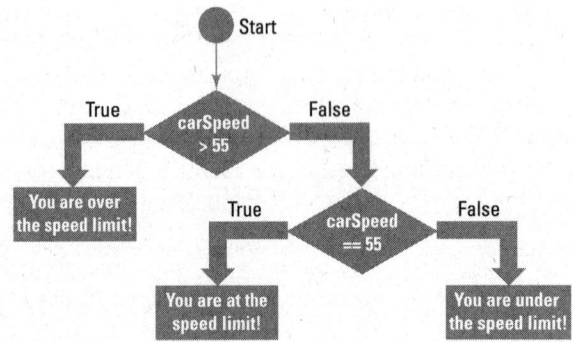

FIGURE 1-1: An if–else statement with an elif.

Input and output

Python can collect input from the user and display output to the user. To collect user input use the raw_input("Prompt") method, which stores the user input as a string. In the following example, the user enters his full name, which is stored in a variable called full_name.

```
full_name = raw_input("What's your full name?")
```

Imagine that the user entered his name as "Jeff Bezos." You can display the value of the variable using `print full_name`, in which case, you will see this:

```
Jeff Bezos
```

Python does not store the newline \n escape sequence after user input.

At this point, you may feel like printing variables and values in a Python interpreter console window is very different from dynamically creating web pages with variables created in Python. Integrating Python into a web page to respond to user requests and generate HTML pages is typically done with a Python web framework, like Django or Flask, which have prewritten code to make the process easier. These frameworks typically require some installation and setup work, and generally separate the data being displayed from templates used to display the page to the user.

Shaping Your Strings

Whenever you collect input from users, you need to clean the input to remove errors and inconsistencies. Here are some common data cleaning tasks:

» Standardizing strings to have consistent uppercase and lowercase

» Removing whitespace from user input

» Inserting a variable's value in strings displayed to the user

Python includes many built-in methods that make processing strings easy.

Dot notation with upper(), lower(), capitalize(), and strip()

Standardizing user input to have proper case and to remove extra whitespace characters is often necessary to easily sort the data later. For example, imagine you are designing a website for the New York Knicks so fans can meet players after the game. The page asks fans to enter their names so that team security can later check fan names against this list before entry. Reviewing past fan entries, you see that fans enter the same name several ways like "Mark," "mark," "marK," and other similar variants that cause issues when the list is sorted alphabetically. To make the input and these names consistent, you could use the string functions described in Table 1-5.

TABLE 1-5 Select Python String Functions

Function Name	Description	Example	Result
string.upper()	Returns all uppercase characters.	"nY".upper()	"NY"
string.lower()	Returns all lowercase characters.	"Hi".lower()	"hi"
string.capitalize()	Capitalizes first letter, lowercases remaining letters.	"wake UP".capitalize()	"Wake up"
string.strip()	Removes leading and trailing whitespaces.	" Ny ".strip()	"Ny"

String formatting with %

To insert variable values into strings shown to the user, you can use the string format operator %. Inserted into the string definition, %d is used to specify integers, %s is used to specify strings, and the variables to format (mapping key) are specified in parenthesis after the string is defined. Here is the example code and result:

Code:

```
yearofbirth = 1990
pplinroom = 20
name = "Mary"
print "Your year of birth is %d. Is this correct?" % (yearofbirth)
print 'Your year of birth is %d. Is this correct?' % (yearofbirth)
print "There are %d women in the room born in %d and %s is one of them."
% (pplinroom/2,
yearofbirth, name)
```

Result:

```
Your year of birth is 1990. Is this correct?
Your year of birth is 1990. Is this correct?
There are 10 women in the room born in 1990 and Mary is one of them.
```

The first string used double quotes, and the variable was inserted into the string and displayed to the user. The second string behaved just like the first string, because defining strings with single quotes does not affect the string formatting. The third string shows that code can be evaluated (pplinroom / 2) and inserted into the string.

The string.format() method is another way to format strings in Python.

Building a Simple Tip Calculator Using Python

Practice your Python online using the Codecademy website. Codecademy is a free website created in 2011 to allow anyone to learn how to code right in the browser, without installing or downloading any software. Practice all the tags (and a few more) that you found in this chapter by following these steps:

1. **Open your browser, go to** www.dummies.com/go/codingaiolinks, **and click the link to Codecademy.**

2. **If you have a Codecademy account, sign in.**

 Signing up is discussed in Book 1, Chapter 3. Creating an account allows you to save your progress as you work, but it's optional.

3. **Navigate to and click Python Syntax to practice some basic Python commands.**

 Background information is presented in the upper-left portion of the site, and instructions are presented in the lower-left portion of the site.

4. **Complete the instructions in the main coding window.**

5. **After you have finished completing the instructions, click the Save and Submit Code button.**

 If you have followed the instructions correctly, a green checkmark appears, and you proceed to the next exercise. If an error exists in your code, a warning appears with a suggested fix. If you run into a problem, or have a bug you cannot fix, click the hint, use the Q&A Forum, or tweet me at @nikhilgabraham and include the hashtag #codingFD. Additionally, you can sign up for book updates and explanations for changes to programming language commands by visiting http://tinyletter.com/codingfordummies.

IN THIS CHAPTER

» Determining which Python distribution to use for machine learning

» Performing a Linux, Mac OS X, and Windows installation

» Obtaining the data sets and example code

Chapter 2
Installing a Python Distribution

"For many people my software is something you install and forget. I like to keep it that way."

— WIETSE VENEMA

Before you can do too much with Python or use it to solve machine learning problems, you need a workable installation. In addition, you need access to the data sets and code used for this book. Downloading the sample code (found at www.dummies.com/go/codingaiodownloads) and installing it on your system is the best way to get a good learning experience from the book. This chapter helps you get your system set up so that you can easily follow the examples in the remainder of the book.

REMEMBER

Using the downloadable source code doesn't prevent you from typing the examples on your own, following them using a debugger, expanding them, or working with the code in all sorts of ways. The downloadable source code is there to help you get a good start with your machine learning and Python learning experience. After you see how the code works when it's correctly typed and configured, you can try to create the examples on your own. If you make a mistake, you can compare what you've typed with the downloadable source code and discover precisely where the error exists. You can find the downloadable source for this chapter in the ML4D; 06; Sample.ipynb and ML4D; 06; Dataset Load.ipynb files.

CHAPTER 2 **Installing a Python Distribution** 367

> ## USING PYTHON 2.7.X FOR THIS BOOK
>
> There are currently two parallel Python developments. Most books rely on the newest version of a language for examples. Actually, however, two new versions of Python exist that you can use as of this writing: 2.7.13 and 3.6.0. Python is unique in that some groups use one version and other groups use the other version. Because data scientists and others who perform machine learning tasks mainly use the 2.7.x version of Python, this book concentrates on that version. (Eventually, all development tasks will move to the 3.x version of the product.) Using the 2.7.x version means that you're better able to work with other people who perform machine learning tasks when you complete this book. If the book used the 3.6.x version instead, you might find it hard to understand examples that you see in real-world applications.
>
> If you truly want to use the 3.6.x version with this book, you can do so, but you need to understand that the examples may not always work as written. For example, when using the Python 2.7 `print()` function, you don't absolutely need to include parentheses. The Python 3.6 version of the same function raises an error unless you do use the parentheses. Even though it seems like a minor difference, it's enough to cause confusion for some people, and you need to keep it in mind as you work through the examples.
>
> Fortunately, you can find a number of online sites that document the version 2.7 and version 3.6 differences:
>
> - One of the easiest sites to understand is nbviewer at `http://nbviewer.ipython.org/github/rasbt/python_reference/blob/master/tutorials/key_differences_between_python_2_and_3.ipynb`.
> - Another good place to look is the DigitalOcean blog at `https://www.digitalocean.com/community/tutorials/python-2-vs-python-3-practical-considerations-2`.
>
> These sites will help you if you choose to use version 3.6 with this book. However, the book supports only version 2.7, and you use version 3.6 at your own risk.

Choosing a Python Distribution with Machine Learning in Mind

It's entirely possible to obtain a generic copy of Python and add all the required machine learning libraries to it. The process can be difficult because you need to ensure that you have all the required libraries in the correct versions to guarantee

success. In addition, you need to perform the configuration required to make sure that the libraries are accessible when you need them. Fortunately, going through the required work is not necessary because a number of Python machine learning products are available for you to use. These products provide everything needed to get started with machine learning projects.

You can use any of the packages mentioned in the following sections to work with the examples in this book. However, the book's source code and downloadable source code rely on Continuum Analytics Anaconda because this particular package works on every platform this book supports: Linux, Mac OS X, and Windows. The book doesn't mention a specific package in the chapters that follow, but all screenshots reflect how things look when using Anaconda on Windows. You may need to tweak the code to use another package, and the screens will look different if you use Anaconda on another platform.

Windows 10 presents some serious installation issues when working with Python. Windows 10 doesn't provide a great environment for Python, because the automatic upgrades mean your system is always changing. If you're working with Windows 10, simply be aware that your road to a Python installation will be a rocky one. If you run into problems, try installing Python 3.x and run the program from the command line instead of from the Start menu.

Getting Continuum Analytics Anaconda

The basic Anaconda package is a free download that you obtain at www.continuum.io/downloads. Simply click Download Anaconda to obtain access to the free product. You do need to provide an email address to get a copy of Anaconda. After you provide your email address, you go to another page, where you can choose your platform and the installer for that platform. Anaconda supports the following platforms:

» Windows 32-bit and 64-bit

The installer may offer you only the 64-bit or 32-bit version, depending on which version of Windows it detects.

» Linux 32-bit and 64-bit

» Mac OS X 64-bit

The code written for this book requires Anaconda 2.1.0 using Python 2.7, which you can download at https://repo.continuum.io/archive (refer to the "Using Python 2.7.x for this book" sidebar for details). You can also choose to install Python 3.5 by clicking one of the links where the filename begins with Anaconda3.

CHAPTER 2 **Installing a Python Distribution** 369

Both Windows and Mac OS X provide graphical installers. When using Linux, you rely on the bash utility.

WARNING

The code exercises and commands in this book will not work as-is if you use the latest version of Anaconda, as a new version is expected to be released during the book's publication with a different command syntax. Make sure you download and use Anaconda 2.1.0.

The Miniconda installer can potentially save time by limiting the number of features you install. However, trying to figure out precisely which packages you do need is an error-prone and time-consuming process. In general, you want to perform a full installation to ensure that you have everything needed for your projects. Even a full install doesn't require much time or effort to download and install on most systems.

The free product is all you need for this book. However, when you look at the site, you see that many other add-on products are available. These products can help you create robust applications. For example, when you add Accelerate to the mix, you obtain the capability to perform multicore and GPU-enabled operations. The use of these add-on products is outside the scope of this book, but the Anaconda site provides details on using them.

TIP

The following Python software packages are alternatives to the basic Anaconda package, but you do not need to install all or even any of these software programs.

Getting Enthought Canopy Express

Enthought Canopy Express is a free product for producing both technical and scientific applications using Python. You can obtain it at www.enthought.com/canopy-express. Click Download Free on the main page to see a listing of the versions that you can download. Only Canopy Express is free; the full Canopy product comes at a cost. However, you can use Canopy Express to work with the examples in this book. Canopy Express supports the following platforms:

» Windows 32-bit and 64-bit

» Linux 32-bit and 64-bit

» Mac OS X 32-bit and 64-bit

Choose the platform and version you want to download. When you click Download Canopy Express, you see an optional form for providing information about yourself. The download starts automatically, even if you don't provide personal information to the company.

One of the advantages of Canopy Express is that Using Python 2.7.*x* for this book is heavily involved in providing support for both students and teachers. People also can take classes, including online classes, that teach the use of Canopy Express in various ways (see https://training.enthought.com/courses).

Getting Python(x,y)

The Python(x,y) Integrated Development Environment (IDE) is a community project hosted on Google at http://python-xy.github.io. It's a Windows-only product, so you can't easily use it for cross-platform needs. (In fact, it supports only Windows Vista, Windows 7, and Windows 8.) However, it does come with a full set of libraries, and you can easily use it for this book if you want.

Because Python(x,y) uses the GNU General Public License (GPL) v3 (see www.gnu.org/licenses/gpl.html), you have no add-ons, training, or other paid features to worry about. No one will come calling at your door hoping to sell you something. In addition, you have access to all the source code for Python(x,y), so you can make modifications if you want.

Getting WinPython

The name tells you that WinPython is a Windows-only product that you can find at winpython.github.io. This product is actually a spin-off of Python(x,y) and isn't meant to replace it. Quite the contrary: WinPython is simply a more flexible way to work with Python(x,y). You can read about the motivation for creating WinPython at https://sourceforge.net/p/winpython/wiki/Roadmap.

The bottom line for this product is that you gain flexibility at the cost of friendliness and a little platform integration. However, for developers who need to maintain multiple versions of an IDE, WinPython may make a significant difference. When using WinPython with this book, make sure to pay particular attention to configuration issues, or you'll find that even the downloadable code has little chance of working.

Installing Python on Linux

You use the command line to install Anaconda on Linux — there is no graphical installation option. Before you can perform the install, you must download a copy of the Linux software from the Continuum Analytics site. You can find the

required download information in the "Getting Continuum Analytics Anaconda" section, earlier in this chapter. The following procedure should work fine on any Linux system, whether you use the 32-bit or 64-bit version of Anaconda:

1. **Open a copy of Terminal.**

 The Terminal window appears.

2. **Change directories to the downloaded copy of Anaconda on your system.**

 The name of this file varies, but normally it appears as Anaconda-2.1.0-Linux-x86.sh for 32-bit systems and Anaconda-2.1.0-Linux-x86_64.sh for 64-bit systems.

 The version number is embedded as part of the filename. In this case, the filename refers to version 2.1.0, which is the version used for this book. If you use some other version, you may experience problems with the source code and need to make adjustments when working with it.

3. **Type** bash Anaconda-2.1.0-Linux-x86.sh **(for the 32-bit version) or** Anaconda-2.1.0-Linux-x86_64.sh **(for the 64-bit version) and press Enter.**

 An installation wizard starts that asks you to accept the licensing terms for using Anaconda.

4. **Read the licensing agreement and accept the terms using the method required for your version of Linux.**

 The wizard asks you to provide an installation location for Anaconda. The book assumes that you use the default location of ~/anaconda. If you choose some other location, you may have to modify some procedures later in the book to work with your setup.

5. **Provide an installation location (if necessary) and press Enter (or click Next).**

 The application extraction process begins. After the extraction is complete, you see a completion message.

6. **Add the installation path to your** PATH **statement using the method required for your version of Linux.**

 You're ready to begin using Anaconda.

Installing Python on Mac OS X

The Mac OS X installation comes in only one form: 64-bit.

Before you can perform the install, you must download a copy of the Mac software from the Continuum Analytics site. You can find the required download information in the "Getting Continuum Analytics Anaconda" section, earlier in this chapter.

The following steps help you install Anaconda 64-bit on a Mac system:

1. **Locate the downloaded copy of Anaconda on your system.**

 The name of this file varies, but normally it appears as Anaconda-2.1.0-MacOSX-x86_64.pkg. The version number is embedded as part of the filename. In this case, the filename refers to version 2.1.0, which is the version used for this book. If you use some other version, you may experience problems with the source code and need to make adjustments when working with it.

2. **Double-click the installation file.**

 An introduction dialog box appears.

3. **Click Continue.**

 The wizard asks whether you want to review the Read Me materials.

 You can read these materials later. For now, you can safely skip the information.

4. **Click Continue.**

 The wizard displays a licensing agreement.

 Be sure to read through the licensing agreement so that you know the terms of usage.

5. **Click I Agree if you agree to the licensing agreement.**

 The wizard asks you to provide a destination for the installation. The destination controls whether the installation is for an individual user or a group.

 You may see an error message stating that you can't install Anaconda on the system. The error message occurs because of a bug in the installer and has nothing to do with your system. To get rid of the error message, choose the Install Only for Me option. You can't install Anaconda for a group of users on a Mac system.

6. **Click Continue.**

 The installer displays a dialog box containing options for changing the installation type. Click Change Install Location if you want to modify where Anaconda is installed on your system. (The book assumes that you use the default path of ~/anaconda.) Click Customize if you want to modify how the installer works. For example, you can choose not to add Anaconda to your PATH statement. However, the book assumes that you have chosen the default install options, and no good reason exists to change them unless you have another copy of Python 2.7 installed somewhere else.

CHAPTER 2 **Installing a Python Distribution** 373

7. **Click Install.**

 The installation begins. A progress bar tells you how the installation process is progressing. When the installation is complete, you see a completion dialog box.

8. **Click Continue.**

 You're ready to begin using Anaconda.

TIP

Continuum also provides a command-line version of the Mac OS X installation. This file has a filename of `Anaconda-2.1.0-MacOSX-x86_64.sh`, and you use the `bash` utility to install it in the same way that you do on any Linux system. However, installing Anaconda from the command line gives you no advantage unless you need to perform it as part of an automated setup. Using the GUI version, as described in this section, is much easier.

Installing Python on Windows

Anaconda comes with a graphical installation application for Windows, so getting a good install means using a wizard, as you would for any other installation. Of course, you need a copy of the installation file before you begin, and you can find the required download information in the "Getting Continuum Analytics Anaconda" section, earlier in this chapter.

The following procedure should work fine on any Windows system, whether you use the 32-bit or the 64-bit version of Anaconda:

1. **Locate the downloaded copy of Anaconda on your system.**

 The name of this file varies, but normally it appears as `Anaconda-2.1.0-Windows-x86.exe` for 32-bit systems and `Anaconda-2.1.0-Windows-x86_64.exe` for 64-bit systems. The version number is embedded as part of the filename. In this case, the filename refers to version 2.1.0, which is the version used for this book. If you use some other version, you may experience problems with the source code and need to make adjustments when working with it.

2. **Double-click the installation file.**

TECHNICAL STUFF

You may see an Open File – Security Warning dialog box that asks whether you want to run this file. Click Run if this dialog box pops up.

You see an Anaconda 2.1.0 Setup dialog box similar to the one shown in Figure 2-1. The exact dialog box that you see depends on which version of the Anaconda installation program you download. If you have a 64-bit operating system, using the 64-bit version of Anaconda is always best so that you obtain

374 BOOK 6 **Selecting Data Analysis Tools**

the best possible performance. This first dialog box tells you when you have the 64-bit version of the product.

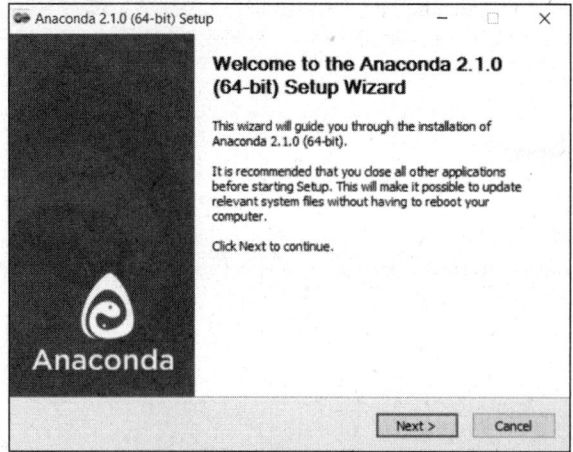

FIGURE 2-1: The setup process begins by telling you whether you have the 64-bit version.

3. **Click Next.**

 The wizard displays a licensing agreement. Be sure to read through the licensing agreement so that you know the terms of usage.

4. **Click I Agree if you agree to the licensing agreement.**

 You're asked what sort of installation type to perform, as shown in Figure 2-2.

 TIP

 In most cases, you want to install the product just for yourself. The exception is if you have multiple people using your system and they all need access to Anaconda.

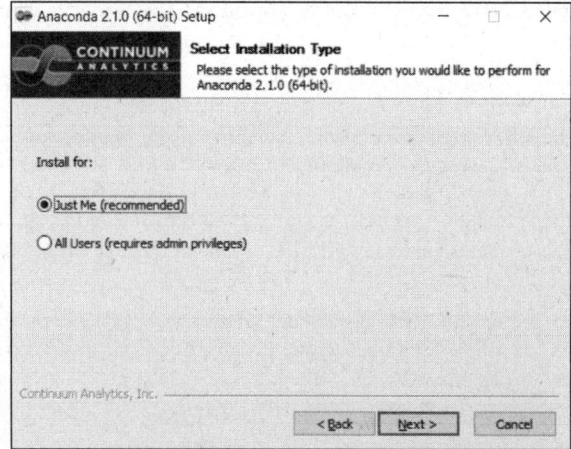

FIGURE 2-2: Tell the wizard how to install Anaconda on your system.

CHAPTER 2 **Installing a Python Distribution** 375

5. **Choose one of the installation types and then click Next.**

 The wizard asks where to install Anaconda on disk, as shown in Figure 2-3.

 The book assumes that you use the default location. If you choose some other location, you may have to modify some procedures later in the book to work with your setup.

FIGURE 2-3: Specify an installation location.

6. **Choose an installation location (if necessary) and then click Next.**

 You see the Advanced Installation Options, shown in Figure 2-4.

 These options are selected by default, and no good reason exists to change them in most cases. You might need to change them if Anaconda won't provide your default Python 2.7 (or Python 3.5) setup. However, the book assumes that you've set up Anaconda using the default options.

7. **Change the advanced installation options (if necessary) and then click Install.**

 You see an Installing dialog box with a progress bar.

 The installation process can take a few minutes, so get yourself a cup of coffee and read the comics for a while.

 When the installation process is over, a Next button is enabled.

8. **Click Next.**

 The wizard tells you that the installation is complete.

9. **Click Finish.**

 You're ready to begin using Anaconda.

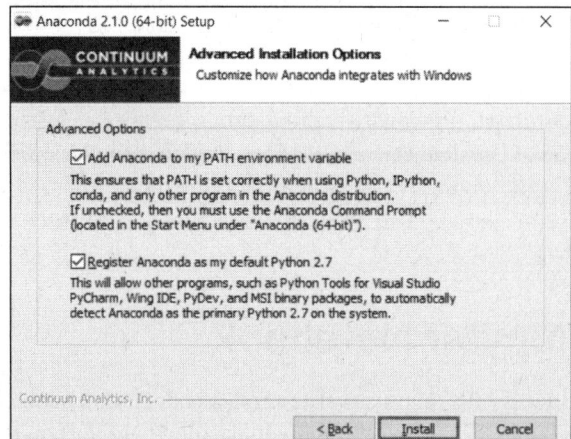

FIGURE 2-4: Configure the advanced installation options.

A WORD ABOUT THE SCREENSHOTS

As you work your way through the book, you use an IDE of your choice to open the Python and Python Notebook files containing the book's source code. Every screenshot that contains IDE-specific information relies on Anaconda because Anaconda runs on all three platforms supported by the book. The use of Anaconda doesn't imply that it's the best IDE; Anaconda simply works well as a demonstration product.

When you work with Anaconda, the name of the graphical (GUI) environment, Jupyter Notebook, is precisely the same across all three platforms, and you won't even see any significant difference in the presentation. Jupyter Notebook is a recent evolution of IPython, so you may see online resources refer to IPython Notebook. The differences that you do see are minor, and you should ignore them as you work through the book. When working on Linux, Mac OS X, or other versions of Windows, you should expect to see some differences in presentation, but these differences shouldn't reduce your ability to work with the examples.

Downloading the Data Sets and Example Code

This book is about using Python to perform machine learning tasks. Of course, you can spend all your time creating the example code from scratch, debugging it, and only then discovering how it relates to machine learning, or you can take the easy way and download the prewritten code at `www.dummies.com/go/codingaiodownloads` so that you can get right to work. Likewise, creating data sets large enough for machine learning purposes would take quite a while. Fortunately, you can access standardized, previously created data sets quite easily using features provided in some of the data science libraries (which also work just fine for machine learning). The following sections help you download and use the example code and data sets so that you can save time and get right to work with data science-specific tasks.

Using Jupyter Notebook

To make working with the relatively complex code in this book easier, you can use Jupyter Notebook. This interface lets you easily create Python notebook files that can contain any number of examples, each of which can run individually. The program runs in your browser, so which platform you use for development doesn't matter; as long as it has a browser, you should be okay.

Starting Jupyter Notebook

Most platforms provide an icon to access Jupyter Notebook. Just open this icon to access Jupyter Notebook. For example, on a Windows system, you choose Start ⇨ All Programs ⇨ Anaconda ⇨ Jupyter Notebook. Figure 2-5 shows how the interface looks when viewed in a Firefox browser. The precise appearance on your system depends on the browser you use and the kind of platform you have installed.

If you have a platform that doesn't offer easy access through an icon, you can use these steps to access Jupyter Notebook:

1. **Open a Command Prompt or Terminal Window on your system.**

 The window opens so that you can type commands.

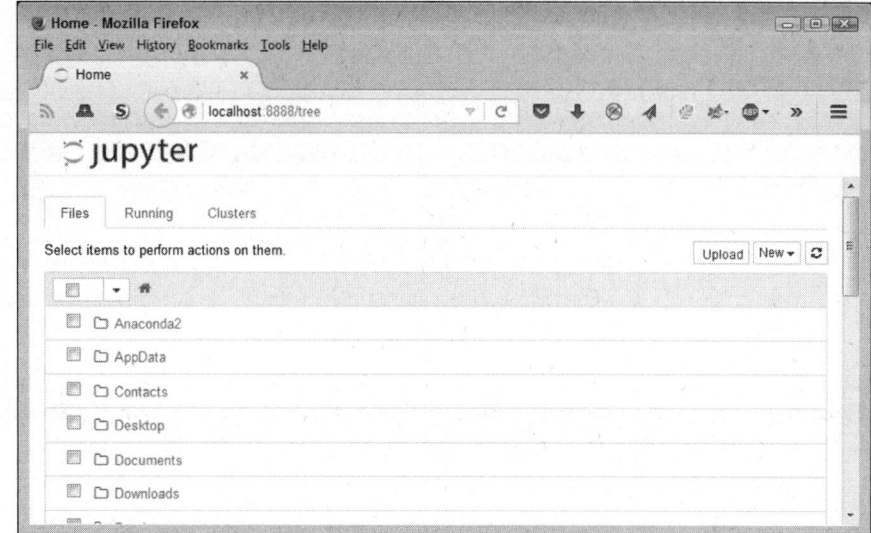

FIGURE 2-5:
Jupyter Notebook provides an easy method to create machine learning examples.

2. **Change directories to the** \Anaconda2\Scripts **directory on your machine.**

 Most systems let you use the CD command for this task.

3. **Type** ..\python ipython2-script.py notebook **and press Enter.**

 The Jupyter Notebook page opens in your browser.

Stopping the Jupyter Notebook server

No matter how you start Jupyter Notebook (or just Notebook, as it appears in the remainder of the book), the system generally opens a command prompt or terminal window to host Jupyter Notebook. This window contains a server that makes the application work. After you close the browser window when a session is complete, select the server window and press Ctrl+C or Ctrl+Break to stop the server.

Defining the code repository

The code you create and use in this book will reside in a repository on your hard drive. Think of a *repository* as a kind of filing cabinet where you put your code. Notebook opens a drawer, takes out the folder, and shows the code to you. You can modify it, run individual examples within the folder, add new examples, and simply interact with your code in a natural manner. The following sections get you started with Notebook so that you can see how this whole repository concept works.

Defining the book's folder

It pays to organize your files so that you can access them easier later. Book 6 keeps its files in the ML4D folder, which stands for Machine Learning for Dummies. Use these steps within Notebook to create a new folder:

1. **Choose New ⇨ Folder.**

 Notebook creates a new folder named Untitled Folder, as shown in Figure 2-6. The file will appear in alphanumeric order, so you may not initially see it. You must scroll down to the correct location.

FIGURE 2-6: New folders will appear with a name of Untitled Folder.

2. **Check the box next to the Untitled Folder entry.**
3. **Click Rename at the top of the page.**

 You see a Rename Directory dialog box like the one shown in Figure 2-7.

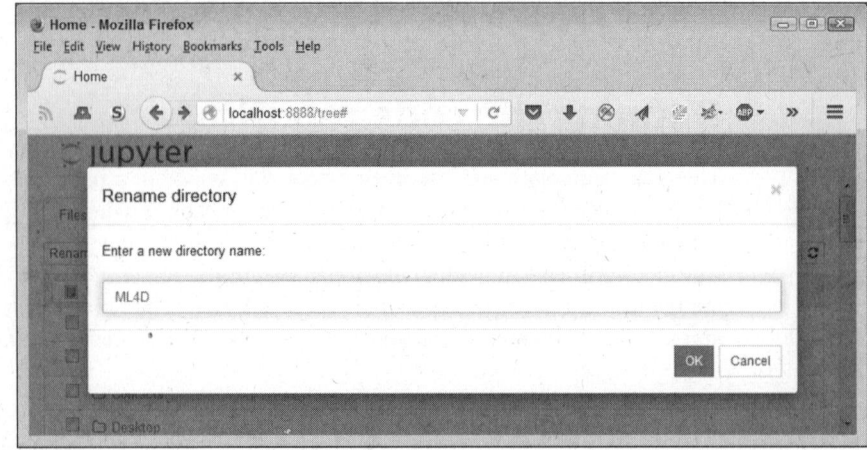

FIGURE 2-7: Rename the folder so that you remember the kinds of entries it contains.

380 BOOK 6 **Selecting Data Analysis Tools**

4. **Type** ML4D **and click OK.**

 Notebook changes the name of the folder for you.

5. **Click the new ML4D entry in the list.**

 Notebook changes the location to the ML4D folder where you perform tasks related to the exercises in this book.

Creating a new notebook

Every new notebook is like a file folder. You can place individual examples within the file folder, just as you would sheets of paper into a physical file folder. Each example appears in a cell.

Use these steps to create a new notebook:

1. **Click New ⇨ Python 2.**

 A new tab opens in the browser with the new notebook, as shown in Figure 2-8. Notice that the notebook contains a cell and that Notebook has highlighted the cell so that you can begin typing code in it. The title of the notebook is Untitled right now. That's not a particularly helpful title, so you need to change it.

2. **Click Untitled on the page.**

 Notebook asks what you want to use as a new name, as shown in Figure 2-9.

3. **Type** ML4D; 06; Sample **and press Enter.**

FIGURE 2-8:
A notebook contains cells that you use to hold code.

CHAPTER 2 **Installing a Python Distribution** 381

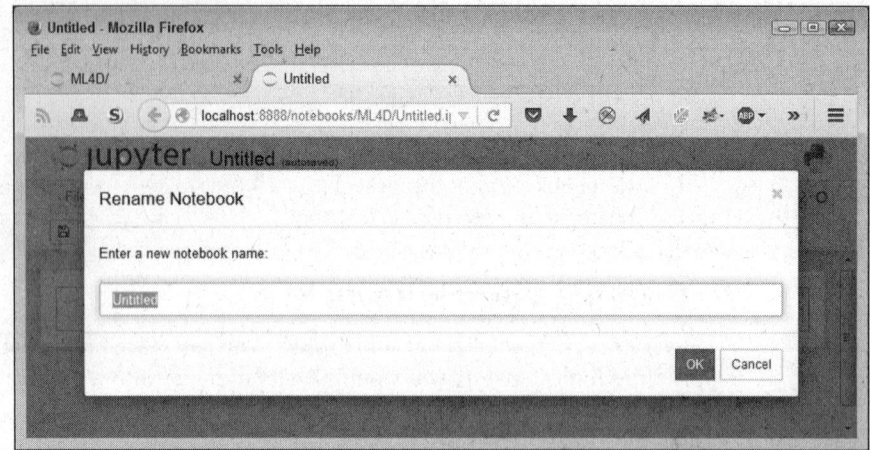

FIGURE 2-9: Provide a new name for your notebook.

Of course, the Sample notebook doesn't contain anything just yet. Place the cursor in the cell, type **print 'Python is really cool!'**, and then click the Run button (the button with the right-pointing arrow on the toolbar). You see the output shown in Figure 2-10. The output is part of the same cell as the code. However, Notebook visually separates the output from the code so that you can tell them apart. Notebook automatically creates a new cell for you.

FIGURE 2-10: Notebook uses cells to store your code.

When you finish working with a notebook, shutting it down is important. To close a notebook, choose File ⇨ Close and Halt. You return to the home page, where you can see the notebook you just created added to the list, as shown in Figure 2-11.

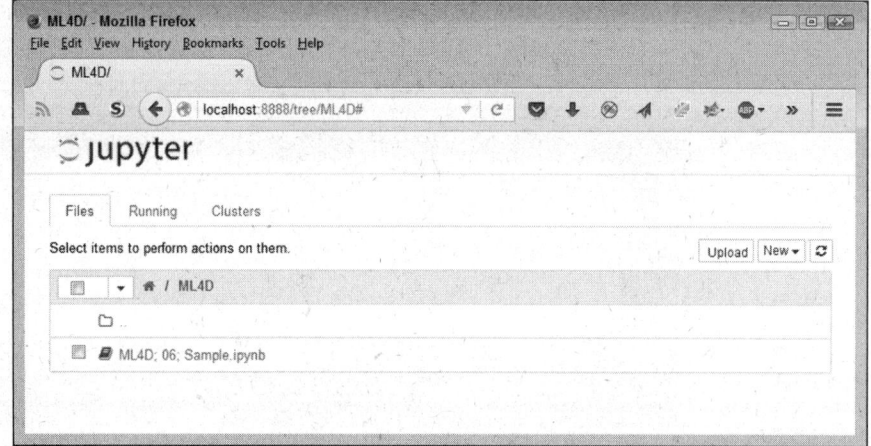

FIGURE 2-11:
Any notebooks you create appear in the repository list.

Exporting a notebook

Creating notebooks and keeping them all to yourself isn't much fun. At some point, you want to share them with other people. To perform this task, you must export your notebook from the repository to a file. You can then send the file to someone else, who will import it into his or her repository.

The previous section shows how to create a notebook named ML4D; 06; Sample. You can open this notebook by clicking its entry in the repository list. The file reopens so that you can see your code again. To export this code, choose File ⇨ Download As ⇨ IPython Notebook. What you see next depends on your browser, but you generally see some sort of dialog box for saving the notebook as a file. Utilize the same method for saving the IPython Notebook file as you do for any other file you save using your browser.

Removing a notebook

Sometimes notebooks get outdated or you simply don't need to work with them any longer. Rather than allow your repository to get clogged with files you don't need, you can remove these unwanted notebooks from the list. Use these steps to remove the file:

1. **Select the box next to the ML4D; 06; Sample.ipynb entry.**
2. **Click the trash can icon (Delete) at the top of the page.**

 You see a Delete notebook warning message like the one shown in Figure 2-12.

3. **Click Delete.**

 The file is removed from the list.

CHAPTER 2 **Installing a Python Distribution** 383

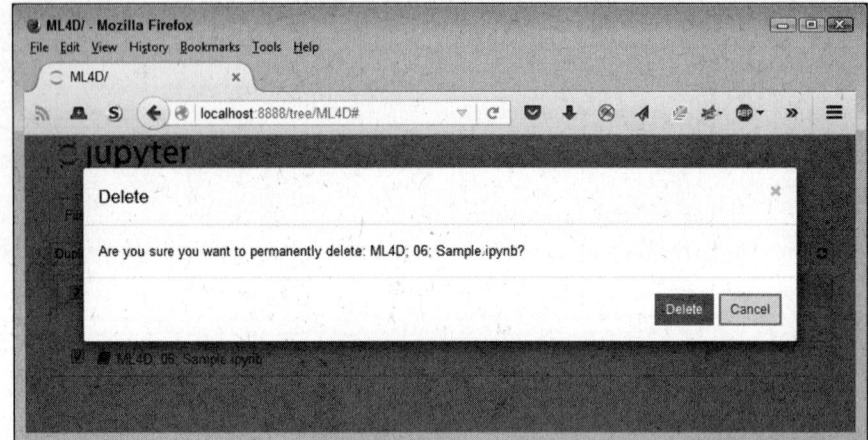

FIGURE 2-12: Notebook warns you before removing any files from the repository.

Importing a notebook

To use the source code from this book, you must import the downloaded files into your repository. The source code comes in an archive file that you extract to a location on your hard drive. The archive contains a list of .ipynb (IPython Notebook) files containing the source code for this book found at www.dummies.com/go/codingaiodownloads. The following steps tell how to import these files into your repository:

1. **Click Upload at the top of the page.**

 What you see depends on your browser. In most cases, you see some type of File Upload dialog box that provides access to the files on your hard drive.

2. **Navigate to the directory containing the files that you want to import into Notebook.**

3. **Highlight one or more files to import and click the Open (or other, similar) button to begin the upload process.**

 You see the file added to an upload list, as shown in Figure 2-13. The file isn't part of the repository yet — you've simply selected it for upload.

4. **Click Upload.**

 Notebook places the file in the repository so that you can begin using it.

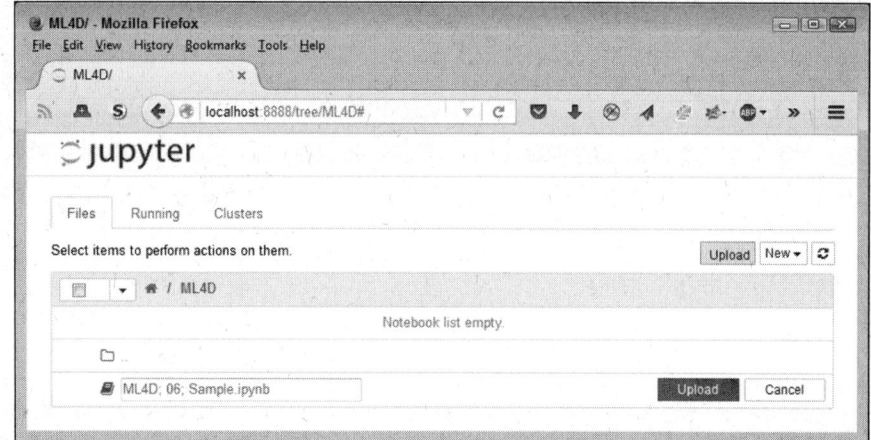

FIGURE 2-13:
The files that you want to add to the repository appear as part of an upload list.

Understanding the data sets used in this book

This book uses a number of data sets, all of which appear in the scikit-learn library. These data sets demonstrate various ways in which you can interact with data, and you use them in the examples to perform a variety of tasks. The following list provides a quick overview of the function used to import each of the data sets into your Python code:

» load_boston(): Regression analysis with the Boston house-prices data set

» load_iris(): Classification with the iris data set

» load_diabetes(): Regression with the diabetes data set

» load_digits([n_class]): Classification with the digits data set

» fetch_20newsgroups(subset='train'): Data from 20 newsgroups

» fetch_olivetti_faces(): Olivetti faces data set from AT&T

The technique for loading each of these data sets is the same across examples. The following example shows how to load the Boston house-prices data set. You can find the code in the ML4D; 06; Dataset Load.ipynb notebook.

```
from sklearn.datasets import load_boston
Boston = load_boston()
print Boston.data.shape
```

To see how the code works, click Run Cell. The output from the print call is (506L, 13L). You can see the output in Figure 2-14.

CHAPTER 2 **Installing a Python Distribution** 385

FIGURE 2-14: The Boston object contains the loaded data set.

> IN THIS CHAPTER
>
> » Manipulating data streams
>
> » Working with flat and unstructured files
>
> » Interacting with relational and NoSQL databases
>
> » Interacting with web-based data

Chapter 3
Working with Real Data

"Real data is a reality check."

— NATE SILVER

Data science applications require data by definition. It would be nice if you could simply go to a data store somewhere, purchase the data you need in an easy-open package, and then write an application to access that data. However, data is messy. It appears in all sorts of places, in many different forms, and you can interpret it in many different ways. Every organization has a different method of viewing data and stores it in a different manner as well. Even when the data management system used by one company is the same as the data management system used by another company, the chances are slim that the data will appear in the same format or even use the same data types. In short, before you can do any data science work, you must discover how to access the data in all its myriad forms. Real data requires a lot of work in order to use it, and fortunately Python is up to the task of manipulating data as needed.

This chapter helps you understand the techniques required to access data in a number of forms and locations. For example, memory streams represent a form of data storage that your computer supports natively; flat files exist on your hard drive; relational databases commonly appear on networks (although smaller relational databases, such as those found in Access, could appear on your hard drive as well); and web-based data usually appears on the Internet. You won't visit every form of data storage available (such as that stored on a point-of-sale, or POS, system). Quite possibly, an entire book on the topic wouldn't suffice to cover

the topic of data formats in any detail. However, the techniques in this chapter do demonstrate how to access data in the formats you most commonly encounter when working with real-world data.

The scikit-learn library includes a number of *toy* data sets (small data sets meant for you to play with). These data sets are complex enough to perform a number of tasks, such as experimenting with Python to perform data science tasks. Because this data is readily available, and making the examples too complicated to understand is a bad idea, this book relies on these toy data sets as input for many of the examples. The toy data sets and techniques shown reduce complexity and make the examples clearer, but the techniques work equally well on real-world data.

You don't have to type the source code for this chapter by hand. In fact, it's a lot easier if you use the downloadable source available at www.dummies.com/go/codingaiodownloads. The source code for this chapter appears in the P4DS4D; 05; Dataset Load.ipynb source code file.

It's essential that the Colors.txt, Titanic.csv, Values.xls, and XMLData.xml files that come with the downloadable source code appear in the same folder (directory) as your IPython Notebook files. Otherwise, the examples in the following sections fail with an input/output (IO) error. The file location varies according to the platform you're using. For example, on a Windows system, you find the notebooks stored in the C:\Users*Username*\My Documents\IPython Notebooks folder, where *Username* is your login name. To make the examples work, simply copy the four files from the downloadable source folder into your IPython Notebook folder.

Uploading, Streaming, and Sampling Data

Storing data in local computer memory represents the fastest and most reliable means to access it. The data could reside anywhere. However, you don't actually interact with the data in its storage location. You load the data into memory from the storage location and then interact with it in memory.

The columns in a database are sometimes called *features* or *variables*. The rows are *cases*. Each row represents a collection of variables that you can analyze.

Uploading small amounts of data into memory

This section uses the Colors.txt file, shown in Figure 3-1, for input.

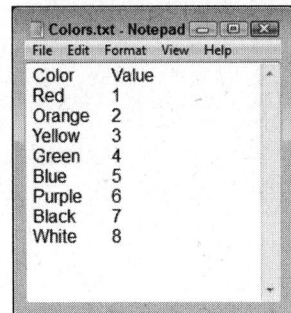

FIGURE 3-1:
Format of the
Colors.txt file.

The example also relies on native Python functionality to get the task done. When you load a file (of any type), the entire data set is available at all times, and the loading process is quite short. Here is an example of how this technique works:

```
with open("Colors.txt", 'rb') as open_file:
    print 'Colors.txt content:\n' + open_file.read()
```

The example begins by using the `open()` method to obtain a `file` object. The `open()` function accepts the filename and an access mode. In this case, the access mode is read binary (rb). (When using Python 3.x, you may have to change the mode to read (r) in order to avoid error messages.) It then uses the `read()` method of the file object to read all the data in the file. If you were to specify a size argument as part of `read()`, such as `read(15)`, Python would read only the number of characters that you specify or stop when it reaches the End Of File (EOF). When you run this example, you see the following output:

```
Colors.txt content:
Color    Value
Red      1
Orange   2
Yellow   3
Green    4
Blue     5
Purple   6
Black    7
White    8
```

WARNING

The entire data set is loaded from the library into free memory. Of course, the loading process will fail if your system lacks sufficient memory to hold the data set. When this problem occurs, you need to consider other techniques for working with the data set, such as streaming it or sampling it. In short, before you use this technique, you must ensure that the data set will actually fit in memory. You won't normally experience any problems when working with the toy data sets in the scikit-learn library.

CHAPTER 3 **Working with Real Data** 389

Streaming large amounts of data into memory

Some data sets will be so large that you won't be able to fit them entirely in memory at one time. In addition, you may find that some data sets load slowly because they reside on a remote site. Streaming answers both needs by making it possible to work with the data a little at a time. You download individual pieces, making it possible to work with just part of the data and to work with it as you receive it, rather than waiting for the entire data set to download. Here's an example of how you can stream data using Python:

```
with open("Colors.txt", 'rb') as open_file:
    for observation in open_file:
        print 'Reading Data: ' + observation
```

This example relies on the `Colors.txt` file, which contains a header, and then a number of records that associate a color name with a value. The `open_file` file object contains a pointer to the open file.

As the code performs data reads in the `for` loop, the file pointer moves to the next record. Each record appears one at a time in `observation`. The code outputs the value in `observation` using a `print` statement. You should receive this output:

```
Reading Data: Color     Value

Reading Data: Red       1

Reading Data: Orange    2

Reading Data: Yellow    3

Reading Data: Green     4

Reading Data: Blue      5

Reading Data: Purple    6

Reading Data: Black     7

Reading Data: White     8
```

Python streams each record from the source. This means that you must perform a read for each record you want.

Sampling data

Data streaming obtains all the records from a data source. You may find that you don't need all the records. You can save time and resources by simply sampling the data. This means retrieving records a set number of records apart, such as every fifth record, or by making random samples. The following code shows how to retrieve every other record in the Colors.txt file:

```
n = 2
with open("Colors.txt", 'rb') as open_file:
    for j, observation in enumerate(open_file):
        if j % n==0:
            print('Reading Line: ' + str(j) +
            ' Content: ' + observation)
```

The basic idea of sampling is the same as streaming. However, in this case, the application uses enumerate() to retrieve a row number. When j % n == 0, the row is one that you want to keep and the application outputs the information. In this case, you see the following output:

```
Reading Line: 0 Content: Color     Value

Reading Line: 2 Content: Orange    2

Reading Line: 4 Content: Green     4

Reading Line: 6 Content: Purple    6

Reading Line: 8 Content: White     8
```

The value of n is important in determining which records appear as part of the data set. Try changing n to 3. The output will change to sample just the header and rows 3 and 6.

TIP

You can perform random sampling as well. All you need to do is randomize the selector, like this:

```
from random import random
sample_size = 0.25
with open("Colors.txt", 'rb') as open_file:
    for j, observation in enumerate(open_file):
        if random()<=sample_size:
            print('Reading Line: ' + str(j) +
            ' Content: ' + observation)
```

To make this form of selection work, you must import the random class. The random() method outputs a value between 0 and 1. However, Python randomizes

CHAPTER 3 **Working with Real Data**

the output so that you don't know what value you receive. The `sample_size` variable contains a number between 0 and 1 to determine the sample size. For example, 0.25 selects 25 percent of the items in the file.

The output will still appear in numeric order. For example, you won't see Green come before Orange. However, the items selected are random, and you won't always get precisely the same number of return values. The spaces between return values will differ as well. Here is an example of what you might see as output (although your output will likely vary):

```
Reading Line: 1 Content: Red     1

Reading Line: 4 Content: Green   4

Reading Line: 8 Content: White   8
```

Accessing Data in Structured Flat-File Form

In many cases, the data you need to work with won't appear within a library, such as the toy data sets in the scikit-learn library. Real-world data usually appears in a file of some type. A flat file presents the easiest kind of file to work with. The data appears as a simple list of entries that you can read one at a time, if desired, into memory. Depending on the requirements for your project, you can read all or part of the file.

A problem with using native Python techniques is that the input isn't intelligent. For example, when a file contains a header, Python simply reads it as yet more data to process, rather than as a header. You can't easily select a particular column of data. The pandas library used in the sections that follow makes it much easier to read and understand flat-file data. Classes and methods in the pandas library interpret (parse) the flat-file data to make it easier to manipulate.

REMEMBER

The least formatted and therefore easiest-to-read flat-file format is the text file. However, a text file also treats all data as strings, so you often have to convert numeric data into other forms. A comma-separated value (CSV) file provides more formatting and more information, but it requires a little more effort to read. At the high end of flat-file formatting are custom data formats, such as an Excel file, which contain extensive formatting and could include multiple data sets in a single file.

The following sections describe these three levels of flat-file data sets and show how to use them. These sections assume that the file structures the data in some

way. For example, the CSV file uses commas to separate data fields. A text file might rely on tabs to separate data fields. An Excel file uses a complex method to separate data fields and to provide a wealth of information about each field. You can work with unstructured data as well, but working with structured data is much easier because you know where each field begins and ends.

Reading from a text file

Text files can use a variety of storage formats. However, a common format is to have a header line that documents the purpose of each field, followed by another line for each record in the file. The file separates the fields using tabs. Refer to Figure 3-1 for an example of the `Colors.txt` file used for the example in this section.

Native Python provides a wide variety of methods you can use to read such a file. However, it's far easier to let someone else do the work. In this case, you can use the pandas library to perform the task. Within the pandas library, you find a set of *parsers*, code used to read individual bits of data and determine the purpose of each bit according to the format of the entire file. Using the correct parser is essential if you want to make sense of file content. In this case, you use the `read_table()` method to accomplish the task, as shown in the following code:

```
import pandas as pd
color_table = pd.io.parsers.read_table("Colors.txt")
print color_table
```

The code imports the pandas library, uses the `read_table()` method to read `Colors.txt` into a variable named `color_table`, and then displays the resulting memory data on-screen using the `print` function. Here's the output you can expect to see from this example:

```
   Color  Value
0     Red      1
1  Orange      2
2  Yellow      3
3   Green      4
4    Blue      5
5  Purple      6
6   Black      7
7   White      8
```

Notice that the parser correctly interprets the first row as consisting of field names. It numbers the records from 0 through 7. Using `read_table()` method arguments, you can adjust how the parser interprets the input file, but the default settings usually work best. You can read more about the `read_table()` arguments at pandas.pydata.org/pandas-docs/dev/generated/pandas.io.parsers.read_table.html#pandas.io.parsers.read_table.

Reading CSV delimited format

A CSV file provides more formatting than a simple text file. In fact, CSV files can become quite complicated. There is a standard that defines the format of CSV files, and you can see it at https://tools.ietf.org/html/rfc4180. The CSV file used for this example is quite simple:

» A header defines each of the fields.

» Fields are separated by commas.

» Records are separated by linefeeds.

» Strings are enclosed in double quotes.

» Integers and real numbers appear without double quotes.

Figure 3-2 shows the raw format for the Titanic.csv file used for this example. You can see the raw format using any text editor.

FIGURE 3-2: The raw format of a CSV file is still text and quite readable.

Applications such as Excel can import and format CSV files so that they become easier to read. Figure 3-3 shows the same file in Excel.

Excel actually recognizes the header as a header. If you were to use features such as data sorting, you could select header columns to obtain the desired result. Fortunately, pandas also makes it possible to work with the CSV file as formatted data, as shown in the following example:

```
import pandas as pd
titanic = pd.io.parsers.read_csv("Titanic.csv")
X = titanic[['age']]
print X
```

FIGURE 3-3:
Use an application such as Excel to create a formatted CSV presentation.

Notice that the parser of choice this time is read_csv(), which understands CSV files and provides you with new options for working with it. (You can read more about this parser at pandas.pydata.org/pandas-docs/dev/io.html#io-read-csv-table.) Selecting a specific field is quite easy — you just supply the field name as shown. The output from this example looks like this (some values omitted for the sake of space):

```
          age
0     29.0000
1      0.9167
2      2.0000
3     30.0000
4     25.0000
5     48.0000
...
1304  14.5000
1305  9999.0000
1306  26.5000
1307  27.0000
1308  29.0000
[1309 rows x 1 columns]
```

TIP

Of course, a human readable output like this one is nice when working through an example, but you might also need the output as a list. To create the output as a list, you simply change the third line of code to read X = titanic[['age']].values. Notice the addition of the values property. The output changes to something like this (some values omitted for the sake of space):

```
[[ 29.        ]
 [  0.91670001]
 [  2.        ]
 ...,
 [ 26.5       ]
 [ 27.        ]
 [ 29.        ]]
```

CHAPTER 3 **Working with Real Data** 395

Reading Excel and other Microsoft Office files

Excel and other Microsoft Office applications provide highly formatted content. You can specify every aspect of the information these files contain. The `Values.xls` file used for this example provides a listing of sine, cosine, and tangent values for a random list of angles. You can see this file in Figure 3-4.

FIGURE 3-4: An Excel file is highly formatted and might contain information of various types.

When you work with Excel or other Microsoft Office products, you begin to experience some complexity. For example, an Excel file can contain more than one worksheet, so you need to tell pandas which worksheet to process. In fact, you can choose to process multiple worksheets, if desired. When working with other Office products, you have to be specific about what to process. Just telling pandas to process something isn't good enough. Here's an example of working with the `Values.xls` file:

```
import pandas as pd
xls = pd.ExcelFile("Values.xls")
trig_values = xls.parse('Sheet1', index_col=None,
                        na_values=['NA'])
print trig_values
```

The code begins by importing the pandas library as normal. It then creates a pointer to the Excel file using the `ExcelFile()` constructor. This pointer, `xls`, lets you access a worksheet, define an index column, and specify how to present empty values. The index column is the one that the worksheet uses to index the records. Using a value of `None` means that pandas should generate an index for you. The `parse()` method obtains the values you request. You can read more about the Excel parser options at pandas.pydata.org/pandas-docs/dev/io.html#io-excel.

TIP You don't absolutely have to use the two-step process of obtaining a file pointer and then parsing the content. You can also perform the task using a single step like this: `trig_values = pd.read_excel("Values.xls", 'Sheet1', index_col=None, na_values=['NA'])`. Because Excel files are more complex, using the two-step process is often more convenient and efficient because you don't have to reopen the file for each read of the data.

Sending Data in Unstructured File Form

Unstructured data files consist of a series of bits. The file doesn't separate the bits from each other in any way. You can't simply look into the file and see any structure because there isn't any to see. Unstructured file formats rely on the file user to know how to interpret the data. For example, each pixel of a picture file could consist of three 32-bit fields. Knowing that each field is 32-bits is up to you. A header at the beginning of the file may provide clues about interpreting the file, but even so, it's up to you to know how to interact with the file.

The example in this section shows how to work with a picture as an unstructured file. The example image is a public domain offering from `https://commons.wikimedia.org/wiki/Main_Page`. To work with images, you need to access the scikit-image library (`scikit-image.org`), which is a free-of-charge collection of algorithms used for image processing. You can find a tutorial for this library at `scipy-lectures.github.io/packages/scikit-image`. The first task is to be able to display the image on-screen using the following code. (This code can require a little time to run. The image is ready when the busy indicator disappears from the IPython Notebook tab.)

```
from skimage.io import imread
from skimage.transform import resize
from matplotlib import pyplot as plt
import matplotlib.cm as cm

example_file = ("http://upload.wikimedia.org/" +
    "wikipedia/commons/7/7d/Dog_face.png")
image = imread(example_file, as_grey=True)
plt.imshow(image, cmap=cm.gray)
plt.show()
```

The code begins by importing a number of libraries. It then creates a string that points to the example file online and places it in `example_file`. This string is part of the `imread()` method call, along with `as_grey`, which is set to `True`. The `as_grey` argument tells Python to turn color images into grayscale. Any images that are already in grayscale remain that way.

CHAPTER 3 **Working with Real Data** 397

Now that you have an image loaded, it's time to render it (make it ready to display on-screen. The `imshow()` function performs the rendering and uses a grayscale color map. The `show()` function actually displays `image` for you, as shown in Figure 3-5.

FIGURE 3-5: The image appears on-screen after you render and show it.

Close the image when you're finished viewing it. (The asterisk in the `In [*]:` entry tells you that the code is still running and you can't move on to the next step.) The act of closing the image ends the code segment. You now have an image in memory, and you may want to find out more about it. When you run the following code, you discover the image type and size:

```
print("data type: %s, shape: %s" %
      (type(image), image.shape))
```

The output from this call tells you that the image type is a `numpy.ndarray` and that the image size is 90 pixels by 90 pixels. The image is actually an array of pixels that you can manipulate in various ways. For example, if you want to crop the image, you can use the following code to manipulate the image array:

```
image2 = image[5:70,0:70]
plt.imshow(image2, cmap=cm.gray)
plt.show()
```

The `numpy.ndarray` in `image2` is smaller than the one in `image`, so the output is smaller as well. Figure 3-6 shows typical results. The purpose of cropping the image is to make it a specific size. Both images must be the same size for you to analyze them. Cropping is one way to ensure that the images are the correct size for analysis.

FIGURE 3-6:
Cropping the image makes it smaller.

Another method that you can use to change the image size is to resize it. The following code resizes the image to a specific size for analysis:

```
image3 = resize(image2, (30, 30), mode='nearest')
plt.imshow(image3, cmap=cm.gray)
print("data type: %s, shape: %s" %
    (type(image3), image3.shape))
```

The output from the `print()` function tells you that the image is now 30 pixels by 30 pixels in size. You can compare it to any image with the same dimensions.

After you have all the images in the right size, you need to flatten them. A data set row is always a single dimension, not two dimensions. The image is currently an array of 30 pixels by 30 pixels, so you can't make it part of a data set. The following code flattens `image3` so that it becomes an array of 900 elements that is stored in `image_row`:

```
image_row = image3.flatten()
print("data type: %s, shape: %s" %
    (type(image_row), image_row.shape))
```

Notice that the type is still a `numpy.ndarray`. You can add this array to a data set and then use the data set for analysis purposes. The size is 900 elements, as anticipated.

CHAPTER 3 **Working with Real Data** 399

Managing Data from Relational Databases

Databases come in all sorts of forms. However, the vast majority of data used by organizations rely on relational databases because these databases provide the means for organizing massive amounts of complex data in a manner that makes the data easy to manipulate. The goal of a database manager is to make data easy to manipulate. The focus of most data storage is to make data easy to retrieve.

REMEMBER

Relational databases accomplish both the manipulation and data retrieval objectives with relative ease. However, because data storage needs come in all shapes and sizes for a wide range of computing platforms, there are many different relational database products. The proliferation of different Database Management Systems (DBMSs) using various data layouts is one of the main problems you encounter with creating a comprehensive data set for analysis.

The one common denominator between many relational databases is that they all rely on a form of the same language to perform data manipulation, which does make the programmer's job easier. The Structured Query Language (SQL) lets you perform all sorts of management tasks in a relational database, retrieve data as needed, and even shape it in a particular way so that the need to perform additional shaping is unnecessary.

Creating a connection to a database can be a complex undertaking. For one thing, you need to know how to connect to that particular database. However, you can divide the process into smaller pieces. The first step is to gain access to the database engine. You use two lines of code similar to the following code (but the code presented here is not meant to execute and perform a task):

```
from sqlalchemy import create_engine
engine = create_engine('sqlite:///:memory:')
```

After you have access to an engine, you can use the engine to perform tasks specific to that DBMS. The output of a read method is always a DataFrame object that contains the requested data. To write data, you must create a DataFrame object or use an existing DataFrame object. You normally use these methods to perform most tasks:

- » read_sql_table(): Reads data from a SQL table to a DataFrame object.
- » read_sql_query(): Reads data from a database using a SQL query to a DataFrame object.
- » read_sql(): Reads data from either a SQL table or query to a DataFrame object.

» `DataFrame.to_sql()`: Writes the content of a `DataFrame` object to the specified tables in the database.

The SQLAlchemy library provides support for a broad range of SQL databases. The following list contains just a few of them:

» SQLite

» MySQL

» PostgreSQL

» SQL Server

» Other relational databases, such as those you can connect to using Open Database Connectivity (ODBC)

You can discover more about working with databases at `pandas.pydata.org/pandas-docs/dev/io.html#sql-queries`. The techniques that you discover in this book using the toy databases also work with relational databases.

Interacting with Data from NoSQL Databases

In addition to standard relational databases that rely on SQL, you find a wealth of databases of all sorts that don't have to rely on SQL. These "Not only SQL" (NoSQL) databases are used in large data storage scenarios in which the relational model can become overly complex or can break down in other ways. The databases generally don't use the relational model. Of course, you find fewer of these DBMSs used in the corporate environment because they require special handling and training. Still, some common DBMSs are used because they provide special functionality or meet unique requirements. The process is essentially the same for using NoSQL databases as it is for relational databases:

1. Import required database engine functionality.
2. Create a database engine.
3. Make any required queries using the database engine and the functionality supported by the DBMS.

The details vary quite a bit, and you need to know which library to use with your particular database product. For example, when working with MongoDB

CHAPTER 3 **Working with Real Data** 401

(www.mongodb.org), you must obtain a copy of the PyMongo library (https://api.mongodb.org/python/current) and use the `MongoClient` class to create the required engine. The MongoDB engine relies heavily on the `find()` function to locate data. Here's a pseudo-code example of a MongoDB session:

```
import pymongo
import pandas as pd
from pymongo import Connection
connection = Connection()
db = connection.database_name
input_data = db.collection_name
data = pd.DataFrame(list(input_data.find()))
```

Accessing Data from the Web

It would be incredibly difficult (perhaps impossible) to find an organization today that doesn't rely on some sort of web-based data. Most organizations use web services of some type. A *web service* is a kind of web application that provides a means to ask questions and receive answers. Web services usually host a number of input types. In fact, a particular web service may host entire groups of query inputs.

APIs AND OTHER WEB ENTITIES

A programmer may have a reason to rely on various web application programming interfaces (APIs) to access and manipulate data. Each API is unique, and APIs operate outside the normal scope of what a programmer might do. For example, you might use a product such as jQuery (jquery.com) to access data and manipulate it in various ways when working with a web application. However, the techniques for doing so are more along the lines of writing an application than employing a data analysis technique.

It's important to realize that APIs can be data sources and that you might need to use one to achieve some data input or data-shaping goals. In fact, you find many data entities that resemble APIs but don't appear in this book. Windows developers can create Component Object Model (COM) applications that output data onto the web that you could possibly use for analysis purposes. In fact, the number of potential sources is nearly endless. This book focuses on the sources that you use most often and in the most conventional manner. Keeping your eyes open for other possibilities, though, is always a good idea.

Another type of query system is the microservice. Unlike the web service, *microservices* have a specific focus and provide only one specific query input and output. Using microservices has specific benefits that are outside the scope of this book, but essentially they work like tiny web services, so that's how this book addresses them.

One of the most beneficial data access techniques to know when working with web data is accessing XML or Extensible Markup Language, a popular web data format. All sorts of content types rely on XML, even some web pages. Working with web services and microservices means working with XML. With this in mind, the example in this section works with XML data found in the XMLData.xml file, shown in Figure 3-7. In this case, the file is simple and uses only a couple of levels. XML is hierarchical and can become quite a few levels deep.

```
<MyDataset>
    <Record>
        <Number>1</Number>
        <String>First</String>
        <Boolean>True</Boolean>
    </Record>
    <Record>
        <Number>2</Number>
        <String>Second</String>
        <Boolean>False</Boolean>
    </Record>
    <Record>
        <Number>3</Number>
        <String>Third</String>
        <Boolean>True</Boolean>
    </Record>
    <Record>
        <Number>4</Number>
        <String>Fourth</String>
        <Boolean>False</Boolean>
    </Record>
</MyDataset>
```

FIGURE 3-7: XML is a hierarchical format that can become quite complex.

The technique for working with XML, even simple XML, can be a bit harder than anything else you've worked with so far. Here's the code for this example:

```python
from lxml import objectify
import pandas as pd

xml = objectify.parse(open('XMLData.xml'))
root = xml.getroot()

df = pd.DataFrame(columns=('Number', 'String', 'Boolean'))
```

CHAPTER 3 **Working with Real Data** 403

```
for i in range(0,4):
    obj = root.getchildren()[i].getchildren()
    row = dict(zip(['Number', 'String', 'Boolean'],
                   [obj[0].text, obj[1].text,
                    obj[2].text]))
    row_s = pd.Series(row)
    row_s.name = i
    df = df.append(row_s)
print df
```

The example begins by importing libraries and parsing the data file using the `objectify.parse()` method. Every XML document must contain a root node, which is `<MyDataset>` in this case. The root node encapsulates the rest of the content, and every node under it is a child. To do anything practical with the document, you must obtain access to the root node using the `getroot()` method.

The next step is to create an empty `DataFrame` object that contains the correct column names for each record entry: `Number`, `String`, and `Boolean`. As with all other pandas data handling, XML data handling relies on a `DataFrame`. The `for` loop fills the `DataFrame` with the four records from the XML file (each in a `<Record>` node).

The process looks complex but follows a logical order. The `obj` variable contains all the children for one `<Record>` node. These children are loaded into a dictionary object in which the keys are `Number`, `String`, and `Boolean` to match the `DataFrame` columns.

There is now a dictionary object that contains the row data. The code creates an actual row for the `DataFrame` next. It gives the row the value of the current `for` loop iteration. It then appends the row to the `DataFrame`. To see that everything worked as expected, the code prints the result, which looks like this:

	Number	String	Boolean
0	1	First	True
1	2	Second	False
2	3	Third	True
3	4	Fourth	False

7 Evaluating Data

Contents at a Glance

CHAPTER 1: Conditioning Your Data 407
- Juggling between NumPy and pandas 408
- Validating Your Data .. 409
- Manipulating Categorical Variables 414
- Dealing with Dates in Your Data 419
- Dealing with Missing Data 421
- Slicing and Dicing: Filtering and Selecting Data 424
- Concatenating and Transforming 426
- Aggregating Data at Any Level 430

CHAPTER 2: Shaping Data .. 433
- Working with HTML Pages 434
- Working with Raw Text .. 436
- Using the Bag of Words Model and Beyond 442
- Working with Graph Data .. 447

CHAPTER 3: Getting a Crash Course in MatPlotLib 451
- Starting with a Graph .. 452
- Setting the Axis, Ticks, Grids 455
- Defining the Line Appearance 458
- Using Labels, Annotations, and Legends 462

CHAPTER 4: Visualizing the Data 467
- Choosing the Right Graph 468
- Creating Advanced Scatterplots 475
- Plotting Time Series ... 478
- Plotting Geographical Data 481
- Visualizing Graphs ... 483

CHAPTER 5: Exploring Data Analysis 489
- The EDA Approach ... 490
- Defining Descriptive Statistics for Numeric Data ... 491
- Counting for Categorical Data 495
- Creating Applied Visualization for EDA 498
- Understanding Correlation 504
- Modifying Data Distributions 508

CHAPTER 6: Exploring Four Simple and Effective Algorithms ... 511
- Guessing the Number: Linear Regression 512
- Moving to Logistic Regression 515
- Making Things as Simple as Naïve Bayes 518
- Learning Lazily with Nearest Neighbors 522

IN THIS CHAPTER

» Working with NumPy and pandas

» Knowing your data

» Working with symbolic variables

» Fixing missing data

» Creating data slices

» Adding data elements and modifying data type

Chapter 1
Conditioning Your Data

"In God we trust. All others must bring data."

— W. EDWARDS DEMING

The characteristics, content, type, and other elements that define your data in its entirety is the data *shape*. The shape of your data determines the kinds of tasks you can perform with it. In order to make your data amenable to certain types of analysis, you must shape it into a different form. Think of the data as clay and you as the potter, because that's the sort of relationship that exists. However, instead of using your hands to shape the data, you rely on functions and algorithms to perform the task. This chapter helps you understand the tools you have available to shape data and the ramifications of shaping it.

Also in this chapter, you consider the problems associated with shaping. For example, you need to know what to do when data is missing from a data set. It's important to shape the data correctly or you end up with an analysis that simply doesn't make sense. Likewise, some data types, such as dates, can present problems. Again, you need to tread carefully to ensure that you get the desired result so that the data set becomes more useful and amenable to analysis of various sorts.

The goal of some types of data shaping is to create a larger data set. In many cases, the data you need to perform an analysis on doesn't appear in a single database or in a particular form. You need to shape the data and then combine it so that you have a single data set in a known format before you can begin the analysis. Combining data successfully can be an art form because data often defies simple analysis or quick fixes.

You don't have to type the source code for this chapter by hand. In fact, it's a lot easier if you use the downloadable source. The source code for this chapter appears in the `P4DS4D; 06; Getting Your Data in Shape.ipynb` source code file available at `www.dummies.com/go/codingaiodownloads`.

Juggling between NumPy and pandas

There is no question that you need NumPy at all times. The pandas library is actually built on top of NumPy. However, you do need to make a choice between NumPy and pandas when performing tasks. You need the low-level functionality of NumPy to perform some tasks, but pandas makes things so much easier that you want to use it as often as possible. The following sections describe when to use each library in more detail.

Knowing when to use NumPy

It's essential to realize that developers built pandas on top of NumPy. As a result, every task you perform using pandas also goes through NumPy. To obtain the benefits of pandas, you pay a performance penalty that some testers say is 100 times slower than NumPy for a similar task (see `https://penandpants.com/2014/09/05/performance-of-pandas-series-vs-numpy-arrays`). Given that computer hardware can make up for a lot of performance differences today, the speed issue may not be a concern at times, but when speed is essential, NumPy is always the better choice.

Knowing when to use pandas

You use pandas to make writing code easier and faster. Because pandas does a lot of the work for you, you could make a case for saying that using pandas also reduces the potential for coding errors. The essential consideration, though, is that the pandas library provides rich time-series functionality, data alignment, NA-friendly statistics, groupby, merge, and join methods. Normally, you need to code these features when using NumPy, which means you keep reinventing the wheel.

> ## IT'S ALL IN THE PREPARATION
>
> This book may seem to spend a lot of time massaging data and little time on actually analyzing it. However, the majority of a data scientist's time is actually spent preparing data because the data is seldom in any order to actually perform analysis. To prepare data for use, a data scientist must
>
> - Get the data.
> - Aggregate the data.
> - Create data subsets.
> - Clean the data.
> - Develop a single data set by merging various data sets together.
>
> Fortunately, you don't need to die of boredom while wading your way through these various tasks. Using Python and the various libraries it provides makes the task a lot simpler, faster, and more efficient. The better you know how to use Python to speed your way through these repetitive tasks, the sooner you begin having fun performing various sorts of analysis on the data.

As the book progresses, you discover just how useful pandas can be performing such tasks as *binning* (a data preprocessing technique designed to reduce the effect of observational errors) and working with a *dataframe* (a two-dimensional labeled data structure with columns that can potentially contain different data types) so that you can calculate statistics on it. Book 7, Chapter 5 shows actual binning examples, such as obtaining a frequency for each categorical variable of a data set. In fact, many of the examples in Book 7, Chapter 5 don't work without binning. In other words, don't worry too much right now about knowing precisely what binning is or why you need to use it — examples later in the book discuss the topic in detail. All you really need to know is that pandas does make your work considerably easier.

Validating Your Data

When it comes to data, no one really knows what a large database contains. Yes, everyone has seen bits and pieces of it, but when you consider the size of some databases, viewing it all would be physically impossible. Because you don't know what's in there, you can't be sure that your analysis will actually work as desired and provide valid results. In short, you must validate your data before you use it

to ensure that the data is at least close to what you expect it to be. This means performing tasks such as removing duplicate records before you use the data for any sort of analysis (duplicates would unfairly weight the results).

However, you do need to consider what validation actually does for you. It doesn't tell you that the data is correct or that there won't be values outside the expected range. What validation does is ensure that you can perform an analysis of the data and reasonably expect that analysis to succeed. Later, you need to perform additional massaging of the data to obtain the sort of results that you need in order to perform the task you set out to perform in the first place.

Figuring out what's in your data

Figuring out what your data contains is important because checking data by hand is sometimes simply impossible due to the number of observations and variables. In addition, hand verifying the content is time consuming, error prone, and, most important, really boring. Finding duplicates is important because you end up

- » Spending more computational time to process duplicates, which slows your algorithms down.
- » Obtaining false results because duplicates implicitly overweight the results. Because some entries appear more than once, the algorithm considers these entries more important.

As a data scientist, you want your data to enthrall you, so it's time to get it to talk to you — not figuratively, of course, but through the wonders of pandas, as shown in the following example:

```
from lxml import objectify
import pandas as pd

xml = objectify.parse(open('XMLData2.xml'))
root = xml.getroot()
df = pd.DataFrame(columns=('Number', 'String', 'Boolean'))

for i in range(0,4):
    obj = root.getchildren()[i].getchildren()
    row = dict(zip(['Number', 'String', 'Boolean'],
                   [obj[0].text, obj[1].text,
                    obj[2].text]))
    row_s = pd.Series(row)
    row_s.name = i
    df = df.append(row_s)

search = pd.DataFrame.duplicated(df)
```

```
print df
print
print search[search == True]
```

This example shows how to find duplicate rows. It relies on a modified version of the XMLData.xml file, XMLData2.xml, which contains a simple repeated row in it. A real data file contains thousands (or more) of records and possibly hundreds of repeats, but this simple example does the job. The example begins by reading the data file into memory using the same technique you explore in Book 6, Chapter 2. It then places the data into a DataFrame.

Place the data file XMLData2.xml in the same directory as your Python program.

At this point, your data is corrupted because it contains a duplicate row. However, you can get rid of the duplicated row by searching for it. The first task is to create a search object containing a list of duplicated rows by calling pd.DataFrame.duplicated(). The duplicated rows contain a True next to their row number.

Of course, now you have an unordered list of rows that are and aren't duplicated. The easiest way to determine which rows are duplicated is to create an index in which you use search == True as the expression. Following is the output you see from this example. Notice that row 1 is duplicated in the DataFrame output and that row 1 is also called out in the search results:

```
   Number  String  Boolean
0       1   First     True
1       1   First     True
2       2  Second    False
3       3   Third     True
1    True
dtype: bool
```

Removing duplicates

To get a clean data set, you want to remove the duplicates. Fortunately, you don't have to write any weird code to get the job done — pandas does it for you, as shown in the following example:

```
from lxml import objectify
import pandas as pd

xml = objectify.parse(open('XMLData2.xml'))
root = xml.getroot()
df = pd.DataFrame(columns=('Number', 'String', 'Boolean'))
```

```
for i in range(0,4):
    obj = root.getchildren()[i].getchildren()
    row = dict(zip(['Number', 'String', 'Boolean'],
                   [obj[0].text, obj[1].text,
                    obj[2].text]))
    row_s = pd.Series(row)
    row_s.name = i
    df = df.append(row_s)

print df.drop_duplicates()
```

As with the previous example, you begin by creating a `DataFrame` that contains the duplicate record. To remove the errant record, all you need to do is call `drop_duplicates()`. Here's the result you get:

```
  Number  String  Boolean
0      1   First     True
2      2  Second    False
3      3   Third     True
```

Creating a data map and data plan

You need to know about your data set — that is, how it looks statically. A *data map* is an overview of the data set. You use it to spot potential problems in your data, such as

- » Redundant variables
- » Possible errors
- » Missing values
- » Variable transformations

Checking for these problems goes into a *data plan*, which is a list of tasks you have to perform to ensure the integrity of your data. The following example shows a data map, A, with two data sets, B and C:

```
import pandas as pd

df = pd.DataFrame({'A': [0,0,0,0,0,1,1],
                   'B': [1,2,3,5,4,2,5],
                   'C': [5,3,4,1,1,2,3]})

a_group_desc = df.groupby('A').describe()
print a_group_desc
```

In this case, the data map uses 0s for the first series and 1s for the second series. The `groupby()` function places the data sets, B and C, into groups. To determine whether the data map is viable, you obtain statistics using `describe()`. What you end up with is a data set B, series 0 and 1, and data set C, series 0 and 1, as shown in the following output:

```
              B         C
A
0 count   5.000000  5.000000
  mean    3.000000  2.800000
  std     1.581139  1.788854
  min     1.000000  1.000000
  25%     2.000000  1.000000
  50%     3.000000  3.000000
  75%     4.000000  4.000000
  max     5.000000  5.000000
1 count   2.000000  2.000000
  mean    3.500000  2.500000
  std     2.121320  0.707107
  min     2.000000  2.000000
  25%     2.750000  2.250000
  50%     3.500000  2.500000
  75%     4.250000  2.750000
  max     5.000000  3.000000
```

These statistics tell you about the two data set series. The breakup of the two data sets using specific cases is the *data plan*. As you can see, the statistics tell you that this data plan may not be viable because some statistics are relatively far apart.

The output from `describe()` can be hard to read. The data is crammed together, but you can break it apart, as shown here:

```
unstacked = a_group_desc.unstack()
print unstacked
```

Using `unstack()` creates a new presentation. Here's the output formatted nicely so that you can see it better:

```
      B
  count mean    std      min  25%   50%  75%   max
A
0   5   3.0   1.581139    1   2.00  3.0  4.00   5
1   2   3.5   2.121320    2   2.75  3.5  4.25   5
```

CHAPTER 1 Conditioning Your Data 413

```
              C
      count mean      std min  25%  50%  75%  max
A
0         5  2.8 1.788854   1 1.00  3.0 4.00    5
1         2  2.5 0.707107   2 2.25  2.5 2.75    3
```

Of course, you may not want all the data that describe() provides. Perhaps you really just want to see the number of items in each series and their mean. Here's how you reduce the size of the information output:

```
print unstacked.loc[:,(slice(None),['count','mean']),]
```

Using loc lets you obtain specific columns. Here's the final output from the example showing just the information you absolutely need to make a decision:

```
       B          C
   count mean count mean
A
0      5  3.0     5  2.8
1      2  3.5     2  2.5
```

Manipulating Categorical Variables

In data science, a *categorical variable* is one that has a specific value from a limited selection of values. The number of values is usually fixed. Many developers will know categorical variables by the moniker *enumerations*. Each of the potential values that a categorical variable can assume is a *level*.

To understand how categorical variables work, say that you have a variable expressing the color of an object, such as a car, and that the user can select blue, red, or green. To express the car's color in a way that computers can represent and effectively compute, an application assigns each color a numeric value, so blue is 1, red is 2, and green is 3. Normally when you print each color, you see the value rather than the color.

If you use pandas.DataFrame (pandas-docs.github.io/pandas-docs-travis/generated/pandas.DataFrame.html#pandas.DataFrame), you can still see the symbolic value (blue, red, and green), even though the computer stores it as a numeric value. Sometimes you need to rename and combine these named values to create new symbols. Symbolic variables are just a convenient way of representing and storing qualitative data.

> **CHECKING YOUR VERSION OF PANDAS**
>
> The categorical variable examples in this section depend on your having a minimum version of pandas 0.15.0 installed on your system (using pandas 0.16.0 or above is actually better because it includes a large number of bug fixes). To check your version of pandas, type **import pandas as pd** and press Enter; then, type **print pd.version.version** and press Enter. You see the version number of pandas you have installed. The Anaconda 2.1.0 software package includes pandas 0.14.1, but you should update to pandas 0.16.0. You can upgrade to this version after installing Anaconda 2.1.0 by typing **conda install pandas=0.16.0** in the command line.
>
> For detailed installation instructions, review the instructions at `pandas.pydata.org/pandas-docs/version/0.16.0/install.html#installing-pandas-with-miniconda`.

When using categorical variables for machine learning, it's important to consider the algorithm used to manipulate the variables. Some algorithms can work directly with the numeric variables behind the symbols, while other algorithms require that you encode the categorical values into binary variables. For example, if you have three levels for a color variable (blue, red, and green), you have to create three binary variables:

» One for blue (1 when the value is blue, 0 when it is not)

» One for red (1 when the value is red, 0 when it is not)

» One for green (1 when the value is green, 0 when it is not)

Creating categorical variables

Categorical variables have a specific number of values, which makes them incredibly valuable in performing a number of data science tasks. For example, imagine trying to find values that are out of range in a huge data set. In this example, you see one method for creating a categorical variable and then using it to check whether some data falls within the specified limits.

```
import pandas as pd

car_colors = pd.Series(['Blue', 'Red', 'Green'], dtype='category')

car_data = pd.Series(
    pd.Categorical(['Yellow', 'Green', 'Red', 'Blue', 'Purple'],
                   categories=car_colors, ordered=False))
```

CHAPTER 1 **Conditioning Your Data** 415

```
find_entries = pd.isnull(car_data)

print car_colors
print
print car_data
print
print find_entries[find_entries == True]
```

WARNING

You must have at least pandas 0.15.0 for this code to work. If you are receiving an error here, make sure to follow the preceding instructions on updating your version of pandas.

The example begins by creating a categorical variable, car_colors. The variable contains the values Blue, Red, and Green as colors that are acceptable for a car. Notice that you must specify a dtype property value of category.

The next step is to create another series. This one uses a list of actual car colors, named car_data, as input. Not all the car colors match the predefined acceptable values. When this problem occurs, pandas outputs Not a Number (NaN) instead of the car color.

Of course, you could search the list manually for the nonconforming cars, but the easiest method is to have pandas do the work for you. In this case, you ask pandas which entries are null using isnull() and place them in find_entries. You can then output just those entries that are actually null. Here's the output you see from the example:

```
0    Blue
1    Red
2    Green
dtype: category
Categories (3, object): [Blue, Green, Red]

0    NaN
1    Green
2    Red
3    Blue
4    NaN
dtype: category
Categories (3, object): [Blue, Red, Green]

0    True
4    True
dtype: bool
```

Looking at the list of car_data outputs, you can see that entries 0 and 4 equal NaN. The output from find_entries verifies this fact for you. If this were a large data set, you could quickly locate and correct errant entries in the data set before performing an analysis on it.

Renaming levels

There are times when the naming of the categories you use is inconvenient or otherwise wrong for a particular need. Fortunately, you can rename the categories as needed using the technique shown in the following example:

```
import pandas as pd

car_colors = pd.Series(['Blue', 'Red', 'Green'],
                       dtype='category')
car_data = pd.Series(
    pd.Categorical(
        ['Blue', 'Green', 'Red', 'Blue', 'Red'],
        categories=car_colors, ordered=False))

car_colors.cat.categories = ["Purple", "Yellow", "Mauve"]
car_data.cat.categories = car_colors

print car_data
```

All you really need to do is set the cat.categories property to a new value, as shown. Here is the output from this example:

```
0    Purple
1    Yellow
2     Mauve
3    Purple
4     Mauve
dtype: category
Categories (3, object): [Purple, Mauve, Yellow]
```

Combining levels

A particular categorical level might be too small to offer significant data for analysis. Perhaps there are only a few of the values, which may not be enough to create a

statistical difference. In this case, combining several small categories might offer better analysis results. The following example shows how to combine categories:

```
import pandas as pd

car_colors = pd.Series(['Blue', 'Red', 'Green'],
                       dtype='category')
car_data = pd.Series(
    pd.Categorical(
        ['Blue', 'Green', 'Red', 'Green', 'Red', 'Green'],
        categories=car_colors, ordered=False))

car_data.cat.categories = ["Blue_Red", "Red", "Green"]
print car_data.ix[car_data.isin(['Red'])]

car_data.ix[car_data.isin(['Red'])] = 'Blue_Red'

print
print car_data
```

What this example shows you is that there is only one Blue item and only two Red items, but there are three Green items, which places Green in the majority. Combining Blue and Red together is a two-step process. First, you change the Blue category to the Blue_Red category so that when you see the output, you know that the two are combined. Then you change the Red entries to Blue_Red, which creates the combined category.

However, before you can change the Red entries to Blue_Red entries, you must find them. This is where a combination of calls to isin(), which locates the Red entries, and ix[], which obtains their index, provides precisely what you need. The first print statement shows the result of using this combination. Here's the output from this example:

```
2       Red
4       Red
dtype: category
Categories (3, object): [Blue_Red, Red, Green]

0       Blue_Red
1       Green
2       Blue_Red
3       Green
4       Blue_Red
5       Green
dtype: category
Categories (3, object): [Blue_Red, Red, Green]
```

Notice that there are now three `Blue_Red` entries and three `Green` entries. The `Blue` category no longer exists, and the `Red` category is no longer in use. The result is that the levels are now combined as expected.

Dealing with Dates in Your Data

Dates can present problems in data. For one thing, dates are stored as numeric values. However, the precise value of the number depends on the representation for the particular platform and could even depend on the users' preferences. For example, Excel users can choose to start dates in 1900 or 1904 (https://support.microsoft.com/en-us/kb/180162). The numeric encoding for each is different, so the same date can have two numeric values depending on the starting date.

In addition to problems of representation, you also need to consider how to work with time values. Creating a time value format that represents a value the user can understand is hard. For example, you might need to use Greenwich Mean Time (GMT) in some situations but a local time zone in others. Transforming between various times is also problematic. With this in mind, the following sections provide you with details on dealing with time issues.

Formatting date and time values

Obtaining the correct date and time representation can make performing analysis a lot easier. For example, you often have to change the representation to obtain a correct sorting of values. Python provides two common methods of formatting date and time. The first technique is to call `str()`, which simply turns a `datetime` value into a string without any formatting. The `strftime()` function requires more work because you must define how you want the `datetime` value to appear after conversion. When using `strftime()`, you must provide a string containing special directives that define the formatting. You can find a listing of these directives at `strftime.org`.

Now that you have some idea of how time and date conversions work, it's time to see an example. The following example creates a `datetime` object and then converts it into a string using two different approaches:

```
import datetime as dt

now = dt.datetime.now()

print str(now)
print now.strftime('%a, %d %B %Y')
```

CHAPTER 1 **Conditioning Your Data** 419

In this case, you can see that using `str()` is the easiest approach. However, as shown by the following output, it may not provide the output you need. Using `strftime()` is infinitely more flexible.

```
2017-01-16 17:26:45.986000
Mon, 16 January 2017
```

Using the right time transformation

Time zones and differences in local time can cause all sorts of problems when performing analysis. For that matter, some types of calculations simply require a time shift in order to get the right results. No matter what the reason, you may need to transform one time into another time at some point. The following examples show some techniques you can employ to perform the task.

```
import datetime as dt

now = dt.datetime.now()
timevalue = now + dt.timedelta(hours=2)

print now.strftime('%H:%M:%S')
print timevalue.strftime('%H:%M:%S')
print timevalue - now
```

The `timedelta()` function makes the time transformation straightforward. You can use any of these parameter names with `timedelta()` to change a time and date value:

- » days
- » seconds
- » microseconds
- » milliseconds
- » minutes
- » hours
- » weeks

You can also manipulate time by performing addition or subtraction on time values. You can even subtract two time values to determine the difference between them. Here's the output from this example:

```
17:44:40
19:44:40
2:00:00
```

Notice that now is the local time, timevalue is two time zones different from this one, and there is a two-hour difference between the two times. You can perform all sorts of transformations using these techniques to ensure that your analysis always shows precisely the time-oriented values you need.

Dealing with Missing Data

Sometimes the data you receive is missing information in specific fields. For example, a customer record might be missing an age. If enough records are missing entries, any analysis you perform will be skewed and the results of the analysis weighted in an unpredictable manner. Having a strategy for dealing with missing data is important. The following sections give you some ideas on how to work through these issues and produce better results.

Finding the missing data

It's essential to find missing data in your data set to avoid getting incorrect results from your analysis. The following code shows how you could obtain a listing of missing values without too much effort:

```
import pandas as pd
import numpy as np

s = pd.Series([1, 2, 3, np.NaN, 5, 6, None])

print s.isnull()

print
print s[s.isnull()]
```

A data set could represent missing data in several ways. In this example, you see missing data represented as np.NaN (NumPy Not a Number) and the Python None value.

Use the isnull() method to detect the missing values. The output shows True when the value is missing. By adding an index into the data set, you obtain just the entries that are missing. The example shows the following output:

```
0    False
1    False
2    False
3     True
4    False
```

```
5    False
6    True
dtype: bool

3    NaN
6    NaN
dtype: float64
```

Encoding missingness

After you figure out that your data set is missing information, you need to consider what to do about it. The three possibilities are to ignore the issue, fill in the missing items, or remove (drop) the missing entries from the data set. Ignoring the problem could lead to all sorts of problems for your analysis, so it's the option you use least often. The following example shows one technique for filling in missing data or dropping the errant entries from the data set:

```
import pandas as pd
import numpy as np

s = pd.Series([1, 2, 3, np.NaN, 5, 6, None])

print s.fillna(int(s.mean()))
print
print s.dropna()
```

The two methods of interest are `fillna()`, which fills in the missing entries, and `dropna()`, which drops the missing entries. When using `fillna()`, you must provide a value to use for the missing data. This example uses the mean of all the values, but you could choose a number of other approaches. Here's the output from this example:

```
0    1
1    2
2    3
3    3
4    5
5    6
6    3
dtype: float64

0    1
1    2
2    3
4    5
5    6
dtype: float64
```

TECHNICAL STUFF

Working with a series is straightforward because the data set is so simple. When working with a DataFrame, however, the problem becomes significantly more complicated. You still have the option of dropping the entire row. When a column is sparsely populated, you might drop the column instead. Filling in the data also becomes more complex because you must consider the data set as a whole, in addition to the needs of the individual feature.

Imputing missing data

The previous section hints at the process of imputing missing data (ascribing characteristics based on how the data is used). The technique you use depends on the sort of data you're working with. The following example shows a technique you can use to impute missing data values:

```
import pandas as pd
import numpy as np
from sklearn.preprocessing import Imputer

s = pd.Series([1, 2, 3, np.NaN, 5, 6, None])

imp = Imputer(missing_values='NaN',
              strategy='mean', axis=0)

imp.fit([1, 2, 3, 4, 5, 6, 7])

x = pd.Series(imp.transform(s).tolist()[0])

print x
```

In this example, s is missing some values. The code creates an Imputer to replace these missing values. The missing_values parameter defines what to look for, which is NaN (Not a Number). You set the axis parameter to 0 to impute along columns and 1 to impute along rows. The strategy parameter defines how to replace the missing values (you can discover more about the Imputer parameters at scikit-learn.org/stable/modules/generated/sklearn.preprocessing.Imputer.html):

- » mean: Replaces the values by using the mean along the axis.
- » median: Replaces the values by using the medium along the axis.
- » most_frequent: Replaces the values by using the most frequent value along the axis.

Before you can impute anything, you must provide statistics for the Imputer to use by calling fit(). The code then calls transform() on s to fill in the missing

values. However, the output is no longer a series. To create a series, you must convert the `Imputer` output to a list and use the resulting list as input to `Series()`. Here's the result of the process with the missing values filled in:

```
0    1
1    2
2    3
3    4
4    5
5    6
6    7
dtype: float64
```

Slicing and Dicing: Filtering and Selecting Data

You may not need to work with all the data in a data set. In fact, looking at just one particular column might be beneficial, such as age, or a set of rows with a significant amount of information. You perform two steps to obtain just the data you need to perform a particular task:

1. Filter rows to create a subject of the data that meets the criterion you select (such as all the people between the ages of 5 and 10).

2. Select data columns that contain the data you need to analyze. For example, you probably don't need the individuals' names unless you want to perform some analysis based on name.

The act of slicing and dicing data gives you a subset of the data suitable for analysis. The following sections describe various ways to obtain specific pieces of data to meet particular needs.

Slicing rows

Slicing can occur in multiple ways when working with data, but the technique of interest in this section is to slice data from a row of 2D or 3D data. A 2D array may contain temperatures (x axis) over a specific timeframe (y axis). Slicing a row would mean seeing the temperatures at a specific time. In some cases, you might associate rows with cases in a data set.

A 3D array might include an axis for place (x axis), product (y axis), and time (z axis) so that you can see sales for items over time. Perhaps you want to track

whether sales of an item are increasing, and specifically where they are increasing. Slicing a row would mean seeing all the sales for one specific product for all locations at any time. The following example demonstrates how to perform this task:

```
x = np.array([[[1, 2, 3],   [4, 5, 6],   [7, 8, 9],],
              [[11,12,13], [14,15,16], [17,18,19],],
              [[21,22,23], [24,25,26], [27,28,29]]])

x[1]
```

In this case, the example builds a 3D array. It then slices row 1 of that array to produce the following output:

```
array([[11, 12, 13],
       [14, 15, 16],
       [17, 18, 19]])
```

Slicing columns

Using the examples from the previous section, slicing columns would obtain data at a 90-degree angle from rows. In other words, when working with the 2D array, you would want to see the times at which specific temperatures occurred. Likewise, you might want to see the sales of all products for a specific location at any time when working with the 3D array. In some cases, you might associate columns with features in a data set. The following example demonstrates how to perform this task using the same array as in the previous section:

```
x = np.array([[[1, 2, 3],   [4, 5, 6],   [7, 8, 9],],
              [[11,12,13], [14,15,16], [17,18,19],],
              [[21,22,23], [24,25,26], [27,28,29]]])

x[:,1]
```

Notice that the indexing now occurs at two levels. The first index refers to the row. Using the colon (:) for the row means to use all the rows. The second index refers to a column. In this case, the output will contain column 1. Here's the output you see:

```
array([[ 4,  5,  6],
       [14, 15, 16],
       [24, 25, 26]])
```

REMEMBER

This is a 3D array. Therefore each of the columns contains all the z axis elements. What you see is every row — 0 through 2 for column 1 with every z axis element 0 through 2 for that column.

CHAPTER 1 **Conditioning Your Data** 425

Dicing

The act of dicing a data set means to perform both row and column slicing such that you end up with a data wedge. For example, when working with the 3D array, you might want to see the sales of a specific product in a specific location at any time. The following example demonstrates how to perform this task using the same array as in the previous two sections:

```
x = np.array([[[1, 2, 3],  [4, 5, 6],  [7, 8, 9],],
              [[11,12,13], [14,15,16], [17,18,19],],
              [[21,22,23], [24,25,26], [27,28,29]]])

print x[1,1]
print x[:,1,1]
print x[1,:,1]
print
print x[1:3, 1:3]
```

This example dices the array in four different ways. First, you get row 1, column 1. Of course, what you may actually want is column 1, z axis 1. If that's not quite right, you could always request row 1, z axis 1 instead. Then again, you may want rows 1 and 2 of columns 1 and 2. Here's the output of all four requests:

```
[14 15 16]
[ 5 15 25]
[12 15 18]

[[[14 15 16]
  [17 18 19]]

 [[24 25 26]
  [27 28 29]]]
```

Concatenating and Transforming

Data used for data science purposes seldom comes in a neat package. You may need to work with multiple databases in various locations — each of which has its own data format. It's impossible to perform analysis on such disparate sources of information with any accuracy. To make the data useful, you must create a single data set (by *concatenating*, or combining, the data from various sources).

Part of the process is to ensure that each field you create for the combined data set has the same characteristics. For example, an age field in one database might

appear as a string, but another database could use an integer for the same field. For the fields to work together, they must appear as the same type of information.

The following sections help you understand the process involved in concatenating and transforming data from various sources to create a single data set. After you have a single data set from these sources, you can begin to perform tasks such as analysis on the data. Of course, the trick is to create a single data set that truly represents the data in all those disparate data sets — modifying the data would result in skewed results.

Adding new cases and variables

You often find a need to combine data sets in various ways or even to add new information for the sake of analysis purposes. The result is a combined data set that includes either new cases or variables. The following example shows techniques for performing both tasks:

```
import pandas as pd

df = pd.DataFrame({'A': [2,3,1],
                   'B': [1,2,3],
                   'C': [5,3,4]})

df1 = pd.DataFrame({'A': [4],
                    'B': [4],
                    'C': [4]})

df = df.append(df1)
df = df.reset_index(drop=True)
print df

df.loc[df.last_valid_index() + 1] = [5, 5, 5]
print
print df

df2 = pd.DataFrame({'D': [1, 2, 3, 4, 5]})

df = pd.DataFrame.join(df, df2)
print
print df
```

The easiest way to add more data to an existing `DataFrame` is to rely on the `append()` method. You can also use the `concat()` method (a technique shown in Book 7, Chapter 5). In this case, the three cases found in `df` are added to the single case found in `df1`. To ensure that the data is appended as anticipated, the columns in `df` and `df1` must match. When you append two `DataFrame` objects in

this manner, the new `DataFrame` contains the old index values. Use the `reset_index()` method to create a new index to make accessing cases easier.

You can also add another case to an existing `DataFrame` by creating the new case directly. Any time you add a new entry at a position that is one greater than the `last_valid_index()`, you get a new case as a result.

Sometimes you need to add a new variable (column) to the `DataFrame`. In this case, you rely on `join()` to perform the task. The resulting `DataFrame` will match cases with the same index value, so indexing is important. In addition, unless you want blank values, the number of cases in both `DataFrame` objects must match. Here's the output from this example:

```
   A  B  C
0  2  1  5
1  3  2  3
2  1  3  4
3  4  4  4

   A  B  C
0  2  1  5
1  3  2  3
2  1  3  4
3  4  4  4
4  5  5  5

   A  B  C  D
0  2  1  5  1
1  3  2  3  2
2  1  3  4  3
3  4  4  4  4
4  5  5  5  5
```

Removing data

At some point, you may need to remove cases or variables from a data set because they aren't required for your analysis. In both cases, you rely on the `drop()` method to perform the task. The difference in removing cases or variables is in how you describe what to remove, as shown in the following example:

```
import pandas as pd

df = pd.DataFrame({'A': [2,3,1],
                   'B': [1,2,3],
                   'C': [5,3,4]})
```

```
df = df.drop(df.index[[1]])
print df

df = df.drop('B', 1)
print
print df
```

The example begins by removing a case from df. Notice how the code relies on an index to describe what to remove. You can remove just one case (as shown), ranges of cases, or individual cases separated by commas. The main concern is to ensure that you have the correct index numbers for the cases you want to remove.

Removing a column is different. This example shows how to remove a column using a column name. You can also remove a column by using an index. In both cases, you must specify an axis as part of the removal process (normally 1). Here's the output from this example:

```
   A  B  C
0  2  1  5
2  1  3  4

   A  C
0  2  5
2  1  4
```

Sorting and shuffling

Sorting and shuffling are two ends of the same goal — to manage data order. In the first case, you put the data into order, while in the second, you remove any systematic patterning from the order. In general, you don't sort data sets for the purpose of analysis because doing so can cause you to get incorrect results. However, you might want to sort data for presentation purposes. The following example shows both sorting and shuffling:

```
import pandas as pd
import numpy as np

df = pd.DataFrame({'A': [2,1,2,3,3,5,4],
                   'B': [1,2,3,5,4,2,5],
                   'C': [5,3,4,1,1,2,3]})

df = df.sort_index(by=['A', 'B'], ascending=[True, True])
df = df.reset_index(drop=True)
print df
```

CHAPTER 1 **Conditioning Your Data** 429

```
index = df.index.tolist()
np.random.shuffle(index)
df = df.ix[index]
df = df.reset_index(drop=True)
print
print df
```

It turns out that sorting the data is a bit easier than shuffling it. To sort the data, you use the sort_index() method and define which columns to use for indexing purposes. You can also determine whether the index is in ascending or descending order. Make sure to always call reset_index() when you're done so that the index appears in order for analysis or other purposes.

To shuffle the data, you first acquire the current index using df.index.tolist() and place it in index. A call to random.shuffle() creates a new order for the index. You then apply the new order to df using ix[]. As always, you call reset_index() to finalize the new order. Here's the output from this example:

```
   A  B  C
0  1  2  3
1  2  1  5
2  2  3  4
3  3  4  1
4  3  5  1
5  4  5  3
6  5  2  2

   A  B  C
0  2  3  4
1  3  5  1
2  3  4  1
3  1  2  3
4  4  5  3
5  5  2  2
6  2  1  5
```

Aggregating Data at Any Level

Aggregation is the process of combining or grouping data together into a set, bag, or list. The data may or may not be alike. However, in most cases, an aggregation function combines several rows together statistically using algorithms such as average, count, maximum, median, minimum, mode, or sum. There are several reasons to aggregate data:

» Make it easier to analyze.

» Reduce the ability of anyone to deduce the data of an individual from the data set for privacy or other reasons.

» Create a combined data element from one data source that matches a combined data element in another source.

The most important use of data aggregation is to promote anonymity in order to meet legal or other concerns. Sometimes even data that should be anonymous turns out to provide identification of an individual using the proper analysis techniques. For example, researchers have found that it's possible to identify individuals based on just three credit card purchases (see http://www.computerworld.com/article/2877935/how-three-small-credit-card-transactions-could-reveal-your-identity.html). Here's an example that shows how to perform aggregation tasks:

```
import pandas as pd

df = pd.DataFrame({'Map': [0,0,0,1,1,2,2],
                   'Values': [1,2,3,5,4,2,5]})

df['S'] = df.groupby('Map')['Values'].transform(np.sum)
df['M'] = df.groupby('Map')['Values'].transform(np.mean)
df['V'] = df.groupby('Map')['Values'].transform(np.var)

print df
```

In this case, you have two initial features for this `DataFrame`. The values in `Map` define which elements in `Values` belong together. For example, when calculating a sum for `Map` index 0, you use the `Values` 1, 2, and 3.

To perform the aggregation, you must first call `groupby()` to group the `Map` values. You then index into `Values` and rely on `transform()` to create the aggregated data using one of several algorithms found in NumPy, such as `np.sum`. Here are the results of this calculation:

```
   Map  Values  S    M    V
0   0      1   6  2.0  1.0
1   0      2   6  2.0  1.0
2   0      3   6  2.0  1.0
3   1      5   9  4.5  0.5
4   1      4   9  4.5  0.5
5   2      2   7  3.5  4.5
6   2      5   7  3.5  4.5
```

CHAPTER 1 **Conditioning Your Data** 431

> **IN THIS CHAPTER**
>
> » Manipulating HTML data
>
> » Manipulating raw text
>
> » Discovering the bag of words model and other techniques
>
> » Manipulating graph data

Chapter 2
Shaping Data

> *"It is a capital mistake to theorize before one has data."*
> — SHERLOCK HOLMES

Book 7, Chapter 1 demonstrates techniques for working with data as an entity — as something you work with in Python. However, data doesn't exist in a vacuum. It doesn't just suddenly appear within Python for absolutely no reason at all. As demonstrated in Book 6, Chapter 3, you load the data. However, loading may not be enough — you may have to shape the data as part of loading it. That's the purpose of this chapter. You discover how to work with a variety of container types in a way that makes it possible to load data from a number of complex container types, such as HTML pages. In fact, you even work with graphics, images, and sounds.

REMEMBER

As you progress through the book, you discover that data takes all kinds of forms and shapes. As far as the computer is concerned, data consists of 0s and 1s. Humans give the data meaning by formatting, storing, and interpreting it in a certain way. The same group of 0s and 1s could be a number, date, or text, depending on the interpretation. The data container provides clues as to how to interpret the data, so that's why this chapter is so important as you use Python to discover data patterns. You will find that you can discover patterns in places where you might have thought patterns couldn't exist.

You don't have to type the source code for this chapter manually. In fact, it's a lot easier if you use the downloadable source available at `www.dummies.com/go/codingaiodownloads`. The source code for this chapter appears in the P4DS4D; 07; Shaping Data.ipynb source code file.

Working with HTML Pages

HTML pages contain data in a hierarchical format. You often find HTML content in a strict HTML form or as XML. The HTML form can present problems because it doesn't always necessarily follow strict formatting rules. XML does follow strict formatting rules because of the standards used to define it, which makes it easier to parse. However, in both cases, you use similar techniques to parse a page. The first section that follows describes how to parse HTML pages in general.

Sometimes you don't need all the data on a page. Instead you need specific data, which is where XPath comes into play. You can use XPath to locate specific data on the HTML page and extract it for your particular needs.

Parsing XML and HTML

Simply extracting data from an XML file as you do in Book 6, Chapter 3 may not be enough. The data may not be in the correct format. Using the approach in Book 6, Chapter 3, you end up with a DataFrame containing three columns of type str. Obviously, you can't perform much data manipulation with strings. The following example shapes the XML data from Book 6, Chapter 3 to create a new DataFrame containing just the <Number> and <Boolean> elements in the correct format.

```
from lxml import objectify
import pandas as pd
from distutils import util

xml = objectify.parse(open('XMLData.xml'))
root = xml.getroot()
df = pd.DataFrame(columns=('Number', 'Boolean'))

for i in range(0,4):
    obj = root.getchildren()[i].getchildren()
    row = dict(zip(['Number', 'Boolean'],
                   [obj[0].pyval,
                    bool(util.strtobool(obj[2].text))]))
    row_s = pd.Series(row)
    row_s.name = obj[1].text
    df = df.append(row_s)

print type(df.ix['First']['Number'])
print type(df.ix['First']['Boolean'])
```

Obtaining a numeric value from the <Number> element consists of using the pyval output, rather than the text output. The result isn't an int, but it is numeric.

The conversion of the <Boolean> element is a little harder. You must convert the string to a numeric value using the strtobool() function in distutils.util. The output is a 0 for False values and a 1 for True values. However, that's still not a Boolean value. To create a Boolean value, you must convert the 0 or 1 using bool().

TIP

This example also shows how to access individual values in the DataFrame. Notice that the name property now uses the <String> element value for easy access. You provide an index value using ix and then access the individual feature using a second index. The output from this example is

```
<type 'numpy.float64'>
<type 'bool'>
```

Using XPath for data extraction

Using XPath to extract data from your data set can greatly reduce the complexity of your code and potentially make it faster as well. The following example shows an XPath version of the example in the previous section. Notice that this version is shorter and doesn't require the use of a for loop.

```
from lxml import objectify
import pandas as pd
from distutils import util

xml = objectify.parse(open('XMLData.xml'))
root = xml.getroot()

data = zip(map(int, root.xpath('Record/Number')),
           map(bool, map(util.strtobool,
               map(str, root.xpath('Record/Boolean')))))

df = pd.DataFrame(data,
                  columns=('Number', 'Boolean'),
                  index=map(str,
                      root.xpath('Record/String')))

print df
print type(df.ix['First']['Number'])
print type(df.ix['First']['Boolean'])
```

The example begins just like the previous example, with the importing of data and obtaining of the root node. At this point, the example creates a data object that contains record number and Boolean value pairs. Because the XML file entries are all strings, you must use the map() function to convert the strings to the appropriate values. Working with the record number is straightforward — all you do is

map it to an `int`. The `xpath()` function accepts a path from the root node to the data you need, which is `'Record/Number'` in this case.

Mapping the Boolean value is a little more difficult. As in the previous section, you must use the `util.strtobool()` function to convert the string Boolean values to a number that `bool()` can convert to a Boolean equivalent. However, if you try to perform just a double mapping, you'll encounter an error message saying that lists don't include a required function, `tolower()`. To overcome this obstacle, you perform a triple mapping and convert the data to a string using the `str()` function first.

Creating the `DataFrame` is different, too. Instead of adding individual rows, you add all the rows at one time by using `data`. Setting up the column names is the same as before. However, now you need some way of adding the row names, as in the previous example. This task is accomplished by setting the `index` parameter to a mapped version of the `xpath()` output for the `'Record/String'` path. Here's the output you can expect:

```
        Number Boolean
First        1    True
Second       2   False
Third        3    True
Fourth       4   False
<type 'numpy.int64'>
<type 'numpy.bool_'>
```

Working with Raw Text

Even though it might seem as if raw text wouldn't present a problem in parsing because it doesn't contain any special formatting, you do have to consider how the text is stored and whether it contains special words within it. The multiple forms of Unicode can present interpretation problems that you need to consider as you work through the text. Using regular expressions can help you locate specific information within a raw-text file. You can use regular expressions for both data cleaning and pattern matching. The following sections help you understand the techniques used to shape raw-text files.

Dealing with Unicode

Text files are pure text — this much is certain. The way the text is encoded can differ. For example, a character can use either seven or eight bits for encoding

purposes. The use of special characters can differ as well. In short, the interpretation of bits used to create characters differs from encoding to encoding. You can see a host of encodings at www.i18nguy.com/unicode/codepages.html.

Sometimes you need to work with encodings other than the default encoding set within the Python environment. When working with Python 3.x, you must rely on Universal Transformation Format 8-bit (UTF-8) as the encoding used to read and write files. This environment is always set for UTF-8, and trying to change it causes an error message. However, when working with Python 2.x, you can choose other encodings. In this case, the default encoding is the American Standard Code for Information Interchange (ASCII), but you can change it to some other encoding.

You can use this technique in any IPython Notebook file, but you won't actually see output from it. In order to see output, you need to work with the IPython prompt. The following steps help you see how to deal with Unicode characters, but only when working with Python 2.x (these steps will cause errors in the Python 3.x environment).

1. **Open a copy of the IPython command prompt.**

 You see the IPython window.

2. **Type the following code, pressing Enter after each line.**

   ```
   import sys
   sys.getdefaultencoding()
   ```

 You see the default encoding for Python, which is ASCII in most cases.

3. **Type** reload(sys) **and press Enter.**

 Python reloads the sys module and makes a special function available.

4. **Type** sys.setdefaultencoding('utf-8') **and press Enter.**

 Python does change the encoding, but you won't know that for certain until after the next step.

5. **Type** sys.getdefaultencoding() **and press Enter.**

 You see that the default encoding has now changed to utf-8.

Changing the default encoding at the wrong time and in the incorrect way can prevent you from performing tasks such as importing modules. Make sure to test your code carefully and completely to ensure that any change in the default encoding won't affect your ability to run the application. Good additional articles to read on this topic appear at http://blog.notdot.net/2010/07/Getting-unicode-right-in-Python and http://web.archive.org/web/20120722170929/http://boodebr.org/main/python/all-about-python-and-unicode.

CHAPTER 2 **Shaping Data** 437

Stemming and removing stop words

Stemming is the process of reducing words to their stem (or root) word. This task isn't the same as understanding that some words come from Latin or other roots, but instead it makes like words equal to each other for the purpose of comparison or sharing. For example, the words *cats*, *catty*, and *catlike* all have the stem *cat*. The act of stemming helps you analyze sentences by tokenizing them.

Removing suffixes to create stem words and generally tokenizing sentences are only two parts of the process, however, of creating something like a natural language interface. Languages include a great number of glue words that don't mean much to a computer but have significant meaning to humans, such as *a*, *as*, *the*, *that*, and so on in English. These short, less useful words are *stop* words. Sentences don't make sense without them to humans, but for your computer, they can act as a means of stopping sentence analysis.

The act of stemming and removing stop words simplifies the text and reduces the number of textual elements so that just the essential elements remain. In addition, you keep just the terms that are nearest to the true sense of the phrase. By reducing phrases in such a fashion, a computational algorithm can work faster and process the text more effectively.

This example requires the use of the Natural Language Toolkit (NLTK), which may not be part of Anaconda's default install. To use this example, you must download and install NLTK using the instructions found at www.nltk.org/install.html for your platform. If you have multiple versions of Python installed on your system, make certain that you install the NLTK for whatever version of Python you're using for this book. After you install NLTK, you must also install the packages associated with it. The instructions at www.nltk.org/data.html tell you how to perform this task (install all the packages to ensure you have everything).

After the NLTK library is installed, you can install all the associated packages from the Python interpreter by opening a terminal window and typing three lines:

```
python
import nltk
nltk.download('all')
```

The following example demonstrates how to perform stemming and remove stop words from a sentence. It begins by training an algorithm to perform the required analysis using a test sentence. Afterward, the example checks a second sentence for words that appear in the first.

```
import sklearn.feature_extraction.text as ext
from nltk import word_tokenize
from nltk.stem.porter import PorterStemmer
```

```
stemmer = PorterStemmer()

def stem_tokens(tokens, stemmer):
    stemmed = []
    for item in tokens:
        stemmed.append(stemmer.stem(item))
    return stemmed

def tokenize(text):
    tokens = word_tokenize(text)
    stems = stem_tokens(tokens, stemmer)
    return stems

vocab = ['Sam loves swimming so he swims all the time']
vect = ext.CountVectorizer(tokenizer=tokenize,
                           stop_words='english')
vec = vect.fit(vocab)

sentence1 = vec.transform(['George loves swimming too!'])

print vec.get_feature_names()
print sentence1.toarray()
```

At the outset, the example creates a vocabulary using a test sentence and places it in vocab. It then creates a CountVectorizer, vect, to hold a list of stemmed words, but excludes the stop words. The tokenizer parameter defines the function used to stem the words. The stop_words parameter refers to a pickle file that contains stop words for a specific language, which is English in this case. There are also files for other languages, such as French and German. (You can see other parameters for the CountVectorizer() at http://scikit-learn.org/stable/modules/generated/sklearn.feature_extraction.text.CountVectorizer.html.) The vocabulary is fitted into another CountVectorizer, vec, which is used to perform the actual transformation on a test sentence using the transform() function. Here's the output from this example:

```
[u'love', u'sam', u'swim', u'time']
[[1 0 1 0]]
```

The first output shows the stemmed words. Notice that the list contains only *swim*, not *swimming* and *swims*. All the stop words are missing as well. For example, you don't see the words *so*, *he*, *all*, or *the*.

The second output shows how many times each stemmed word appears in the test sentence. In this case, a *love* variant appears once and a *swim* variant appears once as well. The words *sam* and *time* don't appear in the second sentence, so those values are set to 0.

Introducing regular expressions

Regular expressions present an interesting array of tools for parsing raw text. At first, it may seem daunting to figure out precisely how regular expressions work. However, sites such as `regexr.com` let you play with regular expressions so that you can see how the use of various expressions performs specific types of pattern matching. Of course, the first requirement is to discover *pattern matching*, which is the use of special characters to tell a parsing engine what to find in the raw text file. Table 2-1 provides a list of pattern-matching characters and tells you how to use them.

TABLE 2-1 Pattern-Matching Characters Used in Python

Character	Interpretation
`(re)`	Groups regular expressions and remembers the matched text.
`(?: re)`	Groups regular expressions without remembering matched text.
`(?#...)`	Indicates a comment, which isn't processed.
`re?`	Matches 0 or 1 occurrence of preceding expression (but no more than 0 or 1 occurrence).
`re*`	Matches 0 or more occurrences of the preceding expression.
`re+`	Matches 1 or more occurrences of the preceding expression.
`(?> re)`	Matches an independent pattern without backtracking.
`.`	Matches any single character except the newline (\n) character (adding the m option allows it to match the newline character as well).
`[^...]`	Matches any single character or range of characters not found within the brackets.
`[...]`	Matches any single character or range of characters that appears within the brackets.
`re{ n, m}`	Matches at least n and at most m occurrences of the preceding expression.
`\n, \t, etc.`	Matches control characters such as newlines (\n), carriage returns (\r), and tabs (\t).
`\d`	Matches digits (which is equivalent to using [0-9]).
`a\|b`	Matches either a or b.
`re{ n}`	Matches exactly the number of occurrences of preceding expression specified by n.
`re{ n,}`	Matches n or more occurrences of the preceding expression.

Character	Interpretation
\D	Matches nondigits.
\S	Matches nonwhitespace.
\B	Matches nonword boundaries.
\W	Matches nonword characters.
\1...\9	Matches nth grouped subexpression.
\10	Matches nth grouped subexpression if it matched already (otherwise the pattern refers to the octal representation of a character code).
\A	Matches the beginning of a string.
^	Matches the beginning of the line.
\z	Matches the end of a string.
\Z	Matches the end of string (when a newline exists, it matches just before newline).
$	Matches the end of the line.
\G	Matches the point where the last match finished.
\s	Matches whitespace (which is equivalent to using [\t\n\r\f]).
\b	Matches word boundaries when outside the brackets; matches the backspace (0x08) when inside the brackets.
\w	Matches word characters.
(?= re)	Specifies a position using a pattern (this pattern doesn't have a range).
(?! re)	Specifies a position using pattern negation (this pattern doesn't have a range).
(?-imx)	Toggles the i, m, or x options temporarily off within a regular expression (when this pattern appears in parentheses, only the area within the parentheses is affected).
(?imx)	Toggles the i, m, or x options temporarily on within a regular expression (when this pattern appears in parentheses, only the area within the parentheses is affected).
(?-imx: re)	Toggles the i, m, or x options within parentheses temporarily off.
(?imx: re)	Toggles the i, m, or x options within parentheses temporarily on.

Using regular expressions helps you manipulate complex text before using other techniques described in this chapter. In the following example, you see how to extract a telephone number from a sentence no matter where the telephone number appears. This sort of manipulation is helpful when you have to work with text of various origins and in irregular format. You can see some additional

telephone number manipulation routines at www.diveintopython.net/regular_
expressions/phone_numbers.html. The big thing is that this example helps you
understand how to extract the text you need from the text you don't.

```
import re

data1 = 'My phone number is: 800-555-1212.'
data2 = '800-555-1234 is my phone number.'

pattern = re.compile(r'(\d{3})-(\d{3})-(\d{4})')

dmatch1 = pattern.search(data1).groups()
dmatch2 = pattern.search(data2).groups()

print dmatch1
print dmatch2
```

The example begins with two telephone numbers placed in sentences in various locations. Before you can do much, you need to create a pattern. Always read a pattern from left to right. In this case, the pattern is looking for three digits, followed by a dash, three more digits, followed by another dash, and finally four digits.

To make the process faster and easier, the code calls the `compile()` function to create a compiled version of the pattern so that Python doesn't have to re-create the pattern every time you need it. The compiled pattern appears in `pattern`.

The `search()` function looks for the pattern in each of the test sentences. It then places any matched text that it finds into groups and outputs a tuple into one of two variables. Here's the output from this example:

```
('800', '555', '1212')
('800', '555', '1234')
```

Using the Bag of Words Model and Beyond

The goal of most data imports is to perform some type of analysis. Before you can perform analysis on textual data, you must tokenize every word within the data set. The act of tokenizing the words creates a *bag of words*. You can then use the bag of words to train *classifiers*, a special kind of algorithm used to break words down into categories. The following section provides additional insights into the bag of words model and shows how to work with it.

> ## GETTING THE 20 NEWSGROUPS DATA SET
>
> The examples in the sections that follow rely on the 20 Newsgroups data set (qwone.com/~jason/20Newsgroups) that's part of the Scikit-learn installation. The host site provides some additional information about the data set, but essentially it's a good data set to use to demonstrate various kinds of text analysis.
>
> You don't have to do anything special to work with the data set because Scikit-learn already knows about it. However, when you run the first example, you see the message "WARNING:sklearn.datasets.twenty_newsgroups:Downloading dataset from http://people.csail.mit.edu/jrennie/20Newsgroups/20news-bydate.tar.gz (14 MB)." All this message tells you is that you need to wait for the data download to complete. There is nothing wrong with your system. Look at the left side of the code cell in IPython Notebook and you see the familiar In [*]: entry. When this entry changes to show a number, the download is complete. The message doesn't go away until the next time you run the cell.

Understanding the bag of words model

In order to perform textual analysis of various sorts, you need to first tokenize the words and create a bag of words from them. The bag of words uses numbers to represent words, word frequencies, and word locations that you can manipulate mathematically to see patterns in the way that the words are structured and used. The bag of words model ignores grammar and even word order — the focus is on simplifying the text so that you can easily analyze it.

The creation of a bag of words revolves around Natural Language Processing (NLP) and Information Retrieval (IR). Before you perform this sort of processing, you normally remove any special characters (such as HTML formatting from a web source), remove the stop words, and possibly perform stemming as well (as described in the "Stemming and removing stop words" section, earlier this chapter). For the purpose of this example, you use the 20 Newsgroups data set directly. Here's an example of how you can obtain textual input and create a bag of words from it:

```
from sklearn.datasets import fetch_20newsgroups
import sklearn.feature_extraction.text as ext

categories = ['comp.graphics', 'misc.forsale',
              'rec.autos', 'sci.space']
```

```
twenty_train = fetch_20newsgroups(subset='train',
                                  categories=categories,
                                  shuffle=True,
                                  random_state=42)

count_vect = ext.CountVectorizer()
X_train_counts = count_vect.fit_transform(
    twenty_train.data)

print X_train_counts.shape
```

REMEMBER

A number of the examples you see online are unclear as to where the list of categories they use come from. The host site at http://qwone.com/~jason/20Newsgroups provides you with a listing of the categories you can use. The category list doesn't come from a magic hat somewhere, but many examples online simply don't bother to document some information sources. Always refer to the host site when you have questions about issues such as data set categories.

The call to fetch_20newsgroups() loads the data set into memory. You see the resulting training object, twenty_train, described as a *bunch*. At this point, you have an object that contains a listing of categories and associated data, but the application hasn't tokenized the data, and the algorithm used to work with the data isn't trained.

Now that you have a bunch of data to use, you can begin creating a bag of words with it. The bag of words process begins by assigning an integer value (an index of a sort) to each unique word in the training set. In addition, each document receives an integer value. The next step is to count every occurrence of these words in each document and create a list of document and count pairs so that you know which words appear how often in each document.

Naturally, some words from the master list aren't used in some documents, thereby creating a *high-dimensional sparse data set*. The scipy.sparse matrix is a data structure that lets you store only the nonzero elements of the list in order to save memory. When the code makes the call to count_vect.fit_transform(), it places the resulting bag of words into X_train_counts. You can see the resulting number of entries by accessing the shape property. The result, using the categories defined for this example, is

```
(2356, 34750)
```

Working with n-grams

An *n-gram* is a continuous sequence of items in the text you want to analyze. The items are phonemes, syllables, letters, words, or base pairs. The *n* in n-gram refers to a size. An n-gram that has a size of one, for example, is a unigram. The example in this section uses a size of three, making a trigram. You use n-grams in a probabilistic manner to perform tasks such as predicting the next sequence in a series, which wouldn't seem very useful until you start thinking about applications such as search engines that try to predict the word you want to type based on the previous letters you've supplied. However, the technique has all sorts of applications, such as in DNA sequencing and data compression. The following example shows how to create n-grams from the 20 Newsgroups data set.

```
from sklearn.datasets import fetch_20newsgroups
import sklearn.feature_extraction.text as ext

categories = ['sci.space']

twenty_train = fetch_20newsgroups(subset='train',
        categories=categories,
        remove=('headers', 'footers', 'quotes'),
        shuffle=True,
        random_state=42)

count_chars = ext.CountVectorizer(analyzer='char_wb',
        ngram_range=(3,3),
        max_features=10).fit(twenty_train['data'])
count_words = ext.CountVectorizer(analyzer='word',
        ngram_range=(2,2),
        max_features=10,
        stop_words='english').fit(twenty_train['data'])
X = count_chars.transform(twenty_train.data)

print count_words.get_feature_names()
print X[1].todense()
print count_words.get_feature_names()
```

The beginning code is the same as in the previous section. You still begin by fetching the data set and placing it into a bunch. However, in this case, the vectorization process takes on new meaning. The arguments process the data in a special way.

In this case, the `analyzer` parameter determines how the application creates the n-grams. You can choose words (`word`), characters (`char`), or characters within word boundaries (`char_wb`). The `ngram_range` parameter requires two inputs in the form of a tuple: The first determines the minimum n-gram size and the second determines the maximum n-gram size. The third argument, `max_features`,

determines how many features the vectorizer returns. In the second vectorizer call, the `stop_words` argument removes the terms contained in the English pickle (see the "Stemming and removing stop words" section, earlier in the chapter, for details). At this point, the application fits the data to the transformation algorithm.

The example provides three outputs. The first shows the top ten trigrams for characters from the document. The second is the n-gram for the first document. It shows the frequency of the top ten trigrams. The third is the top ten trigrams for words. Here's the output from this example:

```
[u'ax ax', u'ax max', u'distribution world', u'don know',
 u'edu organization', u'max ax', u'nntp posting',
 u'organization university', u'posting host',
 u'writes article']
[[0 0 5 1 0 0 4 2 5 1]]
[u'ax ax', u'ax max', u'distribution world', u'don know',
 u'edu organization', u'max ax', u'nntp posting',
 u'organization university', u'posting host',
 u'writes article']
```

Implementing TF-IDF transformations

The *term frequency-inverse document frequency* (*TF-IDF*) transformation is a technique used to help compensate for the lengths of different documents. A short document and a long document might discuss the same topics, but the long document will have higher bag of word counts because it contains more words. When performing a comparison between the short and long document, the long document will receive unfair weighting without this transformation. Search engines often need to weigh documents equally, so you see this transformation used quite often in search engine applications.

However, what this transformation is really telling you is the importance of a particular word to a document. The greater the frequency of a word in a document, the more important it is to that document. However, the measurement is offset by the document size — the total number of words the document contains. The TF part of the equation determines how frequently the term appears in the document, while the IDF part of the equation determines the term's importance. You can see some actual calculations of this particular measure at www.tfidf.com. Here's an example of how you'd calculate TF-IDF using Python:

```
from sklearn.datasets import fetch_20newsgroups
import sklearn.feature_extraction.text as ext

categories = ['sci.space']
```

```
twenty_train = fetch_20newsgroups(subset='train',
        categories=categories,
        remove=('headers', 'footers', 'quotes'),
        shuffle=True,
        random_state=42)
count_vect = ext.CountVectorizer()
X_train_counts = count_vect.fit_transform(
    twenty_train.data)

tfidf = ext.TfidfTransformer().fit(X_train_counts)
X_train_tfidf = tfidf.transform(X_train_counts)

print X_train_tfidf.shape
```

This example begins much like the other examples in this section have, by fetching the 20 Newsgroups data set. It then creates a word bag, much like the example in the "Understanding the bag of words model" section, earlier in this chapter. However, now you see something you can do with the word bag.

In this case, the code calls upon `TfidfTransformer()` to convert the raw newsgroup documents into a matrix of TF-IDF features. The `use_idf` controls the use of inverse-document-frequency reweighting, which it turned on in this case. The vectorized data is fitted to the transformation algorithm. The next step, calling `tfidf.transform()`, performs the actual transformation process. Here's the result you get from this example:

```
(593, 13564)
```

TF-IDF helps you to locate the most important word or n-grams and exclude the least important ones. It is also very helpful as an input for linear models, because they work better with TF-IDF scores than word counts. At this point, you normally train a classifier and perform various sorts of analysis. In Book 7, Chapter 6, you begin working with classifiers in earnest.

Working with Graph Data

Imagine data points that are connected to other data points, such as how one web page is connected to another web page through hyperlinks. Each of these data points is a *node*. The nodes connect to each other using *links*. Not every node links to every other node, so the node connections become important. By analyzing the nodes and their links, you can perform all sorts of interesting tasks in data science, such as defining the best way to get from work to your home using streets and highways. The following sections describe how graphs work and how to perform basic tasks with them.

Understanding the adjacency matrix

An *adjacency matrix* represents the connections between nodes of a graph. When there is a connection between one node and another, the matrix indicates it as a value greater than 0. The precise representation of connections in the matrix depends on whether the graph is directed (where the direction of the connection matters) or undirected.

A problem with many online examples is that the authors keep them simple for explanation purposes. However, real-world graphs are often immense and defy easy analysis simply through visualization. Just think about the number of nodes that even a small city would have when considering street intersections (with the links being the streets themselves). Many other graphs are far larger, and simply looking at them will never reveal any interesting patterns. Data scientists call the problem in presenting any complex graph using an adjacency matrix a *hairball*.

One key to analyzing adjacency matrices is to sort them in specific ways. For example, you might choose to sort the data according to properties other than the actual connections. A graph of street connections might include the date the street was last paved, making it possible for you to look for patterns that direct someone based on the streets that are in the best repair. In short, making the graph data useful becomes a matter of manipulating the organization of that data in specific ways.

Using NetworkX basics

Working with graphs could become difficult if you had to write all the code from scratch. Fortunately, the NetworkX package for Python makes it easy to create, manipulate, and study the structure, dynamics, and functions of complex networks (or graphs). Even though this book covers only graphs, you can use the package to work with digraphs and multigraphs as well.

The main emphasis of NetworkX is to avoid the whole issue of hairballs. The use of simple calls hides much of the complexity of working with graphs and adjacency matrices from view. The following example shows how to create a basic adjacency matrix from one of the NetworkX-supplied graphs:

```
import networkx as nx

G = nx.cycle_graph(10)
A = nx.adjacency_matrix(G)

print(A.todense())
```

The example begins by importing the required package. It then creates a graph using the `cycle_graph()` template. The graph contains ten nodes. Calling `adjacency_matrix()` creates the adjacency matrix from the graph. The final step is to print the output as a matrix, as shown here:

```
[[0 1 0 0 0 0 0 0 0 1]
 [1 0 1 0 0 0 0 0 0 0]
 [0 1 0 1 0 0 0 0 0 0]
 [0 0 1 0 1 0 0 0 0 0]
 [0 0 0 1 0 1 0 0 0 0]
 [0 0 0 0 1 0 1 0 0 0]
 [0 0 0 0 0 1 0 1 0 0]
 [0 0 0 0 0 0 1 0 1 0]
 [0 0 0 0 0 0 0 1 0 1]
 [1 0 0 0 0 0 0 0 1 0]]
```

TIP

You don't have to build your own graph from scratch for testing purposes. The NetworkX site documents a number of standard graph types that you can use, all of which are available within IPython. The list appears at https://networkx.github.io/documentation/development/reference/generators.html.

It's interesting to see how the graph looks after you generate it. The following code displays the graph for you. Figure 2-1 shows the result of the plot.

```
import matplotlib.pyplot as plt
nx.draw_networkx(G)
plt.show()
```

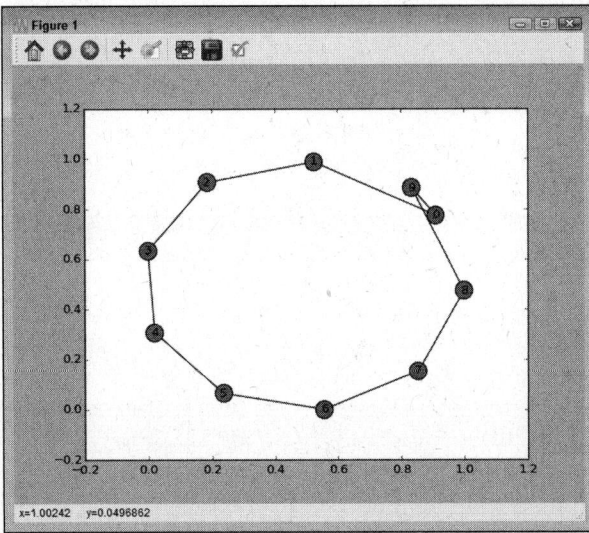

FIGURE 2-1: Plotting the original graph.

CHAPTER 2 **Shaping Data** 449

The plot shows that you can add an edge between nodes 1 and 5. Here's the code needed to perform this task using the add_edge() function. Figure 2-2 shows the result.

```
G.add_edge(1,5)
nx.draw_networkx(G)
plt.show()
```

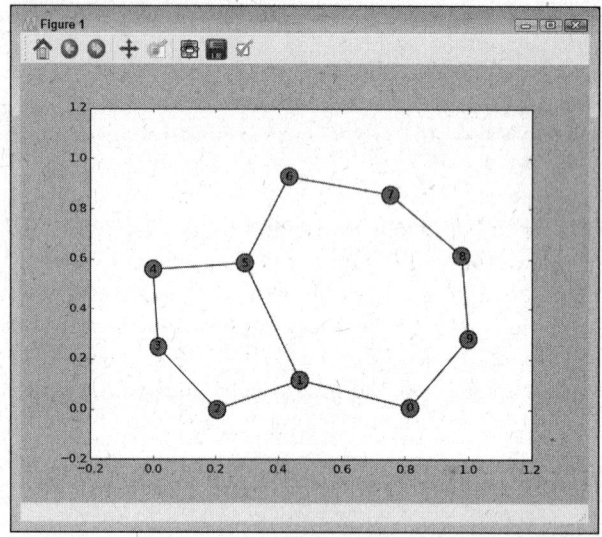

FIGURE 2-2:
Plotting the graph addition.

> **IN THIS CHAPTER**
>
> » Creating a basic graph
>
> » Adding measurement lines to your graph
>
> » Dressing your graph up with styles and color
>
> » Documenting your graph with labels, annotations, and legends

Chapter 3
Getting a Crash Course in MatPlotLib

"If we have data, let's look at data. If all we have are opinions, let's go with mine."

— JIM BARKSDALE

Most people visualize information better when they see it in graphic, versus textual, format. Graphics help people see relationships and make comparisons with greater ease. Even if you can deal with the abstraction of textual data with ease, performing data analysis is all about communication. Unless you can communicate your ideas to other people, the act of obtaining, shaping, and analyzing the data has little value beyond your own personal needs. Fortunately, Python makes the task of converting your textual data into graphics relatively easy using MatPlotLib, which is actually a simulation of the MATLAB application. You can see a comparison of the two at www.pyzo.org/python_vs_matlab.html.

TIP

If you already know how to use MATLAB, moving over to MatPlotLib is relatively easy because they both use the same sort of state machine to perform tasks and have a similar method of defining graphic elements. A number of people feel that MatPlotLib is superior to MATLAB because you can do things like perform tasks using less code when working with MatPlotLib than when using MATLAB

(see `http://phillipmfeldman.org/Python/Advantages_of_Python_Over_Matlab.html`). Others have noted that the transition from MATLAB to MatPlotLib is relatively straightforward (see `https://vnoel.wordpress.com/2008/05/03/bye-matlab-hello-python-thanks-sage`). However, what matters most is what you think. You may find that you like to experiment with data using MATLAB and then create applications based on your findings using Python with MatPlotLib. It's a matter of personal taste rather than one of a strictly correct answer.

This chapter focuses on getting you up to speed quickly with MatPlotLib. You do use MatPlotLib quite a few times later in the book, so this short overview of how it works is important, even if you already know how to work with MATLAB. That said, the MATLAB experience will be incredibly helpful as you progress through the chapter, and you may find that you can simply skim through some sections. Make sure to keep this chapter in mind as you start working with MatPlotLib in more detail later in the book.

REMEMBER

You don't have to type the source code for this chapter manually. In fact, it's a lot easier if you use the downloadable source code available at `www.dummies.com/go/codingaiodownloads`. The source code for this chapter appears in the `P4DS4D; 09; Getting a Crash Course in MatPlotLib.ipynb` source code.

Starting with a Graph

A graph or chart is simply a visual representation of numeric data. MatPlotLib makes a large number of graph and chart types available to you. Of course, you can choose any of the common graph and graph types such as bar charts, line graphs, or pie charts. As with MATLAB, you also have access to a huge number of statistical plot types, such as boxplots, error bar charts, and histograms. You can see a gallery of the various graph types that MatPlotLib supports at `http://matplotlib.org/gallery.html`. However, it's important to remember that you can combine graphic elements in an almost infinite number of ways to create your own presentation of data no matter how complex that data might be. The following sections describe how to create a basic graph, but remember that you have access to a lot more functionality than these sections tell you about.

Defining the plot

Plots show graphically what you've defined numerically. To define a plot, you need some values, the `matplotlib.pyplot` module, and an idea of what you want to display, as shown in the following code.

```
values = [1, 5, 8, 9, 2, 0, 3, 10, 4, 7]
import matplotlib.pyplot as plt
plt.plot(range(1,11), values)
plt.show()
```

In this case, the code tells the `plt.plot()` function to create a plot using x-axis values between 1 and 11 and y-axis values as they appear in values. Calling `plot.show()` displays the plot in a separate dialog box, as shown in Figure 3-1. Notice that the output is a line graph. Book 7, Chapter 4 shows you how to create other chart and graph types.

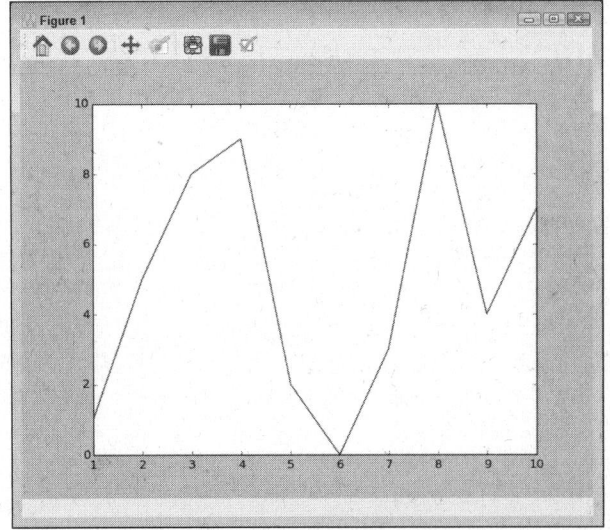

FIGURE 3-1: Creating a basic plot that shows just one line.

Drawing multiple lines and plots

You encounter many situations in which you must use multiple plot lines, such as when comparing two sets of values. To create such plots using MatPlotLib, you simply call `plt.plot()` multiple times — once for each plot line, as shown in the following example:

```
values = [1, 5, 8, 9, 2, 0, 3, 10, 4, 7]
values2 = [3, 8, 9, 2, 1, 2, 4, 7, 6, 6]
import matplotlib.pyplot as plt
plt.plot(range(1,11), values)
plt.plot(range(1,11), values2)
plt.show()
```

CHAPTER 3 **Getting a Crash Course in MatPlotLib** 453

When you run this example, you see two plot lines, as shown in Figure 3-2. Even though you can't see it in the printed book, the line graphs are different colors so that you can tell them apart.

Saving your work

Often you need to save a copy of your work to disk for later reference or to use as part of a larger report. The easiest way to accomplish this task is to click Save the Figure (the floppy disk icon in Figure 3-2). You see a dialog box that you can use to save the figure to disk.

FIGURE 3-2: Defining a plot that contains multiple lines.

However, you sometimes need to save the graphic automatically rather than wait for the user to do it. In this case, you can save it programmatically using the `plt.savefig()` function, as shown in the following code:

```
values = [1, 5, 8, 9, 2, 0, 3, 10, 4, 7]
import matplotlib.pyplot as plt
plt.plot(range(1,11), values)
plt.savefig('MySamplePlot.png', format='png')
```

In this case, you must provide a minimum of two inputs. The first input is the filename. You may optionally include a path for saving the file. The second input is the file format. In this case, the example saves the file in Portable Network Graphic (PNG) format, but you have other options: Portable Document Format (PDF), Postscript (PS), Encapsulated Postscript (EPS), and Scalable Vector Graphics (SVG).

Setting the Axis, Ticks, Grids

It's hard to know what the data actually means unless you provide a unit of measure or at least some means of performing comparisons. The use of axes, ticks, and grids make it possible to illustrate graphically the relative size of data elements so that the viewer gains an appreciation of comparative measure. You won't use these features with every graphic, and you may employ the features differently based on viewer needs, but it's important to know that these features exist and how you can use them to help document your data within the graphic environment.

Getting the axes

The axes define the x and y plane of the graphic. The x-axis runs horizontally, and the y-axis runs vertically. In many cases, you can allow MatPlotLib to perform any required formatting for you. However, sometimes you need to obtain access to the axes and format them manually. The following code shows how to obtain access to the axes for a plot:

```
values = [0, 5, 8, 9, 2, 0, 3, 10, 4, 7]
import matplotlib.pyplot as plt
ax = plt.axes()
plt.plot(range(1,11), values)
plt.show()
```

The reason you place the axes in a variable, ax, instead of manipulating them directly is to make writing the code simpler and more efficient. In this case, you simply turn on the default axes by calling plt.axes(); then you place a handle to the axes in ax. A *handle* is a sort of pointer to the axes. Think of it as you would a frying pan. You wouldn't lift the frying pan directly but would instead use its handle when picking it up.

Formatting the axes

Simply displaying the axes won't be enough in many cases. You want to change the way MatPlotLib displays them. For example, you may not want the highest value t to reach to the top of the graph. The following example shows just a small number of tasks you can perform after you have access to the axes:

```
values = [0, 5, 8, 9, 2, 0, 3, 10, 4, 7]
import matplotlib.pyplot as plt
ax = plt.axes()
ax.set_xlim([0, 11])
ax.set_ylim([-1, 11])
ax.set_xticks([1, 2, 3, 4, 5, 6, 7, 8, 9, 10])
ax.set_yticks([0, 1, 2, 3, 4, 5, 6, 7, 8, 9, 10])
plt.plot(range(1,11), values)
plt.show()
```

In this case, the set_xlim() and set_ylim() calls change the axes limits — the length of each axis. The set_xticks() and set_yticks() calls change the ticks used to display data. The ways in which you can change a graph using these calls can become quite detailed. For example, you can choose to change individual tick labels if you want. Figure 3-3 shows the output from this example. Notice how the changes affect how the line graph displays.

FIGURE 3-3: Specifying how the axes should appear to the viewer.

Adding grids

Grid lines make it possible to see the precise value of each element of a graph. You can more quickly determine both the x- and y-coordinate, which allow you to perform comparisons of individual points with greater ease. Of course, grids also add noise and make seeing the actual flow of data harder. The point is that you can use grids to good effect to create particular effects. The following code shows how to add a grid to the graph in the previous section:

```
values = [0, 5, 8, 9, 2, 0, 3, 10, 4, 7]
import matplotlib.pyplot as plt
ax = plt.axes()
ax.set_xlim([0, 11])
ax.set_ylim([-1, 11])
ax.set_xticks([1, 2, 3, 4, 5, 6, 7, 8, 9, 10])
ax.set_yticks([0, 1, 2, 3, 4, 5, 6, 7, 8, 9, 10])
ax.grid()
plt.plot(range(1,11), values)
plt.show()
```

All you really need to do is call the `grid()` function. As with many other MatPlotLib functions, you can add parameters to create the grid precisely as you want to see it. For example, you can choose whether to add the x grid lines, y grid lines, or both. The output from this example appears in Figure 3-4.

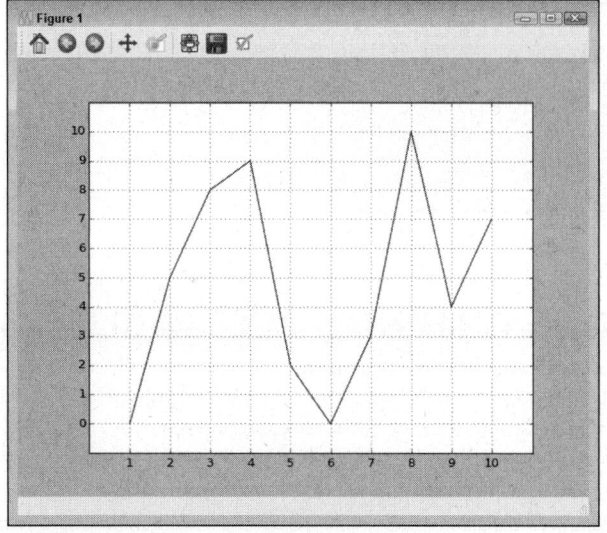

FIGURE 3-4: Adding grids makes the values easier to read.

CHAPTER 3 **Getting a Crash Course in MatPlotLib** 457

Defining the Line Appearance

Just drawing lines on a page won't do much for you if you need to help the viewer understand the importance of your data. In most cases, you need to use different line styles to ensure that the viewer can tell one data grouping from another. However, to emphasize the importance or value of a particular data grouping, you need to employ color. The use of color communicates all sorts of ideas to the viewer. For example, green often denotes that something is safe, while red communicates danger. The following sections help you understand how to work with line style and color to communicate ideas and concepts to the viewer without using any text.

Working with line styles

Line styles help differentiate graphs by drawing the lines in various ways. Using a unique presentation for each line helps you distinguish each line so that you can call it out (even when the printout is in shades of gray). You could also call out a particular line graph by using a different line style for it (and using the same style for the other lines). Table 3-1 shows the various MatPlotLib line styles.

TABLE 3-1 MatPlotLib Line Styles

Character	Line Style
'-'	Solid line
'--'	Dashed line
'-.'	Dash-dot line
':'	Dotted line

MAKING GRAPHICS ACCESSIBLE

Avoiding assumptions about someone's ability to see your graphic presentation is essential. For example, someone who is color blind may not be able to tell that one line is green and the other red. Likewise, someone with low-vision problems may not be able to distinguish between a line that is dashed and one that has a combination of dashes and dots. Using multiple methods to distinguish each line helps ensure that everyone can see your data in a manner that is comfortable to each person.

The line style appears as a third argument to the `plot()` function call. You simply provide the desired string for the line type, as shown in the following example:

```
values = [1, 5, 8, 9, 2, 0, 3, 10, 4, 7]
values2 = [3, 8, 9, 2, 1, 2, 4, 7, 6, 6]
import matplotlib.pyplot as plt
plt.plot(range(1,11), values, '--')
plt.plot(range(1,11), values2, ':')
plt.show()
```

In this case, the first line graph uses a dashed line style, while the second line graph uses a dotted line style. You can see the results of the changes in Figure 3-5.

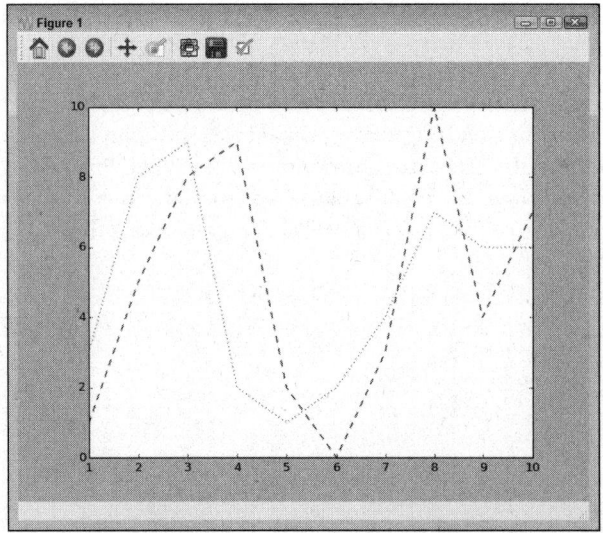

FIGURE 3-5: Line styles help differentiate between plots.

Using colors

Color is another way in which to differentiate line graphs. Of course, this method has certain problems. The most significant problem occurs when someone makes a black-and-white copy of your colored graph — hiding the color differences as shades of gray. Another problem is that someone with color blindness may not be able to tell one line from the other. All this said, color does make for a brighter, eye-grabbing presentation. Table 3-2 shows the colors that MatPlotLib supports.

TABLE 3-2 MatPlotLib Colors

Character	Color
'b'	Blue
'g'	Green
'r'	Red
'c'	Cyan
'm'	Magenta
'y'	Yellow
'k'	Black
'w'	White

As with line styles, the color appears in a string as the third argument to the `plot()` function call. In this case, the viewer sees two lines — one in red and the other in magenta. The actual presentation looks like Figure 3-2, but with specific colors, rather than the default colors used in that screenshot. If you're reading the printed version of the book, Figure 3-2 actually uses shades of gray.

```
values = [1, 5, 8, 9, 2, 0, 3, 10, 4, 7]
values2 = [3, 8, 9, 2, 1, 2, 4, 7, 6, 6]
import matplotlib.pyplot as plt
plt.plot(range(1,11), values, 'r')
plt.plot(range(1,11), values2, 'm')
plt.show()
```

Adding markers

Markers add a special symbol to each data point in a line graph. Unlike line style and color, markers tend to be a little less susceptible to accessibility and printing issues. Even when the specific marker isn't clear, people can usually differentiate one marker from the other. Table 3-3 shows the list of markers that MatPlotLib provides.

TABLE 3-3 MatPlotLib Markers

Character	Marker Type	
'.'	Point	
','	Pixel	
'o'	Circle	
'v'	Triangle 1 down	
'^'	Triangle 1 up	
'<'	Triangle 1 left	
'>'	Triangle 1 right	
'1'	Triangle 2 down	
'2'	Triangle 2 up	
'3'	Triangle 2 left	
'4'	Triangle 2 right	
's'	Square	
'p'	Pentagon	
'*'	Star	
'h'	Hexagon style 1	
'H'	Hexagon style 2	
'+'	Plus	
'x'	X	
'D'	Diamond	
'd'	Thin diamond	
'	'	Vertical line
'_'	Horizontal line	

As with line style and color, you add markers as the third argument to a `plot()` call. In the following example, you see the effects of combining line style with a marker to provide a unique line graph presentation:

```
values = [1, 5, 8, 9, 2, 0, 3, 10, 4, 7]
values2 = [3, 8, 9, 2, 1, 2, 4, 7, 6, 6]
import matplotlib.pyplot as plt
plt.plot(range(1,11), values, 'o--')
plt.plot(range(1,11), values2, 'v:')
plt.show()
```

Notice how the combination of line style and marker makes each line stand out in Figure 3-6. Even when printed in black and white, you can easily differentiate one line from the other, which is why you may want to combine presentation techniques.

FIGURE 3-6: Markers help to emphasize individual values.

Using Labels, Annotations, and Legends

To fully document your graph, you usually have to resort to labels, annotations, and legends. Each of these elements has a different purpose, as follows:

» **Label:** Provides positive identification of a particular data element or grouping. The purpose is to make it easy for the viewer to know the name or kind of data illustrated.

» **Annotation:** Augments the information the viewer can immediately see about the data with notes, sources, or other useful information. In contrast to a label, the purpose of annotation is to help extend the viewer's knowledge of the data rather than simply identify it.

» **Legend:** Presents a listing of the data groups within the graph and often provides cues (such as line type or color) to make identification of the data group easier. For example, all the red points may belong to group A, while all the blue points may belong to group B.

The following sections help you understand the purpose and usage of various documentation aids provided with MatPlotLib. These documentation aids help you create an environment in which the viewer is certain as to the source, purpose, and usage of data elements. Some graphs work just fine without any documentation aids, but in other cases, you might find that you need to use all three in order to communicate with your viewer fully.

Adding labels

Labels help people understand the significance of each axis of any graph you create. Without labels, the values portrayed don't have any significance. In addition to a moniker, such as rainfall, you can also add units of measure, such as inches or centimeters, so that your audience knows how to interpret the data shown. The following example shows how to add labels to your graph:

```
values = [1, 5, 8, 9, 2, 0, 3, 10, 4, 7]
import matplotlib.pyplot as plt
plt.xlabel('Entries')
plt.ylabel('Values')
plt.plot(range(1,11), values)
plt.show()
```

The call to `xlabel()` documents the x-axis of your graph, while the call to `ylabel()` documents the y-axis of your graph. Figure 3-7 shows the output of this example.

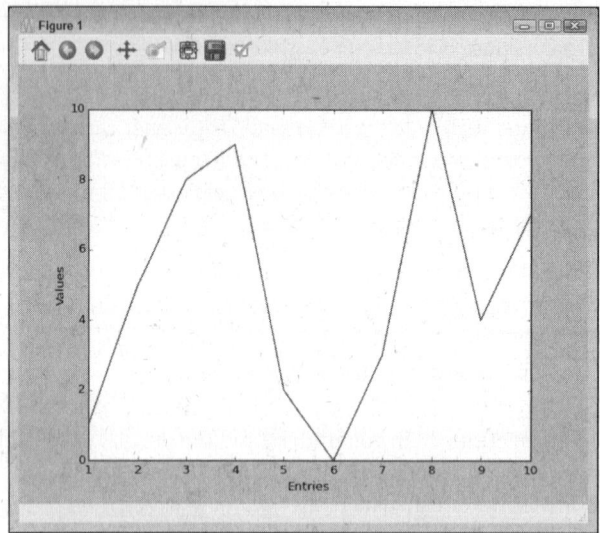

FIGURE 3-7:
Use labels to identify the axes.

Annotating the chart

You use annotation to draw special attention to points of interest on a graph. For example, you may want to point out that a specific data point is outside the usual range expected for a particular data set. The following example shows how to add annotation to a graph.

```
values = [1, 5, 8, 9, 2, 0, 3, 10, 4, 7]
import matplotlib.pyplot as plt
plt.annotate(xy=[1,1], s='First Entry')
plt.plot(range(1,11), values)
plt.show()
```

The call to `annotate()` provides the labeling you need. You must provide a location for the annotation by using the xy parameter, as well as provide text to place at the location by using the s parameter. The `annotate()` function also provides other parameters that you can use to create special formatting or placement on-screen. Figure 3-8 shows the output from this example.

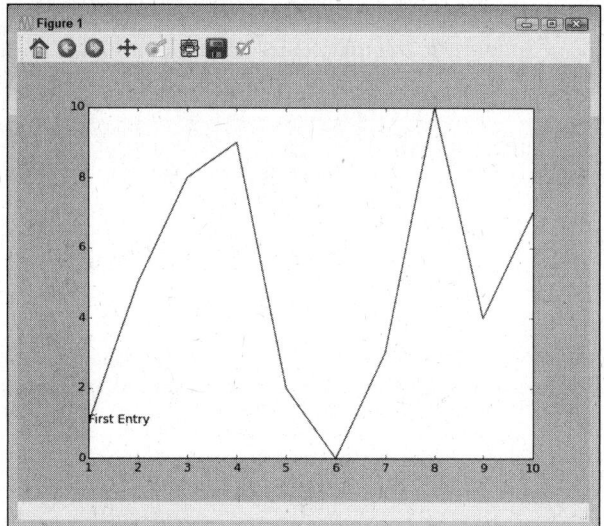

FIGURE 3-8:
Annotation can identify points of interest.

Creating a legend

A legend documents the individual elements of a plot. Each line is presented in a table that contains a label for it so that people can differentiate between each line. For example, one line may represent sales from the first store location and another line may represent sales from a second store location, so you include an entry in the legend for each line that is labeled first and second. The following example shows how to add a legend to your plot:

```
values = [1, 5, 8, 9, 2, 0, 3, 10, 4, 7]
values2 = [3, 8, 9, 2, 1, 2, 4, 7, 6, 6]
import matplotlib.pyplot as plt
line1 = plt.plot(range(1,11), values)
line2 = plt.plot(range(1,11), values2)
plt.legend(['First', 'Second'], loc=4)
plt.show()
```

The call to legend() occurs after you create the plots, not before, as with some of the other functions described in this chapter. You must provide a handle to each of the plots. Notice how line1 is set equal to the first plot() call and line2 is set equal to the second plot() call.

 TIP The default location for the legend is the upper-right corner of the plot, which proved inconvenient for this particular example. Adding the `loc` parameter lets you place the legend in a different location. See the `legend()` function documentation at http://matplotlib.org/api/pyplot_api.html#matplotlib.pyplot.legend for additional legend locations. Figure 3-9 shows the output from this example.

FIGURE 3-9: Use legends to identify individual lines.

> IN THIS CHAPTER
>
> » Selecting the right graph for the job
> » Working with advanced scatterplots
> » Exploring time-related data
> » Exploring geographical data
> » Creating graphs

Chapter 4
Visualizing the Data

"It is a capital mistake to theorize before one has data."
— SHERLOCK HOLMES

Book 7, Chapter 3 helped you understand the mechanics of working with MatPlotLib, which is an important first step toward using it. This chapter takes the next step in helping you use MatPlotLib to perform useful work. The main goal of this chapter is to help you visualize your data in various ways. Creating a graphic presentation of your data is essential if you want to help other people understand what you're trying to say. Even though you can see what the numbers mean in your mind, other people will likely need graphics to see what point you're trying to make by manipulating data in various ways.

The chapter starts by looking at some basic graph types that MatPlotLib supports. You don't find the full list of graphs and plots listed in this chapter — it would take an entire book to explore them all in detail. However, you do find the most common types.

In this chapter, you begin exploring specific sorts of plotting as it relates to data science. Of course, no book on data science would be complete without exploring scatterplots, which are used to help people see patterns in seemingly unrelated data points. Because much of the data that you work with today is time-related or geographic in nature, the chapter devotes two special sections to these topics. You also get to work with both directed and undirected graphs, which is fine for social media analysis.

 REMEMBER You don't have to type the source code for this chapter manually. In fact, it's a lot easier if you use the downloadable source available at www.dummies.com/go/codingaiodownloads. The source code for this chapter appears in the P4DS4D; 10; Visualizing the Data.ipynb source code.

Choosing the Right Graph

The kind of graph you choose determines how people view the associated data, so choosing the right graph from the outset is important. For example, if you want to show how various data elements contribute toward a whole, you really need to use a pie chart. On the other hand, when you want people to form opinions on how data elements compare, you use a bar chart. The idea is to choose a graph that naturally leads people to draw the conclusion that you need them to draw about the data that you've carefully massaged from various data sources. (You also have the option of using line graphs — a technique demonstrated in Book 7, Chapter 3.) The following sections describe the various graph types and provide you with basic examples of how to use them.

Showing parts of a whole with pie charts

Pie charts focus on showing parts of a whole. The entire pie would be 100 percent. The question is how much of that percentage each value occupies. The following example shows how to create a pie chart with many of the special features in place:

```
import matplotlib.pyplot as plt

values = [5, 8, 9, 10, 4, 7]
colors = ['b', 'g', 'r', 'c', 'm', 'y']
labels = ['A', 'B', 'C', 'D', 'E', 'F']
explode = (0, 0.2, 0, 0, 0, 0)

plt.pie(values, colors=colors, labels=labels,
        explode=explode, autopct='%1.1f%%',
        counterclock=False, shadow=True)
plt.title('Values')

plt.show()
```

468 BOOK 7 **Evaluating Data**

The essential part of a pie chart is the values. You could create a basic pie chart using just the values as input.

The colors parameter lets you choose custom colors for each pie wedge. You use the labels parameter to identify each wedge. In many cases, you need to make one wedge stand out from the others, so you add the explode parameter with a list of explode values. A value of 0 keeps the wedge in place — any other value moves the wedge out from the center of the pie.

Each pie wedge can show various kinds of information. This example shows the percentage occupied by each wedge with the autopct parameter. You must provide a format string to format the percentages.

TIP

Some parameters affect how the pie chart is drawn. Use the counterclock parameter to determine the direction of the wedges. The shadow parameter determines whether the pie appears with a shadow beneath it (for a 3D effect). You can find other parameters at http://matplotlib.org/api/pyplot_api.html.

In most cases, you also want to give your pie chart a title so that others know what it represents. You do this using the title() function. Figure 4-1 shows the output from this example.

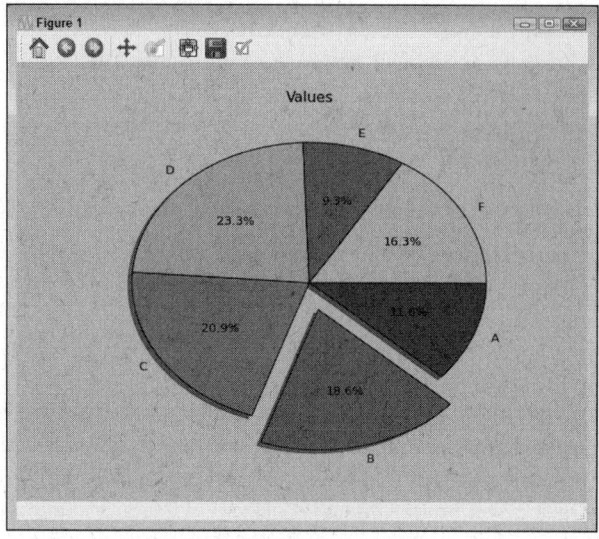

FIGURE 4-1: Pie charts show a percentage of the whole.

CHAPTER 4 **Visualizing the Data** 469

Creating comparisons with bar charts

Bar charts make comparing values easy. The wide bars and segregated measurements emphasize the differences between values, rather than the flow of one value to another as a line graph would do. Fortunately, you have all sorts of methods at your disposal for emphasizing specific values and performing other tricks. The following example shows just some of the things you can do with a vertical bar chart:

```
import matplotlib.pyplot as plt

values = [5, 8, 9, 10, 4, 7]
widths = [0.7, 0.8, 0.7, 0.7, 0.7, 0.7]
colors = ['b', 'r', 'b', 'b', 'b', 'b']

plt.bar(range(0, 6), values, width=widths,
        color=colors, align='center')

plt.show()
```

To create even a basic bar chart, you must provide a series of x-coordinates and the heights of the bars. The example uses the `range()` function to create the x-coordinates, and the `values` variable contains the heights.

Of course, you may want more than a basic bar chart, and MatPlotLib provides a number of ways to get the job done. In this case, the example uses the `width` parameter to control the width of each bar, emphasizing the second bar by making it slightly larger. The larger width would show up even in a black-and-white printout. It also uses the `color` parameter to change the color of the target bar to red (the rest are blue).

As with other chart types, the bar chart provides some special features that you can use to make your presentation stand out. The example uses the `align` parameter to center the data on the x-coordinate (the standard position is to the left). You can also use other parameters, such as `hatch`, to enhance the visual appearance of your bar chart. Figure 4-2 shows the output of this example.

TIP

This chapter helps you get started using MatPlotLib to create a variety of chart and graph types. Of course, more examples are better, so you can also find some more advanced examples on the MatPlotLib site at http://matplotlib.org/1.2.1/examples/index.html. Some of the examples, such as those that demonstrate animation techniques, become quite advanced, but with practice you can use any of them to improve your own charts and graphs.

FIGURE 4-2:
Bar charts make it easier to perform comparisons.

Showing distributions using histograms

Histograms categorize data by breaking it into *bins*, where each bin contains a subset of the data range. A histogram then displays the number of items in each bin so that you can see the distribution of data and the progression of data from bin to bin. In most cases, you see a curve of some type, such as a bell curve. The following example shows how to create a histogram with randomized data:

```
import numpy as np
import matplotlib.pyplot as plt

x = 20 * np.random.randn(10000)

plt.hist(x, 25, range=(-50, 50), histtype='stepfilled',
         align='mid', color='g', label='Test Data')
plt.legend()
plt.title('Step Filled Histogram')
plt.show()
```

In this case, the input values are a series of random numbers. The distribution of these numbers should show a type of bell curve. As a minimum, you must provide a series of values, x in this case, to plot. The second argument contains the number of bins to use when creating the data intervals. The default value is 10. Using the `range` parameter helps you focus the histogram on the relevant data and exclude any outliers.

You can create multiple histogram types. The default setting creates a bar chart. You can also create a stacked bar chart, stepped graph, or filled stepped graph (the type shown in the example). In addition, it's possible to control the orientation of the output, with vertical as the default.

As with most other charts and graphs in this chapter, you can add special features to the output. For example, the `align` parameter determines the alignment of each bar along the baseline. Use the `color` parameter to control the colors of the bars. The `label` parameter doesn't actually appear unless you also create a legend (as shown in this example). Figure 4-3 shows typical output from this example.

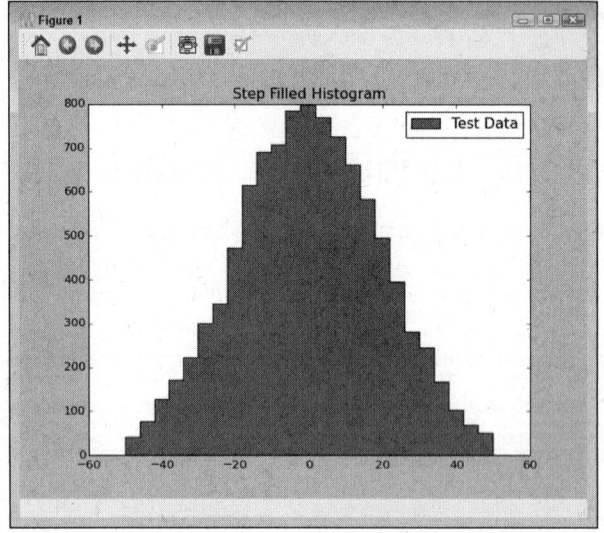

FIGURE 4-3: Histograms let you see distributions of numbers.

REMEMBER

Data generated using the random function changes with every call. Every time you run the example, you see slightly different results because the random-generation process differs.

Depicting groups using boxplots

Boxplots provide a means of depicting groups of numbers through their *quartiles* (three points dividing a group into four equal parts). A boxplot may also have lines, called *whiskers,* indicating data outside the upper and lower quartiles. The spacing shown within a boxplot helps indicate the skew and dispersion

of the data. The following example shows how to create a boxplot with randomized data:

```
import numpy as np
import matplotlib.pyplot as plt

spread = 100 * np.random.rand(100)
center = np.ones(50) * 50
flier_high = 100 * np.random.rand(10) + 100
flier_low = -100 * np.random.rand(10)
data = np.concatenate((spread, center,
                       flier_high, flier_low))

plt.boxplot(data, sym='gx', widths=.75, notch=True)
plt.show()
```

To create a usable data set, you need to combine several different number-generation techniques, as shown at the beginning of the example. Here are how these techniques work:

» `spread`: Contains a set of random numbers between 0 and 100.

» `center`: Provides 50 values directly in the center of the range of 50.

» `flier_high`: Simulates outliers between 100 and 200.

» `flier_low`: Simulates outliers between 0 and -100.

The code combines all these values into a single data set using `concatenate()`. Being randomly generated with specific characteristics (such as a large number of points in the middle), the output will show specific characteristics but will work fine for the example.

The call to `boxplot()` requires only `data` as input. All other parameters have default settings. In this case, the code sets the presentation of outliers to green Xs by setting the `sym` parameter. You use `widths` to modify the size of the box (made extra large in this case to make the box easier to see). Finally, you can create a square box or a box with a notch using the `notch` parameter (which normally defaults to False). Figure 4-4 shows typical output from this example.

The box shows the three data points as the box, with the line in the middle being the median. The two black horizontal lines connected to the box by whiskers show the upper and lower limits (for four quartiles). The outliers appear above and below the upper and lower limit lines as Xs.

CHAPTER 4 **Visualizing the Data** 473

FIGURE 4-4:
Use boxplots to present groups of numbers.

Seeing data patterns using scatterplots

Scatterplots show clusters of data rather than trends (as with line graphs) or discrete values (as with bar charts). The purpose of a scatterplot is to help you see data patterns. The following example shows how to create a scatterplot using randomized data:

```
import numpy as np
import matplotlib.pyplot as plt

x1 = 5 * np.random.rand(40)
x2 = 5 * np.random.rand(40) + 25
x3 = 25 * np.random.rand(20)
x = np.concatenate((x1, x2, x3))

y1 = 5 * np.random.rand(40)
y2 = 5 * np.random.rand(40) + 25
y3 = 25 * np.random.rand(20)
y = np.concatenate((y1, y2, y3))

plt.scatter(x, y, s=[100], marker='^', c='m')
plt.show()
```

The example begins by generating random x- and y-coordinates. For each x-coordinate, you must have a corresponding y-coordinate. It's possible to create a scatterplot using just the x- and y-coordinates.

It's possible to dress up a scatterplot in a number of ways. In this case, the s parameter determines the size of each data point. The marker parameter determines the data point shape. You use the c parameter to define the colors for all the data points, or you can define a separate color for individual data points. Figure 4-5 shows the output from this example.

FIGURE 4-5: Use scatterplots to show groups of data points and their associated patterns.

Creating Advanced Scatterplots

Scatterplots are especially important for data science because they can show data patterns that aren't obvious when viewed in other ways. You can see data groupings with relative ease and help the viewer understand when data belongs to a particular group. You can also show overlaps between groups and even demonstrate when certain data is outside the expected range. Showing these various kinds of relationships in the data is an advanced technique that you need to know in order to make the best use of MatPlotLib. The following sections demonstrate how to perform these advanced techniques on the scatterplot you created earlier in the chapter.

Depicting groups

Color is the third axis when working with a scatterplot. Using color lets you highlight groups so that others can see them with greater ease. The following example shows how you can use color to show groups within a scatterplot:

```
import numpy as np
import matplotlib.pyplot as plt

x1 = 5 * np.random.rand(50)
x2 = 5 * np.random.rand(50) + 25
x3 = 30 * np.random.rand(25)
x = np.concatenate((x1, x2, x3))

y1 = 5 * np.random.rand(50)
y2 = 5 * np.random.rand(50) + 25
y3 = 30 * np.random.rand(25)
y = np.concatenate((y1, y2, y3))

color_array = ['b'] * 50 + ['g'] * 50 + ['r'] * 25

plt.scatter(x, y, s=[50], marker='D', c=color_array)
plt.show()
```

The example works essentially the same as the scatterplot example in the previous section, except that this example uses an array for the colors. Unfortunately, if you're seeing this in the printed book, the differences between the shades of gray in Figure 4-6 will be hard to see. However, the first group is blue, followed by green for the second group. Any outliers appear in red.

FIGURE 4-6:
Color arrays can make the scatterplot groups stand out better.

476 BOOK 7 **Evaluating Data**

Showing correlations

In some cases, you need to know the general direction that your data is taking when looking at a scatterplot. Even if you create a clear depiction of the groups, the actual direction that the data is taking as a whole may not be clear. In this case, you add a trend line to the output. Here's an example of adding a trend line to a scatterplot that includes groups but isn't quite as clear as the scatterplot shown previously in Figure 4-6.

```
import numpy as np
import matplotlib.pyplot as plt
import matplotlib.pylab as plb

x1 = 15 * np.random.rand(50)
x2 = 15 * np.random.rand(50) + 15
x3 = 30 * np.random.rand(30)
x = np.concatenate((x1, x2, x3))

y1 = 15 * np.random.rand(50)
y2 = 15 * np.random.rand(50) + 15
y3 = 30 * np.random.rand(30)
y = np.concatenate((y1, y2, y3))

color_array = ['b'] * 50 + ['g'] * 50 + ['r'] * 25

plt.scatter(x, y, s=[90], marker='*', c=color_array)

z = np.polyfit(x, y, 1)
p = np.poly1d(z)
plb.plot(x, p(x), 'm-')

plt.show()
```

The code for creating the scatterplot is essentially the same as in the example in the "Depicting groups" section, earlier in the chapter, but the plot doesn't define the groups as clearly. Adding a trend line means calling the NumPy polyfit() function with the data, which returns a vector of coefficients, p, that minimizes the least squares error. Least square regression is a method for finding a line that summarizes the relationship between two variables, x and y in this case, at least within the domain of the explanatory variable x. The third polyfit() parameter expresses the degree of the polynomial fit.

The vector output of polyfit() is used as input to poly1d(), which calculates the actual y-axis data points. The call to plot() creates the trend line on the scatterplot. You can see a typical result of this example in Figure 4-7.

FIGURE 4-7: Scatterplot trend lines can show you the general data direction.

Plotting Time Series

Nothing is truly static. When you view most data, you see an instant of time — a snapshot of how the data appeared at one particular moment. Of course, such views are both common and useful. However, sometimes you need to view data as it moves through time — to see it as it changes. Only by viewing the data as it changes can you expect to understand the underlying forces that shape it. The following sections describe how to work with data on a time-related basis.

Representing time on axes

Many times, you need to present data over time. The data could come in many forms, but generally you have some type of time tick (one unit of time), followed by one or more features that describe what happens during that particular tick. The following example shows a simple set of days and sales on those days for a particular item in whole (integer) amounts:

```
import datetime as dt
import pandas as pd
import matplotlib.pyplot as plt

df = pd.DataFrame(columns=('Time', 'Sales'))

start_date = dt.datetime(2016, 7,1)
end_date = dt.datetime(2016, 7,10)
daterange = pd.date_range(start_date, end_date)
```

```
for single_date in daterange:
    row = dict(zip(['Time', 'Sales'],
                   [single_date,
                    int(50*np.random.rand(1))]))
    row_s = pd.Series(row)
    row_s.name = single_date.strftime('%b %d')
    df = df.append(row_s)

df.ix['Jul 01':'Jul 07', ['Time', 'Sales']].plot()
plt.ylim(0, 50)
plt.xlabel('Sales Date')
plt.ylabel('Sale Value')
plt.title('Plotting Time')
plt.show()
```

The example begins by creating a `DataFrame` to hold the information. The source of the information could be anything, but in this example, the data is generated randomly. Notice that the example creates a `date_range` to hold the starting and ending date time frame for easier processing using a `for` loop.

An essential part of this example is the creation of individual rows. Each row has an actual time value so that you don't lose information. However, notice that the index (`row_s.name` property) is a string. This string should appear in the form that you want the dates to appear when presented in the plot.

Using `ix[]` lets you select a range of dates from the total number of entries available. Notice that this example uses only some of the generated data for output. It then adds some amplifying information about the plot and displays it on-screen. Figure 4-8 shows typical output from the randomly generated data.

FIGURE 4-8: Use line graphs to show the flow of data over time.

Plotting trends over time

As with any other data presentation, sometimes you really can't see what direction the data is headed in without help. The following example starts with the plot from the previous section and adds a trend line to it:

```
import datetime as dt
import pandas as pd
import matplotlib.pyplot as plt
import numpy as np
import matplotlib.pylab as plb

df = pd.DataFrame(columns=('Time', 'Sales'))

start_date = dt.datetime(2016, 7,1)
end_date = dt.datetime(2016, 7,10)
daterange = pd.date_range(start_date, end_date)

for single_date in daterange:
    row = dict(zip(['Time', 'Sales'],
                   [single_date,
                    int(50*np.random.rand(1))]))

    row_s = pd.Series(row)
    row_s.name = single_date.strftime('%b %d')
    df = df.append(row_s)

df.ix['Jul 01':'Jul 10', ['Time', 'Sales']].plot()

z = np.polyfit(range(0, 10),
               df.as_matrix(['Sales']).flatten(), 1)

p = np.poly1d(z)
plb.plot(df.as_matrix(['Sales']),
         p(df.as_matrix(['Sales'])), 'm-')

plt.ylim(0, 50)
plt.xlabel('Sales Date')
plt.ylabel('Sale Value')
plt.title('Plotting Time')
plt.legend(['Sales', 'Trend'])
plt.show()
```

The technique for adding the trend line is the same as for the example in the "Showing correlations" section, earlier in this chapter, with some interesting differences. Because the data appears within a DataFrame, you must export it using

as_matrix() and then flatten the resulting array using flatten() before you can use it as input to polyfit(). Likewise, you must export the data before you can call plot() to display the trend line on-screen.

When you plot the initial data, the call to plot() automatically generates a legend for you. MatPlotLib doesn't automatically add the trend line, so you must also create a new legend for the plot. Figure 4-9 shows typical output from this example using randomly generated data.

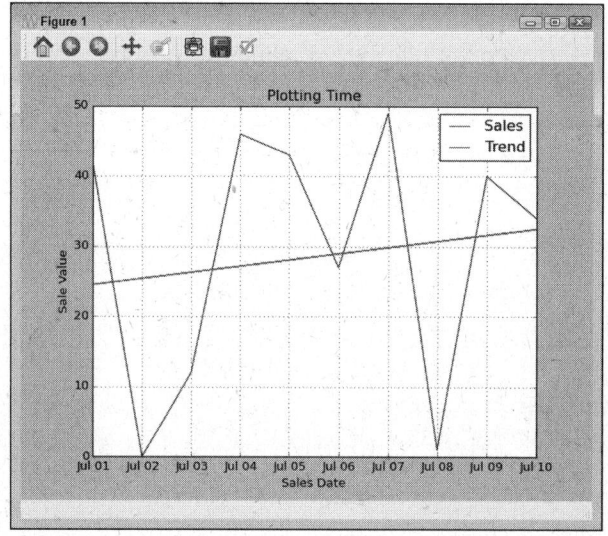

FIGURE 4-9: Add a trend line to show the average direction of change in a chart or graph.

Plotting Geographical Data

Knowing where data comes from or how it applies to a specific place can be important. For example, if you want to know where food shortages have occurred and plan how to deal with them, you need to match the data you have to geographical locations. The same holds true for predicting where future sales will occur. You may find that you need to use existing data to determine where to put new stores. Otherwise, you could put a store in a location that won't receive much in the way of sales, and the effort will lose money rather than make it. The following example shows how to draw a map and place pointers to specific locations.

TIP

If you are using Anaconda, you can install Basemap Toolkit by opening a terminal window and typing **conda install –c anaconda basemap**.

CHAPTER 4 **Visualizing the Data** 481

GETTING THE BASEMAP TOOLKIT

Before you can work with mapping data, you need a library that supports the required mapping functionality. A number of such packages are available, but the easiest to work with and install is the Basemap Toolkit. You can obtain this toolkit from http://matplotlib.org/basemap/users/intro.html. The site includes supplementary information about the toolkit and provides download instructions. Unlike some other packages, this one does include instructions for Mac, Windows, and Linux users. In addition, you can obtain a Windows-specific installer. Make sure to also check out the usage video at http://nbviewer.ipython.org/github/mqlaql/geospatial-data/blob/master/Geospatial-Data-with-Python.ipynb.

```
import numpy as np
import matplotlib.pyplot as plt
from mpl_toolkits.basemap import Basemap

austin = (-97.75, 30.25)
hawaii = (-157.8, 21.3)
washington = (-77.01, 38.90)
chicago = (-87.68, 41.83)
losangeles = (-118.25, 34.05)

m = Basemap(projection='merc',llcrnrlat=10,urcrnrlat=50,
            llcrnrlon=-160,urcrnrlon=-60)

m.drawcoastlines()
m.fillcontinents(color='lightgray',lake_color='lightblue')
m.drawparallels(np.arange(-90.,91.,30.))
m.drawmeridians(np.arange(-180.,181.,60.))
m.drawmapboundary(fill_color='aqua')

m.drawcountries()

x, y = m(*zip(*[hawaii, austin, washington,
                chicago, losangeles]))
m.plot(x, y, marker='o', markersize=6,
       markerfacecolor='red', linewidth=0)

plt.title("Mercator Projection")
plt.show()
```

The example begins by defining the longitude and latitude for various cities. It then creates the basic map. The `projection` parameter defines the basic map appearance. The next four parameters, `llcrnrlat`, `urcrnrlat`, `llcrnrlon`, and `urcrnrlon`, define the sides of the map. You can define other parameters, but these parameters generally create a useful map.

The next set of calls defines the map particulars. For example, `drawcoastlines()` determines whether the coastlines are highlighted to make them easy to see. To make landmasses easy to discern from water, you want to call `fillcontinents()` with the colors of your choice. When working with specific locations, as the example does, you want to call `drawcountries()` to ensure that the country boundaries appear on the map. At this point, you have a map that's ready to fill in with data.

In this case, the example creates x- and y-coordinates using the previously stored longitude and latitude values. It then plots these locations on the map in a contrasting color so that you can easily see them. The final step is to display the map, as shown in Figure 4-10.

FIGURE 4-10: Maps can illustrate data in ways other graphics can't.

Visualizing Graphs

A *graph* is a depiction of data showing the connections between data points using lines. The purpose is to show that some data points relate to other data points, but not all the data points that appear on the graph. Think about a map of a subway system. Each of the stations connects to other stations, but no single station

connects to all the stations in the subway system. Graphs are a popular data science topic because of their use in social media analysis. When performing social media analysis, you depict and analyze networks of relationships, such as friends or business connections, from social hubs such as Facebook, Google+, Twitter, or LinkedIn.

REMEMBER

The two common depictions of graphs are *undirected*, where the graph simply shows lines between data elements, and *directed*, where arrows added to the line show that data flows in a particular direction. For example, consider a depiction of a water system. The water would flow in just one direction in most cases, so you could use a directed graph to depict not only the connections between sources and targets for the water but also to show water direction by using arrows. The following sections help you understand the two types of graphs better and show you how to create them.

Developing undirected graphs

As previously stated, an undirected graph simply shows connections between nodes. The output doesn't provide a direction from one node to the next. For example, when establishing connectivity between web pages, no direction is implied. The following example shows how to create an undirected graph.

```
import networkx as nx
import matplotlib.pyplot as plt

G = nx.Graph()
H = nx.Graph()
G.add_node(1)
G.add_nodes_from([2, 3])
G.add_nodes_from(range(4, 7))
H.add_node(7)
G.add_nodes_from(H)

G.add_edge(1, 2)
G.add_edge(1, 1)
G.add_edges_from([(2,3), (3,6), (4,6), (5,6)])
H.add_edges_from([(4,7), (5,7), (6,7)])
G.add_edges_from(H.edges())

nx.draw_networkx(G)
plt.show()
```

In contrast to the canned example found in Book 7, Chapter 2, this example builds the graph using a number of different techniques. It begins by importing the NetworkX package you use in Book 7, Chapter 2. To create a new undirected

484 BOOK 7 **Evaluating Data**

graph, the code calls the `Graph()` constructor, which can take a number of input arguments to use as attributes. However, you can build a perfectly usable graph without using attributes, which is what this example does.

The easiest way to add a node is to call `add_node()` with a node number. You can also add a list, dictionary, or `range()` of nodes using `add_nodes_from()`. In fact, you can import nodes from other graphs if you want.

REMEMBER

Even though the nodes used in the example rely on numbers, you don't have to use numbers for your nodes. A node can use a single letter, a string, or even a date. Nodes do have some restrictions. For example, you can't create a node using a Boolean value.

Nodes don't have any connectivity at the outset. You must define connections (edges) between them. To add a single edge, you call `add_edge()` with the numbers of the nodes that you want to add. As with nodes, you can use `add_edges_from()` to create more than one edge using a list, dictionary, or another graph as input. Figure 4-11 shows the output from this example (your output may differ slightly but should have the same connections).

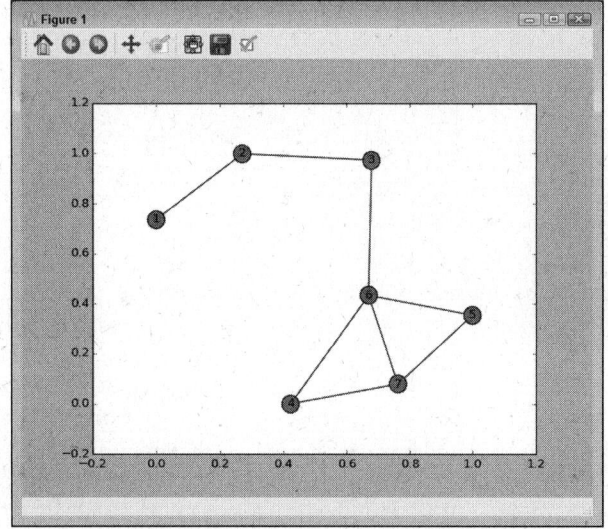

FIGURE 4-11: Undirected graphs connect nodes together to form patterns.

Developing directed graphs

You use directed graphs when you need to show a direction, say from a start point to an end point. When you get a map that shows you how to get from one specific point to another, the starting node and ending node are marked as such, and the lines between these nodes (and all the intermediate nodes) show direction.

CHAPTER 4 **Visualizing the Data** 485

TIP Your graphs need not be boring. You can dress them up in all sorts of ways so that the viewer gains additional information. For example, you can create custom labels, use specific colors for certain nodes, or rely on color to help people see the meaning behind your graphs. You can also change edge line weight and use other techniques to mark a specific path between nodes as the better one to choose. The following example shows many (but not nearly all) the ways in which you can dress up a directed graph and make it more interesting:

```
import networkx as nx
import matplotlib.pyplot as plt

G = nx.DiGraph()

G.add_node(1)
G.add_nodes_from([2, 3])
G.add_nodes_from(range(4, 6))
G.add_path([6, 7, 8])

G.add_edge(1, 2)
G.add_edges_from([(1,4), (4,5), (2,3), (3,6), (5,6)])

colors = ['r', 'g', 'g', 'g', 'g', 'm', 'm', 'r']
labels = {1:'Start', 2:'2', 3:'3', 4:'4',
          5:'5', 6:'6', 7:'7', 8:'End'}
sizes = [800, 300, 300, 300, 300, 600, 300, 800]

nx.draw_networkx(G, node_color=colors, node_shape='D',
                 with_labels=True, labels=labels,
                 node_size=sizes)
plt.show()
```

The example begins by creating a directional graph using the `DiGraph()` constructor. You should note that the NetworkX package also supports `MultiGraph()` and `MultiDiGraph()` graph types. You can see a listing of all the graph types at http://networkx.readthedocs.io/en/stable/reference/classes.html.

Adding nodes is much like working with an undirected graph. You can add single nodes using `add_node()` and multiple nodes using `add_nodes_from()`. The `add_path()` call lets you create nodes and edges at the same time. The order of nodes in the call is important. The flow from one node to another is from left to right in the list supplied to the call.

REMEMBER Adding edges is much the same as working with an undirected graph, too. You can use `add_edge()` to add a single edge or `add_edges_from()` to add multiple edges at one time. However, the order of the node numbers is important. The flow goes from the left node to the right node in each pair.

This example adds special node colors, labels, shape (only one shape is used), and sizes to the output. You still call on `draw_networkx()` to perform the task. However, adding the parameters shown changes the appearance of the graph. Note that you must set `with_labels` to `True` in order to see the labels provided by the `labels` parameter. Figure 4-12 shows the output from this example.

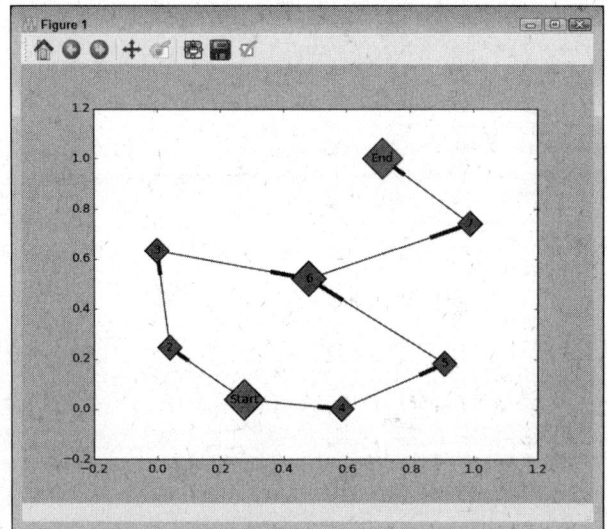

FIGURE 4-12: Use directed graphs to show direction between nodes.

IN THIS CHAPTER

» Understanding the exploratory data analysis (EDA) philosophy

» Describing numeric and categorical distributions

» Estimating correlation and association

» Testing mean differences in groups

» Visualizing distributions, relationships, and groups

Chapter **5**

Exploring Data Analysis

"If you torture the data long enough, it will confess."

— RONALD COASE

Data science relies on complex algorithms for building predictions and spotting important signals in data, and each algorithm presents different strong and weak points. In short, you select a range of algorithms, you have them run on the data, you optimize their parameters as much as you can, and finally you decide which one will best help you build your data product or generate insight into your problem.

It sounds a little bit automatic and, partially, it is, thanks to powerful analytical software and scripting languages like Python. Learning algorithms are complex, and their sophisticated procedures naturally seem automatic and a bit opaque to you. However, even if some of these tools seem like black or even magic boxes, keep this simple acronym in mind: GIGO. GIGO stands for "Garbage In/Garbage Out." It has been a well-known adage in statistics (and computer science) for a long time. No matter how powerful the machine learning algorithms you use, you won't obtain good results if your data has something wrong in it.

Exploratory data analysis (EDA) is a general approach to exploring data sets by means of simple summary statistics and graphic visualizations in order to gain a deeper understanding of data. EDA helps you become more effective in the subsequent data analysis and modeling. In this chapter, you discover all the necessary and indispensable basic descriptions of the data and see how those descriptions can help you decide how to proceed using the most appropriate data transformation and solutions.

You don't have to type the source code for this chapter manually. In fact, it's a lot easier if you use the downloadable source available at www.dummies.com/go/codingaiodownloads. The source code for this chapter appears in the P4DS4D; 13; Exploring Data Analysis.ipynb source code file.

The EDA Approach

EDA was developed at Bell Labs by John Tukey, a mathematician and statistician who wanted to promote more questions and actions on data based on the data itself (the exploratory motif) in contrast to the dominant confirmatory approach of the time. A confirmatory approach relies on the use of a theory or procedure — the data is just there for testing and application. EDA emerged at the end of the '70s, long before the big data flood appeared. Tukey could already see that certain activities, such as testing and modeling, were easy to make automatic. In one of his famous writings, Tukey said

> The only way humans can do BETTER than computers is to take a chance of doing WORSE than them.

This statement explains why your role and tools aren't limited to automatic learning algorithms but also to manual and creative exploratory tasks. Computers are unbeatable at optimizing, but humans are strong at discovery by taking unexpected routes and trying unlikely but very effective solutions.

EDA goes beyond the basic assumptions about data workability, which actually comprises the Initial Data Analysis (IDA). Up to now, the book has shown how to

» Complete observations or mark missing cases by appropriate features.

» Transform text or categorical variables.

» Create new features based on domain knowledge of the data problem.

» Have at hand a numeric data set where rows are observations and columns are variables.

EDA goes further than IDA. It's moved by a different attitude: going beyond basic assumptions. With EDA, you

- Describe of your data.
- Closely explore data distributions.
- Understand the relations between variables.
- Notice unusual or unexpected situations.
- Place the data into groups.
- Notice unexpected patterns within groups.
- Take note of group differences.

Defining Descriptive Statistics for Numeric Data

The first actions that you can take with the data are to produce some synthetic measures to help figure out what is going in it. You acquire knowledge of measures such as maximum and minimum values, and you define which intervals are the best place to start.

During your exploration, you use a simple but useful data set called the Fisher's Iris data set, which contains flower measurements of a sample of 150 irises. You can load it from the Scikit-learn package by using the following code:

```
from sklearn.datasets import load_iris
iris = load_iris()
```

Having loaded the Iris data set into a variable of a custom Scikit-learn class, you can derive a NumPy nparray and a pandas DataFrame from it:

```
import pandas as pd
import numpy as np
print 'Your pandas version is: %s' % pd.__version__
print 'Your NumPy version is %s' % np.__version__
iris_nparray = iris.data
iris_dataframe = pd.DataFrame(iris.data, columns=iris.feature_names)
```

```
iris_dataframe['group'] = pd.Series([iris.target_names[k] for k in iris.target],
    dtype="category")

Your pandas version is: 0.16.0
Your NumPy version is 1.9.0
```

NumPy, Scikit-learn, and especially pandas are packages under constant development, so before you start working with EDA, it's a good idea to check the product version numbers. Using an old version could cause your output to differ from that shown in the book or cause some commands to fail.

This chapter presents a series of pandas and NumPy commands that help you explore the structure of data. Even though applying single explorative commands grants you more freedom in your analysis, it's nice to know that you can obtain most of these statistics using the `describe` method applied to your pandas `DataFrame`, such as `print iris_dataframe.describe()`, when you're in a hurry.

Measuring central tendency

Mean and median are the first measures to calculate for numeric variables when starting EDA. The output from these functions provides an estimate of when the variables are centered and somehow symmetric.

Using pandas, you can quickly compute both means and medians. Here is the command for getting the mean from the Iris `DataFrame`:

```
print iris_dataframe.mean(numeric_only=True)

sepal length (cm)    5.843333
sepal width (cm)     3.054000
petal length (cm)    3.758667
petal width (cm)     1.198667
```

Similarly, here is the command that will output the median:

```
print iris_dataframe.median(numeric_only=True)

sepal length (cm)    5.80
sepal width (cm)     3.00
petal length (cm)    4.35
petal width (cm)     1.30
```

The median provides the central position in the series of values. When creating a variable, the median unlike the mean is a measure less influenced by anomalous cases or by an asymmetric distribution of values. What you should notice here is that the means are not centered (no variable is zero mean) and that the median of petal length is quite different from the mean, requiring further inspection.

When checking for central tendency measures, you should

- Verify whether means are zero.
- Check whether they are different from each other.
- Notice whether the median is different from the mean.

Measuring variance and range

As a next step, you should check the variance by squaring the value of its standard deviation. The variance is a good indicator of whether a mean is a suitable indicator of the variable distribution.

```
print iris_dataframe.std()

sepal length (cm)    0.828066
sepal width (cm)     0.433594
petal length (cm)    1.764420
petal width (cm)     0.763161
```

In addition, the range, which is the difference between the maximum and minimum value for each quantitative variable, is quite informative.

```
print iris_dataframe.max(numeric_only=True)-iris_dataframe.min
    (numeric_only=True)

sepal length (cm)    3.6
sepal width (cm)     2.4
petal length (cm)    5.9
petal width (cm)     2.4
```

Take notice of the standard deviation and the range with respect to the mean and median. A standard deviation or range that is too high with respect to the measures of centrality (mean and median) may point to a possible problem, with extremely unusual values affecting the calculation.

Working with percentiles

Because the median is the value in the central position of your distribution of values, you may need to consider other notable positions. Apart from the minimum and maximum, the position at 25 percent of your values (the lower quartile) and the position at 75 percent (the upper quartile) are useful for figuring how the data distribution works, and they are the basis of an illustrative graph called a *boxplot*, which is one of the topics covered in this chapter.

```
print iris_dataframe.quantile(np.array([0,.25,.50,.75,1]))

      sepal length (cm)  sepal width (cm)  petal length (cm)  petal width (cm)
0.00                4.3               2.0               1.00               0.1
0.25                5.1               2.8               1.60               0.3
0.50                5.8               3.0               4.35               1.3
0.75                6.4               3.3               5.10               1.8
1.00                7.9               4.4               6.90               2.5
```

The difference between the upper and lower percentile constitutes the interquartile range (IQR), which is a measure of the scale of variables that are of highest interest. You don't need to calculate it, but you will find it in the boxplot because it helps to determinate the plausible limits of your distribution. What lies between the lower quartile and the minimum, and the upper quartile and the maximum, are exceptionally rare values that can negatively affect the results of your analysis. Such rare cases are outliers.

Defining measures of normality

The last indicative measures of how the numeric variables used for these examples are structured are skewness and kurtosis:

- » *Skewness* defines the asymmetry of data with respect to the mean. If the skew is negative, the left tail is too long and the mass of the observations are on the right side of the distribution. If the skew is positive, the mass of the observations are on the left side of the distribution.

- » *Kurtosis* shows whether the data distribution, especially the peak and the tails, are of the right shape. If the kurtosis is above zero, the distribution has a marked peak. If it is below zero, the distribution is too flat.

Although reading the numbers can help you determine the shape of the data, taking notice of such measures presents a formal test to select the variables that may need some adjustment or transformation in order to become more similar to the Gaussian distribution. Remember that you also visualize the data later, so this is a first step in a longer process.

As an example, the output shown in the "Measuring central tendency" section earlier in this chapter shows that the petal length feature presents differences between the mean and the median. In this section, you test the same example for kurtosis and skewness in order to determine whether the variable requires intervention.

When performing the kurtosis and skewness tests, you determine whether the p-value is less than or equal 0.05. If so, you have to reject normality, which implies that you could obtain better results if you try to transform the variable into a normal one. The following code shows how to perform the required test:

```
from scipy.stats import kurtosis, kurtosistest

k = kurtosis(iris_dataframe['petal length (cm)'])
zscore, pvalue = kurtosistest(iris_dataframe['petal length (cm)'])
print 'Kurtosis %0.3f z-score %0.3f p-value %0.3f' % (k, zscore, pvalue)

Kurtosis -1.395 z-score -14.811 p-value 0.000

from scipy.stats import skew, skewtest

s = skew(iris_dataframe['petal length (cm)'])
zscore, pvalue = skewtest(iris_dataframe['petal length (cm)'])
print 'Skewness %0.3f z-score %0.3f p-value %0.3f' % (s, zscore, pvalue)

Skewness -0.272 z-score -1.398 p-value 0.162
```

The test results tell you that the data is slightly skewed to the left, but not enough to make it unusable. The real problem is that the curve is much too flat to be bell-shaped, so you should investigate the matter further.

It's a good practice to test all variables for kurtosis and skewness automatically. You should then proceed to inspect those whose values are the highest visually. Non-normality of a distribution may also conceal different issues, such as outliers to groups that you can perceive only by a graphical visualization.

Counting for Categorical Data

The Iris data set is made of four metric variables and a qualitative target outcome. Just as you use means and variance as descriptive measures for metric variables, so do frequencies strictly relate to qualitative ones.

Because the data set is made up of metric measurements (width and lengths in centimeters), you must render it qualitative by dividing it into bins according

to specific intervals. The pandas package features two useful functions, cut and qcut, that can transform a metric variable into a qualitative one:

- » cut expects a series of edge values used to cut the measurements or an integer number of groups used to cut the variables into equal-width bins.
- » qcut expects a series of percentiles used to cut the variable.

You can obtain a new categorical DataFrame using the following command, which concatenates a binning for each variable:

```
iris_binned = pd.concat([
pd.qcut(iris_dataframe.ix[:,0], [0, .25, .5, .75, 1]),
pd.qcut(iris_dataframe.ix[:,1], [0, .25, .5, .75, 1]),
pd.qcut(iris_dataframe.ix[:,2], [0, .25, .5, .75, 1]),
pd.qcut(iris_dataframe.ix[:,3], [0, .25, .5, .75, 1]),
], join='outer', axis = 1)
```

TIP

This example relies on binning. However, it could also help to explore when the variable is above or below a singular hurdle value, usually the mean or the median. In this case, you set pd.qcut to the 0.5 percentile or pd.cut to the mean value of the variable.

REMEMBER

Binning transforms numerical variables into categorical ones. This transformation can improve your understanding of data and the machine learning phase that follows by reducing the noise (outliers) or nonlinearity of the transformed variable.

Understanding frequencies

You can obtain a frequency for each categorical variable of the data set, both for the predictive variable and for the outcome, by using the following code:

```
print iris_dataframe['group'].value_counts()

virginica     50
versicolor    50
setosa        50

print iris_binned['petal length (cm)'].value_counts()

[1, 1.6]      44
(4.35, 5.1]   41
(5.1, 6.9]    34
(1.6, 4.35]   31
```

This example provides you with some basic frequency information as well, such as the number of unique values in each variable and the mode of the frequency (top and freq rows in the output).

```
print iris_binned.describe()

        sepal length (cm)  sepal width (cm)  petal length (cm)  petal width (cm)
count                 150               150                150               150
unique                  4                 4                  4                 4
top            [4.3, 5.1]          [2, 2.8]           [1, 1.6]        [0.1, 0.3]
freq                   41                47                 44                41
```

Frequencies can signal a number of interesting characteristics of qualitative features:

» The mode of the frequency distribution that is the most frequent category

» The other most frequent categories, especially when they are comparable with the mode (bimodal distribution) or if there is a large difference between them

» The distribution of frequencies among categories, if rapidly decreasing or equally distributed

» Rare categories that gather together

Creating contingency tables

By matching different categorical frequency distributions, you can display the relationship between qualitative variables. The pandas.crosstab function can match variables or groups of variables, helping to locate possible data structures or relationships.

In the following example, you check how the outcome variable is related to petal length and observe how certain outcomes and petal binned classes never appear together:

```
print pd.crosstab(iris_dataframe['group'], iris_binned['petal length (cm)'])

petal length (cm)  (1.6, 4.35]  (4.35, 5.1]  (5.1, 6.9]  [1, 1.6]
group
setosa                       6            0           0        44
versicolor                  25           25           0         0
virginica                    0           16          34         0
```

WARNING The pandas.crosstab function ignores categorical variable ordering and always displays the row and column categories according to their alphabetical order. This nuisance is still present in the pandas version used for this book, 0.16.0, but it may be resolved in the future.

Creating Applied Visualization for EDA

Up to now, the chapter has explored variables by looking at each one separately. Technically, if you've followed along with the examples, you have created a *univariate* (that is, you've paid attention to stand-alone variations of the data only) description of the data. The data is rich in information because it offers a perspective that goes beyond the single variable, presenting more variables with their reciprocal variations. The way to use more of the data is to create a *bivariate* (seeing how couples of variables relate to each other) exploration. This is also the basis for complex data analysis based on a *multivariate* (simultaneously considering all the existent relations between variables) approach.

If the univariate approach inspected a limited number of descriptive statistics, then matching different variables or groups of variables increases the number of possibilities. The different tests and bivariate analysis can be overwhelming, and using visualization is a rapid way to limit test and analysis to only interesting traces and hints. Visualizations, using a few informative graphics, can convey the variety of statistical characteristics of the variables and their reciprocal relationships with greater ease.

Inspecting boxplots

Boxplots provide a way to represent distributions and their extreme ranges, signaling whether some observations are too far from the core of the data — a problematic situation for some learning algorithms. The following code shows how to create a basic boxplot using the Iris data set:

```
boxplots = iris_dataframe.boxplot(return_type='axes')
```

In Figure 5-1, you see the structure of each variable's distribution at its core, represented by the 25° and 75° percentile (the sides of the box) and the median (at the center of the box). The lines, the so-called whiskers, represent 1.5 times the IQR (difference between upper and lower quartile) from the box sides (or by the distance to the most extreme value, if within 1.5 times the IQR). The boxplot marks every observation outside the whisker, which is deemed an unusual value.

FIGURE 5-1: A boxplot arranged by variables.

Boxplots are also extremely useful for visually checking group differences. Note in Figure 5-2 how a boxplot can hint that the three groups, setosa, versicolor, and virginica, have different petal lengths, with only partially overlapping values at the fringes of the last two of them.

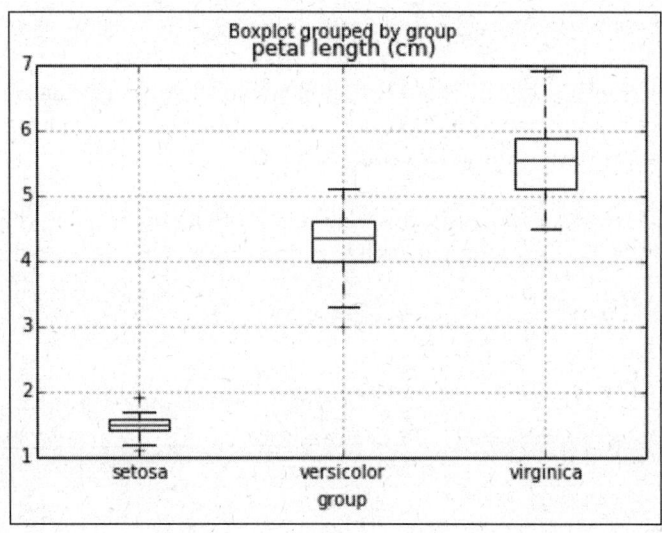

FIGURE 5-2: A boxplot arranged by groups.

Performing t-tests after boxplots

After you have spotted a possible group difference relative to a variable, a t-test (you use a t-test in situations in which the sampled population has an exact

normal distribution) or a one-way analysis of variance (ANOVA) can provide you with a statistical verification of the significance of the difference between the groups' means.

```
from scipy.stats import ttest_ind
group0 = iris_dataframe['group'] == 'setosa'
group1 = iris_dataframe['group'] == 'versicolor'
group2 = iris_dataframe['group'] == 'virginica'
print 'var1 %0.3f var2 %03f' % (iris_dataframe['petal length (cm)']
   [group1].var(),

   iris_dataframe['petal length (cm)'][group2].var())

var1 0.221 var2 0.304588
```

The t-test compares two groups at a time, and it requires that you define whether the groups have similar variance or not. So it is necessary to calculate the variance beforehand, like this:

```
t, pvalue = ttest_ind(iris_dataframe[sepal width (cm)'][group1],
   iris_dataframe['sepal width (cm)'][group2], axis=0, equal_var=False)
print 't statistic %0.3f p-value %0.3f' % (t, pvalue)

t statistic -3.206 p-value 0.002
```

You interpret the `pvalue` as the probability that the calculated t statistic difference is just due to chance. Usually, when it is below 0.05, you can confirm that the groups' means are significantly different.

You can simultaneously check more than two groups using the one-way ANOVA test. In this case, the `pvalue` has an interpretation similar to the t-test:

```
from scipy.stats import f_oneway
f, pvalue = f_oneway(iris_dataframe['sepal width (cm)'][group0],
                    iris_dataframe['sepal width (cm)'][group1],
                    iris_dataframe['sepal width (cm)'][group2])
print "One-way ANOVA F-value %0.3f p-value %0.3f" % (f,pvalue)

One-way ANOVA F-value 47.364 p-value 0.000
```

Observing parallel coordinates

Parallel coordinates can help spot which groups in the outcome variable you could easily separate from the other. It is a truly multivariate plot, because at a glance

it represents all your data at the same time. The following example shows how to use parallel coordinates.

```
from pandas.tools.plotting import parallel_coordinates
iris_dataframe['labels'] = [iris.target_names[k] for k in
iris_dataframe['group']]
pll = parallel_coordinates(iris_dataframe,'labels')
```

As shown in Figure 5-3, on the x-axis, you find all the quantitative variables aligned. On the y-axis, you find all the observations, carefully represented as parallel lines, each one of a different color given its ownership to a different group.

If the parallel lines of each group stream together along the visualization in a separate part of the graph far from other groups, the group is easily separable. The visualization also provides the means to assert the capability of certain features to separate the groups.

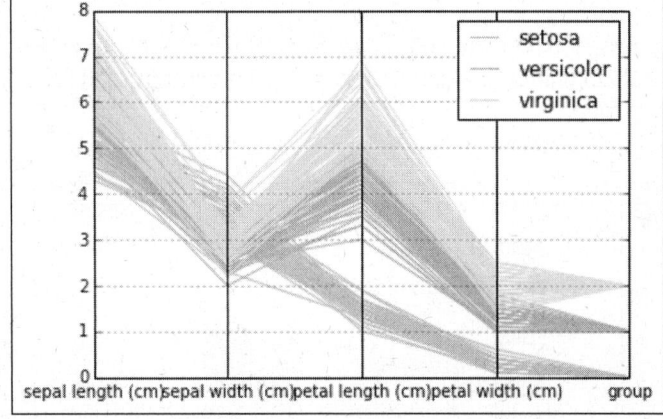

FIGURE 5-3: Parallel coordinates anticipate whether groups are easily separable.

Graphing distributions

You usually render the information that boxplot and descriptive statistics provide into a curve or a histogram, which shows an overview of the complete distribution of values. The output shown in Figure 5-4 represents all the distributions in the data set. Different variable scales and shapes are immediately visible, such as the fact that petals' features display two peaks.

```
densityplot = iris_dataframe[iris_dataframe.columns[:4]].plot(kind='density')
```

FIGURE 5-4: Features' distribution and density.

Histograms present another, more detailed, view over distributions:

```
single_distribution = iris_dataframe['petal length (cm)'].plot(kind='hist')
```

Figure 5-5 shows the histogram of petal length. It reveals a gap in the distribution that could be a promising discovery if you can relate it to a certain group of Iris flowers.

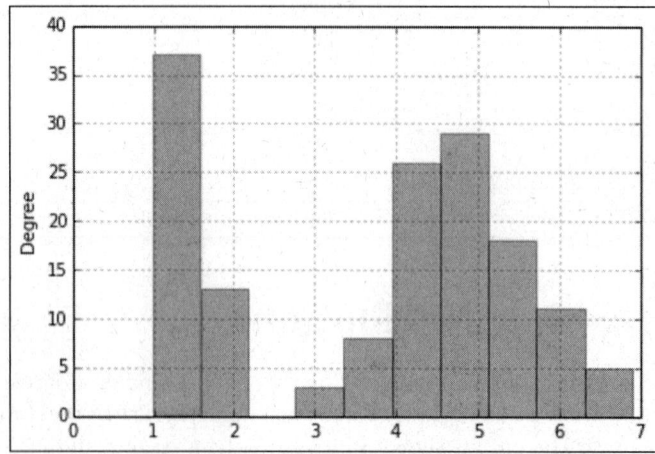

FIGURE 5-5: Histograms can detail better distributions.

Plotting scatterplots

In scatterplots, the two compared variables provide the coordinates for plotting the observations as points on a plane. The result is usually a cloud of points. When the cloud is elongated and resembles a line, you can perceive the variables as correlated. The following example demonstrates this principle.

```
colors_palette = {0: 'red', 1: 'yellow', 2:'blue'}
colors = [colors_palette[c] for c in iris_dataframe['group']]
simple_scatterplot = iris_dataframe.plot(kind='scatter',
    x='petal length (cm)', y='petal width (cm)', c=colors)
```

This simple scatterplot, represented in Figure 5-6, compares length and width of petals. The scatterplot highlights different groups using different colors. The elongated shape described by the points hints at a strong correlation between the two observed variables, and the division of the cloud into groups suggests a possible separability of the groups.

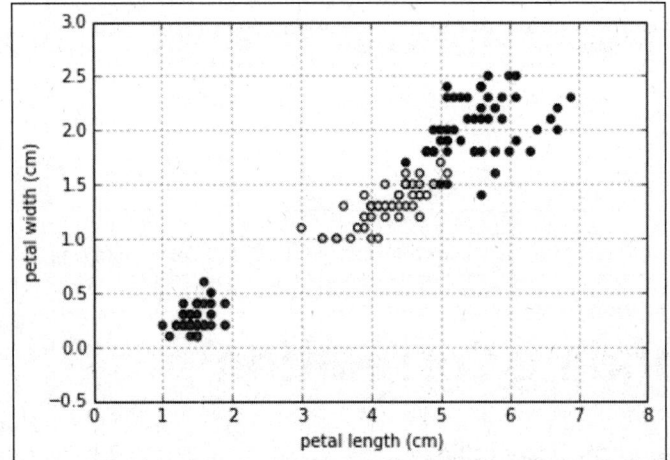

FIGURE 5-6: A scatterplot reveals how two variables relate to each other.

Because the number of variables isn't too large, you can also generate all the scatterplots automatically from the combination of the variables. This representation is a matrix of scatterplots. The following example demonstrates how to create one:

```
from pandas.tools.plotting import scatter_matrix
colors_palette = {0: "red", 1: "yellow", 2: "blue"}
colors = [colors_palette[c] for c in iris_dataframe['group']]
matrix_of_scatterplots = scatter_matrix(iris_dataframe,
    figsize=(6, 6), color=colors, diagonal='kde')
```

In Figure 5-7, you can see the resulting visualization for the Iris data set. The diagonal representing the density estimation can be replaced by a histogram using the parameter diagonal='hist'.

CHAPTER 5 **Exploring Data Analysis** 503

FIGURE 5-7:
A matrix of scatterplots displays more information at one time.

Understanding Correlation

Just as the relationship between variables is graphically representable, it is also measurable by a statistical estimate. When working with numeric variables, the estimate is a correlation, and the Pearson correlation is the most famous. The Pearson correlation is the foundation for complex linear estimation models. When you work with categorical variables, the estimate is an association, and the chi-square statistic is the most frequently used tool for measuring association between features.

Using covariance and correlation

Covariance is the first measure of the relationship of two variables. It determines whether both variables have similar behavior with respect to their mean. If the single values of two variables are usually above or below their respective averages, the two variables have a positive association. It means that they tend to agree, and you can figure out the behavior of one of the two by looking at the other. In such a case, their covariance will be a positive number, and the higher the number, the higher the agreement.

If, instead, one variable is usually above and the other variable usually below their respective averages, the two variables are negatively associated. Even though the two disagree, it's an interesting situation for making predictions, because by observing the state of one of them, you can figure out the likely state of the other (albeit they're opposite). In this case, their covariance will be a negative number.

A third state is that the two variables don't systematically agree or disagree with each other. In this case, the covariance will tend to be zero, a sign that the variables don't share much and have independent behaviors.

Ideally, when you have a numeric target variable, you want the target variable to have a high positive or negative covariance with the predictive variables. Having a high positive or negative covariance among the predictive variables is a sign of information redundancy. *Information redundancy* signals that the variables point to the same data — that is, the variables are telling us the same thing in slightly different ways.

Computing a covariance matrix is straightforward using pandas. You can immediately apply it to the `DataFrame` of the Iris data set as shown here:

```
print iris_dataframe.cov()
                   sepal length (cm)  sepal width (cm)  petal length (cm)  \
sepal length (cm)           0.685694         -0.039268           1.273682
sepal width (cm)           -0.039268          0.188004          -0.321713
petal length (cm)           1.273682         -0.321713           3.113179
petal width (cm)            0.516904         -0.117981           1.296387

                   petal width (cm)
sepal length (cm)          0.516904
sepal width (cm)          -0.117981
petal length (cm)          1.296387
petal width (cm)           0.582414
```

This matrix output shows variables present on both rows and columns. By observing different row and column combinations, you can determine the value of covariance between the variables chosen. After observing these results, you can immediately understand that little relationship exists between sepal length and sepal width, meaning that they're different informative values. However, there could be a special relationship between petal width and petal length, but the example doesn't tell what this relationship is because the measure is not easily interpretable.

CHAPTER 5 **Exploring Data Analysis** 505

The scale of the variables you observe influences covariance, so you should use a different, but standard, measure. The solution is to use correlation, which is the covariance estimation after having standardized the variables. Here is an example of obtaining a correlation using a simple pandas method:

```
print iris_dataframe.corr()
                  sepal length (cm)  sepal width (cm)  petal length (cm)  \
sepal length (cm)           1.000000         -0.109369           0.871754
sepal width (cm)           -0.109369          1.000000          -0.420516
petal length (cm)           0.871754         -0.420516           1.000000
petal width (cm)            0.817954         -0.356544           0.962757

                  petal width (cm)
sepal length (cm)          0.817954
sepal width (cm)          -0.356544
petal length (cm)          0.962757
petal width (cm)           1.000000
```

Now that's even more interesting, because correlation values are bound between values of –1 and +1, so the relationship between petal width and length is positive and, with a 0.96, it is almost the maximum possible.

You can compute covariance and correlation matrices also by means of NumPy commands, as shown here:

```
covariance_matrix = np.cov(iris_nparray, rowvar=0, bias=1)
correlation_matrix= np.corrcoef(iris_nparray, rowvar=0, bias=1)
```

REMEMBER

In statistics, this kind of correlation is a *Pearson correlation*, and its coefficient is a *Pearson's r*.

TIP

Another nice trick is to square the correlation. By squaring it, you lose the sign of the relationship. The new number tells you the percentage of the information shared by two variables. In this example, a correlation of 0.96 implies that 96 percent of the information is shared. You can obtain a squared correlation matrix using this command: `print iris_dataframe.corr()**2`.

TECHNICAL STUFF

Something important to remember is that covariance and correlation are based on means, so they tend to represent relationships that you can express using linear formulations. Variables in real-life data sets usually don't have nice linear formulations. Instead they are highly nonlinear, with curves and bends. You can rely on mathematical transformations to make the relationships linear between variables anyway. A good rule to remember is to use correlations only to assert relationships between variables, not to exclude them.

Using nonparametric correlation

Correlations can work fine when your variables are numeric and their relationship is strictly linear. Sometimes, your feature could be ordinal (a numeric variable but with orderings) or you may suspect some nonlinearity due to non-normal distributions in your data. A possible solution is to test the doubtful correlations with a nonparametric correlation, such as a Spearman correlation (which means that it has fewer requirements in terms of distribution of considered variables). A *Spearman correlation* transforms your numeric values into rankings and then correlates the rankings, thus minimizing the influence of any nonlinear relationship between the two variables under scrutiny.

As an example, you verify the relationship between sepals' length and width whose Pearson correlation was quite weak:

```
from scipy.stats import spearmanr
from scipy.stats.stats import pearsonr
spearmanr_coef, spearmanr_p = spearmanr(iris_dataframe['sepal length (cm)'],
    iris_dataframe['sepal width (cm)'])
pearsonr_coef, pearsonr_p = pearsonr(iris_dataframe['sepal length (cm)'],
    iris_dataframe['sepal width (cm)'])
print 'Pearson correlation %0.3f | Spearman correlation %0.3f' % (pearsonr_coef,
    spearmanr_coef)
Pearson correlation -0.109 | Spearman correlation -0.159
```

In this case, the code confirms the weak association between the two variables using the nonparametric test.

Considering chi-square for tables

You can apply another nonparametric test for relationship when working with cross tables. This test is applicable to both categorical and numeric data (after it has been discretized into bins). The chi-square statistic tells you when the table distribution of two variables is statistically comparable to a table in which the two variables are hypothesized as not related to each other (the so-called independence hypothesis). Here is an example of how you use this technique:

```
from scipy.stats import chi2_contingency
table = pd.crosstab(iris_dataframe['group'], iris_binned['petal length (cm)'])
chi2, p, dof, expected = chi2_contingency(table.values)
print 'Chi-square %0.2f p-value %0.3f' % (chi2, p)

Chi-square 212.43 p-value 0.000
```

As seen before, the p-value is the chance that the chi-square difference is just by chance.

The chi-square measure value depends on how many cells the table has. Do not use the chi-square measure to compare different chi-square tests unless you know for sure that the tables in comparison share the same structure.

The chi-square is particularly interesting for assessing the relationships between binned numeric variables, even in the presence of strong nonlinearity that can fool Person's r. Contrary to correlation measures, it can inform you of a possible association, but it won't provide clear details of its direction or absolute magnitude.

Modifying Data Distributions

As a by-product of data exploration, in an EDA phase, you can do the following:

» Obtain new feature creations from the combination of different but related variables.

» Spot hidden groups or strange values lurking in your data.

» Try some useful modifications of your data distributions by binning (or other discretizations such as binary variables).

When performing EDA, you need to consider the importance of data transformation in preparation for the learning phase, which also means using certain mathematical formulas. The following sections present an overview of the most common mathematical formulas used for EDA (such as linear regression). The data transformation you choose depends on the distribution of your data, with a normal distribution being the most common. In addition, these sections highlight the need to match the transformation process to the mathematical formula you use.

Using the normal distribution

The normal, or Gaussian, distribution is the most useful distribution in statistics thanks to its frequent recurrence and particular mathematical properties. It's essentially the foundation of many statistical tests and models, with some of them, such as the linear regression, widely used in data science.

During data science practice, you'll meet with a wide range of different distributions — with some of them named by probabilistic theory, others not. For some distributions, the assumption that they should behave as a normal distribution may hold, but for others, it may not, and that could be a problem depending on what algorithms you use for the learning process. As a general rule, if your model is a linear regression or part of the linear model family because it boils down to a summation of coefficients, then both variable standardization and distribution transformation should be considered.

Creating a z-score standardization

In your EDA process, you may have realized that your variables have different scales and are heterogeneous in their distributions. As a consequence of your analysis, you need to transform the variables in a way that makes them easily comparable:

```
from sklearn.preprocessing import scale
stand_sepal_width = scale(iris_dataframe['sepal width (cm)'])
```

Transforming other notable distributions

When you check variables with high skewness and kurtosis for their correlation, the results may disappoint you. As you find out earlier in this chapter, using a nonparametric measure of correlation, such as Spearman's, may tell you more about two variables than Pearson's r may tell you. In this case, you should transform your insight into a new, transformed feature:

```
tranformations = {'x': lambda x: x, '1/x': lambda x: 1/x, 'x**2': lambda x: x**2,

    'x**3': lambda x: x**3, 'log(x)': lambda x: np.log(x)}
for transformation in tranformations:
    pearsonr_coef, pearsonr_p = pearsonr(iris_dataframe['sepal length (cm)'],
        tranformations[transformation](iris_dataframe['sepal width (cm)']))
    print 'Transformation: %s \t Pearson\'s r: %0.3f' % (transformation,
    pearsonr_coef)

Transformation: x        Pearson's r: -0.109
Transformation: x**2     Pearson's r: -0.122
Transformation: x**3     Pearson's r: -0.131
Transformation: log(x)   Pearson's r: -0.093
Transformation: 1/x      Pearson's r:  0.073
```

In exploring various possible transformations, using a `for` loop may tell you that a power transformation will increase the correlation between the two variables, thus increasing the performance of a linear machine learning algorithm. You may also try other, further transformations such as square root `np.sqrt(x)`, exponential `np.exp(x)`, and various combinations of all the transformations, such as log inverse `np.log(1/x)`.

IN THIS CHAPTER

» Using linear and logistic regression

» Understanding Bayes theorem and using it for naïve classification

» Predicting on the basis of cases being similar with kNN

Chapter **6**

Exploring Four Simple and Effective Algorithms

"The goal is to turn data into information, and information into insight."
— CARLY FIORINA

In this chapter, you start to explore all the algorithms and tools necessary for learning from data (the training phase) and being capable of predicting a numeric estimate (for example, house pricing) or a class (for instance, the species of an Iris flower) given a new example that you didn't have before. In this chapter, you start with the simplest algorithms and work toward more complex ones.

REMEMBER

Simple and complex aren't absolute values in machine learning — they're relative to the algorithm's construction. Some algorithms are simple summations while others require complex calculations (and Python deals with both the simple and complex algorithms for you). It's the data that makes the difference: For some problems, simple algorithms are better; other problems may instead require complex algorithms.

REMEMBER

You don't have to type the source code for this chapter manually. In fact, it's a lot easier if you use the downloadable source available at www.dummies.com/go/codingaiodownloads. The source code for this chapter appears in the P4DS4D; 17; Exploring Four Simple and Effective Algorithms.ipynb source code file.

CHAPTER 6 **Exploring Four Simple and Effective Algorithms** 511

Guessing the Number: Linear Regression

Regression has a long history in statistics, from building simple but effective linear models of economic, psychological, social, or political data, to hypothesis testing for understanding group differences, to modeling more complex problems with ordinal values, binary and multiple classes, count data, and hierarchical relationships.

Regression is also a common tool in data science. Stripped of most of its statistical properties, data science practitioners see linear regression as a simple, understandable, yet effective algorithm for estimations, and, in its logistic regression version, for classification as well.

Defining the family of linear models

Linear regression is a statistical model that defines the relationship between a target variable and a set of predictive features. It does so using a formula of the following type:

```
y = a + bx
```

You can translate this formula into something readable and useful for many problems. For instance, if you're trying to guess your sales based on historical results and available data about advertising expenditures, the preceding formula becomes

```
sales = a + b * (advertising expenditure)
```

You may already have encountered this formula during high school because it's also the formula of a line in a bidimensional plane, which is made of an x-axis (the abscissa) and a y-axis (the ordinate).

You can demystify the formula by explaining its components: a is the value of the intercept (the value of y when x is zero), and b is a coefficient that expresses the slope of the line (the relationship between x and y). If b is positive, y increases and decreases as x increases and decreases — when b is negative, y behaves in the opposite manner. You can understand b as the unit change in y given a unit change in x. When the value of b is near zero, the effect of x on y is slight, but if the value of b is high, either positive or negative, the effect of changes in x on y is great.

Linear regression, therefore, can find the best y = a + bx and represent the relationship between your target variable, y, with respect to your predictive feature, x. Both a (alpha) and b (beta coefficient) are estimated on the basis of the data, and

they are found using the linear regression algorithm so that the difference between all the real y target values and all the y values derived from the linear regression formula are the minimum possible.

You can express this relationship graphically as the sum of the square of all the vertical distances between all the data points and the regression line. Such a sum is always the minimum possible when you calculate the regression line correctly using an estimation called ordinary least squares, which is derived from statistics or the equivalent gradient descent, a machine learning method. The differences between the real y values and the regression line (the predicted y values) are defined as residuals (because they are what are left after a regression: the errors).

Using more variables

When using a single variable for predicting y, you use simple linear regression, but when working with many variables, you use multiple linear regression. When you have many variables, their scale isn't important in creating precise linear regression predictions. But a good habit is to standardize x values because the scale of the variables is quite important for some variants of regression (that you see later on), and it is insightful for your understanding of data to compare coefficients according to their impact on y.

The following example relies on the Boston data set from scikit-learn. It tries to guess Boston housing prices using a linear regression. The example also tries to determine which variables influence the result more, so the example standardizes the predictors.

```
from sklearn.datasets import load_boston
from sklearn.preprocessing import scale
boston = load_boston()
X, y = scale(boston.data), boston.target
```

The regression class in scikit-learn is part of the `linear_model` module. Having previously scaled the x variable, you have no other preparations or special parameters to decide when using this algorithm.

```
from sklearn.linear_model import LinearRegression
regression = LinearRegression()
regression.fit(X,y)
```

Now that the algorithm is fitted, you can use the `score` method to report the $R2$ measure, which is a measure that ranges from 0 to 1 and points out how using a particular regression model is better in predicting y than using a simple mean would be. You can also see R2 as being the quantity of target information explained

by the model (the same as the squared correlation), so getting near 1 means being able to explain most of the y variable using the model.

```
print regression.score(X,y)

0.740607742865
```

In this case, R2 on the previously fitted data is 0.74, a good result for a simple model.

Calculating R2 on the same set of data used for the training is common in statistics. In data science and machine learning, it's always better to test scores on data that has not been used for training. Algorithms of greater complexity can memorize the data better than they learn from it, but this statement can be also true sometimes for simpler models, such as linear regression.

To understand what drives the estimates in the multiple regression model, you have to look at the coefficients_ attribute, which is an array containing the regression beta coefficients. Printing the variable names at the same time as the coefficients using the boston.DESCR attribute helps you understand which variable the coefficients reference. The zip function will generate an iterable of both attributes, and you can print it for reporting.

```
print [a+':'+str(round(b,1)) for a, b in zip(
    boston.feature_names, regression.coef_,)]

['CRIM:-0.9', 'ZN:1.1', 'INDUS:0.1', 'CHAS:0.7',
 'NOX:-2.1', 'RM:2.7', 'AGE:0.0', 'DIS:-3.1',
 'RAD:2.7', 'TAX:-2.1', 'PTRATIO:-2.1', 'B:0.9',
 'LSTAT:-3.7']
```

DIS is the weighted distances to five employment centers. It shows the major absolute unit change. For example, in real estate, a house that's too far from people's interests (such as work) lowers the value. As a contrast, AGE and INDUS, with both proportions describing building age and showing whether nonretail activities are available in the area, don't influence the result as much because the absolute value of their beta coefficients is lower than DIS.

Understanding limitations and problems

Although linear regression is a simple yet effective estimation tool, it has quite a few problems. The problems can reduce the benefit of using linear regressions in some cases, but it really depends on the data. You determine whether any problems exist by employing the method and testing its efficacy. Still, you may encounter these limitations:

- » Linear regression can model only quantitative data. When modeling categories as response, you need to modify the data into a logistic regression.

- » If data is missing and you don't deal with it properly, the model stops working. It's important to impute the missing values or, using the value of zero for the variable, to create an additional binary variable pointing out that a value is missing.

- » Also, outliers are quite disruptive for a linear regression because linear regression tries to minimize the square value of the residuals, and outliers have big residuals, forcing the algorithm to focus more on them than on the mass of regular points.

- » The relation between the target and each predictor variable is based on a single coefficient — there isn't an automatic way to represent complex relations like a parabola (there is a unique value of x maximizing y) or exponential growth. The only way you can manage to model such relations is to use mathematical transformations of x (and sometimes y) or add new variables.

- » The greatest limitation is that linear regression provides a summation of terms, which can vary independently of each other. It's hard to figure out how to represent the effect of certain variables that affect the result in very different ways according to their value. In short, you can't represent complex situations with your data, just simple ones.

Moving to Logistic Regression

Linear regression is well suited for estimating values, but it isn't the best tool for predicting the class of an observation. In spite of the statistical theory that advises against it, you can actually try to classify a binary class by scoring one class as 1 and the other as 0. The results are disappointing most of the time, so the statistical theory wasn't wrong!

The fact is that linear regression works on a continuum of numeric estimates. In order to classify correctly, you need a more suitable measure, such as the probability of class ownership. Thanks to the following formula, you can transform a linear regression numeric estimate into a probability that is more apt to describe how a class fits an observation:

```
probability of a class =  exp(r) / (1+exp(r))
```

r is the regression result (the sum of the variables weighted by the coefficients), and exp is the exponential function. exp(r) corresponds to Euler's number e elevated to the power of r. A linear regression using such a formula (also called a link function) for transforming its results into probabilities is a logistic regression.

Applying logistic regression

Logistic regression is similar to linear regression, with the only difference being the y data, which should contain integer values indicating the class relative to the observation. Using the Iris data set from the Scikit-learn datasets module, you can use the values 0, 1, and 2 to denote three classes that correspond to three species:

```
from sklearn.datasets import load_iris
iris = load_iris()
X, y = iris.data[:-1,:], iris.target[:-1]
```

To make the example easier to work with, leave a single value out so that later you can use this value to test the efficacy of the logistic regression model on it.

```
from sklearn.linear_model import LogisticRegression
logistic = LogisticRegression()
logistic.fit(X,y)
print 'Predicted class %s, real class %s' % (
    logistic.predict(iris.data[-1,:]),iris.target[-1])
print 'Probabilities for each class from 0 to 2: %s'
    % logistic.predict_proba(iris.data[-1,:])

Predicted class [2], real class 2
Probabilities for each class from 0 to 2:
  [[ 0.00168787  0.28720074  0.71111138]]
```

Contrary to linear regression, logistic regression doesn't just output the resulting class (in this case, the class 2), but it also estimates the probability of the observation's being part of all three classes. Based on the observation used for prediction, logistic regression estimates a probability of 71 percent of its being from class 2 — a high probability, but not a perfect score, therefore leaving a margin of uncertainty.

TIP

Using probabilities lets you guess the most probable class, but you can also order the predictions with respect to being part of that class. This is especially useful for medical purposes: Ranking a prediction in terms of likelihood with respect to others can reveal which patients are at most risk of getting or already having a disease.

Considering when classes are more

The previous problem, logistic regression, automatically handles a multiple class problem (it started with three Iris species to guess). Most algorithms provided by scikit-learn that predict probabilities or a score for class can automatically handle multiclass problems using two different strategies:

- » **One versus rest:** The algorithm compares every class with all the remaining classes, building a model for every class. If you have ten classes to guess, you have ten models. This approach relies on the OneVsRestClassifier class from scikit-learn.

- » **One versus one:** The algorithm compares every class against every individual remaining class, building a number of models equivalent to n * (n–1) / 2, where n is the number of classes. If you have ten classes, you have 45 models. This approach relies on the OneVsOneClassifier class from Scikit-learn.

In the case of logistic regression, the default multiclass strategy is the one versus rest. The example in this section shows how to use both the strategies with the handwritten digit data set, containing a class for numbers from 0 to 9. The following code loads the data and places it into variables.

```
from sklearn.datasets import load_digits
digits = load_digits()
X, y = digits.data[:1700,:], digits.target[:1700]
tX, ty = digits.data[1700:,:], digits.target[1700:]
```

The observations are actually a grid of pixel values. The grid's dimensions are 8 pixels by 8 pixels. To make the data easier to learn by machine learning algorithms, the code aligns them into a list of 64 elements. The example reserves a part of the available examples for a test.

```
from sklearn.multiclass import OneVsRestClassifier
from sklearn.multiclass import OneVsOneClassifier
OVR = OneVsRestClassifier(LogisticRegression()).fit(X,y)
OVO = OneVsOneClassifier(LogisticRegression()).fit(X,y)
print 'One vs rest accuracy: %.3f' % OVR.score(tX,ty)
print 'One vs one accuracy: %.3f' % OVO.score(tX,ty)

One vs rest accuracy: 0.938
One vs one accuracy: 0.969
```

The two multiclass classes OneVsRestClassifier and OneVsOneClassifier operate by incorporating the estimator (in this case, LogisticRegression) when building the model. Interestingly, the one-versus-one strategy obtained the best accuracy thanks to its high number of models in competition.

TECHNICAL STUFF

When working with Anaconda and Python version 3.4, you may receive a deprecation warning when working with this example. You're safe to ignore the deprecation warning — the example should work as normal. All the deprecation warning tells you is that one of the features used in the example is due for an update or will become unavailable in a future version of Python.

Making Things as Simple as Naïve Bayes

You might wonder why anyone would name an algorithm Naïve Bayes. The naïve part comes from its formulation — it makes some extreme simplifications to standard probability calculations. The reference to Bayes in its name relates to the Reverend Bayes and his theorem on probability.

Reverend Thomas Bayes was a statistician and a philosopher who formulated his theorem during the first half of the eighteenth century. The theorem was never published while he was alive. It has deeply revolutionized the theory of probability by introducing the idea of conditional probability — that is, probability conditioned by evidence.

Of course, it helps to start from the beginning — probability itself. Probability tells you the likelihood of an event and is expressed in a numeric form. The probability of an event is measured in the range from 0 to 1 (from 0 percent to 100 percent), and it's empirically derived from counting the number of times the specific event happened with respect to all the events. You can calculate it from data!

When you observe events (for example, when a feature has a certain characteristic), and you want to estimate the probability associated with the event, you count the number of times the characteristic appears in the data and divide that figure by the total number of observations available. The result is a number ranging from 0 to 1, which expresses the probability.

When you estimate the probability of an event, you tend to believe that you can apply the probability in each situation. The term for this belief is *a priori* because it constitutes the first estimate of probability with regard to an event (the one that comes to mind first). For example, if you estimate the probability of a person being a female, you might say, after some counting, that it's 50 percent, which is the prior, the first probability you will stick with.

The prior probability can change in the face of evidence, that is, something that can radically modify your expectations. For example, the evidence of whether a person is male or female could be that the person's hair is long or short. You can estimate having long hair as an event with 35 percent probability for the general

population, but within the female population, it's 60 percent. If the percentage is so high in the female population, contrary to the general probability (the prior for having long hair), there should be some useful information that you can use!

Imagine that you have to guess whether a person is male or female and the evidence is that the person has long hair. This sounds like a predictive problem, and in the end, this situation is really similar to predicting a categorical variable from data: We have a target variable with different categories, and you have to guess the probability of each category on the basis of evidence, the data. Reverend Bayes provided a useful formula:

$$P(A|B) = P(B|A)*P(A) / P(B)$$

The formula looks like statistical jargon and is a bit counterintuitive, so it needs to be explained in depth. Reading the formula using the previous example as input makes the meaning behind the formula quite a bit clearer:

» $P(A|B)$ is the probability of being a female (event A) given long hair (evidence B). This part of the formula defines what you want to predict. In short, it says to predict y given x where y is an outcome (male or female) and x is the evidence (long or short hair).

» $P(B|A)$ is the probability of having long hair when the person is a female. In this case, you already know that it's 60 percent. In every data problem, you can obtain this figure easily by simple cross-tabulation of the features against the target outcome.

» $P(A)$ is the probability of being a female, a 50 percent general chance (a prior).

» $P(B)$ is the probability of having long hair, which is 35 percent (another prior).

TIP

When reading parts of the formula such as $P(A|B)$, you should read them as follows: probability of A given B. The | symbol translates as given. A probability expressed in this way is a conditional probability, because it's the probability of A conditioned by the evidence presented by B. In this example, plugging the numbers into the formula translates into: 60% * 50% / 35% = 85.7%.

Therefore, even if being a female is a 50 percent probability, just knowing evidence like long hair takes it up to 85.7 percent, which is a more favorable chance for the guess. You can be more confident in guessing that the person with long hair is a female because you have a bit less than a 15 percent chance of being wrong.

Finding out that Naïve Bayes isn't so naïve

Naive Bayes, leveraging the simple Bayes' rule, takes advantage of all the evidence available in order to modify the prior base probability of your predictions.

CHAPTER 6 **Exploring Four Simple and Effective Algorithms** 519

Because your data contains so much evidence — that is, it has many features — the data makes a big sum of all the probabilities derived from a simplified Naïve Bayes formula.

REMEMBER

As discussed in the "Guessing the Number: Linear Regression" section, earlier in this chapter, summing variables implies that the model takes them as separate and unique pieces of information. But this isn't true in reality, because applications exist in a world of interconnections, with every piece of information connecting to many other pieces. Using one piece of information more than once means giving more emphasis to that particular piece.

Because you don't know (or simply ignore) the relationships between each piece of evidence, you probably just plug all of them into Naïve Bayes. The simple and naïve move of throwing everything that you know at the formula works well indeed, and many studies report good performance despite the fact that you make a naïve assumption. It's okay to use everything for prediction, even though it seems as though it shouldn't be okay given the strong association between variables. Here are some of the ways in which you commonly see Naïve Bayes used:

» Building spam detectors (catching all annoying emails in your inbox)

» Sentiment analysis (guessing whether a text contains positive or negative attitudes with respect to a topic, and detecting the mood of the speaker)

» Text-processing tasks such as spell correction, or guessing the language used to write or classify the text into a larger category

Naïve Bayes is also popular because it doesn't need as much data to work. It can naturally handle multiple classes. With some slight variable modifications (transforming them into classes), it can also handle numeric variables. Scikit-learn provides three Naïve Bayes classes in the `sklearn.naive_bayes` module:

» `MultinomialNB`: Uses the probabilities derived from a feature's presence. When a feature is present, it assigns a certain probability to the outcome, which the textual data indicates for the prediction.

» `BernoulliNB`: Provides the multinomial functionality of Naïve Bayes, but it penalizes the absence of a feature. It assigns a different probability when the feature is present than when it's absent. In fact, it treats all features as dichotomous variables (the distribution of a dichotomous variable is a Bernoulli distribution). You can also use it with textual data.

» `GaussianNB`: Defines a version of Naïve Bayes that expects a normal distribution of all the features. Hence this class is suboptimal for textual data in which words are sparse (use the multinomial or Bernoulli distributions instead). If your variables have positive and negative values, this is the best choice.

Predicting text classifications

Naïve Bayes is particularly popular for document classification. In textual problems, you often have millions of features involved, one for each word spelled correctly or incorrectly. Sometimes the text is associated with other nearby words in *n-grams*, that is, sequences of consecutive words. Naïve Bayes can learn the textual features quickly and provide fast predictions based on the input.

This section tests text classifications using the binomial and multinomial Naïve Bayes models offered by scikit-learn. The examples rely on the 20newsgroups data set, which contains a large number of posts from 20 kinds of newsgroups. The data set is divided into a training set, for building your textual models, and a test set, which comprises posts that temporally follow the training set. You use the test set to test the accuracy of your predictions.

```
from sklearn.datasets import fetch_20newsgroups
newsgroups_train = fetch_20newsgroups(subset='train',
    remove=('headers', 'footers', 'quotes'))
newsgroups_test = fetch_20newsgroups(subset='test',
    remove=('headers', 'footers', 'quotes'))
```

After loading the two sets into memory, you import the two Naïve Bayes and instantiate them. At this point, you set alpha values, which are useful for avoiding a zero probability for rare features (a zero probability would exclude these features from the analysis). You typically use a small value for alpha, as shown in the following code:

```
from sklearn.naive_bayes import BernoulliNB, MultinomialNB
Bernoulli = BernoulliNB(alpha=0.01)
Multinomial = MultinomialNB(alpha=0.01)
```

You can use two different hashing tricks, one counting the words (for the multinomial approach) and one recording whether a word appeared in a binary variable (the binomial approach). You can also remove *stop words*, that is, common words found in the English language, such as "a," "the," "in," and so on.

```
import sklearn.feature_extraction.text as txt
multinomial_hashing_trick = txt.HashingVectorizer(
    stop_words='english', binary=False, norm=None,
    non_negative=True)
binary_hashing_trick = txt.HashingVectorizer(
    stop_words='english', binary=True, norm=None,
    non_negative=True)
```

At this point, you can train the two classifiers and test them on the test set, which is a set of posts that temporally appears after the training set. The test measure is accuracy, which is the percentage of right guesses that the algorithm makes.

```
Multinomial.fit(multinomial_hashing_trick.transform(
    newsgroups_train.data), newsgroups_train.target)
Bernoulli.fit(binary_hashing_trick.transform(
    newsgroups_train.data), newsgroups_train.target)
from sklearn.metrics import accuracy_score
for m, h in [(Bernoulli, binary_hashing_trick),
    (Multinomial, multinomial_hashing_trick)]:
    print 'Accuracy for %s: %.3f' % (m,
        accuracy_score(y_true=newsgroups_test.target,
            y_pred=m.predict(h.transform(
                newsgroups_test.data))))

Accuracy for BernoulliNB(alpha=0.01, binarize=0.0,
    class_prior=None, fit_prior=True): 0.570
Accuracy for MultinomialNB(alpha=0.01, class_prior=None,
    fit_prior=True): 0.651
```

You might notice that it won't take long for both models to train and report their predictions on the test set. Consider that the training set is made up of more than 11,000 posts containing 300,000 words, and the test set contains about 7,500 other posts.

```
print 'number of posts in training: %i' % len(
    newsgroups_train.data)
D={word:True for post in newsgroups_train.data for word
    in post.split(' ')}
print 'number of distinct words in training: %i' % len(D)
print 'number of posts in test: %i' % len(
    newsgroups_test.data)
number of posts in training: 11314
number of distinct words in training: 300972
number of posts in test: 7532
```

Learning Lazily with Nearest Neighbors

k-Nearest Neighbors (kNN) is not about building rules from data based on coefficients or probability. kNN works on the basis of similarities. When you have to predict something like a class, it may be best to find the observations most similar to the one you want to classify or estimate. You can then derive the answer you need from the similar cases.

Observing how many observations are similar doesn't imply learning something, but rather measuring. Because kNN isn't learning anything, it's considered lazy, and you'll hear it referenced as a lazy learner or an instance-based learner. The idea is that similar premises usually provide similar results, and it's important not to forget to get such low-hanging fruit before trying to climb the tree!

The algorithm is fast during training because it only has to memorize data about the observations. It actually calculates more during predictions. When there are too many observations, the algorithm can become slow and memory-consuming. You're best advised not to use it with big data, or it may take almost forever to predict anything! Moreover, this simple and effective algorithm works better when you have distinct data groups without too many variables involved because the algorithm is also sensitive to the dimensionality curse.

The curse of dimensionality happens as the number of variables increases. Consider a situation in which you're measuring the distance between observations and, as the space becomes larger and larger, it becomes difficult to find real neighbors — a problem for kNN, which sometimes mistakes a far observation for a near one. Rendering the idea is just like playing chess on a multidimensional chessboard. When playing on the classic 2D board, most pieces are near, and you can more easily spot opportunities and menaces for your pawns when you have 32 pieces and 64 positions. However, when you start playing on a 3D board, such as those found in some sci-fi films, your 32 pieces can become lost in 512 possible positions. Now just imagine playing with a 12D chessboard. You can easily misunderstand what is near and what is far, which is what happens with kNN.

TIP

You can still make kNN smart in detecting similarities between observations by removing redundant information.

Predicting after observing neighbors

For an example showing how to use kNN, you can start with the digit data set again. kNN is particularly useful, just like Naïve Bayes, when you have to predict many classes, or in situations that would require you to build too many models or rely on a complex model.

```
from sklearn.datasets import load_digits
from sklearn.decomposition import PCA
digits = load_digits()
pca = PCA(n_components=25)
pca.fit(digits.data[:1700,:])
X, y = pca.transform(digits.data[:1700,:]),
    digits.target[:1700]
tX, ty = pca.transform(digits.data[1700:,:]),
    digits.target[1700:]
```

kNN is an algorithm that's quite sensitive to outliers. Moreover, you have to rescale your variables and remove some redundant information. In this example, you use PCA. Rescaling is not necessary because the data represents pixels, which means that it's already scaled.

TIP

You can avoid the problem with outliers by keeping the neighborhood small, that is, by not looking too far for similar examples.

TIP

Knowing the data type can save you a lot of time and many mistakes. For example, in this case, you know that the data represents pixel values. Doing EDA (as described in Book 7, Chapter 5) is always the first step and can provide you with useful insights, but getting additional information about how the data was obtained and what the data represents is also a good practice and can be just as useful. To see this task in action, you reserve cases in tX and try a few cases that kNN won't look up when looking for neighbors.

```
from sklearn.neighbors import KNeighborsClassifier
kNN = KNeighborsClassifier(n_neighbors=5)
kNN.fit(X,y)
```

kNN uses a distance measure in order to determine which observations to consider as possible neighbors for the target case. You can easily change the predefined distance using the p parameter:

» When p is 2, use the Euclidean distance.

» When p is 1, use the Manhattan distance metric, which is the absolute distance between observations. In a 2D square, when you go from one corner to the opposite one, the Manhattan distance is the same as walking the perimeter, whereas Euclidean is like walking on the diagonal. Although the Manhattan distance isn't the shortest route, it's a more realistic measure than Euclidean distance, and it's less sensitive to noise and high dimensionality.

Usually, the Euclidean distance is the right measure, but sometimes it can give you worse results, especially when the analysis involves many correlated variables. The following code shows that the analysis seems fine with it.

```
print 'Accuracy: %.3f' % kNN.score(tX,ty)
print 'Prediction: %s actual: %s' %
    (kNN.predict(tX[:10,:]),ty[:10])

Accuracy: 0.990
Prediction: [5 6 5 0 9 8 9 8 4 1]
    actual: [5 6 5 0 9 8 9 8 4 1]
```

Choosing your k parameter wisely

A critical parameter that you have to define in kNN is k. As k increases, kNN considers more points for its predictions, and the decisions are less influenced by noisy instances that could exercise an undue influence. Your decisions are based on an average of more observations, and they become more solid. When the k value you use is too large, you start considering neighbors that are too far, sharing less and less with the case you have to predict.

It's an important trade-off. When the value of k is less, you consider a more homogeneous pool of neighbors but can more easily make an error by taking the few similar cases for granted. When the value of k is more, you consider more cases at a higher risk of observing neighbors that are too far or that are outliers. Getting back to the previous example with handwritten digit data, you can experiment with changing the k value, as shown in the following code:

```
for k in [1, 5, 10, 100, 200]:
    kNN = KNeighborsClassifier(n_neighbors=k).fit(X,y)
    print 'for k= %3i accuracy is %.3f' % 
        (k, kNN.score(tX,ty))

for k=   1 accuracy is 0.979
for k=   5 accuracy is 0.990
for k=  10 accuracy is 0.969
for k= 100 accuracy is 0.959
for k= 200 accuracy is 0.907
```

Through experimentation, you find that setting n_neighbors (the parameter representing k) to 5 is the optimum choice, resulting in the highest accuracy. Using just the nearest neighbor (n_neighbors =1) isn't a bad choice, but setting the value above 5 instead brings decreasing results in the classification task.

TIP

As a rule of thumb, when your data set doesn't have many observations, set k as a number near the squared number of available observations. However, there is no general rule, and trying different k values is always a good way to optimize your kNN performance. Always start from low values and work toward higher values.

8 Essentials of Machine Learning

Contents at a Glance

CHAPTER 1: Introducing How Machines Learn............529
 Getting the Real Story about AI............530
 Learning in the Age of Big Data............541

CHAPTER 2: Demystifying the Math behind Machine Learning............553
 Working with Data............554
 Exploring the World of Probabilities............563
 Describing the Use of Statistics............568

CHAPTER 3: Descending the Right Curve............571
 Interpreting Learning as Optimization............572
 Exploring Cost Functions............576
 Descending the Error Curve............578
 Updating by Mini-Batch and Online............581

CHAPTER 4: Validating Machine Learning............585
 Checking Out-of-Sample Errors............586
 Getting to Know the Limits of Bias............589
 Keeping Model Complexity in Mind............591
 Keeping Solutions Balanced............592
 Training, Validating, and Testing............595
 Resorting to Cross-Validation............596
 Looking for Alternatives in Validation............597
 Optimizing Cross-Validation Choices............598
 Avoiding Sample Bias and Leakage Traps............601

IN THIS CHAPTER

» Defining the dream of AI, and comparing AI to machine learning

» Understanding the engineering portion of AI and machine learning

» Considering how statistics and big data work together in machine learning

» Defining the role of algorithms in machine learning

» Determining how training works with algorithms in machine learning

Chapter 1
Introducing How Machines Learn

"A breakthrough in machine learning would be worth ten Microsofts."

— BILL GATES

Artificial Intelligence (AI) is a huge topic today, and it's getting bigger all the time thanks to the success of technologies such as Siri (www.apple.com/ios/siri). Talking to your smartphone is both fun and helpful to find out things like the location of the best sushi restaurant in town or to discover how to get to the concert hall. As you talk to your smartphone, it learns more about the way you talk and makes fewer mistakes in understanding your requests. The capability of your smartphone to learn and interpret your particular way of speaking is an example of an AI, and part of the technology used to make it happen is machine learning. You likely make use of machine learning and AI all over the place today without really thinking about it. For example, the capability to speak to devices and have them actually do what you intend is an example of machine learning at work. Likewise, recommender systems, such as those found

on Amazon, help you make purchases based on criteria such as previous product purchases or products that complement a current choice. The use of both AI and machine learning will only increase with time.

In this chapter, you delve into AI and discover what it means from several perspectives, including how it affects you as a consumer and as a scientist or engineer. You also discover that AI doesn't equal machine learning, even though the media often confuse the two. Machine learning is definitely different from AI, even though the two are related.

You will also understand the fuel that powers both AI and machine learning — big data. Algorithms, lines of computer code based on statistics, turn big data into information and eventually insight. Through this process, you will be amazed by how AI and machine learning help computers excel at tasks that used to be done only by humans.

Getting the Real Story about AI

For many years, people understood AI based on Hollywood. Robots enhanced human abilities in TV shows like *The Jetsons* or *Knight Rider,* and in movies like *Star Wars* and *Star Trek*. Recent developments like powerful computers that can fit in your pocket and cheap storage to collect massive amounts of data have moved real-life reality closer to the on-screen fiction.

This section separates hype from reality, and explores a few actual applications in machine learning and AI.

Moving beyond the hype

As any technology becomes bigger, so does the hype, and AI certainly has a lot of hype surrounding it. For one thing, some people have decided to engage in fear mongering rather than science. Killer robots, such as those found in the film *The Terminator,* really aren't going to be the next big thing. Your first real experience with an android AI is more likely to be in the form a health-care assistant (www.good.is/articles/robots-elder-care-pepper-exoskeletons-japan) or possibly as a coworker (www.computerworld.com/article/2990849/robotics/meet-the-virtual-woman-who-may-take-your-job.html). The reality is that you already interact with AI and machine learning in far more mundane ways. Part of the reason you need to read this chapter is to get past the hype and discover what AI can do for you today.

REMEMBER

You may also have heard machine learning and AI used interchangeably. AI includes machine learning, but machine learning doesn't fully define AI. This chapter helps you understand the relationship between machine learning and AI.

Machine learning and AI both have strong engineering components. That is, you can quantify both technologies precisely based on *theory* (substantiated and tested explanations) rather than simply *hypothesis* (a suggested explanation for a phenomenon). In addition, both have strong science components, through which people test concepts and create new ideas of how expressing the thought process might be possible. Finally, machine learning also has an artistic component, and this is where a talented scientist can excel. In some cases, AI and machine learning both seemingly defy logic, and only the true artist can make them work as expected.

YES, FULLY AUTONOMOUS WEAPONS EXIST

It's true — some people are working on autonomous weapon technologies. You'll find some discussions of the ethics of AI in this book, but for the most part, the book focuses on positive, helpful uses of AI to aid humans, rather than kill them, because most AI research reflects these uses. You can find articles on the pros and cons of AI online, such as the *Guardian* article at www.theguardian.com/technology/2015/jul/27/musk-wozniak-hawking-ban-ai-autonomous-weapons. However, remember that these people are guessing — they don't actually know what the future of AI holds.

If you really must scare yourself, you can find all sorts of sites, such as www.reachingcriticalwill.org/resources/fact-sheets/critical-issues/7972-fully-autonomous-weapons, that discuss the issue of fully autonomous weapons in some depth. Sites such as Campaign to Stop Killer Robots (www.stopkillerrobots.org) can also fill in some details for you. We do encourage you to sign the letter banning autonomous weapons at https://futureoflife.org/open-letter-autonomous-weapons — there truly is no need for them.

However, it's important to remember that bans against space-based, chemical, and certain laser weapons all exist. Countries recognize that these weapons don't solve anything. Countries will also likely ban fully autonomous weapons simply because the citizenry won't stand for killer robots. The bottom line is that the focus of this book is on helping you understand machine learning in a positive light.

CHAPTER 1 **Introducing How Machines Learn** 531

Dreaming of electric sheep

Androids (a specialized kind of robot that looks and acts like a human, such as Data in *Star Trek*) and some types of *humanoid robots* (a kind of robot that has human characteristics but is easily distinguished from a human, such as C-3PO in *Star Wars*) have become the poster children for AI. They present computers in a form that people can anthropomorphize (for example, make human). In fact, it's entirely possible that one day you won't be able to distinguish between human and artificial life with ease. Science fiction authors, such as Philip K. Dick, have long predicted such an occurrence, and it seems all too possible today. The story *Do Androids Dream of Electric Sheep?* discusses the whole concept of more real than real. The idea appears as part of the plot in the movie *Blade Runner* (www.warnerbros.com/blade-runner). The sections that follow help you understand how close technology currently gets to the ideals presented by science fiction authors and the movies.

TECHNICAL STUFF

The current state of the art is lifelike, but you can easily tell that you're talking to an android. Viewing videos online can help you understand that androids that are indistinguishable from humans are nowhere near any sort of reality today. Check out the Japanese robots at www.youtube.com/watch?v=MaTfzYDZG8c and www.nbcnews.com/tech/innovation/humanoid-robot-starts-work-japanese-department-store-n345526. One of the more lifelike examples is Amelia (https://vimeo.com/166359613). Her story appears in *Computerworld* at www.computerworld.com/article/2990849/robotics/meet-the-virtual-woman-who-may-take-your-job.html. The point is, technology is just starting to get to the point where people may eventually be able to create lifelike robots and androids, but they don't exist today.

Understanding the history of AI and machine learning

There is a reason, other than anthropomorphization, that humans see the ultimate AI as one that is contained within some type of android. Ever since the ancient Greeks, humans have discussed the possibility of placing a mind inside a mechanical body. One such myth is that of a mechanical man called Talos (www.ancient-wisdom.com/greekautomata.htm). The fact that the ancient Greeks had complex mechanical devices, only one of which still exists (read about the Antikythera mechanism at www.ancient-wisdom.com/antikythera.htm), makes it quite likely that their dreams were built on more than just fantasy. Throughout the centuries, people have discussed mechanical persons capable of thought (such as Rabbi Judah Loew's Golem, www.nytimes.com/2009/05/11/world/europe/11golem.html).

AI is built on the hypothesis that mechanizing thought is possible. During the first millennium, Greek, Indian, and Chinese philosophers all worked on ways to

perform this task. As early as the seventeenth century, Gottfried Leibniz, Thomas Hobbes, and René Descartes discussed the potential for rationalizing all thought as simply math symbols. Of course, the complexity of the problem eluded them, and still eludes us today. The point is that the vision for AI has been around for an incredibly long time, but the implementation of AI is relatively new.

The true birth of AI as we know it today began with Alan Turing's publication of "Computing Machinery and Intelligence" in 1950. In this paper, Turing explored the idea of how to determine whether machines can think. Of course, this paper led to the Imitation Game involving three players. Player A is a computer and Player B is a human. Each must convince Player C (a human who can't see either Player A or Player B) that they are human. If Player C can't determine who is human and who isn't on a consistent basis, the computer wins.

A continuing problem with AI is too much optimism. The problem that scientists are trying to solve with AI is incredibly complex. However, the early optimism of the 1950s and 1960s led scientists to believe that the world would produce intelligent machines in as little as 20 years. After all, machines were doing all sorts of amazing things, such as playing complex games. AI currently has its greatest success in areas such as logistics, data mining, and medical diagnosis.

Exploring what machine learning can do for AI

Machine learning relies on algorithms to analyze huge data sets. Currently, machine learning can't provide the sort of AI that the movies present. Even the best algorithms can't think, feel, present any form of self-awareness, or exercise free will. What machine learning can do is perform predictive analytics far faster than any human can. As a result, machine learning can help humans work more efficiently. The current state of AI, then, is one of performing analysis, but humans must still consider the implications of that analysis — making the required moral and ethical decisions. The "Considering the relationship between AI and machine learning" section later in this chapter delves more deeply into precisely how machine learning contributes to AI as a whole. The essence of the matter is that machine learning provides just the learning part of AI, and that part is nowhere near ready to create an AI of the sort you see in films.

REMEMBER

The main point of confusion between learning and intelligence is that people assume that simply because a machine gets better at its job (learning) it's also aware (intelligence). Nothing supports this view of machine learning. The same phenomenon occurs when people assume that a computer is purposely causing problems for them. The computer can't (currently) assign emotions and therefore acts only upon the input provided and the instruction contained within an application to process that input. A true AI will eventually occur when computers can finally emulate the clever combination used by nature:

CHAPTER 1 **Introducing How Machines Learn** 533

» **Genetics:** Slow learning from one generation to the next

» **Teaching:** Fast learning from organized sources

» **Exploration:** Spontaneous learning through media and interactions with others

Considering the goals of machine learning

At present, AI is based on machine learning, and machine learning is essentially different from statistics. Yes, machine learning has a statistical basis, but it makes some different assumptions than statistics do because the goals are different. Table 1-1 lists some features to consider when comparing AI and machine learning to statistics.

TABLE 1-1 Comparing Machine Learning to Statistics

Technique	Machine Learning	Statistics
Data handling	Works with big data in the form of networks and graphs; raw data from sensors or the web text is split into training and test data.	Models are used to create predictive power on small samples.
Data input	The data is sampled, randomized, and transformed to maximize accuracy scoring in the prediction of out-of-sample (or completely new) examples.	Parameters interpret real-world phenomena and provide a stress on magnitude.
Result	Probability is taken into account for comparing what could be the best guess or decision.	The output captures the variability and uncertainty of parameters.
Assumptions	The scientist learns from the data.	The scientist assumes a certain output and tries to prove it.
Distribution	The distribution is unknown or ignored before learning from data.	The scientist assumes a well-defined distribution.
Fitting	The scientist creates a best fit, but generalizable, model.	The result is fit to the present data distribution.

Defining machine learning limits based on hardware

Huge data sets require huge amounts of memory. Unfortunately, the requirements don't end there. When you have huge amounts of data and memory, you must also have processors with multiple cores and high speeds. One of the problems that scientists are striving to solve is how to use existing hardware more efficiently. In some cases, waiting for days to obtain a result to a machine learning problem

simply isn't possible. The scientists who want to know the answer need it quickly, even if the result isn't quite right. With this in mind, investments in better hardware also require investments in better science. This book considers some of the following issues as part of making your machine learning experience better:

» **Obtaining a useful result:** As you work through the book, you discover that you need to obtain a useful result first, before you can refine it. In addition, sometimes tuning an algorithm goes too far, and the result becomes quite fragile (and possibly useless outside a specific data set).

» **Asking the right question:** Many people get frustrated in trying to obtain an answer from machine learning because they keep tuning their algorithm without asking a different question. To use hardware efficiently, sometimes you must step back and review the question you're asking. The question might be wrong, which means that even the best hardware will never find the answer.

» **Relying on intuition too heavily:** All machine learning questions begin as a hypothesis. A scientist uses intuition to create a starting point for discovering the answer to a question. Failure is more common than success when working through a machine learning experience. Your intuition adds the art to the machine learning experience, but sometimes intuition is wrong and you have to revisit your assumptions.

TECHNICAL STUFF

When you begin to realize the importance of environment to machine learning, you can also begin to understand the need for the right hardware and in the right balance to obtain a desired result. The current state-of-the-art systems actually rely on graphical processing units (GPUs) to perform machine learning tasks. Relying on GPUs does speed the machine learning process considerably. A full discussion of using GPUs is outside the scope of this book, but you can read more about the topic at `https://devblogs.nvidia.com/parallelforall/bidmach-machine-learning-limit-gpus`.

Overcoming AI fantasies

As with many other technologies, AI and machine learning both have their fantasy or fad uses. For example, some people are using machine learning to create Picasso-like art from photos. You can read all about it at `www.washingtonpost.com/news/innovations/wp/2015/08/31/this-algorithm-can-create-a-new-van-gogh-or-picasso-in-just-an-hour`. As the article points out, the computer can copy only an existing style at this stage — not create an entirely new style of its own. The following sections discuss AI and machine learning fantasies of various sorts.

Discovering the fad uses of AI and machine learning

AI is entering an era of innovation that you used to read about only in science fiction. It can be hard to determine whether a particular AI use is real or simply the dream child of a determined scientist. For example, *The Six Million Dollar Man* (https://en.wikipedia.org/wiki/The_Six_Million_Dollar_Man) is a television series that looked fanciful at one time. When it was introduced, no one actually thought that we'd have real-world bionics at some point. However, Hugh Herr has other ideas — bionic legs really are possible now (www.smithsonianmag.com/innovation/future-robotic-legs-180953040). Of course, they aren't available for everyone yet; the technology is only now becoming useful. Muddying the waters is another television series, *The Six Billion Dollar Man* (www.cinemablend.com/new/Mark-Wahlberg-Six-Billion-Dollar-Man-Just-Made-Big-Change-91947.html). The fact is that AI and machine learning will both present opportunities to create some amazing technologies and that we're already at the stage of creating those technologies, but you still need to take what you hear with a huge grain of salt.

REMEMBER

To make the future uses of AI and machine learning match the concepts that science fiction has presented over the years, real-world programmers, data scientists, and other stakeholders need to create tools. Most of these tools are still rudimentary. Nothing happens by magic, even though it may look like magic when you don't know what's happening behind the scenes. In order for the fad uses for AI and machine learning to become real-world uses, developers, data scientists, and others need to continue building real-world tools that may be hard to imagine at this point.

Considering the true uses of AI and machine learning

You find AI and machine learning used in a great many applications today. The only problem is that the technology works so well that you don't know that it even exists. In fact, you might be surprised to find that many devices in your home already make use of both technologies. Both technologies definitely appear in your car and most especially in the workplace. In fact, the uses for both AI and machine learning number in the millions — all safely out of sight even when they're quite dramatic in nature.

Here are just a few of the ways in which you might see AI used:

> » **Fraud detection:** You get a call from your credit card company asking whether you made a particular purchase. The credit card company isn't being nosy; it's simply alerting you to the fact that someone else could be making a

purchase using your card. The AI embedded within the credit card company's code detected an unfamiliar spending pattern and alerted someone to it.

- » **Resource scheduling:** Many organizations need to schedule the use of resources efficiently. For example, a hospital may have to determine where to put a patient based on the patient's needs, availability of skilled experts, and the amount of time the doctor expects the patient to be in the hospital.

- » **Complex analysis:** Humans often need help with complex analysis because there are literally too many factors to consider. For example, the same set of symptoms could indicate more than one problem. A doctor or other expert might need help making a diagnosis in a timely manner to save a patient's life.

- » **Automation:** Any form of automation can benefit from the addition of AI to handle unexpected changes or events. A problem with some types of automation today is that an unexpected event, such as an object in the wrong place, can actually cause the automation to stop. Adding AI to the automation can allow the automation to handle unexpected events and continue as if nothing happened.

- » **Customer service:** The customer service line you call today may not even have a human behind it. The automation is good enough to follow scripts and use various resources to handle the vast majority of your questions. With good voice inflection (provided by AI as well), you may not even be able to tell that you're talking with a computer.

- » **Safety systems:** Many of the safety systems found in machines of various sorts today rely on AI to take over the vehicle in a time of crisis. For example, many automatic braking systems rely on AI to stop the car based on all the inputs that a vehicle can provide, such as the direction of a skid.

- » **Machine efficiency:** AI can help control a machine in such a manner as to obtain maximum efficiency. The AI controls the use of resources so that the system doesn't overshoot speed or other goals. Every ounce of power is used precisely as needed to provide the desired services.

This list doesn't even begin to scratch the surface. You can find AI used in many other ways. However, it's also useful to view uses of machine learning outside the normal realm that many consider the domain of AI. Here are a few uses for machine learning that you might not associate with an AI:

- » **Access control:** In many cases, access control is a yes or no proposition. An employee smart card grants access to a resource much in the same way that people have used keys for centuries. Some locks do offer the capability to set times and dates that access is allowed, but the coarse-grained control doesn't really answer every need. By using machine learning, you can determine whether an employee should gain access to a resource based on role and

need. For example, an employee can gain access to a training room when the training reflects an employee role.

- **Animal protection:** The ocean might seem large enough to allow animals and ships to cohabitate without problem. Unfortunately, many animals get hit by ships each year. A machine learning algorithm could allow ships to avoid animals by learning the sounds and characteristics of both the animal and the ship.

- **Predicting wait times:** Most people don't like waiting when they have no idea of how long the wait will be. Machine learning allows an application to determine waiting times based on staffing levels, staffing load, complexity of the problems the staff is trying to solve, availability of resources, and so on.

Being useful; being mundane

Even though the movies make it sound like AI is going to make a huge splash, and you do sometimes see some incredible uses for AI in real life, the fact of the matter is that most uses for AI are mundane, even boring. For example, a recent article details how Verizon uses AI to analyze security breach data (www.computerworld.com/article/3001832/data-analytics/how-verizon-analyzes-security-breach-data-with-r.html). The act of performing this analysis is dull when compared to other sorts of AI activities, but the benefits are that Verizon saves money performing the analysis, and the results are better as well.

In addition, Python developers have a huge array of libraries available to make machine learning easy. In fact, Kaggle (www.kaggle.com/competitions) provides competitions to allow developers to hone their machine learning skills in creating practical applications. The results of these competitions often appear later as part of products that people actually use. Additionally, the developer community is particularly busy creating new libraries to make complex data science and machine learning applications easier to program (see www.kdnuggets.com/2015/06/top-20-python-machine-learning-open-source-projects.html for the top 20 Python libraries in use today).

Considering the relationship between AI and machine learning

Machine learning is only part of what a system requires to become an AI. The machine learning portion of the picture enables an AI to perform these tasks:

- Adapt to new circumstances that the original developer didn't envision.
- Detect patterns in all sorts of data sources.

- Create new behaviors based on the recognized patterns.
- Make decisions based on the success or failure of these behaviors.

The use of algorithms to manipulate data is the centerpiece of machine learning. To prove successful, a machine learning session must use an appropriate algorithm to achieve a desired result. In addition, the data must lend itself to analysis using the desired algorithm, or it requires a careful preparation by scientists.

AI encompasses many other disciplines to simulate the thought process successfully. In addition to machine learning, AI normally includes

- **Natural language processing:** The act of allowing language input and putting it into a form that a computer can use
- **Natural language understanding:** The act of deciphering the language in order to act upon the meaning it provides
- **Knowledge representation:** The ability to store information in a form that makes fast access possible
- **Planning (in the form of goal seeking):** The ability to use stored information to draw conclusions in *near real time* (almost at the moment it happens, but with a slight delay, sometimes so short that a human won't notice, but the computer can)
- **Robotics:** The ability to act upon requests from a user in some physical form

TECHNICAL STUFF

In fact, you might be surprised to find that the number of disciplines required to create an AI is huge. Consequently, this book exposes you to only a portion of what an AI contains. However, even the machine learning portion of the picture can become complex because understanding the world through the data inputs that a computer receives is a complex task. Just think about all the decisions that you constantly make without thinking about them. For example, just the concept of seeing something and knowing whether you can interact successfully with it can become a complex task.

Considering AI and machine learning specifications

As scientists continue to work with a technology and turn hypotheses into theories, the technology becomes related more to *engineering* (where theories are implemented) than *science* (where theories are created). As the rules governing a technology become clearer, groups of experts work together to define these rules

CHAPTER 1 **Introducing How Machines Learn** 539

in written form. The result is *specifications* (a group of rules that everyone agrees upon).

Eventually, implementations of the specifications become *standards* that a governing body, such as the IEEE (Institute of Electrical and Electronics Engineers) or a combination of the ISO/IEC (International Organization for Standardization/International Electrotechnical Commission), manages. AI and machine learning have both been around long enough to create specifications, but you currently won't find any standards for either technology.

The basis for machine learning is math. Algorithms determine how to interpret big data in specific ways. The math basics for machine learning appear in Book 8, Chapter 2. You discover that algorithms process input data in specific ways and create predictable outputs based on the data patterns. What isn't predictable is the data itself. The reason you need AI and machine learning is to decipher the data in such a manner to be able to see the patterns in it and make sense of them.

You see the specifications detailed in Book 8, Chapter 4 in the form of algorithms used to perform specific tasks. When you get to Book 9, you begin to see the reason that everyone agrees to specific sets of rules governing the use of algorithms to perform tasks. The point is to use an algorithm that will best suit the data you have in hand to achieve the specific goals you've created. Professionals implement algorithms using languages that work best for the task. Machine learning relies on Python and R, and to some extent MATLAB, Java, Julia, and C++. (See the discussion at `www.quora.com/What-is-the-best-language-to-use-while-learning-machine-learning-for-the-first-time` for details.)

Defining the divide between art and engineering

The reason that AI and machine learning are both sciences and not engineering disciplines is that both require some level of art to achieve good results. The artistic element of machine learning takes many forms. For example, you must consider how the data is used. Some data acts as a baseline that trains an algorithm to achieve specific results. The remaining data provides the output used to understand the underlying patterns. No specific rules governing the balancing of data exist; the scientists working with the data must discover whether a specific balance produces optimal output.

REMEMBER

Cleaning the data also lends a certain amount of artistic quality to the result. The manner in which a scientist prepares the data for use is important. Some tasks, such as removing duplicate records, occur regularly. However, a scientist may also choose to filter the data in some ways or look at only a subset of the data. As a

result, the cleaned data set used by one scientist for machine learning tasks may not precisely match the cleaned data set used by another.

You can also tune the algorithms in certain ways or refine how the algorithm works. Again, the idea is to create output that truly exposes the desired patterns so that you can make sense of the data. For example, when viewing a picture, a robot may have to determine which elements of the picture it can interact with and which elements it can't. The answer to that question is important if the robot must avoid some elements to keep on track or to achieve specific goals.

When working in a machine learning environment, you also have the problem of input data to consider. For example, the microphone found in one smartphone won't produce precisely the same input data that a microphone in another smartphone will. The characteristics of the microphones differ, yet the result of interpreting the vocal commands provided by the user must remain the same. Likewise, environmental noise changes the input quality of the vocal command, and the smartphone can experience certain forms of electromagnetic interference. Clearly, the variables that a designer faces when creating a machine learning environment are both large and complex.

The art behind the engineering is an essential part of machine learning. The experience that a scientist gains in working through data problems is essential because it provides the means for the scientist to add values that make the algorithm work better. A finely tuned algorithm can make the difference between a robot successfully threading a path through obstacles and hitting every one of them.

Learning in the Age of Big Data

Computers manage data through applications that perform tasks using algorithms of various sorts. A simple definition of an *algorithm* is a systematic set of operations to perform on a given data set — essentially a procedure. The four basic data operations are create, read, update, and delete (CRUD). This set of operations may not seem complex, but performing these essential tasks is the basis of everything you do with a computer. As the data set becomes larger, the computer can use the algorithms found in an application to perform more work. The use of immense data sets, known as *big data*, enables a computer to perform work based on pattern recognition in a nondeterministic manner. In short, to create a computer setup that can learn, you need a data set large enough for the algorithms to manage in a manner that allows for pattern recognition, and this pattern recognition needs to use a simple subset to make predictions (statistical analysis) of the data set as a whole.

Big data exists in many places today. Obvious sources are online databases, such as those created by vendors to track consumer purchases. However, you find many non-obvious data sources, too, and often these non-obvious sources provide the greatest resources for doing something interesting. Finding appropriate sources of big data lets you create machine learning scenarios in which a machine can learn in a specified manner and produce a desired result.

Statistics, one of the methods of machine learning that you consider in this book, is a method of describing problems using math. By combining big data with statistics, you can create a machine learning environment in which the machine considers the probability of any given event. However, saying that statistics is the only machine learning method is incorrect. This chapter also introduces you to the other forms of machine learning currently in place.

Algorithms determine how a machine interprets big data. The algorithm used to perform machine learning affects the outcome of the learning process and, therefore, the results you get. This chapter helps you understand the five main techniques for using algorithms in machine learning.

Before an algorithm can do much in the way of machine learning, you must train it. The training process modifies how the algorithm views big data. The final section of this chapter helps you understand that *training* is actually using a subset of the data as a method for creating the patterns that the algorithm needs to recognize specific cases from the more general cases that you provide as part of the training.

Defining big data

Big data is substantially different from being just a large database. Yes, big data implies lots of data, but it also includes the idea of complexity and depth. A big data source describes something in enough detail that you can begin working with that data to solve problems for which general programming proves inadequate. For example, consider Google's self-driving cars. The car must consider not only the mechanics of the car's hardware and position with space but also the effects of human decisions, road conditions, environmental conditions, and other vehicles on the road. The data source contains many variables — all of which affect the vehicle in some way. Traditional programming might be able to crunch all the numbers, but not in real time. You don't want the car to crash into a wall and have the computer finally decide five minutes later that the car is going to crash into a wall. The processing must prove timely so that the car can avoid the wall.

JUST HOW BIG IS BIG?

Big data can really become quite big. For example, suppose that your Google self-driving car has a few HD cameras and a couple hundred sensors that provide information at a rate of 100 times/s. What you might end up with is a raw data set with input that exceeds 100 Mbps. Processing that much data is incredibly hard.

Part of the problem right now is determining how to control big data. Currently, the attempt is to log everything, which produces a massive, detailed data set. However, this data set isn't well formatted, again making it quite hard to use. As this book progresses, you discover techniques that help control both the size and the organization of big data so that the data becomes useful in making predictions.

The acquisition of big data can also prove daunting. The sheer bulk of the data set isn't the only problem to consider — also essential is to consider how the data set is stored and transferred so that the system can process it. In most cases, developers try to store the data set in memory to allow fast processing. Using a hard drive to store the data would prove too costly, time-wise.

REMEMBER

When thinking about big data, you also consider anonymity. Big data presents privacy concerns. However, because of the way machine learning works, knowing specifics about individuals isn't particularly helpful anyway. Machine learning is all about determining patterns — analyzing training data in such a manner that the trained algorithm can perform tasks that the developer didn't originally program it to do. Personal data has no place in such an environment.

Finally, big data is so large that humans can't reasonably visualize it without help. Part of what defined big data as big is the fact that a human can learn something from it, but the sheer magnitude of the data set makes recognition of the patterns impossible (or would take a really long time to accomplish). Machine learning helps humans make sense and use of big data.

Considering the sources of big data

Before you can use big data for a machine learning application, you need a source for big data. Of course, the first thing that most developers think about is the huge, corporate-owned database, which could contain interesting information, but it's just one source. The fact of the matter is that your corporate databases might not even contain particularly useful data for a specific need. The following sections describe locations you can use to obtain additional big data.

Building a new data source

To create viable sources of big data for specific needs, you might find that you actually need to create a new data source. Developers built existing data sources around the needs of the client-server architecture in many cases, and these sources may not work well for machine learning scenarios because they lack the required depth (being optimized to save space on hard drives does have disadvantages). In addition, as you become more adept in using machine learning, you find that you ask questions that standard corporate databases can't answer. With this in mind, the following sections describe some interesting new sources for big data.

OBTAINING DATA FROM PUBLIC SOURCES

Governments, universities, nonprofit organizations, and other entities often maintain publicly available databases that you can use alone or combined with other databases to create big data for machine learning. For example, you can combine several geographic information systems (GIS) to help create the big data required to make decisions such as where to put new stores or factories. The machine learning algorithm can take all sorts of information into account — everything from the amount of taxes you have to pay to the elevation of the land (which can contribute to making your store easier to see).

The best part about using public data is that it's usually free, even for commercial use (or you pay a nominal fee for it). In addition, many of the organizations that created them maintain these sources in nearly perfect condition because the organization has a mandate, uses the data to attract income, or uses the data internally. When obtaining public source data, you need to consider a number of issues to ensure that you actually get something useful. Here are some of the criteria you should think about when making a decision:

- » The cost, if any, of using the data source
- » The formatting of the data source
- » Access to the data source (which means having the proper infrastructure in place, such as an Internet connection when using Twitter data)
- » Permission to use the data source (some data sources are copyrighted)
- » Potential issues in cleaning the data to make it useful for machine learning

OBTAINING DATA FROM PRIVATE SOURCES

You can obtain data from private organizations such as Amazon and Google, both of which maintain immense databases that contain all sorts of useful information. In this case, you should expect to pay for access to the data, especially when used in a commercial setting. You may not be allowed to download the data to your

personal servers, so that restriction may affect how you use the data in a machine learning environment. For example, some algorithms work slower with data that they must access in small pieces.

The biggest advantage of using data from a private source is that you can expect better consistency. The data is likely cleaner than from a public source. In addition, you usually have access to a larger database with a greater variety of data types. Of course, it all depends on where you get the data.

CREATING NEW DATA FROM EXISTING DATA

Your existing data may not work well for machine learning scenarios, but that doesn't keep you from creating a new data source using the old data as a starting point. For example, you might find that you have a customer database that contains all the customer orders, but the data isn't useful for machine learning because it lacks tags required to group the data into specific types. One of the new job types that you can expect to create is people who massage data to make it better suited for machine learning — including the addition of specific information types such as tags.

REMEMBER

Machine learning will have a significant effect on your business. The article at www.computerworld.com/article/3007053/big-data/how-machine-learning-will-affect-your-business.html describes some of the ways in which you can expect machine learning to change how you do business. One of the points in this article is that machine learning typically works on 80 percent of the data. In 20 percent of the cases, you still need humans to take over the job of deciding just how to react to the data and then act upon it. The point is that machine learning saves money by taking over repetitious tasks that humans don't really want to do in the first place (making them inefficient). However, machine learning doesn't get rid of the need for humans completely, and it creates the need for new types of jobs that are a bit more interesting than the ones that machine learning has taken over. Also important to consider is that you need more humans at the outset until the modifications they make train the algorithm to understand what sorts of changes to make to the data.

Using existing data sources

Your organization has data hidden in all sorts of places. The problem is in recognizing the data as data. For example, you may have sensors on an assembly line that track how products move through the assembly process and ensure that the assembly line remains efficient. Those same sensors can potentially feed information into a machine learning scenario because they could provide inputs on how product movement affects customer satisfaction or the price you pay for postage. The idea is to discover how to create mashups that present existing data as a new kind of data that lets you do more to make your organization work well.

CHAPTER 1 **Introducing How Machines Learn** 545

REMEMBER

Big data can come from any source, even your email. A recent article discusses how Google uses your email to create a list of potential responses for new emails. (See the article at www.semrush.com/blog/deep-learning-an-upcoming-gmail-feature-that-will-answer-your-emails-for-you.) Instead of having to respond to every email individually, you can simply select a canned response at the bottom of the page. This sort of automation isn't possible without the original email data source. Looking for big data in specific locations will blind you to the big data sitting in common places that most people don't think about as data sources. Tomorrow's applications will rely on these alternative data sources, but to create these applications, you must begin seeing the data hidden in plain view today.

Some of these applications already exist, and you're completely unaware of them. The video at www.research.microsoft.com/apps/video/default.aspx?id=256288 makes the presence of these kinds of applications more apparent. By the time you complete the video, you begin to understand that many uses of machine learning are already in place and users already take them for granted (or have no idea that the application is even present).

Locating test data sources

As you progress through Book 8, you discover the need to teach whichever algorithm you're using (don't worry about specific algorithms; you see a number of them in Book 9) how to recognize various kinds of data and then to do something interesting with it. This training process ensures that the algorithm reacts correctly to the data it receives after the training is over. Of course, you also need to test the algorithm to determine whether the training is a success. In many cases, Book 8 helps you discover ways to break a data source into training and testing data components in order to achieve the desired result. Then, after training and testing, the algorithm can work with new data in real time to perform the tasks that you verified it can perform.

In some cases, you might not have enough data at the outset for both training (the essential initial test) and testing. When this happens, you might need to create a test setup to generate more data, rely on data generated in real time, or create the test data source artificially. You can also use similar data from existing sources, such as a public or private database. The point is that you need both training and testing data that will produce a known result before you unleash your algorithm into the real world of working with uncertain data.

Specifying the role of statistics in machine learning

Some sites online would have you believe that statistics and machine learning are two completely different technologies. For example, when you read *Statistics vs.*

Machine Learning, fight! (http://brenocon.com/blog/2008/12/statistics-vs-machine-learning-fight/), you get the idea that the two technologies are not only different, but downright hostile toward each other. The fact is that statistics and machine learning have a lot in common and that statistics represents one of the five *tribes* (schools of thought) that make machine learning feasible. The five tribes are

>> **Symbolists:** The origin of this tribe is in logic and philosophy. This group relies on inverse deduction to solve problems.

>> **Connectionists:** The origin of this tribe is in neuroscience. This group relies on backpropagation to solve problems.

>> **Evolutionaries:** The origin of this tribe is in evolutionary biology. This group relies on genetic programming to solve problems.

>> **Bayesians:** This origin of this tribe is in statistics. This group relies on probabilistic inference to solve problems.

>> **Analogizers:** The origin of this tribe is in psychology. This group relies on kernel machines to solve problems.

The ultimate goal of machine learning is to combine the technologies and strategies embraced by the five tribes to create a single algorithm (the *master algorithm*) that can learn anything. Of course, achieving that goal is a long way off. Even so, scientists such as Pedro Domingos (homes.cs.washington.edu/~pedrod/) are currently working toward that goal.

Book 9 follows the Bayesian tribe strategy, for the most part, in that you solve most problems using some form of statistical analysis. You do see strategies embraced by other tribes described, but the main reason you begin with statistics is that the technology is already well established and understood. In fact, many elements of statistics qualify more as *engineering* (in which theories are implemented) than *science* (in which theories are created). The next section of the chapter delves deeper into the five tribes by viewing the kinds of algorithms each tribe uses. Understanding the role of algorithms in machine learning is essential to defining how machine learning works.

Understanding the role of algorithms

Everything in machine learning revolves around algorithms. An *algorithm* is a procedure or formula used to solve a problem. The problem domain affects the kind of algorithm needed, but the basic premise is always the same — to solve some sort of problem, such as driving a car or playing dominoes. In the first case, the problems are complex and many, but the ultimate problem is one of getting a

passenger from one place to another without crashing the car. Likewise, the goal of playing dominoes is to win. The following sections discuss algorithms in more detail.

Defining what algorithms do

An algorithm is a kind of container. It provides a box for storing a method to solve a particular kind of a problem. Algorithms process data through a series of well-defined states. The states need not be deterministic, but the states are defined nonetheless. The goal is to create an output that solves a problem. In some cases, the algorithm receives inputs that help define the output, but the focus is always on the output.

Algorithms must express the transitions between states using a well-defined and formal language that the computer can understand. In processing the data and solving the problem, the algorithm defines, refines, and executes a function. The function is always specific to the kind of problem being addressed by the algorithm.

Considering the five main techniques

As described in the previous section, each of the five tribes has a different technique and strategy for solving problems that result in unique algorithms. Combining these algorithms should lead eventually to the master algorithm that will be able to solve any given problem. The following sections provide an overview of the five main algorithmic techniques.

SYMBOLIC REASONING

The term *inverse deduction* commonly appears as induction. In symbolic reasoning, deduction expands the realm of human knowledge, while induction raises the level of human knowledge. Induction commonly opens new fields of exploration, while deduction explores those fields. However, the most important consideration is that induction is the science portion of this type of reasoning, while deduction is the engineering. The two strategies work hand in hand to solve problems by first opening a field of potential exploration to solve the problem and then exploring that field to determine whether it does, in fact, solve it.

As an example of this strategy, deduction would say that if a tree is green and that green trees are alive, the tree must be alive. When thinking about induction, you would say that the tree is green and that the tree is also alive; therefore, green trees are alive. Induction provides the answer to what knowledge is missing given a known input and output.

CONNECTIONS MODELLED ON THE BRAIN'S NEURONS

The connectionists are perhaps the most famous of the five tribes. This tribe strives to reproduce the brain's functions using silicon instead of neurons. Essentially, each of the neurons (created as an algorithm that models the real-world counterpart) solves a small piece of the problem, and the use of many neurons in parallel solves the problem as a whole.

The use of *backpropagation,* or backward propagation of errors, seeks to determine the conditions under which errors are removed from networks built to resemble the human neurons by changing the *weights* (how much a particular input figures into the result) and *biases* (which features are selected) of the network. The goal is to continue changing the weights and biases until such time as the actual output matches the target output. At this point, the artificial neuron fires and passes its solution along to the next neuron in line. The solution created by just one neuron is only part of the whole solution. Each neuron passes information to the next neuron in line until the group of neurons creates a final output.

EVOLUTIONARY ALGORITHMS THAT TEST VARIATION

The evolutionaries rely on the principles of evolution to solve problems. In other words, this strategy is based on the survival of the fittest (removing any solutions that don't match the desired output). A fitness function determines the viability of each function in solving a problem.

Using a tree structure, the solution method looks for the best solution based on function output. The winner of each level of evolution gets to build the next-level functions. The idea is that the next level will get closer to solving the problem but may not solve it completely, which means that another level is needed. This particular tribe relies heavily on recursion and languages that strongly support recursion to solve problems. An interesting output of this strategy has been algorithms that evolve: One generation of algorithms actually builds the next generation.

BAYESIAN INFERENCE

The Bayesians use various statistical methods to solve problems. Given that statistical methods can create more than one apparently correct solution, the choice of a function becomes one of determining which function has the highest probability of succeeding. For example, when using these techniques, you can accept a set of symptoms as input and decide the probability that a particular disease will result from the symptoms as output. Given that multiple diseases have the same symptoms, the probability is important because a user will see some in which a lower probability output is actually the correct output for a given circumstance.

Ultimately, this tribe supports the idea of never quite trusting any hypothesis (a result that someone has given you) completely without seeing the evidence used to make it (the input the other person used to make the hypothesis). Analyzing the evidence proves or disproves the hypothesis that it supports. Consequently, it isn't possible to determine which disease someone has until you test all the symptoms.

One of the most recognizable outputs from this tribe is the spam filter used in many popular email applications.

SYSTEMS THAT LEARN BY ANALOGY

The analogyzers use kernel machines to recognize patterns in data. By recognizing the pattern of one set of inputs and comparing it to the pattern of a known output, you can create a problem solution. The goal is to use similarity to determine the best solution to a problem. It's the kind of reasoning that determines that using a particular solution worked in a given circumstance at some previous time; therefore using that solution for a similar set of circumstances should also work. One of the most recognizable outputs from this tribe is recommender systems. For example, when you get on Amazon and buy a product, the recommender system comes up with other, related products that you might also want to buy.

Defining what training means

Many people are somewhat used to the idea that applications start with a function, accept data as input, and then provide a result. For example, a programmer might create a function called Add() that accepts two values as input, such as 1 and 2. The result of Add() is 3. The output of this process is a value. In the past, writing a program meant understanding the function used to manipulate data to create a given result with certain inputs.

Machine learning turns this process around. In this case, you know that you have inputs, such as 1 and 2. You also know that the desired result is 3. However, you don't know what function to apply to create the desired result. Training provides a learner algorithm with all sorts of examples of the desired inputs and results expected from those inputs. The learner then uses this input to create a function. In other words, training is the process whereby the learner algorithm maps a flexible function to the data. The output is typically the probability of a certain class or a numeric value.

A single learner algorithm can learn many different things, but not every algorithm is suited for certain tasks. Some algorithms are general enough that they can play chess, recognize faces on Facebook, and diagnose cancer in patients. An algorithm reduces the data inputs and the expected results of those inputs to a

550 BOOK 8 **Essentials of Machine Learning**

function in every case, but the function is specific to the kind of task you want the algorithm to perform.

The secret to machine learning is generalization. The goal is to generalize the output function so that it works on data beyond the training set. For example, consider a spam filter. Your dictionary contains 100,000 words (actually a small dictionary). A limited training data set of 4,000 or 5,000 word combinations must create a generalized function that can then find spam in the 2^100,000 combinations that the function will see when working with actual data.

When viewed from this perspective, training might seem impossible and learning even worse. However, to create this generalized function, the learner algorithm relies on just three components:

- » **Representation:** The learner algorithm creates a *model*, which is a function that will produce a given result for specific inputs. The representation is a set of models that a learner algorithm can learn. In other words, the learner algorithm must create a model that will produce the desired results from the input data. If the learner algorithm can't perform this task, it can't learn from the data, and the data is outside the hypothesis space of the learner algorithm. Part of the representation is to discover which *features* (data elements within the data source) to use for the learning process.

- » **Evaluation:** The learner can create more than one model. However, it doesn't know the difference between good and bad models. An evaluation function determines which of the models works best in creating a desired result from a set of inputs. The evaluation function scores the models because more than one model could provide the required results.

- » **Optimization:** At some point, the training process produces a set of models that can generally output the right result for a given set of inputs. At this point, the training process searches through these models to determine which one works best. The best model is then output as the result of the training process.

Much of Book 8 and Book 9 focuses on representation. For example, in Book 9, Chapter 2 you discover how to work with the k-Nearest Neighbor (KNN) algorithm. However, the training process is more involved than simply choosing a representation. All three steps come into play when performing the training process. Fortunately, you can start by focusing on representation and allow the various libraries discussed in Book 9 to do the rest of the work for you.

IN THIS CHAPTER

» Figuring out why you need a matrix

» Computing with matrix calculus to your advantage

» Getting a glance at how probability works

» Explaining the Bayesian point of view on probability

» Describing observations using statistical measures

Chapter **2**

Demystifying the Math behind Machine Learning

"With me, everything turns into mathematics."

— RENÉ DESCARTES

If you want to implement existing machine learning algorithms from scratch or you need to devise new ones, you will require some knowledge of probability, linear algebra, linear programming, and multivariable calculus. You also need to know how to translate math into working code. This chapter begins by helping you understand the mechanics of machine learning math and describes how to translate math basics into usable code.

If you want to apply existing machine learning for practical purposes instead, you can leverage existing R and Python software libraries using a basic knowledge of math and statistics. In the end, you can't avoid having some of these skills because machine learning has strong roots in both math and statistics, but

you don't need to overdo it. After you get some math basics down, the chapter shows how even simple Bayesian principles can help you perform some interesting machine learning tasks.

Even though this introductory chapter focuses on machine learning experiments using R and Python, in the text you still find many references to vectors, matrices, variables, probabilities, and their distributions. Book 8 and Book 9 sometimes use descriptive statistics as well. Consequently, it helps to know what a mean, a median, and a standard deviation are in order to understand what happens under the hood of the software you use. This knowledge makes it easier to learn how to use the software better. The chapter also demonstrates how machine learning can help you make better predictions, even when you don't quite have all the information you need.

Working with Data

Machine learning is so appealing because it allows machines to learn from real-world examples (such as sales records, signals from sensors, and textual data streaming from the Internet) and determine what such data implies. Common outputs from a machine learning algorithm are predictions of the future, prescriptions to act on now, or new knowledge in terms of examples categorized by groups. Many useful applications have already become a reality by leveraging these results:

- » Diagnosing hard-to-find diseases
- » Discovering criminal behavior and detecting criminals in action
- » Recommending the right product to the right person
- » Filtering and classifying data from the Internet at an enormous scale
- » Driving a car autonomously

The mathematical and statistical basis of machine learning makes outputting such useful results possible. Using math and statistics in this way enables the algorithms to understand anything with a numerical basis.

To begin the process, you represent the solution to the problem as a number. For example, if you want to diagnose a disease using a machine learning algorithm, you can make the response a 1 or a 0 (a binary response) to indicate whether the person is ill, with a 1 stating simply that the person is ill. Alternatively, you can use a number between 0 and 1 to convey a less definite answer. The value can

represent the probability that the person is ill, with 0 indicating that the person isn't ill and 1 indicating that the person definitely has the disease.

A machine learning algorithm can provide an answer (predictions) when supported by the required information (sample data) and an associated response (examples of the predictions that you want to be able to guess). Information can include facts, events, observations, counts, measurements, and so on. Any information used as input is a *feature* or *variable* (a term taken from statistics). Effective features describe the values that relate to the response and help the algorithm guess a response using the function it creates given similar information in other circumstances.

There are two types of features: quantitative and qualitative. *Quantitative features* are perfect for machine learning because they define values as numbers such as integers, floats, counts, rankings, or other measures. Qualitative features are usually labels or symbols that convey useful information in a nonnumeric way, a way that you can define as more humanlike such as words, descriptions, or concepts.

You can find a classic example of qualitative features in the paper "Induction of Decision Trees" by John Ross Quinlan (http://dl.acm.org/citation.cfm?id=637969), a computer scientist who contributed to the development of decision trees in a fundamental way. Decision trees are one of the most popular machine learning algorithms to date. In his paper, Quinlan describes a set of information useful for deciding whether to play tennis outside or not, something a machine can learn using the proper technique. The set of features described by Quinlan is as follows:

» **Outlook:** Sunny, overcast, or rain
» **Temperature:** Cool, mild, hot
» **Humidity:** High or normal
» **Windy:** True or false

A machine learning algorithm cannot really digest such information. You must first transform the information into numbers. Many ways are available to do so, but the simplest is *one-hot encoding*, which turns every feature into a new set of binary (values 0 or 1) features for all its symbolic values. For instance, consider the outlook variable, which becomes three new features, as follows: outlook:sunny, outlook:overcast, and outlook:rain. Each one will have a numeric value of 1 or 0 depending on whether the implied condition is present. So when the day is sunny, outlook:sunny has a value of 1 and outlook:overcast and outlook:rain have a value of 0.

In addition to one-hot encoding, you can use a few other techniques to turn qualitative features into numbers, especially when a feature is made of words, such as a tweet from Twitter, a chunk of text from an online review, or a news feed. In Book 9, you have occasion to discuss other ways to effectively transform words and concepts into meaningful numbers that are understandable by a machine learning algorithm when dealing with textual analysis.

REMEMBER

No matter what the information is, for a machine learning algorithm to correctly process the information, it should always be transformed into a number.

Creating a matrix

After you make all the data numeric, the machine learning algorithm requires that you turn the individual features into a matrix of features and the individual responses into a vector or a matrix (when there are multiple responses). A *matrix* is a collection of numbers, arranged in rows and columns, much like the squares in a chessboard. However, unlike a chessboard, which is always square, matrices can have a different number of rows and columns.

By convention, a matrix used for machine learning relies on rows to represent examples and columns to represent features. So, as in the example for learning the best weather conditions to play tennis, you would construct a matrix that uses a new row for each day and columns containing the different values for outlook, temperature, humidity, and wind. Typically, you represent a matrix as a series of numbers enclosed by square brackets, as shown here:

$$X = \begin{bmatrix} 1.1 & 1 & 545 & 1 \\ 4.6 & 0 & 345 & 2 \\ 7.2 & 1 & 754 & 3 \end{bmatrix}$$

In this example, the matrix called X contains three rows and four columns, so you can say that the matrix has dimensions of 3 by 4 (also written as 3 x 4). To quote the number of the rows in a formula, you commonly use the letter n and the letter m for the number of columns. Knowing the size of a matrix is fundamental for correctly operating on it.

Operating on a matrix also requires being able to retrieve a number or a portion of a matrix for specific calculations. You use *indexes*, numbers that tell the position of an element in a matrix to perform this task. Indexes point out the row and column number that correspond to the location of a values of interest. Usually you use *i* for the row index and *j* for the column index. Both i and j indexes start counting rows and columns beginning with the number 0 *(0-indexed)* or 1 *(1-indexed)*.

REMEMBER

R matrices are 1-indexed, whereas matrices in Python are 0-indexed. The use of different index starting points can prove confusing, so you need to know how the language operates.

When viewing the example matrix, the element 2,3 is the element located in the second row intersecting with the third column, that is, 345 (assuming that the matrix is 1-index). Therefore, if you need to express three different elements of matrix X, you can use the following notation:

```
X1,1=1.1, X2,3=345, X3,4=3
```

Sometimes multiple matrices are stacked in slices of a more complex data structure called an *array*. An array is a collection of numeric data having more than two dimensions. As an example, you can have three-dimensional arrays where each matrix represents a different timeframe, and the matrices are then stacked together as the slices of a cake. A case for such an array happens when you continuously record medical data, perhaps from a scanner recording body functions such as brain activity. In this case, rows are still examples and columns are features — with the third dimension representing time.

A matrix that has a single feature is a special case called a *vector*. Vector is a term used in different scientific disciplines, from physics, to medical disciplines, to mathematics, so some confusion may arise depending on your previous expertise. In machine learning, a vector is simply a matrix of dimension n by 1, and that's all.

Vectors are lists of consecutive values. You have to represent and treat them as single columns when compared to a two-dimensional matrix. When working with a vector, you have a single positional index, *i*, which tells you the location of the value you want to access in the element sequence. You mostly use vectors when talking about response values *(response vector)* or when dealing with the internal coefficients of some algorithms. In this case, you call them a *vector of coefficients*.

$$y = \begin{bmatrix} 44 \\ 21 \\ 37 \end{bmatrix} \quad y_1 = 44, y_2 = 21, y_3 = 37$$

WARNING

In machine learning, the matrix of features usually appears as *X* and the corresponding vector of responses as *y*. More generally, matrices usually use a capital letter and vectors use a lowercase letter for identification. In addition, you use lowercase letters for constants, so you need to exercise care when determining whether a letter is a vector or a constant, because the set of possible operations is quite different.

You use matrices in machine learning quite often because they allow you to rapidly organize, index, and retrieve large amounts of data in a uniform and meaningful way. For every example i in the X feature matrix, you can then determine the i-th row of the matrix expressing its features and the i-th element on the response vector telling you the results that a specific set of features implies. This strategy allows the algorithm to look up data and make product predictions quickly.

Matrix notation also allows you to perform systematic operations on the entire matrix or portions of it quickly. Matrices are also useful for writing and executing programs in a speedy way because you can use computer commands to execute matrix operations.

Understanding basic operations

The basic matrix operations are addition, subtraction, and scalar multiplication. They are possible only when you have two matrices of the same size and the result is a new matrix of the same dimensions. If you have two matrices of the same shape, you just have to apply the operation to each corresponding position in the two matrices. Therefore, to perform addition, you start summing the values in the first row and first column of the two source matrices and place the resulting value in the same position of the resulting matrix. You continue the process for each paired element in the two matrices until you complete all the operations. The same process holds true for subtraction, as shown in the following example:

$$\begin{bmatrix} 1 & 1 \\ 1 & 0 \end{bmatrix} - \begin{bmatrix} 1 & 0 \\ 0 & 1 \end{bmatrix} = \begin{bmatrix} 0 & 1 \\ 1 & -1 \end{bmatrix}$$

In scalar multiplication, you instead take a single numeric value (the *scalar*) and multiply it for each element of the matrix. If your value is fractional, such as ½ or ¼, your multiplication turns into division. In the previous example, you can multiply the resulting matrix by −2:

$$\begin{bmatrix} 0 & 1 \\ 1 & -1 \end{bmatrix} * -2 = \begin{bmatrix} 0 & -2 \\ -2 & 2 \end{bmatrix}$$

You can also perform scalar addition and subtraction. In this case, you add or subtract a single value from all the elements of a matrix.

Performing matrix multiplication

Using indexes and basic matrix operations, you can express quite a few operations in a compact way. The combination of indexes and operations allows you to

» Slice a part of a matrix.

» Mask a part of matrix, reducing it to zero.

» Center the values of a matrix by removing a value from all elements.

» Rescale the values of a matrix, changing its range of values.

However, you can achieve the largest number of operations at one time only when you multiply a matrix against a vector or against another matrix. You perform these tasks often in machine learning, and multiplying a matrix by a vector occurs frequently. Many machine learning algorithms rely on finding a vector of coefficients that, multiplied by the matrix of features, can result in an approximation of the vector of response values. In such models, you have formulations like

$$y = Xb$$

where y is the response vector, X the feature matrix, and b a vector of coefficients. Often, the algorithm also includes a scalar named a to add to the result. In this example, you can imagine it as being zero, so it isn't present. As a result, y is a vector constituted by three elements:

$$y = \begin{bmatrix} 2 \\ -2 \\ 3 \end{bmatrix}$$

With this in mind, you can express the multiplication between X and b as

$$Xb = \begin{bmatrix} 4 & 5 \\ 2 & 4 \\ 3 & 3 \end{bmatrix} \begin{bmatrix} 3 \\ -2 \end{bmatrix}$$

TIP

To express multiplication when vectors or matrices are involved, the standard notation is to write them side by side. Whether you write them within parentheses or express them in letter form doesn't matter. This is a common way to point out matrix multiplication (called *implicit* because there is no sign marking the operation). As an alternative, you sometimes find an explicit dot format for the operation, such as in A·B. The use of the asterisk is limited to scalar products such as A*2 or A*b, where b is a constant.

Next, you need to know how X multiplied by b can result in y. As a check of being able to perform the multiplication, the matrix and the vector involved in the multiplication should have compatible sizes. In fact, the number of columns of the matrix should equal the number of rows in the vector. In this case, there is a match because X is 3 by 2 and b is 2 by 1. Knowing the shapes of the terms, you

can figure out in advance the shape of the resulting matrix, which is given by the rows of the matrix and the columns of the vector, or 3 by 1.

Matrix vector multiplication works as a series of summed vector-vector multiplications. Multiplication treats each row of the X matrix as a vector and multiplies it by the b vector. The result becomes the corresponding row element of the resulting vector. For instance, the first row [4,5] is multiplied by [3,−2] resulting in a vector [12,−10], whose elements summed result in a value of 2. This first summed multiplication corresponds to the first row of the resulting vector and then all the other calculations follow:

```
sum([4*3, 5*-2]) = 2
sum([2*3, 4*-2]) = -2
sum([3*3, 3*-2]) = 3
```

The resulting vector is [2, −2, 3]. Things get a little bit more tricky when multiplying two matrices, but you can perform the operation as a series of matrix-vector multiplications, just as in the previous example, by viewing the second matrix as a series of feature vectors. By multiplying the first matrix by the m vectors, you obtain a single column of the resulting matrix for each multiplication.

An example can clarify the steps in obtaining a matrix by matrix multiplication. The following example multiplies X by B, which is a square matrix 2 x 2:

$$XB = \begin{bmatrix} 4 & 5 \\ 2 & 4 \\ 3 & 3 \end{bmatrix} \begin{bmatrix} 3 & -2 \\ -2 & 5 \end{bmatrix}$$

You can divide the operation into two distinct matrices by vector multiplications by splitting the matrix B into column vectors.

$$\begin{bmatrix} 4 & 5 \\ 2 & 4 \\ 3 & 3 \end{bmatrix} \begin{bmatrix} 3 \\ -2 \end{bmatrix} = \begin{bmatrix} 2 \\ -2 \\ 3 \end{bmatrix}$$

$$\begin{bmatrix} 4 & 5 \\ 2 & 4 \\ 3 & 3 \end{bmatrix} \begin{bmatrix} -2 \\ 5 \end{bmatrix} = \begin{bmatrix} 17 \\ 16 \\ 9 \end{bmatrix}$$

Now all you have to do is take the resulting column vectors and use them to rebuild the output matrix using the multiplication of the first column vector as the first column in the new matrix and so on.

$$XB = \begin{bmatrix} 4 & 5 \\ 2 & 4 \\ 3 & 3 \end{bmatrix} \begin{bmatrix} 3 & -2 \\ -2 & 5 \end{bmatrix} = \begin{bmatrix} 2 & 17 \\ -2 & 16 \\ 3 & 9 \end{bmatrix}$$

In matrix multiplication, because of matrix shapes, order matters. Consequently, you cannot invert terms, as you would do in a multiplication of scalar numbers. Multiplying 5*2 or 2*5 is the same thing, because of the commutative property of scalar multiplication, but Ab is not the same as bA because sometimes the multiplication isn't possible (because the shapes of the matrices are incompatible), or, worse, it produces a different result. When you have a series of matrix multiplications, such as ABC, the order of the terms doesn't matter; whether you go with AB first or BC first, you get the same result because, like scalars, matrix multiplication is associative.

Glancing at advanced matrix operations

You may encounter two important matrix operations in some algorithm formulations. They are the transpose and inverse of a matrix. *Transposition* occurs when a matrix of shape n x m is transformed into a matrix m x n by exchanging the rows with the columns. Most tests indicate this operation using the superscript T, as in A^T. You see this operation used most often for multiplication, in order to obtain the right dimensions.

You apply *matrix inversion* to matrices of shape m x m, which are square matrices that have the same number of rows and columns. This operation is quite important because it allows the immediate resolution of equations involving matrix multiplication, such as y=bX, where you have to discover the values in the vector b. Because most scalar numbers (exceptions include zero) have a number whose multiplication results in a value of 1, the idea is to find a matrix inverse whose multiplication will result in a special matrix called the identity matrix, whose elements are zero, except the diagonal elements (the elements in positions where the index I is equal to the index j). Finding the inverse of a scalar is quite easy (the scalar number n has an inverse of n^{-1} that is 1/n). It's a different story for a matrix. Matrix inversion involves quite a large number of computations, so special math functions perform the calculations in R or Python. The inverse of a matrix A is indicated as A^{-1}.

Sometimes, finding the inverse of a matrix is impossible. When a matrix cannot be inverted, it is referred to as a *singular matrix* or a *degenerate matrix*. Singular matrices aren't the norm; they're quite rare.

Using vectorization effectively

If performing matrix operations, such as matrix by vector multiplication, seems a bit hard, consider that your computer does all the hard work. All you have to do is determine in a theoretical formulation what happens to the numbers as you put them into matrices, vectors, and constants, and then you sum, subtract, divide, or multiply them.

TIP Understanding what happens in a machine learning algorithm will give you an edge in using the algorithm because you'll understand how it digests and processes data. To get a correct result, you need to feed the right data to the right algorithm, according to the manner in which it works with data.

In Python, the NumPy package offers all the functionality needed to create and manipulate matrices. The ndarray objects allow fast creation of an array, such as a multidimensional matrix, by starting with data queued into lists.

TIP The term *ndarray* means "n-dimensional array," implying that you can create arrays of multiple dimensions, not just row-by-column matrices. Using a simple list, ndarray can quickly create a vector, as shown in the Python example here:

```
import numpy as np
y = np.array([44,21,37])
print (y)
print (y.shape)

[44 21 37]
(3,)
```

The method shape can promptly inform you about the shape of a matrix. In this case, it reports only three rows and no columns, which means that the object is a vector.

To create matrices made of rows and columns, you can use a list of lists. The contents of the lists inside the main list are the rows of your matrix.

```
X = np.array([[1.1, 1, 545, 1],[4.6, 0, 345, 2],
              [7.2, 1, 754, 3]])
print (X)

[[   1.1    1.   545.    1. ]
 [   4.6    0.   345.    2. ]
 [   7.2    1.   754.    3. ]]
```

You can also obtain the same result by using a single list, which creates a vector that you can reshape into the desired number of rows and columns. Numbers are filled into the new matrix row by row, starting from the element (0,0) down to the last one.

```
X = np.array([1.1, 1, 545, 1, 4.6, 0, 345, 2,
              7.2, 1, 754, 3]).reshape(3,4)
```

562 BOOK 8 **Essentials of Machine Learning**

Operations with addition and subtraction with scalars using NumPy `ndarray` are straightforward. You just sum, subtract, multiply, or divide using the standard operators:

```
a = np.array([[1, 1],[1, 0]])
b = np.array([[1, 0],[0, 1]])
print (a - b)

[[ 0  1]
 [ 1 -1]]

a = np.array([[0, 1],[1, -1]])
print (a * -2)

[[ 0 -2]
 [-2  2]]
```

To perform multiplication on vectors and matrices, you use the `np.dot` function instead. The input for this function is two arrays of compatible sizes to multiply according to the given order.

```
X = np.array([[4, 5],[2, 4],[3, 3]])
b = np.array([3,-2])
print(np.dot(X, b))

[ 2 -2  3]

B = np.array([[3, -2],[-2, 5]])
print (np.dot(X, B))

[[ 2 17]
 [-2 16]
 [ 3  9]]
```

Exploring the World of Probabilities

Probability tells you the likelihood of an event, and you express it as a number. The probability of an event is measured in the range from 0 (no probability that an event occurs) to 1 (certainty that an event occurs). Intermediate values, such as 0.25, 0.5, and 0.75, say that the event will happen with a certain frequency when tried enough times. If you multiply the probability by an integer number representing the number of trials you're going to try, you'll get an estimate of how many times an event should happen on average if all the trials are tried.

CHAPTER 2 **Demystifying the Math behind Machine Learning** 563

For instance, if you have an event occurring with probability p=0.25 and you try 100 times, you're likely to witness that event happening 0.25 * 100 = 25 times. This is, for example, the probability of picking a certain suit when choosing a card randomly from a deck of cards. French playing cards make a classic example of explaining probabilities. The deck contains 52 cards equally divided into four suits: clubs and spades, which are black, and diamonds and hearts, which are red. So if you want to determine the probability of picking an ace, you must consider that there are four aces of different suits. The answer in terms of probability is p=4/52=0.077.

REMEMBER

Probabilities are between 0 and 1; no probability can exceed such boundaries. You define probabilities empirically from observations. Simply count the number of times a specific event happens with respect to all the events that interest you. For example, say that you want to calculate the probability of how many times fraud happens when doing banking transactions or how many times people get a certain disease in a particular country. After witnessing the event, you can estimate the probability associated with it by counting the number of times the event occurs and dividing by the total number of events.

You can count the number of times the fraud or the disease happens using recorded data (mostly taken from databases) and then divide that figure by the total number of generic events or observations available. Therefore you divide the number of frauds by the number of transactions in a year, or you count the number of people who fell ill during the year with respect to the population of a certain area. The result is a number ranging from 0 to 1, which you can use as your baseline probability for a certain event given certain circumstances.

REMEMBER

Counting all the occurrences of an event is not always possible, so you need to know about sampling. By sampling, which is an act based on certain probability expectations, you can observe a small part of a larger set of events or objects, yet be able to infer correct probabilities for an event, as well as exact measures such as quantitative measurements or qualitative classes related to a set of objects.

For instance, if you want to track the sales of cars in the United States for the last month, you don't need to track every sale in the country. Using a sample comprising the sales from a few car sellers around the country, you can determine quantitative measures, such as the average price of a car sold, or qualitative measures, such as the car model sold most often.

Operating on probabilities

Operations on probabilities are indeed a bit different from numeric operations. Because they always have to be in the range of 0 to 1, you must rely on particular rules in order for the operation to make sense. For example, summations between

probabilities are possible if the events are *mutually exclusive* (they can't happen together). Say that you want to know the probability of drawing a spade or a diamond from a deck of cards. You can sum the probability of drawing a spade and the probability of drawing a diamond this way: p=0.25+0.25=0.5.

You use subtraction (difference) to determine the probability of events that are different from the probability of an event that you have already computed. For instance, to determine the probability of drawing a card that isn't a diamond from the deck, you just subtract from the probability of drawing any kind of card, which is p=1, the probability of drawing a diamond, like so: p=1−0.25=0.75. You get the *complement* of a probability when you subtract a probability from 1.

Multiplication helps you compute the intersection of independent events. *Independent events* are events that do not influence each other. For instance, if you play a game of dice and you throw two die, the probability of getting two sixes is 1/6 (the probability of getting six from the first dice) multiplied by 1/6 (the probability of getting six from the second dice), which is p=1/6 * 1/6=0.028. This means that if you throw the dice one hundred times, you can expect two sixes to come up only two or three times.

Using summation, difference, and multiplication, you can get the probability of most complex situations dealing with events. For instance, you can now compute the probability getting at least a six from two thrown dice, which is a summation of mutually exclusive events:

» The probability of having two sixes: p=1/6 * 1/6
» The probability of having a six on the first dice and something other than a six on the second one: p= 1/6 * (1−1/6)
» The probability of having a six on the second dice and something other than a six on the first one: p= 1/6 * (1−1/6)

Your probability of getting at least one six from two thrown dice is p=1/6 * 1/6 + 2 * 1/6 * (1−1/6)=0.306.

Conditioning chance by Bayes' theorem

Probability makes sense in terms of time and space, but some other conditions also influence the probability you measure. The context is important. When you estimate the probability of an event, you may (sometimes wrongly) tend to believe that you can apply the probability you calculated to each possible situation. The term to express this belief is *a priori probability*, meaning the general probability of an event.

For example, when you toss a coin, if the coin is fair, the a priori probability of a head is 50 percent. No matter how many times you toss the coin, when faced with a new toss, the probability for heads is still 50 percent. However, there are other situations in which, if you change the context, the a priori probability is not valid anymore because something subtle happened and changed it. In this case, you can express this belief as an *a posteriori* probability, which is the a priori probability after something happened to modify the count.

For instance, the a priori probability of a person being female is roughly about 50 percent. However, the probability may differ drastically if you consider only specific age ranges, because females tend to live longer, and after a certain age there are more females than males. As another example related to gender, if you examine the presence of women in certain faculties at a university, you notice that fewer females are engaged in the scientific faculties than males. Therefore, given these two contexts, the a posteriori probability is different from the expected a priori one. In terms of gender distribution, nature and culture can both create a different a posteriori probability.

You can view such cases as *conditional probability,* and express it as $p(y|x)$, which is read as *the probability of event y happening given that x has happened.* Conditional probabilities are a very powerful tool for machine learning. In fact, if the a priori probability can change so much because of certain circumstances, knowing the possible circumstances can boost your chances of correctly predicting an event by observing examples — exactly what machine learning is intended to do. For example, as previously mentioned, generally the expectation of a random person's being a male or a female is 50 percent. But what if you add the evidence that the person's hair is long or short? You can estimate the probability of having long hair as being 35 percent of the population; yet, if you observe only the female population, the probability rises to 60 percent. If the percentage is so high in the female population, contrary to the a priori probability, a machine learning algorithm can benefit from knowing whether the person's hair is long or short.

In fact, the Naïve Bayes algorithm can really take advantage of boosting the chance of making a correct prediction by knowing the circumstances surrounding the prediction, as explained in Book 9, Chapter 1, which covers the first, simplest learners. Everything starts with Reverend Bayes and his revolutionary theorem of probabilities. In fact, one of the machine learning tribes (see Book 8, Chapter 1) is named after him. Also, there are great expectations for the development of advanced algorithms based on Bayesian probability; MIT's *Technology Review* magazine mentioned Bayesian machine learning as an emerging technology that will change our world (www2.technologyreview.com/news/402435/10-emerging-technologies-that-will-change-your). Yet the foundations of the theorem aren't all that complicated (although they may be a bit counterintuitive if you normally consider just prior probabilities without considering posterior ones).

Reverend Thomas Bayes was a statistician and a philosopher who formulated his theorem during the first half of the eighteenth century. The theorem was never published while he was alive. Its publication revolutionized the theory of probability by introducing the idea of conditional probability just mentioned.

Thanks to Bayes' theorem, predicting the probability of a person being male or female becomes easier if the evidence is that the person has long hair. The formula used by Thomas Bayes is quite useful:

```
P(B|E) = P(E|B)*P(B) / P(E)
```

Reading the formula using the previous example as input can provide a better understanding of an otherwise counterintuitive formula:

- **P(B|E):** The probability of a belief (B) given a set of evidence (E) (posterior probability). Read "belief" as an alternative way to express a *hypothesis*. In this case, the hypothesis is that a person is a female and the evidence is long hair. Knowing the probability of such a belief given evidence can help to predict the person's gender with some confidence.

- **P(E|B):** The probability of having long hair when the person is a female. This term refers to the probability of the evidence in the subgroup, which is itself a conditional probability. In this case, the figure is 60 percent, which translates to a value of 0.6 in the formula (prior probability).

- **P(B):** The general probability of being a female; that is, the a priori probability of the belief. In this case, the probability is 50 percent, or a value of 0.5 (likelihood).

- **P(E):** The general probability of having long hair. Here it is another a priori probability, this time related to the observed evidence. In this formula, it is a 35 percent probability, which is a value of 0.35 (evidence).

If you solve the previous problem using the Bayes' formula and the values you have singled out, the result is 0.6 * 0.5 / 0.35 = 0.857. That is a high percentage of likelihood, which leads you to affirm that given such evidence, the person is probably a female.

Another common example, which can raise some eyebrows and is routinely found in textbooks and scientific magazines, is that of the positive medical test. It is quite interesting for a better understanding of how prior and posteriori probabilities may indeed change a lot under different circumstances.

Say that you're worried that you have a rare disease experienced by 1 percent of the population. You take the test and the results are positive. Medical tests are

CHAPTER 2 **Demystifying the Math behind Machine Learning** 567

never perfectly accurate, and the laboratory tells you that when you are ill, the test is positive in 99 percent of the cases, whereas when you are healthy, the test will be negative in 99 percent of the cases.

Now, using these figures, you immediately believe that you're certainly ill, given the high percentage of positive tests when a person is ill (99 percent). However, the reality is quite different. In this case, the figures to plug into the Bayes' theorem are as follows:

> 0.99 as P(E|B)

> 0.01 as P(B)

> 0.01*0.99 + 0.99*0.01 = 0.0198 as P(E)

The calculations are then 0.01*0.99 / 0.0198 = 0.5, which corresponds to just a 50 percent probability that you're ill. In the end, your chances of not being ill are more than you expected. You may wonder how this is possible. The fact is that the number of people seeing a positive response from the test is as follows:

- **Who is ill and gets the correct answer from the test:** This group is the *true positives*, and it amounts to 99 percent of the 1 percent of the population who gets the illness.

- **Who isn't ill and gets the wrong answer from the test:** This group is the 1 percent of the 99 percent of the population who gets a positive response even though they aren't ill. Again, this is a multiplication of 99 percent and 1 percent. This group corresponds to the *false positives*.

If you look at the problem using this perspective, it becomes evident why, when limiting the context to people who get a positive response to the test, the probability of being in the group of the true positives is the same as that of being in the false positives.

Describing the Use of Statistics

As a concluding topic related to probability, it's important to skim through some basic statistical concepts related to probability and statistics and understand how they can better help you describe the information used by machine learning algorithms. Previous sections discuss probability in ways that come in handy because sampling, statistical distributions, and statistical descriptive measures are all, in one way or another, based on concepts of probability.

Here, the matter is not simply about how to describe an event by counting its occurrences; it's about describing an event without counting all the times it occurs in a reliable way. For example, if you want an algorithm to learn how to detect a disease or criminal intent, you have to face the fact that you can't create a matrix comprising all the occurrences of the disease or the crime, so the information that you'll elaborate will be necessarily partial. Moreover, if you measure something in the real world, you often don't get the exact measurements because of some error in the procedure, imprecision in the instrument you use, or simply because of a random nuisance disturbing the process of recording the measure. A simple measure such as your weight, for example, will differ every time you get on the scale, slightly oscillating around what you believe to be your true weight. If you were to take this measurement on a larger scale, such as by weighing all the people who live in your city on one huge scale, you would get a picture of how difficult it is to measure accurately (because error occurs) and completely (because it is difficult to measure everything).

Having partial information, especially if what you want to describe is quite complex, isn't a completely negative condition, because you can use smaller matrices, thereby implying fewer computations. Sometimes you can't even get a sample of what you want to describe and learn for certain problems, because the event is complex and has a great variety of features. As another example, consider learning how to determine sentiment from a text taken from the Internet, such as from Twitter tweets. Apart from retweets, you're unlikely to see an identical tweet (expressing the same sentiment using precisely the same words for precisely the same topic) by another person in a lifetime. You may happen to see something somehow similar, but never identical. Therefore it's impossible to know in advance all the possible tweets that associate certain words to sentiments. In short, you have to use a sample and derive general rules from a partial set.

Even given such practical restrictions and the impossibility of getting all the possible data, you can still grasp what you want to describe and learn from it. Sampling is a part of the statistical practice. When using samples, you choose your examples according to certain criteria. When done carefully, you have a certain probability that your partial view resembles the global view well.

In statistics, *population* refers to all the events and objects you want to measure, and a *sample* is a part of it chosen by certain criteria. Using random sampling, which is picking the events or objects to represent randomly, helps you create a set of examples for machine learning to learn as it would learn from all the possible examples. The sample works because the value distributions in the sample are similar to those in the population, and that's enough.

TIP
Random sampling isn't the only possible approach. You can also apply *stratified sampling*, through which you can control some aspects of the random sample in order to avoid picking too many or too few events of a certain kind. After all, random is random, and you have no absolute assurance of always replicating the exact distribution of the population.

A *distribution* is a statistical formulation describing how to observe an event or a measure by telling you the probability of witnessing a certain value. Distributions are described in mathematical formula (a topic not covered in the book) and can be graphically described using charts such as histograms or distribution plots. The information you put into your matrix has a distribution, and you may find that distributions of different features are related. A distribution naturally implies a variation, and when dealing with numeric values, it is important to figure out a center of variation, which is often the statistical mean, calculated by summing all your values and dividing the sum by the number of values you considered.

The *mean* is a descriptive measure, telling you the value to expect the most, considering all the possible cases. The mean is best suited for a symmetrical and bell-shaped distribution (so that when values are above the mean, the distribution is similarly shaped as for the values below). A famous distribution, the normal or Gaussian distribution, is shaped just like that, but in the real world, you can also find many skewed distributions that have extreme values only on one side of the distribution, thereby influencing the mean too much.

The *median* is a measure that takes the value in the middle after you order all your observations from the smallest to the largest. Being based on the value order, the median is insensible to values in the distribution and can represent a fairer descriptor than the average in certain cases. The significance of the mean and median descriptors is that they describe a value in the distribution around which there is a variation, and machine learning algorithms do care about such a variation. Most people call the variation a *variance*. Because variance is a squared number, there is also a root equivalent, termed the *standard deviation*. Machine learning takes into account the variance in every single variable (univariate distributions) and in all features together (multivariate distributions) to determine how such variation impacts the response.

In other words, statistics matter in machine learning because they convey the idea that features have a distribution. Distribution implies variation, and variation is like a quantification of information — the more variance in your features, the more information that can be matched to the response in order to draw a rule from certain types of information to certain responses. You can then use statistics to assess the quality of your feature matrix and even to leverage statistical measures to build effective machine learning algorithms, as discussed in Book 9, where matrix operations, sampling from distributions, statistics, and probability all contribute to solutions and have computers effectively learn from data.

> **IN THIS CHAPTER**
>
> » Understanding how machine learning works under the hood
>
> » Recognizing the different parts of a learning process
>
> » Defining the most common error functions
>
> » Deciding which error function is best for your problem
>
> » Glancing at the steps in machine learning optimization when using gradient descent
>
> » Distinguishing between batch, mini-batch, and online learning

Chapter **3**

Descending the Right Curve

"Those who only think in straight lines cannot see around a curve."
— ROMINA RUSSELL

Machine learning may appear as a kind of magic trick to a newcomer to the discipline — something to expect from any application of advanced scientific discovery, as Arthur C. Clarke, the futurist and author of popular sci-fi stories (one of which became the landmark movie *2001: A Space Odyssey*), expressed by his third law: "*any sufficiently advanced technology is indistinguishable from magic.*" However, machine learning isn't magic at all. It's the application of mathematical formulations to how we view the human learning process.

Expecting that the world itself is a representation of mathematical and statistical formulations, machine learning algorithms strive to learn about such formulations

by tracking them back from a limited number of observations. Just as you don't need to see all the trees in the world to learn to recognize one (because humans can understand the distinguishing characteristics of trees), so machine learning algorithms can use the computational power of computers and the wide availability of data to learn how to solve a large number of important and useful problems.

Although machine learning is inherently complex, humans devised it, and in its initial inception, it simply started mimicking the way we learn from the world. We can express simple data problems and basic learning algorithms based on how a child perceives and understands the world, or solve a challenging learning problem by using the analogy of descending from the top of a mountain by taking the right slope. This chapter helps you understand machine learning as a technology rather than as magic. To that end, the following sections offer some basic theory and then delve into some simple problems that demonstrate the theory.

Interpreting Learning as Optimization

Learning comes in many different flavors, depending on the algorithm and its objectives. You can divide machine learning algorithms into three main groups based on their purpose:

» Supervised learning
» Unsupervised learning
» Reinforcement learning

Supervised learning

Supervised learning occurs when an algorithm learns from example data and associated target responses that can consist of numeric values or string labels, such as classes or tags, in order to later predict the correct response when posed with new examples. The supervised approach is indeed similar to human learning under the supervision of a teacher. The teacher provides good examples for the student to memorize, and the student then derives general rules from these specific examples. You need to distinguish between regression problems, whose target is a numeric value, and classification problems, whose target is a qualitative variable, such as a class or a tag. Referring to the examples used in the book, a regression task determines the average prices of houses in the Boston area, and a classification task distinguishes between kinds of iris flowers based on their sepal and petal measures.

Unsupervised learning

Unsupervised learning occurs when an algorithm learns from plain examples without any associated response, leaving it up to the algorithm to determine the data patterns on its own. This type of algorithm tends to restructure the data into something else, such as new features that may represent a class or a new series of uncorrelated values. They are quite useful in providing humans with insights into the meaning of data and new useful inputs to supervised machine learning algorithms. As a kind of learning, it resembles the methods humans use to figure out that certain objects or events are from the same class, such as by observing the degree of similarity between objects. Some recommendation systems that you find on the web in the form of marketing automation are based on this type of learning. The marketing automation algorithm derives its suggestions from what you've bought in the past. The recommendations are based on an estimation of what group of customers you resemble the most and then an inference about your likely preferences based on that group.

Reinforcement learning

Reinforcement learning occurs when you present the algorithm with examples that lack labels, as in unsupervised learning. However, you can accompany an example with positive or negative feedback according to the solution the algorithm proposes. Reinforcement learning is connected to applications for which the algorithm must make decisions (so the product is prescriptive, not just descriptive, as in unsupervised learning), and the decisions bear consequences. In the human world, it is just like learning by trial and error. Errors help you learn because they have a penalty added (cost, loss of time, regret, pain, and so on), teaching you that a certain course of action is less likely to succeed than others. An interesting example of reinforcement learning occurs when computers learn to play video games by themselves. In this case, an application presents the algorithm with examples of specific situations, such as having the gamer stuck in a maze while avoiding an enemy. The application lets the algorithm know the outcome of actions it takes, and learning occurs while trying to avoid what it discovers to be dangerous and pursuing survival. You can have a look at how the company Google DeepMind has created a reinforcement learning program that plays old Atari's video games at www.youtube.com/watch?v=V1eYniJ0Rnk. When watching the video, notice how the program is initially clumsy and unskilled but steadily improves with training until it becomes a champion.

The learning process

REMEMBER

Even though supervised learning is the most popular and frequently used of the three types, all machine learning algorithms respond to the same logic. The central idea is that you can represent reality using a mathematical function that the algorithm doesn't know in advance but can guess after having seen some data.

You can express reality and all its challenging complexity in terms of unknown mathematical functions that machine learning algorithms find and make advantageous. This concept is the core idea for all kinds of machine learning algorithms. To create clear examples, this chapter focuses on supervised classification as the most emblematic of all the learning types and provides explanations of its inner functioning that you can extend later to other types of learning approaches.

The objective of a supervised classifier is to assign a class to an example after having examined some characteristics of the example itself. Such characteristics are called *features*, and they can be both quantitative (numeric values) or qualitative (string labels). To assign classes correctly, the classifier must first closely examine a certain number of known examples (examples that already have a class assigned to them), each one accompanied by the same kinds of features as the examples that don't have classes. The training phase involves observation of many examples by the classifier that helps it learn so that it can provide an answer in terms of a class when it sees an example without a class later.

To give an idea of what happens in the training process, imagine a child learning to distinguish trees from other objects. Before the child can do so in an independent fashion, a teacher presents the child with a certain number of tree images, complete with all the facts that make a tree distinguishable from other objects of the world. Such facts could be features such as its material (wood), its parts (trunk, branches, leaves or needles, roots), and location (planted into the soil). The child produces an idea of what a tree looks like by contrasting the display of tree features with the images of other different objects, such as pieces of furniture that are made of wood but do not share other characteristics with a tree.

A machine learning classifier works in the same way. It builds its cognitive capabilities by creating a mathematical formulation that includes all the given features in a way that creates a function that can distinguish one class from another. Pretend that a mathematical formulation, also called *target function*, exists to express the characteristics of a tree. In such a case, a machine learning classifier can look for its representation as a replica or as an approximation (a different function that works alike). Being able to express such mathematical formulation is the representation capability of the classifier.

REMEMBER

From a mathematical perspective, you can express the representation process in machine learning using the equivalent term *mapping*. Mapping happens when you discover the construction of a function by observing its outputs. A successful mapping in machine learning is similar to a child internalizing the idea of an object. She understands the abstract rules derived from the facts of the world in an effective way so that when she sees a tree, for example, she immediately recognizes it.

Such a representation (abstract rules derived from real-world facts) is possible because the learning algorithm has many internal parameters (constituted of vectors and matrices of values), which equate to the algorithm's memory for ideas that are suitable for its mapping activity that connects features to response classes. The dimensions and type of internal parameters delimit the kind of target functions that an algorithm can learn. An optimization engine in the algorithm changes parameters from their initial values during learning to represent the target's hidden function.

During optimization, the algorithm searches among the possible variants of its parameter combinations in order to find the one that best allows the correct mapping between the features and classes during training. This process evaluates many potential candidate target functions from among those that the learning algorithm can guess. The set of all the potential functions that the learning algorithm can figure out is called the *hypothesis space*. You can call the resulting classifier with all its set parameters a *hypothesis*, a way in machine learning to say that the algorithm has set parameters to replicate the target function and is now ready to work out correct classifications (a fact demonstrated later).

The hypothesis space must contain all the parameter variants of all the machine learning algorithms that you want to try to map to an unknown function when solving a classification problem. Different algorithms can have different hypothesis spaces. What really matters is that the hypothesis space contains the target function (or its approximation, which is a different but similar function).

You can imagine this phase as the time when a child, in an effort to figure out her own idea of a tree, experiments with many different creative ideas by assembling her own knowledge and experiences (an analogy for the given features). Naturally, the parents are involved in this phase, and they provide relevant environmental inputs. In machine learning, someone has to provide the right learning algorithms, supply some nonlearnable parameters (called *hyper-parameters*), choose a set of examples to learn from, and select the features that accompany the examples. Just as a child can't always learn to distinguish between right and wrong if left alone in the world, so machine learning algorithms need human beings to learn successfully.

Even after completing the learning process, a machine learning classifier often can't univocally map the examples to the target classification function because many false and erroneous mappings are also possible, as shown in Figure 3-1. In many cases, the algorithm lacks enough data points to discover the right function. Noise mixed with the data can also cause problems, as shown in Figure 3-2.

Noise in real-world data is the norm. Many extraneous factors and errors that occur when recording data distort the values of the features. A good machine learning algorithm should distinguish the signals that can map back to the target function from extraneous noise.

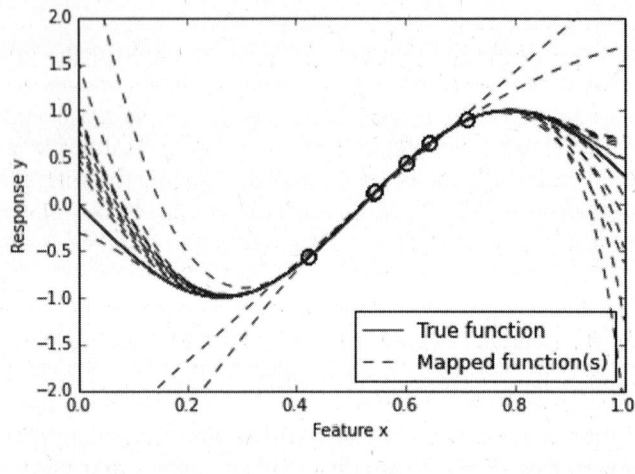

FIGURE 3-1:
A lack of evidence makes it hard to map back to the target function.

FIGURE 3-2:
Noise can cause mismatches in the data points.

Exploring Cost Functions

The driving force behind optimization in machine learning is the response from a function internal to the algorithm, called the *cost function.* You may see other terms used in some contexts, such as *loss function, objective function, scoring function,* or *error function,* but the cost function is an evaluation function that measures how well the machine learning algorithm maps the target function that it's striving to guess. In addition, a cost function determines how well a machine learning algorithm performs in a supervised prediction or an unsupervised optimization problem.

The evaluation function works by comparing the algorithm predictions against the actual outcome recorded from the real world. Comparing a prediction against its real value using a cost function determines the algorithm's error level. Because it's a mathematical formulation, the cost function expresses the error level in a numerical

576 BOOK 8 **Essentials of Machine Learning**

form, thereby keeping errors low. The cost function transmits what is actually important and meaningful for your purposes to the learning algorithm. As a result, you must choose, or accurately define, the cost function based on an understanding of the problem you want to solve or the level of achievement you want to reach.

As an example, when considering stock market forecasting, the cost function expresses the importance of avoiding incorrect predictions. In this case, you want to make money by avoiding big losses. In forecasting sales, the concern is different because you need to reduce the error in common and frequent situations, not in the rare and exceptional ones, so you use a different cost function.

When the problem is to predict who will likely become ill from a certain disease, you prize algorithms that can score a high probability of singling out people who have the same characteristics and actually did become ill later. Based on the severity of the illness, you may also prefer that the algorithm wrongly chooses some people who don't get ill after all rather than miss the people who actually do get ill.

The cost function is what truly drives the success of a machine learning application. It's as critical to the learning process as representation (the capability to approximate certain mathematical functions) and optimization (how the machine learning algorithms set their internal parameters). Most algorithms optimize their own cost function, and you have little choice but to apply them as they are. Some algorithms allow you to choose among a certain number of possible functions, providing more flexibility. When an algorithm uses a cost function directly in the optimization process, the cost function is used internally. Given that algorithms are set to work with certain cost functions, the optimization objective may differ from your desired objective. In such a case, you measure the results using an external cost function that, for clarity of terminology, you call an *error function* or *loss function* (if it has to be minimized) or a *scoring function* (if it has to be maximized).

TIP

With respect to your target, a good practice is to define the cost function that works the best in solving your problem, and then to figure out which algorithms work best in optimizing it to define the hypothesis space you want to test. When you work with algorithms that don't allow the cost function you want, you can still indirectly influence their optimization process by fixing their hyper-parameters and selecting your input features with respect to your cost function. Finally, when you've gathered all the algorithm results, you evaluate them by using your chosen cost function and then decide on the final hypothesis with the best result from your chosen error function.

When an algorithm learns from data, the cost function guides the optimization process by pointing out the changes in the internal parameters that are the most beneficial for making better predictions. The optimization continues as the cost function response improves iteration by iteration. When the response stalls or

worsens, it's time to stop tweaking the algorithm's parameters because the algorithm isn't likely to achieve better prediction results. When the algorithm works on new data and makes predictions, the cost function helps you evaluate whether it's working properly and is indeed effective.

Deciding on the cost function is an underrated activity in machine learning. It's a fundamental task because it determines how the algorithm behaves after learning and how it handles the problem you want to solve. Never rely on default options, but always ask yourself what you want to achieve using machine learning and check what cost function can best represent the achievement.

In Book 9, Chapters 1 through 4, you find out about some machine learning algorithms, and in Book 9, Chapter 5, you see how to apply theory to real problems, introducing classification problems for scoring text and sentiments. If you need to pick a cost function, machine learning explanations and examples introduce a range of error functions for regression and classification, comprising root mean squared errors, log loss, accuracy, precision, recall, and area under the curve (AUC). (Don't worry if these terms aren't quite clear right now; they're explained in detail in Book 9.)

Descending the Error Curve

The gradient descent algorithm offers a perfect example of how machine learning works, and it sums up the concepts expressed so far in Book 8 because you can provide it with an intuitive image, not just a mathematical formulation. Moreover, though it is just one of many possible methods, gradient descent is a widely used approach that's applied to a series of machine learning algorithms presented in Book 9, such as linear models, neural networks, and gradient boosting machines.

Gradient descent works out a solution by starting from a random solution when given a set of parameters (a data matrix made of features and a response). It then proceeds in various iterations using the feedback from the cost function, thus changing its parameters with values that gradually improve the initial random solution and lower the error. Even though the optimization may take a large number of iterations before reaching a good mapping, it relies on changes that improve the response cost function most (lower error) during each iteration. Figure 3-3 shows an example of a complex optimization process with many local minima (the minimum points on the curve marked with letters) where the process can get stuck (it no longer continues after the deep minimum marked with an asterisk) and cannot continue its descent.

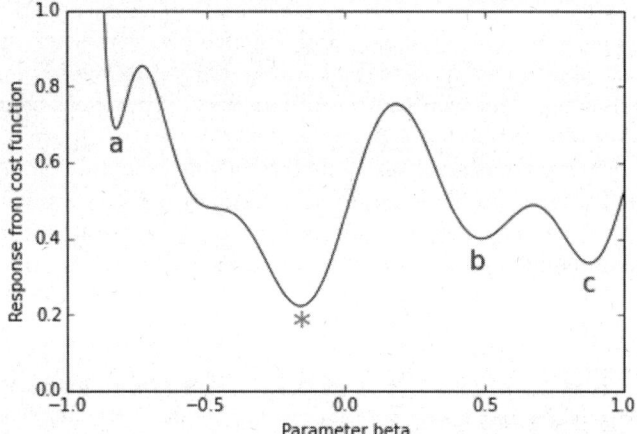

FIGURE 3-3:
A plotting of parameter data against the output of the cost function.

You can visualize the optimization process as a walk in high mountains, with the parameters being the different paths to descend to the valley. A gradient descent optimization occurs at each step. At each iteration, the algorithm chooses the path that reduces error the most, regardless of the direction taken. The idea is that if steps aren't too large (causing the algorithm to jump over the target), always following the most downward direction will result in finding the lowest place. Unfortunately, this result doesn't always occur because the algorithm can arrive at intermediate valleys, creating the illusion that it has reached the target. However, in most cases, gradient descent leads the machine learning algorithm to discover the right hypothesis for successfully mapping the problem. Figure 3-4 shows how a different starting point can make the difference. Starting point x1 ends toward a local minimum, whereas points x2 and x3 reach the global minimum.

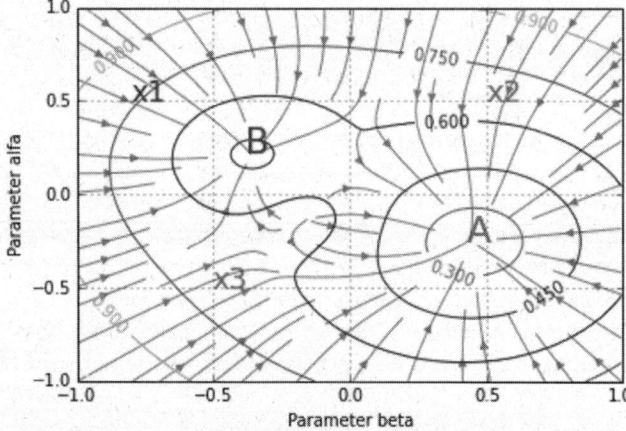

FIGURE 3-4:
Visualizing the effect of starting point on outcome.

CHAPTER 3 **Descending the Right Curve** 579

TIP

In an optimization process, you distinguish between different optimization outcomes. You can have a global minimum that's truly the minimum error from the cost function, and you can have many local minima — solutions that *seem* to produce the minimum error but actually don't (the intermediate valleys where the algorithm gets stuck). As a remedy, given the optimization process's random initialization, running the optimization many times is good practice. This means trying different sequences of descending paths and not getting stuck in the same local minimum.

MARKETING IN THE MOMENT WITH ROCKET FUEL

Online machine learning is more common than you may think. The constant flow of information available on the Internet increases as the world becomes more digitized. One of the more interesting applications that feature online machine learning is Rocket Fuel (https://rocketfuel.com), which provides a useful and unique programmatic trading platform.

Programmatic trading involves buying large amounts of goods or services automatically based on a combination of machine-based transactions, algorithms, and data. When used for advertising, the sector in which Rocket Fuel operates, the object of programmatic trading is to align the selling side, represented by online publishers (websites on which the advertising is placed), to the buying side, represented by advertisers and advertising agencies. This approach helps advertising to reach people who are interested in it. Rocket Fuel relies on Real Time Bidding (RTB) platforms (see https://adexchanger.com/online-advertising/real-time-bidding and http://digiday.com/platforms/what-is-real-time-bidding) as a smart approach that uses machine learning to connect the dots. Machine learning determines how best to match the audience of a website to a specific piece of advertising.

The machine learning part of this approach relies on linear and logistic regressions, as well as neural networks trained with online learning (because information flow on the web is continuous, and the advertising scenery is changeable). The algorithms determine whether a person will accept a particular piece of advertising based on the huge amount of data that the person produces online, such as interests hinted at by website behaviors and social networks (see www.pnas.org/content/110/15/5802.full), site-provided social and demographic information, and e-commerce website preferences and intentions. For instance, by using machine learning techniques, Rocket Fuel can determine the right moment to offer a person information on a product or a service (https://rocketfuel.com/how-it-works), thus optimizing communication between companies and consumers without wasting effort and attention.

Updating by Mini-Batch and Online

Machine learning boils down to an optimization problem in which you look for a global minimum given a certain cost function. Consequently, working out an optimization using all the data available is clearly an advantage, because it allows checking, iteration by iteration, to determine the amount of minimization with respect to all the data. That's the reason that most machine learning algorithms prefer to use all data available, and they want it accessible inside the computer memory.

Learning techniques based on statistical algorithms use calculus and matrix algebra, and they need all data in memory. Simpler algorithms, such as those based on a step-by-step search of the next best solution by proceeding iteration by iteration through partial solution (such as the gradient descent discussed in the previous section), can gain an advantage when developing a hypothesis based on all data because they can catch weaker signals on the spot and avoid being fooled by noise in data.

When operating with data within the limits of the computer's memory (assuming about 4GB or 8GB), you're working in *core memory*. You can solve most machine learning problems using this approach. Algorithms that work with core memory are called *batch algorithms* because, as in a factory where machines process single batches of materials, such algorithms learn to handle and predict a single data batch at a time, represented by a data matrix.

However, sometimes data can't fit into core memory because it's too big. Data derived from the web is a typical example of information that can't fit easily into memory. In addition, data generated from sensors, tracking devices, satellites, and video monitoring are often problematic because of their dimensions when compared to computer RAM; however, they can be stored easily on a hard disk, given the availability of cheap and large storage devices that easily hold terabytes of data.

A few strategies can save the day when data is too big to fit into the standard memory of a single computer. A first solution you can try is to subsample. Data is reshaped by a selection of cases (and sometimes even features) based on statistical sampling into a more manageable, yet reduced, data matrix. Clearly, reducing the amount of data can't always provide exactly the same results as when globally analyzing it. Working on less than the available data can even produce less powerful models. Yet, if subsampling is executed properly, the approach can generate almost equivalent and still reliable results. A successful subsampling must correctly use statistical sampling, by employing random or stratified sample drawings.

REMEMBER

In random sampling, you create a sample by randomly choosing the examples that appear as part of the sample. The larger the sample, the more likely the sample will resemble the original structure and variety of data, but even with few drawn examples, the results are often acceptable, both in terms of representation of the original data and for machine learning purposes.

REMEMBER

In stratified sampling, you control the final distribution of the target variable or of certain features in data that you deem critical for successfully replicating the characteristics of your complete data. A classic example is to draw a sample in a classroom made up of different proportions of males and females in order to guess the average height. If females are, on average, shorter than and in smaller proportion to males, you want to draw a sample that replicates the same proportion in order to obtain a reliable estimate of the average height. If you sample only males by mistake, you'll overestimate the average height. Using prior insight with sampling (such as knowing that gender can matter in height guessing) helps a lot in obtaining samples that are suitable for machine learning, as explained in Book 9, Chapter 2.

After you choose a sampling strategy, you have to draw a subsample of enough examples, given your memory limitations, to represent the variety of data. Data with high dimensionality, characterized by many cases and many features, is more difficult to subsample because it needs a much larger sample, which may not even fit into your core memory.

Beyond subsampling, a second possible solution to fitting data in memory is to leverage *network parallelism*, which splits data into multiple computers that are connected in a network. Each computer handles part of the data for optimization. After each computer has done its own computations and all the parallel optimization jobs have been reduced into a single elaboration, a solution is achieved.

To understand how this solution works, compare the process of building a car piece by piece using a single worker to having many workers working separately on car part aggregates — leaving a single worker to perform the final assembly. Apart from having a faster assembly execution, you don't have to keep all the parts in the factory at the same time. Similarly, you don't have to keep all the data parts in a single computer, but you can take advantage of their being processed separately in different computers, thus overcoming core memory limitations.

This approach is the basis of the map-reduce technology and cluster-computer frameworks, Apache Hadoop and Apache Spark, which are focused on mapping a problem onto multiple machines and finally reducing their output into the desired solution. Unfortunately, you can't easily split all machine learning algorithms into separable processes, and this problem limits the usability of such an approach. More important, you encounter significant cost and time overhead in setup and

maintenance when you keep a network of computers ready for such data processing, thereby limiting the applicability of this approach to only large organizations.

A third solution is to rely on out-of-core algorithms, which work by keeping data on the storage device and feeding it in chunks into computer memory for processing. The feeding process is called *streaming*. Because the chunks are smaller than core memory, the algorithm can handle them properly and use them for updating the machine learning algorithm optimization. After the update, the system discards them in favor of new chunks, which the algorithm uses for learning. This process goes on repetitively until there are no more chunks. Chunks can be small (depending on core memory), and the process is called *mini-batch learning*, or they can even be constituted by just a single example, called *online learning*.

The previously described gradient descent, as with other iterative algorithms, can work fine with such an approach; however, reaching an optimization takes longer because the gradient's path is more erratic and nonlinear with respect to a batch approach. The algorithm can reach a solution using fewer computations with respect to its in-memory version.

When working with repeated updates of its parameters based on mini-batches and single examples, the gradient descent takes the name *stochastic gradient descent*. It will reach a proper optimization solution given two prerequisites:

» The examples streamed are randomly extracted (hence the stochastic, recalling the idea of a random extraction from a distribution of examples).

» A proper learning rate is defined as fixed or flexible according to the number of observations or other criteria.

Disregarding the first prerequisite implies that you must also consider the ordering of the examples — a sometimes undesirable effect. The learning rate makes the learning more or less open to updates, rendering the learning itself more or less flexible in dealing with the characteristics of examples, which are seen later in the stream.

TIP

The learning parameter can make a difference in the quality of the optimization because a high learning rate, though faster in the optimization, can constrain the parameters to the effects of noisy or erroneous examples seen at the beginning of the stream. A high learning rate also renders the algorithm insensible to the latter streamed observations, which can prove to be a problem when the algorithm is learning from sources that are naturally evolving and mutable, such as data from the digital advertising sector, where new advertising campaigns often start mutating the level of attention and response of targeted individuals.

IN THIS CHAPTER

» Explaining how correct sampling is critical in machine learning

» Highlighting errors dictated by bias and variance

» Proposing different approaches to validation and testing

» Warning against biased samples, overfitting, underfitting, and snooping

Chapter 4
Validating Machine Learning

"I'm not running around looking for love and validation . . ."
— SOPHIE B. HAWKINS

Having examples (in the form of data sets) and a machine learning algorithm at hand doesn't assure that solving a learning problem is possible or that the results will provide the desired solution. For example, if you want your computer to distinguish a photo of a dog from a photo of a cat, you can provide it with good examples of dogs and cats. You then train a dog versus cat classifier based on some machine learning algorithm that could output the probability that a given photo is a dog or a cat. Of course, the output is a probability — not an absolute assurance that the photo is a dog or cat.

Based on the probability that the classifier reports, you can decide the class (dog or cat) of a photo based on the estimated probability calculated by the algorithm. When the probability is higher for a dog, you can minimize the risk of making a wrong assessment by choosing the higher chances favoring a dog. The greater the probability difference between the likelihood of a dog against that of a cat, the higher the confidence you can have in your choice. A close choice likely occurs

because of some ambiguity in the photo (the photo is not clear or the dog is actually a bit cattish). For that matter, it might not even be a dog — and the algorithm doesn't know anything about the raccoon, which is what the picture actually shows.

Such is the power of training a classifier: You pose the problem; you offer the examples, with each one carefully marked with the label or class that the algorithm should learn; your computer trains the algorithm for a while; and finally you get a resulting model, which provides you with an answer or probability. (Labeling is a challenging activity in itself, as you discover in Book 9.) In the end, a probability is just an opportunity (or a risk, from another perspective) to propose a solution and get a correct answer. At this point, you may seem to have addressed every issue and believe that the work is finished, but you must still validate the results. This chapter helps you discover why machine learning isn't just a push-the-button-and-forget-it activity.

Checking Out-of-Sample Errors

When you first receive the data used to train the algorithm, the data is just a data sample. Unless the circumstances are quite rare, the data you receive won't be all the data that you could possibly get. For instance, if you receive sales data from your marketing department, the data you receive is not all the possible sales data because unless sales are stopped, there will always be new data representing new sales in the future.

If your data is not all the data possible, you must call it a sample. A sample is a selection, and as with all selections, the data could reflect different motivations as to why someone selected it in such a way. Therefore, when you receive data, the first question you have to consider is how someone has selected it. If someone selected it randomly, without any specific criteria, you can expect that, if things do not change from the past, future data won't differ too much from the data you have at hand.

REMEMBER

Statistics expects that the future won't differ too much from the past. Thus you can base future predictions on past data by employing random sampling theory. If you select examples randomly without a criterion, you do have a good chance of choosing a selection of examples that won't differ much from future examples, or in statistical terms, you can expect that the distribution of your present sample will closely resemble the distribution of future samples.

However, when the sample you receive is somehow special, it could present a problem when training the algorithm. In fact, the special data could force your

algorithm to learn a different mapping to the response than the mapping it might have created by using random data. As an example, if you receive sales data from just one shop or only the shops in a single region (which is actually a specific sample), the algorithm may not learn how to forecast the future sales of all the shops in all the regions. The specific sample causes problems because other shops may be different and follow different rules from the ones you're observing.

REMEMBER

Ensuring that your algorithm is learning correctly from data is the reason you should always check what the algorithm has learned from *in-sample* data (the data used for training) by testing your hypothesis on some out-of-sample data. *Out-of-sample* data is data you didn't have at learning time, and it should represent the kind of data you need to create forecasts.

Looking for generalization

Generalization is the capability to learn from data at hand the general rules that you can apply to all other data. Out-of-sample data therefore becomes essential to figuring out whether learning from data is possible, and to what extent.

No matter how big your in-sample data set is, bias created by some selection criteria still makes seeing similar examples frequently and systematically highly unlikely in reality. For example, in statistics, there is an anecdote about inferring from biased samples. It involves the 1936 US presidential election between Alfred Landon and Franklin D. Roosevelt in which the *Literary Digest* used biased poll information to predict the winner.

At that time, the *Literary Digest,* a respectable and popular magazine, polled its readers to determine the next president of the United States, a practice that it had performed successfully since 1916. The response of the poll was strikingly in favor of Landon, with more than a 57 percent consensus on the candidate. The magazine also used such a huge sample — more than 10 million people (with only 2.4 million responding) — that the result seemed unassailable: A large sample coupled with a large difference between the winner and the loser tends not to raise many doubts. Yet the poll was completely unsuccessful. In the end, the margin of error was 19 percent, with Landon getting only 38 percent of the vote and Roosevelt getting 62 percent. This margin is the largest error ever for a public opinion poll.

What happened? Well, simply put, the magazine questioned people whose names were pulled from every telephone directory in United States, as well as from the magazine's subscription list and from rosters of clubs and associations, gathering more than ten million names. Impressive, but at the end of the Great Depression, having a telephone, subscribing to a magazine, or being part of a club meant that you were rich, so the sample was made of only affluent voters and completely ignored lower-income voters, who happen to represent the majority (thereby

CHAPTER 4 **Validating Machine Learning** 587

resulting in a *selection bias*). In addition, the poll suffered from a *nonresponsive bias* because only 2.4 million people responded, and people who respond to polls tend to differ from those who don't. (You can read more about the faulty *Literary Digest* poll at `www.math.upenn.edu/~deturck/m170/wk4/lecture/case1.html`.) The magnitude of error for this particular incident ushered in the beginning of a more scientific approach to sampling.

REMEMBER

Such classical examples of selection bias point out that if the selection process biases a sample, the learning process will have the same bias. However, sometimes bias is unavoidable and difficult to spot. As an example, when you go fishing with a net, you can see only the fish you catch and that didn't pass through the net itself.

Another example comes from World War II. At that time, designers constantly improved US war planes by adding extra armor plating to the parts that took the most hits upon returning from bombing runs. It took the reasoning of the mathematician Abraham Wald to point out that designers actually needed to reinforce the places that *didn't* have bullet holes on returning planes. These locations were likely so critical that a plane hit there didn't return home, and consequently no one could observe its damage (a kind of *survivorship bias* where the survivors skew the data). Survivorship bias is still a problem today. In fact, you can read about how this story has shaped the design of Facebook at `www.fastcodesign.com/1671172/how-a-story-from-world-war-ii-shapes-facebook-today`.

Preliminary reasoning on your data and testing results with out-of-sample examples can help you spot or at least have an intuition of possible sampling problems. However, receiving new out-of-sample data is often difficult, costly, and requires investment in terms of timing. In the sales example discussed earlier, you have to wait for a long time to test your sales forecasting model — maybe an entire year — in order to find out whether your hypothesis works. In addition, making the data ready for use can consume a great deal of time. For example, when you label photos of dogs and cats, you need to spend time labeling a larger number of photos taken from the web or from a database.

A possible shortcut to expending additional effort is getting out-of-sample examples from your available data sample. You reserve a part of the data sample based on a separation between training and testing data dictated by time or by random sampling. If time is an important component in your problem (as it is in forecasting sales), you look for a time label to use as separator. Data before a certain date appears as in-sample data; data after that date appears as out-of-sample data. The same happens when you choose data randomly: What you extracted as in-sample data is just for training; what is left is devoted to testing purposes and serves as your out-of-sample data.

Getting to Know the Limits of Bias

Now that you know more about the in-sample and out-of-sample portions of your data, you also know that learning depends a lot on the in-sample data. This portion of your data is important because you want to discover a point of view of the world, and as with all points of view, it can be wrong, distorted, or just merely partial. You also know that you need an out-of-sample example to check whether the learning process is working. However, these aspects form only part of the picture. When you make a machine learning algorithm work on data in order to guess a certain response, you are effectively taking a gamble, and that gamble is not just because of the sample you use for learning. There's more. For the moment, imagine that you freely have access to suitable, unbiased, in-sample data, so data is not the problem. Instead you need to concentrate on the method for learning and predicting.

First, you must consider that you're betting that the algorithm can reasonably guess the response. You can't always make this assumption because figuring out certain answers isn't possible no matter what you know in advance. For instance, you can't fully determine the behavior of human beings by knowing their previous history and behavior. Maybe a random effect is involved in the generative process of our behavior (the irrational part of us, for instance), or maybe the issue comes down to free will (the problem is also a philosophical/religious one, and there are many discordant opinions). Consequently, you can guess only some types of responses, and for many others, such as when you try to predict people's behavior, you have to accept a certain degree of uncertainty which, with luck, is acceptable for your purposes.

Second, you must consider that you're betting that the relationship between the information you have and the response you want to predict can be expressed as a mathematical formula of some kind, and that your machine learning algorithm is actually capable of guessing that formula. The capacity of your algorithm to guess the mathematical formula behind a response is intrinsically embedded in the nuts and bolts of the algorithm. Some algorithms can guess almost everything; others actually have a limited set of options. The range of possible mathematical formulations that an algorithm can guess is the set of its possible hypotheses. Consequently, a hypothesis is a single algorithm, specified in all its parameters and therefore capable of a single, specific formulation.

Mathematics is fantastic. It can describe much of the real world by using some simple notation, and it's the core of machine learning because any learning algorithm has a certain capability to represent a mathematical formulation. Some algorithms, such as linear regression, explicitly use a specific mathematical formulation for representing how a response (for instance, the price of a house) relates to a set of predictive information (such as market information, house location, surface of the estate, and so on).

CHAPTER 4 **Validating Machine Learning** 589

Some formulations are so complex and intricate that even though representing them on paper is possible, doing so is too difficult in practical terms. Some other sophisticated algorithms, such as decision trees (a topic of Book 9, Chapter 4), don't have an explicit mathematical formulation, but are so adaptable that they can be set to approximate a large range of formulations easily. As an example, consider a simple and easily explained formulation. The linear regression is just a line in a space of coordinates given by the response and all the predictors. In the easiest example, you can have a response, y, and a single predictor, x, with a formulation of

$$y = \beta_1 x_1 + \beta_0$$

In a simple situation of a response predicted by a single feature, such a model is perfect when your data arranges itself as a line. However, what happens if it doesn't and instead shapes itself like a curve? To represent the situation, just observe the following bidimensional representations, as shown in Figure 4-1.

FIGURE 4-1: Example of a linear model struggling to map a curve function.

When points resemble a line or a cloud, some error occurs when you're figuring out that the result is a straight line; therefore the mapping provided by the preceding formulation is somehow imprecise. However, the error doesn't appear systematically but rather randomly because some points are above the mapped line and others are below it. The situation with the curved, shaped cloud of points

is different, because this time, the line is sometimes exact but at other times is systematically wrong. Sometimes points are always above the line; sometimes they are below it.

Given the simplicity of its mapping of the response, your algorithm tends to systematically overestimate or underestimate the real rules behind the data, representing its bias. The bias is characteristic of simpler algorithms that can't express complex mathematical formulations.

Keeping Model Complexity in Mind

Just as simplicity of formulations is a problem, automatically resorting to mapping very intricate formulations doesn't always provide a solution. In fact, you don't know the true complexity of the required response mapping (such as whether it fits in a straight line or in a curved one). Therefore, just as simplicity may create an unsuitable response (refer to Figure 4-1), it's also possible to represent the complexity in data with an overly complex mapping. In such cases, the problem with a complex mapping is that it has many terms and parameters — and in some extreme cases, your algorithm may have more parameters than your data has examples. Because you must specify all the parameters, the algorithm then starts memorizing everything in the data — not just the signals but also the random noise, the errors, and all the slightly specific characteristics of your sample.

In some cases, it can even just memorize the examples as they are. However, unless you're working on a problem with a limited number of simple features with few distinct values (basically a toy data set, that is, a data set with few examples and features, thus simple to deal with and ideal for examples), you're highly unlikely to encounter the same example twice, given the enormous number of possible combinations of all the available features in the data set.

When memorization happens, you may have the illusion that everything is working well because your machine learning algorithm seems to have fitted the in-sample data so well. Instead, problems can quickly become evident when you start having it work with out-of-sample data and you notice that it produces errors in its predictions as well as errors that actually change a lot when you relearn from the same data with a slightly different approach. *Overfitting* occurs when your algorithm has learned too much from your data, up to the point of mapping curve shapes and rules that do not exist, as shown in Figure 4-2. Any slight change in the procedure or in the training data produces erratic predictions.

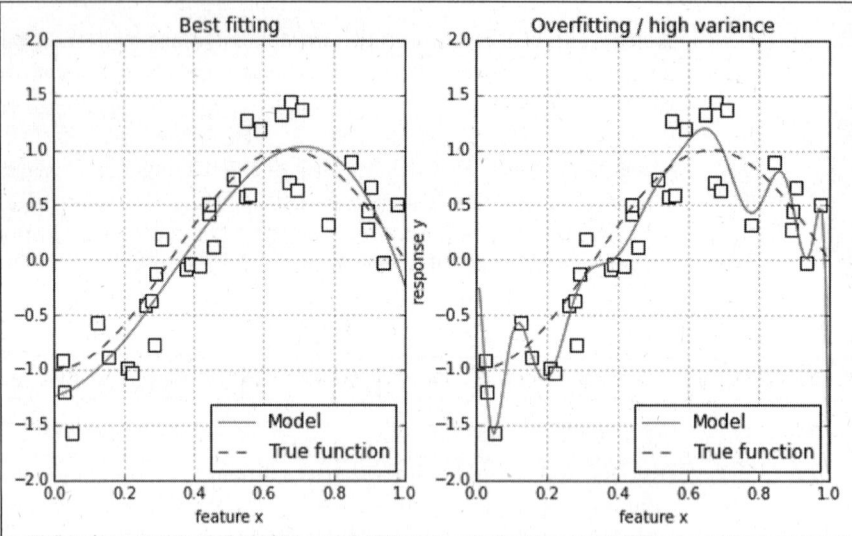

FIGURE 4-2: Example of a linear model going right and becoming too complex while trying to map a curve function.

Keeping Solutions Balanced

To create great solutions, machine learning models trade off between simplicity (implying a higher bias) and complexity (generating a higher variance of estimates). If you intend to achieve the best predictive performance, you do need to find a solution in the middle by understanding what works better, which you do by using trial and error on your data. Because data is what dictates the most suitable solution for the prediction problem, you have neither a panacea nor an easy recurrent solution for solving all your machine learning dilemmas.

REMEMBER

A commonly referred to theorem in the mathematical folklore is the no-free-lunch theorem by David Wolpert and William Macready, which states that "any two optimization algorithms are equivalent when their performance is averaged across all possible problems" (see `https://en.wikipedia.org/wiki/No_free_lunch_theorem` for details). If the algorithms are equivalent in the abstract, no one is superior to the other unless proved in a specific, practical problem. (See the discussion at `www.no-free-lunch.org` for more details about no-free-lunch theorems; two of them are actually used for machine learning.)

In particular, in his article "The Lack of A Priori Distinctions Between Learning Algorithms," Wolpert discussed the fact that there are no *a priori* distinctions between algorithms, no matter how simple or complex they are (you can obtain the article at `http://citeseerx.ist.psu.edu/viewdoc/summary?doi=10.1.1.51.9734`). Data dictates what works and how well it works. In the end, you cannot always rely on a single machine learning algorithm, but you have to test many and find the best one for your problem.

Besides being led into machine learning experimentation by the try-everything principle of the no-free-lunch theorem, you have another rule of thumb to consider: Occam's razor, which is attributed to William of Occam, a scholastic philosopher and theologian who lived in the fourteenth century (see http://math.ucr.edu/home/baez/physics/General/occam.html for details). The Occam's razor principle states that theories should be cut down to the minimum in order to plausibly represent the truth (hence the razor). The principle doesn't state that simpler solutions are better but that, between a simple solution and a more complex solution offering the same result, the simpler solution is always preferred. The principle is at the very foundations of our modern scientific methodology, and even Albert Einstein seems to have often referred to it, stating that "everything should be as simple as it can be, but not simpler" (see http://quoteinvestigator.com/2011/05/13/einstein-simple for details). Summarizing the evidence so far:

» To get the best machine learning solution, try everything you can on your data and represent your data's performance with learning curves.

» Start with simpler models, such as linear models, and always prefer a simpler solution when it performs nearly as well as a complex solution. You benefit from the choice when working on out-of-sample data from the real world.

» Always check the performance of your solution using out-of-sample examples, as discussed in the preceding sections.

Depicting learning curves

To visualize the degree to which a machine learning algorithm is suffering from bias or variance with respect to a data problem, you can take advantage of a chart type named learning curve. *Learning curves* are displays in which you plot the performance of one or more machine learning algorithms with respect to the quantity of data they use for training. The plotted values are the prediction error measurements, and the metric is measured both as in-sample and cross-validated or out-of-sample performance.

REMEMBER

If the chart depicts performance with respect to the quantity of data, it's a learning curve chart. When it depicts performance with respect to different hyper-parameters or a set of learned features picked by the model, it's a validation curve chart instead. To create a learning curve chart, you must do the following:

» Divide your data into in-sample and out-of-sample sets (a train/test split of 70/30 works fine, or you can use cross-validation).

» Create portions of your training data of growing size. Depending on the size of the data that you have available for training, you can use 10 percent portions

CHAPTER 4 **Validating Machine Learning** 593

or, if you have a lot of data, grow the number of examples on a power scale such as 10^3, 10^4, 10^5, and so on.

- » Train models on the different subsets of the data. Test and record their performance on the same training data and on the out-of-sample set.

- » Plot the recorded results on two curves, one for the in-sample results and the other for the out-of-sample results (see Figure 4-3). If instead of a train/test split you use cross-validation, you can also draw boundaries expressing the stability of the result across multiple validations (confidence intervals) based on the standard deviation of the results themselves.

Ideally, you should obtain two curves with different starting error points: higher for the out-of-sample; lower for the in-sample. As the size of the training set increases, the difference in space between the two should reduce until, at a certain number of observations, they become close to a common error value.

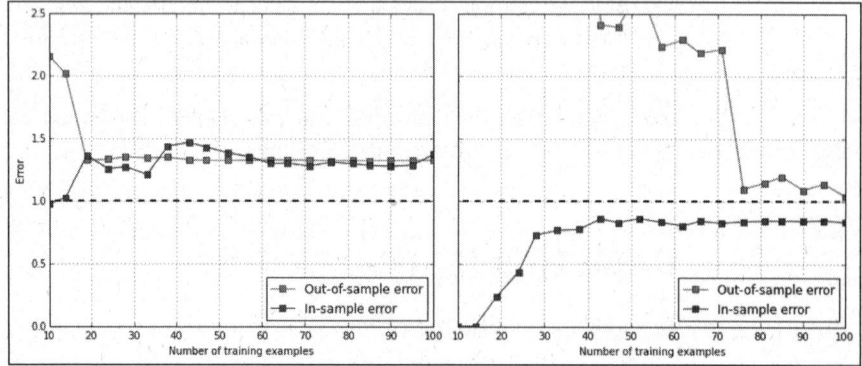

FIGURE 4-3: Examples of learning curves affected by bias (left) and variance (right).

Noticeably, after you print your chart, problems arise when

- » **The two curves tend to converge, but you can't see on the chart that they get near each other because you have too few examples.** This situation gives you a strong hint to increase the size of your data set if you want to successfully learn with the tested machine learning algorithm.

- » **The final convergence point between the two curves has a high error, so consequently your algorithm has too much bias.** Adding more examples here does not help because you have a convergence with the amount of data you have. You should increase the number of features or use a more complex learning algorithm as a solution.

- » **The two curves do not tend to converge because the out-of-sample curve starts to behave erratically.** Such a situation is clearly a sign of high variance of the estimates, which you can reduce by increasing the number of

examples (at a certain number, the out-of-sample error will start to decrease again), reducing the number of features, or, sometimes, just fixing some key parameters of the learning algorithm.

Python provides learning curves as part of the scikit-learn package using the `learning_curve` function that prepares all the computations for you (see the details at http://scikit-learn.org/stable/modules/generated/sklearn.learning_curve.learning_curve.html).

Training, Validating, and Testing

In a perfect world, you could perform a test on data that your machine learning algorithm has never learned from before. However, waiting for fresh data isn't always feasible in terms of time and costs. As a first simple remedy, you can randomly split your data into training and test sets. The common split is from 25 to 30 percent for testing and the remaining 70 to 75 percent for training. You split your data consisting of your response and features at the same time, keeping correspondence between each response and its features.

The second remedy occurs when you need to tune your learning algorithm. In this case, the test split data isn't a good practice because it causes another kind of overfitting called snooping (see more on this topic later in the chapter). To overcome snooping, you need a third split, called a validation set. A suggested split is to have your examples partitioned in thirds: 70 percent for training, 20 percent for validation, and 10 percent for testing.

You should perform the split randomly, that is, regardless of the initial ordering of the data. Otherwise, your test won't be reliable, because ordering could cause *overestimation* (when there is some meaningful ordering) or *underestimation* (when distribution differs by too much). As a solution, you must ensure that the test set distribution isn't very different from the training distribution, and that sequential ordering occurs in the split data. For example, check whether identification numbers, when available, are continuous in your sets. Sometimes, even if you strictly abide by random sampling, you can't always obtain similar distributions among sets, especially when your number of examples is small.

TIP

When your number of examples n is high, such as n>10,000, you can quite confidently create a randomly split data set. When the data set is smaller, comparing basic statistics such as mean, mode, median, and variance across the response and features in the training and test sets will help you understand whether the test set is unsuitable. When you aren't sure that the split is right, just recalculate a new one.

Resorting to Cross-Validation

A noticeable problem with the train/test set split is that you're actually introducing bias into your testing because you're reducing the size of your in-sample training data. When you split your data, you may be actually keeping some useful examples out of training. Moreover, sometimes your data is so complex that a test set, though apparently similar to the training set, is not really similar because combinations of values are different (which is typical of highly dimensional data sets). These issues add to the instability of sampling results when you don't have many examples. The risk of splitting your data in an unfavorable way also explains why the train/test split isn't the favored solution by machine learning practitioners when you have to evaluate and tune a machine learning solution.

Cross-validation based on k-folds is actually the answer. It relies on random splitting, but this time it splits your data into a number k of *folds* (portions of your data) of equal size. Then each fold is held out in turn as a test set and the others are used for training. Each iteration uses a different fold as a test, which produces an error estimate. In fact, after completing the test on one fold against the others used as training, a successive fold, different from the previous, is held out and the procedure is repeated in order to produce another error estimate. The process continues until all the k-folds are used once as a test set and you have a k number of error estimates that you can compute into a mean error estimate (the cross-validation score) and a standard error of the estimates. Figure 4-4 shows how this process works.

	FOLD 1	FOLD 2	FOLD 3	FOLD 4	FOLD 5
ITERATION 1	TRAIN	TRAIN	TRAIN	TRAIN	TEST
ITERATION 2	TRAIN	TRAIN	TRAIN	TEST	TRAIN
ITERATION 3	TRAIN	TRAIN	TEST	TRAIN	TRAIN
ITERATION 4	TRAIN	TEST	TRAIN	TRAIN	TRAIN
ITERATION 5	TEST	TRAIN	TRAIN	TRAIN	TRAIN

DATASET PARTITIONED INTO FOLDS

FIGURE 4-4: A graphical representation of how cross-validation works.

This procedure provides the following advantages:

>> It works well regardless of the number of examples, because by increasing the number of used folds, you are actually increasing the size of your training set (larger k, larger training set, reduced bias) and decreasing the size of the test set.

- » Differences in distribution for individual folds don't matter as much. When a fold has a different distribution compared to the others, it's used just once as a test set and is blended with others as part of the training set during the remaining tests.

- » You are actually testing all the observations, so you are fully testing your machine learning hypothesis using all the data you have.

- » By taking the mean of the results, you can expect a predictive performance. In addition, the standard deviation of the results can tell you how much variation you can expect in real out-of-sample data. Higher variation in the cross-validated performances informs you of extremely variegated data that the algorithm is incapable of properly catching.

REMEMBER

Using k-fold cross-validation is always the optimal choice unless the data you're using has some kind of order that matters. For instance, it could involve a time series, such as sales. In that case, you shouldn't use a random sampling method but instead rely on a train/test split based on the original sequence so that the order is preserved and you can test on the last examples of that ordered series.

Looking for Alternatives in Validation

You have a few alternatives to cross-validation, all of which are derived from statistics. The first one to consider — but only if you have an in-sample made of few examples — is the leave-one-out cross-validation (LOOCV). It is analogous to k-folds cross-validation, with the only difference being that k, the number of folds, is exactly n, the number of examples. Therefore, in LOOCV, you build n models (which may turn into a huge number when you have many observations) and test each one on a single out-of-sample observation. Apart from being computationally intensive and requiring that you build many models to test your hypothesis, the problem with LOOCV is that it tends to be pessimistic (making your error estimate higher). It's also unstable for a small number of n, and the variance of the error is much higher. All these drawbacks make comparing models difficult.

Another alternative from statistics is *bootstrapping*, a method long used to estimate the sampling distribution of statistics, which are presumed not to follow a previously assumed distribution. Bootstrapping works by building a number (the more the better) of samples of size n (the original in-sample size) drawn with repetition. To *draw with repetition* means that the process could draw an example multiple times to use it as part of the bootstrapping resampling. Bootstrapping has the advantage of offering a simple and effective way to estimate the true error measure. In fact, bootstrapped error measurements usually have much less

variance than cross-validation ones. On the other hand, validation becomes more complicated due to the sampling with replacement, so your validation sample comes from the out-of-bootstrap examples. Moreover, using some training samples repeatedly can lead to a certain bias in the models built with bootstrapping.

REMEMBER

If you are using out-of-bootstrapping examples for your test, you'll notice that the test sample can be of various sizes, depending on the number of unique examples in the in-sample, likely accounting for about a third of your original in-sample size. This simple Python code snippet demonstrates randomly simulating a certain number of bootstraps:

```
from random import randint
import numpy as np
n = 1000 # number of examples
# your original set of examples
examples = set(range(n))
results = list()
for j in range(10000):
    # your bootstrapped sample
    chosen = [randint(0,n) for k in range(n)]
    # out-of-sample
    results.append((1000-len(set(chosen)&examples))
                    /float(n))
print ("Out-of-bootstrap: %0.1f %%" %
       (np.mean(results)*100))

Out-of-bootstrap: 36.8 %
```

Running the experiment may require some time, and your results may be different due to the random nature of the experiment. However, you should see an output of around 36.8 percent.

Optimizing Cross-Validation Choices

Being able to validate a machine learning hypothesis effectively allows further optimization of your chosen algorithm. As discussed in the previous sections, the algorithm provides most of the predictive performance on your data, given its ability to detect signals from data and fit the true functional form of the predictive function without overfitting and generating much variance of the estimates. Not every machine learning algorithm is a best fit for your data, and no single algorithm can suit every problem. It's up to you to find the right one for a specific problem.

A second source of predictive performance is the data itself when appropriately transformed and selected to enhance the learning capabilities of the chosen algorithm.

The final source of performance derives from fine-tuning the algorithm's *hyper-parameters*, which are the parameters that you decide before learning happens and that aren't learned from data. Their role is in defining *a priori* a hypothesis, whereas other parameters specify it *a posteriori,* after the algorithm interacts with the data and, by using an optimization process, finds that certain parameter values work better in obtaining good predictions. Not all machine learning algorithms require much hyper-parameter tuning, but some of the most complex ones do, and though such algorithms still work out of the box, pulling the right levers may make a large difference in the correctness of the predictions. Even when the hyper-parameters aren't learned from data, you should consider the data you're working on when deciding hyper-parameters, and you should make the choice based on cross-validation and careful evaluation of possibilities.

Complex machine learning algorithms, the ones most exposed to variance of estimates, present many choices expressed in a large number of parameters. Twiddling with them makes them adapt more or less to the data they are learning from. Sometimes too much hyper-parameter twiddling may even make the algorithm detect false signals from the data. That makes hyper-parameters themselves an undetected source of variance if you start manipulating them too much based on some fixed reference like a test set or a repeated cross-validation schema.

Python offers slicing functionalities that slice your input matrix into train, test, and validation parts. In particular, for more complex testing procedures, such as cross-validation or bootstrapping, the Scikit-learn package offers an entire module (http://scikit-learn.org/stable/modules/classes.html#module-sklearn.cross_validation). In Book 9, you discover how to apply machine learning to real problems, including some practical examples using both these packages.

Exploring the space of hyper-parameters

The possible combinations of values that hyper-parameters may form make deciding where to look for optimizations hard. As described when discussing gradient descent, an optimization space may contain value combinations that perform better or worse. Even after you find a good combination, you're not assured that it's the best option. (This is the problem of getting stuck in local minima when minimizing the error, an issue described in Book 8, Chapter 3 when talking about gradient descent's problems.)

As a practical way of solving this problem, the best way to verify hyper-parameters for an algorithm applied to specific data is to test them all by cross-validation,

and to pick the best combination. This simple approach, called *grid-search*, offers indisputable advantages by allowing you to sample the range of possible values to input into the algorithm systematically and to spot when the general minimum happens. On the other hand, grid-search also has serious drawbacks because it's computationally intensive (you can easily perform this task in parallel on modern multicore computers) and quite time-consuming. Moreover, systematic and intensive tests enhance the possibility of incurring error because some good but fake validation results can be caused by noise present in the data set.

Some alternatives to grid-search are available. Instead of testing everything, you can try exploring the space of possible hyper-parameter values guided by computationally heavy and mathematically complex nonlinear optimization techniques (like the Nelder-Mead method), using a Bayesian approach (where the number of tests is minimized by taking advantage of previous results), or using random search.

Surprisingly, random search works incredibly well, is simple to understand, and isn't just based on blind luck, though it may initially appear to be. In fact, the main point of the technique is that if you pick enough random tests, you actually have enough possibilities to spot the right parameters without wasting energy on testing slightly different combinations of similarly performing combinations.

The graphical representation shown in Figure 4-5 explains why random search works well. A systematic exploration, though useful, tends to test every combination, which turns into a waste of energy if some parameters don't influence the result. A random search actually tests fewer combinations but more in the range of each hyper-parameter, a strategy that proves winning if, as often happens, certain parameters are more important than others.

FIGURE 4-5: Comparing grid-search to random search.

TIP For randomized search to perform well, you should make from 15 to a maximum of 60 tests. It does make sense to resort to random search if a grid-search requires a larger number of experiments.

Avoiding Sample Bias and Leakage Traps

On a final note, it's important to mention a possible remedy to in-sampling bias. In-sampling bias can happen to your data before machine learning is put into action, and it causes high variance of the following estimates. In addition, this section provides a warning about leakage traps that can occur when some information from the out-of-sample passes to in-sample data. This issue can arise when you prepare the data or after your machine learning model is ready and working.

The remedy, which is called ensembling of predictors, works perfectly when your training sample is not completely distorted and its distribution is different from the out-of-sample, but not in an irremediable way, such as when all your classes are present but not in the right proportion (as an example). In such cases, your results are affected by a certain variance of the estimates that you can possibly stabilize in one of several ways: by resampling, as in bootstrapping; by subsampling (taking a sample of the sample); or by using smaller samples (which increases bias).

To understand how ensembling works so effectively, visualize the image of a bull's eye. If your sample is affecting the predictions, some predictions will be exact and others will be wrong in a random way. If you change your sample, the right predictions will keep on being right, but the wrong ones will start being variations between different values. Some values will be the exact prediction you are looking for; others will just oscillate around the right one.

By comparing the results, you can guess that what is recurring is the right answer. You can also take an average of the answers and guess that the right answer should be in the middle of the values. With the bull's-eye game, you can visualize superimposing photos of different games: If the problem is variance, ultimately you will guess that the target is in the most frequently hit area or at least at the center of all the shots.

In most cases, such an approach proves to be correct and improves your machine learning predictions a lot. When your problem is bias and not variance, using ensembling really doesn't cause harm unless you subsample too few samples. A good rule of thumb for subsampling is to take a sample from 70 to 90 percent compared to the original in-sample data.

TIP

If you want to make ensembling work, you should do the following:

1. Iterate a large number of times through your data and models (from just a minimum of three iterations to ideally hundreds of times of them).

2. Every time you iterate, subsample (or else bootstrap) your in-sample data.

3. Use machine learning for the model on the resampled data, and predict the out-of-sample results. Store those results away for later use.

4. At the end of the iterations, for every out-of-sample case you want to predict, take all its predictions and average them if you are doing a regression. Take the most frequent class if you are doing a classification.

Watching out for snooping

Leakage traps can surprise you because they can prove to be an unknown and undetected source of problems with your machine learning processes. The problem is *snooping*, or otherwise observing the out-of-sample data too much and adapting to it too often. In short, snooping is a kind of overfitting — and not just on the training data but also on the test data, making the overfitting problem itself harder to detect until you get fresh data. Usually you realize that the problem is snooping when you already have applied the machine learning algorithm to your business or to a service for the public, making the problem an issue that everyone can see.

You can avoid snooping in two ways. First, when operating on the data, take care to neatly separate training, validation, and test data. Also, when processing, never take any information from validation or test, even the most simple and innocent-looking examples. Worse still is to apply a complex transformation using all the data. In finance, for instance, it is well known that calculating the mean and the standard deviation (which can actually tell you a lot about market conditions and risk) from all training and testing data can leak precious information about your models. When leakage happens, machine learning algorithms perform predictions on the test set rather than the out-of-sample data from the markets, which means that they didn't work at all.

Check the performance of your out-of-sample examples. In fact, you may bring back some information from your snooping on the test results to help you determine that certain parameters are better than others, or lead you to choose one machine learning algorithm instead of another. For every model or parameter, apply your choice based on cross-validation results or from the validation sample. Never fall for getting takeaways from your out-of-sample data, or you'll regret it later.

9 Applying Machine Learning

Contents at a Glance

CHAPTER 1: Starting with Simple Learners 605
Discovering the Incredible Perceptron 606
Growing Greedy Classification Trees 610
Taking a Probabilistic Turn 615

CHAPTER 2: Leveraging Similarity 623
Measuring Similarity between Vectors 624
Using Distances to Locate Clusters 626
Tuning the K-Means Algorithm 630
Searching for Classification by k-Nearest Neighbors 637
Leveraging the Correct K Parameter 638

CHAPTER 3: Hitting Complexity with Neural Networks 643
Learning and Imitating from Nature 644
Struggling with Overfitting 653
Introducing Deep Learning 657

CHAPTER 4: Resorting to Ensembles of Learners 661
Leveraging Decision Trees 662
Working with Almost Random Guesses 670
Boosting Smart Predictors 673
Averaging Different Predictors 676

CHAPTER 5: Real-World Applications 677
Classifying Images .. 677
Scoring Opinions and Sentiments 691
Using Scoring and Classification 703
Recommending Products and Movies 710

IN THIS CHAPTER

» Partitioning recursively training data by decision trees

» Discovering the rules behind playing tennis and surviving the *Titanic*

» Leveraging Bayesian probability to analyze textual data

Chapter 1
Starting with Simple Learners

"We learn from failure, not from success."

— DRACULA

Beginning with this chapter, the examples start illustrating the basics of how to learn from data. The plan is to touch some of the simplest learning strategies first — providing some formulas (just those that are essential), intuitions about their functioning, and examples in R and Python for experimenting with some of their most typical characteristics. The chapter begins by reviewing the use of the perceptron to separate classes.

At the root of all principal machine learning techniques presented in the book, there is always an algorithm based on somewhat interrelated linear combinations, variations of the sample splitting of decision trees, or some kind of Bayesian probabilistic reasoning. This chapter uses classification trees to demonstrate the technique. The only exception is the k-Nearest Neighbors (kNN) algorithm, which, based on analogical reasoning, is treated apart in a special chapter devoted to detection of similarity in data (see Book 9, Chapter 2).

Getting a grasp on these basic techniques means being able to deal with more complex learning techniques later and being able to understand (and use) them better. It may appear incredible now, but you can create some of the most effective

algorithms using ensembles of the simplest algorithms — those viewed as weak learners. In this chapter, you see how to use various techniques to predict when playing tennis is appropriate based on weather conditions.

At the end of the journey, no algorithm will appear as a black box anymore. Machine learning has a strong intuitive and human component because it is a human creation (at least for the moment), and it is based on analogies of how we learn from the world or on the imitation of nature (for instance, on how we know the brain works). If core ideas of the discipline are conveyed, no algorithm is really too difficult to understand. The chapter demonstrates this approach using Bayesian probability to analyze text samples.

Discovering the Incredible Perceptron

You can start the journey toward discovering how machine learning algorithms work by looking at models that figure out their answers using lines and surfaces to divide examples into classes or to estimate value predictions. These are *linear models*, and this chapter presents one of the earliest linear algorithms used in machine learning: the perceptron.

Falling short of a miracle

Frank Rosenblatt at the Cornell Aeronautical Laboratory devised the perceptron in 1957 under the sponsorship of the US Naval Research Laboratory. Rosenblatt was a psychologist and pioneer in the field of artificial intelligence. Proficient in cognitive science, it was his idea to create a computer that could learn by trial and error, just as a human does.

The idea was successfully developed, and at the beginning, the perceptron wasn't conceived as just a piece of software; it was created as software running on dedicated hardware. The use of the combination allowed faster and more precise recognition of complex images than any other computer could do at the time. The new technology raised great expectations and caused a huge controversy when Rosenblatt affirmed that the perceptron was the embryo of a new kind of computer that would be able to walk, talk, see, write, and even reproduce itself and be conscious of its existence. If true, it would have been a powerful tool, and it introduced the world to AI.

Needless to say, perceptron didn't realize the expectations of its creator. It soon displayed a limited capacity, even in its image-recognition specialization.

The general disappointment ignited the first AI Winter and the temporary abandonment of connectionism until the 1980s.

REMEMBER

Connectionism is the approach to machine learning that is based on neuroscience as well as the example of biologically interconnected networks. You can retrace the root of connectionism to the perceptron. (See the "Specifying the role of statistics in machine learning" section of Book 8, Chapter 1 for a discussion of the five tribes of machine learning.)

The perceptron is an iterative algorithm that strives to determine, by successive and reiterative approximations, the best set of values for a vector, w, which is also called the *coefficient vector*. Vector w can help predict the class of an example when you multiply it by the matrix of features, X (containing the information in numeric values) and then add it to a constant term, called the bias. The output is a prediction in the sense that the previously described operations output a number whose sign should be able to predict the class of each example exactly.

The natural specialty of the perceptron is binary classification. However, you can use it to predict multiple classes using more models (one for each class guess, a training strategy called one-versus-all or OVA). Apart from classification, the perceptron can't provide much more information. For instance, you can't use it to estimate the probability of being exact in predictions. In mathematical terms, the perceptron tries to minimize the following cost function formulation, but it does so only for the examples that are misclassified (in other words, whose sign doesn't correspond to the right class):

$$Error = -\sum_{i \in M} y_i \left(x_i^T w + b \right)$$

The formula, which is an example of a cost function as defined in Book 8, Chapter 3, involves only the examples of the matrix X, which, under the current set of w, have been assigned a misclassified sign. To understand the function of the formula, you have to consider that there are only two classes. The examples from the first class are expressed as a +1 value in response to vector y, whereas the examples from the other class are consequently coded as −1. The misclassified examples are deemed part of the set M (summations consider just the i-th example as being part of M). The formula picks up each of the misclassified examples and, in turn, multiplies their features by the vector w, and then adds the bias.

Because the multiplication of misclassified examples, X, by the weight vector, w, within the parenthesis is a multiplication of vectors, you should transpose the x vector of features of an example so that the result of the multiplication with w is a number. This is an aspect of matrix multiplication covered in Book 8, Chapter 2.

REMEMBER

Multiplying two vectors is the same as creating a weighted sum of the values of the first vector using the values in the second vector as the weights. Therefore, if x_i has five features and the vector w has five coefficients, the result of their multiplication is the sum of all five features, each one first multiplied by its respective coefficient. Matrix multiplication makes the procedure compact to express in formula, but in the end, the operation doesn't differ from a weighted average.

After getting the result of the multiplication of vectors, you sum the values to the bias and multiply everything to the value that you should have predicted (which is +1 for the first class and −1 for the second one). Because you're working only with misclassified examples, the result of the operation is always negative because the multiplication of two sign-mismatched values is always negative.

Finally, after running the same computation for all the misclassified examples, you pool all the results together and sum them. The result is a negative number that becomes positive because of the negative sign at the head of the formulation (which is like multiplying everything by −1). The size of the result increases as the number of perceptron errors becomes larger.

By observing the results carefully, you realize that the formula is devised in a smart way (although far from being a miracle). The output is smaller when the number of errors is smaller. When you have no misclassification, the summation (result) turns to zero. By putting the formula in this form, you tell the computer to try to achieve perfect classification and never give up. The idea is that when it finds the right values of the vector w, and there aren't any prediction errors, all that's left to do is to apply the following formula:

$$\hat{y} = sign(Xw + q)$$

Running the formula outputs a vector of predictions (\hat{y}) containing a sequence of +1 and −1 values that correspond to the expected classes.

Touching the nonseparability limit

The secret to perceptron calculations is in how the algorithm updates the vector w values. Such updates happen by randomly picking one of the misclassified examples (call it x_t) and changing the w vector using a simple weighted addition:

$$w = w + \eta(x_t * y_t)$$

The Greek letter eta (η) is the *learning rate*. It's a floating number between 0 and 1. When you set this value near zero, it can limit the ability of the formula to update the vector w too much, whereas setting the value near one makes the update process fully impact the w vector values. Setting different learning rates can speed

up or slow down the learning process. Many other algorithms use this strategy, and lower eta is used to improve the optimization process by reducing the number of sudden w value jumps after an update. The trade-off is that you have to wait longer before getting the concluding results.

The update strategy provides intuition about what happens when using a perceptron to learn the classes. If you imagine the examples projected on a Cartesian plane, the perceptron is nothing more than a line trying to separate the positive class from the negative one. As you may recall from linear algebra, everything expressed in the form of $y = xb+a$ is actually a line in a plane.

Initially, when w is set to zero or to random values, the separating line is just one of the infinite possible lines found on a plane, as shown in Figure 1-1. The updating phase defines it by forcing it to become nearer to the misclassified point. Using multiple iterations to define the errors places the line at the exact border between the two classes.

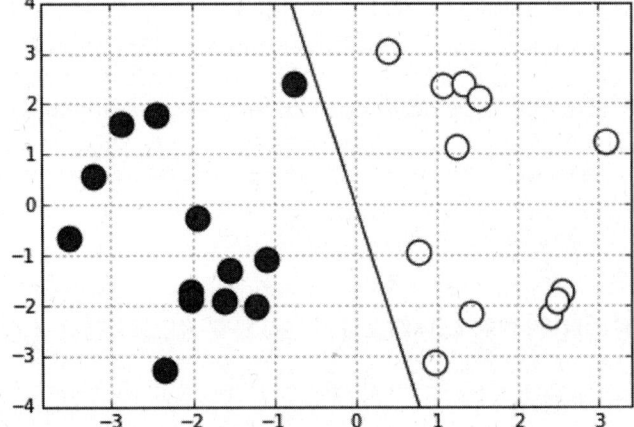

FIGURE 1-1: The separating line of a perceptron across two classes.

In spite of being such a smart algorithm, perceptron showed its limits quite soon. Apart from being capable of guessing two classes using only quantitative features, it had an important limit: If two classes had no border due to mixing, the algorithm couldn't find a solution and kept updating itself infinitively.

REMEMBER

If you can't divide two classes spread on two or more dimensions by any line or plane, they're *nonlinearly separable*. Overcoming data's being nonlinearly separable is one of the challenges that machine learning has to accomplish in order to become effective against complex problems based on real data, not just on artificial data created for academic purposes.

CHAPTER 1 **Starting with Simple Learners** 609

When the nonlinear separability matter came under scrutiny and practitioners started losing interest in the perceptron, experts quickly theorized that they could fix the problem by creating a new feature space in which previously inseparable classes are tuned to become separable. Thus the perceptron would be as fine as before. Unfortunately, creating new feature spaces is a challenge because it requires computational power that's only partially available to the public today.

In recent years, the algorithm has had a revival thanks to big data: A perceptron, in fact, doesn't need to work with all the data in memory, but it can do fine using single examples (updating its coefficient vector only when a misclassified case makes it necessary). It's therefore a perfect algorithm for online learning, such as learning from big data an example at a time.

Growing Greedy Classification Trees

Decision trees have a long history. The first algorithm of their kind dates back to the 1970s, but if you consider experiments and first original research, the use of decision trees goes back even earlier. As core algorithms of the symbolists tribe, decision trees have enjoyed a long popularity because of their intuitive algorithm. Their output is easily translated into rules and is therefore quite understandable by humans. They're also extremely easy to use. All these characteristics make them an effective and appealing no-brainer with respect to models that require complex mathematical transformations of the input data matrix or extremely accurate tuning of their hyper-parameters.

Predicting outcomes by splitting data

Using a sample of observations as a starting point, the algorithm retraces the rules that generated the output classes (or the numeric values when working through a regression problem) by dividing the input matrix into smaller and smaller partitions until the process triggers a rule for stopping. Such retracing from particular toward general rules is typical of human inverse deduction, as treated by logic and philosophy. In a machine learning context, such inverse reasoning is achieved by applying a search among all the possible ways to split the training in-sample and decide, in a greedy way, to use the split that maximizes statistical measurements on the resulting partitions.

REMEMBER

An algorithm is *greedy* when it always chooses its move to maximize the result in each step along the optimization process, regardless of what could happen in the following steps. In other words, the algorithm looks to maximize the current step without looking forward toward achieving a global optimization.

The division occurs to enforce a simple principle: Each partition of the initial data must make it easier to predict the target outcome, which is characterized by a different and more favorable distribution of classes (or values) than the original sample. The algorithm creates partitions by splitting the data. It determines the data splits by first evaluating the features and then the values in the features that could bring the maximum improvement of a special statistical measure that plays the role of the cost function in a decision tree.

A number of statistical measurements determine how to make the splits in a decision tree. All abide by the idea that a split must improve on the original sample, or another possible split, when it makes prediction safer. Among the most used measurements are *gini impurity, information gain,* and *variance reduction* (for regression problems). These measurements operate similarly, so this chapter focuses on information gain because it's the most intuitive measurement and conveys how a decision tree can detect an increased predictive ability (or a reduced risk) in the easiest way for a certain split. Ross Quinlan created a decision tree algorithm based on information gain (ID3) in the 1970s, and it's still quite popular thanks to its recent upgraded version to C4.5. Information gain relies on the formula for *informative entropy*, a generalized formulation that describes the expected value from the information contained in a message:

$$Entropy = \sum -p_i \log_2 p_i$$

In the formula, p is the probability for a class (expressed in the range of 0 to 1) and \log_2 is the base 2 logarithm. Starting with a sample in which you want to classify two classes having the same probability (a 50/50 distribution), the maximum possible entropy is

```
Entropy = -0.5*log₂(0.5) -0.5*log₂(0.5) = 1.0
```

However, when the decision tree algorithm detects a feature that can split the data set into two partitions, where the distribution of the two classes is 40/60, the average informative entropy diminishes:

```
Entropy = -0.4*log₂(0.4) -0.6*log₂(0.6) = 0.97
```

Note the entropy sum for all the classes. Using the 40/60 split, the sum is less than the theoretical maximum of 1 (diminishing the entropy). Think of the entropy as a measure of the mess in data: the less mess, the more order, and the easier it is to guess the right class. After a first split, the algorithm tries to split the obtained partitions further using the same logic of reducing entropy. It progressively splits any successive data partition until no more splits are possible because the subsample is a single example or because it has met a stopping rule.

REMEMBER

Stopping rules are limits to the expansion of a tree. These rules work by considering three aspects of a partition: initial partition size, resulting partition size, and information gain achievable by the split. Stopping rules are important because decision tree algorithms approximate a large number of functions; however, noise and data errors can easily influence this algorithm. Consequently, depending on the sample, the instability and variance of the resulting estimates affect decision tree predictions.

As an example, take a look at what a decision tree can achieve using one of the original Ross Quinlan data sets that present and describe the ID3 algorithm in "Induction of Decision Trees" (1986) (dl.acm.org/citation.cfm?id=637969). The data set is quite simple, consisting of only 14 observations relative to the weather conditions, with results that say whether it's appropriate to play tennis. The example contains four features: outlook, temperature, humidity, and wind, all expressed using qualitative classes instead of measurements (you could express temperature, humidity, and wind strength numerically) to convey a more intuitive understanding of how the features relate to the outcome. The following example uses R to create a data.frame containing the play tennis data:

```
weather <- expand.grid(Outlook = c("Sunny","Overcast","Rain"), Temperature = c("Hot","Mild","Cool"), Humidity=c("High","Normal"), Wind=c("Weak","Strong"))

response <- c(1, 19, 4, 31, 16, 2, 11, 23, 35, 6, 24, 15, 18, 36)

play <- as.factor(c("No", "No", "No", "Yes", "Yes", "Yes", "Yes", "Yes", "Yes", "No", "Yes", "Yes", "No"))

tennis <- data.frame(weather[response,],play)
```

To create a decision tree, the example uses the rpart library and sets the parameters necessary to have a tree fully grown by information gain as the split criteria:

```
library(rpart)
tennis_tree <- rpart(play ~ ., data=tennis, method="class",
parms=list(split="information"), control=rpart.control(minsplit=1))
```

After creating the tree, you can inspect it using a simple `print` command or the `summary` command for a more detailed and verbose report about its construction. Different implementations can have different outputs, as you can see from the rpart output.

ON THE WEB

In addition to rpart, you have other R implementation options for working with decision trees, such as the packages tree, party, and a few others that you can discover in this blog post: www.r-bloggers.com/a-brief-tour-of-the-trees-and-forests. Python also provides a Scikit-learn described at scikit-learn.org/stable/modules/tree.html. However, if the tree isn't too complex, a visual representation can immediately reveal how the tree works no matter what implementation you use. You can represent trees made by rpart using the rpart.plot package. Download the package from CRAN. The paper "rpart.plot: Plot rpart Models" by Stephen Milborrow at www.milbo.org/rpart-plot describes the package in detail (you can click the rpart plot link on the page to begin the download). After installing the package, you run it and plot the representation of the tree, as shown in Figure 1-2:

```
library(rpart.plot)
prp(tennis_tree, type=0, extra=1, under=TRUE, compress=TRUE)
```

FIGURE 1-2: A visualization of the decision tree built from the play tennis data set.

To read the nodes of the tree, just start from the topmost node, which corresponds to the original training data, and then start reading the rules. Note that each node has two derivations: The left branch means that the upper rule is true (stated as yes in a square box), and the right one means that it is false (stated as no in a square box).

On the right of the first rule, you see an important terminal rule (a *terminal leaf*), in a circle, stating a positive result, Yes, that you can read as play tennis=True. According to this node, when the outlook isn't sunny (Snn) or rainy (Ran), it's possible to play. (The numbers under the terminal leaf show four examples affirming this rule and zero denying it.) Please note that you could understand the rule better if the output simply stated that when the outlook is overcast, play is possible. Frequently, decision tree rules aren't immediately usable, and you need

to interpret them before use. However, they are clearly intelligible (and much better than a coefficient vector of values).

On the left, the tree proceeds with other rules related to Humidity. Again, on the left, when humidity is high and outlook is sunny, most terminal leaves are negative, except when wind isn't strong. When you explore the branches on the right, you see that the tree reveals that play is always possible when wind isn't strong, or when the wind is strong but it doesn't rain.

Pruning overgrown trees

Even though the play tennis data set in the previous section illustrates the nuts and bolts of a decision tree, it has little probabilistic appeal because it proposes a set of *deterministic actions* (there are no conflicting instructions). Training with real data usually doesn't feature such sharp rules, thereby providing room for ambiguity and hopeful likelihood.

Another, more realistic example, is a data set describing the survival rates of passengers from the *RMS Titanic*, the British passenger liner that sank in the North Atlantic Ocean in April 1912 after colliding with an iceberg. Various versions of the data set exist — the R version used in the example is made of cross tabulations of gender, age, and survival. The example transforms the tables into a matrix and learns rules using the rpart package as previously done with the play tennis data set.

```
data(Titanic, package = "datasets")
dataset <- as.data.frame(Titanic)
library(rpart)

titanic_tree <- rpart(Survived ~ Class + Sex + Age, data=dataset, weights=Freq,
method="class", parms=list(split="information"),
control=rpart.control(minsplit=5))

pruned_titanic_tree <- prune(titanic_tree, cp=0.02)
```

Decision trees have more variance than bias in their estimations. To overfit the data less, the example specifies that the minimum split has to involve at least five examples; also, it prunes the tree. Pruning happens when the tree is fully grown. Starting from the leaves, the example *prunes* the tree of branches, showing little improvement in the reduction of information gain. By initially letting the tree expand, branches with little improvement are tolerated because they can unlock more interesting branches and leaves. Retracing from leaves to root and keeping only branches that have some predictive value reduces the variance of the model, making the resulting rules more strict.

 TIP For a decision tree, pruning is just like brainstorming. First, the code generates all possible ramifications of the tree (as with ideas in a brainstorming session). Second, when the brainstorming concludes, the code keeps only what really works. A chart of the tree structure (see Figure 1-3) reveals that only two rules matter in survival: gender (being male penalizes survival) and not being in third class (the poorest).

```
library(rpart.plot)
prp(pruned_titanic_tree, type=0, extra=1, under=TRUE, compress=TRUE)
```

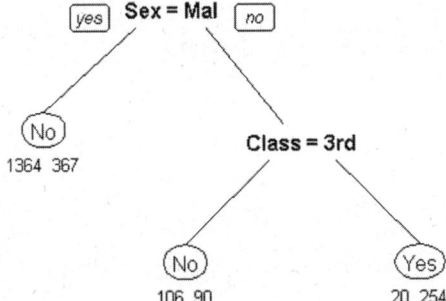

FIGURE 1-3: A visualization of the pruned decision tree build from the Titanic data set.

Taking a Probabilistic Turn

Naïve Bayes, another basic learning algorithm, is more similar to the previously discussed perceptron than the decision tree because it is based on a set of values being put together to obtain a prediction. As with the perceptron and decision trees, Naïve Bayes is a historical algorithm used since the 1950s, although under different names and slightly different forms. Moreover, Naïve Bayes is famed for being an effective algorithm for learning from text, and it clearly appeals to the Bayesian tribe. Given its simplicity and the fact that it works with little preprocessing, it has become the baseline for most textual problems in machine learning before testing more complex solutions.

Understanding Naïve Bayes

As with the perceptron, Naïve Bayes requires values that are probabilities of an outcome given a certain context (a *conditional probability*). Moreover, you multiply the values instead of summing them. Naïve Bayes is powered by computations on probability, and it consequently requires typical operations on probabilities.

REMEMBER

As seen in Book 8, Chapter 2, when probabilities are multiplied, it means that the events, whose likelihood we are considering, are independent and not influencing each other in any way. Such an assumption, though deemed simplistic and naïve, is frequent in many basic machine learning algorithms because it's unbelievably effective when working with a lot of data.

By summing values or multiplying probabilities, you treat each piece of information as a separate contribution to the answer. It's an unrealistic assumption sometimes because reality points to a world of interconnections. However, in spite of the lack of realism, Naïve Bayes can outperform most complex techniques, as described by two researchers from Microsoft, Banko and Brill, in their memorable paper "Scaling to Very Very Large Corpora for Natural Language Disambiguation" (www.microsoft.com/en-us/research/wp-content/uploads/2016/02/acl2001.pdf).

Naïve Bayes relates to the Bayes' theorem discussed in Book 8, Chapter 2. It represents a simplified form of the theorem itself. To answer the class of an example, the algorithm does the following:

1. Learns the probabilities connecting the features to each of the possible classes.
2. Multiplies all the probabilities related to each resulting class.
3. Normalizes the probabilities by dividing each of them by their total sum.
4. Takes the class featuring the highest probability as the answer.

For instance, in the previous example of the play tennis data set, you observe that the different distributions of the sunny, overcast, and rain outlooks connect to the positive and negative answer of whether to play tennis. Using R can provide you with a quick check on that observation:

```
print (table(tennis$Outlook, tennis$play))

           No Yes
  Sunny     3   2
  Overcast  0   4
  Rain      2   3
```

The output shows nine positive responses and five negative ones. By analyzing the positive responses, you see that given a positive response, the outlook is sunny two times out of nine (probability = 2/9 = 0.22); overcast four times out of nine (probability = 4/9 = 0.44); and rainy three times out of nine (probability = 3/9 = 0.33). You can repeat the same procedure using the negative responses with probabilities of 3/5, 0/5, and 2/5, respectively, for sunny, overcast, and rainy when you can't play tennis. Using the Bayes' theorem, you can determine that the

probabilities that you calculated are actually P(E|B), which is the probability that given a certain belief (such as whether to play tennis), you have certain evidence (which is weather, in this case):

```
P(B|E) = P(E|B)*P(B) / P(E)
```

The formula provides the answer you need, because it is the probability of a certain belief (to play or not to play) given certain evidence (the weather conditions). If you estimate the probabilities for every belief, you can choose the belief that has the highest probability, thus minimizing the risk of predicting something incorrectly. P(E|B) then becomes critical for estimating the probabilities because P(B) is the general probability of a positive or negative answer (the prior probability) and it's easy to determine. In this case, you have nine positive outcomes and five negative ones. Thus P(B) is 9/(9+5) = 0.64 for positive and 0.36 for negative.

When you have many pieces of evidence, as in this example, P(E|B) is a compound of all the single P(E|B) probabilities on hand. This example has sets of probabilities for outlook, temperature, humidity, and wind. Putting them together isn't easy unless you presume that they affect the response separately. As mentioned previously, probabilities of independent events are simply multiplied together, and the overall P(E|B) turns out to be the multiplication of all the P(E|B) for each feature.

TIP

It may happen that you don't have evidence for a response. For instance, in this example, you don't have cases of not playing tennis when the sky is overcast. The result is a zero probability, and in a multiplication, a zero probability always returns zero no matter what other probabilities are involved. A lack of evidence for a response can occur when you don't sample enough examples. A good practice is to modify observed probabilities by a constant, called a *Laplace correction*, which consists of adding fictitious evidence when estimating the probability. Using such a correction in this example, you'd find that the probability of 0/5 would become (0+1)/(5+1) = 0.17.

P(E) isn't a big deal for this example, and you should ignore it. The reason P(E) doesn't matter is that it represents the probability of seeing a certain set of features in reality and it naturally varies from example to example (for instance, your location could make certain weather conditions rare). However, you're not comparing probabilities across examples. You're comparing probabilities within each example to determine the most likely prediction for that example. Within the same example, the probability of a certain set of evidence is the same because you have only that set for every possible outcome. Whether the set of evidence is rare doesn't matter; in the end, you have to predict that example in isolation from the others, so you can safely rule out P(E) by making it a value of 1. The following

example shows that how to use R determines the numbers to plug in the formulation for getting a prediction given certain weather conditions:

```
outcomes      <- table(tennis$play)
prob_outcomes <- outcomes / sum(outcomes)
outlook       <- t(as.matrix(table(tennis$Outlook, tennis$play))) / as.vector(outcomes)
temperature   <- t(as.matrix(table(tennis$Temperature, tennis$play))) /
    as.vector(outcomes)
humidity      <- t(as.matrix(table(tennis$Humidity, tennis$play))) /
    as.vector(outcomes)
wind          <- t(as.matrix(table(tennis$Wind, tennis$play))) / (as.vector(outcomes))
```

After running the previous code snippet, you have all the elements needed to figure out a prediction. Pretend that you to need to guess the following condition:

```
Outlook = Sunny, Temperature = Mild, Humidity = Normal, Wind = Weak
```

To obtain the required information, you first compute the probability for a positive outcome:

```
p_positive <- outlook["Yes","Sunny"] * temperature["Yes","Mild"] *
humidity["Yes","Normal"] * wind["Yes","Weak"] * prob_outcomes["Yes"]
```

If you print p_positive, you can see that the probability is 0.02821869. Now you can check for a negative outcome:

```
p_negative <- outlook["No","Sunny"] * temperature["No","Mild"] *
humidity["No","Normal"] * wind["No","Weak"] * prob_outcomes["No"]
```

The result in terms of probability for a negative response is 0.006857143. Finally, you can obtain the guess using a Boolean check:

```
print (p_positive &gt;= p_negative)
```

The positive result, TRUE, confirms that given such conditions, the algorithm predicts that you can play tennis.

Estimating response with Naïve Bayes

Now that you know how it works, Naïve Bayes should appear quite simple and strongly naïve in its assumption. You should also know that multiplying probabilities is fine. You also need to consider these issues:

- » Fixing zero probabilities using the Laplace correction
- » Converting numeric features into qualitative variables because estimating probability for classes comprising ranges of numbers is easier
- » Using counted features only (values equal to or above zero) — although some algorithm variants can deal with binary features and negative values
- » Imputing values in missing features (when you're missing an important probability in the computation), along with removing redundant and irrelevant features (keeping such features would make estimation by Naïve Bayes more difficult)

In particular, irrelevant features can affect results a lot. When you are working with a few examples with many features, an unlucky probability can really skew your result. As a solution, you can select features, filtering only the most important ones. When you have enough examples and you spend some time fixing features, Naïve Bayes renders effective solutions to many prediction problems involving the analysis of textual input such as:

- » **Email spam detection:** Allows you to place only useful information in your Inbox.
- » **Text classification:** No matter the source (online news, tweets, or other textual feeds), you can correctly arrange text into the right category (such as sports, politics, foreign affairs, and economy).
- » **Text-processing tasks:** Lets you perform spelling correction or guess the language of a text.
- » **Sentiment analysis:** Detects the sentiment behind written text (positive, negative, neutral, or one of the basic human emotions).

As an example of a practical application, you can use R and the klaR library, which contains the `NaiveBayes` function. This library offers an interesting data set containing selected features for detecting whether an inbound email should be considered spam. Because klarR and kernlab are nonstandard libraries, the first time you run the code, you have to install them:

```
install.packages(c("klaR","kernlab"))
```

After doing so, you are ready to run the example code:

```
library(klaR)
data(spam, package = "kernlab")
```

Hewlett-Packard Labs collected the data set and classified 4,601 emails as spam or nonspam, using 57 features. You can also find the spam data set on the free UCI machine learning repository at https://archive.ics.uci.edu/ml/datasets/Spambase.

If you upload the spam data set and check its features (using the command head(spam), for instance), you notice that some features are words, whereas others point to the presence of certain characters or writing styles (such as capital letters). More noticeably, some of the features aren't integer numbers representing counts but rather are floats ranging from 0 to 100. They represent the presence of each feature in the text as a percentage (for instance, the variable charDollar represents the percentage of dollar sign characters in the phrase and ranges from 0 to 6).

Features expressed as percentages of certain words or characters in text represent a wise strategy to balance the higher likelihood of finding certain elements if the text is long. Using percentages instead of counts normalizes the texts and lets you view them as being of the same length.

Applying a Naïve Bayes model in R requires just a few commands. You can set the Laplace correction using the fL parameter (the example keeps it set to zero) and defining different *a priori* probabilities, P(B), using the prior parameter and providing a vector of probabilities. In this example, we set the probability of an email's being nonspam to 90 percent:

```
set.seed(1234)
train_idx <- sample(1:nrow(spam), ceiling(nrow(spam)*3/4), replace=FALSE)
naïve <- NaiveBayes(type ~ ., data=spam[train_idx,], prior = c(0.9,0.1), fL = 0)
```

The code doesn't use all the examples at hand, but instead keeps a quarter of them for testing the results out-of-sample. NaiveBayes automatically translates the numeric features into features suitable for the algorithm, thus leaving little more to do than to ask the model to scan the out-of-sample data and generate predictions that you check in order to know how well the model works. (Don't worry about the warnings you see from the confusionMatrix function found in the caret library — what you care about is the confusion matrix output.)

The caret library is used for error estimation, and is a powerful tool supporting you in many operations for validating and evaluating machine learning algorithm, but you must install it first:

```
install.packages("caret")
```

Installation will take some time because the library has many dependencies (it requires many other R libraries, such as the e1071 library, a package for supporting vector machines). After completing the installation, you can proceed with the example.

```
library(caret)
predictions <- predict(naïve, spam[-train_idx,])
confusionMatrix(predictions$class, spam[-train_idx,"type"])
```

REMEMBER

The example shows that `NaiveBayes` takes longer to predict than to train. The increased prediction time happens because training the algorithm involves counting only the occurrences in the features and stores the results. The real computations happen when the algorithm is predicting, making it fast to train and slow to predict. Here's the output you see from this example:

```
Prediction nonspam spam
   nonspam     403   24
   spam        293  430
```

It seems that, as often happens, an algorithm can catch almost all the spam, but does so at the cost of putting some regular email into the spam box. The code can report such problems using a score measure such as accuracy, which you can split further into accuracy for the positive and the negative classes, respectively:

```
Accuracy : 0.7243
Pos Pred Value : 0.9438
Neg Pred Value : 0.5947
```

Catching spam isn't that difficult; the problem is to avoid discarding important emails in the process (false positives, where a positive is a spam email).

TIP

There are quite a few kinds of Naïve Bayes models. The model you just used is called multinomial. However, there is also a Bernoulli version, suitable for binary indicators (you don't count words but instead check to determine whether they're present) and a Gaussian version (which expects normally distributed features — having both positive and negative values). Python, contrary to R, offers a complete range of Naïve Bayes models in the Scikit-learn package at `scikit-learn.org/stable/modules/naive_bayes.html`.

IN THIS CHAPTER

» Understanding differences between examples

» Clustering data into meaningful groups

» Classifying and regressing after looking for data neighbors

» Grasping the difficulties of working in a high-dimensional data space

Chapter 2
Leveraging Similarity

"A rose by any other name would smell as sweet."
— JULIET, *ROMEO AND JULIET*

A rose is a rose. A tree is a tree. A car is a car. Even though you can make simple statements like this, one example of each kind of item doesn't suffice to identify all the items that fit into that classification. After all, many species of trees and many kinds of roses exist. If you evaluate the problem under a machine learning framework in the examples, you find features whose values change frequently and features that somehow systematically persist (a tree is always made of wood and has a trunk and roots, for instance). When you look closely for the features' values that repeat constantly, you can guess that certain observed objects are of much the same kind.

So children can figure out by themselves what cars are by looking at the features. After all, cars all have four wheels and run on roads. But what happens when a child sees a bus or a truck? Luckily, someone is there to explain the big cars and open the child's world to larger definitions. In this chapter, you explore how machines can learn by exploiting similarity in

» **A supervised way:** Learning from previous examples. For example, a car has four wheels; therefore if a new object has four wheels, it could be a car.

> **An unsupervised way:** Inferring a grouping without any label to learn from. For example, a list of items all have roots and are made of wood, so they should go into the same group even though they lack a name.

Both our topic algorithms, K-means, an unsupervised clustering algorithm, and k-Nearest Neighbors, a supervised regression and classification algorithm, work by leveraging similarities among examples. They offer a good glance at the advantages and disadvantages of ordering the world in items that are more or less similar.

Measuring Similarity between Vectors

You can easily compare examples from your data using calculations if you think of each of them as a vector. The following sections describe how to measure similarity between vectors to perform tasks such as computing the distance between vectors for learning purposes.

Understanding similarity

In a vector form, you can see each variable in your examples as a series of coordinates, with each one pointing to a position in a different space dimension, as shown in Figure 2-1. If a vector has two elements, that is, it has just two variables, working with it is just like checking an item's position on a map by using the first number for the position on the East-West axis and the second on the North-South axis.

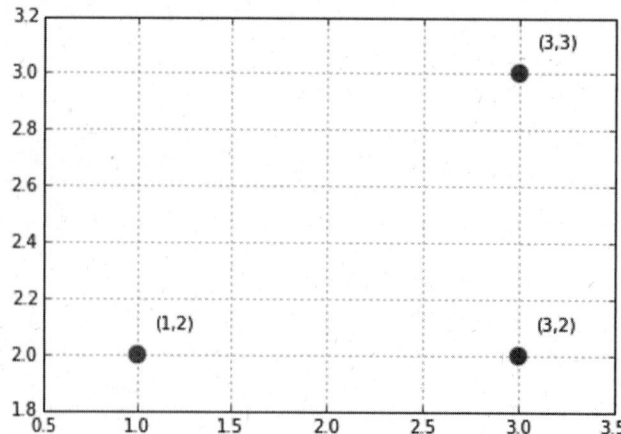

FIGURE 2-1: Examples of values plotted as points on a chart.

For instance, the numbers between parentheses (1,2) (3,2), and (3,3) are all examples of points. Each example is an ordered list of values (called a tuple) that can be easily located and printed on a map using the first value of the list for x (the horizontal axis) and the second for y (the vertical axis). The result is a scatterplot, and you find examples of them in this chapter.

If your data set, in matrix form, has many numeric features (the columns), ideally the number of the features represents the dimensions of the data space, while the rows (the examples) represent each point, which mathematically is a vector. When your vector has more than two elements, visualization becomes troublesome because representing dimensionalities above the third isn't easy (after all, we live in a three-dimensional world). However, you can strive to convey more dimensionalities by some expedient, such as by using size, shape, or color for other dimensions. Clearly, that's not an easy task, and often the result is far from being intuitive. However, you can grasp the idea of where the points would be in your data space by systematically printing many graphs while considering the dimensions two by two. Such plots are called matrices of scatterplots.

Don't worry about multidimensionality. You extend the rules you learned in two or three dimensions to multiple dimensions, so if a rule works in a bidimensional space, it also works in a multiple one. Therefore all the examples first refer to bidimensional examples.

Computing distances for learning

An algorithm can learn by using vectors of numbers that use distance measurements. Often the space implied by your vectors is a metric one that is a space whose distances respect certain specific conditions:

» No negative distances exist, and your distance is zero only when the starting point and ending point coincide (called *nonnegativity*).

» The distance is the same going from a point to another and vice versa (called *symmetry*).

» The distance between an initial point and a final one is always greater than, or at worse the same as, the distance going from the initial to a third point and from there to the final one (called *triangle inequality* — which means that there are no shortcuts).

Distances that measure a metric space are the Euclidean distance, the Manhattan distance, and the Chebyshev distance. These are all distances that can apply to numeric vectors.

CHAPTER 2 **Leveraging Similarity** 625

Euclidean distance

The most common is the Euclidean distance, also described as the l2 norm of two vectors (you can find a discussion of l1, l2, and linfinity norms at `https://rorasa.wordpress.com/2012/05/13/l0-norm-l1-norm-l2-norm-l-infinity-norm`). In a bidimensional plane, the Euclidean distance refigures as the straight line connecting two points, and you calculate it as the square root of the sum of the squared difference between the elements of two vectors. In the previous plot, the Euclidean distance between points (1,2) and (3,3) can be computed in R as sqrt((1-3)^2+(2-3)^2), which results in a distance of about 2.236.

Manhattan distance

Another useful measure is the Manhattan distance (also described as the l1 norm of two vectors). You calculate the Manhattan distance by summing the absolute value of the difference between the elements of the vectors. If the Euclidean distance marks the shortest route, the Manhattan distance marks the longest route, resembling the directions of a taxi moving in a city. (The distance is also known as taxicab or city-block distance.) For instance, the Manhattan distance between points (1,2) and (3,3) is abs(1-3) and abs(2-3), which results in 3.

Chebyshev distance

The Chebyshev distance or maximum metric takes the maximum of the absolute difference between the elements of the vectors. It is a distance measure that can represent how a king moves in the game of chess or, in warehouse logistics, the operations required by an overhead crane to move a crate from one place to another. In machine learning, the Chebyshev distance can prove useful when you have many dimensions to consider and most of them are just irrelevant or redundant (in Chebyshev, you just pick the one whose absolute difference is the largest). In the example used in previous sections, the distance is simply 2, the max between (1-3) and abs(2-3).

Using Distances to Locate Clusters

Working with a well-ordered space, you naturally find similar items next to each other, such as books about the same topic in a library. In a library, similar books stand in the same bookshelf, in the same bookcase, and in the same section. Imagine, for instance, being a librarian who is tasked with gathering all the books on the same topic without any helpful indication of a preexisting index or label. Grouping similar objects or examples in this case is clustering. In machine

learning, it is an unsupervised task. It allows you to create labels when no labeling is available, or when creating new labeling empirically is helpful.

With the library example, a good solution to the lack of an index or labels would be picking books here and there at random, each one located in a different bookcase and bookshelf, and then looking for similar books in all directions. You could go as far from the original book as makes sense. In a short time, based on the books' locations, you could partition your library into homogeneous areas of books around similar topics. After reading a single representative book from each area, you could easily and confidently label all the books located there by topic.

Based on this same idea (starting from an example and looking in all directions within a given range), an entire series of statistical algorithms, called partition algorithms, help you explore data dimensions around starting examples by aggregating the ones that are similar. Among partition algorithms, K-means is the most well-known and popular one. It usually works out good solutions by leveraging the nearness of similar examples in a data space, drawing the boundaries of classes, and ultimately recovering any unknown group structure. K-means allows labeling, summarization, and sometimes a deeper understanding of hidden dynamics of data. K-means can help you achieve the following:

>> Labeling examples into separated groups

>> Creating new features (the labels of the groups) for use in supervised learning tasks (labels from a cluster analysis are very helpful as new features when learning from text and images)

>> Grouping anomalous examples into groups of their own, thus helping you to locate them easily

K-means is not the only algorithm capable of performing clustering tasks. Clustering (also known as cluster analysis) has a long history, and algorithms of different kinds exist for performing it. There are clustering methods that arrange the examples into tree-like structures (hierarchical clustering) and others that look for parts of the data space where examples are denser (DBSCAN). Others figure out whether any cluster is derivable from certain statistical distributions, such as a Gaussian. Among so many choices, K-means has become a very successful algorithm in machine learning for good reasons:

>> It's easy and intuitive to understand.

>> It can be fast and scales nicely to large amounts of data.

>> It does not require keeping too much information in memory.

>> Its output is useful as an input to other machine learning algorithms.

CHAPTER 2 **Leveraging Similarity** 627

Checking assumptions and expectations

K-means relies on assumptions that some people dispute and that you need to know about. First, the algorithm assumes that your data has groups called *clusters*. It also assumes that the groups are made of similar examples, with the starting example, called the *prototype* or the *centroid*, in the center of the cluster. Finally, it assumes that, in the data space, groups have a rigorously spherical-like shape. Therefore, regretfully, K-means doesn't allow strange shapes, which can be a weakness of the technique because the real world isn't always geometrically shaped. These are all theoretical assumptions. (The algorithm can work well when the data meets the conditions; otherwise, you must check the result closely.)

K-means works with a numeric measure, the Euclidean distance. All your data has to be in the form of a number representing a measure (technically called a metric measure; for instance, everyday metrics measures are meters and kilos). You can't use variables whose values are assigned arbitrarily; the measure should have some relation to reality. However, even though it's not ideal, you can use ordinal numbers (like 1st, 2nd, 3rd, and so on, because they have a measure-like order). You can also use binary variables (1 or 0).

REMEMBER

The Euclidean distance is the root of a big sum, so all your variables have to be of the same scale, or the variables with the larger range will dominate the distance (and you'll create clusters on just those variables). The same domination also occurs if some variables are correlated; that is, they share a part of their informative content (variance). Again, you have some variables influencing the result more than others do. One solution is to transform your data before the K-means by statistically standardizing all the variables and transforming them into components with a dimensionality reduction algorithm such as principal component analysis (PCA), which is discussed later in this chapter.

K-means also expects you to already know how many clusters your data contains. However, it isn't a big problem if you don't know, because you can guess or try many solutions, starting from the desirable ones. Because the algorithm makes so many theoretical and practical assumptions, it always comes up with a solution (which is why everyone loves it so much). When you work with data with no clusters or ask for the wrong number of clusters, it can provide you with some misleading results. You can distinguish good results from bad ones based on the following:

» **Heuristics:** You can measure the quality of the clustering.

» **Reproducibility:** Random results cannot be replicated.

» **Understandability:** Absurd solutions are seldom real solutions.

» **Usability:** You care about how machine learning practically solves problems and aren't concerned about its correctness in terms of assumptions.

REMEMBER

The K-means algorithm is an unsupervised algorithm, so unless you know the cluster solution beforehand, you don't have any error to measure in terms of deviance or accuracy. After getting a solution, always do a reality check with the clustering quality measures to see whether the result is reproducible under different conditions, makes sense, and can help with your problem.

Inspecting the gears of the algorithm

The K-means algorithm performs tasks in a specific way. By understanding the procedure that the algorithm uses to perform tasks, you can better understand how to employ the K-means algorithm. You can detail the procedure that the algorithm uses in a few steps:

1. After you instruct the algorithm that there are k clusters in the data (where k is an integer number), the algorithm picks k random examples as the original centroids of your k clusters.

2. The algorithm assigns all the examples to each of the k clusters based on their Euclidian distance to each one's centroid. The nearest centroid wins the example, which then becomes part of its cluster.

3. After assigning all the examples to the clusters, the algorithm recalculates the new centroid of each one by averaging all the examples that are part of the group. After the first round, the new centroids likely won't coincide with a real example anymore. At this point, when thinking of centroids, consider them as ideal examples (actually, *prototypes*).

4. If it is not the first round, after averaging, the algorithm checks how much the position of centroids has changed in the data space. If it has not changed all that much from the previous round, the algorithm assumes a stable solution and returns the solution to you. Otherwise, the algorithm repeats Steps 2 and 3. Having changed the position of centroids, the algorithm reassigns part of the examples to a different cluster, which likely leads to a change in the centroid position.

Given the jumps between Steps 2 and 4 until the output meets a certain convergence condition, the K-means algorithm is iterative. Iteration after iteration, the initial centroids, which the algorithm chooses randomly, move their position until the algorithm finds a stable solution. (The examples don't move anymore between clusters, or at least few do.) At that point, after the algorithm has converged, you can expect that

>> All your data is separated into clusters (so each example will have one and just one cluster label).

>> All the clusters tend to have the maximum internal cohesion possible. You can compute the cohesion for every cluster by subtracting the centroid position from the position of each example, then squaring the result of each subtraction (so you remove the sign), and finally summing all the results. Thus you obtain the cohesion, which in a cluster analysis, always tends to be the minimum possible (called *within-cluster sum of squares* or *WSS*).

>> All the clusters have the maximum external difference possible. This means that if you take the difference of each centroid with the average of the data space (the grand centroid), square each difference, multiply each of them by their respective cluster's number of examples, and then sum all results together, the result is the maximum possible (*between-cluster sum of squares* or *BSS*).

Because the between-cluster sum of squares is dependent on the result of the within-cluster calculation, you need to look at only one of them (usually WSS will suffice). Sometimes the starting position is an unlucky one, and the algorithm doesn't converge at a proper solution. The data is always partitioned, so you can only guess that the algorithm has performed the work acceptably by calculating the within-cluster sum of squares of the solution and comparing it with previous calculations.

If you run the K-means a few times and record the results, you can easily spot algorithm runs that had a higher within-cluster sum of squares and a lower between-cluster result as the solution that you can't trust. Depending on your computational power at hand and the data set size, running many trials can consume a lot of time, and you have to decide how to trade time for safety in choosing a good solution.

Tuning the K-Means Algorithm

To get the best possible results from the K-means algorithm, you must tune it. Tuning a K-means algorithm requires clear ideas about its purpose:

>> **If the purpose is explorative,** stop at the number of clusters when the solution makes sense and you can determine which clusters to use by naming them.

>> **If you are working with abstract data,** looking at the within-cluster sum of squares or at some other tuning measure can help hint at the right solution.

>> **If you need the cluster results to feed a supervised algorithm,** use cross-validation to determine the solution that brings more predictive power.

The next step requires you to decide on an implementation. The Python language offers two versions of the algorithm in the scikit-learn package. The first one is the classical algorithm, `sklearn.cluster.KMeans`. You can also use a mini-batch version, `sklearn.cluster.MiniBatchKMeans`, which differs from the standard K-means because it can compute new centroids and reassign all previous cluster labels on portions of the data (instead of making all the computations after evaluating all the data sample).

The advantage of the mini-batch is that it can process data that won't fit in the available memory of your computer by fetching examples in small chunks from disk. The algorithm processes each chunk, updates the clusters, and then loads the next chunk. The only possible bottleneck is the speed of data transfer. The process takes more time than the classical algorithm, but when it's finished computing (and it may take a few passages on all your data), you'll have a complete model that's not much different from the model you could have obtained using the standard algorithm.

`sklearn.cluster.MiniBatchKMeans` has two fit methods:

» `fit`: Works with data in memory and stops after it processes the information available based on the batch size that you set using the `batch_size` parameter.

» `partial_fit`: Processes the data in memory, but then remains open to start again when presented with new data, so it's perfect for streaming data in blocks from disk or from a network such as the Internet.

`sklearn.cluster.KMeans` offers all the standard parameters discussed earlier: the number of clusters (`n_clusters`) and the initialization method (`init`). Moreover, it offers the possibility to precompute distances (`precompute_distances`). If the number of effective iterations is high, `sklearn.cluster.KMeans` calculates the distances repetitively, wasting time. If you have memory and need speed, just set `precompute_distances` to `TRUE`, which stores all the calculations in advance. You can also instruct the algorithm to work in parallel (setting `n_job` to –1) when it has to create many solutions simultaneously (because of different random initializations). Precomputing distances and parallel computation make the Python implementation currently the fastest available.

Experimenting K-means reliability

The nuances of K-means can be seen using the Iris data set, a popular example data set about three species of iris flowers that had their petals and sepals (part of the flower, supporting the petals when in bloom) measured. Introduced by the statistician Ronald Fisher in one of his papers in 1936 to demonstrate linear

discriminant analysis (a statistical predictive analysis), the tricky thing about this data set is that two iris species (*Virginica* and *Versicolor*) need combined measurements to aid in distinguishing one from the other (in supervised learning). You can't resolve labeling in unsupervised learning by using just the given information. The Iris data set is also a balanced data set because you use the same number of examples for each of the three iris species, as shown in the following Python example:

```
from sklearn.datasets import load_iris
data = load_iris()
print ("Features :%s" % data.feature_names)
features = data.data
labels = data.target

Features :['sepal length (cm)', 'sepal width (cm)',
          'petal length (cm)', 'petal width (cm)']
```

The experiment uses both of the two available K-means versions in scikit-learn: the standard algorithm and the mini-batch version. In the scikit-learn package, you must define a variable for each learning algorithm in advance, specifying its parameters. Therefore you define two variables, k_means and mb_k_means, which requires three clusters, a smart initialization procedure (called 'k-means++'), and raising the number of maximum iterations to a high figure (don't worry, usually the algorithm is quite fast). Finally, you fit the features, and after a short delay, the computations complete.

```
from sklearn.cluster import MiniBatchKMeans, KMeans
k_means = KMeans(n_clusters=3, init='k-means++',
                 max_iter=999, n_init=1, random_state=101)
mb_k_means = MiniBatchKMeans(n_clusters=3, init='k-means++',
         max_iter=999, batch_size=10, n_init=1, random_state=101)

k_means.fit(features)
mb_k_means.fit(features)
```

The following code prints a nice plot on your screen of how points (our examples of flowers) distribute on a map made of sepal length and width, as shown in Figure 2-2. If you're working with IPython Notebook, %matplotlib inline displays the chart inside your notebook.

```
%matplotlib inline
import matplotlib.pyplot as plt
plt.scatter(features[:,0], features[:,1], s=2**7, c=labels,
            edgecolors='white', alpha=0.85, cmap='autumn')
plt.grid() # adds a grid
plt.xlabel(data.feature_names[0]) # adds label to x axis
```

```
plt.ylabel(data.feature_names[1]) # adds label to y axis
# Printing centroids, first of regular K-means, then of mini-batch
plt.scatter(k_means.cluster_centers_[:,0], k_means.cluster_centers_[:,1],
            s=2**6, marker='s', c='white')
plt.scatter(mb_k_means.cluster_centers_[:,0],
            mb_k_means.cluster_centers_[:,1], s=2**8,
            marker='*', c='white')
for class_no in range(0,3): # We just annotate a point for each class
    plt.annotate(data.target_names[class_no],
                 (features[3+50*class_no,0],features[3+50*class_no,1]))
plt.show() # Showing the result
```

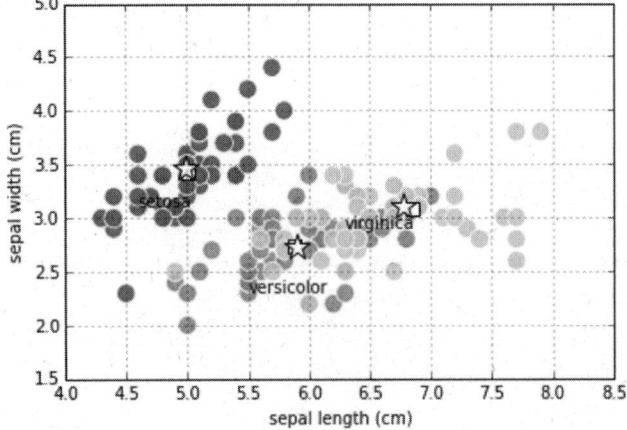

FIGURE 2-2: Clusters of iris species plotted on a chart based on sepal length and width.

What is noticeable about the plot is that it also displays the centroids — those from the standard algorithm as squares; those from the mini-batch version as stars — and they don't differ all that much. This fact demonstrates how the different learning procedures lead to almost identical conclusions. Sometimes it's amazing to see how even algorithms that are different may arrive at the same conclusions. When that doesn't happen, you might have too much variance in the estimates, and each algorithm could have a very different learning strategy; yet you'll notice that machine learning algorithms often tend to get the same strong signals (though in the end they make different use of them).

All the information about the algorithm is now stored in the variables. For instance, by typing **k_means.cluster_centers_**, you can get all the coordinates of the centroids elaborated by the K-means procedure.

Experimenting with how centroids converge

Though you can now compute the result and know that the different versions and runs of K-means tend to arrive at similar solutions, you still need to grasp how you reach the result. In this section's experiment, you follow how a centroid (the second one) changes along iterations by visualizing its vector of coordinates step by step along the optimization.

```
import numpy as np
np.set_printoptions(precision=3, suppress=True) # sets output 3 dec points
for iteration in range(1, 10):
    k_means = KMeans(n_clusters=3, init='random',
                    max_iter=iteration, n_init=1, random_state=101)
    k_means.fit(features)
    print ("Iteration: % - 2nd centroid: %s" %
           (iteration, k_means.cluster_centers_[1]))

Iteration: 1 - 2nd centroid: [ 5.362  3.763  1.512  0.275]
Iteration: 2 - 2nd centroid: [ 4.959  3.352  1.47   0.246]
Iteration: 3 - 2nd centroid: [ 4.914  3.268  1.539  0.275]
Iteration: 4 - 2nd centroid: [ 4.878  3.188  1.58   0.295]
Iteration: 5 - 2nd centroid: [ 4.833  3.153  1.583  0.294]
Iteration: 6 - 2nd centroid: [ 4.8    3.109  1.606  0.303]
Iteration: 7 - 2nd centroid: [ 4.783  3.087  1.62   0.307]
Iteration: 8 - 2nd centroid: [ 4.776  3.072  1.621  0.297]
Iteration: 9 - 2nd centroid: [ 4.776  3.072  1.621  0.297]
```

Observing the adjusting values as iterations proceed, the rate of change diminishes until later iterations, when the change from each passage is so small that you can't see it without using many decimal places.

The clustering module in scikit-learn contains all the presented versions of K-means plus other clustering algorithms. You can find it at http://scikit-learn.org/stable/modules/classes.html#module-sklearn.cluster. In addition, R has a rich and efficient implementation of K-means. You can find it in the library stats (https://stat.ethz.ch/R-manual/R-devel/library/stats/html/kmeans.html).

The next experiment, which uses R, aims to check how good the K-means algorithm is at guessing the real clusters in the Iris data set. This experiment is a challenging task because various studies say that it isn't possible to achieve it accurately (see https://en.wikipedia.org/wiki/Iris_flower_data_set for details).

```
# We call the libraries
library(datasets)
library(class)

# We divide our dataset into answer and features
answer <- iris[,5]
features <- iris[,1:4]
X <- princomp(features)$scores

clustering <- kmeans(x=X, centers=3, iter.max = 999, nstart = 10,
        algorithm = "Hartigan-Wong")

print (clustering$tot.withinss)
table(answer, clustering$cluster)

answer         1  2  3
  setosa       0 50  0
  versicolor   2  0 48
  virginica   36  0 14
```

Working with the Iris data set allows tests on both real data using a ground truth (which is another way of saying that the examples are labeled). This example first creates a principal component analysis (PCA) solution and then computes a three-cluster solution. The PCA removes the correlations and standardizes the variables at the same time, so you can be confident that the Euclidean distance measurement that K-means computes works well. Finally, you print a confusion matrix, a matrix representation of where the correct answers are in the rows and the predicted ones are in columns. Glancing at the confusion matrix, you notice that 14 flowers of the *Virginica* species are classified as *Versicolor.* K-means wasn't able to recover the correct natural classes at this time. Usually, increasing the number of clusters solves such problems, although doing so may generate many clusters that differ only slightly from each other. From a machine learning point of view, having more clusters is not all that much fuss, but for humans, it may render understanding more complicated. This experiment tests different clustering solutions in an iterative loop with the output shown in Figure 2-3.

```
w <- rep(0,10)
for (h in 1:10) {
  clustering <- kmeans(x=X, centers=h, iter.max = 999, nstart = 10,
                algorithm = "Hartigan-Wong")
  w[h] <- clustering$tot.withinss
}

plot(w, type='o')
```

```
clustering <- kmeans(x=X, centers=8, iter.max = 999, nstart = 10,
             algorithm = "Hartigan-Wong")

table(answer, clustering$cluster)

answer        1  2  3  4  5  6  7  8
  setosa     22 28  0  0  0  0  0  0
  versicolor  0  0  3 20  0  9 18  0
  virginica   0  0 15  1 22  0  0 12

plot(X[,c(1,2)], col = clustering$cluster)
points(clustering$centers[,c(1,2)], col = 1:8,
    pch = 15, cex = 1.2)
```

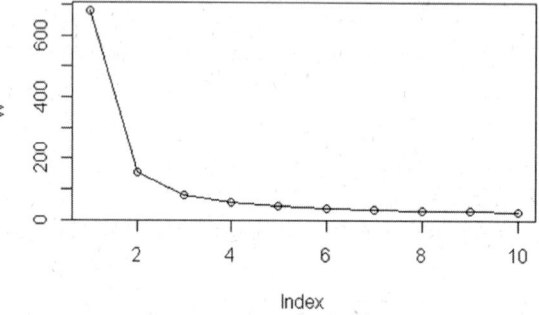

FIGURE 2-3: Plot of a within-cluster sum of squares regarding different cluster solutions.

A loop over many solutions reveals that after a four-cluster solution, improvements are slight. Such is a quite common (and disappointing) situation, and the best heuristic is to see when the WSS curve flattens out. In this case, the right solution is eight clusters because you can test it and visually confirm that this solution is the best in separating classes, as shown in Figure 2-4.

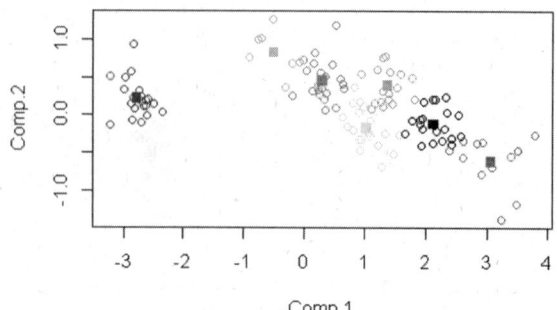

FIGURE 2-4: Iris species represented by eight clusters.

REMEMBER

When working with real data, you rarely have a ground truth to check. Trust your intuition and the cluster quality measures if you can't rely on a test. If you're not satisfied with the solutions, look for ways to add and remove one or more of your features.

Searching for Classification by k-Nearest Neighbors

No matter if the problem is to guess a number or a class, the idea behind the learning strategy of the k-Nearest Neighbors (kNN) algorithm is always the same. The algorithm finds the most similar observations to the one you have to predict and from which you derive a good intuition of the possible answer by averaging the neighboring values, or by picking the most frequent answer class among them.

The learning strategy in a kNN is more like memorization. It's just like remembering what the answer should be when the question has certain characteristics (based on circumstances or past examples) rather than really knowing the answer, because you understand the question by means of specific classification rules. In a sense, kNN is often defined as a lazy algorithm because no real learning is done at the training time, just data recording.

Being a lazy algorithm implies that kNN is quite fast at training but very slow at predicting. (Most of the searching activities and calculations on the neighbors is done at that time.) It also implies that the algorithm is quite memory-intensive because you have to store your data set in memory (which means that there's a limit to possible applications when dealing with big data). Ideally, kNN can make the difference when you're working on classification and you have many labels to deal with (for instance, when a software agent posts a tag on a social network or when proposing a selling recommendation). kNN can easily deal with hundreds of labels, whereas other learning algorithms have to specify a different model for each label.

Usually, kNN works out the neighbors of an observation after using a measure of distance such as Euclidean (the most common choice) or Manhattan (works better when you have many redundant features in your data). No absolute rules exist concerning what distance measure is best to use. It really depends on the implementation you have. You also have to test each distance as a distinct hypothesis and verify by cross-validation as to which measure works better with the problem you're solving.

Leveraging the Correct K Parameter

The k parameter is the one you can work on tuning to make a kNN algorithm perform well in prediction and regression. The following sections describe how to use the k parameter to tune the kNN algorithm.

Understanding the k parameter

The k value, an integer number, is the number of neighbors that the algorithm has to consider in order to figure out an answer. The smaller the k parameter, the more the algorithm will adapt to the data you are presenting, risking overfitting but nicely fitting complex separating boundaries between classes. The larger the k parameter, the more it abstracts from the ups and downs of real data, which derives nicely smoothed curves between classes in data, but does so at the expense of accounting for irrelevant examples.

TIP

As a rule of thumb, first try the nearest integer of the square root of the number of examples available as a k parameter in kNN. For instance, if you have 1,000 examples, start with k = 31 and then decrease the value in a grid search backed up by cross-validation.

Using irrelevant or unsuitable examples is a risk that a kNN algorithm takes as the number of examples it uses for its distance function increases. The previous illustration of the problem of data dimensions shows how to compute a well-ordered data space as a library in which you could look for similar books in the same bookshelf, bookcase, and section. However, things won't look so easy when the library has more than one floor. At that point, books upstairs and downstairs are not necessarily similar; therefore being near but on a different floor won't assure that the books are similar. Adding more dimensions weakens the role of useful ones, but that is just the beginning of your trouble.

Now imagine having more than the three dimensions in daily life (four if you consider time). The more dimensions, the more space you gain in your library. (As in geometry, you multiply dimensions to get an idea of the volume.) At a certain point, you will have so much space that your books will fit easily with space left over. For instance, if you have 20 binary variables representing your library, you could have 2 raised to the 20^{th} power combinations, that is, 1,048,576 possible different bookcases. It's great to have a million bookcases, but if you don't have a million books to fill them, most of your library will be empty. So you obtain a book and then look for similar books to place it with. All your nearby bookcases are actually empty, so you have to go far before finding another nonempty bookcase. Think about it: You start with *The Hitchhiker's Guide to the Galaxy* and end up having a book on gardening as its nearest neighbor. This is the curse of dimensionality.

The more dimensions, the more likely you are to experience some false similarity, misunderstanding far for near.

Using the right-sized k parameters alleviates the problem because the more neighbors you have to find, the further kNN has to look — but you have other remedies. Principal component analysis (PCA) can compress the space, making it denser and removing noise and irrelevant, redundant information. In addition, feature selection can do the trick, selecting only the features that can really help kNN find the right neighbors.

As explained in Book 8, Chapter 4 about validating machine learning tasks, a stepwise selection, checked by cross-validation, can make a kNN work well because it keeps only the features that are truly functional for the task.

kNN is an algorithm that's sensitive to outliers. Neighbors on the boundaries of your data cloud in the data space could be outlying examples, causing your predictions to become erratic. You need to clean your data before using it. Running a K-means first can help you identify outliers gathered into groups of their own. (Outliers love to stay in separate groups; you can view them as the hermit types in your data.) Also, keeping your neighborhood large can help you minimize (but sometimes not avoid completely) the problem at the expense of a lower fit to the data (more bias than overfitting).

Experimenting with a flexible algorithm

The kNN algorithm has slightly different implementations in R and Python. In R, the algorithm is found in the library class. The function is just for classification and uses only the Euclidean distance for locating neighbors. It does offer a convenient version with automatic cross-validation for discovering the best k value. There's also another R library, FNN (https://cran.r-project.org/web/packages/FNN/index.html), which contains one kNN variant for classification and another for regression problems. The peculiarity of the FNN functions is that they can deal with the complexity of distance computations using different algorithms, but the Euclidean distance is the only distance available.

Choosing and testing k values

The following R code experiment uses the cross-validated kNN from the library class. It looks for the best k value by cross-validation and then tests it on an out-of-sample portion of the data. Learning the correct hyper-parameters using cross-validation guarantees that you find the best value, not just for the single analyzed data but also for any other possible data arriving from the same source. Testing using out-of-sample data offers a realistic evaluation of the accuracy of

the learned model because the data was never used for any setting during the learning phase.

```
set.seed(seed=101)
out_of_sample <- sample(x=length(answer),25)

# in a loop we try values of k ranging from 1 to 15
for (h in 1:15) {
  in_sample_pred <- knn.cv(train=features[-out_of_sample,],
                      cl=answer[-out_of_sample],
                      k = h, l = 0, prob = FALSE, use.all = TRUE)
  # After getting the cross-validated predictions,
  # we calculate the accuracy
  accuracy <- sum(answer[-out_of_sample]==in_sample_pred) /
    length(answer[-out_of_sample])
  # We print the result
  print (paste("for k=",h," accuracy is:",accuracy))
}

[1] "for k= 1   accuracy is: 0.952"
[1] "for k= 2   accuracy is: 0.968"
[1] "for k= 3   accuracy is: 0.96"
[1] "for k= 4   accuracy is: 0.96"
[1] "for k= 5   accuracy is: 0.952"
[1] "for k= 6   accuracy is: 0.952"
[1] "for k= 7   accuracy is: 0.968"
[1] "for k= 8   accuracy is: 0.968"
[1] "for k= 9   accuracy is: 0.968"
[1] "for k= 10  accuracy is: 0.968"
[1] "for k= 11  accuracy is: 0.976"
[1] "for k= 12  accuracy is: 0.968"
[1] "for k= 13  accuracy is: 0.968"
[1] "for k= 14  accuracy is: 0.968"
[1] "for k= 15  accuracy is: 0.96"

out_sample_pred <- knn(train=features[-out_of_sample,],
                   test=features[out_of_sample,],
                   cl=answer[-out_of_sample], k = 11,
                   l = 0, prob = TRUE, use.all = TRUE)

print (table(answer[out_of_sample], out_sample_pred))
            out_sample_pred
            setosa versicolor virginica
            setosa versicolor virginica

  setosa         7          0         0
  versicolor     0         10         1
  virginica      0          0         7
```

The cross-validated search indicates that setting k to value 11 scores the best accuracy. The example then predicts a result using the untouched test set and verifies the results using a confusion matrix by cross-validating on rows containing real values against estimated values on columns. The performance is high, as expected, with just an Iris *Versicolor* example misclassified as an Iris *Virginica*.

Finding shapes in data

The second experiment with kNN uses the Python class from scikit-learn and demonstrates how such a simple algorithm is quite apt at learning shapes and nonlinear arrangements of examples in the data space. The block of code prepares a tricky data set: In two dimensions, two classes are arranged in bull's-eye concentric circles, as shown in Figure 2-5.

```
import numpy as np
from sklearn.datasets import make_circles, make_blobs
strange_data  = make_circles(n_samples=500, shuffle=True,
                             noise=0.15, random_state=101,
                             factor=0.5)
center = make_blobs(n_samples=100, n_features=2,
                    centers=1, cluster_std=0.1,
                    center_box=(0, 0))
first_half    = np.row_stack((strange_data[0][:250,:],
                center[0][:50,:]))
first_labels  = np.append(strange_data[1][:250],
                np.array([0]*50))
second_half   = np.row_stack((strange_data[0][250:,:],
                center[0][50:,:]))
second_labels = np.append(strange_data[1][250:],
                np.array([0]*50))

%matplotlib inline
import matplotlib.pyplot as plt
plt.scatter(first_half[:,0], first_half[:,1], s=2**7,
    c=first_labels, edgecolors='white',
         alpha=0.85, cmap='winter')
plt.grid() # adds a grid
plt.show() # Showing the result
```

After having built the data set, you can test the experiment by setting the classification algorithm to learn the patterns in data after fixing a neighborhood of 3 and set weights to be uniform (scikit-learn allows you to weight less distant observations when it's time to average them or pick the most frequent observations), and the Euclidean distance as metric. scikit-learn algorithms, in fact, allow you to both regress and classify using different metrics, such as Euclidean, Manhattan, or Chebyshev, as shown in this Python code.

FIGURE 2-5: The bull's-eye data set, a nonlinear cloud of points that is difficult to learn.

```
from sklearn.neighbors import KNeighborsClassifier
from sklearn.metrics import accuracy_score
kNN = KNeighborsClassifier(n_neighbors=3,
                           weights='uniform',
                           algorithm='auto',
                           metric='euclidean')
kNN.fit(first_half,first_labels)
print ("Learning accuracy score:%0.3f" %
       accuracy_score(y_true=second_labels,
                      y_pred=kNN.predict(second_half)))

Learning accuracy score:0.937
```

IN THIS CHAPTER

» Upgrading the perceptron to the interconnection paradigm

» Structuring neural architectures made of nodes and connections

» Getting a glimpse of the backpropagation algorithm

» Understanding what deep learning is and what it can achieve

Chapter 3
Hitting Complexity with Neural Networks

"Computers will overtake humans... within the next 100 years. When that happens, we need to make sure the computers have goals that align with ours."
— STEPHEN HAWKING

As you journey in the world of machine learning, you often see metaphors from the natural world to explain the details of algorithms. This chapter presents a family of learning algorithms that directly derives inspiration from how the brain works. They are neural networks, the core algorithms of the connectionists' tribe.

Starting with the idea of reverse-engineering how a brain processes signals, the connectionists base neural networks on biological analogies and their components, using brain terms such as neurons and axons as names. However, you'll discover that neural networks resemble nothing more than a sophisticated kind of linear regression when you check their math formulations. Yet these algorithms are extraordinarily effective against complex problems such as image and sound recognition, or machine language translation. They also execute quickly when predicting.

Well-devised neural networks use the name *deep learning* and are behind such power tools as Siri and other digital assistants. They are behind the more astonishing machine learning applications as well. For instance, you see them at work in this incredible demonstration by Microsoft CEO Rick Rashid, who is speaking in English while being simultaneously translated into Chinese: www.youtube.com/watch?v=Nu-nlQqFCKg.

If an AI revolution is about to happen, the increased learning capabilities of neural networks will likely drive it.

Learning and Imitating from Nature

The core neural network algorithm is the *neuron* (also called a *unit*). Many neurons arranged in an interconnected structure make up a neural network, with each neuron linking to the inputs and outputs of other neurons. Thus a neuron can input features from examples or the results of other neurons, depending on its location in the neural network.

Something similar to the neuron, the perceptron, appears in Book 9, Chapter 1, although it uses a simpler structure and function. When the psychologist Rosenblatt conceived the perceptron, he thought of it as a simplified mathematical version of a brain neuron. A perceptron takes values as inputs from the nearby environment (the data set), weights them (as brain cells do, based on the strength of the in-bound connections), sums all the weighted values, and activates when the sum exceeds a threshold. This threshold outputs a value of 1; otherwise, its prediction is 0. Unfortunately, a perceptron can't learn when the classes it tries to process aren't linearly separable. However, scholars discovered that even though a single perceptron couldn't learn the logical operation XOR shown in Figure 3-1 (the exclusive or, which is true only when the inputs are dissimilar), two perceptrons working together could.

Neurons in a neural network are a further evolution of the perceptron: They take many weighted values as inputs, sum them, and provide the summation as the result, just as a perceptron does. However, they also provide a more sophisticated transformation of the summation, something that the perceptron can't do. In observing nature, scientists noticed that neurons receive signals but don't always release a signal of their own. It depends on the amount of signal received. When a neuron acquires enough stimuli, it fires an answer; otherwise, it remains silent. In a similar fashion, algorithmic neurons, after receiving weighted values, sum them and use an *activation function* to evaluate the result, which transforms it in a nonlinear way. For instance, the activation function can release a zero value unless the input achieves a certain threshold, or it can dampen or enhance a value by nonlinearly rescaling it, thus transmitting a rescaled signal.

FIGURE 3-1: Learning logical XOR using a single separating line isn't possible.

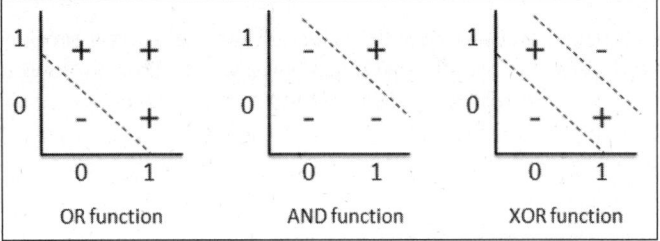

A neural network has different activation functions, as shown in Figure 3-2. The linear function doesn't apply any transformation, and it's seldom used because it reduces a neural network to a regression with polynomial transformations. Neural networks commonly use the sigmoid or the hyperbolic tan.

FIGURE 3-2: Plots of different activation functions.

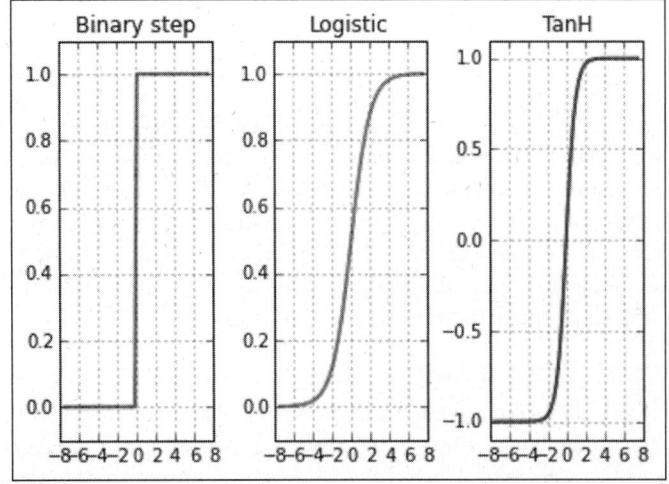

The figure shows how an input (expressed on the horizontal axis) can transform an output into something else (expressed on the vertical axis). The examples show a binary step, a logistic, and a tangent hyperbolic activation function.

TIP

You learn more about activation functions later in the chapter, but note for now that activation functions clearly work well in certain ranges of x values. For this reason, you should always rescale inputs to a neural network using statistical standardization (zero mean and unit variance) or normalize the input in the range from 0 to 1 or from −1 to 1.

Going forth with feed-forward

In a neural network, you have first to consider the architecture, which is how the neural network components are arranged. Contrary to other algorithms, which

CHAPTER 3 **Hitting Complexity with Neural Networks** 645

have a fixed pipeline that determines how algorithms receive and process data, neural networks require you to decide how information flows by fixing the number of units (the neurons) and their distribution in layers, as shown in Figure 3-3.

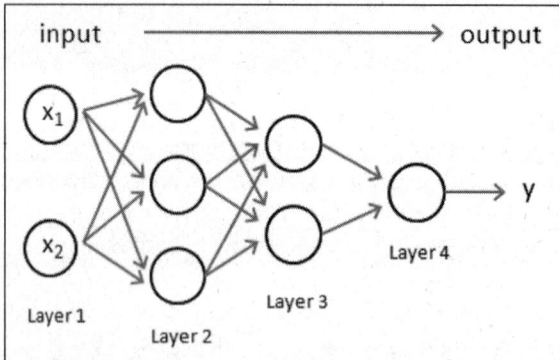

FIGURE 3-3: An example of the architecture of a neural network.

The figure shows a simple neural architecture. Note how the layers filter information in a progressive way. This is a feed-forward input because data feeds one way forward into the network. Connections exclusively link the units in one layer with the units in the following layer (information flow from left to right). No connections exist between units in the same layer or with units outside the next layer. Moreover, the information pushes forward (from the left to the right). Processed data never returns to previous neuron layers.

Using a neural network is like using a stratified filtering system for water: You pour the water from above, and the water is filtered at the bottom. The water has no way to go back; it just goes forward and straight down, and never laterally. In the same way, neural networks force data features to flow through the network and mix with each other only according to the network's architecture. By using the best architecture to mix features, the neural network creates new composed features at every layer and helps achieve better predictions. Unfortunately, there is no way to determine the best architecture without empirically trying different solutions and testing whether output data helps predict your target values after flowing through the network.

The first and last layers play an important role. The first layer, called the *input layer*, picks up the features from each data example processed by the network. The last layer, called the *output layer*, releases the results.

A neural network can process only numeric, continuous information; it can't be constrained to work with qualitative variables (for example, labels indicating a quality such as red, blue, or green in an image). You can process qualitative variables by transforming them into a continuous numeric value, such as a series of

binary values, as discussed in Book 8, Chapter 2 in the material about working with data. When a neural network processes a binary variable, the neuron treats the variable as a generic number and turns the binary values into other values, even negative ones, by processing across units.

Note the limitation of dealing only with numeric values, because you can't expect the last layer to output a nonnumeric label prediction. When dealing with a regression problem, the last layer is a single unit. Likewise, when you're working with a classification and you have output that must choose from a number n of classes, you should have n terminal units, each one representing a score linked to the probability of the represented class. Therefore, when classifying a multi-class problem such as iris species (as in the Iris data set demonstration found in Book 9, Chapter 2), the final layer has as many units as species. For instance, in the classical iris classification example, created by the famous statistician Fisher, you have three classes: setosa, versicolor, and virginica. In a neural network based on the Iris data set, you therefore have three units representing one of the three iris species. For each example, the predicted class is the one that gets the higher score at the end.

In some neural networks, there are special final layers, called a softmax, which can adjust the probability of each class based on the values received from a previous layer.

In classification, the final layer may represent both a partition of probabilities thanks to softmax (a multiclass problem in which total probabilities sum to 100 percent) or an independent score prediction (because an example can have more classes, which is a multilabel problem in which summed probabilities can be more than 100 percent). When the classification problem is a binary classification, a single node suffices. Also, in regression, you can have multiple output units, each one representing a different regression problem (for instance, in forecasting, you can have different predictions for the next day, week, month, and so on).

Going even deeper down the rabbit hole

Neural networks have different layers, each one having its own weights. Because the neural network segregates computations by layers, knowing the reference layer is important because it means accounting for certain units and connections. Thus you can refer to every layer using a specific number and generically talk about each layer using the letter l.

Each layer can have a different number of units, and the number of units located between two layers dictates the number of connections. By multiplying the number of units in the starting layer with the number in the following layer, you can determine the total number of connections between the two: *number of connections*$^{(l)}$ = *units*$^{(l)}$*units*$^{(l+1)}$.

A matrix of weights, usually named with the uppercase Greek letter theta (Θ), represents the connections. For ease of reading, the book uses the capital letter W, which is a fine choice because it is a matrix. Thus you can use W^1 to refer to the connection weights from layer 1 to layer 2, W^2 for the connections from layer 2 to layer 3, and so on.

REMEMBER

You may see references to the layers between the input and the output as *hidden layers* and count layers starting from the first hidden layer. This is just a different convention from the one used in the book. The examples in the book always start counting from the input layer, so the first hidden layer is layer number 2.

Weights represent the strength of the connection between neurons in the network. When the weight of the connection between two layers is small, it means that the network dumps values flowing between them and signals that taking this route won't likely influence the final prediction. On the contrary, a large positive or negative value affects the values that the next layer receives, thus determining certain predictions. This approach is clearly analogous to brain cells, which don't stand alone but are in connection with other cells. As someone grows in experience, connections between neurons tend to weaken or strengthen to active or deactivate certain brain network cell regions, causing other processing or an activity (a reaction to a danger, for instance, if the processed information signals a life-threatening situation).

Now that you know some conventions regarding layers, units, and connections, you can start examining the operations that neural networks execute in detail. First, you can call inputs and outputs in different ways:

» **a:** The result stored in a unit in the neural network after being processed by the activation function (called *g*). This is the final output that is sent further along the network.

» **z:** The multiplication between a and the weights from the W matrix. z represents the signal going through the connections, analogous to water in pipes that flows at a higher or lower pressure depending on the pipe thickness. In the same way, the values received from the previous layer get higher or lower values because of the connection weights used to transmit them.

Each successive layer of units in a neural network progressively processes the values taken from the features, same as in a conveyor belt. As data transmits in the network, it arrives into each unit as a value produced by the summation of the values present in the previous layer and weighted by connections represented in the matrix W. When the data with added bias exceeds a certain threshold, the activation function increases the value stored in the unit; otherwise, it extinguishes the signal by reducing it. After processing by the activation function, the result

is ready to push forward to the connection linked to the next layer. These steps repeat for each layer until the values reach the end and you have a result, as shown in Figure 3-4.

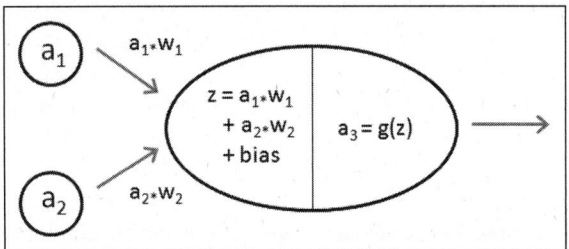

FIGURE 3-4: A detail of the feed-forward process in a neural network.

The figure shows a detail of the process that involves two units pushing their results to another unit. This event happens in every part of the network. When you understand the passage from two neurons to one, you can understand the entire feed-forward process, even when more layers and neurons are involved. For more explanation, here are the six steps used to produce a prediction in a neural network made of four layers (like the one shown earlier in Figure 3-3):

1. The first layer (notice the superscript 1 on a) loads the value of each feature in a different unit:

 $a^{(1)} = X$

 The weights of the connections bridging the input layer with the second layer are multiplied by the values of the units in the first layer. A matrix multiplication weights and sums the inputs for the second layer together.

 $z^{(2)} = W^{(1)} a^{(1)}$

2. The algorithm adds a bias constant to layer two before running the activation function. The activation function transforms the second-layer inputs. The resulting values are ready to pass to the connections.

 $a^{(2)} = g(z^{(2)} + bias^{(2)})$

3. The third-layer connections weigh and sum the outputs of layer two.

 $z^{(3)} = W^{(2)} a^{(2)}$

4. The algorithm adds a bias constant to layer three before running the activation function. The activation function transforms the layer-three inputs.

 $a^{(3)} = g(z^{(3)} + bias^{(3)})$

CHAPTER 3 Hitting Complexity with Neural Networks

5. The layer-three outputs are weighted and summed by the connections to the output layer.

 $$z^{(4)} = W^{(3)}a^{(3)}$$

6. Finally, the algorithm adds a bias constant to layer four before running the activation function. The output units receive their inputs and transform the input using the activation function. After this final transformation, the output units are ready to release the resulting predictions of the neural network.

 $$a^{(4)} = g(z^{(4)} + bias^{(4)})$$

The activation function plays the role of a signal filter, helping to select the relevant signals and avoid the weak and noisy ones (because it discards values below a certain threshold). Activation functions also provide nonlinearity to the output because they enhance or damp the values passing through them in a nonproportional way.

REMEMBER

The weights of the connections provide a way to mix and compose the features in a new way, creating new features in a way not too different from a polynomial expansion. The activation renders nonlinear the resulting recombination of the features by the connections. Both of these neural network components enable the algorithm to learn complex target functions that represent the relationship between the input features and the target outcome.

Getting back with backpropagation

From an architectural perspective, a neural network does a great job of mixing signals from examples and turning them into new features to achieve an approximation of complex nonlinear functions (functions that you can't represent as a straight line in the features' space). To create this capability, neural networks work as *universal approximators* (for more details, go to https://en.wikipedia.org/wiki/Universal_approximation_theorem), which means that they can guess any target function. However, you have to consider that one aspect of this feature is the capacity to model complex functions *(representation capability)*, and another aspect is the capability to learn from data effectively. Learning occurs in a brain because of the formation and modification of synapses between neurons, based on stimuli received by trial-and-error experience. Neural networks provide a way to replicate this process as a mathematical formulation called *backpropagation*.

Since its early appearance in the 1970s, the backpropagation algorithm has been given many fixes. Each neural network learning process improvement resulted in new applications and a renewed interest in the technique. In addition, the current deep learning revolution, a revival of neural networks, which were abandoned at the beginning of the 1990s, is due to key advances in the way neural networks

learn from their errors. As seen in other algorithms, the cost function activates the necessity to learn certain examples better (large errors correspond to high costs). When an example with a large error occurs, the cost function outputs a high value that is minimized by changing the parameters in the algorithm.

In linear regression, finding an update rule to apply to each parameter (the vector of beta coefficients) is straightforward. However, in a neural network, things are a bit more complicated. The architecture is variable, and the parameter coefficients (the connections) relate to each other because the connections in a layer depend on how the connections in the previous layers recombined the inputs. The solution to this problem is the backpropagation algorithm. Backpropagation is a smart way to propagate the errors back into the network and make each connection adjust its weights accordingly. If you initially feed-forward propagated information to the network, it's time to go backward and give feedback on what went wrong in the forward phase.

Discovering how backpropagation works isn't complicated, even though demonstrating how it works using formulas and mathematics requires derivatives and the proving of some formulations, which is quite tricky and beyond the scope of this book. To get a sense of how backpropagation operates, start from the end of the network, just at the moment when an example has been processed and you have a prediction as an output. At this point, you can compare it with the real result and, by subtracting the two results, get the difference, which is the error. Now that you know the mismatch of the results at the output layer, you can progress backward in order to distribute it along all the units in the network.

The cost function of a neural network for classification is based on cross-entropy (as seen in logistic regression):

$$Cost = y * \log(h_W(X)) + (1-y) * \log(1 - h_W(X))$$

This is a formulation involving logarithms. It refers to the prediction produced by the neural network and expressed as $h_W(X)$ (which reads as the result of the network given connections W and X as input). To make things easier, when thinking of the cost, it helps to simply think of the formulation as computing the offset between the expected results and the neural network output.

The first step in transmitting the error back into the network relies on backward multiplication. Because the values fed to the output layer are made of the contributions of all units, proportional to the weight of their connections, you can redistribute the error according to each contribution. For instance, the vector of errors of a layer n in the network, a vector indicated by the Greek letter delta (δ), is the result of the following formulation:

$$\delta^{(n)} = W^{(n)T} * \delta^{(n+1)}$$

This formula says that, starting from the final delta, you can continue redistributing delta going backward in the network and using the weights you used to push forward the value to partition the error to the different units. In this way, you can get the terminal error redistributed to each neural unit, and you can use it to recalculate a more appropriate weight for each network connection to minimize the error. To update the weights W of layer l, you just apply the following formula:

$$W^{(l)} = W^{(l)} + \eta * \delta^{(l)} * g'(z^{(l)}) * a^{(l)}$$

It may appear to be a puzzling formula at first sight, but it is a summation, and you can discover how it works by looking at its elements. First, look at the function g'. It's the first derivative of the activation function g, evaluated by the input values z. In fact, this is the gradient descent method. Gradient descent determines how to reduce the error measure by finding, among the possible combinations of values, the weights that most reduce the error.

The Greek letter eta (η), sometimes also called alpha (α) or epsilon (ε) depending on the textbook you consult, is the learning rate. As found in other algorithms, it reduces the effect of the update suggested by the gradient descent derivative. In fact, the direction provided may be only partially correct or just roughly correct. By taking multiple small steps in the descent, the algorithm can take a more precise direction toward the global minimum error, which is the target you want to achieve (that is, a neural network producing the least possible prediction error).

Different methods are available for setting the right eta value, because the optimization largely depends on it. One method sets the eta value starting high and reduces it during the optimization process. Another method variably increases or decreases eta based on the improvements obtained by the algorithm: Large improvements call a larger eta (because the descent is easy and straight); smaller improvements call a smaller eta so that the optimization will move slower, looking for the best opportunities to descend. Think of it as being on a tortuous path in the mountains: You slow down and try not to be struck or thrown off the road as you descend.

TIP

Most implementations offer an automatic setting of the correct eta. You need to note this setting's relevance when training a neural network because it's one of the important parameters to tweak to obtain better predictions, together with the layer architecture.

Weight updates can happen in different ways with respect to the training set of examples:

» **Online mode:** The weight update happens after every example traverses the network. In this way, the algorithm treats the learning examples as a stream

from which to learn in real time. This mode is perfect when you have to learn *out-of-core,* that is, when the training set can't fit into RAM memory. However, this method is sensitive to outliers, so you have to keep your learning rate low. (Consequently, the algorithm is slow to converge to a solution.)

» **Batch mode:** The weight update happens after seeing all the examples in the training set. This technique makes optimization fast and less subject to having variance appear in the example stream. In batch mode, the backpropagation considers the summed gradients of all examples.

» **Mini-batch (or stochastic) mode:** The weight update happens after the network has processed a subsample of randomly selected training set examples. This approach mixes the advantages of online mode (low memory usage) and batch mode (a rapid convergence), while introducing a random element (the subsampling) to avoid having the gradient descent stuck in a local minima.

Struggling with Overfitting

Given the neural network architecture, you can imagine how easily the algorithm could learn almost anything from data, especially if you added too many layers. In fact, the algorithm does so well that its predictions are often affected by a high estimate variance called *overfitting*. Overfitting causes the neural network to learn every detail of the training examples, which makes it possible to replicate them in the prediction phase. But apart from the training set, it won't ever correctly predict anything different. The following sections discuss some of the issues with overfitting in more detail.

Understanding the problem

When you use a neural network for a real problem, you have to take some cautionary steps in a much stricter way than you do with other algorithms. Neural networks are frailer and more prone to relevant errors than other machine learning solutions.

First, you carefully split your data into training, validation, and test sets. Before the algorithm learns from data, you must evaluate the goodness of your parameters: architecture (the number of layers and nodes in them); activation functions; learning parameter; and number of iterations. In particular, the architecture offers great opportunities to create powerful predictive models at a high risk of overfitting. The learning parameter controls how fast a network learns from data, but it may not suffice in preventing overfitting the training data.

You have two possible solutions to this problem:

» The first solution is *regularization*, as in linear and logistic regression. You can sum all connection coefficients, squared or in absolute value, to penalize models with too many coefficients with high values (achieved by L2 regularization) or with values different from zero (achieved by L1 regularization).

» The second solution is also effective because it controls when overfitting happens. It's called *early-stop* and works by checking the cost function on the validation set as the algorithm learns from the training set.

TIP

You may not realize when your model starts overfitting. The cost function calculated using the training set keeps improving as optimization progresses. However, as soon as you start recording noise from the data and stop learning general rules, you can check the cost function on an out-of-sample (the validation sample). At some point, you'll notice that it stops improving and starts worsening, which means that your model has reached its learning limit.

Opening the black box

The best way to learn how to build a neural network is to build one. Python offers a wealth of possible implementations for neural networks and deep learning. Python has libraries such as Theano (http://deeplearning.net/software/theano), which allows complex computations at an abstract level, and more practical packages, such as Lasagne (https://github.com/Lasagne/Lasagne), which allows you to build neural networks, though it still requires some abstractions. For this reason, you need wrappers, such as nolearn, which is compatible with scikit-learn (https://github.com/dnouri/nolearn), or Keras (https://github.com/fchollet/keras), which can also wrap the TensorFlow (https://github.com/tensorflow/tensorflow) library released by Google that has the potential to replace Theano as a software library for neural computation.

R provides libraries that are less complicated and more accessible, such as nnet (https://cran.r-project.org/web/packages/nnet/), AMORE (https://cran.r-project.org/web/packages/AMORE/), and neuralnet (https://cran.r-project.org/web/packages/neuralnet/). These brief examples in R show how to train both a classification network (on the Iris data set) and a regression network (on the Boston data set). Starting from classification, the following code loads the data set and splits it into training and test sets:

```
library(neuralnet)

target <- model.matrix( ~ Species&#x00A0;- 1, data=iris )
colnames(target) <- c("setosa", "versicolor", "virginica")
```

```
set.seed(101)
index <- sample(1:nrow(iris), 100)

train_predictors <- iris[index, 1:4]
test_predictors  <- iris[-index, 1:4]
```

Because neural networks rely on gradient descent, you need to standardize or normalize the inputs. Normalizing is better so that the minimum is zero and the maximum is one for every feature. Naturally, you learn how to make the numeric conversion using the training set only in order to avoid any chance of using information from the test out-of-sample.

```
min_vector   <- apply(train_predictors, 2, min)
range_vector <- apply(train_predictors, 2, max) -
  apply(train_predictors, 2, min)

train_scaled <- cbind(scale(train_predictors,
                            min_vector, range_vector),
                            target[index,])
test_scaled  <- cbind(scale(test_predictors,
                            min_vector, range_vector),
                            target[-index,])

summary(train_scaled)
```

When the training set is ready, you can train the model to guess three binary variables, with each one representing a class. The output is a value for each class proportional to its probability of being the real class. You pick a prediction by taking the highest value. You can also visualize the network by using the internal plot and thus seeing the neural network architecture and the assigned weights, as shown in Figure 3-5.

```
set.seed(102)
nn_iris <- neuralnet(setosa + versicolor + virginica ~
                     Sepal.Length + Sepal.Width
                     + Petal.Length + Petal.Width,
                     data=train_scaled, hidden=c(2),
                     linear.output=F)

plot(nn_iris)

predictions <- compute(nn_iris, test_scaled[,1:4])
y_predicted <- apply(predictions$net.result,1,which.max)
y_true <- apply(test_scaled[,5:7],1,which.max)
confusion_matrix <- table(y_true, y_predicted)
accuracy <- sum(diag(confusion_matrix)) /
  sum(confusion_matrix)
```

```
print (confusion_matrix)
print (paste("Accuracy:",accuracy))
```

FIGURE 3-5:
You can plot a trained neural network.

The following example demonstrates how to predict house values in Boston, using the Boston data set. The procedure is the same as in the previous classification, but here you have a single output unit. The code also plots the test set's predicted results against the real values to verify the good fit of the model.

```
no_examples <- nrow(Boston)
features <- colnames(Boston)

set.seed(101)
index <- sample(1:no_examples, 400)

train <- Boston[index,]
test  <- Boston[-index,]

min_vector <- apply(train,2,min)
range_vector <- apply(train,2,max) - apply(train,2,min)
scaled_train <- scale(train,min_vector,range_vector)
scaled_test  <- scale(test, min_vector,range_vector)

formula = paste("medv ~", paste(features[1:13],
                                collapse='+'))
nn_boston <- neuralnet(formula, data=scaled_train,
                       hidden=c(5,3), linear.output=T)
predictions <- compute(nn_boston, scaled_test[,1:13])
predicted_values <- (predictions$net.result *
                     range_vector[14]) + min_vector[14]
```

```
RMSE <- sqrt(mean((test[,14] - predicted_values)^2))
print (paste("RMSE:",RMSE))
plot(test[,14],predicted_values, cex=1.5)
abline(0,1,lwd=1)
```

Introducing Deep Learning

After backpropagation, the next improvement in neural networks led to deep learning. Research continued in spite of AI winter and neural networks started to take advantage of the developments in CPUs and GPUs (the graphic processing units better known for their application in gaming but which are actually powerful computing units for matrix and vector calculations). These technologies make training neural networks an achievable task in a shorter time and accessible to more people. Research also opened a world of new applications. Neural networks can learn from huge amounts of data, and because they're more prone to high variance than to bias, they can take advantage of big data, creating models that continuously perform better, depending on the amounts of data you feed them. However, you need large, complex networks for certain applications (to learn complex features, such as the characteristics of a series of images) and thus incur problems like the vanishing gradient.

In fact, when training a large network, the error redistributes among the neurons favoring the layers nearest to the output layer. Layers that are further away receive smaller errors, sometimes too small, making training slow if not impossible. Thanks to the studies of scholars such as Geoffrey Hinton, new turnarounds help avoid the problem of the vanishing gradient. The result definitely helps a larger network, but deep learning isn't just about neural networks with more layers and units.

In addition, something inherently qualitative changed in deep learning as compared to shallow neural networks, shifting the paradigm in machine learning from feature creation (features that make learning easier) to feature learning (complex features automatically created on the basis of the actual features). Big players such as Google, Facebook, Microsoft, and IBM spotted the new trend and since 2012 have started acquiring companies and hiring experts (Hinton now works with Google; LeCun leads Facebook AI research) in the new fields of deep learning. The Google Brain project, run by Andrew Ng and Jeff Dean, put together 16,000 computers to calculate a deep learning network with more than a billion weights, thus enabling unsupervised learning from YouTube videos.

There is a reason why the quality of deep learning is different. Of course, part of the difference is the increased usage of GPUs. Together with parallelism (more

computers put in clusters and operating in parallel), GPUs allow you to successfully apply pretraining, new activation functions, convolutional networks, and *drop-out*, a special kind of regularization different from L1 and L2. In fact, it has been estimated that a GPU can perform certain operations 70 times faster than any CPU, allowing a cut in training times for neural networks from weeks to days or even hours (for reference, see http://robotics.stanford.edu/~ang/papers/icml09-LargeScaleUnsupervisedDeepLearningGPU.pdf).

Both pretraining and new activation functions help solve the problem of the vanishing gradient. New activation functions offer better derivative functions, and pretraining helps start a neural network with better initial weights that require just a few adjustments in the latter parts of the network. Advanced pretraining techniques such as restricted Boltzmann machines (https://en.wikipedia.org/wiki/Restricted_Boltzmann_machine), autoencoders (https://en.wikipedia.org/wiki/Autoencoder), and deep belief networks (https://en.wikipedia.org/wiki/Deep_belief_network) elaborate data in an unsupervised fashion by establishing initial weights that don't change much during the training phase of a deep learning network. Moreover, they can produce better features representing the data and thus achieve better predictions.

Given the high reliance on neural networks for image recognition tasks, deep learning has achieved great momentum thanks to a certain type of neural network, the convolutional neural networks. Discovered in the 1980s, such networks now bring about astonishing results because of the many deep learning additions (for reference, see http://rodrigob.github.io/are_we_there_yet/build/classification_datasets_results.html).

To understand the idea behind convolutional neural networks, think about the convolutions as filters that, when applied to a matrix, transform certain parts of the matrix, make other parts disappear, and make other parts stand out. You can use convolution filters for borders or for specific shapes. Such filters are also useful for finding details in images that determine what the image shows. Humans know that a car is a car because it has a certain shape and certain features, not because they have previously seen every type of car possible. A standard neural network is tied to its input, and if the input is a pixel matrix, it recognizes shapes and features based on their position on the matrix. Convolution neural networks can elaborate images better than a standard neural network because

- » The network specializes particular neurons to recognize certain shapes (thanks to convolutions), so that same capability to recognize a shape doesn't need to appear in different parts of the network.

- » By sampling parts of an image into a single value (a task called *pooling*), you don't need to strictly tie shapes to a certain position (which would make it impossible to rotate them). The neural network can recognize the shape in

every rotation or distortion, thus assuring a high capacity of generalization of the convolutional network.

Finally, *drop-out* is a new type of regularization that is particularly effective with deep convolutional networks, but it also works with all deep learning architectures, which acts by temporarily and randomly removing connections between the neurons. This approach removes connections that collect only noise from data during training. Also, this approach helps the network learn to rely on critical information coming from different units, thus increasing the strength of the correct signals passed along the layers.

> **IN THIS CHAPTER**
>
> » Discovering why many guesses are better than one
>
> » Making uncorrelated trees work well together in Random Forests
>
> » Learning to map complex target functions piece by piece using boosting
>
> » Getting better predictions by averaging models

Chapter 4
Resorting to Ensembles of Learners

"Prediction is very difficult, especially if it's about the future."

— NILS BOHR

After discovering so many complex and powerful algorithms, you might be surprised to discover that a summation of simpler machine learning algorithms can often outperform the most sophisticated solutions. Such is the power of *ensembles*, groups of models made to work together to produce better predictions. The amazing thing about ensembles is that they are made up of groups of singularly nonperforming algorithms.

Ensembles don't work much differently from the collective intelligence of crowds, through which a set of wrong answers, if averaged, provides the right answer. Sir Francis Galton, the English Victorian age statistician known for having formulated the idea of correlation, narrated the anecdote of a crowd in a county fair that could guess correctly the weight of an ox after all the people's previous answers were averaged. You can find similar examples everywhere and easily re-create the experiment by asking friends to guess the number of sweets in a jar and averaging their answers. The more friends who participate in the game, the more precise the averaged answer.

Luck isn't what's behind the result — it's simply the *law of large numbers* in action (see more at `https://en.wikipedia.org/wiki/Law_of_large_numbers`). Even though an individual has a slim chance of getting the right answer, the guess is better than a random value. By cumulating guesses, the wrong answers tend to distribute themselves around the right one. Opposite wrong answers cancel each other when averaging, leaving the pivotal value around which all answers are distributed, which is the right answer. You can employ such an incredible fact in many practical ways (consensus forecasts in economics and political sciences are examples) and in machine learning.

Leveraging Decision Trees

Ensembles are based on a recent idea (formulated around 1990), but they leverage older tools, such as decision trees, which have been part of machine learning since 1950. As covered in Book 9, Chapter 1, decision trees at first looked quite promising and appealing to practitioners because of their ease of use and understanding. After all, a decision tree can easily do the following:

- » Handle mixed types of target variables and predictors, with very little or no feature preprocessing (missing values are handled almost automatically).
- » Ignore redundant variables and select only the relevant features.
- » Work out of the box, with no complex hyper-parameters to fix and tune.
- » Visualize the prediction process as a set of recursive rules arranged in a tree with branches and leaves, thus offering ease of interpretation.

Given the range of positive characteristics, you may wonder why practitioners slowly started distrusting this algorithm after a few years. The main reason is that the resulting models often have high variance in the estimates.

To grasp the critical problem of decision trees better, you can consider the problem visually. Think of the tricky situation of the bull's-eye problem that requires a machine learning algorithm to approximate nonlinear functions (as neural networks do) or to transform the feature space (as when using linear model with polynomial expansion or kernel functions in support vector machines). Figure 4-1 shows the squared decision boundary of a single decision tree (on the left) as compared to an ensemble of decision trees (on the right).

Decision trees partition the feature space into boxes and then use the boxes for classification or regression purposes. When the decision boundary that separates classes in a bull's-eye problem is an ellipse, decision trees can approximate it by using a certain number of boxes.

FIGURE 4-1: Comparing a single decision tree output (left) to an ensemble of decision trees (right).

The visual example seems to make sense and might give you confidence when you see the examples placed far from the decision boundary. However, in proximity of the boundary, things are quite different from how they appear. The decision boundary of the decision tree is very imprecise and its shape is extremely rough and squared. The issue is visible on bidimensional problems. It decisively worsens as feature dimensions increase and in the presence of noisy observations (observations that are somehow randomly scattered around the feature space). You can improve decision trees using some interesting heuristics that stabilize results from trees:

» Keep only the correctly predicted cases to retrain the algorithm.

» Build separate trees for misclassified examples.

» Simplify trees by pruning the less decisive rules.

Apart from these heuristics, the best trick is to build multiple trees using different samples and then compare and average their results. The example in Figure 4-1, shown previously, indicates that the benefit is immediately visible. As you build more trees, the decision boundary gets smoother, slowly resembling the hypothetical target shape.

Growing a forest of trees

Improving a decision tree by replicating it many times and averaging results to get a more general solution sounded like such a good idea that it spread, and practitioners created various solutions. When the problem is a regression, the technique averages results from the ensemble. However, when the trees deal with a classification task, the technique can use the ensemble as a voting system, choosing the most frequent response class as an output for all its replications.

TIP

When using an ensemble for regression, the standard deviation, calculated from all the ensemble's estimates for an example, can provide you with an estimate of how confident you can be about the prediction. The standard deviation shows how good a mean is. For classification problems, the percentage of trees predicting a

CHAPTER 4 **Resorting to Ensembles of Learners** 663

certain class is indicative of the level of confidence in the prediction, but you can't use it as a probability estimate because it's the outcome of a voting system.

Deciding on how to compute the solution of an ensemble happened quickly; finding the best way to replicate the trees in an ensemble required more research and reflection. The first solution is *pasting,* that is, sampling a portion of your training set. Initially proposed by Leo Breiman, pasting reduces the number of training examples, which can become a problem for learning from complex data. It shows its usefulness by reducing the learning sample noise (sampling fewer examples reduces the number of outliers and anomalous cases). After pasting, Professor Breiman also tested the effects of bootstrap sampling (sampling with replacement), which not only leaves out some noise (when you bootstrap, on average you leave out 37 percent of your initial example set) but, thanks to sampling repetition, also creates more variation in the ensembles, improving the results. This technique is called *bagging* (also known as *bootstrap aggregation*).

Bootstrapping appears in Book 8, Chapter 4 as part of validation alternatives. In bootstrapping, you sample the examples from a set to create a new set, allowing the code to sample the examples multiple times. Therefore, in a bootstrapped sample, you can find the same example repeated from one to many times.

Breiman noticed that results of an ensemble of trees improved when the trees differ significantly from each other (statistically, they're *uncorrelated*), which leads to the last technique transformation — the creation of mostly uncorrelated ensembles of trees. This approach performs predictions better than bagging. The transformation tweak samples both features and examples. Breiman, in collaboration with Adele Cutler, named the new ensemble Random Forests (RF).

Random Forests is a trademark of Leo Breiman and Adele Cutler. For this reason, open source implementations often have different names, such as `randomForest` in R or `RandomForestClassifier` in Python's scikit-learn.

RF is a classification (naturally multiclass) and regression algorithm that uses a large number of decision tree models built on different sets of bootstrapped examples and subsampled features. Its creator strove to make an algorithm that is easy to use (little preprocessing and few hyper-parameters to try) and understandable (the decision tree basis) and that can democratize the access of machine learning to nonexperts. In other words, because of its simplicity and immediate usage, RF can allow anyone to apply machine learning successfully. The algorithm works through a few repeated steps:

1. Bootstrap the training set multiple times. The algorithm obtains a new set to use to build a single tree in the ensemble during each bootstrap.

2. Randomly pick a partial feature selection in the training set to use for finding the best split variable every time you split the sample in a tree.

3. Create a complete tree using the bootstrapped examples. Evaluate new subsampled features at each split. Don't limit the full tree expansion to allow the algorithm to work better.

4. Compute the performance of each tree using examples you didn't choose in the bootstrap phase (out-of-bag estimates, or OOB). OOB examples provide performance metrics without cross-validation or using a test set (equivalent to out-of-sample).

5. Produce feature importance statistics and compute how examples associate in the tree's terminal nodes.

6. Compute an average or a vote on new examples when you complete all the trees in the ensemble. Declare for each of them the average estimate or the winning class as a prediction.

All these steps reduce both the bias and the variance of the final solution because the solution limits the bias. The solution builds each tree to its maximum possible extension, thus allowing a fine fitting of even complex target functions, which means that each tree is different from the others. It's not just a matter of building on different bootstrapped example sets: Each split taken by a tree is strongly randomized — the solution considers only a random feature selection. Consequently, even if an important feature dominates the others in terms of predictive power, the times a tree doesn't contain the selection allows the tree to find different ways of developing its branches and terminal leaves.

The main difference with bagging is this opportunity to limit the number of features to consider when splitting the tree branches. If the number of selected features is small, the complete tree will differ from others, thus adding uncorrelated trees to the ensemble. On the other hand, if the selection is small, the bias increases because the fitting power of the tree is limited. As always, determining the right number of features to consider for splitting requires that you use cross-validation or OOB estimate results.

GETTING MORE RANDOM FORESTS INFORMATION

You can find more information on Random Forests in Python at http://scikit-learn.org/stable/modules/ensemble.html#forest. The R version appears at https://cran.r-project.org/web/packages/randomForest/randomForest.pdf. For a general discussion of the algorithm, the best resource is the manual by Leo Breiman and Adele Cutler at www.stat.berkeley.edu/~breiman/RandomForests.

No problem arises in growing a high number of trees in the ensemble. You do need to consider the cost of the computational effort (completing a large ensemble takes a long time). A simple demonstration conveys how a Random Forests algorithm can solve a simple problem using a growing number of trees. Both R and Python offer good implementations of the algorithm. The R implementation has more parameters; the Python's implementation is easier to parallelize.

Because the test is computationally expensive, the example starts with the Python implementation and uses the digits data set.

```
import numpy as np
from sklearn import datasets
from sklearn.learning_curve import validation_curve
from sklearn.ensemble import RandomForestClassifier

digits = datasets.load_digits()
X,y = digits.data, digits.target
series = [10, 25, 50, 100, 150, 200, 250, 300]
RF = RandomForestClassifier(random_state=101)
train_scores, test_scores = validation_curve(RF,
        X, y, 'n_estimators', param_range=series,
            cv=10, scoring='accuracy',n_jobs=-1)
```

The example begins by importing functions and classes from scikit-learn: `numpy`, `datasets` module, `validation_curve` function, and `RandomForestClassifier`. The last item is scikit-learn's implementation of Random Forests for classification problems. The `validation_curve` function is particularly useful for the tests because it returns the cross-validated results of multiple tests performed on ensembles made of differing numbers of trees (similar to learning curves).

TIP

The example will build almost 11,000 decision trees. To make the example run faster, the code sets the `n_jobs` parameter to –1, allowing the algorithm to use all available CPU resources. This setting may not work on some computer configurations, which means setting `n_jobs` to 1. Everything will work, but it takes longer.

After completing the computations, the code outputs a plot that reveals how the Random Forests algorithm converges to a good accuracy after building a few trees, as shown in Figure 4-2. It also shows that adding more trees isn't detrimental to the results, although you may see some oscillations in accuracy due to estimate variances that even the ensemble can't control fully.

```
import matplotlib.pyplot as plt
%matplotlib inline
plt.figure()
plt.plot(series, np.mean(test_scores,axis=1), '-o')
plt.xlabel('number of trees')
```

```
plt.ylabel('accuracy')
plt.grid()
plt.show()
```

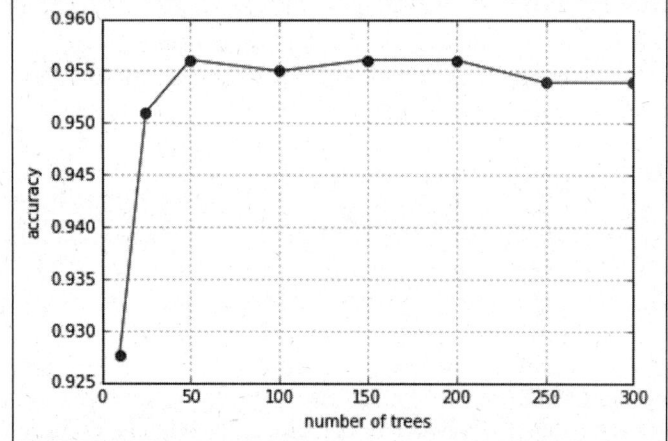

FIGURE 4-2:
Seeing the accuracy of ensembles of different sizes.

Understanding the importance measures

Random Forests have these benefits:

» Fit complex target functions, but have little risk in overfitting.

» Select the features they need automatically (although the random subsampling of features in branch splitting influences the process).

» Are easy to tune up because they have only one hyper-parameter, the number of subsampled features.

» Offer OOB error estimation, saving you from setting up verification by cross-validation or test set.

Note that each tree in the ensemble is independent from the others (after all, they should be uncorrelated), which means that you can build each tree in parallel to the others. Given that all modern computers have multiprocessor and multithread functionality, they can perform computations of many trees at the same time, which is a real advantage of RF over other machine learning algorithms.

A Random Forests ensemble can also provide additional output that could be helpful when learning from data. For example, it can tell you which features are more important than others. You can build trees by optimizing a purity measure (entropy or gini index) so that each split chooses the feature that improves the

measure the most. When the tree is complete, you check which features the algorithm uses at each split and sum the improvement when the algorithm uses a feature more than once. When working with an ensemble of trees, simply average the improvements that each feature provides in all the trees. The result shows you the ranking of the most important predictive features.

Practitioners call importance evaluation *gini importance* or *mean decrease impurity*. You can compute it in both R and Python algorithm implementations. Another way to estimate feature importance is *mean decrease accuracy,* and you obtain it as an output of the `randomForest` function in R. In this estimation, after the algorithm builds each tree, it replaces each feature with junk data and records the decrease in predictive power after doing so. If the feature is important, crowding it with casual data harms the prediction, but if it's irrelevant, the predictions are unchanged. Reporting the average performance decrease in all trees due to randomly changing the feature is a good indicator of a feature's importance.

TIP

You can use importance output from Random Forests to select features to use in the Random Forests or in another algorithm, such as a linear regression. The scikit-learn algorithm version offers a *tree-based feature selection,* which provides a way to select relevant features using the results from a decision tree or an ensemble of decision trees. You can use this kind of feature selection by employing the `SelectFromModel` function found in the `feature_selection` module (see http://scikit-learn.org/stable/modules/generated/sklearn.feature_selection.SelectFromModel.html).

To provide an interpretation of importance measures derived from Random Forests, this example tests the R implementation on the air quality data set, which reports the ozone level in the air of New York from May to September 1973. To make the example work, you must install the `randomForest` library. The following R example also uses the caret library, so if you haven't installed it yet, this is the right time to do so.

```
install.packages("randomForest")
install.packages("caret")
```

As a first step, the example uploads the data set and filters the examples whose ozone level data isn't missing.

```
library(caret)
library(randomForest)

# Data preparation
data(airquality, package="datasets")
dataset <- airquality[!(is.na(airquality$Ozone)),]
dataset[is.na(dataset)] <- -1
```

After filtering, the example finds all the missing data set values and sets them to −1. Because all the predictors (solar radiation, wind, temperature, month, and day) are positive, using a negative replacement value tells the Random Forests decision trees to split when the information that a value is missing is somehow predictive.

```
# Optimizing a tree
rf_grid <- expand.grid(.mtry=c(2,3,5))
rf_model<-train(Ozone ~ ., data=dataset, method="rf",
            trControl=trainControl(method="cv",number=10),
            metric = "RMSE",
            ntree=500,
            importance = TRUE)
print (rf_model)
```

The caret package provides a cross-validate check on the mtry hyper-parameter, which represents the number of features that each tree in the ensemble considers to be possible candidates at each split. Having the RMSE (root mean squared error) as a cost function, the caret output specifies the optimal choice is mtry=2. The train function of caret also provides the best model, whose importance rankings you can question using the importance function.

```
# Evaluate the importance of predictors
print (importance(rf_model$finalModel))

          %IncMSE IncNodePurity
Solar.R 10.624739     13946.509
Wind    20.944030     40084.320
Temp    39.697999     49512.349
Month    7.660438      4777.895
Day      3.911277      9845.365
```

You can read the importance output according to two measures: the cost function percentage increase, which is based on testing garbage data using the final model performance; and increased node purity, which is based on the internal improvement of the branch splits of the trees.

TIP

Sometimes the two rankings agree; sometimes they don't. The cost function percentage increase is a sensitivity analysis and is representative of the general feature importance. Thus you can use it in other models or for communicating insights. Increased node impurity is mostly focused on what the algorithm deems important, so it's excellent for feature selection to improve the ensemble.

Working with Almost Random Guesses

Thanks to bootstrapping, bagging produces variance reduction by inducing some variations in otherwise similar predictors. Bagging is most effective when the models created are different from each other and, though it can work with different kinds of models, it mostly performs with decision trees.

Bagging and its evolution, the Random Forests, aren't the only ways to leverage an ensemble. Instead of striving for ensemble elements' independence, a totally contrarian strategy is to create interrelated ensembles of simple machine learning algorithms in order to solve complex target functions. This approach is called *boosting*, which works by building models sequentially and training each model using information from the previous one.

Contrary to bagging, which prefers working with fully grown trees, boosting uses biased models, which are models that can predict simple target functions well. Simpler models include decision trees with a single split branch (called stumps), linear models, perceptrons, and Naïve Bayes algorithms. These models may not perform well when the target function to guess is complex (they're weak learners), but they can be trained fast and perform at least slightly better than a random lucky guess (which means that they can model a part of the target function).

Each algorithm in the ensemble guesses a part of the function well, so when summed together, they can guess the entire function. It's a situation not too different from the story of the blind men and the elephant (https://en.wikipedia.org/wiki/Blind_men_and_an_elephant). In the story, a group of blind men needs to discover the shape of an elephant, but each man can feel only a part of the whole animal. One man touches the tusk, one the ears, one the proboscides, one the body, and one the tail, which are different parts of the entire elephant. Only when they put what each one learned separately together can they figure out the elephant's shape. The information for the target function to guess is transmitted from one model to the other by modifying the original data set so that the ensemble can concentrate on the parts of the data set that have yet to be learned.

Bagging predictors with Adaboost

The first boosting algorithm formulated in 1995 was Adaboost (short for Adaptive Boosting) by Yoav Freund and Robert Schapire. Here is the Adaboost formulation:

$$H(X) = sign\left(\sum_{m=1}^{M} \alpha_m H_m(X)\right)$$

You may think that the Adaboost formulation is quite complicated at first sight, but you can make it simpler by examining it piece by piece. H(X) represents the prediction function, which transforms the features, the X matrix, into predictions. As an ensemble of models, the prediction function is a weighted summation of models similar to linear models.

The H(X) function provides results as a vector of signs (positive or negative) that point out classes in a binary prediction. (Adaboost is a binary prediction algorithm.) The signs derive from the summation of M models, each one distinguishable by a different m index (the generic model is $H_m(X)$). M is an integer number that you determine when training from data. (Deciding by testing on a validation set or using cross-validation is better.) In principle, each model fits a portion of the data, and having too many models means fitting the data too well, which is a kind of memorization that leads to overfitting, high variance of estimates, and, consequently, bad predictions. The number of added models is therefore a critical hyper-parameter.

Note that the algorithm multiplies each model $H_m(X)$ by an alpha value, which differs for each model. This is the weight of the model in the ensemble, and alpha is devised in a smart way because its value is related to the capacity of the model to produce the fewest prediction errors possible. You calculate alpha as follows:

$$\alpha_m = \frac{1}{2} * \log\left((1 - err_m)/err_m\right)$$

Alpha, according to this formulation, gets a larger value as the error of the model $H_m(X)$, pointed out by the notation err_m, gets smaller. The algorithm multiplies models with fewer errors by larger alpha values and thus such models play a more important role in the summation at the core of the Adaboost algorithm. Models that produce more prediction errors are weighted less.

The role of the coefficient alpha doesn't end with model weighting. Errors output by a model in the ensemble don't simply dictate the importance of the model in the ensemble itself but also modify the relevance of the training examples used for learning. Adaboost learns the data structure by using a simple algorithm a little at a time; the only way to focus the ensemble on different parts of the data is to assign weights. Assigning weights tells the algorithm to count an example according to its weight; therefore a single example can count the same as two, three, or even more examples. You can also make an example disappear from the learning process by making it count less and less. When considering weights, it becomes easier to reduce the cost function of the learning function by working on the examples that weigh more (more weight = more cost function reduction). Using weights effectively guides the learning process.

Initially, the examples, as in all the other learning algorithms seen so far, have the same contribution in the construction of the model. The optimization happens as usual. After creating the first model and estimating a total error, the algorithm checks each example to determine whether the prediction is correct. If correctly predicted, nothing happens; each example's weight remains the same as before. If misclassified, each example has its weight increased, and in the next iteration, examples with larger weight influence the model, placing a greater emphasis on finding a solution for the larger example.

At each iteration, the Adaboost algorithm is guided by weights to work on the part of data that's less predictable. In fact, you don't need to work on data that the algorithm can predict well. Weighting is a smart solution for conditioning learning, and gradient boosting machines refine and improve the process. Notice that the strategy here is different from RF. In RF, the goal is to create independent predictions; here, the predictors are chained together because earlier predictors determine how later predictors work. Because boosting algorithms rely on a chain of calculations, you can't easily parallelize the computations, so they're slower. You can express the formulation of the weight update in this way:

$$w_i = w_i * exp\left(\alpha_m * I\left(y_i \neq H_m(x_i)\right)\right)$$

The $I(y_i \neq H_m(x_i))$ function outputs 0 if the inequality is false and 1 if true. When true, the previous example weight is multiplied by the exponential of alpha. The algorithm modifies the resulting vector w by overweighting single misclassified cases by the most recent learning algorithm in the ensemble. Figuratively, learning in such a way is like taking a small improvement step each time toward the goal of a working predicting ensemble, and doing so without looking back, because after learning algorithms are summed, you can't change them anymore.

Remember the kinds of learning algorithms that work well with Adaboost. Usually they are weak learners, which means that they don't have much predictive power. Because Adaboost approximates complex functions using an ensemble of its parts, using machine learning algorithms that train quickly and have a certain bias makes sense, so the parts are simple. It's just like drawing a circle using a series of lines: Even though the line is straight, all you have to do is draw a polygon with as many sides as possible to approximate the circle. Commonly, decision stumps are the favorite weak learner for an Adaboost ensemble, but you can also successfully use linear models or Naïve Bayes algorithms. The following example leverages the bagging function provided by scikit-learn to determine whether decision trees, perceptron, or the k-Nearest Neighbors algorithm is best for handwritten digits recognition.

```
import numpy as np
from sklearn.ensemble import AdaBoostClassifier
from sklearn.tree import DecisionTreeClassifier
```

```
from sklearn.linear_model import Perceptron
from sklearn.naive_bayes import BernoulliNB
from sklearn.cross_validation import cross_val_score
from sklearn import datasets
digits = datasets.load_digits()
X,y = digits.data, digits.target

DT = cross_val_score(AdaBoostClassifier(
        DecisionTreeClassifier(),
        random_state=101) ,X, y,
        scoring='accuracy',cv=10)
P = cross_val_score(AdaBoostClassifier(
        Perceptron(), random_state=101,
        algorithm='SAMME') ,X, y,
        scoring='accuracy',cv=10)
NB = cross_val_score(AdaBoostClassifier(
        BernoulliNB(), random_state=101)
        ,X,y,scoring='accuracy',cv=10)

print ("Decision trees: %0.3f\nPerceptron: %0.3f\n"
        "Naive Bayes: %0.3f" %
        (np.mean(DT),np.mean(P), np.mean(NB)))
```

TIP

You can improve the performance of Adaboost by increasing the number of elements in the ensemble until the cross-validation won't report worsening results. The parameter you can increase is n_estimators, and it's currently set to 50. The weaker your predictor is, the larger your ensemble should be in order to perform the prediction well.

Boosting Smart Predictors

The Adaboost, previously discussed in this chapter, explains how the learning procedure creates a function after moving step by step toward a target, an analogy that's similar to the gradient descent described in Book 8, Chapter 3. This section describes the gradient boosting machines (GBM) algorithm, which uses gradient descent optimization to determine the right weights for learning in the ensemble. The resulting performances are indeed impressive, making GBM one of the most powerful predictive tools that you can learn to use in machine learning. Here is the GBM formulation:

$$f(x) = \sum_{m=1}^{M} v * h_m(x; w_m)$$

As in Adaboost, you start from the formulation. The GBM formulation requires that the algorithm make a weighted sum of multiple models. In fact, what changes the most is not the principle of how boosting works but rather the optimization process for getting the weight and the power of the summed functions, which weak learners can't determine.

In the preceding formula, M represents the number of total models and h represents the final function, which is the sum of a series of M models. Each model is different, hence the notation h_m, which translates into h1, h2, and so on. The difference between the learning functions of the series occurs because the models depend on both the features X and the examples weighted by the values of the vector w, which actually changes for every model.

Meeting again with gradient descent

Up to now, things aren't all that different from Adaboost. However, note that the algorithm weights each model by a constant factor, v, the shrinkage factor. This is where you start noticing the first difference between Adaboost and GBM. The fact is that v is just like alpha. However, here it's fixed and forces the algorithm to learn in any case, no matter the performance of the previously added learning function. Considering this difference, the algorithm builds the chain by reiterating the following sequence of operations:

$$f_m(x) = f_{m-1}(x) + v * h_m(x; w_m)$$

Look at the formula as it develops during training. After each iteration m, the algorithm sums the result of the previous models with a new model built on the same features, but on a differently weighted series of examples. This is represented in the form of the function h(X,w). The function shows the other difference with respect to Adaboost: The vector w isn't determined by the misclassified errors from the previous model but rather derives from a gradient descent optimization, which assigns weights with respect to a cost function, optionally of different kinds.

GBM can take on different problems: regression, classification, and ranking (for ordering examples), with each problem using a particular cost function. Gradient descent helps discover the set of vector w values that reduce the cost function. This calculation is equivalent to selecting the best examples to use to obtain a better prediction. The algorithm calculates vector w multiple times as the function h uses it, and each time, the algorithm adds the resulting function to the previous ones. The secret of GBM's performance lies in weights optimized by gradient descent, as well as in these three smart tricks:

- **Shrinkage:** Acts as a learning rate in the ensemble. As in gradient descent, you must fix an adequate learning rate to avoid jumping too far from the solution, which is the same as in GBM. Small shrinkage values lead to better predictions.

- **Subsampling:** Emulates the pasting approach. If each subsequent tree builds on a subsample of the training data, the result is a stochastic gradient descent. For many problems, the pasting approach helps reduce noise and influence by outliers, thus improving the results.

- **Trees of fixed size:** Fixing the tree depth used in boosting is like fixing a complexity limit to learning functions that you put into the ensemble, yet relying on more sophisticated trees than the stumps used in Adaboost. Depth acts like power in a polynomial expansion: The deeper the tree, the larger the expansion, thus increasing both the ability to intercept complex target functions and the risk of overfitting.

Both R and Python implement GBM using all the characteristics described in the chapter so far. You can learn more about the R implementation by reading about the gbm package at https://cran.r-project.org/web/packages/gbm/gbm.pdf. Python relies on an implementation in scikit-learn, which is discussed at http://scikit-learn.org/stable/modules/ensemble.html#gradient-boosting. The following example continues the previous test. In this case, you create a GBM classifier for the handwritten digits data set and test its performance (this example may run for a long time):

```python
import numpy as np
from sklearn.ensemble import GradientBoostingClassifier
from sklearn.cross_validation import cross_val_score
from sklearn import datasets
digits = datasets.load_digits()
X,y = digits.data, digits.target

GBM = cross_val_score(
    GradientBoostingClassifier(n_estimators=300,
        subsample=0.8, max_depth=2, learning_rate=0.1,
        random_state=101), X, y, scoring='accuracy',cv=10)

print ("GBM: %0.3f" % (np.mean(GBM)))
```

Averaging Different Predictors

Up to this section, the chapter discusses ensembles made of the same kind of machine learning algorithms, but both averaging and voting systems can also work fine when you use a mix of different machine learning algorithms. This is the *averaging* approach, and it's widely used when you can't reduce the estimate variance.

As you try to learn from data, you have to try different solutions, thus modeling your data using different machine learning solutions. It's good practice to check whether you can put some of them successfully into ensembles using prediction averages or by counting the predicted classes. The principle is the same as in bagging noncorrelated predictions, when models mixed together can produce less variance-affected predictions. To achieve effective averaging, you have to

1. Divide your data into training and test sets.
2. Use the training data with different machine learning algorithms.
3. Record predictions from each algorithm and evaluate the viability of the result using the test set.
4. Correlate all the predictions available with each other.
5. Pick the predictions that least correlate and average their result. Or, if you're classifying, pick a group of least correlated predictions and, for each example, pick as a new class prediction the class that the majority of them predicted.
6. Test the newly averaged or voted-by-majority prediction against the test data. If successful, you create your final model by averaging the results of the models part of the successful ensemble.

To understand which models correlate the least, take the predictions one by one, correlate each one against the others, and average the correlations to obtain an averaged correlation. Use the averaged correlation to rank the selected predictions that are most suitable for averaging.

> IN THIS CHAPTER
>
> » Handling images with Python
>
> » Performing image classification tasks on images of faces
>
> » Considering Natural Language Processing (NLP)
>
> » Defining how machines can understand text
>
> » Obtaining rating data

Chapter **5**

Real-World Applications

"In the realm of ideas everything depends on enthusiasm . . . in the real world all rests on perseverance."

— JOHANN WOLFGANG VON GOETHE

Beginners become experts and develop mastery of a skill by applying two themes: *preparation* and *practice*. This chapter shows you how to apply machine learning theory to solve real-world problems and provides practice in classifying images, scoring sentiment, and creating recommendations.

While developers have made great progress creating these algorithms and implementing feasible solutions, these problems are far from solved and continue to evolve and update every day. This chapter shows you how to turn artificial intelligence and machine learning knowledge into something useful.

Classifying Images

Among the five senses, sight is certainly the most powerful in conveying knowledge and information derived from the world outside. Many people feel that the gift of sight helps children know about the different things and persons around

them. In addition, humans receive and transmit knowledge across time by means of pictures, visual arts, and textual documents.

Because sight is so important and precious, it's similarly invaluable for a machine learning algorithm because sight opens the algorithm to new capabilities. Most information today is available in digital form (text, music, photos, and videos), yet being able to read visual information in a binary format doesn't help you to understand it and to use it properly. In recent years, one of the more important uses of vision in machine learning is to classify images for all sorts of reasons.

For example, robots need to know which objects they should avoid and which objects they need to work with, yet without image classification, the task is impossible. Humans also rely on image classification to perform tasks such as handwriting recognition and finding particular individuals in a crowd. Here's a smattering of other vital tasks of image classification: conducting medical scans; detecting pedestrians (an important feature to implement in cars and that could save thousands of lives); and helping farmers determine where fields need the most water. Check out the state of the art in image classification at http://rodrigob.github.io/are_we_there_yet/build.

Working with a set of images

At first sight, image files appear as unstructured data made up of a series of bits. The file doesn't separate the bits from each other in any way. You can't simply look into the file and see an image structure because none exists. As with other file formats, image files rely on the user to know how to interpret the data. For example, each pixel of a picture file could consist of three 32-bit fields. Knowing that each field is 32 bits is up to you. A header at the beginning of the file may provide clues about interpreting the file, but even so, it's up to you to know how to interact with the file using the right package or library.

You use scikit-image for the following examples. It's a Python package dedicated to processing images, picking them up from files, and handling them using NumPy arrays. By using scikit-image, you can obtain all the skills needed to load and transform images for any machine learning algorithm. This package also helps you upload all the necessary images, resize or crop them, and flatten them into a vector of features in order to transform them for learning purposes.

Scikit-image isn't the only package that can help you deal with images in Python. There are also other packages, such as the following:

» **scipy.ndimage** (https://docs.scipy.org/doc/scipy/reference/ndimage.html): Allows you to operate on multidimensional images

» **Mahotas** (http://mahotas.readthedocs.org/en/latest): A fast C++-based processing library

» **OpenCV** (https://opencv-python-tutroals.readthedocs.org): A powerful package that specializes in computer vision

» **ITK** (https://itk.org): Designed to work on 3D images for medical purposes

The example in this section shows how to work with a picture as an unstructured file. The example image is a public domain offering from https://commons.wikimedia.org/wiki/Main_Page. To work with images, you need to access the scikit-image library (http://scikit-image.org), which is an algorithm collection used for image processing. You can find a tutorial for this library at http://scipy-lectures.github.io/packages/scikit-image. The first task is to display the image on-screen using the following code. (Be patient: The image is ready when the busy indicator disappears from the IPython Notebook tab.)

```
from skimage.io import imread
from skimage.transform import resize
from matplotlib import pyplot as plt
import matplotlib.cm as cm

%matplotlib inline

example_file = ("http://upload.wikimedia.org/" +
    "wikipedia/commons/7/7d/Dog_face.png")
image = imread(example_file, as_grey=True)
plt.imshow(image, cmap=cm.gray)
plt.show()
```

The code begins by importing a number of libraries. It then creates a string that points to the example file online and places it in `example_file`. This string is part of the `imread()` method call, along with `as_grey`, which is set to `True`. The `as_grey` argument tells Python to turn any color images into grayscale. Any images that are already in grayscale remain that way.

After you have an image loaded, you render it (make it ready to display on-screen). The `imshow()` function performs the rendering and uses a grayscale color map. The `show()` function actually displays `image` for you, as shown in Figure 5-1.

FIGURE 5-1: The image appears on-screen after you render and show it.

Sometimes images aren't perfect; they can present noise or other granularity. You must smooth the erroneous and unusable signals. Filters can help you achieve that smoothing without hiding or modifying important characteristics of the image, such as the edges. If you're looking for an image filter, you can clean up your images using the following:

» **Median filter:** Based on the idea that the true signal comes from a median of a neighborhood of pixels. A function disk provides the area used to apply the median, which creates a circular window on a neighborhood.

» **Total variation denoising:** Based on the idea that noise is variance and this filter reduces the variance.

» **Gaussian filter:** Uses a Gaussian function to define the pixels to smooth.

The following code provides you with an idea of the effect every filter has on the final image, with the effects shown in Figure 5-2:

```
import warnings
warnings.filterwarnings("ignore")
from skimage import filters, restoration
from skimage.morphology import disk
median_filter = filters.rank.median(image, disk(1))
tv_filter = restoration.denoise_tv_chambolle(image,
                                             weight=0.1)
gaussian_filter = filters.gaussian_filter(image,
                                          sigma=0.7)
```

Don't worry if a warning appears when you're running the code. It happens because the code converts some number during the filtering process and the new numeric form isn't as rich as before.

```
fig = plt.figure()
for k,(t,F) in enumerate((('Median filter',median_filter),
            ('TV filter',tv_filter),
            ('Gaussian filter', gaussian_filter))):
    f=fig.add_subplot(1,3,k+1)
    plt.axis('off')
    f.set_title(t)
    plt.imshow(F, cmap=cm.gray)
plt.show()
```

FIGURE 5-2: Different filters for different noise cleaning.

If you aren't working in IPython (or you aren't using the magic command %matplotlib inline), just close the image when you're finished viewing it after filtering noise from the image.

In the IPython command line, the asterisk in the In [*]: entry tells you that the code is still running and you can't move on to the next step.

The act of closing the image ends the code segment. You now have an image in memory, and you may want to find out more about it. When you run the following code, you discover the image type and size:

```
print("data type: %s, shape: %s" %
        (type(image), image.shape))
```

The output from this call tells you that the image type is a numpy.ndarray and that the image size is 90 pixels by 90 pixels. The image is actually an array of pixels that you can manipulate in various ways. For example, if you want to crop the image, you can use the following code to manipulate the image array:

```
image2 = image[5:70,0:70]
plt.imshow(image2, cmap=cm.gray)
plt.show()
```

The numpy.ndarray in image2 is smaller than the one in image, so the output is smaller as well. Figure 5-3 shows typical results. The purpose of cropping the

image is to make it a specific size. Both images must be the same size for you to analyze them. Cropping is one way to ensure that the images are the correct size for analysis.

FIGURE 5-3: Cropping the image makes it smaller.

Another method that you can use to change the image size is to resize it. The following code resizes the image to a specific size for analysis:

```
image3 = resize(image2, (30, 30), mode='nearest')
plt.imshow(image3, cmap=cm.gray)
print("data type: %s, shape: %s" %
      (type(image3), image3.shape))
```

The output from the `print()` function tells you that the image is now 30 pixels by 30 pixels in size. You can compare it to any image with the same dimensions.

After you have cleaned up all the images and made them the right size, you need to flatten them. A data set row is always a single dimension, not two or more dimensions. The image is currently an array of 30 pixels by 30 pixels, so you can't make it part of a data set. The following code flattens `image3`, so it becomes an array of 900 elements stored in `image_row`.

```
image_row = image3.flatten()
print("data type: %s, shape: %s" %
      (type(image_row), image_row.shape))
```

Notice that the type is still a `numpy.ndarray`. You can add this array to a data set and then use the data set for analysis purposes. The size is 900 elements, as anticipated.

682 BOOK 9 **Applying Machine Learning**

Extracting visual features

Machine learning on images works because it can rely on features to compare pictures and associate an image with another one (because of similarity) or to a specific label (guessing, for instance, the represented objects). Humans can easily choose a car or a tree when we see one in a picture. Even if it's the first time that we see a certain kind of tree or car, we can correctly associate it with the right object *(labeling)* or compare it with similar objects in memory *(image recall)*.

In the case of a car, having wheels, doors, a steering wheel, and so on are all elements that help you categorize a new example of a car among other cars. It happens because you see shapes and elements beyond the image itself; thus no matter how unusual a tree or a car may be, if it owns certain characteristics, you can figure out what it is.

An algorithm can infer elements (shapes, colors, particulars, relevant elements, and so on) directly from pixels only when you prepare data for it. Apart from special kinds of neural networks, called convolutional networks (discussed in Book 9, Chapter 3 as part of deep learning), which rank as the state of the art in image recognition because they can extract useful features from raw images by themselves, it's always necessary to prepare the right features when working with images.

Feature preparation from images is like playing with a jigsaw — you have to figure out any relevant particular, texture, or set of corners represented inside the image in order to re-create a picture from its details. All this information serves as the image features and makes up a precious element for any machine learning algorithm to complete its job.

Convolutional neural networks filter information across multiple layers, training the parameters of their convolutions (kinds of image filters); thus they can filter out only the features relevant to the images and the tasks they're trained to perform. Other special layers, called *pooling layers,* help the neural net catch these features in the case of translation (they appear in unusual parts of the image) or rotation.

Applying deep learning requires special techniques and machines able to sustain the heavy computational workload. The Caffe library, developed by Yangqing Jia from the Berkeley Vision and Learning Center, allows building such neural networks but also leverages existing pretrained ones (http://caffe.berkeleyvision.org/model_zoo.html). A pretrained neural network is a convolutional network trained on a large number of varied images, thus learning how to filter out a large variety of features for classification purpose. The pretrained network lets you input your images and obtain a large number of values that correspond to a score on a certain kind of feature previously learned by the network as an output. The features may correspond to a certain shape or texture. What matters to

your machine learning objectives is that the most revealing features for your purpose are among those produced by the pretrained network, so you must choose the right features by making a selection using another neural network, an SVM, or a simple regression model.

When you can't use a convolutional neural network or pretrained library (because of memory or CPU constraints), OpenCV (opencv-python-tutroals. readthedocs.org/en/latest/py_tutorials/py_feature2d/py_table_of_ contents_feature2d/py_table_of_contents_feature2d.html) or some scikit-image functions can still help. For instance, to emphasize the borders of an image, you can apply a simple process using scikit-image, as shown here:

```
from skimage import measure
contours = measure.find_contours(image, 0.55)
plt.imshow(image, cmap=cm.gray)
for n, contour in enumerate(contours):
    plt.plot(contour[:, 1], contour[:, 0], linewidth=2)
plt.axis('image')
plt.show()
```

You can read more about finding contours and other algorithms for feature extraction (histograms; corner and blob detection) in the tutorials at http:// scikit-image.org/docs/dev/auto_examples.

Recognizing faces using eigenfaces

The capability to recognize a face in the crowd has become an essential tool for many professions. For example, both the military and law enforcement rely on it heavily. Of course, facial recognition has uses for security and other needs as well. This example looks at facial recognition in a more general sense. You may have wondered how social networks manage to tag images with the appropriate label or name. The following example demonstrates how to perform this task by creating the right features using eigenfaces.

Eigenfaces is an approach to facial recognition based on the overall appearance of a face, not on its particular details. By means of a technique that can intercept and reshape the variance present in the image, the reshaped information is treated like the DNA of a face, thus allowing recovery of similar faces (because they have similar variances) in a host of facial images. It's a less effective technique than extracting features from the details of an image, yet it works, and you can implement it quickly on your computer. This approach demonstrates how machine learning can operate with raw pixels, but it's more effective when you change image data into another kind of data. You can learn more about eigenfaces at https://en.wikipedia.org/wiki/Eigenface or by trying the tutorial that

explores variance decompositions in scikit-learn at `http://scikit-learn.org/stable/auto_examples/decomposition/plot_faces_decomposition.html`.

In this example, you use eigenfaces to associate images present in a training set with those in a test set, initially using some simple statistical measures.

```
import numpy as np
from sklearn.datasets import fetch_olivetti_faces
dataset = fetch_olivetti_faces(shuffle=True,
                               random_state=101)
train_faces = dataset.data[:350,:]
test_faces  = dataset.data[350:,:]
train_answers = dataset.target[:350]
test_answers  = dataset.target[350:]
```

The example begins by using the Olivetti faces data set, a public domain set of images readily available from scikit-learn. For this experiment, the code divides the set of labeled images into a training and a test set. You need to pretend that you know the labels of the training set but don't know anything from the test set. As a result, you want to associate images from the test set to the most similar image from the training set.

```
print (dataset.DESCR)
```

The Olivetti data set consists of 400 photos taken from 40 people (so there are 10 photos of each person). Even though the photos represent the same person, each photo has been taken at different times during the day, with different light and facial expressions or details (for example, with glasses and without). The images are 64 x 64 pixels, so unfolding all the pixels into features creates a data set made of 400 cases and 4,096 variables. It seems like a high number of features, and actually, it is. Using `RandomizedPCA`, you can reduce them to a smaller and more manageable number.

```
from sklearn.decomposition import RandomizedPCA
n_components = 25
Rpca = RandomizedPCA(n_components=n_components,
            whiten=True,
            random_state=101).fit(train_faces)
print ('Explained variance by %i components: %0.3f' %
       (n_components,
        np.sum(Rpca.explained_variance_ratio_)))
compressed_train_faces = Rpca.transform(train_faces)
compressed_test_faces  = Rpca.transform(test_faces)

Explained variance by 25 components: 0.794
```

The `RandomizedPCA` class is an approximate PCA version, which works better when the data set is large (has many rows and variables). The decomposition creates 25 new variables (`n_components` parameter) and whitening (`whiten=True`), removing some constant noise (created by textual and photo granularity) and irrelevant information from images in a different way from the filters just discussed. The resulting decomposition uses 25 components, which is about 80 percent of the information held in 4,096 features.

```
import matplotlib.pyplot as plt
photo = 17 # This is the photo in the test set
print ('We are looking for face id=%i'
       % test_answers[photo])
plt.subplot(1, 2, 1)
plt.axis('off')
plt.title('Unknown face '+str(photo)+' in test set')
plt.imshow(test_faces[photo].reshape(64,64),
           cmap=plt.cm.gray, interpolation='nearest')
plt.show()
```

Figure 5-4 shows the chosen photo, subject number 34, from the test set.

FIGURE 5-4: The example application would like to find similar photos.

After the decomposition of the test set, the example takes the data relative only to photo 17 and subtracts it from the decomposition of the training set. Now the training set is made of differences with respect to the example photo. The code squares them (to remove negative values) and sums them by row, which results in a series of summed errors. The most similar photos are the ones with the least squared errors, that is, the ones whose differences are the least.

```
#Just the vector of value components of our photo
mask = compressed_test_faces[photo,]
squared_errors = np.sum((compressed_train_faces -
                        mask)**2,axis=1)
```

```
minimum_error_face = np.argmin(squared_errors)
most_resembling = list(np.where(squared_errors < 20)[0])
print ('Best resembling face in train test: %i' %
       train_answers[minimum_error_face])

Best resembling face in train test: 34
```

As it did before, the code can now display photo 17, which is the photo that best resembles images from the train set. Figure 5-5 shows typical output from this example.

```
import matplotlib.pyplot as plt
plt.subplot(2, 2, 1)
plt.axis('off')
plt.title('Unknown face '+str(photo)+' in test set')
plt.imshow(test_faces[photo].reshape(64,64),
           cmap=plt.cm.gray, interpolation='nearest')
for k,m in enumerate(most_resembling[:3]):
    plt.subplot(2, 2, 2+k)
    plt.title('Match in train set no. '+str(m))
    plt.axis('off')
    plt.imshow(train_faces[m].reshape(64,64),
               cmap=plt.cm.gray, interpolation='nearest')
plt.show()
```

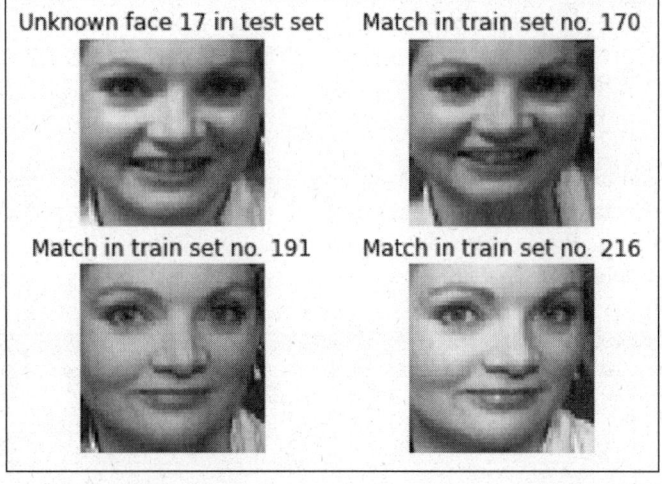

FIGURE 5-5: The output shows the results that resemble the test image.

Even though the most similar photo is similar (it's just scaled slightly differently), the other two photos are quite different. However, even though those photos don't match the test image as well, they really do show the same person as in photo 17.

Classifying images

This section adds to your knowledge of facial recognition, this time applying a learning algorithm to a complex set of images, called the Labeled Faces in the Wild data set that contains images of famous people collected over the Internet: http://scikit-learn.org/stable/datasets/labeled_faces.html. You must download the data set from the Internet, using the scikit-learn package in Python. The package mainly contains photos of well-known politicians.

```
import warnings
warnings.filterwarnings("ignore")
from sklearn.datasets import fetch_lfw_people
lfw_people = fetch_lfw_people(min_faces_per_person=60,
                              resize=0.4)
X = lfw_people.data
y = lfw_people.target
target_names = [lfw_people.target_names[a] for a in y]
n_samples, h, w = lfw_people.images.shape
from collections import Counter
for name, count in Counter(target_names).items():
    print ("%20s %i" % (name, count))

        Ariel Sharon 77
   Junichiro Koizumi 60
        Colin Powell 236
    Gerhard Schroeder 109
          Tony Blair 144
         Hugo Chavez 71
       George W Bush 530
     Donald Rumsfeld 121
```

As an example of data set variety, after dividing the examples into training and test sets, you can display a sample of pictures from both sets depicting Junichiro Koizumi, Prime Minister of Japan from 2001 to 2006. Figure 5-6 shows the output of the following code.

```
from sklearn.cross_validation import
    StratifiedShuffleSplit
train, test = list(StratifiedShuffleSplit(target_names,
        n_iter=1, test_size=0.1, random_state=101))[0]

plt.subplot(1, 4, 1)
plt.axis('off')
for k,m in enumerate(X[train][y[train]==6][:4]):
    plt.subplot(1, 4, 1+k)
    if k==0:
        plt.title('Train set')
```

```
    plt.axis('off')
    plt.imshow(m.reshape(50,37),
            cmap=plt.cm.gray, interpolation='nearest')
plt.show()

for k,m in enumerate(X[test][y[test]==6][:4]):
    plt.subplot(1, 4, 1+k)
    if k==0:
        plt.title('Test set')
    plt.axis('off')
    plt.imshow(m.reshape(50,37),
            cmap=plt.cm.gray, interpolation='nearest')
plt.show()
```

FIGURE 5-6:
Examples from the training and test sets do differ in pose and expression.

As you can see, the photos have quite a few variations, even among photos of the same person, which makes the task challenging: expression, pose, different light, and quality of the photo. For this reason, the example that follows applies the eigenfaces method described in the previous section, using different kinds of decompositions and reducing the initial large vector of pixel features (1850) to a simpler set of 150 features. The example uses PCA, the variance decomposition technique; Non-Negative Matrix Factorization (NMF), a technique for decomposing images into only positive features; and FastIca, an algorithm for Independent Component Analysis, an analysis that extracts signals from noise and other separated signals (the algorithm is successful at handling problems

like the cocktail party problem described at https://en.wikipedia.org/wiki/Cocktail_party_effect).

```
from sklearn import decomposition
n_components = 50
pca = decomposition.RandomizedPCA(
        n_components=n_components,
        whiten=True).fit(X[train,:])
nmf = decomposition.NMF(n_components=n_components,
                        init='nndsvda',
                        tol=5e-3).fit(X[train,:])
fastica = decomposition.FastICA(n_components=n_components,
                        whiten=True).fit(X[train,:])
eigenfaces = pca.components_.reshape((n_components, h, w))
X_dec = np.column_stack((pca.transform(X[train,:]),
        nmf.transform(X[train,:]),
        fastica.transform(X[train,:])))
Xt_dec = np.column_stack((pca.transform(X[test,:]),
        nmf.transform(X[test,:]),
        fastica.transform(X[test,:])))
y_dec = y[train]
yt_dec = y[test]
```

After extracting and concatenating the image decompositions into a new training and test set of data examples, the code applies a grid search for the best combinations of parameters for a classification support vector machine to perform a correct problem classification.

```
from sklearn.grid_search import GridSearchCV
from sklearn.svm import SVC
param_grid = {'C': [0.1, 1.0, 10.0, 100.0, 1000.0],
              'gamma': [0.0001, 0.001, 0.01, 0.1], }
clf = GridSearchCV(SVC(kernel='rbf'), param_grid)
clf = clf.fit(X_dec, y_dec)
print ("Best parameters: %s" % clf.best_params_)

Best parameters: {'gamma': 0.01, 'C': 100.0}
```

After finding the best parameters, the code checks for accuracy — the percentage of correct answers in the test set — and obtains an estimate of about 0.82 (the measure may change when you run the code on your computer).

```
from sklearn.metrics import accuracy_score
solution = clf.predict(Xt_dec)
print("Achieved accuracy: %0.3f"
      % accuracy_score(yt_dec, solution))

Achieved accuracy: 0.815
```

More interestingly, you can ask for a confusion matrix that shows the correct classes along the rows and the predictions in the columns. When a character in a row has counts in columns different from its row number, the code has mistakenly attributed one of the photos to someone else. In the case of the former Prime Minister of Japan, the example actually gets a perfect score (notice that the output shows a 6 in row 6, column 6, and zeroes in the remainder of the entries for that row).

```
from sklearn.metrics import confusion_matrix
confusion = str(confusion_matrix(yt_dec, solution))
print (' '*26+ ' '.join(map(str,range(8))))
print (' '*26+ '-'*22)
for n, (label, row) in enumerate(
                zip(lfw_people.target_names,
                    confusion.split('\n'))):
    print ('%s %18s > %s' % (n, label, row))

                           0  1  2  3  4  5  6  7
                          ----------------------
0        Ariel Sharon > [[ 6  0  1  0  1  0  0  0]
1        Colin Powell > [ 0 22  0  2  0  0  0  0]
2     Donald Rumsfeld > [ 0  0  8  2  1  0  0  1]
3       George W Bush > [ 1  1  2 46  1  0  0  2]
4    Gerhard Schroeder > [ 0  0  2  1  6  1  0  1]
5        Hugo Chavez > [ 0  0  0  0  1  5  0  1]
6    Junichiro Koizumi > [ 0  0  0  0  0  0  6  0]
7          Tony Blair > [ 0  0  0  1  2  0  0 11]]
```

Scoring Opinions and Sentiments

Many people have the idea that somehow computers can understand text. The fact is that computers don't even have a way in which to represent text — it's all numbers to the computer.

This section helps you understand three phases of working with text to score opinions and sentiments: using Natural Language Processing (NLP) to parse the text; performing the actual task of understanding the text; and then performing scoring and classification tasks to interact with the text meaningfully.

Introducing natural language processing

As human beings, understanding language is one of our first achievements, and associating words to their meaning seems natural. It's also automatic to handle

discourses that are ambiguous, unclear, or simply have a strong reference to the context of where we live or work (such as dialect, jargon, or terms family or associates understand). In addition, humans can catch subtle references to feelings and sentiments in text, enabling people to understand polite speech that hides negative feelings and irony. Computers don't have this ability but can rely on NLP, a field of computer science concerned with language understanding and language generation between a machine and a human being. Since Alan Turing first devised the Turing Test in 1950, which aims at spotting an artificial intelligence based on how it communicates with humans (`https://en.wikipedia.org/wiki/Turing_test`), NLP experts have developed a series of techniques that define the state of the art in computer-human interaction by text.

A computer powered with NLP can successfully spot spam in your email, tag the part of a conversation that contains a verb or a noun, and spot an entity like the name of a person or a company (called *named entity recognition*; see `https://en.wikipedia.org/wiki/Named-entity_recognition`). All these achievements have found application in tasks such as spam filtering, predicting the stock market using news articles, and de-duplicating redundant information in data storage.

Things get more difficult for NLP when translating a text from another language and understanding who the subject is in an ambiguous phrase. For example, consider the sentence, "John told Luca he shouldn't do that again." In this case, you can't really tell whether "he" refers to John or Luca. Disambiguating words with many meanings, such as considering whether the word *mouse* in a phrase refers to an animal or a computer device, can prove difficult. Obviously, the difficulty in all these problems arises because of the context.

As humans, we can easily resolve ambiguity by examining the text for hints about elements like place and time that express the details of the conversation (such as understanding what happened between John and Luca, or whether the conversation is about a computer when mentioning the mouse). Relying on additional information for understanding is part of the human experience. This sort of analysis is somewhat difficult for computers. Moreover, if the task requires critical contextual knowledge or demands that the listener resort to common sense and general expertise, the task becomes daunting. Simply put, NLP still has a lot of ground to cover in order to discover how to extract meaningful summaries from text effectively or how to complete missing information from text.

Understanding how machines read

Before a computer can do anything with text, it must be able to read the text in some manner. You can prepare data to deal with categorical variables, such as a feature representing a color (for instance, representing whether an example relates to the colors red, green, or blue). Categorical data is a type of short text

that you represent using binary variables, that is, variables coded using one or zero values according to whether a certain value is present in the categorical variable. Not surprisingly, you can represent complex text using the same logic.

Therefore, just as you transform a categorical color variable, having values such as red, green, and blue, into three binary variables, each one representing one of the three colors, so too can you transform a phrase like "The quick brown fox jumps over the lazy dog" using nine binary variables, one for each word that appears in the text ("The" is considered distinct from "the" because of its initial capital letter). This is the *Bag of Words* (BoW) form of representation. In its simplest form, BoW shows whether a certain word is present in the text by flagging a specific feature in the data set. Take a look at an example using Python and its scikit-learn package.

The input data is three phrases, `text_1`, `text_2`, and `text_3`, placed in a list, `corpus`. A *corpus* is a set of homogeneous documents put together for NLP analysis:

```
text_1 = 'The quick brown fox jumps over the lazy dog.'
text_2 = 'My dog is quick and can jump over fences.'
text_3 = 'Your dog is so lazy that it sleeps all the day.'
corpus = [text_1, text_2, text_3]
```

TIP

When you need to analyze text using a computer, you load the documents from disk or scrape them from the web and place each of them into a string variable. If you have multiple documents, you store them all in a list, the corpus. When you have a single document, you can split it using chapters, paragraphs, or simply the end of each line. After splitting the document, place all its parts into a list and apply analysis as if the list were a corpus of documents.

Now that you have a corpus, you use a class from the `feature_extraction` module in scikit-learn, `CountVectorizer`, which easily transforms texts into BoW like this:

```
from sklearn.feature_extraction import text
vectorizer = text.CountVectorizer(binary=True).fit(corpus)
vectorized_text = vectorizer.transform(corpus)
print(vectorized_text.todense())

[[0 0 1 0 0 1 0 1 0 0 0 1 1 0 1 1 0 0 0 1 0]
 [0 1 0 1 0 1 1 0 1 0 1 0 0 1 1 1 0 0 0 0 0]
 [1 0 0 0 1 1 0 0 1 1 0 0 1 0 0 0 1 1 1 1 1]]
```

The `CountVectorizer` class learns the corpus content using the `fit` method and then turns it (using the `transform` method) into a list of lists. As discussed in Book 8, Chapter 2, a list of lists is nothing more than a matrix in disguise, so what the class returns is actually a matrix made of three rows (the three documents, in the same order as the corpus) and 21 columns representing the content.

CHAPTER 5 **Real-World Applications** 693

The BoW representation turns words into the column features of a document matrix, and these features have a nonzero value when present in the processed text. For instance, consider the word *dog*. The following code shows its representation in the BoW:

```
print(vectorizer.vocabulary_)

{'day': 4, 'jumps': 11, 'that': 18, 'the': 19, 'is': 8,
 'fences': 6, 'lazy': 12, 'and': 1, 'quick': 15, 'my': 13,
 'can': 3, 'it': 9, 'so': 17, 'all': 0, 'brown': 2,
 'dog': 5, 'jump': 10, 'over': 14, 'sleeps': 16,
 'your': 20, 'fox': 7}
```

Asking the `CountVectorizer` to print the vocabulary learned from text reports that it associates *dog* with the number five, which means that *dog* is the fifth element in the BoW representations. In fact, in the obtained BoW, the fifth element of each document list always has a value of 1 because *dog* is the only word present in all the tree documents.

REMEMBER

Storing documents in a document matrix form can be memory-intensive because you must represent each document as a vector of the same length as the dictionary that created it. The dictionary in this example is quite limited, but when you use a larger corpus, you discover that a dictionary of the English language contains well over a million terms. The solution is to use sparse matrices. A sparse matrix is a way to store a matrix in your computer's memory without having zero values occupying memory space. You can read more about sparse matrices here: https://en.wikipedia.org/wiki/Sparse_matrix.

Processing and enhancing text

Marking whether a word is present or not in a text is indeed a good start, but sometimes it is not enough. The BoW model has its own limits. As if you were putting stuff randomly into a bag, in a BoW, words lose their order relationship with each other. For instance, in the phrase *My dog is quick and can jump over fences*, you know that *quick* refers to *dog* because it is glued to it by the form *is* of the verb *to be*. In a BoW, however, everything is mixed and some internal references are lost. Further processing can help prevent such. The following sections discuss how to process and enhance text.

Considering basic processing tasks

Instead of marking the presence or absence of an element of the phrase (technically called a *token*), you can instead count how many times it occurs, as shown in the following code:

```
text_4 = 'A black dog just passed by but my dog is brown.'
corpus.append(text_4)
vectorizer = text.CountVectorizer().fit(corpus)
vectorized_text = vectorizer.transform(corpus)
print(vectorized_text.todense()[-1])

[[0 0 1 1 1 1 0 0 2 0 0 1 0 0 0 1 0 1 0 1 0 0 0 0 0 0]]
```

This code modifies the previous example by adding a new phrase with the word *dog* repeated two times. The code appends the new phrase to the `corpus` and retrains the `vectorizer`, but it omits the `binary=True` setting this time. The resulting vector for the last inserted document clearly shows a 2 value in the ninth position, thus the `vectorizer` counts the word *dog* twice.

Counting tokens helps make important words stand out. Yet it's easy to repeat phrase elements, such as articles, that aren't important to the meaning of the expression. In the next section, you discover how to exclude less important elements, but for the time being, the example underweights them using the term frequency-inverse document frequency (TF-IDF) transformation.

The TF-IDF transformation is a technique that, after counting how many times a token appears in a phrase, divides the value by the number of documents in which the token appears. Using this technique, the vectorizer deems a word less important, even if it appears many times in a text, when it also finds that word in other texts. In the example corpus, the word *dog* appears in every text. In a classification problem, you can't use the word to distinguish between texts because it appears everywhere in the corpus. The word *fox* appears only in one phrase, making it an important classification term.

You commonly apply a number of transformations when applying TF-IDF, with the most important transformation normalizing the text length. Clearly, a longer text has more chances to have more words that are distinctive when compared to a shorter text. For example, when the word *fox* appears in a short text, it can be relevant to the meaning of that expression because *fox* stands out among few other words. However, when the word *fox* appears once in a long text, its presence might not matter much because it's a single word among many others. For this reason, the transformation divides the total tokens by the count of each token for each phrase. Treating a phrase like this turns token counting into a token percentage, so TF-IDF no longer considers how many times the word *fox* appears, but instead considers the percentage of times the word *fox* appears among all the tokens. The following example demonstrates how to complete the previous example using a combination of normalization and TF-IDF.

```
TfidF = text.TfidfTransformer(norm='l1')
tfidf = TfidF.fit_transform(vectorized_text)
```

```
phrase = 3 # choose a number from 0 to 3
total = 0
for word in vectorizer.vocabulary_:
    pos = vectorizer.vocabulary_[word]
    value = list(tfidf.toarray()[phrase])[pos]
    if value !=0:
        print ("%10s: %0.3f" % (word, value))
        total += value
print ('\nSummed values of a phrase: %0.1f' % total)

        is: 0.077
        by: 0.121
     brown: 0.095
       dog: 0.126
      just: 0.121
        my: 0.095
     black: 0.121
    passed: 0.121
       but: 0.121

Summed values of a phrase: 1.0
```

Using this new TF-IDF model rescales the values of important words and makes them comparable between each text in the corpus. To recover part of the ordering of the text before the BoW transformation, adding n-grams (https://en.wikipedia.org/wiki/N-gram) is also useful. An *n-gram* is a continuous sequence of tokens in the text that you use as a single token in the BoW representation. For instance, in the phrase *The quick brown fox jumps over the lazy dog*, a *bigram* — that is, a sequence of two tokens — transforms *brown fox* and *lazy dog* into single tokens. A *trigram* may create a single token from *quick brown fox*. An n-gram is a powerful tool, but it has a drawback because it doesn't know which combinations are important to the meaning of a phrase. N-grams create all the contiguous sequences of size N. The TF-IDF model can underweight the less useful n-grams, but only projects like Google's NGram viewer (you learn more about this viewer later in the chapter) can tell you which n-grams are useful in NLP with any certainty. The following example uses CountVectorizer to model n-grams in the range of (2, 2), that is, bigrams.

```
bigrams = text.CountVectorizer(ngram_range=(2,2))
print (bigrams.fit(corpus).vocabulary_)

{'can jump': 6, 'by but': 5, 'over the': 21,
 'it sleeps': 13, 'your dog': 31, 'the quick': 30,
 'and can': 1, 'so lazy': 26, 'is so': 12, 'dog is': 7,
 'quick brown': 24, 'lazy dog': 17, 'fox jumps': 9,
 'is brown': 10, 'my dog': 19, 'passed by': 22,
 'lazy that': 18, 'black dog': 2, 'brown fox': 3,
```

```
'that it': 27, 'quick and': 23, 'the day': 28,
'just passed': 16, 'dog just': 8, 'jump over': 14,
'sleeps all': 25, 'over fences': 20, 'jumps over': 15,
'the lazy': 29, 'but my': 4, 'all the': 0,
'is quick': 11}
```

TIP

Setting different ranges lets you use both *unigrams* (single tokens) and n-grams in your NLP analysis. For instance the setting `ngram_range=(1,3)` creates all tokens, all bigrams, and all trigrams. You usually never need more than trigrams in an NLP analysis. Increasing the number of n-grams is slightly beneficial after trigrams and sometimes even just after bigrams, depending on the corpus size and the NLP problem.

Stemming and removing stop words

Stemming is the process of reducing words to their stem (or root) word. This task isn't the same as understanding that some words come from Latin or other roots, but instead makes similar words equal to each other for the purpose of comparison or sharing. For example, the words *cats, catty,* and *catlike* all have the stem *cat.* The act of stemming helps you analyze sentences when tokenizing them because words having the same stem should have the same meaning (represented by a single feature).

Creating stem words by removing suffixes to make tokenizing sentences easier isn't the only way to make the document matrix simpler. Languages include many glue words that don't mean much to a computer but have significant meaning to humans, such as *a, as, the, that,* and so on in English. They make the text flow and concatenate in a meaningful way. Yet, the BoW approach doesn't care much about how you arrange words in a text. Thus removing such words is legitimate. These short, less useful words are called *stop words.*

The act of stemming and removing stop words simplifies the text and reduces the number of textual elements so that only the essential elements remain. In addition, you keep just the terms that are nearest to the true sense of the phrase. By reducing the number of tokens, a computational algorithm can work faster and process the text more effectively when the corpus is large.

This example requires the use of the Natural Language Toolkit (NLTK), which Anaconda doesn't install by default. To use this example, you must download and install NLTK using the instructions found at `www.nltk.org/install.html` for your platform. Make certain that you install the NLTK for whatever version of Python you're using for this book when you have multiple versions of Python installed on your system. After you install NLTK, you must also install the packages associated with it. The instructions at `www.nltk.org/data.html` tell you how to perform this task. (Install all the packages to ensure that you have everything.)

The following example demonstrates how to perform stemming and remove stop words from a sentence. It begins by training an algorithm to perform the required analysis using a test sentence. Afterward, the example checks a second sentence for words that appear in the first.

```
from sklearn.feature_extraction import text

import nltk
from nltk import word_tokenize
from nltk.stem.porter import PorterStemmer
nltk.download('punkt')

stemmer = PorterStemmer()

def stem_tokens(tokens, stemmer):
    stemmed = []
    for item in tokens:
        stemmed.append(stemmer.stem(item))
    return stemmed

def tokenize(text):
    tokens = word_tokenize(text)
    stems = stem_tokens(tokens, stemmer)
    return stems

vocab = ['Sam loves swimming so he swims all the time']
vect = text.CountVectorizer(tokenizer=tokenize,
                            stop_words='english')
vec = vect.fit(vocab)

sentence1 = vec.transform(['George loves swimming too!'])

print (vec.get_feature_names())
print (sentence1.toarray())
```

At the outset, the example creates a vocabulary using a test sentence and places it in the variable vocab. It then creates a CountVectorizer, vect, to hold a list of stemmed words, but it excludes the stop words. The tokenizer parameter defines the function used to stem the words. The stop_words parameter refers to a pickle file that contains stop words for a specific language, which is English in this case. There are also files for other languages, such as French and German. (You can see other parameters for the CountVectorizer() at scikit-learn.org/stable/modules/generated/sklearn.feature_extraction.text.CountVectorizer.html.) The vocabulary is fitted into another CountVectorizer, vec, which is used to perform the actual transformation on a test sentence using the transform() function. Here's the output from this example:

```
[nltk_data] Downloading package punkt to
[nltk_data]     C:\Users\Luca\AppData\Roaming\nltk_data...
[nltk_data]     Unzipping tokenizers\punkt.zip.
['love', 'sam', 'swim', 'time']
[[1 0 1 0]]
```

The first output shows the stemmed words. Notice that the list contains only *swim*, not *swimming* or *swims*. All the stop words are missing as well. For example, you don't see the words *so, he, all,* or *the*.

The second output shows how many times each stemmed word appears in the test sentence. In this case, a *love* variant appears once and a *swim* variant appears once as well. The words *sam* and *time* don't appear in the second sentence, so those values are set to 0.

Scraping textual data sets from the web

Given NLP's capabilities, building complete language models is just a matter of gathering large text collections. Digging through large amounts of text enables machine learning algorithms using NLP to discover connections between words and derive useful concepts relative to specific contexts. For instance, when discussing a mouse in the form of a device or an animal, a machine learning algorithm powered by NLP text processing can derive the precise topic from other hints in the phrase. Humans decipher these hints by having lived, seen, or read about the topic of the conversation.

Computers also have the opportunity to see and read a lot. The web offers access to millions of documents, most of them freely accessible without restrictions. Web scraping allows machine learning algorithms to automatically feed their NLP processes and learn new capabilities in recognizing and classifying text. Developers have already done much to create NLP systems capable of understanding textual information better by leveraging the richness of the web.

For instance, by using free text acquired from the web and other open text sources, such as dictionaries, scientists at Microsoft Research have developed various versions of MindNet, a semantic network, which is a network of words connected by meaning. MindNet can find related words through synonyms, parts, causes, locations, and sources. For instance, when you ask for the word *car,* MindNet provides answers such as *vehicle* (a synonym) and then connects *vehicle* to *wheel* because it is a specific part of a car, thus providing knowledge directly derived from text without anyone's having specifically instructed MindNet about cars or how they're made. You can read more about MindNet at https://research.microsoft.com/en-us/projects/mindnet/default.aspx.

Google developed something similar based on its Google Books project, helping build better language models for all Google's applications. A public API based on Google's work is the Ngram Viewer, which can explore how frequently certain combinations of tokens up to five grams have appeared over time: https://books.google.com/ngrams.

Being able to retrieve information from the web allows even greater achievements. For example, you could build a dictionary of positive or negative words based on associated emoticons or emoji (https://en.wikipedia.org/wiki/Emoji).

Web scraping is a complex subject that could require an entire book to explain. This chapter provides you with an example of web scraping and an overview of what to expect. You need to install the Beautiful Soup package when using Python to perform web scraping (www.crummy.com/software/BeautifulSoup). This package should already be part of your Anaconda installation, but if not, you can easily install it on your system by opening a command shell and issuing the command:

```
pip install beautifulsoup4
```

Beautiful Soup is a package created by Leonard Richardson and is an excellent tool for scraping data from HTML or XML files retrieved from the web, even if they are malformed or written in a nonstandard way. The package name refers to the fact that HTML documents are made of tags, and when they are a mess, many developers idiomatically call the document a *tag soup*. Thanks to Beautiful Soup, you can easily navigate in a page to locate the objects that matter and extract them as text, tables, or links.

This example demonstrates how to download a table from a Wikipedia page containing all the major US cities. Wikipedia (www.wikipedia.org) is a free-access and free-content Internet encyclopedia, enjoyed by millions of users every day, all around the world. Because its knowledge is free, open, and, most important, well structured, it's a precious resource for learning from the web.

WARNING

Most publishers and many college instructors view Wikipedia as being a dubious source of information. Anyone can edit the entries it contains, and sometimes people do so in ways that slant the information politically or socially, or simply reflect a lack of knowledge (see www.foxbusiness.com/features/2015/09/02/just-how-accurate-is-wikipedia.html and isites.harvard.edu/icb/icb.do?keyword=k70847&pageid=icb.page346376). This means that the information you receive may not reflect reality. However, many studies show that the community effort behind creating Wikipedia (see www.livescience.com/32950-how-accurate-is-wikipedia.html, www.cnet.com/news/study-wikipedia-as-accurate-as-britannica/, and www.zmescience.com/science/study-wikipedia-25092014) does tend to mitigate this issue partially. Even so, you need to exercise some level

of care in taking Wikipedia entries at face value, just as you would any Internet content. Just because someone tells you something is so doesn't make it true (no matter what form that information source might take). You need to cross-reference the information and verify the facts before accepting any Internet information source as factual, even Wikipedia. This said, the authors have verified every Wikipedia source used in this book as much as possible to ensure that you receive accurate information.

REMEMBER

Wikipedia has its own rules and terms of service, which you may read at https://meta.wikimedia.org/wiki/Bot_policy#Unacceptable_usage. The terms of service forbid the use of bots for automated tasks, such as modifying the website (corrections and automatic posting), and bulk downloads (downloading massive amounts of data). Yet Wikipedia is a great source for NLP analysis because you can download all its English articles at https://dumps.wikimedia.org/enwiki. Other languages also are available for download. Just consult https://dumps.wikimedia.org for further information.

```
from bs4 import BeautifulSoup
import pandas as pd
try:
    import urllib2 # Python 2.7.x
except:
    import urllib.request as urllib2 # Python 3.x

wiki = "https://en.wikipedia.org/wiki/\
List_of_United_States_cities_by_population"
header = {'User-Agent': 'Mozilla/5.0'}
query = urllib2.Request(wiki, headers=header)
page = urllib2.urlopen(query)
soup = BeautifulSoup(page, "lxml")
```

After you upload the Beautiful Soup package, the code defines a header (stating that you are a human user using a browser) and a target page. The target page is a document containing a list of major US cities: https://en.wikipedia.org/wiki/List_of_United_States_cities_by_population. The list also contains information about population and surface of the city.

```
table = soup.find("table",
    { "class" : "wikitable sortable" })
final_table = list()
for row in table.findAll('tr'):
    cells = row.findAll("td")
    if len(cells) >=6:
        v1 = cells[1].find(text=True)
        v2 = cells[2].find(text=True)
        v3 = cells[3].find(text=True)
```

CHAPTER 5 **Real-World Applications** 701

```
            v4 = cells[4].find(text=True)
            v5 = cells[6].findAll(text=True)
            v5 = v5[2].split()[0]
            final_table.append([v1, v2, v3, v4, v5])
cols = ['City','State','Population_2014','Census_2010'
            ,'Land_Area_km2']
df = pd.DataFrame(final_table, columns=cols)
```

After downloading the page into the variable named soup, using the find() and findAll() methods, you can look for a table (the <tr> and <td> tags). The cells variable contains a number of cell entries, each of which can contain text. The code looks inside each cell for textual information (v1 through v5) that it stores in a list (final_table). It then turns the list into a pandas DataFrame for further processing later. For example, you can use the DataFrame, df, to turn strings into numbers. Simply printing df outputs the resulting table.

Handling problems with raw text

Even though raw text wouldn't seem to present a problem in parsing because it doesn't contain any special formatting, you do have to consider how the text is stored and whether it contains special words within it. The multiple forms of encoding present on web pages can present interpretation problems that you need to consider as you work through the text.

For example, the way the text is encoded can differ because of different operating systems, languages, and geographical areas. Be prepared to find a host of different encodings as you recover data from the web. Human language is complex, and the original ASCII coding, comprising just unaccented English letters, can't represent all the different alphabets. That's why so many encodings appeared with special characters. For example, a character can use either seven or eight bits for encoding purposes. The use of special characters can differ as well. In short, the interpretation of bits used to create characters differs from encoding to encoding. You can see a host of encodings at www.i18nguy.com/unicode/codepages.html.

REMEMBER

Sometimes you need to work with encodings other than the default encoding set within the Python environment. When working with Python 3.*x*, you must rely on Universal Transformation Format 8-bit (UTF-8) as the encoding used to read and write files. This environment is always set for UTF-8, and trying to change it causes an error message. However, when working with Python 2.*x*, you can choose other encodings. In this case, the default encoding is the American Standard Code for Information Interchange (ASCII), but you can change it to some other encoding.

You can use this technique in any Python script. It can save your day when your code won't work because of errors when Python can't encode a character. However, working at the IPython prompt is actually easier in this case. The following steps help you see how to deal with Unicode characters, but only when working with Python 2.x. (These steps are unnecessary and cause errors in the Python 3.x environment.)

1. **Open a copy of the IPython command prompt.**

 You see the IPython window.

2. **Type the following code, pressing Enter after each line.**

   ```
   import sys
   sys.getdefaultencoding()
   ```

 You see the default encoding for Python, which is ascii in Python 2.x (in Python 3.x, it's utf-8 instead). If you really do want to work with Jupyter Notebook, create a new cell after this step.

3. **Type** reload(sys) **and press Enter.**

 Python reloads the sys module and makes a special function available.

4. **Type** sys.setdefaultencoding('utf-8') **and press Enter.**

 Python does change the encoding, but you won't know that for certain until after the next step. If you really do want to work with Jupyter Notebook, create a new cell after this step.

5. **Type** sys.getdefaultencoding() **and press Enter.**

 You see that the default encoding has now changed to utf-8.

WARNING

Changing the default encoding at the wrong time and in the incorrect way can prevent you from performing tasks such as importing modules. Make sure to test your code carefully and completely to ensure that any change in the default encoding won't affect your ability to run the application. Good additional articles to read on this topic appear at http://blog.notdot.net/2010/07/Getting-unicode-right-in-Python and http://web.archive.org/web/20120722170929/http://boodebr.org/main/python/all-about-python-and-unicode.

Using Scoring and Classification

The previous NLP discussions in this chapter show how a machine learning algorithm can read text (after scraping it from the web) using the BoW representation and how NLP can enhance its understanding of text using text length

normalization, TF-IDF model, and n-grams. The following sections demonstrate how to put text processing into use by learning to solve two common problems in textual analysis: classification and sentiment analysis.

Performing classification tasks

When you classify texts, you assign a document to a class because of the topics it discusses. You can discover the topics in a document in different ways. The simplest approach is prompted by the idea that if a group of people talks or writes about a topic, the people tend to use words from a limited vocabulary because they refer or relate to the same topic. When you share some meaning or are part of the same group, you tend to use the same language. Consequently, if you have a collection of texts and don't know what topics the text references, you can reverse the previous reasoning — you can simply look for groups of words that tend to associate, so their newly formed group by dimensionality reduction may hint at the topics you'd like to know about. This is a typical unsupervised learning task.

This learning task is a perfect application for the singular value decomposition (SVD) family of algorithms because by reducing the number of columns, the features (which, in a document, are the words) will gather in dimensions, and you can discover the topics by checking high-scoring words. SVD and principal components analysis (PCA) provide features to relate both positively and negatively to the newly created dimensions. So a resulting topic may be expressed by the presence of a word (high positive value) or by the absence of it (high negative value), making interpretation both tricky and counterintuitive for humans. The scikit-learn package includes the Non-Negative Matrix Factorization (NMF) decomposition class, which allows an original feature to relate only positively with the resulting dimensions.

This example starts with a new experiment after loading the `20newsgroups` data set, a data set collecting newsgroup postings scraped from the web, selecting only the posts regarding objects for sale and automatically removing headers, footers, and quotes. You may receive a warning message to the effect of, `WARNING:sklearn.datasets.twenty_newsgroups:Downloading dataset from ...`, with the URL of the site used for the download when working with this code.

```
import warnings
warnings.filterwarnings("ignore")
from sklearn.datasets import fetch_20newsgroups
dataset = fetch_20newsgroups(shuffle=True,
    categories = ['misc.forsale'],
    remove=('headers', 'footers', 'quotes'), random_state=101)
print ('Posts: %i' % len(dataset.data))

Posts: 585
```

The `TfidVectorizer` class is imported and set up to remove stop words (common words such as *the* or *and*) and keep only distinctive words, producing a matrix whose columns point to distinct words.

```
from sklearn.feature_extraction.text import TfidfVectorizer
vectorizer = TfidfVectorizer(max_df=0.95,
            min_df=2, stop_words='english')
tfidf = vectorizer.fit_transform(dataset.data)
from sklearn.decomposition import NMF
n_topics = 5
nmf = NMF(n_components=n_topics, random_state=101).fit(tfidf)
```

REMEMBER

As noted earlier in the chapter, the term frequency-inverse document frequency (TF-IDF) is a simple calculation based on the frequency of a word in the document. It is weighted by the rarity of the word between all the documents available. Weighting words is an effective way to rule out words that cannot help you to classify or identify the document when processing text. For example, you can eliminate common parts of speech or other common words.

As with other algorithms from the `sklearn.decomposition` module, the `n_components` parameter indicates the number of desired components. If you'd like to look for more topics, you use a higher number. As the required number of topics increases, the `reconstruction_err_` method reports lower error rates. It's up to you to decide when to stop given the trade-off between more time spent on computations and more topics.

The last part of the script outputs the resulting five topics. By reading the printed words, you can decide on the meaning of the extracted topics, thanks to product characteristics (for instance, the words *drive, hard, card,* and *floppy* refer to computers) or the exact product (for instance, *comics, car, stereo, games*).

```
feature_names = vectorizer.get_feature_names()
n_top_words = 15
for topic_idx, topic in enumerate(nmf.components_):
    print ("Topic #%d:" % (topic_idx+1),)
    print (" ".join([feature_names[i] for i in
                    topic.argsort()[:-n_top_words - 1:-1]]))

Topic #1:
drive hard card floppy monitor meg ram disk motherboard vga scsi brand
 color internal modem
Topic #2:
00 50 dos 20 10 15 cover 1st new 25 price man 40 shipping comics
Topic #3:
condition excellent offer asking best car old sale good new miles 10 000
 tape cd
```

```
Topic #4:
email looking games game mail interested send like thanks price package
 list sale want know
Topic #5:
shipping vcr stereo works obo included amp plus great volume vhs unc mathes
 gibbs radley
```

You can explore the resulting model by looking into the attribute components_ from the trained NMF model. It consists of a NumPy ndarray holding positive values for words connected to the topic. By using the argsort method, you can get the indexes of the top associations, whose high values indicate that they are the most representative words.

```
print (nmf.components_[0,:].argsort()[:-n_top_words-1:-1])
# Gets top words for topic 0

[1337 1749  889 1572 2342 2263 2803 1290 2353 3615 3017  806 1022 1938
 2334]
```

Decoding the words' indexes creates readable strings by calling them from the array derived from the get_feature_names method applied to the TfidfVectorizer that was previously fitted.

```
print (vectorizer.get_feature_names()[1337])
# Transforms index 1337 back to text

drive
```

Analyzing reviews from e-commerce

Sentiment is difficult to catch because humans use the same words to express even opposite sentiments. The expression you convey is a matter of how you construct your thoughts in a phrase, not simply the words used. Even though dictionaries of positive and negative words do exist and are helpful, they aren't decisive because word context matters. You can use these dictionaries as a way to enrich textual features, but you have to rely more on machine learning if you want to achieve good results.

TIP

It's a good idea to see how positive and negative word dictionaries work. The AFINN-111 dictionary contains 2,477 positive and negative words and phrases (www2.imm.dtu.dk/pubdb/views/publication_details.php?id=6010). Another good choice is the larger opinion lexicon by Hu and Liu that appears at www.cs.uic.edu/~liub/FBS/sentiment-analysis.html#lexicon. Both dictionaries contain English words.

Using labeled examples that associate phrases to sentiments can create more effective predictors. In this example, you create a machine learning model based on a data set containing reviews from Amazon, Yelp, and IMDB that you can find at the UCI, the machine learning repository, https://archive.ics.uci.edu/ml/datasets/Sentiment+Labelled+Sentences.

This data set was created for the paper "From Group to Individual Labels Using Deep Features," by Kotzias et al., for KDD 2015. The data set contains 3,000 labeled reviews equally divided from the three sources, and the data has a simple structure. Some text is separated by a tab from a binary sentiment label where 1 is a positive sentiment and 0 a negative one. You can download the data set and place it in your Python working directory using the following commands:

```
try:
    import urllib2 # Python 2.7.x
except:
    import urllib.request as urllib2 # Python 3.x
import requests, io, os, zipfile

UCI_url = 'https://archive.ics.uci.edu/ml/\
machine-learning-databases/00331/sentiment%20\
labelled%20sentences.zip'

response = requests.get(UCI_url)
compressed_file = io.BytesIO(response.content)
z = zipfile.ZipFile(compressed_file)
print ('Extracting in %s' %  os.getcwd())
for name in z.namelist():
    filename = name.split('/')[-1]
    nameOK = ('MACOSX' not in name and '.DS' not in name)
    if filename and nameOK:
            newfile = os.path.join(os.getcwd(),
                                   os.path.basename(filename))
            with open(newfile, 'wb') as f:
                f.write(z.read(name))
            print ('\tunzipping %s' % newfile)
```

TIP

In case the previous script doesn't work, you can download the data (in zip format) directly from https://archive.ics.uci.edu/ml/machine-learning-databases/00331 and expand it using your favorite unzipper. You'll find the imdb_labelled.txt file inside the newly created sentiment labelled sentences directory. After downloading the files, you can upload the IMDB file to a pandas DataFrame by using the read_csv function.

```
import numpy as np
import pandas as pd
```

CHAPTER 5 **Real-World Applications** 707

```
dataset = 'imdb_labelled.txt'
data = pd.read_csv(dataset, header=None, sep=r"\t",
                   engine='python')
data.columns = ['review','sentiment']
```

Exploring the textual data is quite interesting. You'll find all short phrases such as "Wasted two hours" or "It was so cool." Some are clearly ambiguous for a computer, such as "Waste your money on this game." Even though waste has a negative meaning, the imperative makes the phrase sound positive. A machine learning algorithm can learn to decipher ambiguous phrases like these only after seeing many variants. The next step is to build the model by splitting the data into training and test sets.

```
from sklearn.cross_validation import train_test_split
corpus, test_corpus, y, yt = train_test_split(
    data.ix[:,0], data.ix[:,1],
    test_size=0.25, random_state=101)
```

After splitting the data, the code transforms the text using most of the NLP techniques described in this chapter: token counts, unigrams and bigrams, stop words removal, text length normalization, and TF-IDF transformation.

```
from sklearn.feature_extraction import text
vectorizer = text.CountVectorizer(ngram_range=(1,2),
                    stop_words='english').fit(corpus)
TfidF = text.TfidfTransformer()
X = TfidF.fit_transform(vectorizer.transform(corpus))
Xt = TfidF.transform(vectorizer.transform(test_corpus))
```

After the text for both the training and test sets is ready, the algorithm can learn sentiment using a linear support vector machine. This kind of support vector machine supports L2 regularization, so the code must search for the best C parameter using the grid search approach.

```
from sklearn.svm import LinearSVC
from sklearn.grid_search import GridSearchCV
param_grid = {'C': [0.01, 0.1, 1.0, 10.0, 100.0]}
clf = GridSearchCV(LinearSVC(loss='hinge',
                    random_state=101), param_grid)
clf = clf.fit(X, y)
print ("Best parameters: %s" % clf.best_params_)

Best parameters: {'C': 1.0}
```

Now that the code has determined the best hyper-parameter for the problem, you can test performance on the test set using the *accuracy measure*, the percentage of correct times the code can guess the correct sentiment.

```
from sklearn.metrics import accuracy_score
solution = clf.predict(Xt)
print("Achieved accuracy: %0.3f" %
      accuracy_score(yt, solution))

Achieved accuracy: 0.816
```

The results indicate accuracy of higher than 80 percent, but determining which phrases tricked the algorithm into making a wrong prediction is interesting. You can print the misclassified texts and consider what the learning algorithm is missing in terms of learning from text.

```
print(test_corpus[yt!=solution])

601     There is simply no excuse for something this p...
32      This is the kind of money that is wasted prope...
887     At any rate this film stinks, its not funny, a...
668     Speaking of the music, it is unbearably predic...
408            It really created a unique feeling though.
413          The camera really likes her in this movie.
138     I saw "Mirrormask" last night and it was an un...
132     This was a poor remake of "My Best Friends Wed...
291                              Rating: 1 out of 10.
904     I'm so sorry but I really can't recommend it t...
410     A world better than 95% of the garbage in the ...
55      But I recommend waiting for their future effor...
826     The film deserves strong kudos for taking this...
100           I don't think you will be disappointed.
352                                    It is shameful.
171     This movie now joins Revenge of the Boogeyman ...
814     You share General Loewenhielm's exquisite joy ...
218     It's this pandering to the audience that sabot...
168     Still, I do like this movie for it's empowerme...
479                         Of course, the acting is blah.
31                      Waste your money on this game.
805     The only place good for this film is in the ga...
127     My only problem is I thought the actor playing...
613                                        Go watch it!
764                        This movie is also revealing.
107     I love Lane, but I've never seen her in a movi...
674     Tom Wilkinson broke my heart at the end... and...
30      There are massive levels, massive unlockable c...
667                                      It is not good.
```

```
823    I struggle to find anything bad to say about i...
739         What on earth is Irons doing in this film?
185                            Highly unrecommended.
621    A mature, subtle script that suggests and occa...
462    Considering the relations off screen between T...
595    Easily, none other cartoon made me laugh in a ...
8                                   A bit predictable.
446    I like Armand Assante & my cable company's sum...
449    I won't say any more - I don't like spoilers, ...
715    Im big fan of RPG games too, but this movie, i...
241    This would not even be good as a made for TV f...
471    At no point in the proceedings does it look re...
481    And, FINALLY, after all that, we get to an end...
104                           Too politically correct.
522    Rating: 0/10 (Grade: Z) Note: The Show Is So B...
174            This film has no redeeming features.
491    This movie creates its own universe, and is fa...
Name: review, dtype: object
```

Recommending Products and Movies

One of the oldest and most common sales techniques is to recommend something to a customer based on what you know about the customer's needs and wants. If people buy one product, they might buy another associated product if given a good reason to do so. They may not even have thought about the need for the second product until the salesperson recommends it, yet they really do need to have it in order to use the primary product. For this reason alone, most people actually like to get recommendations. Given that web pages now serve as a salesperson in many cases, recommender systems are a necessary part of any serious sales effort on the web. The rest of this chapter helps you better understand the significance of the recommender revolution in all sorts of venues.

Recommender systems serve all sorts of other needs. For example, you might see an interesting movie title, read the synopsis, and still not know whether you're likely to find it a good movie. Watching the trailer might prove equally fruitless. Only after you see the reviews provided by others do you feel you have enough information to make a good decision. You also find methods for obtaining and using rating data in this chapter.

Gathering, organizing, and ranking such information is hard, though, and information overflow is the bane of the Internet. A recommender system can perform all the required work for you in the background, making the work of getting to

a decision a lot easier. You may not even realize that search engines are actually huge recommender systems. The Google search engine, for instance, can provide personalized search results based on your previous search history.

Recommender systems do more than just make recommendations. After reading images and texts, machine learning algorithms can also read a person's personality, preferences, and needs and act accordingly. The rest of this chapter helps you understand how all these activities take place by exploring techniques such as singular value decomposition (SVD).

Realizing the revolution

A recommender system can suggest items or actions of interest to a user, after having learned the user's preferences over time. The technology, which is based on data and machine learning techniques (both supervised and unsupervised), has appeared on the Internet for about two decades. Today you can find recommender systems almost everywhere, and they're likely to play an even larger role in the future under the guise of personal assistants, such as Siri or some other artificial intelligence-based digital assistant.

The drivers for users and companies to adopt recommender systems are different but complementary. Users have a strong motivation to reduce the complexity of the modern world (regardless of whether the issue is finding the right product or a place to eat) and avoid information overload. Companies, on the other hand, find that recommender systems provide a practical way to communicate in a personalized way with their customers and successfully push sales.

Recommender systems actually started as a means to handle information overload. The Xerox Palo Alto Research Center built the first recommender in 1992. Named Tapestry, it handled the increasing number of emails received by center researchers. The idea of collaborative filtering was born (learned from users by leveraging similarities in preferences), and the GroupLens project soon extended it to news selection and movie recommendations (the MovieLens project, whose data you use in this chapter).

When giant players in the e-commerce sector, such as Amazon, started adopting recommender systems, the idea went mainstream and spread widely in e-commerce. Netflix did the rest by promoting recommenders as a business tool and sponsoring a competition to improve its recommender system (https://en.wikipedia.org/wiki/Netflix_Prize) that involved various teams for quite a long time. The result is an innovative recommender technology that uses SVD and Restricted Boltzmann Machines (a kind of unsupervised neural network discussed in Book 9, Chapter 3).

However, recommender systems aren't limited to promoting products. Since 2002, a new kind of Internet service has made its appearance: social networks such as Friendster, Myspace, Facebook, and LinkedIn. These services promote link exchanges between users and share information such as posts, pictures, and videos. In addition, search engines such as Google amassed user response information to offer more personalized services and understand how to better match users' desires when responding to users' queries (`https://en.wikipedia.org/wiki/RankBrain`).

Recommendations have become so pervasive in guiding people's daily life that experts now worry about the impact on our ability to assume independent decisions and perceive the world in freedom. You can read about this concern in the article at `https://en.wikipedia.org/wiki/Filter_bubble`. The history of recommender systems is one of machines striving to learn about our minds and hearts, to make our lives easier, and to promote the business of their creators.

Downloading rating data

Getting good rating data can be hard. Later in this chapter, you use the MovieLens data set to see how SVD can help you in creating movie recommendations. However, you have other databases at your disposal. The following sections describe the MovieLens data set and the data logs contained in MSWeb — both of which work quite well when experimenting with recommender systems.

Trudging through the MovieLens data set

The MovieLens site (`https://movielens.org`) is all about helping you find a movie you might like. After all, with millions of movies out there, finding something new and interesting could take time that you don't want to spend. The setup works by asking you to input ratings for movies that you already know about. The MovieLens site then makes recommendations for you based on your ratings. In short, your ratings teach an algorithm what to look for, and then the site applies this algorithm to the entire data set.

You can obtain the MovieLens data set at `https://grouplens.org/datasets/movielens`. The interesting thing about this site is that you can download all or part of the data set based on how you want to interact with it. You can find downloads in the following sizes:

- 100,000 ratings from 700 users on 9,000 movies
- 1 million ratings from 6,000 users on 4,000 movies

- 10 million ratings and 100,000 tag applications applied to 10,000 movies by 72,000 users
- 20 million ratings and 465,000 tag applications applied to 27,000 movies by 138,000 users
- MovieLens's latest data set in small or full sizes (At this writing, the full size contained 20,000,000 ratings and 470,000 tag applications applied to 27,000 movies by 138,000 users; its size increase.)

This data set presents you with an opportunity to work with user-generated data using both supervised and unsupervised techniques. The large data sets present special challenges that only big data can provide. You can find some starter information for working with supervised and unsupervised techniques in Book 9, Chapter 1 and Book 9, Chapter 2.

The following example uses a version called the MovieLense ratings data set found in the R recommenderlab library.

After calling the library from R (and installing it if it isn't already available on your system), the code uploads the library into memory and starts exploring the data.

```
if (!"recommenderlab" %in% rownames(installed.packages()))
         {install.packages("recommenderlab")}
library("recommenderlab")
data(MovieLense)
print(MovieLense)

943 x 1664 rating matrix of class 'realRatingMatrix' with
 99392 ratings.
```

Printing the data set doesn't print any data but reports to you that the data set is a matrix of 943 rows (the users) and 1664 columns (the movies), containing 99392 ratings. MovieLense is actually a *sparse matrix*, a matrix that compresses the data by removing most of the zero values. You can normally operate on a sparse matrix as you would when using a standard matrix. When necessary, you can convert it into a standard dense matrix for specific statistics by using code like the following:

```
print(table(as.vector(as(MovieLense, "matrix"))))

    1     2     3     4     5
 6059 11307 27002 33947 21077
```

The output displays the rankings distribution. Rankings range from 1 to 5, and there are more positive rankings than negative ones. This often happens with rating data: It has some imbalance in favor of positive data because users tend to buy

or watch what they believe they will like. Disappointment mostly motivates negative ratings because expectations aren't satisfied. You can also report how many films each user has rated on average and how many users have rated each film:

```
summary(colCounts(MovieLense))
   Min. 1st Qu.  Median    Mean 3rd Qu.    Max.
   1.00    7.00   27.00   59.73   80.00  583.00
summary(rowCounts(MovieLense))
   Min. 1st Qu.  Median    Mean 3rd Qu.    Max.
   19.0    32.0    64.0   105.4   147.5   735.0
```

It is also quite easy to go into deeper detail and find how users rank a particular film.

```
average_ratings <- colMeans(MovieLense)

print(average_ratings[50])
Star Wars (1977)
        4.358491

print (colCounts(MovieLense[,50]))
Star Wars (1977)
             583
```

In this example, 583 users have rated the fiftieth movie, the original *Star Wars* from 1977, which scored an average rating of 4.36.

Navigating through anonymous web data

Another interesting data set that you can use to learn from preferences is the MSWeb data set. It consists of a week's worth of anonymously recorded data from the Microsoft website. In this case, the recorded information is about a behavior, not a judgment, thus values are expressed in a binary form. As with the MovieLens data set, you can download the MSWeb data set from the R recommenderlab library, get information about its structure, and explore how its values are distributed.

```
data(MSWeb)
print(MSWeb)
32710 x 285 rating matrix of class 'binaryRatingMatrix'
 with 98653 ratings.

print(table(as.vector(as(MSWeb, "matrix"))))

  FALSE    TRUE
9223697   98653
```

The data set, stored in a sparse matrix, consists of 32710 randomly selected Microsoft website users, and the columns represent 285 Vroots. A Vroot is a series of grouped website pages. Together they constitute an area of the website. The binary values show whether someone has visited a certain area. (You just see a flag; you don't see how many times the user has actually visited that website area.)

The idea is that a user's visit to a certain area indicates a specific interest. For instance, when a user visits pages to learn about productivity software along with visits to a page containing terms and prices, this behavior indicates an interest in acquiring the productivity software soon. Useful recommendations can be based on such inferences about a user's desire to buy certain versions of the productivity software or bundles of different software and services.

The remainder of the chapter uses the MovieLense data set exclusively. However, you should use the knowledge gained in this chapter to explore the MSWeb data set using the same methodologies because they apply equally to rating data and binary data.

Encountering the limits of rating data

For recommender systems to work well, they need to know about you as well as other people, both like you and different from you. Acquiring rating data allows a recommender system to learn from the experiences of multiple customers. Rating data could derive from a judgment (such as rating a product using stars or numbers) or a fact (a binary 1/0 that simply states that you bought the product, saw a movie, or stopped browsing at a certain web page).

No matter the data source or type, rating data is always about behaviors. To rate a movie, you have to decide to see it, watch it, and then rate it based on your experience of seeing the movie. Actual recommender systems learn from rating data in different ways:

» **Collaborative filtering:** Matches raters based on movie or product similarities used in the past. You can get recommendations based on items liked by people similar to you or on items similar to those you like.

» **Content-based filtering:** Goes beyond the fact that you watched a movie. It examines the features relative to you and the movie to determine whether a match exists based on the larger categories that the features represent. For instance, if you are a female who likes action movies, the recommender will look for suggestions that include the intersection of these two categories.

» **Knowledge-based recommendations:** Based on metadata, such as preferences expressed by users and product descriptions. It relies on machine

CHAPTER 5 **Real-World Applications** 715

learning and is effective when you do not have enough behavioral data to determine user or product characteristics. This is called a *cold start* and represents one of the most difficult recommender tasks because you don't have access to either collaborative filtering or content-based filtering.

When using collaborative filtering, you need to calculate similarity (see Book 9, Chapter 2 for a discussion of the use of similarity measures). Apart from Euclidean, Manhattan, and Chebyshev distances, the remainder of this section discusses cosine similarity. *Cosine similarity* measures the angular cosine distance between two vectors, which may seem like a difficult concept to grasp but is just a way to measure angles in data spaces.

Imagine a space made of features and having two points. Using the formulations found in Book 9, Chapter 2, you can measure the distance between the points. For instance, you could use the Euclidean distance, which is a perfect choice when you have few dimensions, but which fails miserably when you have multiple dimensions because of the curse of dimensionality (https://en.wikipedia.org/wiki/Curse_of_dimensionality).

The idea behind the cosine distance is to use the angle created by the two points connected to the space origin (the point where all dimensions are zero) instead. If the points are near, the angle is narrow, no matter how many dimensions are there. If they are far away, the angle is quite large. Cosine similarity implements the cosine distance as a percentage and is quite effective in telling whether a user is similar to another or whether a film can be associated to another because the same users favor it. The following example locates the movies that are the most similar movies to movie 50, *Star Wars*.

```
print (colnames(MovieLense[,50]))
[1] "Star Wars (1977)"

similar_movies <- similarity(MovieLense[,50],
                             MovieLense[,-50],
                             method ="cosine",
                             which = "items")
colnames(similar_movies)[which(similar_movies>0.70)]
[1] "Toy Story (1995)"
    "Empire Strikes Back, The (1980)"
[3] "Raiders of the Lost Ark (1981)"
    "Return of the Jedi (1983)"
```

Leveraging SVD

A property of SVD is to compress the original data at such a level and in such a smart way that, in certain situations, the technique can actually create new

meaningful and useful features, not just compressed variables. The following sections help you understand what role SVD plays in recommender systems.

Considering the origins of SVD

SVD is a method from linear algebra that can decompose an initial matrix into the multiplication of three derived matrices. The three derived matrices contain the same information as the initial matrix, but in a way that expresses any redundant information (expressed by statistical variance) only once. The benefit of the new variable set is that the variables have an orderly arrangement according to the initial variance portion contained in the original matrix.

SVD builds the new features using a weighted summation of the initial features. It places features with the most variance leftmost in the new matrix, whereas features with the least or no variance appear on the right side. As a result, no correlation exists between the features. (Correlation between features is an indicator of information redundancy, as explained in the previous paragraph.) Here's the formulation of SVD:

$$A = U * D * V^T$$

For compression purposes, you need to know only about matrices U and D, but examining the role of each resulting matrix helps, starting with the origin. A is a matrix n*p, where n is the number of examples and p is the number of variables. As an example, consider a matrix containing the purchase history of n customers, who bought something in the p range of available products. The matrix values are populated with quantities that customers purchased. As another example, imagine a matrix in which rows are individuals, columns are movies, and the content of the matrix is a movie rating (which is exactly what the MovieLens data set contains).

After the SVD computation completes, you obtain the U, S, and V matrices. U is a matrix of dimensions n by k, where k is p, exactly the same dimensions of the original matrix. It contains the information about the original rows on a reconstructed set of columns. Therefore, if the first row on the original matrix is a vector of items that Mr. Smith bought, the first row of the reconstructed U matrix will still represent Mr. Smith, but the vector will have different values. The new U matrix values are a weighted combination of the values in the original columns.

Of course, you might wonder how the algorithm creates these combinations. The combinations are devised to concentrate the most variance possible on the first column. The algorithm then concentrates most of the residual variance in the second column with the constraint that the second column is uncorrelated with the first one, distributing the decreasing residual variance to each column in succession. By concentrating the variance in specific columns, the original features

that were correlated are summed into the same columns of the new U matrix, thus cancelling any previous redundancy present. As a result, the new columns in U don't have any correlation between themselves, and SVD distributes all the original information in unique, nonredundant features. Moreover, given that correlations may indicate causality (but correlation isn't causation; it can simply hint at it — a necessary but not sufficient condition), cumulating the same variance creates a rough estimate of the variance's root cause.

V is the same as the U matrix, except that its shape is p*k and it expresses the original features with new cases as a combination of the original examples. This means that you'll find new examples composed of customers with the same buying habits. For instance, SVD compresses people buying certain products into a single case that you can interpret as a homogeneous group or as an archetypal customer.

In such reconstruction, D, a diagonal matrix (only the diagonal has values) contains information about the amount of variance computed and stored in each new feature in the U and V matrices. By cumulating the values along the matrix and making a ratio with the sum of all the diagonal values, you can see that the variance is concentrated on the first leftmost features, while the rightmost are almost zero or an insignificant value. Therefore an original matrix with 100 features can be decomposed and have an S matrix whose first 10 new reconstructed features represent more than 90 percent of the original variance.

SVD has many optimizing variants with slightly different objectives. The core functions of these algorithms are similar to SVD. Principal component analysis (PCA) focuses on common variance. It's the most popular algorithm and is used in machine learning preprocessing applications.

TIP

A great SVD property is that the technique can create new meaningful and useful features, not just compressed variables, as a byproduct of compression in certain situations. In this sense, you can consider SVD a feature creation technique.

Understanding the SVD connection

If your data contains hints and clues about a hidden cause or motif, an SVD can put them together and offer you proper answers and insights. That is especially true when your data is made up of interesting pieces of information like the ones in the following list:

>> **Text in documents hints at ideas and meaningful categories.** Just as you can make up your mind about discussion topics by reading blogs and newsgroups, so can SVD help you deduce a meaningful classification of groups of documents or the specific topics being written about in each of them.

» **Reviews of specific movies or books hint at your personal preferences and larger product categories.** If you say on a rating site that you loved the original *Star Trek* series collection, the algorithm can easily determine what you like in terms of other films, consumer products, or even personality types.

An example of a method based on SVD is latent semantic indexing (LSI), which has been successfully used to associate documents and words based on the idea that words, though different, tend to have the same meaning when placed in similar contexts. This type of analysis suggests not only synonymous words but also higher grouping concepts. For example, an LSI analysis on some sample sports news may group baseball teams of the Major League based solely on the co-occurrence of team names in similar articles, without any previous knowledge of what a baseball team or the Major League is.

Other interesting applications for data reduction are systems for generating recommendations about the things you may like to buy or know more about. You likely have quite a few occasions to see recommenders in action. On most e-commerce websites, after logging in, visiting some product pages, and rating or putting a product into your electronic basket, you see other buying opportunities based on other customers' previous experiences. (As mentioned previously, this method is called *collaborative filtering*.) SVD can implement collaborative filtering in a more robust way, relying not just on information from single products but also on the wider information of a product in a set. For example, collaborative filtering can determine not only that you liked the film *Raiders of the Lost Ark* but also that you generally like all action and adventure movies.

You can implement collaborative recommendations based on simple means or frequencies calculated on other customers' sets of purchased items or on ratings using SVD. This approach helps you reliably generate recommendations even in the case of products that the vendor seldom sells or that are quite new to users.

Seeing SVD in action

For the example in this section, you use the MovieLense data set described in the "Trudging through the MovieLens data set" section, earlier in the chapter. After uploading it, you choose settings to work with users and movies with a minimum number of available ratings:

```
ratings_movies <- MovieLense[rowCounts(MovieLense) > 10,
                             colCounts(MovieLense) > 50]
```

After you filter the useful profiles, you center the ratings of each user. You subtract the mean from the rating values for each user to center the rating. This operation lessens the effect of extreme ratings (giving only highest or lowest ratings).

It also makes assigning missing values easy because each user can rate only a few movies. The missing ratings, which SVD requires to complete its computations, are determined using an average, which means zero values after mean centering.

```
ratings_movies_norm <- normalize(ratings_movies, row=TRUE)
densematrix <- as(ratings_movies_norm, "matrix")
densematrix[is.na(densematrix)] <- 0
```

After normalizing, setting the missing ratings to zero, and making the matrix dense (you're not using a sparse matrix anymore), the code uploads the irlba library (https://cran.r-project.org/web/packages/irlba/index.html). If the library isn't present on your system, you can use the following code snippet to install it:

```
if (!"irlba" %in% rownames(installed.packages()))
  {install.packages("irlba")}
library("irlba")
SVD <- irlba(densematrix, nv = 50, nu = 50)
```

The library's core algorithm is the augmented *implicitly restarted Lanczos bidiagonalization algorithm* (IRLBA), which computes an approximate SVD limited to a certain number of reconstructed dimensions. By computing just the required dimensions, it saves times and enables you to apply SVD even to immense matrices. The Netflix Prize successfully used the algorithm, and it works best when computing few SVD dimensions (www.youtube.com/watch?feature=player_embedded&v=ipkuRqYT8_I).

The following code explores the matrices extracted by the `irlba` function and uses them as a smaller data set with similar informative content to the original sparse matrix. Notice how the matrix u has the same number of rows as the initial movie matrix, while the matrix v has the number of rows equal to the number of columns of the original matrix. Columns are always 50, the number of dimensions requested as part of the `irlba` call.

```
print(attributes(SVD))
$names
[1] "d"     "u"     "v"     "iter"  "mprod"

print(dim(densematrix))
[1] 943 591

print(dim(SVD$u))
[1] 943 50

print(dim(SVD$v))
[1] 591 50
```

```
print(length(SVD$d))
[1] 50
```

The example doesn't stop at learning from data using an unsupervised approach. It can also learn the likelihood of a user's having seen a certain film from the data, that is, you can determine whether a person has seen a film or not based on movie interests, thanks to the SVD reconstruction. To make this analysis possible, the code selects a film, extracts it from the data set, and recomputes the SVD decomposition. This way, the output doesn't have any hints about the specific film inside the reconstructed matrices.

```
chosen_movie <- 45
print (paste("Chosen film:",
             colnames(densematrix)[chosen_movie]))
answer <- as.factor(as.numeric(
  densematrix[,chosen_movie]!=0))
SVD <- irlba(densematrix[,-chosen_movie], nv=50, nu=50)
rotation <- data.frame(movies=colnames(
  densematrix[,-chosen_movie]),SVD$v)

[1] "Chosen film: Pulp Fiction (1994)"
```

Before proceeding to learn from data, the example takes advantage of the v matrix produced from the SVD. The v matrix, the item matrix, contains information about the films, and it tells how SVD calculates the features in the matrix u (user matrix). For learning tasks, the example uses the matrix u and its reconstructed 50 components. As a machine learning tool, the example relies on a Random Forest ensemble of decision tree models.

```
if (!"randomForest" %in% rownames(installed.packages()))
   {install.packages("randomForest")}
library("randomForest")
train <- sample(1:length(answer),500)
user_matrix <- as.data.frame(SVD$u[train,])
target_matrix <- as.data.frame(SVD$u[-train,])
model <- randomForest(answer[train] ~., data=user_matrix,
                      importance=TRUE)
```

To test the learned model effectively, the example uses 500 users as a training set. The example uses the remaining users to test the prediction accuracy.

```
response <- predict(model, newdata=target_matrix,
                    n.trees=model$n.trees)
confusion_matrix <- table(answer[-train],response)
precision <- confusion_matrix[2,2] /
  sum(confusion_matrix[,2])
```

```
recall      <- confusion_matrix[2,2] /
  sum(confusion_matrix[2,])
print (confusion_matrix)
print(paste("Precision:",round(precision,3),
            "Recall:",round(recall,3)))

   response
      0   1
  0 214  50
  1  36 143

[1] "Precision: 0.741 Recall: 0.799"
```

By arranging the predictions on the test set in a confusion matrix, you can observe that the precision is quite high, as is the recall. Precision is the percentage of correct predictions. The Random Forest predicts that 193 users have seen the film in the test set and predicts a true assertion for 143 users of them, which amounts to a precision of 74.1 percent. Checking the true total of users who have seen the film (the previous figure was predicted) shows that 179 users watched the film. Because 143 predicted users equates to 79.9 percent of the 179 users, the model has a recall of 79.9 percent, which is the capability of predicting all the positive users.

The model that you prepared can also provide insight about reconstructed features that helps determine which users have seen a certain film. You can inspect the information by printing the importance derived from the Random Forest model, as shown in Figure 5-7.

```
varImpPlot(model,n.var=10)
```

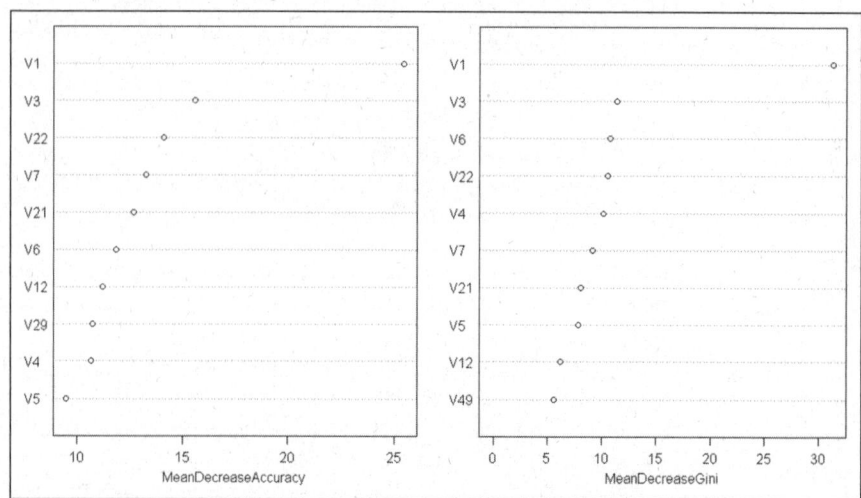

FIGURE 5-7: Importance measures derived from Random Forest.

According to the plotted importance, the first component of the u matrix derived from the SVD is the most predictive in determining whether a user has seen the movie. To determine what this component means, you can print its ordered elements from the one contributing the most in a positive fashion to the one contributing the most in a negative one.

```
rotation[order(rotation[,2]),1:2]
```

The resulting output is a long enumeration of films. At the start of the vector, in the negative range, you find films such as *Star Wars, The Godfather, Raiders of the Lost Ark,* and *The Silence of the Lambs.* At the end of the vector, in the positive sector, you see films such as *Liar Liar, Mars Attacks!,* and *Broken Arrow.* Because the negative values are stronger in absolute value than the positive ones, these values seem to convey more sense to the SVD component. Thus users who see blockbusters such as *Star Wars, The Godfather,* or *Raiders of the Lost Ark* are also likely to see a film like *Pulp Fiction.* You can test the theory directly by seeing how similar they are to the target film using the cosine distance.

```
similarity(ratings_movies[,45], ratings_movies[,145],
        method ="cosine", which = "items")

Raiders of the Lost Ark (1981)
Pulp Fiction (1994)                    0.7374849

similarity(ratings_movies[,45], ratings_movies[,82],
        method ="cosine", which = "items")

Silence of the Lambs, The (1991)
Pulp Fiction (1994)                    0.7492093
```

As shown in the output, users who see films such as *Raiders of the Lost Ark* or *The Silence of the Lambs* are also likely to see *Pulp Fiction.*

TIP

Interpreting results from an SVD is quite an art and requires a lot of domain knowledge (in this case, that means having movie experts). SVD puts sets of users and items together in the u and v matrices. It's up to you to use them for building recommendations and, if necessary, to provide them with an explanation about their reconstructed features based on your knowledge and intuition.

REMEMBER

SVD always finds the best way to relate a row or column in your data, discovering complex interactions or relations that you didn't imagine before. You don't need to imagine anything in advance; it's a fully data-driven approach.

Index

Special Characters & Numbers

':' character, 458
'-' character, 458
'--' character, 458
'-.' character, 458
: (colon), 133, 141, 357
\' or \" escape sequence, 360
\n escape sequence, 360
\t escape sequence, 360
_ (underscore) character, 358
+ operator, 261
== (equality) operator, 255, 257, 362
-moz-box-orient attribute, 225, 226
-ms-box-orient attribute, 226
-webkit-box-orient attribute, 226
!= (inequality) operator, 255, 362
!DOCTYPE html, 100
(hashtag), 162
symbol, 359
#id selector, 299
$ alias, 297
% operator, string formatting with, 364
[attribute] selector, 299
{ } (curly brackets), 132, 252, 350
< (left-angle bracket), 97, 98, 350
< (less than) operator, 255, 362
< and > (angle bracket), 350
<= (less than or equal to) operator, 255, 362
> (greater than) operator, 255, 362
> (right-angle bracket), 97, 98, 350
>= (greater than or equal to) operator, 245, 255, 362
2D array, 424, 425
3D array, 424–425

A

a posteriori probability, 566
a priori probability, 565, 566
<a> (anchor tag), 105, 106, 140
absLayout.css style sheet, 210
abs(n) function, 359
absolute positioning
　adding position guidelines, 203–204
　building page layouts with, 208–212
　overview, 209
　setting up HTML, 202–203
　using, 204–205
absolute value, position attribute, 205, 209
absolute value and rounding, 359
abstraction, 337
access control, AI used for, 537–538
accuracy measure, 709
action attribute, of <form> tag, 126, 127
activation functions, 644, 648, 650
active state, anchor tag (<a>), 140
ad blockers, 23
Adaboost, 670–673
add_path() function, 486
add_edge() function, 450, 485, 486
add_edges_from() function, 485, 486
add_node() function, 485, 486
add_nodes_from() function, 485, 486
addEventListener method, 270
addictive websites and apps, characteristics of, 13
addition, using matrices, 558
<address> tag, 184
adjacency matrix, 448
adjacency_matrix() function, 449
Adobe Photoshop app, 36
advertising, coding and, 11–12

AFINN-111 dictionary, 706
after() method, 302
aggregating data, at any level, 430–431
agile process, 34–35, 316
AI. *See* artificial intelligence
Airbnb, 11
AJAX (asynchronous JavaScript and XML)
　examples of, 280–282
　jQuery with, 309–310
　overview, 250–251, 279–289
　shorthand methods, 310
　using CORS, 287–288
　using same-origin policy, 287–288
　using XMLHttpRequest object, 285–287
　viewing requests and responses, 282–284
ajax() method, 309
alert() method, 259–260, 337
alerting users, 259–260
algorithms. *See also specific algorithms*
　defined, 541
　definition of, 548
　evolutionary, 549
　flexible, 639–642
　gradient descent, 578–580
　with kNN, 522–525
　learning process, 573–576
　linear regression, 512–515
　logistic regression, 515–518
　Naïve Bayes, 518–522
　reinforcement learning, 573
　supervised learning, 572
　techniques, 548–550
　training, 542
　unsupervised learning, 573
align attribute
　of <table> tag, 122
　of <td> tag, 123–124
　of <tr> tag, 123
align parameter, 470, 472
all div, 197–199, 209, 215, 229
alpha (α), 652
Amelia (robot), 532

American Standard (ASCII) coding, 702
AMORE library, 654
Anaconda-2.1.0-MacOSX-x86_64.sh file, 374
analogies, systems learning by, 550
analogizers, 547, 550
analysis of variance (ANOVA), 500
analytics, 55
analyzer parameter, 445
anchor tag (<a>), 105, 106, 140
Android devices, 56
androids
　artificial intelligence with machine learning, 533–534
　goals of machine learning, 534
　history of artificial intelligence (AI), 532–533
　history of machine learning, 532–533
　machine learning limitations based on hardware, 534–535
angle bracket (< and >), 350
animal protection, AI used for, 537
animate() method, 307
animation methods
　practicing with jQuery, 308–309
　setting arguments for, 307
annotate() function, 464
anonymity, big data and, 543
ANOVA (analysis of variance), 500
Antikythera mechanism, 532
Apache Hadoop, 582
Apache Spark, 582
APIs (application programming interfaces)
　API directories, 334–335
　choosing, 267
　overview, 263–265
　researching, 267
　screen scraping without, 266
append() method, 302, 427
Apple
　App Store, 56
　iPod, design changes, 328–329
　Maps product, 334
　programmers hired by, 87

application programming interfaces.
 See APIs
applications. *See also* mobile applications; web applications
 addictive, characteristics of, 13
 designing, 36–37
 planning, 316–318
 testing, 57
`argsort` method, 706
arrays, 557
`<article>` tag, 184, 229
artificial intelligence (AI)
 androids and, 532–535
 art and engineering divide, 540–541
 current uses of, 536–538
 facts versus fiction, 530–531
 fad uses of, 535–538
 history of, 532–533
 machine learning with, 533–534, 538–539
 mundane uses of, 538
 specifications of, 539–540
`as_grey` argument, 679
`as_matrix()` function, 481
ASCII (American Standard) coding, 702
`<aside>` tag, 184
assembly language, 15
Associate of Arts (AA) degree, 64
asynchronous JavaScript and XML. *See* AJAX
`attr()` method, 300
`[attribute]` selector, 299
attributes
 making changes with jQuery, 300
 overview, 98–99
`auto` value, of `backgroundsize` property, 143
autoencoders, 658
automation, AI used for, 537
autonomous weapon technologies, 531
`autopct` parameter, 469
averaging predictors, 676
awareness, computers and, 533
`ax` variable, 455

axes
 formatting, 456
 obtaining, 455
 representing time on, 478–479
 setting, 455–457
`axis` parameter, 423
Axure prototyping tool, 47

B

Bachelor of Arts (BA) degree, 59, 60
back end, 24–25
back-end developers
 careers as, 54–56
 overview, 38
 of web applications, 321
background colors, temporary, 177–179, 188
background images, 142–146
`background-attachment` property, 144–146
`backgroundattachment` property, 142
`background-image` property, 142–143, 154
`background-position` property, 144
`backgroundposition` property, 142
`background-repeat` property, 144
`backgroundrepeat` property, 142
`background-size` property, 143–144
`backgroundsize` property, 142
backpropagation, 549, 650–653
Bag of Words (BoW)
 implementing TF-IDF transformations, 446–447
 machine reading and, 693, 694
 n-grams, 445–446
 overview, 442–444
bagging, 664, 665, 670–673
Balsamiq tool, 36
bar charts, 471–472
Barksdale, Jim, 451
Basemap Toolkit, 481, 482
`bash` utility, 370
basic effects, in jQuery, 306
batch algorithms, 581
batch mode, for weight updates, 653
Bayes' theorem, 565–568, 616–617

Index 727

Bayesian inference, 549–550
Bayesian probability, 566–568
Bayesians, 547, 549–550
Beautiful Soup package, 700, 701
`before()` method, 302
between-cluster sum of squares (BSS), 630
biases
 backpropagation and, 549
 learning curves affected by, 594
 limits of, 589–591
 Literary Digest anecdote and, 587–588
 sample, avoiding, 601–602
big data
 algorithms in, 547–550
 defining training, 550–551
 definition of, 542–543
 overview, 541–542
 privacy and, 543
 size of, 543
 sources of, 543–546
 statistics in machine learning, 546–547
bigrams, 696
binary step, 645
binary values, neural networks and, 647
binary variables, 693
binning, 409, 496
bins, 471
bivariates, 498
Black Girls Who Code (organization), 90
`blacktie.co`, 240
blind men and elephant story, 670
blogs, 334
body tags, 100–101
`<body>` tag, 100, 158
bold (``) tag, 107–108
Boltzmann machines, restricted, 658
`bool()` function, 435, 436
`<Boolean>` element, 434, 435
boosting, 670–673
boot camps, 78
`Bootply.com`, 239
`bootsnipp.com`, 240

Bootstrap. *See* Twitter Bootstrap
bootstrapping, 597–598, 664
`bootstrapzero.com`, 240
`bootswatch.com`, 240
`border` attribute, 122
`border` property, 155, 156, 166, 167, 168
`border-collapse` property, 157
borders
 adjusting, 180–181
 emphasizing, 684
Boston data set, 656
BoW. *See* Bag of Words
box display type, 222
boxes
 overview, 167–168
 positioning, 169–171
`box-flex` attribute, 222, 225
Box.net, 118
`box-ordinal-group` attribute, 223, 225
`box-orient` attribute, 222, 224
`boxplot()` function, 473
boxplots
 basis of, 494
 depicting groups using, 472–474
 inspecting, 498–499
 performing t-tests after, 499–500
braces. *See* curly brackets (`{ }`)
broadband connectivity, 10
browsers
 cross-browser testing, 53–54
 most popular, 20
 overview, 39
 support for various, 318
BSS (between-cluster sum of squares), 630
`btn-defaultbtn-primarybtnsuccessbtn-danger` class prefix, 243
`btn-lgbtn-defaultbtn-sm` class prefix, 243
bugs. *See* debugging
BuiltWith website, 354
bull's-eye data set, 642
`<button>` tag, 243
buttons, designing, 243–244

C

c parameter, 475
Caffe library, 683
Cal Hacks hackathon, 63
callbacks
 overview, 269–273
 passing functions as arguments, 270
 using named functions as, 271–273
 writing functions with, 270–271
`capitalize()` string function, dot notation with, 363–364
`<caption>` tag, 157
careers
 augmenting existing job, 46–52
 finding new job, 52–58
 misconceptions about, 83–91
 overview, 45
`caret dropdown-menu` class prefix, 245
caret library, 620
Cascading Style Sheets. *See* CSS
cases
 adding new to data, 427–428
 in databases, 388
categorical data
 creating contingency tables, 497–498
 frequencies, 496–497
 overview, 495–496, 692–693
categorical variables
 creating, 415–419
 manipulating, 414–419
cells, aligning, 121–124
`cells` variable, 702
`center`, 473
centered fixed-width layouts
 creating surrogate body with `all div`, 197–198
 jello layouts, 198–200
 overview, 196–197
central tendency, measuring, 492–493
centroids, 628, 629, 633, 634–637
certificates, from schools of continuing education, 64–65
chaining, 297–298

charts, annotations, 464–465
Cheat Sheet for this book, 4
Chebyshev distance, 626
child selector, 160
chi-square statistic, 504, 507–508
Chrome browser
 HTML and, 96
 Inspect Element feature, 135
 installing latest, 20
 required, 3
`class` attribute, 162–163, 170, 242, 243
`.class` selector, 299
classification
 analyzing reviews from e-commerce, 706–709
 of images, 677–684
 searching by k-Nearest Neighbor, 637
 tasks, 704–706
classifiers, 442
ClassTranscribe project, 70
`clear` property, 169, 170
clients
 deliverables to, 318
 goals of, understanding, 317–318
closing tags, 98, 350
closures
 containing secret references to outer function variables, 275–276
 overview, 274–276
 using, 277–278
cluster-computer frameworks, 582
clusters, using distances to locate
 checking assumptions, 628–629
 checking expectations, 628–629
 K-means algorithm procedure, 629–630
 overview, 626–627
code, example
 defining code repository, 379–385
 using Jupyter Notebook, 378–379
Code 2040 (organization), 90
code blocks, 357
code repository. *See* repository
Codecademy.com, 38–41

Codepen.io development environment
 coding steps, 347–349
 overview, 343
 pre-written code in, 343–347
coding
 defined, 8–9
 online tutorials, 9
 tools, 38–39
 trends in, 9–10
 uses of, 9–13
 writing code, 33–38
Coding for Lawyers website, 52
coefficient vector, 557, 607
Coffitivity website, 12–13, 85
collaborative filtering, 711, 715, 719
`collapse` value, of `border-collapse` property, 157
`col-lg-` class prefix, 241
`col-md-` class prefix, 241, 242
colon (:), 133, 141, 357
`color` parameter, 472
`color` property, 133, 134, 136, 137–138, 140
colors
 background, temporary, 177–179
 in graphs, 458–460
`colors` parameter, 469
`col-sm-` class prefix, 241, 242
`colspan` attribute, 120
`col-sx-` class prefix, 241
columns
 CSS3 and, 200
 in database, 388
 floating, 179–180
 slicing, 425
 stretching, 120–121
 using Twitter Bootstrap, 236–239
COM (Component Object Model) applications, 402
comma-separated value (CSV) files, 392, 394–395
comments, 359
companies, enduring, characteristics of, 13

comparison operators, 362
`compile()` function, 442
compiled programming languages, 15
compilers, purpose of, 15
complement of a probability, 565
`complete` argument, 307
complex analysis, AI used for, 537
complexity of programs, lines of code and, 8
Component Object Model (COM) applications, 402
`components_` attribute, 706
computer science curriculum, 60–61, 66–68
Computer Science Education Week, 9
computer vision, 68
`concat()` method, 427
`concatenate()` function, 473
concatenating data
 adding new cases, 427–428
 adding new variables, 427–428
 overview, 426–427
 removing data, 428–429
 shuffling, 429–430
 sorting, 429–430
conditional probability, 566, 615
conditional statements, 254, 337
confusionMatrix function, 620
connectionism, 547, 549, 607
connectivity, broadband, 10
`console.log` statement, 254
`contain` value, of `backgroundsize` property, 143
content class, 221
content div, 219
content services, careers in, 47–48
content updates, 74
content-based filtering, 715
contingency tables, creating, 497–498
continuing education, certificates from, 64–65
Continuum Analytics Anaconda, 369–370
contracting, 88
convolutional neural networks, 658–659, 683
coordinates, parallel, 500–501
core memory, 581

corpus, 693
correlations
 considering chi-square for tables, 507–508
 covariance and, 504–506
 nonparametric, 507
 showing in scatterplots, 477
CORS (Cross-Origin Resource Sourcing), 287–288
cosine similarity, 716
cost functions, 576–579
`count_vect.fit_transform()` function, 444
`counterclock` parameter, 469
`CountVectorizer()` function, 439
`CountVectorizer` class, 693, 694, 696
Course Report, 78
CourseHorse, 78
covariance, correlations and, 504–506
`cover` value, of `backgroundsize` property, 143
`Craigslist.org`, 114, 280
create, read, update, and delete (CRUD), 541
creative design, careers in, 46–47
creators of programming languages, 14
cropping images, 681–682
cross-browser testing, 53–54
Cross-Origin Resource Sourcing (CORS), 287–288
cross-validation
 optimizing, 598–601
 overview, 596–597
CRUD (create, read, update, and delete), 541
CSS (Cascading Style Sheets)
 adding to HTML, 146–148
 adding to static layouts, 210–212
 building sample web page, 148–149
 columns and, 200
 customizing links, 139–141
 designing tables, 155–157
 embedded, 147
 fixing width with, 194–196
 frameworks for, 54
 history of, 130
 incorporating into web pages, 146–149
 laying out elements, 163–171
 in-line, 146
 making changes with jQuery, 300–301
 modifying on web pages, 133–135
 naming elements, 161–163
 as one of first languages to learn, 86
 overview, 26–27, 129–131
 practicing with `Codecademy.com`, 148–149, 172
 precompilers for, 54
 pre-written codes, 344–345
 selecting elements, 157–163
 selectors, 135–146
 in separate style sheets, 147–148
 setting background images, 142–146
 setting fonts, 135–139
 structure of, 131–135
 styling elements, 158–161
 styling lists, 152–155
 time needed to learn, 85
CSV (comma-separated value) files, 392, 394–395
curly brackets ({ }), 132, 252, 350
curriculum, computer science, 60–61, 66–68
cursive font family, 139
`cursive` value, of `font-family` property, 132, 133
custom effects, with `animate()` method, 307
customer service, AI used for, 537
`cut` function, 496
Cutler, Adele, 664
`cycle_graph()` function, 449

D

D3.js library, 268
dashed lines, in graphs, 458
data. *See also* big data; data sets; data shaping, data types; numeric data
 accessing from web, 402–404
 accessing in flat-file form, 392–397
 adding new cases to, 427–428
 adding new variables to, 427–428
 advanced matrix operations, 561
 aggregating at any level, 430–431
 categorical, 495–498
 concatenating, 426–430

data *(continued)*
 creating from existing, 545
 dates in, 419–421
 distributions, 508–510
 extracting, with Xpath, 435–436
 filtering, 424–426
 finding shapes in, 641–642
 geographical, plotting, 481–483
 machines reading, 692–694
 managing from relational databases, 400–401
 manipulating categorical variables, 414–419
 missing, 421–424
 navigating from web, 714–715
 from NoSQL databases, interacting with, 401–402
 obtaining from private sources, 544–545
 obtaining from public sources, 544
 performing matrix multiplication, 558–561
 ratings, 712, 715–716
 removing, 428–429
 sampling, 388–392
 selecting, 424–426
 sending unstructured-file form, 397–399
 shuffling, 429–430
 sorting, 429–430
 sources of, 544–546
 splitting to predict outcomes, 610–614
 storing with variables, 253–254
 streaming, 388–392
 textual sets from the web, 699–702
 transforming, 426–430
 uploading, 388–392
 validating, 409–414
data analysis
 careers in, 57–58
 categorical, 495–498
 correlations, 504–508
 defining descriptive statistics for numeric data, 491–495
 exploratory data analysis (EDA), 490–491, 498–504
 modifying distributions, 508–510

data handling, machine learning vs. statistics at, 534
data input, machine learning vs. statistics at, 534
data retrieval, 74
data sets. *See also specific data sets*
 downloading, 378–386
 overview, 385–386
 time needed to learn about, 85
data shaping
 bag of words model, 442–447
 in graphs, 447–450
 on HTML pages, 434–436
 overview, 433–434
 in raw text files, 436–442
data types, defining in Python, 357–358
data visualization
 with bar charts, 471–472
 with box plots, 472–474
 choosing graphs, 468–475
 graphs, 483–487
 with histograms, 472–474
 overview, 57–58, 467–468
 with pie charts, 468–469
 plotting geographical, 481–483
 plotting time series, 478–481
 with scatterplots, 474–478
Database Management Systems (DBMSs), 400
databases
 early vs. modern, 63
 NoSQL, 401–402
 overview, 54
 relational, 400–401
DataFrame object, SQL, 400
dataframed, 409
DataFrame.to_sql() method, 401
date_range, 479
dates
 formatting time values, 419–420
 formatting values, 419–420
 using time transformations, 420–421
datetime object, 419
DBMSs (Database Management Systems), 400

debugging, 38, 350
decision trees
 adaptability of, 590
 importance measures, 667–679
 overview, 662–663
 predicting outcomes by splitting data, 610–614
 pruning, 614–615
 Quinlan paper on, 555
 Random Forests algorithm, 663–677
declarations, 133
deep belief networks, 658
deep learning, 644, 654, 657–659
degenerate matrices, 561
`` (strikethrough) tag, 107–108
deleted text, 107
deliverables, 318
delta (δ), 651–652
denial of service (DoS) attack, 55–56
deprecated (older) attributes, 121–122
depth, adjusting, 206–207
descendant selector, 160–161
`describe()` method, 413, 414, 492
descriptive statistics
 defining measures of normality, 494–495
 measuring central tendency, 492–493
 measuring range, 493
 measuring variance, 493
 overview, 491–492
 working with percentiles, 494
designers
 responsibilities of, 54
 of web applications, 319–320
 who code, 47
desktops, adapting layouts for, 241–242
Developer Tools panel, Chrome browser, 20
developers
 back-end, 38
 front-end, 38
 full stack, 25, 38
 networking with, 81
 specializations of, 25, 38
 support from while learning to code, 77

development environments, 343
`df.index.tolist()` method, 430
`diagonal='hist'` parameter, 503
dicing, 426
digital designers. *See* designers
`DiGraph()` constructor, 486
directed graphs, 485–487
`display` attribute, 222, 224
display errors, 38
Disrupt hackathon, 70
distances
 computing for machine learning, 625–626
 to locate clusters, 626–630
distributed storage and processing, 58
distribution, machine learning vs. statistics at, 534
distributions
 data, 508–510
 graphing, 501–502
 normal, 508–509
 transforming, 509–510
`distutils.util`, 435
`<div>` tag, 165–167, 175–176, 237–238, 242
DNS (domain name server), 23, 24
doctorate degrees, 66
document ready event, 298
`documentLoader` function, 286
DOM (Document Object Model), 160, 301–302
domain name server (DNS), 23, 24
`doMath` function (example), 270–271
Dorm Room Fund, 62
DoS (denial of service) attack, 55–56
dot notation
 with `capitalize()`, 363–364
 with `lower()`, 363–364
 with `strip()`, 363–364
 with `upper()`, 363–364
dotted line, in graphs, 458
double borders, 180–181
dragging and dropping, to web pages, 239–240
`draw_networkx()` function, 487
`drawcoastlines()` function, 483

drawcountries() function, 483
drawing with repetition, 597
dribbble.com, 330
drop() method, 428
drop_duplicates() method, 412
dropdown class prefix, 245
dropdown-toggle class, 245
dropna() method, 422
drop-out, 658, 659
dtype property, 416
duplicates, data, removing, 412–414
duration argument, 307

E

e1071 library, 621
early-stop, 654
easing argument, 307
e-commerce, analyzing reviews from, 706–709
EDA. *See* exploratory data analysis
editorial services, careers in, 47–48
editors. *See* text editors
education in coding, misconceptions about
 can learn coding in weeks, 85
 must be good at math, 84
 must study engineering, 84
 need great idea to start coding, 85–86
 overview, 83
 Ruby is better than Python, 86–87
effects, jQuery
 basic, 306
 custom, 307
 fading, 306
 overview, 305–306
 practicing with jQuery animations, 308–309
 setting arguments for animation methods, 307
 sliding, 306–307
eigenfaces, 684–687
Element selector, 299
elements, HTML
 choosing, 131–133
 laying out, 163–171
 manipulating in DOM, 301–302
 naming, 161–163
 overview, 97–98
 selecting, 157–163
 styling, 158–161
elif statements, 361–362
else if statement, 256–257
else statement, 256, 361–362
em values, 136–137
 (emphasize) tag, 107, 108
email
 as source of big data, 546
 spam detection, 619
embedded CSS, 147
emphasize () tag, 107, 108
empty() method, 302
encodings, 422–423, 702
English, in programming languages, 14
ensembles
 averaging different predictors, 676
 bagging, 670–673
 boosting, 670–673
 GBM algorithm, 673–675
 leveraging decision trees, 662–669
ensembling of predictors, 601–602
entelo.com, 88
Enthought Canopy Express, 369–370
enumerate() function, in Python, 391
enumerations, 414
environment, importance to machine learning, 535
epsilon (ε), 652
equality (==) operator, 255, 257, 362
error function, 576, 577
errors, 38. *See also* debugging
escape sequences, 360, 361
eta (η), 608, 652
Euclidean distance, 626, 628
evaluation function, 576–577
EventHub platform, 70
evolutionaries, 547
evolutionary algorithms, 549

examples in this book, source code for, 4
Excel files, 393, 396–397
executable files, 15
expectations, checking, 628–629
explode parameter, 469
exploratory data analysis (EDA)
 graphing distributions, 501–502
 inspecting boxplots, 498–499
 observing parallel coordinates, 500–501
 overview, 490–491
 performing t-tests after boxplots, 499–500
 plotting scatterplots, 502–504
exporting, notebooks in Jupyter Notebooks, 383
eXtensible Markup Language. *See* XML
extra content, 4
extracting
 data, with Xpath, 435–436
 visual features, 683–684
extracurricular activities, 61–64

F

Facebook
 native mobile app vs. mobile web app, 31
 programmers hired by, 87
 survivorship bias and, 588
faces recognition, 684–687
`fadeIn()` method, 306
`fadeOut()` method, 306
`fadeTo()` method, 306
`fadeToggle()` method, 306
fading effects, in jQuery, 306
fantasy font family, 139
Farecast algorithm, 68
FarmLogs, 46
FastIca algorithm, 689
feature learning, 657
`feature_extraction` module, 693
`feature_selection` module, 668
feedback, collecting, 330–331, 333
feed-forward, 645–647
Fellig, Sam, 85

fellowships, 69
`fetch_20newsgroups()` function, 444
`fetch_olivetti_faces()` function, 385
`<figcaption>` tag, 184
`<figure>` tag, 184
files
 CSV delimited, 394–395
 Excel, 396–397
 formats of, 331
 Microsoft Office, 396–397
 text, 393, 436–442
`fillcontinents()` function, 483
`fillna()` method, 422
filtering data, 424–426
`find()` function, 402, 702
`findAll()` method, 702
finding missing data, 421–422
Firefox browser, HTML and, 96
Fisher's Iris data set, 491
`fit()` method, 423, 631, 693
fitting, machine learning vs. statistics at, 534
fixed positioning, 216–220
`fixed` value
 `backgroundattachment` property, 145
 `position` attribute, 220
fixed-width layouts
 fixing width with CSS, 194–196
 setting up HTML, 193–194
flat-file data, accessing
 CSV delimited files, 394–395
 Excel files, 396–397
 Microsoft Office files, 396–397
 overview, 392–393
 text file, 393
flat-file formatting, 392
`flatten()` function, 481
flattening images, 682
flexbox layout
 building, 215–216
 designing with percentages, 213–214
 overview, 212–213

flexible algorithms
 choosing k values, 639–641
 finding shapes in data, 641–642
 testing k values, 639–641
Flickr, 106, 143
`flier_high`, 473
`flier_low`, 473
`float` attribute, 188
`float` property, 169, 170
floating columns, setting, 179–180
floating layouts
 centered fixed-width, 196–200
 fixed-width, 193–196
 problems with, 188–189
 three-column, 185–192
 two-column
 adjusting borders, 180–181
 advantages of fluid layouts, 181
 building HTML code, 175–177
 setting floating columns, 179–180
 sketching web pages, 173–175
 using semantic tags, 182–185
 using temporary background colors, 177–179
fluid layouts, advantages of, 181
FNN library, 639
folders, in Jupyter Notebooks, 380–381
`font-family` property, 132, 133, 136, 138–139
fonts, CSS properties for styling
 `color` property, 137–138
 `font-family` property, 138–139
 `font-size` property, 136–137
 `font-style` property, 138
 `font-weight` property, 138
 overview, 135–136
 `text-decoration` property, 139
`<footer>` tag, 184, 229
footers, 179, 188
form, of applications, 328–331, 332–333
`<form>` tag
 attributes of, 125
 defining form with, 126

formatting
 bold, 107–108
 date values, 419–420
 italics, 107–108
 strikethrough, 107–108
 subscript, 108–109
 superscript, 108–109
 time values, 419–420
 underline, 107–108
forms, 124–127
Fortune 1000 companies, programmers hired by, 87–88
frameworks
 for CSS, 54
 for JavaScript, 54
 for mobile web, 30
 overview, 27–28
fraud detection, 536–537
freeCodeCamp, 80
freelancing, 79–80, 88
frequencies, 496–497
front end, 24–25
front-end developers
 careers as, 53–54
 overview, 38
 of web applications, 321
full stack developers, 25, 38
function declarations, 260
function factory, 277
functions
 case of, 347
 creating using functions, 274, 277–278
 named as callbacks, 271–273
 naming code with, 260–261
 passing as arguments, 270
 writing with callbacks, 270–271

G

Garbage In/Garbage Out (GIGO), 489
gasbuddy.com, 290–291
Gaussian distribution, 508–509, 570, 680

GBM (gradient boosting machines) algorithms, 673–675
gbm package, 675
Gecko-based browsers, 225
General Assembly, 77–78
generalizations, 551, 587–588
geographic information systems (GIS), 544
geographical data, plotting, 481–483
geolocation, 335
.get() method, 310
GET value, of method attribute, of <form> tag, 126
get_feature_names method, 706
getbootstrap.com, 245, 247
Getcha-Books website, 61
getElementByID method, 347
.getJSON() method, 310
getlocation() function, 335
getLocation() function, 345
getroot() method, 404
.getScript() method, 310
GIGO (Garbage In/Garbage Out), 489
gini importance, 668
gini impurity, 611
Girls Who Code (organization), 90
GIS (geographic information systems), 544
GitHub, 80
glyphicons.com, 246
glyphs, 246
goals
 of apps, 329
 of clients, 317–318
Google, programmers hired by, 87
Google Brain project, 657
Google Chrome browser. *See* Chrome browser
Google DeepMind, 573
Google Drive, 39
Google Images, 106, 143
Google Made with Code campaign, 90
Google Maps, on Yelp site, 17
Google NGram viewer, 696
Google Play Store, 56
Google self-driving car, 542, 543

Google Sites, 39
GPUs (graphical processing units), 535, 657–658
gradient boosting machines (GBM) algorithms, 673–675
gradient descent, 578–580, 652, 674–675
graduate degrees, 65–68
Graph() constructor, 485
graph data
 adjacency matrix, 448
 overview, 447
 using NetworkX, 448–450
graphical processing units (GPUs), 535, 657–658
graphics-intensive applications, 31
graphs
 bar charts, 471–472
 box plots, 472–474
 defining plots, 452–453
 directed, 485–487
 drawing multiple lines, 453–454
 drawing plots, 453–454
 graphing distributions, 501–502
 histograms, 472–474
 with MatPlotLib, 452–455
 pie charts, 468–469
 saving, 454–455
 scatterplots, 474–475
 undirected, 484–485
 visualizing, 483–487
greater than (>) operator, 255, 362
greater than or equal to (>=) operator, 245, 255, 362
grid() function, 457
grid system, Bootstrap, 236–239
grids, in MatPlotLib
 adding, 457
 setting, 455–457
grid-search, 600
groupby() function, 413, 431
GroupLens project, 711
Groupon, 11
groups, depicting in scatterplots, 476
guidelines, positioning, adding, 203–204

Index 737

H

h1 selector, 132
hackathons, 63
Hadoop, Apache, 582
hairballs, 448
handles, in MatPlotLib, 455
hashtag (#), 162
Haversine formula, 337, 346
`<head>` tag, 100–101, 158
`<header>` tag, 184, 229
headlines
 on web pages, example of, 102
 writing, 103–104
healthcare.gov website, 35
height, 191–192
`height` attribute, 123–124, 205, 209
heuristics, 628
hex code, 137
`hidden` attribute, 99
hidden layers, 648
`hide()` method, 306
high-dimensional sparse data set, 444
high-level programming languages, 14–15
`Hipmunk.com`, 114–115, 330
hiring of programmers, 87–88
histograms, 472–474, 502
"hook model," 13
horizontal navigation, 164, 165
`horizontal` value, of `box-orient` attribute, 224
hotlinking, 106, 143
hover state, anchor tag (`<a>`), 140
HTML (HyperText Markup Language). *See also* CSS (Cascading Style Sheets); elements, HTML
 adding CSS to, 146–148
 attributes, 98–99
 building sample web pages using, 109–111
 building the code, 175–177
 formatting, 107–109
 forms, 124–127
 history of, 101
 HTML5, 101
 lists, 115–117
 as one of first languages to learn, 86
 organizing content on web pages, 113–114
 overview, 95–96
 parsing, 434–435
 practicing with `Codecademy.com`, 127–128
 pre-written codes, 343–344
 setting up, 193–194, 202–203
 shaping data on pages, 434–436
 structure of, 96–101
 tables, 118–124
 tags, 102–107
 time needed to learn, 85
 writing, 210
`html()` method, 302
`<html>` tag, 100, 158
HTTP GET method, 286
Huffington Post website, 134
Huffman, Steve, 355
human resources, careers in, 48–49
humanoid robots, 532
Huxley, Aldous, 233
H(X) function, 671
hyperlinks. *See* links
hyper-parameters, 575, 599–601
HyperText Markup Language. *See* HTML
hypotheses, 575, 589

I

I Quant NY blog, 48
icons, adding, 246–247
`id` attribute, 162, 166, 170
IDA (Initial Data Analysis), 490
identity matrix, 561
IEEE (Institute of Electrical and Electronics Engineers), 540
`if` statements, 361–362
`if-else` statement, 254–257, 337, 348
image (``) tag, 106
image classification
 extracting visual features, 683–684
 overview, 677–678

recognizing faces using eigenfaces, 684–687
working with sets of images, 678–682
image file format, 331
images
 adding, 106
 background, 142–146
 borders of, 684
 cropping, 681–682
 flattening, 682
 resizing, 682
 on web pages, example of, 102, 103
`` (image) tag, 106
`imgur.com`, 106
Imitation Game, 533
implementation, ease of, 338
implicit matrix multiplication, 559
implicitly restarted Lanczos bidiagonalization algorithm (IRLBA), 720
`import math` statement, 359
`import this;` command, 356
importance function, 669
importance measures, 667–679
`import.io`, 266
Imputer parameters, 423
`imread()` method, 397, 679
`imshow()` function, 398, 679
indenting code, 342, 350, 357
independence hypothesis, 508
Independent Component Analysis, 689
independent events, 565
indexes, 556
industry news and blogs, 334
inequality (!=) operator, 255, 362
information gain, 611
information redundancy, 505
Information Retrieval (IR), 443
informative entropy, 611
infrastructure category, of website code, 24, 25
`init` method, 631
Initial Data Analysis (IDA), 490
in-line CSS, 146

`.innerHTML` method, 347
in-person training programs, 76–77
input layer, in neural networks, 646
`<input>` tag, 126
in-sample data, 587, 589, 591
Insight Segmentation and Registration Toolkit (ITK), 679
Inspect Element feature (Developer Tools), Chrome browser, 135
Instagram, 26
Institute of Electrical and Electronics Engineers (IEEE), 540
interaction designers, 320
International Organization for Standardization/ International Electrotechnical Commission (ISO/IEC), 540
Internet, broadband connectivity, 10
Internet Protocol (IP) address, 23
Internet service provider (ISP), 23, 24
internships, 68–72
interpreted programming languages, 15
interpreters, purpose of, 15
interquartile range (IQR), 494, 498
intuition, machine learning and, 535
inverse of a matrix, 561
InVision prototyping tool, 47
iOS devices, 56
IP (Internet Protocol) address, 23
iPod, design changes, 328–329
`.ipynb` files, 384
IPython Notebook, 377, 383, 384
IQR (interquartile range), 494, 498
IR (Information Retrieval), 443
Iris data set, 495, 505, 632, 634, 635, 647
`iris_dataframe.describe()` function, 492
IRLBA (implicitly restarted Lanczos bidiagonalization algorithm), 720
`irlba` function, 720
irlba library, 720
`isin()` method, 418
`isnull()` method, 416, 421
ISO/IEC (International Organization for Standardization/ International Electrotechnical Commission), 540

Index **739**

ISP (Internet service provider), 23, 24
italics text, 107–108
ITK (Insight Segmentation and Registration Toolkit), 679

J

JavaScript. *See also* AJAX
 adding to web pages, 261–262
 alerting users, 259–260
 creator of, 14
 frameworks for, 54
 functions, 260–261
 functions in, case of, 347
 `if-else` statements, 254–257
 libraries, 267–268
 number methods, 258–259
 as one of first languages to learn, 86
 overview, 26–27, 249–251
 practicing with `Codecademy.com`, 263
 pre-written codes, 345–347
 prompting users for input, 259–260
 string methods, 258–259
 structure of, 251–252
 variables, 253–254
 working with APIs, 263–267
JavaScript Object Notation (JSON), 280, 289–293
jello layouts, 198–200
`Jetstrap.com`, 239
`join()` method, 428
jQuery
 with AJAX, 309–310
 document ready event, 298
 effects, 305–309
 getting started, 296–297
 making changes with, 300–302
 objects, 297–298
 overview, 267–268, 295
 selectors, 298–299
jQuery keyword, 297
JSON (JavaScript Object Notation), 280, 289–293
`JSON.parse` method, 293
Jupyter Notebook
 creating folders, 380–381
 creating notebooks, 381–383
 exporting notebooks, 383
 importing notebooks, 384–385
 removing notebooks, 383–384
 starting, 378–379
 stopping, 379

K

k parameters
 choosing, 525
 flexible algorithms, 639–642
 overview, 638–639
k values, 639–641
`k_means` variable, 632
Kaggle library, 538
Keras wrapper, 654
Keynote app, 36
keywords value, of `background-position` property, 144, 145
k-fold cross-validation, 596, 597
klaR library, 619
K-means algorithms
 procedure of, 629–630
 tuning, 630–637
k-means++ initialization procedure, 632
k-Nearest Neighbors (kNN)
 choosing k parameters, 525
 overview, 522–523
 predicting after observing neighbors, 523–524
 searching for classification by, 637
knowledge representation, 539
knowledge-based recommendations, 715–716
kurtosis, 494, 495

L

`label` parameter, 472
Labeled Faces in the Wild data set, 688
labels, in graphs, 463–464
`labels` parameter, 469, 487

language processing, natural, 68, 443, 539, 691–692
Laplace correction, 617
large numbers, law of, 662
Lasagne library, Python, 654
last_valid_index() method, 428
latent semantic indexing (LSI), 719
law of large numbers, 662
layers
 in neural networks, 647–650
 in Photoshop, 36
Layoutit.com, 239
layouts. *See also* floating layouts; positioning
 adapting for desktops, 241–242
 adapting for mobile, 241–242
 adapting for tablets, 241–242
 building with absolute positioning, 208–212
 centered fixed-width, 196–200
 dragging and dropping web pages, 239–240
 fixed-width, 193–196
 flexbox, 212–216
 fluid, 181
 jello, 198–200
 static, 210–212
 three-column, 185–192
 two-column
 adjusting borders, 180–181
 advantages of fluid layouts, 181
 building HTML code, 175–177
 setting floating columns, 179–180
 sketching web pages, 173–175
 using semantic tags, 182–185
 using temporary background colors, 177–179
 using grid system, 236–239
 using predefined templates, 240
leakage traps, avoiding, 602
learning curves, depicting, 593–595
learning rates, 583, 608–609, 652
learning_curve function, 595
leave-one-out cross-validation (LOOCV), 597
left attribute, 205, 209, 221
left navigation toolbar, 164, 165
left-angle bracket (<), 97, 98, 350

legal services, careers in, 51–52
legend() function, 465, 466
legends, in graphs, 465–466
.length method, 259
less than (<) operator, 255, 362
less than or equal to (<=) operator, 255, 362
 (list item) tag, 116, 158, 245
library classes, 79
lifespan of programming languages, 14
lindaliukas.fi website, 27
linear function, 307
linear models, 512–513, 592, 606
linear regression
 bias and, 589, 590
 defining family of linear models, 512–513
 limitations of, 514–515
 neural networks and, 654
 using more variables, 513–514
lines, in MatPlotLib
 defining appearance, 458–462
 multiple, drawing, 453–454
 using styles, 458–459
lines of code, complexity of programs and, 8
link state, anchor tag (<a>), 140
<link> tag, 147
links
 to content, 104–106
 customizing, 139–141
 description of, 105
 destination of, 105
 in graph data, 447
 on web pages, example of, 102, 103
Linux operating system, installing Python on, 371–372
lipsum.org, 238
list item () tag, 116, 158, 245
lists
 nesting, 117
 ordered, 116
 overview, 115–116
 styling, 152–155
 unordered, 116

list-style-image property, 153, 154
list-style-type property, 152–153, 154
Literary Digest poll, 587–588
live data, displaying in web page, 281
LiveScript. *See* JavaScript
LivingLanguage app, 70
llcrnrlat parameter, 483
llcrnrlon parameter, 483
load_boston() function, 385
load_diabetes() function, 385
load_digits([n_class]) function, 385
load_iris() function, 385
location services, 56–57, 342
location-based offers, building applications with, 313–315
logic category, of website code, 24, 25
logic errors, 38
logical operation XOR, 644, 645
logistic regression
 applying, 516
 multiclass problems, 517–518
 overfitting and, 654
 overview, 515–516
LOOCV (leave-one-out cross-validation), 597
Lorem Ipsum text, 176, 238
loss function, 577
lower() string function, dot notation with, 363–364
low-level programming languages, 14–15
LSI (latent semantic indexing), 719
Lynda.com, 76

M

Mac operating system, installing Python on, 372–374
machine code, 14–15
machine efficiency, AI used for, 537
machine learning. *See also* artificial intelligence (AI); big data
 algorithms, 572–576
 choosing Python distribution for, 368–371
 computing distances for, 625–626
 cost functions, 576–578
 current uses of, 536–538
 decision trees, 610–615
 fad uses of, 536
 goals of, 534
 history of, 532–533
 limitations based on hardware, 534–535
 mathematics and
 describing use of statistics, 568–570
 exploring probabilities, 563–568
 overview, 553–554
 working with data, 554–563
 overview, 57
 perceptrons and, 606–610
 probabilities, 563–568, 615–621
 process, 573–576
 role of statistics in, 546–547
 specifications of, 539–540
 taught in college courses, 67
 training defined, 550–551
 updating by mini-batch, 581–583
 updating online, 581–583
 validating
 alternatives, 597–598
 avoiding leakage traps, 602
 avoiding sample bias, 601–602
 balancing solutions, 592–595
 checking out-of-sample errors, 586–588
 considering model complexity, 591–592
 cross-validation, 596–597
 limits of bias, 589–591
 optimizing cross-validation, 598–601
 overview, 585–586
 testing, 595
 training, 595
Made with Code campaign, Google, 90
Mahotas library, 679
mailto value, of action attribute, of <form> tag, 127
Manhattan distance, 626
map() function, 435
mapping, 574

map-reduce technology, 582
Maps product, Apple, 334
`margin` property, 166, 167, 168
`margin-bottom`, 215
`margin-left`, 215, 216
`margin-right`, 215, 216
`margin-top`, 215
marker parameter, 475
markers, adding in MatPlotLib, 460–462
marketing
 careers in, 50–51
 coding and, 12
mashape.com, 335
mashups, big data, 545
master algorithm, 547
master's degree, 65–66
`math.method(variable)` method, 359
`math.ceil(n)` function, 359
mathematics
 computing math in Python, 358–360
 machine learning and
 describing use of statistics, 568–570
 exploring probabilities, 563–568
 overview, 553–554
 working with data, 554–563
`math.floor(n)` function, 359
`math.method(value)` method, 359
MATLAB application, 451–452
MatPlotLib
 annotations, 462–466
 axes, 455–457
 graphs, 452–455
 grids, 455–457
 labels, 462–466
 legends, 462–466
 line appearance, 458–462
 overview, 451–452
 ticks, 455–457
`matplotlib.pyplot` module, 452
matrices
 adjacency, 448
 advanced operations, 561
 basic operations, 558

 creating, 556–558
 defined, 556
 multiplication, 558–561
`max_features` argument, 445–446
`mb_k_means` variable, 632
mean, 570
mean decrease accuracy and impurity, 668
measuring
 central tendency, 492–493
 range, 493
 similarity between vectors, 624–625
 variance, 493
median, 570
Median filter, 680
menu div, 219
menu navigation, 164, 165
`<menu/command>` tag, 184
`<meter>` tag, 184
method attribute, of `<form>` tag, 126
methods, 258
Meyer, Eric, 137
Meyer, Rebecca, 137
microservices, 403
Microsoft, programmers hired by, 87
Microsoft Excel files, 393, 396–397
Microsoft Office files, 396–397
Microsoft Windows operating system, installing Python on, 374–377
MindNet semantic network, 699
`min-height` attribute, 189–191
`min-height` property, specifying, 189–191
mini-batch (stochastic) mode, for weight updates, 653
mini-batches, updating machine learning by, 581–583
Miniconda installer, 370
minimum viable product, 37
missing data
 encoding, 422–423
 finding, 421–422
 imputing, 423–424
`missing_values` parameter, 423
misspelled statements, 350

mobile applications
 coding, 28–32
 coding for practice, 79–80
 defined, 25–26
 development of, careers in, 56–57
 layouts for, 241–242
 native apps, 30–32
 web apps, 29–30
mobile web applications, compared with native mobile applications, 28–29
mockups, 36, 37, 47, 54, 331, 333
modules, 360
MongoClient class, 402
MongoDB, 401–402
monospace font family, 139
MovieLens data sets, 712–714, 719
-moz-box-orient attribute, 225, 226
Mozilla Firefox browser, HTML and, 96
mozilla.org, 163
-ms-box-orient attribute, 226
MSWeb data set, 714–715
mtry hyper-parameter, 669
multiclass, strategies with logistic regression, 517–518
MultiDiGraph() graph type, 486
MultiGraph() graph type, 486
multiplication, on matrices, 558–561
multivariates, 498, 570
mutually exclusive probabilities, 565
<MyDataset> root node, in XML, 404

N

\n escape sequence, 360
n_ components parameter, 705
n_clusters, 631
n_components parameter, 686
n_estimators parameter, 673
n_jobs parameter, 666
Naïve Bayes
 estimating responses with, 618–621
 general discussion, 615–618
 overview, 518–520
 predicting text classifications, 520–522

NaiveBayes function, 619, 620, 621
named entity recognition, 692
named functions, using as callbacks, 271–273
native mobile applications, 25, 28–29
natural language, 15
Natural Language Processing (NLP), 68, 443, 539, 691–692
Natural Language Toolkit (NLTK), 438, 697
natural language understanding, 539
<nav> tag, 184, 229
nav-pills class prefix, 245
ndarray objects, 562, 563
n-dimensional arrays, 562
Nelder-Mead method, 600
nesting
 flexboxes, 222
 lists, 117
network parallelism, 582
network systems, taught in college courses, 67
NetworkX package, 448–450, 484
neural networks
 architecture of, 646
 building, 654–656
 deep learning, 657–659
 imitating nature
 backpropagation algorithms, 650–653
 feed-forward process, 645–647
 layers, 647–650
 overview, 644–645
 overfitting, 653–657
 overview, 643–644
neuralnet library, 654
neurons, 549, 644
newlines, 357, 360
ngram_range parameter, 445
n-grams, 445–446, 696, 697
NLP. *See* Natural Language Processing
NLTK (Natural Language Toolkit), 438, 697
NMF (Non-Negative Matrix Factorization), 689, 704
nodes, 447
no-freelunch theorem, 592–593
noise, 575, 576
nolearn wrapper, 654

None value, in Python, 421
nonlearnable parameters, 575
nonlinear separability, 608–610
Non-Negative Matrix Factorization (NMF), 689, 704
nonnegativity, 625
nonparametric correlation, 507
nonresponsive bias, 588
no-repeat value, of background repeat property, 144
normal distribution, 570
normality, defining measures of, 494–495
NoSQL (not only SQL) databases, 401–402
notch parameter, 473
nparray, 491
np.dot function, 563
np.NaN (NumPy Not a Number), 421
number methods, working with, 258–259
<Number> element, 434
numeric data
 defining measures of normality, 494–495
 measuring central tendency, 492–493
 measuring range, 493
 measuring variance, 493
 overview, 491–492
 working with percentiles, 494
NumPy, 408–409
numpy, datasets module, 666
NumPy Not a Number (np.NaN), 421
NumPy package, 492, 562
numpy.ndarray, 681
NYU (New York University), Certificate in Web Development from, 65

O

objectify.parse() method, 404
Objective-C programming language, 32, 56
Occam's razor, 593
off() method, 304
off() method, 304
 (ordered list) tag, 116, 152
older (deprecated) attributes, 121–122
Olivetti faces data set, 685

on() method, 302–304
onclick attribute, 336
one-hot encoding, 555
online learning, 583
online mode, for weight updates, 652–632
on-the-job training, 75–79
open() method, 389
.open method, 287
OpenCV package, 679, 684
opening tags, 98, 350
OpenOffice, 36
open-source apps, 334
OpenTable app, 36
optimization engine, 575
ordered list () tag, 116, 152
ordered lists, 116, 152–155
oReq object, 286
Outgrow.me, 85–86
out-of-bootstrapping examples, 598
out-of-core algorithms, 583
out-of-sample errors, 587–588
output layer, in neural networks, 646
<output> tag, 184
overestimation, 595
overfitting, 591, 602, 653–657
overflow property, 191–192

P

p selector, 136
<p> (paragraph) tag, 104, 158
padding property, 166, 167, 168
page layouts. *See* layouts
pandas package, 393, 408–409, 415, 496
pandas.crosstab function, 497, 498
paragraph (<p>) tag, 104, 158
paragraphs
 organizing text in, 104
 on web pages, example of, 102, 103
parallel coordinates, 500–501
parallelism, 657–658
parameters, 261

parentheses, using in JavaScript, 252
Parody Tech Twitter accounts, 160–163
`parse()` method, in Python, 396
parsers, 393
parsing
 HTML, 434–435
 XML, 434–435
`partial_fit` method, 631
partition algorithms, 627
pasting, 664
pattern-matching, 440–442
PayScale cost of living calculator, 90
PCA (principal component analysis), 635, 639, 689, 704, 718
`pd.DataFrame.duplicated()` method, 411
Pearson correlation, 504, 506, 507
Pearson's r, 506
percentage-sizing, 136–137
percentiles, defining for numeric data, 494
perceptrons
 neural networks and, 644
 nonlinear separability, 608–610
 overview, 606–608
PhD programs, 66
PhoneGap wrapper, 31
Photoshop app, 36
Photos. See images, 678
PHP, 27–28, 87
pictures. See images
pie charts, 468–469
Pingendo.com, 239
Play Store. See Google Play Store
`plot()` function, 459, 460, 465, 477
`plot.show()` function, 453
plotting
 defining plots, 452–453
 drawing plots, 453–454
 geographical data, 481–483
 scatterplots, 502–504
 time series, 478–481
 trends, 480–481
`plt.axes()` function, 455
`plt.plot()` function, 453

`plt.savefig()` function, 454
PNG (Portable Network Graphic) format, 455
`poly1d()` function, 477
`polyfit()` function, 477, 481
Pong game, 8
pooling, 658–659, 683
population, in statistics, 569
Portable Network Graphic (PNG) format, 455
`position` value, of `backgroundposition` property, 144, 145
positioning. See also layouts
 absolute, 201–205
 fixed, 216–220
 guidelines, adding, 203–204
 `z-index` attribute, 206–208
positive and negative word dictionaries, 706
`.post()` method, 310
POST value, of `method` attribute, of `<form>` tag, 126
PowerPoint app, 36
precompilers, for CSS, 54
predefined templates, 240
predicting
 outcomes, by splitting data, 610–614
 text classifications, 520–522
predictive analytics, 66
predictors, averaging, 676
`prepend()` method, 302
prerequisites, 2–3
pretrained neural networks, 683–684
pre-written codes
 CSS, 344–345
 HTML, 343–344
 JavaScript, 345–347
price, 338
principal component analysis (PCA), 635, 639, 689, 704, 718
privacy, big data and, 543
probabilities
 conditioning chance by Bayes' theorem, 565–568
 Naïve Bayes and, 615–621
 operations on, 564–565

processing, distributed, 58
product managers, 49–50, 54, 322
`programmableweb.com`, 335
programmatic trading, 580
programming. *See* coding
programming languages
 compiled versus interpreted, 15
 creators of, 14
 functionality across, 14
 lifespan of, 14
 low-level versus high-level, 14–15
 overview, 13–16
 syntax and structure of, 14
 for web software, 16
`<progress>` tag, 184
project managers, 38
Project_<code>, 79
`projection` parameter, 483
`prompt()` method, 259–260
prompting users for input, 259–260
properties, 131, 133
prototypes, 47, 74, 628, 629
PSD file format, 331
pseudo-class selectors, 141
public relations, coding and, 12
`publicdomainarchive.com`, 143
`pvalue`, 500
PyMongo library, 402
Python programming language. *See also* scikit-learn package
 collecting input, 362–363
 commands, 361–362
 creator of, 14
 data types, defining, 357–358
 displaying output, 362–363
 distribution for machine learning, choosing, 368–371
 downloading data sets, 378–386
 downloading example code, 378–386
 installing, 371–377
 math computations, 358–360
 matrices in, 557
 NetworkX package for, 448–450
 as one of first languages to learn, 86
 overview, 27–28, 354
 Random Forests in, 665
 required, 3
 versus Ruby, 86–87
 special characters, 360–361
 strings, 360–361, 363–364
 structure of, 355–357
 tip calculator, building, 365
 variables, defining, 357–358
 versions of, 356, 368

Q

`qcut` function, 496
qualitative features, in machine learning, 555
quality assurance, 74, 322–323
quantitative features, in machine learning, 555
quartiles, 472
quotation marks, 360
quotes, in JavaScript, 252

R

R programming language
 kNN algorithm in, 639
 matrices in, 557
 Random Forests in, 665
`random()` method, in Python, 391–392
Random Forests (RF), 663–668, 721–722
random sampling, 569, 582, 586
random search, 600–601
`randomForest` function, 668
`randomForest` library, 664, 668
`RandomForestClassifier`, 666
`RandomizedPCA` class, 685–686
`range()` function, 470, 485
`range` parameter, 471
ranges, measuring, 493
ratings data
 downloading, 712
 limitations of, 715–716

raw text files, shaping data in
 introducing regular expressions, 440–442
 removing stop words, 438–439
 stemming stop words, 438–439
 Unicode, 436–437
raw_input("prompt") method, 362
read() method, in Python, 389
read_csv() method, 395, 707
read_sql() method, 400
read_sql_query() method, 400
read_sql_table() function, 400
read_table() method, in Python, 393
readability, 355
Real Time Bidding (RTB) platforms, 580
recommender systems
 downloading ratings data, 712
 leveraging SVD, 716–723
 limitations of ratings data, 715–716
 MovieLens data sets, 712–714
 navigating anonymous web data, 714–715
 overview, 711–712
recommenderlab library, 713
reconstruction_err_ method, 705
<Record> node, in XML, 404
Reddit.com, 355
RegExr.com, 52
regexr.com, 440
regression
 linear, 512–515
 logistic, 515–518
regular expressions, 51–52, 266, 440–442
regularization, 654
reinforcement learning, 573
rel attribute, of <link> tag, 147
relational databases, managing data from, 400–401
relative positioning, 216
relative value, position attribute, 216, 221
remove() method, 302
Ren, Bob, 70
repeat value, of backgroundrepeat property, 144

repeat-x value, of backgroundrepeat property, 144
repeat-y value, of backgroundrepeat property, 144
repository
 creating folders, 380–381
 creating notebooks, 381–383
 exporting notebooks, 383
 importing notebooks, 384–385
 overview, 379
 removing notebooks, 383–384
representation, 551, 650
reproducibility, 628
reqListener function, 286
researching
 APIs, 267
 for graduate degree programs, 68
 identifying sources, 333–335
 projects, 35–36
 web applications
 choosing solutions for each step, 338–340
 dividing applications into steps, 326–333
 identifying research sources, 333–335
 overview, 325
reset_index() method, 428, 430
resizing images, 682
resource scheduling, AI used for, 537
resources, 4
response vectors, 557, 558
responsive design, 191, 222
responsive website design, 36
restricted Boltzmann machines, 658
results, machine learning vs. statistics at, 534
reviews, from e-commerce, 706–709
RF (Random Forests), 663–668, 721–722
RGB value, 137
right navigation toolbar, 164, 165
right-angle bracket (>), 97, 98, 350
RMSE (root mean squared error), 669
robotics, 532, 539
Rocket Fuel, 580
root mean squared error (RMSE), 669
round (n, d) function, 359

row_s.name property, 479
rows
 in databases, 388
 slicing, 424–425
 stretching, 120–121
rowspan attribute, 120
rpart.plot package, 613
RTB (Real Time Bidding) platforms, 580
Ruby programming language
 creator of, 14, 321, 322
 as one of first languages to learn, 86
 overview, 27–28
 versus Python, 86–87

S

safety systems, AI used for, 537
sales
 careers in, 50–51
 coding and, 12
same-origin policy, 287–288
sample bias, avoiding, 601–602
samples, defined, 586
sampling data, 388–392
sans-serif font family, 139
scalar multiplication, using matrices, 558
scaling, 55
scatterplots
 creating, 475–478
 overview, 474–475
 plotting, 502–504
school-year internships, 69
scikit-image library, 397, 678, 679, 684
scikit-learn package
 feature_extraction module in, 693
 K-means algorithm offered by, 631
 learning_curve function of, 595
 Naïve Bayes models in, 621
 Olivetti faces data set from, 685
 Random Forests and, 666
 tutorial for, 679
SciPy library, 354

scipy.ndimage package, 679
scipy.sparse matrix, 444
scope creep, 17
scoring
 analyzing reviews from e-commerce, 706–709
 enhancing text, 694–699
 machines reading data, 692–694
 natural language processing, 691–692
 problems with raw text, 702–703
 processing text, 694–699
 scraping textual data sets from the web, 699–702
SCOTUS Servo, 52
Scrapy library, 354
screen scraping, 266
<script> tag, embedding JavaScript using, 261–262
scroll value, of backgroundattachment property, 145
search() function, 442
search engine optimization (SEO), 11–12, 53
search engines, researching using, 334
<section> tag, 184, 229
security, 55–56, 67
SelectFromModel function, 668
selection bias, 588
selectors
 background images, 142–146
 child, 160
 customizing links, 139–141
 descendant, 160–161
 fonts, 135–139
 jQuery, 298–299
 writing name correctly, 178
semantic tags, 182–185, 229
semicolons, using in JavaScript, 252
sentiment analysis, 619
SEO (search engine optimization), 53
separability, nonlinear, 608–610
separate style sheets, CSS specified in, 147–148
separate value, of border-collapse property, 157
Series(), 424

Index 749

serif font family, 139
servers, 54
`set_xlim()` function, 456
`set_xticks()` class, 456
`set_ylim()` function, 456
`set_yticks()` function, 456
shape method, 562
shape property, 444
shapes, finding in data, 641–642
shaping data
 bag of words model, 442–447
 in graphs, 447–450
 on HTML pages, 434–436
 overview, 433
 in raw text files, 436–442
Shazam app, 68
shorthand methods, for AJAX, 310
`show()` function, 306, 398, 679–680
`showLocation()` function, 346
shrinkage, 675
shuffling data, 429–430
side projects, 61
sight, 677–678. *See also* images
similarity
 k parameters, 638–642
 measuring between vectors, 624–625
 overview, 624–625
 searching for classification by kNN, 637
 tuning K-means algorithm, 630–637
 using distances to locate clusters, 626–630
single tokens (unigrams), 697
singular matrices, 561
singular value decomposition (SVD)
 in action, 719–723
 classification tasks and, 704
 origins of, 717–718
 overview, 716–718
sketching web pages, 173–175
skewness, 494, 495
`sklearn.cluster.KMeans` algorithm, 631
`sklearn.cluster.MiniBatchKMeans` algorithm, 631
`sklearn.decomposition` module, 705

`slideDown()` method, 307
`slideToggle()` method, 307
`slideUp()` method, 307
sliding effects, in jQuery, 306–307
SnapMeNow app, 70
social networks, recommender systems and, 712
softmax, in neural networks, 647
solid lines, in graphs, 458
solutions, balancing, 592–595
`sort_index()` method, 430
sorting, data, 429–430
source code for examples in this book, 4
spaces
 in HTML, 101
 in Python, 356–357
spam filters, 551
spanning, 120
Spark, Apache, 582
sparse matrices, 694, 713
Spearman correlation, 507
special characters, in Python, 360–361
specializations of website developers, 25, 38
specifications, 540
splitting, data to predict outcomes, 610–614
`spread`, 473
spreadsheet consolidation, 74
SQL (Structured Query Language), 400
SQLAlchemy library, 401
SQLite database, 353
`src` attribute, 106, 262
`stackoverflow.com`, 163
standard deviation, 570
standardization, z-score, 509
standards, 540
`starbucks.com` website, 30
startups, programmers hired by, 88
statements, 8–9
static layouts, adding CSS to, 210–212
statistics. *See also* descriptive statistics
 comparing machine learning to, 534
 defined, 542
 describing use of, 568–570
 role in machine learning, 546–547

750 Coding All-in-One For Dummies

stemming, 438–439, 697–699
stochastic (mini-batch) mode, for weight updates, 653
stochastic gradient descent, 583
stop words
 removing, 438–439, 697–699
 stemming, 438–439, 697–699
`stop_words` parameter, 439, 446, 698
stopping rules, 612
storage, distributed, 58
storage category, of website code, 24, 25
`str()` function, 419, 436
`strategy` parameter, 423
stratified sampling, 570, 582
streaming, 388–392, 583
`strftime()` function, in Python, 419
strikethrough (``) tag, 107–108
string methods, 258–259
`<String>` element, 435
`string.capitalize()` function, 364
`string.format()` method, 364
`string.lower()` function, 364
strings, 252, 360–364
`string.strip()` function, 364
`string.upper()` function, 364
`strip()` string function, 363–364
`` (bold) tag, 107–108
`strtobool()` function, 435
Structured Query Language (SQL), 400
student-run companies, 62
`style` attribute, 154
`<style>` tag, 147, 154
styling, 356–357
subsampling, 675
subscript (`<sub>`) tag, 108–109
subscript text, 108–109
`.substring (start, end)` method, 259
subtraction, using matrices, 558
suffixes, removing from words, 438
`<summary/detail>` tag, 184
summer internships, 69
superscript (`<sup>`) tag, 108–109

supervised classification, 574
supervised learning, 572
surrogate body, creating with `all div`, 197–198
survivorship bias, 588
SVD. *See* singular value decomposition
`<svg>` tag, 184
Swift programming language, 32, 56
`swing` function, 307
Sworkit app, 86
`sym` parameter, 473
symbolic reasoning, 548
symbolic variables, 414
symbolists, 547
symmetry, 625
syntax of programming languages, 14

T

`\t` escape sequence, 360
table heading (`<th>`) tag, 119
table row (`<tr>`) tag, 119–120, 123
`table` selector, 157
`<table>` tag, 118–119, 122
tables
 aligning, 121–124
 basic structure of, 118–120
 cells, aligning, 121–124
 chi-square for, 507–508
 columns, stretching, 120–121
 contingency, creating, 497–498
 designing, 155–157
 rows, stretching, 120–121
tablets, adapting layouts for, 241–242
tabs, 360
tag soup, 700
tags, HTML. *See* elements, HTML
tangent hyperbolic activation function, 645
Tapestry recommender, 711
target functions, 574, 576
tasks, breaking goals into, 329
`td` selector, 157
`<td>` tag, 119, 123

Techcrunch Disrupt hackathon, 70
technical designs and decisions, 37
technology companies, hiring by, 87–88
templates, predefined, 240
temporary background colors, 188
TensorFlow library, 654
term frequency-inverse document frequency (TF-IDF) transformations, 446–447, 695–696, 705
terminal leaf, 613
testing
 k values, 639–641
 machine learning, 595
text
 processing, 694–699
 raw, 436–442, 702–703
text() method, 302
text analysis, 51–52
text classification, 619
text classifications, 520–522
text editors, 39
text encodings, 436–437
text files, accessing data from, 392, 393
text-align attribute, 155, 156
text-align property, table and td selectors, 157
text-decoration property, 136, 139, 140
text-processing tasks, 619
TF-IDF transformations. *See* term frequency-inverse document frequency (TF-IDF) transformations
tfidf.transform() function, 447
TfidfTransformer() function, 447
TfidVectorizer class, 705, 706
<th> (table heading) tag, 119
Theano library, Python, 654
theta (Θ), 648
third-party providers, 17
3D array, 424–425
three-column layouts
 overview, 185–186
 problems with floating layouts, 188–189
 specifying min-height property, 189–191
 styling three-column web pages, 186–188
 using height, 191–192
 using overflow, 191–192
threshold distance, 337, 339
ticks, setting in MatPlotLib, 455–457
time
 formatting values, 419–420
 plotting series, 478–481
 representing on axes, 478–479
 transformations, 420–421
<time> tag, 184
timedelta() function, 420
timeline, 318
tinyletter.com, 263
title() function, 469
title attribute, 98–99
title tags, 100–101
<title> tag, 100, 158
.toFixed(n) method, 259
toggle() method, 306
tokenizer parameter, 698
tokenizing, 442, 697
tokens, 694
tolower() function, 436
toolbars, 244–246
tooltips, 99
top attribute, 205, 209, 221
Torvalds, Linus, 341
toString() method, 274–275
total variation denoising, 680
<tr> (table row) tag, 119–120, 123
training
 by freelancing, 79–80
 by learning after work, 75–79
 by learning at work, 75–79
 machine learning, 550–551, 595
 overview, 73
 by taking work project to next level, 74–75
 by transitioning to new role, 80–82
training algorithms, 542
train/test set split, 596
transform() function, 423, 431, 439, 693, 698

transforming data
 adding new cases, 427–428
 adding new variables, 427–428
 overview, 426–427
 removing data, 428–429
 shuffling, 429–430
 sorting, 429–430
transitioning to new role, 80–82
transpose of a matrix, 561
triangle inequality, 625
trigrams, 696
try-everything principle, of no-free-lunch theorem, 593
t-tests, 499–500
Turing Test, 692
TV filter, 681
`twenty_train` object, 444
Twitter, programmers hired by, 87
Twitter Bootstrap
 coding web page elements, 243–247
 installing, 235–236
 layout options, 236–242
 overview, 233–235
 practicing with Codecademy.com, 247
2D array, 424, 425
two-column layouts
 adjusting borders, 180–181
 advantages of fluid layouts, 181
 building HTML code, 175–177
 setting floating columns, 179–180
 sketching web pages, 173–175
 using semantic tags, 182–185
 using temporary background colors, 177–179
type attribute
 of `<form>` tag, 125
 of `<link>` tag, 147

U

`<u>` (underline) tag, 107, 108
Uber, 11, 50
udacity.com, 77

UI (user interface) designers, 320
`` (unordered list) tag, 116, 117, 158
uncorrelated ensembles of trees., 664
underestimation, 595
undergraduate degees
 computer science curriculum, 60–61
 extracurricular activities, 61–64
 two-year versus four-year school, 64–65
underline (`<u>`) tag, 107, 108
underscore (_) character, 358
understandability, 628
undirected graphs, 484–485
Unicode, 436–437
unicorns, 47
unigrams (single tokens), 697
units. *See* neurons
univariates, 498, 570
universal approximators, 650
Universal Transformation Format 8-bit (UTF-8), 437, 702
unordered list (``) tag, 116, 117, 158
unordered lists
 creating, 116
 using CSS, 152–155
`unstack()` method, 413
unstructured data, sending, 397–399
unsupervised learning, 573
unsupervised tasks, 627
uploading data, 388–389
`upper()` string function, dot notation with, 363–364
Upwork, 88
`urcrnrlat` parameter, 483
`urcrnrlon` parameter, 483
usability, 628
`use_idf`, 447
user experience (UX) designers, 320
user interface (UI) designers, 320
user-generated coding websites, 335
users
 alerting, 259–260
 prompting for input, 259–260

Index 753

UTF-8 (Universal Transformation Format 8-bit), 437, 702
`util.strtobool()` function, 436
UX (user experience) designers, 320

V

`val()` method, 302
validating data, 409–414. *See also* machine learning, validating
validation curve charts, 593
validation sets, 595
`validation_curve` function, 666
`valign` attribute
 of `<td>` tag, 123–124
 of `<tr>` tag, 123
`value` attribute, of `<form>` tag, 125
values, 131, 133
values variable, 470
`var` keyword, 254
variables
 adding new to data, 427–428
 categorical, 414–419
 in databases, 388
 defining in Python, 357–358
 in machine learning, 555
 storing data with, 253–254
 using with algorithms, 513–514
variance decomposition technique, 689
variance measurement, 493
variance reduction, 611
vector of coefficients, 557
vectorization, 561–563
vectors, 557, 624–625
Venema, Wietse, 367
vertical navigation, 164, 165
`vertical` value, of `box-orient` attribute, 224, 225
virtual training resources, 76
`visited` state, anchor tag (`<a>`), 140
visual designers. *See* designers
visual designs, 36
visual features, extracting, 683–684

visualizing data. *See* data visualization
Vroots, 715

W

W matrix, 648
W3C (World Wide Web Consortium), 101
wait times, AI used to predict, 538
waterfall process, 34–35, 316
weapon technologies, autonomous, 531
web
 accessing data from, 402–404
 navigating anonymous data from, 714–715
 textual data sets from, 699–702
web applications
 building, 319–323
 coding
 with CSS, 26–27
 development environments, 343
 with HTML, 26–27
 with JavaScript, 26–27
 with PHP, 27–28
 preparing, 342
 pre-written codes, 343–347
 with Python, 27–28
 with Ruby, 27–28
 steps to follow, 347–349
 debugging, 350
 defined, 25–26
 defining purpose and scope of, 16–17
 example, 16–17
 planning, 316–317
 researching
 choosing solutions for each step, 338–340
 dividing applications into steps, 326–333
 identifying research sources, 333–335
 using third-party providers, 17
web browsers. *See* browsers
web hosts, 39
web pages
 adding JavaScript to, 261–262
 building sample using CSS, 148–149
 building sample using HTML, 109–111

coding basic elements, 243–247
displaying, 20–26
dragging and dropping to, 239–240
incorporating CSS, 146–149
inspecting code, 20–23
modifying CSS on, 133–135
organizing content on, 113–114
organizing data on, 163–165
sketching, 173–175
three-column, 186–188
web scraping. *See* screen scraping
web services, 402
web-based software, 10
WebKit-based browsers, 225
`-webkit-box-orient` attribute, 226
website developers. *See* developers
websites. *See* web pages
Weebly web host, 39
weight updates, 652–653
weights, in neural networks, 648, 650, 651
WhatsApp, 26
whiskers, 472
whitespace, 357, 363
width, fixing with CSS, 194–196
`width` attribute, 122, 123–124, 155, 156, 473
WinPython, 371
wireframes, 36, 37, 330, 333
Wistia code school, 74
within-cluster sum of squares (WSS), 630, 636
Wix web host, 39
Women Who Code (organization), 90
workplace utility apps, coding for practice, 79
World Wide Web Consortium (W3C), 101
`wrapbootstrap.com`, 240
wrappers, 31
WSS (within-cluster sum of squares), 630, 636

X

x-axis, in MatPlotLib, 455
`xlabel()` function, 463
XML (eXtensible Markup Language)
 accessing, 403–404
 parsing, 434–435
 strict formatting in, 434
`XMLHttpRequest` objects, 285–287
XPath, 434, 435–436
`xpath()` function, 436
xy parameter, 464

Y

Yahoo! 87, 116
y-axis, in MatPlotLib, 455
`Yelp.com`, 16–17
Yes We Code (organization), 90
`ylabel()` function, 463

Z

`z-index` attribute, 206–208

About the Authors

Nikhil Abraham is currently the CFO of Udacity, a venture-backed education technology startup that teaches its students how to code and that bridges the gap between real-world skills, relevant education, and employment. Prior to joining Udacity, he worked at Codecademy. At Codecademy, he helped technology, finance, media, and advertising companies teach their employees how to code. With his help, thousands of marketing, sales, and recruiting professionals have written their first lines of code and built functional applications. In addition to his day job, he has lectured at the University of Chicago Law School and created a course that teaches students how to solve legal problems using open data and software.

Prior to joining startups, Nikhil worked in a variety of fields, including management consulting, investment banking, and law; he also founded a Y Combinator-backed technology education startup. He received a JD and MBA from the University of Chicago and a BA in quantitative economics from Tufts University.

Nikhil is a recent transplant from Manhattan, New York, and now lives in Mountain View, California. Content from Nikhil's books *Coding For Dummies* and *Getting a Coding Job For Dummies* appears in this book.

Andrie de Vries started to use R in 2009 to analyze survey data, and he has been continually impressed by the ability of the open-source community to innovate and create phenomenal software. During 2009 he also started PentaLibra, a boutique market research and statistical analysis agency. After getting increasingly involved in the R community, he joined Revolution Analytics to help take R to enterprise customers, helping clients to deal with the challenges of data science and big data. To maintain equilibrium in his life, Andrie is studying and practicing yoga. Content from Andrie's book *R For Dummies, 2nd Edition* appears in this book.

Andy Harris began his teaching life as a special education teacher. He joined the faculty of the Indiana University-Purdue University Indianapolis Computer Science department in 1995. He serves as a Senior Lecturer, teaching the introductory course to freshmen as well as numerous courses on web development, general programming, and game programming. As manager of the Streaming Media Laboratory, he developed a number of online video-based courses, and worked on a number of international distance education projects including helping to start a computer science program in Tetevo, Macedonia FYR, and collaboration with Sun-Yat-Sen University in Guangzhou, China.

Andy is active in home schooling, and is the technology columnist for a national homeschool magazine.

Eva Holland is an experienced writer, trainer, and cofounder of WatzThis?. She excels in presenting complicated subjects in easy-to-understand language for beginners of all levels.

Eva has written, designed, and taught online, in-person, and video courses. She has created curriculum for web development, mobile web development, and search engine optimization (SEO). Prior to founding WatzThis?, Eva served as COO of MWS, where she provided astute leadership, management, and vision that guided the company to its goals. Content from Eva's book *Coding with JavaScript For Dummies* appears in this book.

Luca Massaron is a data scientist and marketing research director who specializes in multivariate statistical analysis, machine learning, and customer insight, with more than a decade of experience in solving real-world problems and generating value for stakeholders by applying reasoning, statistics, data mining, and algorithms. From being a pioneer of web audience analysis in Italy to achieving the rank of top ten Kaggler on kaggle.com, he has always been passionate about everything regarding data and analysis and about demonstrating the potentiality of data-driven knowledge discovery to both experts and nonexperts. Content from Luca's books *Machine Learning For Dummies* and *Python for Data Science For Dummies* appears in this book.

Chris Minnick is an accomplished author, trainer, and web developer. Prior to cofounding WatzThis?, Chris was CEO of Minnick Web Services for 18 years, where he managed and worked on hundreds of web and mobile projects for customers ranging from small businesses to some of the world's largest companies. Content from Chris' book *Coding with JavaScript For Dummies* appears in this book.

Joris Meys, MSc is a statistical consultant, R programmer and R lecturer at Ghent University (Belgium). After earning a master's degree in biology, he worked for six years in environmental research and management before starting an advanced master's degree in statistical data analysis. Joris writes packages for both specific projects and general implementation of methods developed in his department, and he is the maintainer of several packages on R-Forge. He has co-authored a number of scientific papers as a statistical expert. To balance science with culture, Joris spends most of his spare time playing saxophone in a couple of local bands. Content from Joris' book *R For Dummies, 2nd Edition* appears in this book.

John Mueller is a freelance author and technical editor. He has writing in his blood, having produced 100 books and more than 600 articles to date. His technical editing skills have helped more than 63 authors refine the content of their manuscripts. John has provided technical editing services to both *Data Based Advisor* and *Coast Compute* magazines. It was during his time with *Data Based Advisor* that John was first exposed to MATLAB, and he has continued to follow the progress in MATLAB development ever since. During his time at Cubic Corporation, John was exposed to reliability engineering and has continued his interest in probability. Be sure to read John's blog at `http://blog.johnmuellerbooks.com`. Content from John's books *Machine Learning For Dummies* and *Python for Data Science For Dummies* appears in this book.

Dedication

This book is dedicated to my infant son, the ever-energetic Aiden Abraham. Son, someday we'll go through this book together, and you'll learn to code. For now, I'm just happy that you made it on the 16-hour flight from Abu Dhabi to San Francisco without crying so I could finish this book! This book is also dedicated to my amazing wife, Molly Grovak. I am very grateful for all your love and support, and for being an amazing mom to Aiden, especially this last year with weekly bicoastal travels.

— Nikhil Abraham

Author's Acknowledgments

This book was possible with help from a number of people.

Thanks to all the people at Wiley, including Steven Hayes and Pat O'Brien for edits and helpful advice. Also, thank-you to all the technical, editorial, layout, and graphics folks for turning text of variable quality into text of outstanding quality.

Thanks to those of you who helped shape the content in this book online and offline. Thanks to Codecademy for all the freely available online content. Thanks to Douglas Rushkoff for starting a national conversation on whether we as a society should program or be programmed, and for bringing this message to schools, universities, and nonprofits. Thanks to Susan Kish for being the only executive I can find who has spoken publicly about her journey learning how to code (check out her TED Talk!) and for seeing the future of coding in corporations. Thanks to Alia Shafir and Joshua Slusarz at Bloomberg for all the coding sessions you helped organize, leaders you wrangled, rooms you reserved, and laptops you rebooted. Thanks to Melissa Frescholtz and her leadership team at AOL for supporting a culture of code and for taking code education even to places where it's used every day. Thanks to alumni at Cornell University, Northwestern University, University of Virginia, and Yale University for testing early versions of content and helping to make it better. Thanks to the people at Donorschoose.org, including Charles Best and Ali Austerlitz, and at Google.org for shining a bright light on coding for women and girls. Thanks to Code.org for making coding accessible and cool for hundreds of millions of kids in the United States and abroad.

— Nikhil Abraham

Publisher's Acknowledgments

Project Manager: Pat O'Brien
Copy Editor: Melba Hopper
Sr. Editorial Assistant: Cherie Case

Production Editor: Vasanth Koilraj
Cover Image: © maciek905/iStockphoto

Apple & Mac

iPad For Dummies,
6th Edition
978-1-118-72306-7

iPhone For Dummies,
7th Edition
978-1-118-69083-3

Macs All-in-One
For Dummies, 4th Edition
978-1-118-82210-4

OS X Mavericks
For Dummies
978-1-118-69188-5

Blogging & Social Media

Facebook For Dummies,
5th Edition
978-1-118-63312-0

Social Media Engagement
For Dummies
978-1-118-53019-1

WordPress For Dummies,
6th Edition
978-1-118-79161-5

Business

Stock Investing
For Dummies, 4th Edition
978-1-118-37678-2

Investing For Dummies,
6th Edition
978-0-470-90545-6

Personal Finance
For Dummies, 7th Edition
978-1-118-11785-9

QuickBooks 2014
For Dummies
978-1-118-72005-9

Small Business Marketing
Kit For Dummies,
3rd Edition
978-1-118-31183-7

Careers

Job Interviews
For Dummies, 4th Edition
978-1-118-11290-8

Job Searching with Social
Media For Dummies,
2nd Edition
978-1-118-67856-5

Personal Branding
For Dummies
978-1-118-11792-7

Resumes For Dummies,
6th Edition
978-0-470-87361-8

Starting an Etsy Business
For Dummies, 2nd Edition
978-1-118-59024-9

Diet & Nutrition

Belly Fat Diet For Dummies
978-1-118-34585-6

Mediterranean Diet
For Dummies
978-1-118-71525-3

Nutrition For Dummies,
5th Edition
978-0-470-93231-5

Digital Photography

Digital SLR Photography
All-in-One For Dummies,
2nd Edition
978-1-118-59082-9

Digital SLR Video &
Filmmaking For Dummies
978-1-118-36598-4

Photoshop Elements 12
For Dummies
978-1-118-72714-0

Gardening

Herb Gardening
For Dummies, 2nd Edition
978-0-470-61778-6

Gardening with Free-Range
Chickens For Dummies
978-1-118-54754-0

Health

Boosting Your Immunity
For Dummies
978-1-118-40200-9

Diabetes For Dummies,
4th Edition
978-1-118-29447-5

Living Paleo For Dummies
978-1-118-29405-5

Big Data

Big Data For Dummies
978-1-118-50422-2

Data Visualization
For Dummies
978-1-118-50289-1

Hadoop For Dummies
978-1-118-60755-8

Language & Foreign Language

500 Spanish Verbs
For Dummies
978-1-118-02382-2

English Grammar
For Dummies, 2nd Edition
978-0-470-54664-2

French All-in-One
For Dummies
978-1-118-22815-9

German Essentials
For Dummies
978-1-118-18422-6

Italian For Dummies,
2nd Edition
978-1-118-00465-4

e Available in print and e-book formats.

Available wherever books are sold. **For more information or to order direct visit www.dummies.com**

Math & Science

Algebra I For Dummies, 2nd Edition
978-0-470-55964-2

Anatomy and Physiology For Dummies, 2nd Edition
978-0-470-92326-9

Astronomy For Dummies, 3rd Edition
978-1-118-37697-3

Biology For Dummies, 2nd Edition
978-0-470-59875-7

Chemistry For Dummies, 2nd Edition
978-1-118-00730-3

1001 Algebra II Practice Problems For Dummies
978-1-118-44662-1

Microsoft Office

Excel 2013 For Dummies
978-1-118-51012-4

Office 2013 All-in-One For Dummies
978-1-118-51636-2

PowerPoint 2013 For Dummies
978-1-118-50253-2

Word 2013 For Dummies
978-1-118-49123-2

Music

Blues Harmonica For Dummies
978-1-118-25269-7

Guitar For Dummies, 3rd Edition
978-1-118-11554-1

iPod & iTunes For Dummies, 10th Edition
978-1-118-50864-0

Programming

Beginning Programming with C For Dummies
978-1-118-73763-7

Excel VBA Programming For Dummies, 3rd Edition
978-1-118-49037-2

Java For Dummies, 6th Edition
978-1-118-40780-6

Religion & Inspiration

The Bible For Dummies
978-0-7645-5296-0

Buddhism For Dummies, 2nd Edition
978-1-118-02379-2

Catholicism For Dummies, 2nd Edition
978-1-118-07778-8

Self-Help & Relationships

Beating Sugar Addiction For Dummies
978-1-118-54645-1

Meditation For Dummies, 3rd Edition
978-1-118-29144-3

Seniors

Laptops For Seniors For Dummies, 3rd Edition
978-1-118-71105-7

Computers For Seniors For Dummies, 3rd Edition
978-1-118-11553-4

iPad For Seniors For Dummies, 6th Edition
978-1-118-72826-0

Social Security For Dummies
978-1-118-20573-0

Smartphones & Tablets

Android Phones For Dummies, 2nd Edition
978-1-118-72030-1

Nexus Tablets For Dummies
978-1-118-77243-0

Samsung Galaxy S 4 For Dummies
978-1-118-64222-1

Samsung Galaxy Tabs For Dummies
978-1-118-77294-2

Test Prep

ACT For Dummies, 5th Edition
978-1-118-01259-8

ASVAB For Dummies, 3rd Edition
978-0-470-63760-9

GRE For Dummies, 7th Edition
978-0-470-88921-3

Officer Candidate Tests For Dummies
978-0-470-59876-4

Physician's Assistant Exam For Dummies
978-1-118-11556-5

Series 7 Exam For Dummies
978-0-470-09932-2

Windows 8

Windows 8.1 All-in-One For Dummies
978-1-118-82087-2

Windows 8.1 For Dummies
978-1-118-82121-3

Windows 8.1 For Dummies Book + DVD Bundle
978-1-118-82107-7

e Available in print and e-book formats.

 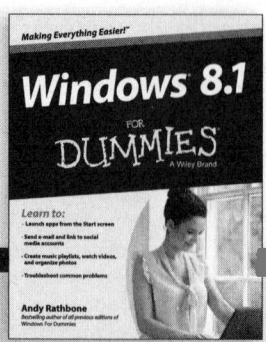

Available wherever books are sold. **For more information or to order direct visit www.dummies.com**

Take Dummies with you everywhere you go!

Whether you are excited about e-books, want more from the web, must have your mobile apps, or are swept up in social media, Dummies makes everything easier.

| Visit Us | Like Us | Follow Us | Watch Us |
|---|---|---|---|
| | | | |
| bit.ly/JE0O | on.fb.me/1f1ThNu | bit.ly/ZDytkR | bit.ly/gbOQHn |
| **Join Us** | **Pin Us** | **Circle Us** | **Shop Us** |
| | | | |
| linkd.in/1gurkMm | bit.ly/16caOLd | bit.ly/1aQTuDQ | bit.ly/4dEp9 |

Leverage the Power

For Dummies is the global leader in the reference category and one of the most trusted and highly regarded brands in the world. No longer just focused on books, customers now have access to the For Dummies content they need in the format they want. Let us help you develop a solution that will fit your brand and help you connect with your customers.

Advertising & Sponsorships

Connect with an engaged audience on a powerful multimedia site, and position your message alongside expert how-to content.

Targeted ads • Video • Email marketing • Microsites • Sweepstakes sponsorship

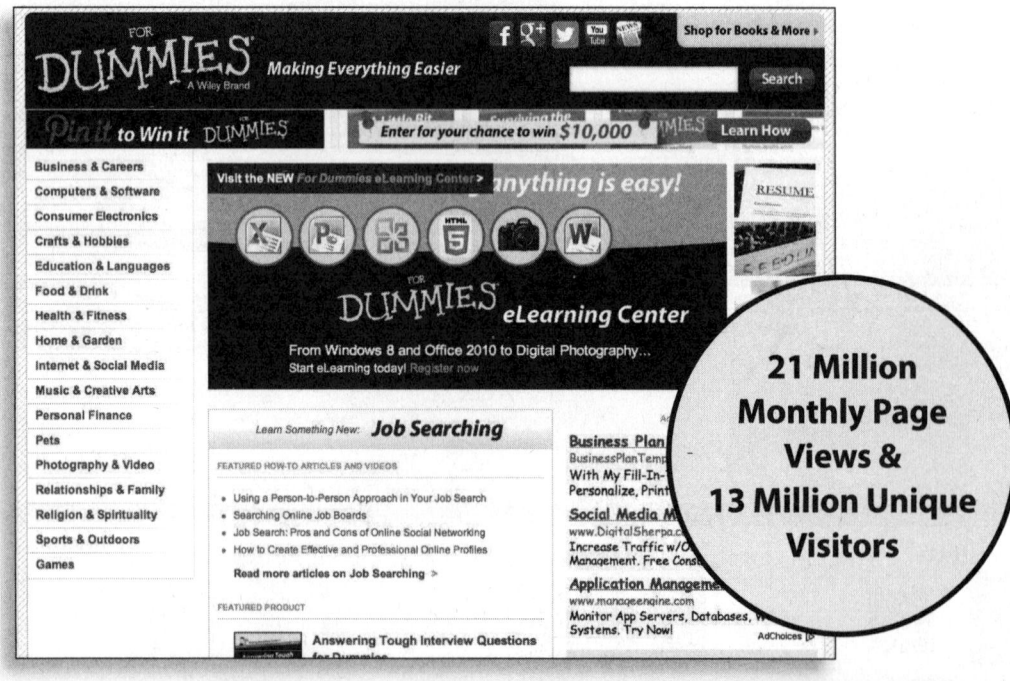

For Dummies is a registered trademark of John Wiley & Sons, Inc.

of For Dummies

Custom Publishing

Reach a global audience in any language by creating a solution that will differentiate you from competitors, amplify your message, and encourage customers to make a buying decision.

Apps • Books • eBooks • Video • Audio • Webinars

 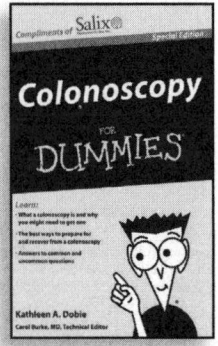

Brand Licensing & Content

Leverage the strength of the world's most popular reference brand to reach new audiences and channels of distribution.

 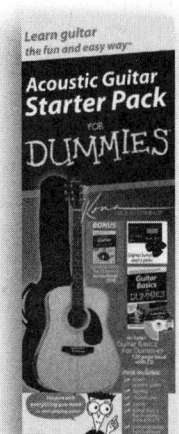

For more information, visit www.Dummies.com/biz

For DUMMIES
A Wiley Brand

Dummies products make life easier!

- DIY
- Consumer Electronics
- Crafts
- Software
- Cookware
- Hobbies
- Videos
- Music
- Games
- and More!

For more information, go to **Dummies.com** and search the store by category.

For Dummies is a registered trademark of John Wiley & Sons, Inc.

FOR DUMMIES
A Wiley Brand